Global Security in an Age of Crisis

GLOBAL SECURITY IN AN AGE OF CRISIS

Edited by Aiden Warren

EDINBURGH
University Press

Edinburgh University Press is one of the leading university presses in the UK. We publish academic books and journals in our selected subject areas across the humanities and social sciences, combining cutting-edge scholarship with high editorial and production values to produce academic works of lasting importance. For more information visit our website: edinburghuniversitypress.com

Edinburgh University Press Ltd
The Tun – Holyrood Road
12(2f) Jackson's Entry
Edinburgh EH8 8PJ

Typeset in 11/13 Sabon by
IDSUK (DataConnection) Ltd, and
printed and bound in Great Britain

A CIP record for this book is available from the British Library

ISBN 978 1 3995 0543 7 (hardback)
ISBN 978 1 3995 0545 1 (webready PDF)
ISBN 978 1 3995 0546 8 (epub)

Contents

Notes on Contributors

Aiden Warren, RMIT University

Dr. Aiden Warren is Associate Professor in Politics and IR at the School of Global, Urban and Social Studies at RMIT University in Melbourne, Australia. His teaching and research interests are in the areas of international security, US national security and foreign policy, US politics (ideas, institutions, contemporary and historical), international relations (especially great power politics), issues associated with weapons of mass destruction (WMD) proliferation, nonproliferation and arms control, and emerging technologies. Dr. Warren is a Fulbright Scholar and has spent extensive time in Washington, DC, completing fellowships at the James Martin Center for Nonproliferation, the Arms Control Association (ACA), and Institute for International Science and Technology Policy (IISTP) at George Washington University. He is the coauthor of *US Foreign Policy and China: Security Challenges across the Bush, Obama and Trump Administrations* (Edinburgh University Press, 2020) and *Understanding Presidential Doctrines: U.S. National Security from George Washington to Joe Biden* (Rowman and Littlefield, 2022).

Christine Agius, Swinburne University

Dr. Christine Agius is Associate Professor in Politics and IR at Swinburne University of Technology, Melbourne, Australia. Her research interests include critical approaches to security, gender, and bordering practices. Recent research has also engaged with drone warfare and the connection between antifeminism and the far right. Dr. Agius is the author of *The Social Construction of Swedish Neutrality: Challenges to Swedish Identity and Sovereignty* (Manchester University Press, 2006), coeditor of *The Politics of*

Identity: Place, Space and Discourse (Manchester University Press, 2018), and coauthor of *The Persistence of Global Masculinism: Discourse, Gender and Neo-colonial Re-articulations of Violence* (Palgrave Macmillan, 2018). She has published articles in *Cooperation and Conflict*, *Security Dialogue*, *Political Geography*, *Postcolonial Studies*, *Australian Journal of International Affairs*, *Review of International Studies*, and *Critical Studies on Terrorism*. She is an associate editor of *Critical Military Studies* and a member of the editorial board of *Global Studies Quarterly*.

Adam Bartley, George Washington University

Dr. Adam Bartley is a visiting research fellow with the Sigur Center for Asian Affairs, George Washington University, and is the 2022 Fulbright Scholar in US-Australia Alliance Studies. His research lies at the intersection of US-China rivalry, emerging security challenges, authoritarianism, and grand strategy. Adam is the coauthor of *US Foreign Policy and China: Security Challenges across the Bush, Obama, and Trump Administrations* (Edinburgh University Press, 2020) and author of *Perceptions of China and White House Decision-Making, 1941–1963: Spears of Promise, Shields of Truth* (Routledge, 2020). Dr. Bartley has previously lectured at Melbourne University, La Trobe University, and RMIT University, where he received his PhD. He is also a nonresident Vasey Fellow with the Pacific Forum where he is researching regional responses to grey zone threats. Adam speaks fluent Mandarin.

Nick Bisley, La Trobe University

Nick Bisley is the Dean of Humanities and Social Sciences and Professor of International Relations at La Trobe University, Melbourne, Australia. His research and teaching expertise is in Asia's international relations, great power politics, and Australian foreign and defense policy. Professor Bisley is a Fellow of the Australian Institute of International Affairs and the Secretary of the Council of Australasian Deans of Arts, Social Sciences and Humanities. He is a member of the advisory board of *China Matters* and a member of the Council for Security and Cooperation in the Asia-Pacific, and he served as the Editor-in-Chief of the *Australian Journal of International Affairs* between 2013 and 2018, the country's oldest scholarly journal in the field of international relations. Professor Bisley has been a senior research associate of the International Institute of Strategic Studies and a visiting fellow at the East-West Center in Washington, DC. Nick is the author of many works on international relations, including *Issues in 21st Century World Politics* (third edition, Palgrave, 2017), *Great Powers in the Changing International Order* (Lynne Rienner, 2012), and *Building Asia's Security* (IISS/Routledge, 2009). He regularly contributes to and is quoted in national and international media including *The Guardian*, the *Wall Street Journal*, CNN, and *Time* magazine.

Mia Bloom, Georgia State University

Mia Bloom is the International Security Fellow at New America, a professor at Georgia State University, and a member of the Evidence-Based Cybersecurity Group at the Andrew Young School of Policy Studies. Professor Bloom conducts research in Europe, the Middle East, and South Asia and speaks eight languages. She is the author or editor of several books and articles on violent extremism, including *Dying to Kill: The Allure of Suicide Terror* (Columbia University Press, 2005), *Living Together after Ethnic Killing: Exploring the Chaim Kaufmann Argument* with Roy Licklider (Routledge, 2007), *Bombshell: Women and Terrorism* (University of Pennsylvania Press, 2011), *Small Arms: Children and Terrorism* with John Horgan (Cornell University Press, 2019), and *Pastels and Pedophiles: Inside the Mind of QAnon* with Sophia Moskalenko (Stanford University Press, 2021). Her next book, *Veiled Threats: Women and Jihad*, is expected in 2022. Professor Bloom is a former term member of the Council on Foreign Relations and has held appointments at Princeton, Cornell, Harvard, and McGill universities. She serves on the Anti-Radicalization Board of the Anti-Defamation League and with the UN Counter-Terrorism Centre Executive Directorate, Women without Borders, and the Women's Alliance for Security Leadership. Professor Bloom has a PhD in political science from Columbia University, a Master's in Arab studies from Georgetown University and a Bachelor's degree from McGill University in Russian, Islamic, and Middle Eastern studies.

Brendon J. Cannon, Khalifa University

Dr. Brendon J. Cannon is Assistant Professor of International Security at Khalifa University, Abu Dhabi, UAE. He previously worked in Nairobi, Kenya, and Hargeisa, Somaliland. Dr. Cannon's research is at the nexus of international relations, security studies, and geopolitics with a particular focus on the interplay between Arab Gulf states and the Horn of Africa. He is the author of multiple articles appearing in

African Security, *Defence Studies*, *Small Wars & Insurgencies* and *Third World Quarterly*.

Cynthia Enloe, Clark University

Cynthia Enloe is a research professor at Clark University, Worcester, Massachusetts. Among the most recent of her fifteen books are *Bananas, Beaches and Bases: Making Feminist Sense of International Politics* (second edition, University of California Press, 2014), *Globalization and Militarism: Feminists Make the Link* (second edition, Rowman and Littlefield, 2016), and *The Big Push: Exposing and Challenging the Persistence of Patriarchy* (University of California Press, 2017). Professor Enloe is also the recipient of the Susan Strange Award and the Susan Northcut Award from the International Studies Association. Among her other recognitions are honorary doctorates from the University of Iceland, the University of Lund, and SOAS, University of London.

Vandra Harris Agisilaou, RMIT University

Dr. Vandra Harris Agisilaou is a senior lecturer in International Development in the School of Global, Urban and Social Studies at RMIT University, Melbourne, Australia. Her research focuses particularly on the interface between different actors in humanitarian spaces, especially militaries, police, and NGOs, and local and international development actors. Vandra has a special interest in humanitarianism(s), children and youth, and ethics in everyday practice. Her most recent research project addressed NGO-military interaction in complex emergencies and disasters, and was funded by the Australian Civil-Military Centre. Vandra has previously worked on ARC research projects on Australia's international policing and on youth recidivism in Australia.

Alek Hillas, RMIT University

Alek Hillas is a researcher in the School of Global, Urban and Social Studies at RMIT University, where he graduated with a first-class honors degree in International Studies and a Diploma of Languages. His research interests are in global security and emerging technologies, including artificial intelligence and lethal robotics. Alek has published articles on lethal autonomous weapons systems (LAWS) with *Yale Journal of International Affairs* (2017), *UCLA Journal of International Law and Foreign Affairs* (2018), *Small Wars &*

Insurgencies (2020), *Georgetown Journal of International Affairs* (2021), *Penn State Journal of Law & International Affairs* (2021), and *Cornell International Affairs Review* (2022). He has contributed chapters to two books published with Routledge (2020). Alek has received two RMIT Vice-Chancellor's List for Academic Excellence awards, first prizes in the National Playwright Competition Youth Award, first place in the German-language Goethe Poetry Competition held at the University of Melbourne, and the Asian Language Award Certificate of Achievement for excellence in Chinese at RMIT University, awarded by the Australian-Asian Association of Victoria.

Jennifer Hunt, Macquarie University

Dr. Jennifer S. Hunt is a security studies scholar at Macquarie University, Sydney, Australia, specializing in the national security of critical systems including cyber and energy. For her work on cyber-conflict and cyber-enabled information warfare, Dr. Hunt has participated in CyCon at the NATO Cyber Centre of Excellence in Estonia and served as a delegate at the Shangri-la Security Dialogue. Since 2020, She has worked closely with civil, military, and health institutions including the WHO to trace and combat COVID-19 disinformation. Dr. Hunt's policy report "Pandemic v Post-truth" (2020), examining the national security ramifications of COVID-19 conspiracy theories and their intersection with extremist recruitment and radicalization, has been downloaded more than 1,500 times via https://ghsn.org/Policy-Reports. She regularly provides expert commentary on the ABC, BBC, SBS and the History Channel. Dr. Hunt holds degrees from the University of Sydney and the University of North Carolina at Chapel Hill where she was captain of the saber fencing team.

Paul James, Western Sydney University

Paul James is Professor of Globalization and Cultural Diversity in the Institute for Culture and Society at Western Sydney University. He is author or editor of over thirty books, including *Globalization Matters: Engaging the Global in Unsettled Times* (with Manfred Steger, Cambridge University Press, 2019). Other books include sixteen volumes mapping the field of globalization (Sage). That collection is the most comprehensive and systematic representation of the field of globalization studies, comprising 3.5 million words. Professor James is Scientific Advisor to the Mayor of Berlin, and to Metropolis, the World

Association of Major Metropolises. He has also been an advisor to a number of other agencies and governments including the Canadian Prime Minister's G20 Forum, and the Commission on Reception, Truth and Reconciliation in Timor Leste. Professor James' work for the Papua New Guinea Minister for Community Development became the basis for the country's Integrated Community Development Policy. From 2007 through 2014 he was Director of the United Nations agency the Global Compact Cities Programme. Professor James has given invited presentations to universities and public institutions in forty-two countries.

Ngoc Nguyen, University of New South Wales

Dr. Ngoc Nguyen was awarded a PhD by UNSW Canberra in 2021 for her thesis titled "Regional Stabiliser: Questioning Middle Power Diplomacy and Collaboration in the Asia-Pacific." Before joining the UNSW, she worked as a research fellow and a lecturer at the Diplomatic Academy of Vietnam, teaching and publishing on Asia-Pacific regional security and great power relations. She also worked on projects that examine the implications of the South China Sea disputes on regional security and international relations. Dr. Nguyen has been a recipient of various awards and scholarships including the UNSW Tuition Fee Scholarship, the Endeavour Award, and the Andrew Dennis Research Grant. She was also a fellow with the Pacific Forum Young Leaders (2010–present) and the Singapore International Foundation ASEAN Fellowship (2003–7).

Peter Phipps, RMIT University

Dr. Peter Phipps is a senior lecturer in global studies at RMIT's School of Global, Urban and Social Studies. He is Director of the Honours program and was a founding member of the Centre for Global Research. Dr. Phipps undertook postgraduate training in cultural anthropology at the University of California Berkeley and completed a PhD on the cultural politics of postcolonial theory in the School of Anthropology, Philosophy and Social Enquiry at the University of Melbourne. He has published broadly on the politics of cultural globalization. Dr. Phipps has consulted to several organizations and government bodies including the PNG Department for Community Development, ATSIC, ATSIAB (Australia Council), and UNDP (Sarajevo), and to the Yothu Yindi Foundation, the City of Melbourne, and the Victorian Multicultural Commission.

Kaye Quek, RMIT University

Dr. Kaye Quek is a senior lecturer in global studies at RMIT's School of Global, Urban and Social Studies. She has a PhD in political science and a BA (Hons.) from the School of Social and Political Sciences at the University of Melbourne. Dr. Quek's research examines gendered abuses of human rights, particularly in the context of harmful marriage practices, domestic violence, and human trafficking. She is the author of *Marriage Trafficking: Women in Forced Wedlock* (Routledge, 2018) and her research has appeared in journals including *Women's Studies International Forum* and the *British Journal of Politics and International Relations*.

Ash Rossiter, Khalifa University

Dr. Ash Rossiter is Assistant Professor of International Security at Khalifa University in Abu Dhabi, UAE. He received his PhD from the University of Exeter in 2014 after earlier completing a MA in war studies at King's College London. Dr. Rossiter is the author of *Security in the Gulf: Local Militaries before British Withdrawal*, published in 2020 by Cambridge University Press. He has published widely on technology and international security, the modern Middle East, strategy, warfare, comparative defense industries, and the changing military balance in the Indo-Pacific. Dr. Rossiter's work has appeared in peer-reviewed journals such as *Intelligence & National Security*, *Defence Studies*, *International Politics*, *Parameters*, and *Middle Eastern Studies*, as well as many other outlets. He has written numerous policy reports and evaluations for several governments. Before entering academia, Dr. Rossiter pursued a career across the Middle East spanning both governmental and private sectors.

Shirley Scott, University of New South Wales

Shirley Scott is Professor of International Law and International Relations at UNSW Canberra and the immediate Past President of the Asian Society of International Law (AsianSIL). Her research lies at the intersection of international law and international relations and she has published widely in leading journals of both disciplines. One of Professor Scott's most significant contributions to scholarship in international law has been her theory of international law as ideology. She has also contributed widely on topics of international security, including in particular the increasing role of the United Nations Security Council in addressing climate security. *Climate Change and the UN Security Council* (Edward Elgar, 2018), which she coedited with Professor Charlotte Ku, was the first book-length treatment of the subject and has been highly influential in ongoing policy debates on the subject.

Erin M. Sorrell, Georgetown University

Dr. Erin M. Sorrell is Director of the Elizabeth R. Griffin Program at the Center for Global Health Science and Security and an assistant professor in the Department of Microbiology and Immunology at Georgetown University. She is also the Director of and teaches in the Biohazardous Threat Agents & Emerging Infectious Diseases MSc program. Dr. Sorrell works with partners across the US government, international organizations, and ministries around the world to identify elements required to support health system strengthening and laboratory capacity building for disease detection, reporting, risk assessment, and response. She is also interested in operational and implementation research questions related to sustainable health system strengthening, with an emphasis on the prevention, management, and control of infectious diseases in humanitarian situations, and particularly countries and regions affected by conflict.

Reuben Steff, University of Waikato

Dr. Reuben Steff is a senior lecturer at the University of Waikato, New Zealand, where he teaches courses on international relations and global security. He is also a member of Te Puna Haumaru / New Zealand Institute for Security and Crime Science. Dr. Steff's academic research stretches across a number of areas and includes the implications of artificial intelligence for the global balance of power and small states, the intersection between nuclear deterrence theory, ballistic missile defense, and the security dilemma, New Zealand and US foreign policy, and great power competition. His two most recent monographs are *Emerging Technologies and International Security: Machines, the State and War* and *US Foreign Policy in the Age of Trump: Drivers, Strategy and Tactics* (both Routledge, 2020). Dr. Steff sits on the editorial board of two security journals (*Defence & Security Analysis* and the *National Security Journal*), is regularly sought after by New Zealand media, industry and government agencies for his input, and has a number of journal articles published in the *Journal of Strategic Studies*, *Pacific Review*, *Contemporary Security Policy*, *Defense and Security Analysis*, *New Zealand International Review*, *National Security*

Journal, *Professional Journal of the Royal New Zealand Navy*, and *Australian Journal of International Affairs*.

Shahrbanou Tadjbakhsh, Sciences Po

Dr. Shahrbanou Tadjbakhsh has been teaching at Sciences Po in Paris courses on human security (since 2004) and understanding and responding to violent extremism (since 2018). She has also taught at Columbia and Georgetown universities and has been a visiting professor at universities in Tehran, Kabul, New Delhi, Pretoria, Moscow, and Dushanbe. Dr. Tadjbakhsh is the author or editor of dozens of publications, including most recently *A Rock between Hard Places: Afghanistan as an Arena of Regional Insecurity* with Kristian Berg Harpviken (Oxford University Press, 2016), *Rethinking the Liberal Peace: External Models and Local Alternatives* (Routledge, 2011), and *Human Security: Concepts and Implications* with Anuradha Chenoy (Routledge, 2007), and she has published extensively on human security, peace building, and radicalization, with geographic specialization on Afghanistan and Central Asia. Between 2010 and 2016 she was a researcher at the Peace Research Institute Oslo (PRIO) working on regional security complexes around Afghanistan and on the ethics of liberal peace. Since 2003, Dr. Tadjbakhsh has been working as a consultant with various UN agencies, among them the UNDP on evaluations of projects to prevent violent extremism and the Office of Counter-Terrorism and the Regional Centre for Preventive Diplomacy in Central Asia on the preparation and then application of the Action Plan for the Implementation of the UN Global Counter-Terrorism Strategy in Central Asia. In 2018, she worked with the permanent mission of Kazakhstan to the United Nations on its presidency of the UN to help with resolutions and statements on counterterrorism and on Afghanistan.

Maria Julia Trombetta, University of Nottingham

Dr. Maria Julia Trombetta is an Associate Professor at the University of Nottingham Ningbo China. Before moving to UNNC, Julia was a post-doctoral researcher at the Delft University of Technology, the Netherlands, where she worked on projects on the geopolitics of energy, energy governance, and energy transitions. Dr. Trombetta taught at Aberystwyth and Oxford Brookes universities. She was awarded a Fulbright Scholarship to study US environmental policy. Working from a critical security studies perspective, Dr. Trombetta has published on the securitization of the environment and of climate change and she is working on the transformations of security discourses and practices in the Anthropocene. She has edited, with Hugh Dyer, the *International Handbook of Energy Security* (Edward Elgar, 2013). Her work has been published in the *Cambridge Review of International Studies*, *Asian Perspective*, and *Critical Studies on Security*. Dr. Trombetta has a PhD in international politics from Aberystwyth University, a Master's in environmental governance from the University of Pavia, Italy (European School for Advanced Studies), and a MSc in economic and social science from Bocconi University, Milan.

Foreword

Embarrassment Is Intellectually Useful

Whoever bothered with the politics of the WHO? As I was, step-by-step, honing skills to make (hopefully) reliable sense of international and national politics, no one ever suggested that I should pay close analytical attention to the WHO—or to national ministers of health, or to pharmaceutical company executives, or, good grief, to nurses. Maybe someone else was minding these actors, but it wasn't on the research or teaching agendas of any of my mentors or colleagues.

That was then.

The COVID-19 global pandemic changed that. Since 2020, state and interstate health officials, along with the health industry's policymakers, and healthcare workers up and down the ladder have belatedly attracted the attention of critical security analysts. The actions of each of these players were materially affecting the daily lives of even the most-comfortable-with-abstraction security specialists. We suddenly were compelled to become curious about spheres we had spent decades leaving to other people to investigate. Many of us have had to run to catch up.

In a double challenge, simultaneously, most of us in security studies today have had to work hard to get up to speed on the globalized political causes and consequences of sea-rise, floods, wildfires and devastating droughts.

It turns out that over the last century's development of International Relations and, within it, Security Studies, most of us had not explicitly prepared ourselves or our students to tackle intellectually either globalized plagues or globalized climate destruction. It's not as if we allowed conventional Security Studies to go unquestioned. Researchers and teachers who created Human Security Studies, Critical Military Studies, and Feminist Security Studies made sure we stayed in a questioning mode.

Still, I wonder: How many of us have stood in front of a classroom filled with eager first-year students and confessed, “Honestly, I’m now starting to realize that, over the years, I have become so deeply militarized that too often I have shrunken security down to the politics of armed conflict, ignoring the politics of both viruses and carbon”?

Offering that sort of *mea culpa* probably takes some courage, a sort of courage that our profession rarely nurtures.

Aiden Warren and his insightful contributors are our tutors in Security Studies catch-up. Each author here is offering us a critical stance from which to make up for woeful shortfalls in both curiosity and skills. This is a book—an intellectual tool kit—for our global times. If we are honest with ourselves, we will read every chapter that follows here in an attitude of humility. That is, we will each gain the most from this volume if we open its covers as embarrassed readers, readers who acknowledge that we have missed the proverbial boat and now need—urgently—to shift our perspectives and expand our fields of investigation in order to remain relevant to this current generation of students.

All of these writers have crafted their interesting analyses in the time of COVID. Their shared awareness of this distinctive era is one of the special strengths of this collection. Every book or article, of course, is written *in* history. That is, every intellectual effort to make sense of this complex, dynamic world is written by someone living and thinking in a particular time. Acknowledging that does not weaken the analysis; it laces that analysis with grit.

As readers, we also live and think *in* history. That means that each of us will be reading and mulling over these valuable chapters in a time of still-morphing, still-spreading COVID infections and deepening droughts and continuing sea-rise. That should infuse our reading with a sense of urgency.

We also, however, will be reading Aiden Warren’s important collection in a time of renewed military conflict, most alarmingly a brutalizing war initiated by Putin’s autocratic Russian regime. It is remarkable how quickly the older, militarized version of Security Studies can reassert its lure. This pull, I’m guessing, will mean that each of us today as we read will have to exert more conscious energy to take on board the crucial security analytical lessons that follow.

Cynthia Enloe
April 2022

Introduction
Global Security in the Postpandemic Age

Aiden Warren

Rationale

This edited collection will seek to unpack the key global security issues and challenges the world is facing in the third decade of the twenty-first century. It will consider the extent to which the omnipresent epochal juncture in the form of the global pandemic will redefine (and amplify) the associated security discourse, the applicable theoretical debates, and responses to the new and ongoing threats to our survival.

The intensification of global security across the first two decades of the twenty-first century has seen the old "compression of time and space" adage go to another level. While debates and realities between new and old wars remain in play, the continuance of environmental degradation and the advent of emerging technologies have contributed to what some analysts have described as a new era of "*super* threat multipliers." Of course, in 2020 the global security environment entered a stage of heightened and protracted volatility, emanating from COVID-19's multifaceted and pervasive ramifications. The pandemic exacerbated prevalent global challenges, further exposing the fundamental triggers of insecurity and social and economic inequality, along with multiple layers of internal/external tensions. As the title of this book illustrates, the world is clearly going through what can be defined by every measure as a great epochal "age of crisis," and so it is only logical to presume that it will be a transforming point in global security and, more broadly, modern history.

The tumultuous global response to the COVID-19 pandemic has challenged the beliefs of even the most fervent internationalists and optimists. Most states, including the world's most influential, reshifted their focus inwardly, embracing travel sanctions in the initial stages, implementing export controls, hoarding or concealing information, and sidelining the World Health Organization (WHO) and other multilateral institutions. The pandemic appears to have uncovered, or perhaps reaffirmed, that the liberal order and the global community are illusions, while also illuminating the terrible effects of waning global cooperation. In more apt terms, the pandemic has clearly exposed both the limits of the present multilateral system and the gruesome, deadly costs of the broader structure's collapse. The conundrum is, of course, that if the contagion does spur policymakers to presume that multilateralism is doomed and encourages them to incite or fast-track its undoing, they will be establishing a platform where humanity will be poised to encounter a plethora of other costly tragedies. Conversely, if the crisis stirs up a reinvigoration to drive and invest in a more effective multilateral system, the world will be much better prepared when the *next* global pandemic transpires, boosting the prospect that the priorities of cooperation will win out over the stresses of competition and turning inward.[1] The reality has seen a different picture come to the fore across the pandemic, where the absence of global cooperation to confront or even limit the ramifications of the virus has been nothing short of disturbing. Many states recoiled toward a narrow position of national self-interest and a transactional approach to their management of information and resources. Others stepped up authoritarian responses that further challenged human rights and the rule of law, and undercut the very foundation of peaceful and robust societies.[2]

In the period since the emergence of COVID-19, analysts and policymakers have varied in their opinions of the kind of world the contagion will leave in its wake. For the most part they have argued that the world we are entering will be profoundly different from what existed before. Some envisage that the pandemic will fast-track a new world order led by China, while concurrently accelerating the demise of the United States' leadership. Some say it will put an end to globalization; others hope it will spur a new age of global collaboration. And still others have argued that it will intensify nationalism, destabilize trade, and lead to regime change in various states and an exacerbation of security fractures—or all of the above. However, it is perhaps worth considering that the world following the pandemic will *not* necessarily be fundamentally different from the one that preceded it. In this regard, COVID-19 will not so much change the rudimentary direction of world history and its core security issues as hasten it. The pandemic response has exposed the underlying characteristics of global politics and security of the contemporary period. As a consequence, the crisis perhaps can be considered to be less of a defining juncture than "a way station along the road that the world has been traveling for the past few decades."[3] In this context, deepening and intensifying tensions are certain to yield a range of security-related ramifications.

As this collection will illustrate across its seventeen chapters, the unparalleled circumstances spurred by the pandemic—taken together with an already complex security environment—have evolved and coalesced with the shifting dynamics of geopolitics, prolonged armed conflicts, large-scale public health emergencies, economic fractures and debt crises, climate shocks, deepening social and economic inequity, food insecurity, mass migration, gendered violence, populism and xenophobia, growing nationalism, and disinformation and cyber insecurity. In more concise terms, according to the United Nations, the pandemic has been more than a global health crisis: "It is a game-changer for international peace and security."[4] It has revealed the precariousness of humanity and exposed the systemic and deep-rooted inequities that are testing the resistance of societies. Further, it has pushed geopolitical disputes and hard security dangers back into the limelight, "exacerbating grievances, undermining social cohesion and fuelling conflicts."[5]

The ongoing contestation in the discourse

Within this global context the discourse pertaining to security will become an even more "essentially" contested concept. Here, security's inner complexity and the disputed principles associated with it will continue to deliver competing adaptations of the concept, which in turn will continue to engender perpetual tussles over its "true" meaning.[6] As early as 1991, Barry Buzan recognized twelve diverse definitions of security that significant analysts had fashioned,[7] one of which was that "security," in "an objective sense, measures the absence of threats to acquired values, [and] in a subjective sense, the absence of fear that such values will be attacked."[8] Not surprisingly, and particularly in the twenty-first century, the definitions of security have proliferated substantially outside the ones identified by Buzan. Some have even gone so far as to describe "security" as "a Tower of Babel,"[9] signifying both the immense mounds of texts and fantastic puzzlement as to the meaning of the theoretical underpinnings at the same time. Given these many interpretations of the concept, security cannot be viewed as a singular entity; it has many overlapping attributes, often dependent on *who* uses the term and for *what purpose*.

While this book in many instances advocates the consideration of more critical approaches—and newer views on how we need to reconceive security, and different referent objects[10] to consider outside the state domain—it needs to be acknowledged that traditional (or orthodox) approaches, as well as associated hybrid forms, continue to remain the "approach of choice" of many state leaders and policymakers today. In this light, the two dominant theoretical traditions in security studies, realism and liberalism, are often obediently adhered to and practiced extensively. While the state remains the defining and sacrosanct referent object to maintain "survival" within these traditions, both embody their own respective broad church and diversity within, where varying theoretical traditions are situated. Evaluating liberal and realist approaches to security, Patrick M. Morgan argues that, for both, "security has long been about the survival and physical safety of the actors and their people; by extension it concerns the deliberate use-of-force by states (and some other actors) for various purposes."[11] While the liberal church generally advocates a much greater adjustment for the prospective limitation of force than realists, their object of concern continues to be essentially the same. Additionally, these viewpoints engage with comparable territory theoretically. With few delineations, the analysis here is characteristically devoted to a positivist method of investigation that predominantly adheres to the notion that states define the "prevailing social and power relationships and the institutions into which they are organized . . . as the given framework for action."[12]

Of course, the different aspects of "critical security studies" which have positioned themselves as formidable alternatives to the traditional theories since the end of the Cold War are prominently featured in this volume across different delineations, including human security, feminist security studies, and postcolonialism (to name a few).[13] Not surprisingly, in an age where globalization, new technologies, and security threats easily transgress porous borders, grand theories appear to be increasingly losing traction in security studies to problem-centered analyses, which attempt to challenge and reconfigure how researchers approach the discipline itself. New and emerging problems, as evident with COVID-19, will necessitate a blend and rethinking of theoretical lenses and the application of methods that empower us to understand how security is experienced. This coincides with what occurs in the policy space. In fact, for many state leaders and policymakers such theoretical discussions have rarely been the defining pillar in the necessity to recognize (and respond to) security issues; it has been the issues themselves. Here, security issues or threats are either a) considered to be "concrete"/material threats by the *traditional approaches* to security, or b) constructed as security issues in a (security) political process by the *critical approaches*, with various outcomes for how they are examined.[14]

Notwithstanding the contested debates on the nature or definitions of security, it is evident that on a broad scale a consensus remains in play on what security entails: in essence, it is to do with threats to survival. In traditional discourse across the twentieth century, the state was deemed to be the inviolable object to be "secured," or what is often referred to as the "referent object." However, with the demise of the Cold War, the acceleration of globalization, the advent of advanced technologies, and the porosity of borders, other security issues emerged and the central conventions about *what* is to be secured, and *how*, came to occupy our thoughts, positing different referent objects and different ways in which we could reconceive security. As alluded to above, there are now wideranging approaches to security, approaches that propose several referent objects and different methods of attaining security, and that imply that previous practice, far from augmenting security, has actually been the source of *in*security.

Despite security being extensively critiqued over the last two decades for being too narrowly defined, a number of contemporary writers continue to press for its expanded conception outward from the restrictions of the narrow state-centric referent to one that encompasses a range of other considerations. Matters previously marginalized in the analysis of security are receiving expanded intellectual consideration where there has been a broadening, deepening, and extension on how we need to reconfigure our views on security. There have also been refreshing assessments of the character and importance of critical security studies, its association with international relations, "traditional" security studies and other disciplinary domains, and how best to unify, blend, and understand the area and its constituent components.[15]

In looking back to (among others) Barry Buzan's study, *People, States and Fear*, and Cynthia Enloe's *Bananas, Beaches and Bases*[16]—two pivotal and influential bodies of work that contended for a vision of security encompassing gender, political, economic, societal, environmental, as well as military aspects of security—this book also aims to elucidate the "new(er) risks and dangers" as we traverse the century's third decade. Of course, some risks and threats to our survival are not necessarily recent developments, particularly those associated with global terrorism, a (potential) collapse of the global monetary system, climate change, and the hazards of nuclear accidents. These threats to security, on a global level, continue to be regarded as universally significant and remain predominantly beyond the control of nation-states. However, the new and great "threat multipliers" in the form of emerging technologies, environmental degradation, and the era-defining issue of an all-pervading global pandemic demand due discussion and a reimagining of how we need to conceive security.

Plan of this book

As the authors in this collection will illustrate and illuminate across a range of chapters, the world in the aftermath of the pandemic is in some ways unlikely to be fundamentally different from the one that preceded it. That is, COVID-19 will not so much redefine the basic trajectory of security, or world history for that matter, as accelerate our progress along it. The pandemic and the responses to it thus far have uncovered and reinforced the fundamental characteristics of geopolitics and global security today. As such, the post-pandemic age promises to be perhaps less of a turning point than a stepping stone on the pathway that the world has been traveling along for the past few decades, where waning leadership, stuttering global cooperation, great power discord, and emerging threats to our survival—which characterized the global environment before the advent of COVID-19—have now been brought into sharper focus than ever. In tackling this evolving area, the structure of this book will be as follows.

Part I (**Approaches**) of the collection will position the variations in discourse across the global security domain. In this regard, it will bring together a wide array of theoretical approaches to security and specific ways in which these approaches are currently extended, and even challenged, given recent global events.

Each chapter aims to provide a clear, concise and accessible introduction to each of these positions. In addition to providing a summary and guide to each approach and its key advocates, the chapters also emphasize the academic traditions that these approaches in turn draw upon. Of course, not all of the approaches surveyed here function along the same intellectual lines; some of them endeavor to broaden the terrain and engage in ideas beyond the more orthodox security studies domains, such as post-Marxist critical theory, feminism, theories of postcolonialism, poststructuralist ideas, and sociology, among others.

In analyzing these distinct political-theoretical underpinnings we can gain a more nuanced understanding of the varied starting points of the different perspectives. In maintaining the sentiments posited in the above, the importance placed here on theoretical complexity will provide readers with new avenues for conceiving the various points of convergence and divergence between the different approaches. Indeed, the theoretical discussions undertaken in this first section cross the thematic chapters vertically, while allowing readers to evaluate the degree to which different perspectives intersect with significant global security issues and challenges, which Part II will address.

As **Part II (Issues and Challenges)** will illustrate through a range of thematic chapters, while war and the threat of the use-of-force remain decisive components of the security calculi, it is not exclusively so: global security now incorporates threats that vary from pandemics and environmental degradation to the more easily coupled security apprehensions of immediate violence, such as terrorism, and intra- and inter-state armed conflict. The topics chosen for consideration in this part illustrate this progression, ranging from "classic" security issues pertaining to war, great power tensions, ethnic and religious violence, and the connection between resources, the environment, and conflict, to a variety of "new" security issues (i.e. cybersecurity, emerging technologies, and pandemics). As such, Part II offers an overview of how the varying approaches play out across a diverse range of global security issues, thereby illuminating how the implementation of different approaches extends the domain of study outside narrow militaristic threats to also encompass a wide range of contemporary problems. In turn, the ways in which different approaches focus upon and analyze these issues will tell us much about how these approaches operate, what they deem to be important, and how they treat the concept of security more broadly.

Overall, all authors and chapters across Parts I and II—whether writing on an approach or on an issue/challenge—will assess where their "area" is situated in the context of COVID-19 and the applicable challenges, transformation, and/or tensions this will present. A century ago, when pandemic influenza attacked a war-torn world, few multilateral institutions existed. States fought their common contagious adversary alone. Today, an assortment of multilateral mechanisms exist to tackle global public health crises and address their related economic, social, and political effects. But the presence of such mechanisms has not prevented most states from taking a unilateral approach. Indeed, as signified earlier, the pandemic has illustrated both the limits of the current multilateral system and the horrendous costs of the system's failure. If the current crisis causes policymakers to determine that multilateralism is hopeless and persuades them to incite its unraveling, they will be setting humanity up for even more devastating tragedies. If the crisis instead provides a wake-up call—a catalyst to invest in a more effective multilateral system—the world will be far better equipped when the next global pandemic hits, increasing the likelihood that the requirements of cooperation will win out over the pressures of competition. Of course, where this epochal contagion intersects with concerns pertaining to global security will be incorporated into each chapter's assessment.

Chapter structure and authors

In Part I (Approaches), the collection begins with Christine Agius's Chapter 1, "Critical Approaches and Security," in which the author argues that the global COVID-19 pandemic has exacerbated existing security issues while also producing new concerns and perhaps a different type of "security." In contrast to the state-centric realist and liberal traditional approaches, the chapter provides an exploration of critical security approaches and how they might help us to think about security in the postpandemic age. In this regard, critical security studies embraces a wider perception of security beyond the state, in which human security is a central focus, while other critical and post-structuralist security approaches focusing on identity, securitization and the referent object of security, language, and discourse are also areas for rethinking. Additionally, critical security approaches in the context of the global pandemic facilitate analysis of how we understand hierarchical relations, identity, bodies, and the relationship between truth and knowledge—*who* benefits and *who* is excluded.

In Chapter 2, "Traditional Approaches and Security," Adam Bartley argues that recent events with COVID-19, US-China rivalry, and the rise of populism in traditional liberal countries have foreshadowed a resurgent interest in the value of realist structuralist assumptions and competing liberal ones. For both, the fundamental concepts of power, the international system, national interest, and security have all remained central to the methods of global political exchange. In evaluating these attributes, the chapter questions the international response to the pandemic. Can vaccine diplomacy, pandemic lockdown, supply chain disruption, and technological progress be better explained as existing in a medium of cooperation or competition? Unmistakably, leaders have turned increasingly inwards, finding solutions in the pathologies of contemporary insecurities in the prescriptive theories. What else could explain Russia's posturing over Ukraine, China's military assertiveness or Britain's exit from the European Union? The liberal institutionalist school by contrast finds that, while the tethers of international institutions have stretched, they have remained intact. Invariably, recent events have presaged less a paradigmatic shift in international security than a return to the familiar trends and behaviors of nations described by the traditional approaches, albeit at an innovatively competitive new level.

In looking at "Globalization and Security," Paul James's Chapter 3 argues that, amid the current global unsettling, the intense search for security, at least in the way that it has come to be figured in the past half century, has become increasingly contradictory. That is, the technoscientific search for increased security now tends to bring about circles of increasing *in*security. Here, the chapter is concerned not just with the extension of social relations across world space (globalization) but with the foundational or ontological unsettling of that space and its consequences for human security in general, including military security. In looking at nuclear security, cybersecurity, financial security, and biosecurity, the chapter argues that the COVID-19 crisis reaffirmed trends, as nation-states closed borders in the name of biosecurity, but failed to focus on the unsettling conditions which provide the basis for zoonotically transferred viral pandemics: global deforestation, industrial agriculture, global inequality, and climate change.

Many debates over the last few years have grappled with the notion of a "new Cold War." In Chapter 4, "Great Power Politics and Security," Reuben Steff argues that in early 2020 a systemic "black swan" phenomenon—the COVID-19 global pandemic—emerged, intersecting with the increasing competition, deepening and intensifying it as Beijing and Washington sought benefit amid the chaos. While much discourse focused on China's rise vis-à-vis the decline of US power, most commentary neglected a systematic empirical account of the implications of the pandemic for the US-China competition. Steff's chapter addresses this gap and tests the accuracy of the predominant narrative. It does so by delineating the US-China relationship's breakdown during the Trump administration and its trajectory during the Biden administration; examining how COVID-19 impacted US-China tensions; and contemplating whether the pandemic altered the relative power balance—comprising economic, military, and ideological metrics—in a structurally significant way.

In Chapter 5, "Gender and Security," Kaye Quek argues that the COVID-19 pandemic has drawn sharper focus on the gendered nature of security, which has been evidenced and theorized by feminist and gender scholars over the course of the last forty years. The pandemic, in fact, provides a useful microcosm for underscoring the ongoing, and even heightened, significance of feminist work in the area of global security, despite positive changes in the discourse in recent decades. The chapter examines the major themes to have emerged from scholarship on gender and security, via the now well-established academic discipline known as feminist security studies. Additionally, it seeks to emphasize several of the gendered challenges to global security that have intensified as a result of state responses to COVID-19, and that can be expected to replicate in its wake. Drawing on case studies, the chapter contends that, more than ever, the role of gendered norms and consequences of policy responses to global security challenges must be considered, in order to cultivate effective strategies and to protect against threats to global security now, but also well into the future.

In Chapter 6, Peter Phipps's discussion on "Postcolonialism and Security" begins by explaining the significance of postcolonialism in helping us reconceive our understanding of domestic and global security in the wake of colonialism and the anticolonial movements. Across the last three decades, postcolonial theories have opened up new interpretations of both intra- and inter-state dynamics as complex, sometimes contradictory sets of relationships founded in deep historical interconnections between colonizing and colonized polities. The COVID-19 pandemic has brought these dynamics into starker contrast, with sobering implications for how we understand security and risk. Utilizing a range of case studies, the chapter illustrates how postcolonial perspectives on security challenges, previously seen as marginal or insignificant, emphasize the contradictions and fractures within settler colonial societies. Amid the global pandemic, such internal fractures and their related security risks of domestic terrorism and perpetual external wars are likely to become more volatile as the larger global power shift plays out.

In building upon the critical approaches posited in this section, Shahrbanou Tadjbakhsh's Chapter 7 on "Human Security" illustrates how traditional security thinking and the tools of security have proved to be unsatisfactory in protecting the lives and well-being of citizens threatened by the COVID-19 pandemic. Given that the state-centric, traditional security paradigm cannot capture such complexity, the chapter calls for a broader conception of "security" which is more specifically relevant to situations of crisis and risk. In positing the significance of the human security approach, Tadjbakhsh argues that in crisis situations (wars, pandemics, forced migration, financial crisis, environmental catastrophes, and so forth) threats often combine to endanger the survival, livelihoods, and dignity of people, much like they threaten the existence, functioning, and sovereignty of nation-states. The chapter examines how, as an approach, human security can evaluate existing and future public policies and programs related to mitigating multidimensional risks stemming from the pandemic.

In Chapter 8 on "Humanitarianism and Security," Vandra Harris Agisilaou argues that much humanitarian practice now takes place in complex environments, in which humanitarian need is exacerbated by conflict. Conflict causes civilian injury and death, and destruction of housing and critical infrastructure and of trading routes and production. This impact is amplified in places where extreme poverty was already pervasive, infrastructure already poor, and extreme weather and natural hazards already creating stress. The intersection of crises here creates urgent human need, known as a complex emergency. After establishing these foundations, the chapter proceeds to examine the existing challenges to humanitarians in conflict environments and asserts that these will be exacerbated by the impact of COVID-19, which has already seen the first rise of global poverty in about a quarter of a century. The increasing humanitarian need will likely encounter a reduction in funding as a result of global economic downturn and/or volatility as a result of the pandemic, as well as greater limitations on the movement of goods and people. The chapter concludes that the pandemic brings to a head a series of challenges already faced by this sector, and will test the agility, creativity, and flexibility of the sector in reimagining lifesaving actions.

After this presentation of some mainstay, alternative, and critical approaches to the ways we need to (re)conceive and reimagine our understanding of security—as well as different and multiple "referent objects" to protect and maintain our survival—the collection will turn to Part II (Issues and Challenges).

In Chapter 9, "Pandemics and Health Security," Erin M. Sorrell argues that the pandemic, coupled with weak health systems, has not only cost lives but poses some of the greatest risks to contemporary security. The effects of health security successes and failures can influence foreign policy, society, and security. Nations cannot shelter in place and avoid an infectious disease. Pandemics have underscored that treating health security as a niche issue for a small number of stakeholders will fail. It takes a global community to prepare and respond. Traditionally, national security has been viewed and defined broadly through a state-centric defense paradigm. As such, the chapter outlines the extent to which pandemics can disrupt national security as destructively as a traditional global enemy, if not more so, highlighting the inextricable links between global security, pandemics, and health security. Lastly, the chapter concludes that health security cannot be treated as the sole responsibility of national ministries of health and international health organizations, nor can it be considered a secondary issue behind transnational threats that claim fewer lives annually. Pandemics will recur.

Aside from the immediate impact deriving from the ramifications of the pandemic, climate change and environmental degradation remain the greatest challenge to our survival. As Maria Julia Trombetta's Chapter 10 on "Environmental Security" argues, the pandemic has exposed many of the limits of existing security discourses. Many of the contradictions have been anticipated in the debate about environmental security. As environmental problems have started to emerge, so have their security implications and appeals to redefine security. Additionally, the chapter examines recurring attempts to conceptualize security in familiar terms, like the debates on environmental conflict, and the resilience of national, defensive, zero-sum approaches in times of crises. At the same time, environmental security has prompted a deeper reworking of security. Within the literature, the environmental security debate has questioned the referent objects, moving from the state to humans and to ecosystems. It has also questioned the logic of security, challenging reactive measures and promoting precautionary ones. In political strategies it has supported the promotion of resilience. The pandemic has outlined how humans are connected to other species and to the environment and has made evident the extent of the human impact on the environment.

The next significant and ongoing issue is discussed in Mia Bloom's Chapter 11, "Global Terrorism and Security." The chapter argues that in the fog of the pandemic, violent extremists have sought to capitalize on the crisis: There has been an opening up of political space which bad actors can fill with misinformation, and where they can foster mistrust in legitimate governments or exacerbate people's fears of "the other." The uncertainty that the pandemic induced in millions of people, and the near paralysis that interrupted the normal daily functioning of society, were perceived by both jihadist and far-right extremist groups as a significant opportunity for recruitment, amplified attacks, and the spreading of chaos and confusion intended to topple governments to achieve the terrorists' notions of "utopia." The conditions of social distancing intensified existing vulnerabilities of groups stuck at home experiencing high anxiety. Additionally, a developing sense of unpredictability, exacerbated by the proliferation of disinformation intended to propagate chaos and confusion, continued to grow divisions in society and spur many levels of polarization.

In Chapter 12, "Emerging Technologies and Security," Aiden Warren and Alek Hillas argue that as the capacity to construct and use new proprietary technologies has become a contested source of economic strength and military power, access to such innovations may disrupt global or regional security architectures in the future. While the dangers of digital-enabled systems and devices are not yet fully realized, policymakers will be compelled to address the threats posed by advanced weapons technologies and formulate international provisions to regulate or mitigate their use. In seeking to unpack recent developments, this chapter provides an overview of the various definitions and security ramifications of four critical emerging technologies: artificial intelligence (AI), drones, lethal autonomous weapons systems (LAWS), and cybersecurity. While each emerging technology poses distinct challenges for policymakers, they can also be considered as a set of interrelated challenges—with AI as a particular enabling capability. Finding viable approaches for the management of weapons systems, including potential options for their governance, remains vital for technologies that are emerging in the twenty-first century, as well as disarmament and arms control issues in continuation since the twentieth century. Following the onset of the COVID-19 pandemic, the relative decline of multilateral institutions has added further strain to diplomacy and international negotiations. In this context, the chapter highlights the growing risks associated with conventional and unconventional weapons, where there has been relative inaction on enacting regulations across the broader milieu of international bodies.

In focusing exclusively on the "Cybersecurity" challenge, Jennifer Hunt's Chapter 13 clearly illustrates that, while in the early stages cybersecurity was exclusively a technical domain, the increasing sophistication and severity of cyberattacks has elevated it on the national security and popular agenda. In the wake of high-profile attacks against state agencies, industries, and critical infrastructure such as hospitals and utilities, cyberattacks now consistently rank in the top five threats in global surveys. In recent times, cyber-intrusion into voter rolls and electoral systems, email hacking of candidates, and algorithmically targeted propaganda and disinformation campaigns launched over social media designed to rupture civil society have become prevalent security features. However, cyber-enabled disinformation as a tool of state-based conflict is not limited to elections: foreign actors have also carried out targeted online disinformation campaigns through social media aimed at stoking confusion about the COVID-19 pandemic and thus undermining state responses. In this regard, the chapter argues, the difficulties of defense have become more acute. That is, while traditional cybersecurity threats exploit the vulnerabilities of the system, these evolving attacks exploit its virtues, harnessing the openness and virality of social media. Such tactics, whether for great power competition or profit, represent a strategic challenge to democracies.

In Chapter 14, "Nuclear Weapons and Security," Aiden Warren argues that, notwithstanding the significant reductions in global nuclear arsenals, the risks deriving from nuclear security have actually expanded. More states in more unstable regions have attained such weapons, terrorists continue to pursue them, and the command-and-control systems in even the most sophisticated nuclear-armed states remain susceptible to not only system and human error but, increasingly, cyberattack. Even a limited regional nuclear war would have calamitous global consequences. Moreover, the chapter argues, the failure of existing nuclear-armed states to disarm, the inability to impede new states obtaining nuclear weapons, the potential of nonstate actors gaining access to such weapons and their concomitant material, and the challenge presented by the expansion of nuclear energy plants, hypersonic weapons, and modernization all present serious security challenges in the twenty-first century. Given the post-COVID-19 inertia and issues deriving from the Russian invasion of Ukraine, the aforesaid nuclear-related security complications will only become further amplified, while potential solutions in the form of arms control/ nonproliferation mechanisms will continue to be hindered.

The next two chapters turn toward two regional security concerns. In Chapter 15, "Security in the Middle East," Ash Rossiter and Brendon J. Cannon argue that in the decade since the so-called 2011 Arab Spring uprisings—themselves a turning point in the region's history—insecurity and instability have become more pronounced. Focused on leaving readers with a better understanding of the Middle East's emerging security landscape, much of the chapter concentrates on—and is organized around—enduring and new security threats facing regional states and their leaders, elected or otherwise. One point that comes out strongly in the analysis throughout this chapter is that the underlying conditions that produced the so-called "Arab uprisings"—the changes they brought, and the deep fissures they exposed—have not disappeared. Neither have the transboundary, ideational forces that have fueled much of the ethnoreligious violence in the region's modern history dissipated. What makes the Middle East especially volatile today, the authors argue, is the additional pressure exerted from structural change at the international system level, that is, a return to multipolarity and the growing frequency of exogenous shocks, including climate change-induced challenges and the COVID-19 pandemic.

In Chapter 16, "The Indo-Pacific and Security," Nick Bisley begins by discussing the "Indo-Pacific" as a relatively new term in global politics; a regional construct that has been created in response to the growing ties that bind the states and societies of the Western Pacific and Indian Ocean regions. Such linkages encompass the flows of energy, commodities, and goods moving along transoceanic sea lanes, but also include security threats and challenges. This chapter examines the key security dynamics and issues in the Indo-Pacific and argues that it is not just security that is at the heart of the idea of the Indo-Pacific, but that the key security concerns of the region entail a new fault line in global security. The chapter begins by introducing the Indo-Pacific construct and showing how security matters are the most important force behind the emergence of and contestation around the idea. It then examines four main security issues in the region: the role and dynamics of great power competition; the part played by alliances, institutions, and strategic geometry in the security landscape; the intersection of economic concerns and security dynamics; and the region's major flashpoints. Lastly, the chapter assesses the pandemic's impact on Indo-Pacific security and the broader future trajectory of the region.

In assessing "The UN Security Council and Climate Security" in Chapter 17, Shirley Scott and Ngoc Nguyen look specifically at the intersection between the United Nations Security Council (UNSC) and climate change. They argue that the issue can be viewed from two distinct perspectives: the security implications arising out of humanity's failure to adequately mitigate climate change; and the council's law and practice to date. Viewed from the first of these perspectives, the UNSC has done little relative to the magnitude of the dangers we are facing. Viewed from the second perspective, however—and what the founders of the UN envisaged the council would be addressing—it is arguably surprising that the council has even considered what the United Nations Framework Convention on Climate Change regime has treated as an issue primarily of sustainable development. In fact, the Council is now taking more visible steps toward assuming a lead role in climate change governance and it is possible that the global COVID-19 pandemic may yet add significant momentum to the process. This is particularly the case if it becomes widely accepted that the pandemic is yet another major world crisis that was made more likely by the advent of climate change and variability.

Final introductory thoughts

When pandemic influenza raced through the war-devastated world 100-plus years ago, there were very few options for mitigation and a small number of multilateral institutions, and states struggled against their common contagious adversary in isolation. While today there appears to be a robust assortment of multilateral instruments to mitigate global public health disasters and respond to the correlating economic, social, and political impacts, the presence of such mechanisms has not prevented most states from adopting unilateral, inward approaches.[17]

That said, even those in the security discipline across the policy, research, analyst, and scholarly spectrum who envisaged the advent of such a crisis being plausible if not inevitable have been taken aback by the way it has been handled. Clearly, the failure to prepare was followed by a failure to contain. The preliminary stages of the crisis saw a brutal political pressure test that only a minority of states passed—encompassing a combination of competency, social trust, and relatively efficient leadership. As these same narrowly defined attributes will be needed to guide and steer us through the long grind ahead, the likelihood of greater failure, political instability, and security volatility around the world in years to come appears inevitable. While many Western states' early responses were impeded by inadequate governance and in some instances federalism, a unified social intent was also lacking. Not surprisingly, a comparable development on the international stage saw a global dash toward stonewalling outsiders, inward self-help, and reproachment rather than invigorated multilateralism.[18]

Of course, the warning signs were there for many to see. In the earlier part of the twenty-first century, after the severe acute respiratory syndrome (SARS) and influenza A virus subtype (H5N1) epidemics, there were calls by many in the security domain to be prepared as there was ample evidence to suggest that it was only a matter of time—amid globalization, global mobility, the transferal of goods, services, and capital, and porous borders—before a global contagion took place. In moving forward to 2017, after Middle East respiratory syndrome (MERS) and Ebola and Zika, further concerns were raised among public health experts who lamented the lack of definitive attention to the matter. It is perhaps easy to presume that multilateral institutions, ostensibly the pillars of the rules-based international system, are at best somewhat less effective than they have been presented and, at worst, destined to flounder when they are required most.[19] The insipid and scattered multilateral response to the pandemic is illustrative to some extent of the decisions of particular leaders, especially Chinese president Xi Jinping and US president Donald J. Trump. Their behavior helps us understand why the WHO struggled in the preliminary phases of the contagion and why mechanisms for multilateral coordination, such as the G7, the G20, and the UNSC, markedly failed in both their capacity and their inclination to step up.[20]

While the pandemic is not the core focus of this book, it would be remiss not to have it as a defining consideration in any contemporary assessment pertaining to global security, referent objects to protect our survival, and the ways we need to reconceive our understanding of security. Clearly, while the older parameters are still very relevant, they need to be readjusted in adapting to this postpandemic age. As this monograph will seek to demonstrate across its seventeen chapters, the incomparable conditions engendered by the pandemic—taken together with an already multifaceted security environment—have evolved and combined with the ever-changing dynamics of geopolitics, protracted armed conflicts, large-scale public health emergencies, economic fissures and debt crises, climate shocks, intensifying social and economic inequity, food insecurity, mass migration, populism and xenophobia, growing nationalism, disinformation, and cyber insecurity.

In this light, the pandemic is much more than a global health crisis; it is a significant juncture in global history and "threat exacerbator" set to challenge the already precarious position that international peace and security were in *before* the pandemic. It has laid bare the vulnerability of humanity and reaffirmed the dichotomous, systemic, and deep-rooted divisions that continue to undermine the resilience of societies. As UN secretary-general António Guterres stated at the General Assembly, "the only certainty is more uncertainty," and as such, states must unite to establish a new, more optimistic, and more even path. In describing the collective effects of a rampant COVID-19 pandemic, an ethically insolvent global financial system, the climate crisis, anarchy in cyberspace, and weakened peace and security, Guterres said: "We face a five-alarm global fire that requires the full mobilization of all countries." Further, while emerging technologies potentially offer extraordinary opportunities for humanity, "growing digital chaos is benefiting the most destructive forces and denying opportunities to ordinary people." Here, states are also encouraged to work toward banning lethal autonomous weapons, or "killer robots," and to initiate new and more agile governance frameworks for biotechnology and neurotechnology.[21]

In what can be considered a colossal task, the talented and cutting-edge group of authors assembled here in this edited collection aim to add much-needed connective tissue and critical analysis to these coalescing global security matters. The collection will seek to unpack the key global security issues and challenges the world is encountering in the third decade of the twenty-first century. It will take into consideration the extent to which the era-defining global pandemic will readjust (and intensify) the associated security discourse and the applicable theoretical debates, and evaluate the responses to new and continuing threats to our survival in an "age of crisis."

Notes

1. Stewart Patrick, "When the System Fails: COVID-19 and the Costs of Global Dysfunction," *Foreign Affairs*, July/August 2020, https://www.foreignaffairs.com/articles/world/2020-06-09/when-system-fails (accessed February 15, 2022).
2. "As COVID-19 Fuels Conflict, Threatens International Security, Global Unity to Fight Terrorism Needed More than Ever, Secretary-General Tells Aqaba Process Meeting," press release, United Nations, September 2, 2020, https://www.un.org/press/en/2020/sgsm20227.doc.htm (accessed February 15, 2022); Sophie Harman, "Threat Not Solution: Gender, Global Health Security and COVID-19," *International Affairs* 97, no. 3 (2021): 601–23.
3. Richard Haass, "The Pandemic Will Accelerate History Rather than Reshape It," *Foreign Affairs*, April 7, 2020, https://www.foreignaffairs.com/articles/united-states/2020-04-07/pandemic-will-accelerate-history-rather-reshape-it (accessed February 15, 2022).
4. "As COVID-19 Fuels Conflict."
5. Ibid.
6. Walter Bryce Gallie, "Essentially Contested Concepts," *Proceedings of the Aristotelian Society* 56 (1956): 167–98.
7. Barry Buzan, *People, States and Fear: An Agenda for International Security Studies in the Post-Cold War Era*, 2nd edn. (Boulder, CO: Lynne Rienner, 1991), 16.
8. Arnold Wolfers, "'National Security' as an Ambiguous Symbol," *Political Science Quarterly* 67, no. 4 (1952): 485; see also Columba Peoples and Nick Vaughan-Williams, *Critical Security Studies: An Introduction*, 2nd edn. (Abingdon, England: Routledge, 2015), 2–3.
9. Edward A. Kolodziej, *Security and International Relations* (Cambridge, England: Cambridge University Press, 2005), 11; see also Peoples and Vaughan-Williams, *Critical Security Studies*, 4–5.
10. A referent object is an entity that is viewed as the focal point for assessment in security studies (e.g., the state, the human, the ecosystem), or, put differently, that which is to be secured.
11. Patrick M. Morgan, "Liberalist and Realist Security Studies at 2000: Two Decades of Progress?" in *Critical Reflections on Security and Change*, ed. Stuart Croft and Terry Terriff (London: Frank Cass, 2000), 40.
12. Robert W. Cox, "Social Forces, States and World Orders: Beyond International Relations Theory," *Millennium* 10, no. 2 (1981): 126–55; see also Peoples and Vaughan-Williams, *Critical Security Studies*, 4–5.
13. Myriam Dunn Cavelty and Thierry Balzacq (eds.), *Routledge Handbook of Security Studies*, 2nd edn. (Abingdon, England: Routledge, 2017), 2–4.
14. Ibid. See also Charles L. Glasner, "Realism," in *Contemporary Security Studies*, ed. Alan Collins, 2nd edn. (Oxford: Oxford University Press, 2010), 16–20; Patrick Morgan, "Liberalism," ibid., 35–47.

15. Peoples and Vaughan-Williams, *Critical Security Studies*, 2–3.
16. See Buzan, *People, States and Fear*; Cynthia Enloe, *Bananas, Beaches and Bases: Making Feminist Sense of International Politics* (Berkeley: University of California Press, 1989).
17. Patrick, "When the System Fails."
18. Gideon Rose, "What Is Killing Us Is Not Connection; It Is Connection without Cooperation," *Foreign Affairs*, July/August 2020, https://www.foreignaffairs.com/issue-packages/2020-06-03/world-after-pandemic.
19. Ibid.
20. Patrick, "When the System Fails"; Edward Newman, "Covid-19: A Human Security Analysis," *Global Society*, December 2021, https://www.tandfonline.com/doi/full/10.1080/13600826.2021.2010034 (accessed February 16, 2022).
21. "UN Chief Calls for Action to Put Out '5-Alarm Global Fire,'" UN News, January 11, 2022, https://news.un.org/en/story/2022/01/1110292 (accessed February 16, 2022).

Part I

Approaches

1

Critical Approaches and Security: Emancipation and Threat Multiplication

Christine Agius

Introduction

The global COVID-19 pandemic presents multiple challenges for international and everyday security, exacerbating existing security tensions while also producing new security concerns. COVID-19 has produced new realities and modes of being and living as the world experiences the varying and uneven effects of the pandemic and efforts to mitigate it. In some ways, it also represents a new epoch as we increasingly speak of a "pre-" or "postpandemic" world, where time is divided into the world before the pandemic, and what a "return to normal" means or might look like. This chapter considers questions of security in the pandemic age through critical approaches to security. Generally, a critical approach to security questions many of the assumptions found in traditional schools such as realism and liberalism. Critical security studies broadly encompass a wide range of schools of thought and ontological and epistemological concerns. The "capital C" Critical Security Studies (CSS) of the Aberystwyth School embraces wider perceptions of security beyond the state, making human security and emancipation a central focus, while other ("small c") critical and poststructuralist security approaches focus on identity, securitization, and the referent object of security, language, discourse, and what constitutes "reality"—themes of major significance in an era of "posttruth" politics.

This chapter will explore the ways in which critical security approaches can analyze and make sense of what we mean by "security" in the pandemic era, and how the pandemic has become a "threat multiplier." Understanding the impact of the pandemic on global security from a range of critical perspectives means addressing human security, biopolitics, language, image, and power. In some cases, the pandemic has solidified existing power relations and given rise to new ones, but it has also prompted debate about how we can or whether we should seek a different type of "security." Critical security approaches will be used to analyze the global pandemic in terms of how we understand hierarchical relations, identity, bodies, and the relationship between truth and knowledge—who benefits and who is excluded.

The global nature of the pandemic permits an opportunity to take an overview of multiple constraints from an international crisis that affects virtually all states and individuals, albeit differently. This differentiation is a central concern of this chapter because, despite the widespread rhetoric that the pandemic means "we are all in this together," some have faced greater insecurity than others. Moreover, the pandemic has provided additional layers of insecurity for those whose security is already precarious. As such, it is possible to see security issues emerge or become exacerbated and to apply relevant critical security perspectives to understand the multiplicity of threats that are part of the pandemic and the responses to it. The analysis will take in the unevenness of the idea of human security, how securitization has worked in the case of COVID-19, and the impact of discourse and language in the construction of threat. Moreover, the relationship between health and security comes together under the responses to the pandemic to further highlight issues related to the emancipatory project that is part of the broader CSS/critical security studies agenda. This prompts speculation about the sort of postpandemic world that will be produced from the crisis, and what critical security approaches can tell us about its possibilities and limitations.

The chapter commences with an overview of critical approaches to security, bringing together a range of perspectives that tend to be housed under the "critical" label, distinguishing between "small c" approaches and CSS. As it turns to the case study of COVID-19, the chapter draws out how the pandemic has amplified the tensions between state and human security and global inequalities, while considering how it has served as a threat multiplier. The chapter will focus on borders, images and narratives of truth and misinformation, and the securitization and militarization of COVID-19, looking at the ways in which the state has played a role in (in)security and how ideas of human security have become enveloped in aspects of individualism, which can be read as highly problematic. Importantly, the pandemic provides insights into how concepts central to critical approaches to security, such as emancipation, have become contested and blurred.

Critical Security Studies/critical security studies

To speak of critical approaches to security is to take on board not simply a disciplinary perspective, but one that is open to a range of viewpoints that originate from outside the realm of what we would consider "traditional" security, with the purpose of questioning the idea of security itself. In this sense, it is difficult to capture exactly what "critical" approaches to security mean. As a field, CSS (or what has come to be known as the Welsh, Paris, and Copenhagen schools[1]) has been concerned with widening and deepening what security means. "Widening" refers to understanding security beyond its narrow military and statist confines, and bringing neglected issues to the fore, such as economic insecurity, transnational crime and terrorism, environmental security, and health as a security issue. "Deepening" refers to the critical approaches and theories used to examine political phenomena.[2] Most important, in terms of CSS as a theoretical approach, security is seen in terms of *emancipation*, meaning the removal of the structural barriers that prevent individuals and communities from being secure; people cannot be "free" or meaningfully secure if war, economic oppression, or other barriers restrict their lives.[3]

While we can identify the foundations of CSS in the Frankfurt School and Marxist perspectives, what we call the critical study of security has "many points of emergence, and a contested history."[4] For some, a CSS approach includes a limited acceptance of capitalism; Ken Booth, for example, called for a "better," more distributive form of capitalism in his 2007 book *Theory of World Security*,[5] which has been critiqued.[6] For others, CSS can be seen as Eurocentric (consider the key focus and case studies pertaining to Europe), Western-centric,[7] and grounded in Enlightenment ideas, or having a concept of emancipation that has limited applicability outside the West.[8] Emancipation can also have connotations of individualism or universalist goals, where those doing the "emancipating" are Western states and institutions.[9] Others see emancipation as an idea that can "travel" and may not necessarily be "[a product] of a single geo-cultural setting."[10] Moreover, there has been lively debate about the merits of CSS that draws into question whether it is "critical" at all (in that security has *always* been a contested concept) or can provide an ethical or political account of security.[11]

In this context, this chapter aims to adopt what Krause and Williams call "small-c" critical security studies, which rather suggests an "orientation towards the discipline than a precise theoretical label."[12] As the CASE Collective also note, critical approaches to security are "dissident" perspectives that aim to engage and critique narratives of modernity, the relationship between power and knowledge, the production of security discourses, and the scholarly limits of the field.[13] Moreover, to take a critical perspective of security is to engage reflexively with the political through questioning given categories of social reality.[14] Over the decades, different approaches to security have become subsumed under a "critical" label and we can consider feminist, political sociology, securitization theory, poststructuralist, postcolonial, visual politics, constructivist, and other approaches as part of critical security studies.[15]

The COVID-19 pandemic presents a case study that joins up multiple dimensions of the critical security studies agenda. At its core, the pandemic foregrounds the importance of health as a human security issue (see Chapters 7 and 9) but goes beyond this to impact economic and societal well-being. While health is the central focus, the way in which a critical lens can elucidate discreet and overt dimensions of the pandemic provides insights that are often glossed over or completely missed among the daily reporting and analysis. This crisis of human security and state power speaks to questions of identity, the power of discourses and narratives, ideas about truth, and muddier questions about "emancipation."

Significantly, the pandemic has also prompted questions about the world that comes next, and what forms of insecurity will persist or emerge. The following sections focus on aspects of the pandemic that bring together a range of different perspectives from critical security studies, paying attention to how differing notions of exclusionary politics have played into debates and policy positions. I focus on questions of inequality that have been amplified by the pandemic and state power, and how the pandemic has become a threat multiplier.

The state is back? Borders, authority, and securing the state in pandemic times

Long before COVID-19, Stefan Elbe argued that health and security had become greatly intertwined, resulting in a securitization of health and an increasing turn to a medicalization of security. This has produced a tension between greater global cooperation and a national framing of security which can result in closed borders to protect the state.[16] The COVID-19 pandemic has had two simultaneous and seemingly contradictory impacts on the state. The first was to show its limitations—or rather, those of the broader global structures and systems into which the state is embedded. As the fragility of supply chains halted the movement of goods and supplies, the impact of a globalized form of capitalism left the state with no power to deliver some basic goods to its citizens. Early in the pandemic, goods necessary to deal with the virus proved difficult to secure; medical staff had to work with shortages of personal protective equipment such as gloves, masks, and gowns; and hand sanitizer and basic household goods such as toilet paper were in scarce supply.

At the same time, measures to tackle the pandemic in many ways seemed to herald the *return* of the state. In the UK, Australia, and the US, it was stimulus packages provided by states—in varying degrees and forms—that gave some economic relief to citizens who had lost employment due to lockdowns and support for businesses. State capitalism—or intervention by the state in the economy and markets in addition to its regulatory role—is said to have increased as states bailed out key industries, invested in sectors such as health and technology, and provided financial support to businesses to weather the impact of the pandemic.[17] Yet, as some have observed, the state's intervention can be explained as a political and ideological choice to "rescue" capital, after decades of neoliberal hollowing out of state institutions and decentralization.[18]

Nonetheless, the state was visible during the pandemic in wider bordering practices, protection of national interests, and vaccine competition. "Hard" borders came into effect, as states cordoned off their boundaries to avoid "contamination," but the pandemic has also revived global divisions, with states engaging in "vaccine nationalism" and competition. An early example of this can be seen in efforts by former US president Donald Trump to buy up global stocks of one of only two COVID drugs available in July 2020.[19] In the following month, the UK, US, Japan, and the EU member states topped the league for the best-supplied nations, with ninety-two low- and middle-income countries and economies at the bottom of the list.[20] Vaccine nationalism was identified in August 2020 by Tedros Adhanom Ghebreyesus, the director of the World Health Organization (WHO), as problematic for global vaccination efforts.[21] It also exacerbated the divide between rich and poor nations. In February 2021, UN Secretary-General António Guterres criticized the "wildly uneven and unfair" distribution of COVID vaccines, noting that just ten countries had acquired 75 percent of available vaccines, with over 130 countries having "not received a single dose."[22] Eric Otieno Sumba noted that in the same month, South Africa had paid twice as much as the EU for a vaccine which was clinically trialed in South Africa.[23] Meanwhile "[a]ccess for most of the Global South remained conditional on varying degrees of philanthropy."[24]

While international efforts to ensure equitable distribution of COVID-19 vaccines were established via COVAX (the COVID-19 Vaccines Global Access initiative, coordinated by Gavi, the Vaccine Alliance, the Coalition for Epidemic Preparedness Innovations, and the WHO), problems soon emerged with rich states accessing COVAX stockpiles for their own populations. As the Morrison government in Australia came under intense criticism for its failure to secure enough vaccines for its population, in August 2021, it took 500,000 doses of Pfizer from the COVAX stockpile, double what all of Africa received in that same month. In October 2021, it was reported that only 8 percent of the sixty million vaccinations the Australian government promised to developing countries in the region had been delivered, and only one in seven of the vaccination doses committed to developing countries through COVAX had been delivered by wealthy nations and pharmaceutical companies.[25] COVAX was intended to ensure that vaccines were accessible to some of the poorest nations at risk from COVID. Yet, by its own admission, it is also "an invaluable insurance policy" for richer nations to ensure their own supply of vaccines, so it can be concluded that such initiatives ultimately benefit richer states.[26] Moreover, the contributions to COVAX by rich Western states have come at the expense of development aid. Australia used its aid budget to fund responses to the pandemic in its region,[27] and the Biden administration's $US3.5 billion donation to COVAX diverted hundreds of millions of dollars allocated to vaccination drives in poorer nations.[28] Rich nations paid high premiums to secure their supplies while delaying financial pledges to COVAX.[29] It has been estimated that more than eighty-five poor nations will not have access to vaccines before 2023.[30]

Furthermore, while it has been positive that vaccine development has been rapid, there has been a seriously underexamined economic dimension, whereby profit and intellectual property rights significantly impact vaccine equality. In addition to "vaccine nationalism," this has affected some of the poorest nations, resulting in a "vaccine apartheid."[31] India and South Africa proposed a temporary intellectual property waiver on COVID-19 medical technologies and tools in October 2020 and, although it has attracted the backing of over 100 countries, the EU Commission and other nations have blocked it.[32] A critical security analysis of how state competition and national interest have featured in global responses to the pandemic reveals that liberal cooperation and multilateralism have been limited in reality, with longstanding divisions of wealth and hierarchy having a real impact on human security.

At the same time, the pandemic provided the opportunity for governments to not only close their borders but also manage those who crossed them. This had a significant impact on refugees and asylum seekers globally, as well as those in war zones. Migrants have long been seen as "unsafe" and risky bodies that threaten the body politic, and the pandemic has provided further justification for some states to enact deeply restrictive policies regarding migrants and extensive policing of migrant bodies. European states serve as prominent examples in this respect. Italy did not permit migrants to disembark at ports, ostensibly for their own safety, and on the Greek islands asylum seekers endured lengthy lockdowns, while tourists and Greek citizens were free to circulate from May 2020. As Martina Tazzioli writes: "[T]his differential measure was taken with the twofold official goal of preventing migrants from becoming vehicles of contagion and, at the same time, not exposing them to the infection."[33] Tazzioli refers to this as a type of "hygienic-sanitary" border, which aims to contain migrants and define their "irresponsible conduct," while juxtaposing the "good behaviours" of citizens.[34] Umut Ozguc also notes that those confined to the refugee camps were "doubly vulnerable": They were not prioritized in terms of status, healthcare, and vaccination,[35] and they had less access to legal support and humanitarian services. Furthermore, far-right movements have exploited the pandemic with claims that illegal migrants spread the virus.[36]

The closure of borders also affected citizens of states. Australia provides an interesting case of the multiplicities of bordering practices under COVID-19, with the federal government responsible for certain areas (such as quarantine, health, and international border controls) and states and territories bearing responsibility for lockdowns, with a newly created National Cabinet to coordinate responses.[37] In Australia, the then Prime Minister Scott Morrison told migrants on temporary visas to "go home" and a high portion of the population supported closing the border to international arrivals, which also left tens of thousands of Australians stranded abroad. When the Delta variant erupted in India, Australia banned all flights from that country, and threatened to jail and/or fine Australian citizens returning from India, attracting criticisms of racism from nearly all parts of the political spectrum.[38] Within Australian cities such as Melbourne and Sydney, suburbs and districts with large migrant communities that are characterized by low income and with a concentration of essential workers faced harsh lockdown conditions; temporary visa holders who carried out some of the lowest-paid jobs in cleaning and food delivery were not supported by the federal government's pandemic welfare programs.

The pandemic also vividly exacerbated racial divides. In an era of populist discourse, the "China virus," as it was called by Trump, drew associations of foreignness and difference globally. As the international community blamed China for the outbreak, Asians were attacked and marginalized. Furthermore, in Chengxin Pan's reading, longstanding assumptions that the West could manage the pandemic exposed a "racialized politics . . . in Western security thinking and practice,"[39] where the West is valorized as peaceful, rational, and secure against dangerous others. What Pan calls "epistemic racism" stretches to knowledge (for example, questioning whether non-Western, namely Chinese, science and knowledge is reliable or trustworthy, resisting the use of face masks in the West although it is common practice in Asia), methods (closing borders to stop the virus being brought in by others, yet seeing lockdowns as "draconian" and anti-democratic in the context of China's response to COVID), and zones of security (assuming the West is clean, that the "China virus" is a disease of nonwhites due to their practices).[40] Pan's criticism goes to the center of some major concerns about rationality and knowledge in Western thought and "critical" approaches to security. This is further highlighted in the following section, which discusses militarized responses to the pandemic; such responses can serve as a distraction from understanding the underlying inadequacies and inequalities that are obscured in state responses to COVID.

The "war" on COVID: militarized responses to the pandemic

There have been several examples of militarized responses to the pandemic; the "war on COVID" has not only been a well-used metaphor but in some cases has involved an overtly militarized response. The intersection of health and security has long been a focus of critical security studies. During a previous era of globalization, with increased travel, the threat of the spread of HIV/AIDS saw the UN Security Council issue Resolution 2000, which declared HIV/AIDS a risk to stability and security, with reference to state security and peacekeeping.[41] Health and disease have increasingly become "securitized." As Colin McInnes has pointed out, the linkage between national security and health has primarily been concerned with health insofar as it affects the state—for example, the physical health of military personnel during operations and the potential for disease to diminish the capacity of a state's military or to produce casualties.[42] But militarized responses to the pandemic are also varied. As Fawzia Gibson-Fall outlines, under COVID-19, three trends in civil-military engagements can be identified. The first is minimal technical military support which is centered on "niche tasks," such as transportation, border control, and supply chains (with Japan, Taiwan, Canada, Sweden, New Zealand, Kerala, and South Korea as examples). The second is a blended civil-military response which includes mobile testing and quarantine and lockdown enforcement (Nigeria, Kenya, France, the USA, the UK, China, Vietnam, South Africa, and Singapore), and the third is a military-led response which assumes control of planning, coordinating, and other tasks (examples of which can be seen in Brazil, Indonesia, the Philippines, Iran, Pakistan, and Peru).[43] Importantly, the implications of greater military involvement in responses to health crises are significant where health systems are weak and top-down responses may not only "entrench militaries" as key health actors but impact community trust and citizenship rights.[44]

Seeing health in securitized and militarized terms goes beyond institutional responses to the pandemic; doing so also conditions understandings of what counts as justified and appropriate responses to the pandemic, as well as delimiting critical engagement with the deeper structural issues involved. As Federica Caso writes, the war metaphor is powerful: "It is an effective, immediate, and emotive tool to communicate urgency to the general public. It also conveys a sense of struggle and righteousness that can justify exceptional measures."[45] In many cases, a militarized response to the pandemic can be interpreted as a performance of state security or an effort to extend power and authority. In the US, former president Trump invoked wartime rhetoric as his approval ratings declined over his handling of the pandemic, stating: "We must sacrifice together, because we are all in this together, and we will come through together. It's the invisible enemy. That's always the toughest enemy, the invisible enemy."[46] In the UK, citizens—including Prime Minister Boris Johnson—applauded nurses, carers, and medical personnel on the "coronavirus frontline."[47]

While Australia locked down its borders, it was hailed early in the pandemic as a success case, with comparatively few cases and fatalities. But poor planning in terms of securing enough vaccines and relying on one single vaccine eventually caused a crisis in its management of the pandemic. In March 2020, at the height of this criticism, Morrison invoked the "ANZAC spirit" and turned to military rhetoric, saying: "We are in a war against this virus and all Australians are enlisted to do the right thing."[48] State responses in Australia have seen certain communities targeted in lockdown measures more than others, with immigrants, Indigenous people and suburbs with low socioeconomic profiles overpoliced compared to more affluent suburbs. In late July 2021 as the Delta variant spread rapidly through Sydney, hundreds of soldiers were deployed to enforce the lockdown in the city's suburbs, in what former defense minister Peter Dutton called a "force multiplier" to increase police presence.[49] A year earlier, 1,000 army personnel were directed to the state of Victoria at the height of its outbreak and state of emergency.[50] Against intense criticism for its vaccine rollout failures, the Morrison government adopted a militarized solution by appointing Lieutenant-General John Frewen to head the taskforce overseeing the vaccine rollout and used army personnel in local responses to enforce lockdown measures. The (late) vaccination campaign urged Australians to "arm yourself" against the virus,[51] despite low supplies of vaccine and limited access to it.

From a critical perspective on security, COVID-19 has raised questions about "whose health is supposed to be secured by the global health security framework, and should we think about health in security terms at all?"[52] Moreover, thinking and speaking of the pandemic in militarized terms and war metaphors produces different types of behaviors and dispositions by states and their citizens. Caso notes that the normalization of post-9/11 surveillance, for example, should be a sign about how accepting (or not) publics are with regard to surveilling the pandemic or deploying the institutions of state authority, such as the police or the military, to manage the pandemic. Citizens can buy into the war rhetoric, stockpiling and hoarding, and seeing enemies that can threaten their health and existence,[53] rather than critically questioning why authorities have failed to contain the pandemic:

> The rhetoric of war against the coronavirus puts the blame for sickness and death onto an external invisible enemy, while masking that in fact our current political and economic system is at the basis of many of the health conditions that make us vulnerable to this virus.[54]

The resort to securitized measures can obscure preexisting inequalities and limit the available tools to deal with global pandemics, which have wider effects and impacts. For Andreas Papamichail, the nexus between health and security "obscures how security thinking and practices fundamentally enable and sustain these dynamics."[55]

Threat multipliers: increased insecurity in a pandemic world

The far-reaching effects of a global pandemic—although uneven in application and intensity—are many and varied, and we have probably not accounted for all its interconnectedness. In this sense, the pandemic serves as a key example of a threat multiplier—a form of insecurity that can exacerbate preexisting problems or produce new security issues in the macro and micro sense; often these threats are linked. First, the COVID-19 pandemic has shown us that the world can come to a standstill—during the pandemic, everything was affected, from the economy to our personal relations. Economic slowdown meant job losses, impacts on workers' rights, and heavier workload burdens for employees. At an individual level, mental health issues, domestic violence, poverty, and health sacrifices have caused insecurity for many. In terms of national security, states that retreated into protecting their own did so at the expense of others who had less power to shoulder the burden of the pandemic. Joanne Wallis and Henrietta McNeil demonstrate how the pandemic can be a threat multiplier in certain parts of the world, affecting different communities unevenly. The impact of COVID-19 in the Pacific shows the tensions between security and development in particular.[56] For those in conflict zones and already enduring hardships, the pandemic has been an additional source of insecurity—at these sites, access to healthcare, hospitals, and vaccines puts already precarious lives at further risk.

The inequalities of neoliberal capitalism in the context of the pandemic also determine the ways in which COVID acts as a threat multiplier. Economic inequality is a central component of critical approaches to security, and links directly to CSS's concern with emancipation. During the pandemic, poverty levels increased, as did the gap between rich and poor. Essential workers are largely from poorer backgrounds and in precarious employment, while middle-class workers could work from the safety of their homes. Economic insecurity has been exacerbated by the pandemic, with an estimated increase of 200–500 million people living in poverty while billionaires have seen their wealth grow.[57] The increased gap between the poor and the rich is likely to be a threat multiplier in various ways, impacting the availability of housing and healthcare, increased crime and violence, reduced life prospects, and further exploitation of employment conditions. Such impacts will have different effects in parts of the world where violence, conflict, and instability are already entrenched in society.

Similarly, there has been extensive debate about the extent to which climate change is connected to the outbreak of the pandemic. Scientists and researchers point to habitat destruction as a connection, bringing humans and animals in closer proximity, and global warming and natural disasters as further vectors for the spread of disease. Zoonotic spillover (where pathogens overcome natural barriers to infect other animal species) can be affected by climate change.[58] While the WHO states that there is no direct connection between climate change and COVID transmission, climate change could "indirectly" affect how we can respond to COVID due to "evidence of increasing human pressure on the natural environment [which] may drive disease emergence."[59]

Greater environmental instability can also lead to competition over resources and violence. While the pandemic can be identified as a threat multiplier for existing problems such as migration, climate change, poverty, and insecure governance, the question of how we can address those problems is further complicated when we turn to our traditional responses, which are often punitive and militarized. Here the vulnerabilities of supply lines, cooperation, and instability also threaten militarized responses and crisis management capabilities. When militaries are called upon to deal with pandemics and related issues such as climate change, they face additional pressures. These are already noted in terms of major security and defense challenges faced by the EU, US, and Australia, for example, not only in responding to the pandemic but also in dealing with preexisting security threats such as those anticipated from China.[60] Militarized approaches to managing the pandemic can also further entrench militarized responses to wider forms of insecurity, which has implications for civil society and power relations. Multilateralism is also seen to be jeopardized, with questions about governance and global leadership viewed as increasingly complex in an era of populism and pandemic.[61]

One of the most significant challenges in contending with critiques in the context of COVID-19 relates to misinformation and vested interests. Arguments about state overreach and authority have also produced at times contradictory narratives and ideas around what it means to be secure. In an era of populism and post-truth politics, opposition to public health measures to counter the spread of the virus has seen alternative narratives of danger and misinformation emerge. The rise of antivaccination groups and those who see health measures as an infringement of personal freedoms has been a key feature of the pandemic. Criticism of medical and health expertise has been a feature of both elites and ordinary people, with Trump, President Jair Bolsonaro of Brazil, and others characterizing the virus as either a myth or "harmless."[62] Different groups have spread misinformation online and organized large protests, which have been seen to be threat multipliers as many of these protests end up being "superspreader events" that increase the number of COVID cases. These divisions also exacerbate tensions in democracy, institutions, and levels of political trust, with societal divisions becoming starker and more fragmented.[63] This final point around misinformation and challenges to authority raises important questions for critical approaches to security: on the one hand, the pandemic has instigated a push by those in authority to exercise emergency measures to manage it, a move which many critical theorists would take issue with. Yet the shape and direction of this represents a more complex set of propositions, which the final section explores.

The purpose of "critical" security studies: imagining a post-COVID world

The pandemic has complicated our understanding of what it means to be secure. Normally, critical security scholars grapple with questions of state power and overreach, questioning metanarratives and truth claims, and offering a healthy skepticism toward emergency measures and powers. Yet the responses to the pandemic have produced strange bedfellows and conundrums. Without public health measures, there is no doubt that COVID would have spread beyond imaginable levels, making it impossible to control or manage. Health systems would be overwhelmed—indeed this is the case in many countries even with measures in place—and the weakest in society would bear the consequences.

While we should be concerned about militarized responses to the pandemic and the invocation of states of emergency, some of the ways in which this has played out must be seen in the context of growing divisions in recent years. The rise of populist politics, the spread of misinformation on social media and the internet, and the reemergence of the far right, signal a very different world from one where the "state of exception" was a major framing for critical perspectives on politics and security. In protest movements against public health measures, we see a cooption of ideas that once animated the push for greater human security and rights. Vaccine skepticism, "freedom of choice," and bodily autonomy have been appropriated to push back against government power. In the context of posttruth politics, questioning the reality of the virus has also featured. In February 2020, when COVID-19 was only beginning to be recognized as an emergency, Giorgio Agamben questioned its reality, calling the epidemic in Italy an "invention" and arguing that the media and Italian authorities were doing "their utmost to create a climate of panic, thus provoking a true state of exception, with severe limitations on movement and the suspension of daily life and work activities for entire regions."[64] He regarded government measures as a "real militarization" of specific sites of outbreaks, governed by a vague formula that could be applied and extended elsewhere. This would cement, in his view, a biopolitics of the state of exception: "[I]n a perverse vicious circle, the limitation of freedom imposed by governments is accepted in the name of a desire for safety, which has been created by the same governments who now intervene to satisfy it."[65]

While some supported Agamben's contention, there was also a strong refutation of his claims, especially as it became clear the virus was indeed very real, and the effects of not responding with lockdowns to contain its spread became starkly apparent in the USA, the UK, and elsewhere as cases reached thousands per day. Panagiotis Sotiris argued that, while China, because of its authoritarian form of governance, could address the pandemic more effectively than liberal democracies, where the individual and individual rights are centered, Agamben's binary of authoritarian biopolitics and freedom was too simple. Public health measures have been used to protect populations, and are important for vulnerable groups, particularly in the context of weakened public health infrastructures in advanced capitalist economies. Without this, bare life would "be closer to the pensioner on a waiting list for a respirator or an ICU bed, because of a collapsed health system, than the intellectual having to do with the practicalities of quarantine measures."[66]

How state power has been amplified and reasserted in response to the pandemic raises serious challenges for critical security thinking. As Bastian Vollmer points out, "the distinction between 'human security' and 'state security' has collapsed"[67] under the pandemic; borders are given a new normative status as positive measures to protect populations from the dangers of infection. Furthermore, the ability of states to control life and lives and use powerful tools to monitor and track populations, or exclude certain populations, requires careful critical attention. The use of surveillance technologies, for example, has differential meaning and effects depending on the communities and states that are its focus; as Sheena Chestnut Greitens argues, the use of such technologies in some democracies has had more impact on democratic institutions and norms than in others.[68]

While critical security studies has been at the forefront of unpacking and interrogating power, constructions of reality, and efforts to imagine a more secure world in the holistic rather than narrow statist sense, in recent years truth claims have become a contentious point in global discourses. More recently, critical theory has either been seen to be a failure in addressing phenomena such as the posttruth world or has in fact been accused of enabling it. But in this regard, the recovery of critical theory's purpose is being debated. Beate Jahn has recently argued that, rather than ushering in an era of "alternative facts," critical theory serves a vital purpose in challenging posttruth politics.[69] The narrative and framing of the pandemic as a particular kind of security problem (for instance, one that cements state authority and power, and denies individual freedoms) must also be open to critique; the emancipatory visions of some produce great insecurity for others. While critical security studies is concerned with challenging prevailing paradigms and power relations, where that challenge comes from and what drives it remain important.

Finally, the COVID-19 pandemic, despite calls for a "return to normal," provides an opportunity to rethink and reconfigure the world. The pandemic has also shed light on how we understand the human and human resilience as a "problematic fiction";[70] neoliberal forms of self-reliance have been dangerous to those who are already vulnerable. *Whose* human security matters and, moreover, the neoliberal emphasis on the interests of the individual that is part of this formulation does not capture how certain communities are based on social attachments rather than individualism; different societies are "resilient" in different ways and can challenge individualized forms of resilience central to the neoliberal understanding.[71] The fragility of capitalism and supply chains, unemployment, and changes to working life show that change is possible and current systems can be questioned and challenged.

What can critical approaches to security tell us about the possibilities of a post-COVID world? The emancipatory ambitions that are part of the CSS agenda provide an opportunity to think about a post-COVID world that is not a "return to normal." If anything, the global pandemic has shown many fault lines on which we need to focus in order to address underlying inequalities and hierarchies. Moreover, preexisting inequalities condition which responses to the pandemic are available. In the US and Australia, the very conditions that support structural inequalities were those that were upheld and protected in government responses. In Australia, no connection had been made with threat multipliers such as climate change and environmental destruction. Instead, the pandemic was interpreted as an opportunity to "defend resource nationalism and petro-masculinity in the face of the 'real' emergency—question marks over Australian fossil fuels' future created by the global turn to renewable energy."[72] In the US, public health measures were "received as posing an implicit limit on White desire."[73] According to Kevin Grove and colleagues, "[o]ne of the paradoxes of COVID-19 response is that the imperative to return to 'normal' typically entails reconstituting patterns of social, ecological, and environmental change that created the conditions for the pandemic and its uneven socio-spatial outcomes."[74]

Conclusion

Positionality and an ethical reflexivity must also figure in grappling with a pandemic that is constructed as "affecting us all" but does so in very different and uneven ways. While the default position on the pandemic is to return as quickly as possible to some state of normalcy—that is, to a pre-pandemic world—many argue that the pandemic presents an opportunity to rethink the world. This, as Annick Wibben reminds us, is an essential task of critical scholarship and political transformation, to "do security" in a way that reveals its political effects and opens new possibilities.[75] While numerous pressures revolve around the pandemic, with its interconnected issues and insecurities, a critical approach to security is important; its purpose, as Beate Jahn reminds us, in the vein of critical theory, lies in its "promise to create the space for political imagination."[76] If this is to be pursued, it is imperative to address the underlying conditions on which insecurity rests.

Notes

1. The Copenhagen School is associated with security as a speech act; and the Welsh School, inspired by the Frankfurt School, is concerned with emancipation and moving away from realism's focus on state security in military terms. The Paris School is associated with political theory and the sociology of policing and migration studies. It is important to note that this categorization can be a little misleading, as dialogue between and across these schools exists and they should not be seen in terms of location. See CASE Collective, "Critical Approaches to Security in Europe: A Networked Manifesto," *Security Dialogue* 37, no. 4 (2006): 444.
2. Richard Wyn Jones, *Security, Strategy, and Critical Theory* (Boulder, CO: Lynne Rienner, 1999).
3. Ken Booth, "Security and Emancipation," *Review of International Studies* 17, no. 4 (1991): 319.
4. David Mutimer, Kyle Grayson, and J. Marshall Beier, "*Critical Studies on Security*: An Introduction," *Critical Studies on Security* 1, no. 1 (2013): 3.
5. Ken Booth, *Theory of World Security* (Cambridge, England: Cambridge University Press, 2007).
6. Rens van Munster, "Book Reviews," *Cambridge Review of International Affairs* 21, no. 3 (2008): 437–50.
7. Samer Abboud et al., "Towards a Beirut School of Critical Security Studies," *Critical Studies on Security* 6, no. 3 (2018): 273–95. See also the controversial debates within International Relations regarding Alison Howell and Melanie Richter-Montpetit's coauthored article that asked if securitization theory was racist and Ole Wæver and Barry

Buzan's response: Alison Howell and Melanie Richter-Montpetit, "Is Securitization Theory Racist? Civilizationism, Methodological Whiteness, and Antiblack Thought in the Copenhagen School," *Security Dialogue* 51, no. 1 (2020): 3–22; Ole Wæver and Barry Buzan, "Racism and Responsibility: The Critical Limits of Deepfake Methodology in Security Studies—A Reply to Howell and Richter-Montpetit," *Security Dialogue* 51, no. 4 (2020): 386–94.

8. Mohammed Ayoob, "Defining Security: A Subaltern Realist Perspective," in *Critical Security Studies: Concepts and Cases*, ed. Keith Krause and Michael C. Williams (Minneapolis: University of Minnesota Press, 1997), 121–46; in the context of securitization theory, see also Claire Wilkinson, "The Copenhagen School on Tour in Kyrgyzstan: Is Securitization Theory Useable outside Europe?" *Security Dialogue* 38, no. 1 (2007): 5–25.
9. Nik Hynek and David Chandler, "No Emancipatory Alternative, No Critical Security Studies," *Critical Studies on Security* 1, no. 1 (2013): 47–8.
10. Pinar Bilgin, "The Continuing Appeal of Critical Security Studies," in *Critical Theory in International Relations and Security Studies: Interviews and Reflections*, ed. Shannon Brincat, Laura Lima, and João Nunes (Abingdon, England: Routledge, 2012), 161.
11. Hynek and Chandler, "No Emancipatory Alternative"; Christopher S. Browning and Matt McDonald, "The Future of Critical Security Studies: Ethics and the Politics of Security," *European Journal of International Relations* 19, no. 2 (2013): 235–55.
12. Michael C. Williams and Keith Krause, "Preface: Toward Critical Security Studies," in *Critical Security Studies: Concepts and Cases*, ed. Keith Krause and Michael C. Williams (London: UCL Press, 1997), x.
13. CASE Collective, "Critical Approaches," 447.
14. Ibid., 476.
15. Mark B. Salter (ed.) et al., "Horizon Scan: Critical Security Studies for the Next 50 Years," *Security Dialogue* 50, no. 4 supplement (2019): 9–37.
16. Stefan Elbe, *Security and Global Health* (Cambridge, England: Polity, 2010); Adam Ferhani and Simon Rushton, "The International Health Regulations, COVID-19, and Bordering Practices: Who Gets In, What Gets Out, and Who Gets Rescued?" *Contemporary Security Policy* 41, no. 3 (2020): 458–77.
17. Mike Wright et al., "State Capitalism in International Context: Varieties and Variations," *Journal of World Business* 56, no. 2 (2021): 101160.
18. Shahar Hameiri, "COVID-19: Time to Bring Back the State," *Progress in Political Economy* (blog), March 19, 2020, https://www.ppesydney.net/covid-19-time-to-bring-back-the-state/ (accessed February 16, 2022); see also Miloš Šumonja, "Neoliberalism Is Not Dead—On Political Implications of Covid-19," Capital & Class 45, no. 2 (2021): 215–27; João Nunes, "The COVID-19 Pandemic: Securitization, Neoliberal Crisis, and Global Vulnerabilization," *Cadernos de Saúde Pública* 36, no. 5 (2020):

e00063120; Matthew Sparke and Owain David Williams, "Neoliberal Disease: COVID-19, Co-pathogenesis and Global Health Insecurities," *Environment and Planning A: Economy and Space* 54, no. 1 (2022): 15–32.

19. Sarah Boseley, "US Secures World Stock of Key Covid-19 Drug Remdesivir," *The Guardian*, June 30, 2020, https://www.theguardian.com/us-news/2020/jun/30/us-buys-up-world-stock-of-key-covid-19-drug (accessed February 16, 2022).
20. Ewen Callaway, "The Unequal Scramble for Coronavirus Vaccines—by the Numbers," *Nature* 584, no. 7822 (2020): 506–7, https://doi.org/10.1038/d41586-020-02450-x (accessed April 20, 2022).
21. Tedros Adhanom Ghebreyesus, "WHO Director-General's Opening Remarks at the Media Briefing on COVID-19—18 August 2020," WHO, August 18, 2020, https://www.who.int/director-general/speeches/detail/who-director-general-s-opening-remarks-at-the-media-briefing-on-covid-19---18-august-2020 (accessed April 20, 2022).
22. "COVID-19 Vaccination 'Wildly Uneven and Unfair': UN Secretary-General," UN News, February 17, 2021, https://news.un.org/en/story/2021/02/1084962 (accessed April 6, 2022).
23. Eric Otieno Sumba, "Necropolitics at Large: Pandemic Politics and the Coloniality of the Global Access Gap," *Critical Studies on Security* 9, no. 1 (2021): 51.
24. Ibid., 49.
25. Caitlin Cassidy, "Australia Has Delivered Just 8% of Covid Vaccinations Promised to Developing Nations," *The Guardian*, October 22, 2021, https://www.theguardian.com/australia-news/2021/oct/22/australia-has-delivered-just-8-of-covid-vaccinations-promised-to-developing-nations (accessed February 16, 2022).
26. Melissa Coade, "Questions as to Whether COVAX Is Benefiting Wealthy Countries like Australia over Developing Nations," *The Mandarin*, August 17, 2021, https://www.themandarin.com.au/166058-questions-as-to-whether-covax-is-benefiting-wealthy-countries-like-australia-over-developing-nations/ (accessed February 16, 2022).
27. Marise Payne and Alex Hawke, "Partnering with Our Neighbours to Respond to COVID-19," joint media release, 29 May 2020, https://www.foreignminister.gov.au/minister/marise-payne/media-release/partnering-our-neighbours-respond-covid-19; Angela Clare, "Australia's Foreign Aid Budget 2020–21," Parliament of Australia, https://www.aph.gov.au/About_Parliament/Parliamentary_Departments/Parliamentary_Library/pubs/rp/BudgetReview202021/AustraliasForeignAidBudget (both accessed February 16, 2022).
28. Benjamin Mueller and Rebecca Robbins, "'COVAX Hasn't Failed but It Is Failing': Global Vaccine Drive Struggles to Compete," *Sydney Morning Herald*, August 3, 2021, https://www.smh.com.au/world/africa/covax-hasn-t-failed-but-it-is-failing-global-vaccine-drive-struggles-to-compete-20210803-p58fc8.html (accessed February 16, 2022).

29. Ibid.
30. "Limited Covid Vaccines for Poor Countries until 2023," Economist Intelligence Unit, January 27, 2021, https://www.eiu.com/n/85-poor-countries-will-not-have-access-to-coronavirus-vaccines/ (accessed February 16, 2022).
31. "World Has Entered Stage of 'Vaccine Apartheid'—WHO Head," Reuters, May 17, 2021, https://www.reuters.com/business/healthcare-pharmaceuticals/world-has-entered-stage-vaccine-apartheid-who-head-2021-05-17/ (accessed February 16, 2022).
32. "Countries Obstructing COVID-19 Patent Waiver Must Allow Negotiations," press release, Médecins Sans Frontières, March 9, 2021, https://www.msf.org/countries-obstructing-covid-19-patent-waiver-must-allow-negotiations; Sam Meredith, "Rich Countries Are Refusing to Waive the Rights on Covid Vaccines as Global Cases Hit Record Levels," CNBC, April 22, 2021, https://www.cnbc.com/2021/04/22/covid-rich-countries-are-refusing-to-waive-ip-rights-on-vaccines.html (both accessed February 16, 2022).
33. Martina Tazzioli, "'Stay Safe, Stay Away, and Put Face Masks On'—The Hygienic-Sanitary Borders of Covid-19," Political Economy Research Centre blog, September 21, 2020, https://www.perc.org.uk/project_posts/stay-safe-stay-away-and-put-face-masks-on-the-hygienic-sanitary-borders-of-covid-19/ (accessed February 16, 2022).
34. Ibid.
35. Umut Ozguc, "Three Lines of Pandemic Borders: From Necropolitics to Hope as a Method of Living," *Critical Studies on Security* 9, no. 1 (2021): 64.
36. Tazzioli, "'Stay Safe.'"
37. Jessica Kirk and Matt McDonald, "The Politics of Exceptionalism: Securitization and COVID-19," *Global Studies Quarterly* 1, no. 3 (2021): ksab024.
38. "Australia's India Ban Criticised as 'Racist' Rights Breach," BBC News, May 3, 2021, https://www.bbc.com/news/world-australia-56967520 (accessed February 16, 2022).
39. Chengxin Pan, "Racialised Politics of (In)Security and the COVID-19 Westfailure," *Critical Studies on Security* 9, no. 1 (2021): 40.
40. Ibid.
41. Colin McInnes, "The Many Meanings of Health Security," in *Routledge Handbook of Global Health Security*, ed. Simon Rushton and Jeremy Youde (Abingdon, England: Routledge, 2014), 8.
42. Ibid.
43. Fawzia Gibson-Fall, "Military Responses to COVID-19, Emerging Trends in Global Civil-Military Engagements," *Review of International Studies* 47, no. 2 (2021): 166.
44. Ibid., 170.
45. Federica Caso, "Are We at War? The Rhetoric of War in the Coronavirus Pandemic," *The Disorder of Things* (blog), April 10, 2020,

https://thedisorderofthings.com/2020/04/10/are-we-at-war-the-rhetoric-of-war-in-the-coronavirus-pandemic/ (accessed February 16, 2022).

46. Cailtin Oprysko and Susannah Luthi, "Trump Labels Himself 'a Wartime President' Combating Coronavirus," *Politico*, March 18, 2020, https://www.politico.com/news/2020/03/18/trump-administration-self-swab-coronavirus-tests-135590 (accessed February 16, 2022).
47. Aamna Mohdin, "Pots, Pans, Passion: Britons Clap Their Support for NHS Workers Again," *The Guardian*, April 2, 2020, https://www.theguardian.com/world/2020/apr/02/pots-pans-passion-britons-clap-their-support-for-nhs-workers-again (accessed February 16, 2022).
48. Amy Haddad, "Metaphorical Militarisation: Covid-19 and the Language of War," *The Strategist*, May 13, 2020, https://www.aspistrategist.org.au/metaphorical-militarisation-covid-19-and-the-language-of-war/ (accessed February 16, 2022).
49. Alison Xiao, "Army to Begin Patrolling Sydney COVID Hotspots to Help Police Enforce Lockdown Rules," ABC News (Australia), July 30, 2021, https://www.abc.net.au/news/2021-07-30/adf-soldiers-to-arrive-in-sydney-covid19-lockdown/100336124 (accessed February 16, 2022).
50. "Coronavirus: Australia Sends 1,000 Army Personnel to Victoria to Fight Outbreak," BBC News, June 25, 2020, https://www.bbc.com/news/world-australia-53174827 (accessed February 16, 2022).
51. Stuart Ralph and Mark Stoové, "Using Military Language and Presence Might Not Be the Best Approach to COVID and Public Health," *The Conversation*, August 17, 2021, http://theconversation.com/using-military-language-and-presence-might-not-be-the-best-approach-to-covid-and-public-health-166019 (accessed February 16, 2022).
52. Andreas Papamichail, "COVID-19 and the Limits of the Health-Security Nexus," in Giovanni Agostinis et al., "Forum: COVID-19 and IR Scholarship: One Profession, Many Voices," *International Studies Review* 23, no. 2 (2021): 304.
53. Caso, "Are We at War?"
54. Ibid.
55. Papamichail, "COVID-19 and the Limits of the Health-Security Nexus," 304.
56. Joanne Wallis and Henrietta McNeill, "The Implications of COVID-19 for Security in the Pacific Islands," *Round Table* 110, no. 2 (2021): 203–16.
57. "COVID Has Worsened Inequality Even as the Rich Thrive: Oxfam," Al Jazeera, January 25, 2021, https://www.aljazeera.com/economy/2021/1/25/covid-19-worsened-global-inequality-even-as-the-rich-bounced-back (accessed February 16, 2022).
58. Xavier Rodó et al., "Changing Climate and the COVID-19 Pandemic: More than Just Heads or Tails," *Nature Medicine* 27, no. 4 (2021): 576–9.

59. "Coronavirus Disease (COVID-19): Climate Change," World Health Organization, April 22, 2020, https://www.who.int/news-room/q-a-detail/coronavirus-disease-covid-19-climate-change (accessed February 16, 2022).
60. Christoph Meyer, Martin Bricknell, and Ramon Pacheco Pardo, *How the COVID-19 Crisis Has Affected Security and Defence-Related Aspects of the EU: In Depth Analysis* (Brussels: European Parliament, 2021).
61. "In Defence of a Renewed Multilateralism to Address the COVID-19 Pandemic and Other Global Challenges: Report" (Geneva: OHCHR, 2021), https://www.ohchr.org/EN/Issues/IntOrder/Pages/covid19-multilateralism.aspx (accessed February 16, 2022).
62. Christine Agius, Annika Bergman Rosamond, and Catarina Kinnvall, "Populism, Ontological Insecurity and Gendered Nationalism: Masculinity, Climate Denial and Covid-19," *Politics, Religion & Ideology* 21, no. 4 (2020): 432–50.
63. Brent J. Steele, "Nowhere to Run To, Nowhere to Hide: Inescapable Dread in the 2020s," *Journal of International Relations and Development* 24, 1037–43 (2021); Matthew Flinders, "Democracy and the Politics of Coronavirus: Trust, Blame and Understanding," *Parliamentary Affairs* 74, no. 2 (2021): 483–502.
64. Giorgio Agamben, "The State of Exception Provoked by an Unmotivated Emergency," *Positions Politics* (blog), February 26, 2020, https://positionspolitics.org/giorgio-agamben-the-state-of-exception-provoked-by-an-unmotivated-emergency/ (accessed February 16, 2022).
65. Ibid.
66. Panagiotis Sotiris, "Against Agamben: Is a Democratic Biopolitics Possible?" *Critical Legal Thinking* (blog), March 14, 2020, https://criticallegalthinking.com/2020/03/14/against-agamben-is-a-democratic-biopolitics-possible/ (accessed February 16, 2022).
67. Bastian A. Vollmer, *Borders Revisited: Discourses on the UK Border* (Cham, Switzerland: Palgrave Macmillan, 2021), 118.
68. Sheena Chestnut Greitens, "Surveillance, Security, and Liberal Democracy in the Post-COVID World," *International Organization* 74, no. S1 (2020): E169–E190.
69. Beate Jahn, "Critical Theory in Crisis? A Reconsideration," *European Journal of International Relations* 27, no. 4 (2021): 1274–99.
70. David Chandler, "Coronavirus and the End of Resilience," *E-International Relations*, March 25, 2020, https://www.e-ir.info/2020/03/25/opinion-coronavirus-and-the-end-of-resilience/ (accessed February 16, 2022).
71. Wallis and McNeill, "The Implications of COVID-19."
72. Kevin Grove at al., "The Uneven Distribution of Futurity: Slow Emergencies and the Event of COVID-19," *Geographical Research* 60, no. 1 (2022): 7.
73. Ibid., 7.

74. Ibid., 11.
75. Annick T. R. Wibben, "Opening Security: Recovering Critical Scholarship as Political," *Critical Studies on Security* 4, no. 2 (2016): 137.
76. Jahn, "Critical Theory in Crisis?" 18.

2

Traditional Approaches and Security: Rethinking Power and Uncertainty

Adam Bartley

Introduction

This chapter considers the ongoing discussion between the two traditional approaches to security—realism and neoliberalism—and the insights gained from the challenges of US-China great power rivalry and the COVID-19 pandemic. In the post-9/11 security account of international relations the focus has been increasingly on the role of nonstate actors, the prevalence of globalization, and the rise of nontraditional security challenges. These trends have also promulgated critical security approaches, widening and deepening the debate on security and on the important questions of what is to be securitized, how security is to be defined, and under what ontological framework.[1] In some ways these questions have involved a presumptive and concomitant weakening of the traditional approaches. In others, they have precipitated a critical rethinking of the practical, conceptual, and theoretical implications of the state. The strides in these areas have in some cases been profound, but the assertion that the critical approaches have replaced the authority of the state and the value of the traditional approaches, the chapter argues, has been oversold.

The suggestion that we now inhabit what the German sociologist Ulrich Beck has called a "world risk society" explains part of this argument. As scientists, politicians, and observers try to make sense of the prevailing social media misinformation climate, great power competition, ethnic conflict, and technological decoupling, among many other uncertainties in the twenty-first century, the trends toward disruption and insecurity seem vast. Writing in 1998, Beck called this phenomenon a "reflexive modernization." Greater individual uncertainties in health, economics, and security were driving a questioning of the foundations of society and subsequently the eruption of new social movements, popular political trends, nativism, and a rejection of authority—implying in many ways the decline of traditional assumptions.[2] These arguments remain unconvincing. What is evident rather is that the significance of the state in risk analyses, along with a declining trust in institutions, norms, and narratives, has once again begun to trend despite the overwhelming challenges of nontraditional insecurities.

While not a main focus of this chapter, it is necessary to mention the February 2022 Russian invasion of Ukraine on this point, and its potential to exacerbate numerous insecurities around nuclear weapons, refugee crises, war crimes, disinformation campaigns, and nationalism (among others). It is clear that, even as the crisis develops, the ability to resolve the many challenges must begin with the state, starting with the end of conflict. The various arguments examined in this chapter bear directly upon the real-time crisis enveloping Ukraine and international relations in 2022.

In looking back, at least over the past two decades, scholars note that the challenges to security promised in the form of climate change, and of human security more generally, have not prompted a move toward more protections for people or more international cooperation in mitigating disasters.[3] Few theorists, with perhaps the exception of realists, some have charged, had prepared their readers for the populist backlash against immigrants and immigration, the rise in the new cynicism concerning human rights, and the ideological attachment to the state above and beyond economic and political self-interest.[4] As we come to terms with the 'pandemic age' of COVID-19 and, more significantly, the syndemic (concerning the biological and social interactions between conditions and states) implications associated with new and uncertain pathogens, the call for new interest and innovations in the traditional approaches has grown.

Indeed, for some, the explanatory power of the traditional approaches had never truly disappeared. Rather, the exceptional period of liberal expansion and cooperation following the Cold War allowed governments and theorists to experiment more broadly, giving rise to the proposition that an international system transcending the state was plausible.[5] For others, over at least the past two decades an increasing connectedness has bounded nations with the dilemma of having to face various threatening headwinds, while also redefining the role of the state and dealing with fragmentation. Still others, remarking on the emerging challenge illustrated in the return to great power politics, have called for an end to the liberal enterprise and a return to a more realpolitik basis for policy as the only means to assure a stabilizing of international order and security.

The aim here is not to recount the former battles between the traditional approaches in explaining the actions and reactions of states to certain phenomena. Rather, the chapter seeks to tease out the subtle changes to and new acceptances of the realist and liberal traditions as scholars try to explain the rise of great power competition and security in an era of COVID-19. On this point, it highlights the definitive roles of power and uncertainty in the assessments of these security challenges.

Conceptually, the chapter adopts a broad approach to defining realism, focusing on core assumptions rather than on taxonomical divisions as expressed in offensive, defensive, or classical varieties. This is done for two reasons, the first being that except for a few differences in questions on power and security maximization and morality, they mostly share overlapping claims. These include the significance of power distribution, the role of the state, the nature of anarchy, the focus on survival, and the prevalence of selfish and zero-sum behaviors.[6] The second reason is that the renewed interest in realism, with a recent surge in the neoclassical and classical forms, highlights the need to address shortcomings in the narrower application of assumptions, particularly as they apply to the role of ideas and movements.[7]

Neoliberal institutionalism, like realism, belongs to a broad church with many overlapping logics between the different liberal subsets.[8] At a fundamental level, proponents view the search for a workable peace as evident in the growth of tolerance, conflict resolution, and the respect for rights, obligations, and rules. As the further growth in economic interdependencies, liberal international institutions, and legal authorities occurs, the more the question of survival fades and is supplanted in the interest of material well-being and social mobility.[9] Under this rubric, liberal policies, grand strategies, and forms of international cooperation can work to socially engineer not just the nation-state, but also the world through institutions designed to make conflict unthinkable or at the very least prohibitively expensive. On this basis, liberalism incorporates the assumptions that the anarchic international system is the driving factor of behavior, and that states are the primary unit of analysis.[10]

Why traditional approaches still matter

The debate between the traditional approaches and its critics has ebbed and flowed over the decades. For the most part, the challenges to liberal and realist applications have often taken place in response to international events, such as the collapse of the Berlin Wall or 9/11, though occasionally innovations in theoretical and conceptual domains have accelerated new debates. For those observing the end of the Cold War and the transition to humanitarian intervention and the rise of "new wars," the logics of self-help, zero-sum, and balance-of-power politics seemed anachronistic. By the 1990s, Robert Jervis was to observe that realism seemed out of date.[11] Meanwhile, the case for liberalism was only beginning to catch up. The explosion of civil society groups, the rise in international agreements, and economic linkages led many to suggest that the fear of anarchy could be ameliorated by increasing levels of cooperation.[12] Others talked about a democratic peace theory and the end of wars as liberalism spread more widely, led by the European Union as the lodestar of integration.

Yet, many continued to critique the traditional approaches as too narrow in their focus on the state. In the post-9/11 era, scholars turned to new paradigms to account for the more ethical, human dimensions of security.[13] In other words, the greater threat often came from internal conflicts, often underpinned by hunger and disease. These paradigms called for reversing the equation of people supporting the state to one of states supporting the people.[14] Indeed, for some, the greater threat was the state itself, which could not seem to meet the more systemic challenges of environmental or climate security, among other nontraditional threats. While states signed up to the Millennium Development Goals, they mostly continued in a fashion seemingly ignorant of the causes of impoverishment and exploitation which were highly correlated with the failures of a state-centered system. Still others called attention to the role of failed states and the emerging significance of terrorism to draw greater connective tissue between globalization, anarchy, and governance.[15]

To be sure, the state has never been too far from the considerations of the human security and globalization paradigms. Theorists, according to Jervis, were unlikely to abandon all of realism's assumptions in the pursuit of "highly productive theories" or for that matter start from their opposites.[16] The emergence of the pandemic and the return to great power politics, at any rate, engendered a reinvigoration of the traditional approaches, sprouting attempts to capture actor behavior under new and seemingly more complex conditions. Some have gone as far as to call the twenty-first century the age of realism, underscoring the rise of "whatever it takes" policies in the defense of the national interest.[17] The invasion of Ukraine by Russia, the cause for which has been, blatantly, a grab for controlling power in Ukraine, has certainly reinforced such perceptions. Meanwhile, in the actions of both Beijing and Washington, a cavalier attitude to others has led to a deep divide in international efforts to meet the challenge of the pandemic, fight together for climate change mitigation, and join in treaties for disarmament.

Others call for new scholarship addressing the interactions between states and the emergence of new infectious diseases. Tiago Correia and Karen Willis, for instance, call for a more critical realist take on the distinction between reality and cognition, particularly as the emerging science of syndemics becomes more critical for treatment and health policy both globally and domestically.[18] Similarly, calls have been made for greater interest in the "softer" positivist approaches to better understand the role of ideas and material interests in the examination of security.[19]

By contrast, the case for a liberal approach to security for many has broken down on several fronts, not least through the difficulties of the pandemic. Not simply have the major actors signaled their contempt for a multilateral approach to addressing security challenges, giving only "a suboptimal amount of attention," writes Damjan Krnjevic Miskovic. Their ability to commit to working in concert toward a more agreeable framework for a workable international system has fallen short even on the fundamental issues of human rights, gender, climate change, and war, among others.[20] For Miskovic, liberal nations continue to remain wedded to an "end of history" *Weltanschauung*, blinding them to the conditions that have brought about the return to great power politics. Meanwhile, challengers to the Western liberal traditions have failed to provide an alternative arrangement whereby the guardrails to anarchy can be firmly established and so conflict avoided.

For some at least, the adoption by institutions of a neoliberal economic framework over time weakened the authority and therefore legitimacy of global institutions as economies crumbled under multiple crises. For Michael Zürn, international actors, particularly after 2008, began to adopt policies and measures that were by nature counterinstitutional in their outlook, as broader international institutional ideals and ideas began to erode.[21] Others have attributed this erosion to an institutional gridlock, where more international actors and a greater heterogeneity of interests have made cooperation on security challenges more diffuse. On this point, even optimists cautioned the prospects for cooperation. While there are avenues "beyond gridlock," David Held was to observe, these may only be partial and will be in some way subject to the role of great powers and their interests in the provision of public goods.[22]

Others, such as Stephen Walt and John J. Mearsheimer, bring attention to the failure of the liberal hegemonic enterprise more specifically, arguing that a return to a more realist setting in foreign policy must now occur given that the constraints of multipolarity have become more acute.[23] The problem is not simply that economic integration and international institutions have failed to transcend the self-help, zero-sum nature of the international system, but that the liberal democratic appeal has eroded more broadly as a result. "US efforts to address important regional problems have repeatedly failed," observes Walt, where "existing global institutions are visibly fraying, and terrorism and nuclear weapons have spread despite extensive US efforts to contain them."[24] Echoing the sentiments of E. H. Carr, both Walt and Mearsheimer charged proponents of the liberal hegemonic project with focusing too keenly on the "shoulds" and "oughts" of international relations in the face of a reality generally distinct from broader liberal principles.[25]

On practice, power, and uncertainty amid COVID and US-China competition

What becomes clear in surveying the shortcomings of the traditional approaches, and indeed more so as we come to the topic of COVID-19 and renewed great power politics, is that the need to define the relationships between power, uncertainty, and practice is acute. If we accept the claim that "theory is always for someone and some purpose," then we must accept the problem-solving case for theory and its utility in practice—and not solely as a value-free theory.[26] My attempt here is to further deepen the interparadigmatic debate and, simultaneously, draw attention to the need to strengthen theoretical and conceptual tools in the traditional approaches. Power and politics in practice make this cause more pertinent. As Stephen Walt exclaims, radical transformations in international orders rarely occur and certainly not in neat theoretical vacuums. Dwelling on ideal possibilities may attract adherents; indeed, politicians find considerable value in trafficking in their high-sounding promises. In reality, identifying an effective course of action often precludes a critical evaluation of what is, what can be done, and what sources of power can be employed to make it happen.[27] What conceptual tools, then, are more useful in explaining responses to the pandemic and US-China relations?

The first concern here is power. Power is central to the study of security yet there is no agreement on how to define it or even operationalize it in a useful sense. For realists, the distribution of power in a state of anarchy is the key to understanding relations and therefore actions with regard to a particular threat. Because states can never be certain about the intentions of others, they will seek security and power, often at the expense and insecurity of others.[28] This is a simplistic formula, to be sure, but there is purpose in simplicity, particularly as it equates with diffuse concepts of power and practice, as discussed below. This is not to say, however, that the logic is seamless or that definitions do not often overlap. Power as a concept is contextual. Definitions may vary in understanding and use, even by the same theorist—thus underscoring that the case for being critical and empirical is still strong.[29]

Writing in 1964 at the height of the Cold War, Kalevi Holsti cautioned against narrowing definitions to one-dimensional units of causation. He conceived that power must be a means to an end, but that it also include capabilities, relationships, and processes, and that it can also be quantifiable.[30] In 2022, despite the obvious absence of the Cold War, we are no nearer to agreeing upon these polymorphous dimensions, even as we have learned more about the "complexities" or "paradoxes" of them.[31] Discussion of "hard" and "soft"[32] forms, later to be joined by "sharp," "useful,"[33] and "protean"[34] counterparts, has permeated the wider theoretical debate on security, expanding across different epistemological and ontological domains as a means to fill logic gaps in the explanation of actor behaviors. Where once these conceptual paradigms complicated the definitional space of "power"—particularly as it occurred for liberals and constructivists—this is no longer as troubling as once imagined. Rather, as Michael Barnett and Raymond Duvall illustrate, scholars are increasingly required to "work with multiple conceptions of power" if they are to avoid conceptual myopia; "to understand power means to understand its various forms." [35]

How then do we understand the varying forms of power at the intersection of great power competition and the COVID-19 pandemic? In terms of US-China strategic competition, there seems to be no doubt that material capabilities have captured much of the attention of observers, particularly in the United States, as the calibrations of American military might are weighed against China's growing naval prowess.[36] One reason for this is that capabilities and resources, in contrast to other notions of influence, control, or even soft power, offer a degree of measurability. Security experts can gauge the competition's strength and determine the probability of attack, making suggestions on the potential use of weapons, systems, or assets to respond. For realists, such calculations derive meaning in relative terms, since states seeking to optimize security need to know what forms of power are deficient or needed, and where. While useful, there are two cautions to this assessment. The first is the predilection for analysts to measure capabilities based on gross indicators—military spending, gross domestic product, composite indicator of national capability—without accounting for net domestic costs. As Michael Beckley states, the result is that measurements can easily and systemically exaggerate capabilities, especially of large-population countries, leading to misinterpretations about intentions.[37] The second is that by concentrating attention on states and their capabilities as the main power units, the search for security ends up becoming excessively competitive—feeding a calculus that ultimately becomes "endlessly self-perpetuating."[38]

Liberal institutionalists to some degree avoid this claim by augmenting the role of institutions and interdependence. With the help of game theory and Robert Axelrod's seminal examination of cooperation under the prisoner's dilemma, neoliberals drew attention to power as a form of socialization under conditions of mutual learning—where over time cooperation in the interest of increasing gains defines the trade-offs to spending on ever-increasing security platforms.[39] Power, then, can also be defined as the ability to shape international politics in line with one's interests and without the anxiety created by a sole reliance on military capabilities. For those looking for empirical legitimization, these forms of power were found to be difficult to systemically observe, not the least since "doing so would require parsing each country's interest in, and influence over, a potentially infinite number of international events."[40] What's more, the ability to measure power could only take place by evaluating outcomes, causing such denominations of power to lose their utility since the observer has to wait for the event, in lieu of preparing for it. Power as an amorphous object, then, makes it harder to operationalize in a more practical sense, but it also suffers from normative deficiencies as patterns of behavior are difficult to evaluate without regularity. This forms part of the difficulty in crediting claims that China's past behavior speaks to its benign intentions and not to any desire for regional hegemonic control, or that power in the context of what Rush Doshi calls "forms of control" (coercion, consent, and legitimacy) can play a definitive role in revising international order.[41] Until it happens, how do we know?

The second concern, then, is the environment of uncertainty which pervades questions of cooperation or competition in security terms. Will China use its impressive military capabilities for good and not conquest? Can we trust health institutions like the World Health Organization (WHO) to deliver timely information and so mitigate an international pandemic? Is the Belt and Road Initiative (BRI) a force for good and not debt diplomacy? These questions seem somewhat redundant in retrospect, but they are critical questions that are evaluated time and again. COVID-19 is not going to be the last pandemic, China's military modernization is still expanding, the BRI is an unparalleled development tool, but it does not adhere to time-tested methods of transparency and lending practice. These questions are also taking place at a time of great technological change and amid the weakening of norms and institutions, meaning that an existential uncertainty increasingly defines the strategic rationality of states.[42]

How do we understand the obvious security implications of these uncertainties? There is no easy answer to this question. For some, traditional security concerns have failed to explain actors' reactions to uncertainties provided by nontraditional security threats, in part because they fail to account for threats endogenous to the structure of the international system.[43] For instance, should China's initial obfuscation of the nature of COVID-19—perhaps leading to the internationalization of the contagion—be assessed on the basis of intentions (based on capabilities) or on the domestic insecurities threatening the authority and legitimacy of the Communist Party? Which power here is more important, political legitimization or national military assets? Realists have trouble with these questions in part because they fail to explain domestic sources of power. Others, such as constructivists, have more leeway in questioning the nature of uncertainty, not just in terms of understanding intentions, but also in determining how to understand the information or signals provided.[44] For instance, we can say it makes little sense to exacerbate a pandemic to the point of world contagion since the forces of Chinese legitimacy are also impacted by economic factors which would be affected by a pandemic-induced supply chain crisis.[45] If we accept that threats to security can also come from within, and shape actions from without, then we must broaden the framework to assess intentions for fear of misinterpreting decisions made for other reasons entirely.

This is a necessary proposition since for realists the considered objectivity of realism's assumptions provides a seemingly easy clarity to understanding uncertainty as a problem that can be simply fixed by gaining more information about the other's intentions.[46] Constructivists are accused of questioning uncertainty and information too broadly, "mak[ing] them less certain about how to respond."[47] For realists, there is certainty in the definition of uncertainty and in the actions required to reduce the insecurity produced by ambiguity. Because states have offensive capabilities and because their intentions can never be guaranteed, anything short of full transparency must be considered suspect.[48] For liberals, this problem of uncertainty is ameliorated by the role of institutions and state interconnectedness; the more linkages there are, the more information is available and thus the less an actor is able to destabilize a critical event, for the principle of surprise is gone. But what happens when the institutions have been compromised by state capture, such as Trump's accusation about the WHO?[49] What happens when states do not participate in information exchange?

In the context of great power competition and COVID-19, discernibly, we need to ask to what extent these assumptions of power prove true and to what extent uncertainty impacts decisions in a complex environment. When the Trump administration published its National Security Strategy in 2017 it very deliberately announced a strategic shift from engagement to competition with China. While this was not a whole-of-society disengagement, it was one in which the sources of Chinese and American capabilities were specifically targeted, producing policies affecting defense spending, cooperation on arms control, alliance partnerships, and decisions about commercial technological transfers, trade, and intellectual property—in other words, the critical units of measurable power. In 2018, the Trump administration further plunged the liberal entanglement thesis into disarray when it unleashed a trade war, albeit on the basis of a faulty economic rationale.[50] What are the sources of these decisions? America's measurement of China's resource capabilities indicated they were significant, to be sure. But the process of learning was also necessarily impactful. The shift toward competition was in no small way justified on the basis that China had failed to integrate and engage in norms of appropriateness. China's ascension to the World Trade Organization in 2000 and its subsequent growth in global trade networks, Elbridge Colby and Wess Mitchell have argued, did not change its discriminatory economic practices so much as reinforce them.[51] Meanwhile, engaging China in regional institutions and assimilating it within the world's key security forums failed to lessen disagreements on security. The Trump administration's justification then was that the US must adjust its own policies to reflect China's actions—indeed its failure to assimilate. The decisions of the Trump administration, as illustrated by the National Security Strategy and other documents, were accumulatively the product of estimates of Chinese measurable powers and both process and social agency.[52]

What can be said of the neoliberal approach? There are sufficient grounds to suggest that even with emerging forms of competition the critical role of institutions and liberal market mechanisms provides a powerful incentive to cooperate over the long term. After all, so the notion is often heard, China's growth could not have been facilitated without the international liberal economic and political institutions in place that were critical to its opening up. For liberals, China's leaders are likely to view a retention of such institutional linkages as counterproductive and even a direct threat to the Communist Party's governing position since enhanced competition and rivalry will force a dissipation of economic gains.[53] That these gains are critical to the legitimacy of the Party's governing regime will ensure the institutions will remain in some form not indifferent to their liberal beginnings.[54] There is some validity to this claim. The rise of an authoritarian alternative to liberal hegemony has not culminated in a concomitant rise in authoritarian institutions. Additionally, the retreat of American liberalism with the Trump administration's hostility to international trade agreements did not lead to a breakdown so much as an increase in their significance. To the contrary, China's paramount leader traveled to the World Economic Forum in January 2017 to reinforce China's commitment, followed in succeeding years by the signing of the Regional Comprehensive Economic Partnership and a commitment to joining the Comprehensive and Progressive Agreement for Trans-Pacific Partnership—the successor to the Trans-Pacific Partnership, which Trump had pulled out of.[55]

Of course, the emergence of COVID-19 has complicated the liberal arguments on the power of integration. Despite the global dimensions of the pandemic, states have turned to self-reinforcing and self-centered responses, seemingly multiplying existing power struggles on the global stage. The WHO's inability to contain the virus, and then its participation in the spread of misinformation about the contagion, fostered an environment of uncertainty and therefore a mistrust that was later reinforced by the internationalization of the pandemic. Indeed, those nations that ignored China's declarations in the beginning, and those of the WHO, and closed their borders were initially successful in containing the crisis.[56] But there was also a breakdown in broader institutions that worked to reinforce the state-centric responses that occurred afterwards. For one, the United Nations Security Council did not sit immediately to decide upon a response; Chinese diplomats blocked a discussion on the issue. The Trump administration exacerbated these failings further by calling for resolutions within the United Nations to single out China for blame for the emerging crisis. According to some, the global response to the COVID-19 pandemic showcased the weaknesses in the UN system across its three core mission areas of human rights, peace and security, and sustainable development.[57]

There are some reasons, however, to be optimistic about cooperation in the future, though this rationale is based on negative feedback. For one point, the inability to work in concert to provide vaccines globally has predictably failed to build a herd immunity, without which the pandemic will likely spread further. Another drawback has been the economic consequences of vaccine nationalism, which has stifled economic development and slowed global GDP in trade by approximately US$1.2 trillion per annum.[58] On this basis, while China and others may derive satisfaction from eradicating the virus through strict control measures, the challenges of COVID-19 will continue to exist, meaning that at some stage effective mitigation measures will require international cooperation not just on vaccines but also on economic matters. The institutions for this do exist in the form of COVAX, a vaccine distribution alliance, but for the time being they rely on individual state donations and are subject to the whims of great power competition.

Conclusion

As global reactions to the global pandemic and the return to power politics demonstrate a return to the state-centric approaches of the traditional security theories, it is important to retrace the major challenges to the assumptions that underscore their popularity. The purpose in this chapter, as such, has been to draw attention to the important aspects of power and uncertainty amid what must be considered two of the most critical security dilemmas of our time—great power competition and COVID-19. Understanding intentions and applying the correct elements of power, whether it be through governance institutions or even economic agreements, will be highly contextual to the problem that must be solved and the relationships that must be exercised to that end. For the traditional approaches, and realism in particular, the danger lies in oversimplifying patterns of behavior and determinants of national strength, though this does not mean such methods should be abandoned. The argument rather is that they must be adaptive, making use of the many conceptual improvements made over the years in identifying, conceptualizing, and defining different forms of power, particularly as they are relevant to domestic sources of contention.

The challenges of COVID-19 and great power competition have made this proposition difficult. There is comfort in sticking with what is known, what is "easy" to understand, and what may seem at the time reliable methods of control. Should it be surprising that the strong reaction to COVID-19 with border lockdowns precipitated in effect an anti-globalization sentiment that has done little to ameliorate the contagion? What has become apparent is that the costs of noncooperation are becoming increasingly problematic as, while states move to fight off contagion individually, the evolution of new strains in other parts of the world is rendering such efforts redundant. If ever there was a symbol for the power of cooperation, the inability of states to address the pandemic individually should be it. Reality in practice is not as simple as reality described in theory. Theoretical approaches must adopt and respond to these problems.

Notes

1. Barry Buzan, Ole Wæver, and Jaap de Wilde, *Security: A New Framework for Analysis* (Boulder, CO: Lynne Rienner, 1998).
2. Ulrich Beck, *World Risk Society* (Cambridge, England: Polity Press, 1998).
3. Edward Newman, "Human Security: Reconciling Critical Aspirations with Political 'Realities,'" *British Journal of Criminology* 56, no. 6 (2016): 1165–83.
4. Robert O. Keohane, "The Global Politics Paradigm: Guide to the Future or Only the Recent Past?" *International Theory* 13, no. 1 (2021): 119; Ivor Crewe and David Sanders (eds.), *Authoritarian Populism and Liberal Democracy* (Cham, Switzerland: Palgrave Macmillan, 2020), 2.
5. Keohane, "The Global Politics Paradigm," 112–21.
6. On realism, see Kenneth N. Waltz, *Theory of International Politics* (Reading, MA: Addison-Wesley, 1979); John J. Mearsheimer, *The Tragedy of Great Power Politics* (New York: W. W. Norton, 2001); Robert Gilpin, "The Richness of the Tradition of Political Realism," *International Organization* 38, no. 2 (1984): 287–304.
7. Robert O. Keohane, "Ideas Part-Way Down," *Review of International Studies* 26, no. 1 (2000): 125–30; J. Samuel Barkin, "Realist Constructivism," *International Studies Review* 5, no. 3 (2003): 325–42.
8. I use "liberal," "liberalism," and "neoliberalism" hereafter interchangeably, although in doing so I refer to the neoliberal institutional variation.
9. Bruce Russett and John R. Oneal, *Triangulating Peace: Democracy, Interdependence, and International Organizations* (New York: W. W. Norton, 2000); Dale C. Copeland, *Economic Interdependence and War* (Princeton, NJ: Princeton University Press, 2015); Michael W. Doyle, "Kant, Liberal Legacies, and Foreign Affairs," part 1, *Philosophy and Public Affairs* 12, no. 3 (1983): 205–35.
10. Robert Axelrod and Robert O. Keohane, "Achieving Cooperation under Anarchy: Strategies and Institutions," *World Politics* 38, no. 1 (1985): 226–54.
11. Robert Jervis, "Theories of War in an Era of Leading-Power Peace: Presidential Address, American Political Science Association," *American Political Science Review* 96, no. 1 (2002): 1–14.
12. David A. Baldwin (ed.), *Neorealism and Neoliberalism: The Contemporary Debate* (New York: Columbia University Press, 1993); Robert O. Keohane, *After Hegemony: Cooperation and Discord in the World Political Economy* (Princeton, NJ: Princeton University Press, 1984); Robert O. Keohane and Lisa Martin, "Institutional Theory as a Research Program," in Colin Elman and Miriam Fendius Elman (eds.), *Progress in*

International Relations Theory: Appraising the Field (Cambridge, MA: MIT Press, 2003).

13. Caroline Thomas, *Global Governance, Development and Human Security: The Challenge of Poverty and Inequality* (London: Pluto Press, 2000).
14. Edward Newman, "Critical Human Security Studies," *Review of International Studies* 36, no. 1 (2010): 77–94.
15. Stewart Patrick, "'Failed' States and Global Security: Empirical Questions and Policy Dilemmas," *International Studies Review* 9, no. 4 (2007): 644–62.
16. Robert Jervis, "Realism in the Study of World Politics," *International Organization* 52, no. 4 (1998): 981.
17. Alasdair Roberts, "'Whatever It Takes': Danger, Necessity, and Realism in American Public Policy," *Administration & Society* 52, no. 7 (2020): 1131–44.
18. Tiago Correia and Karen Willis, "Applying Critical Realism to the COVID-19 Pandemic to Improve Management of Future Public Health Crises," *International Journal of Health Planning and Management* 37, no. 2 (2022): 599–603. See also Richard Horton, "Offline: COVID-19 Is Not a Pandemic," *The Lancet* 396, no. 10255 (2020): 874.
19. Gustav Meibauer, "Interests, Ideas, and the Study of State Behaviour in Neoclassical Realism," *Review of International Studies* 46, no. 1 (2020): 20–36.
20. Damjan Krnjevic Miskovic, "Back with a Vengeance: The Return of Rough and Tumble Geopolitics," *Orbis* 65, no.1 (2020): 118–35.
21. Michael Zürn, *A Theory of Global Governance: Authority, Legitimacy, and Contestation* (Oxford: Oxford University Press, 2018), p. 11.
22. David Held, "Elements of a Theory of Global Governance," *Philosophy and Social Criticism* 42, no. 9 (2016): 844–5; Thomas Hale and David Held (eds.), *Beyond Gridlock* (Cambridge, England: Polity, 2017); Kalevi Holsti, "Change in International Politics: The View from High Altitude," *International Studies Review* 20, no. 2 (2018): 186–94.
23. John Mearsheimer, *The Great Delusion: Liberal Dreams and International Realities* (New Haven, CT: Yale University Press, 2018).
24. See, for instance, Stephen M. Walt, *The Hell of Good Intentions: America's Foreign Policy Elite and the Decline of US Primacy* (New York: Farrar, Straus & Giroux, 2018), 10.
25. E. H. Carr, *The Twenty Years Crisis, 1919–1939* (Basingstoke, England: Palgrave, [1939] 2001).
26. Robert W. Cox, "Social Forces, States and World Orders: Beyond International Relations Theory," *Millennium* 10, no. 2 (1981): 126–55.
27. Stephen M. Walt, "US Grand Strategy after the Cold War: Can Realism Explain It? Should Realism Guide It?" *International Relations* 32, no. 1 (2018): 7.
28. Waltz, *Theory of International Politics*, chapters 5 and 6.

29. Hans Morgenthau, for instance, talked about power as a form of control over people and as a material capability. See Hans Morgenthau, *Politics among Nations: The Struggle for Power and Peace*, 5th edn. (New York: Alfred A. Knopf, 1978), 26, 102.
30. K. J. Holsti, "The Concept of Power in the Study of international Relations," *Background* 7, no. 4 (1964): 182.
31. Joseph S. Nye Jr., *The Paradox of American Power: Why the World's Only Superpower Can't Go It Alone* (New York: Oxford University Press, 2002); Zeev Maoz, *Paradoxes of War: On the Art of National Self-Entrapment* (Boston: Unwin Hyman, 1989).
32. Joseph S. Nye, "Soft Power," *Foreign Policy* 80 (1990): 153–71.
33. See Stanley Hoffman, "Obstinate or Obsolete? The Fate of the Nation-State and the Case of Western Europe," *Dædalus* 95, no. 3 (1966): 862–915; Peter Trubowitz and Peter Harris, "The End of the American Century? Slow Erosion of the Domestic Sources of Usable Power," *International Affairs* 95, no. 3 (2019): 619–39.
34. Peter J. Katzenstein and Lucea A. Seybert (eds.), *Protean Power: Exploring the Uncertain and Unexpected in World Politics* (Cambridge, England: Cambridge University Press, 2018).
35. Michael Barnett and Raymond Duvall, "Power in International Politics," *International Organization* 59, no. 1 (2005): 40, 69.
36. See, for instance, Elbridge A. Colby, *The Strategy of Denial: American Defense in an Age of Great Power Conflict* (New Haven, CT: Yale University Press, 2021).
37. Michael Beckley, "The Power of Nations: Measuring What Matters," *International Security* 43, no. 2 (2018): 7–44.
38. Barry Buzan, "Peace, Power, and Security: Contending Concepts in the Study of International Relations," *Journal of Peace Research* 21, no. 2 (1984): 119.
39. Robert Axelrod, *The Evolution of Cooperation* (New York: Basic, 1984).
40. Beckley, "The Power of Nations," p. 8. See also Tuomas Forsberg, "Power in International Relations: An Interdisciplinary Perspective," in *International Studies: Interdisciplinary Approaches*, ed. Pami Aalto, Viho Harle, and Sami Moisio (Basingstoke, England: Palgrave Macmillan, 2011), 213.
41. See, for instance, Rush Doshi, *The Long Game: China's Grand Strategy to Displace American Order* (New York: Oxford University Press, 2021), 21–2.
42. On this existential uncertainty, see Keohane, "The Global Politics Paradigm," 115–16.
43. Oliver Kessler and Christopher Daase, "From Insecurity to Uncertainty: Risk and the Paradox of Security Politics," *Alternatives* 33, no. 2 (2008): 211–32.
44. Brian C. Rathbun, "Uncertain about Uncertainty: Understanding the Multiple Meanings of a Crucial Concept in International Relations Theory," *International Studies Quarterly* 51, no. 3 (2007): 534.

45. On China's domestic problems of legitimacy and insecurity, see Chris Ogden, "Beyond Succession: China's Internal Security Challenges," *Strategic Analysis* 37, no. 2 (2013): 193–202.
46. Rathbun (2007), "Uncertain about Uncertainty."
47. Ibid.
48. John J. Mearsheimer, "The False Promise of International Institutions," *International Security* 19, no. 3 (1994): 10.
49. Javier C. Hernández, "Trump Slammed the WHO over Coronavirus. He's Not Alone," *New York Times*, April 8, 2020, https://www.nytimes.com/2020/04/08/world/asia/trump-who-coronavirus-china.html; "Coronavirus: Trump Accuses WHO of Being a 'Puppet of China,'" BBC News, May 19, 2020, https://www.bbc.com/news/health-52679329 (both accessed March 1, 2022).
50. For more on the liberal entanglement thesis see Robert S. Ross, "Engagement in US China Policy," in *Engaging China: The Management of an Emerging Power*, ed. Alastair Iain Johnston and Robert S. Ross (Abingdon, England: Routledge, 1999), 185.
51. Elbridge A. Colby and A. Wess Mitchell, "The Age of Great-Power Competition: How the Trump Administration Refashioned American Strategy," *Foreign Affairs*, January/February 2020, https://www.foreignaffairs.com/articles/2019-12-10/age-great-power-competition; see also *Indo-Pacific Strategy Report: Preparedness, Partnerships, and Promoting a Networked Region*, US Department of Defense, June 1, 2019, https://media.defense.gov/2019/Jul/01/2002152311/-1/-1/1/DEPARTMENT-OF-DEFENSE-INDO-PACIFIC-STRATEGY-REPORT-2019.PDF; "A Free and Open Indo-Pacific: Advancing a Shared Vision," US Department of State, November 4, 2019, https://www.state.gov/wp-content/uploads/2019/11/Free-and-Open-Indo-Pacific-4Nov2019.pdf (all accessed March 1, 2022).
52. Barkin, "Realist Constructivism," 337; Stefano Guzzini, "A Reconstruction of Constructivism in International Relations," *European Journal of International Relations* 6, no. 2 (2000): 147–82.
53. David Shambaugh, *China Goes Global: The Partial Power* (New York: Oxford University Press, 2013).
54. Evan A. Feigenbaum, "Reluctant Stakeholder: Why China's Highly Strategic Brand of Revisionism is More Challenging than Washington Thinks," Macro Polo, April 27, 2018, https://macropolo.org/analysis/reluctant-stakeholder-why-chinas-highly-strategic-brand-of-revisionism-is-more-challenging-than-washington-thinks/ (accessed March 1, 2022).
55. Thomas E. Kellogg, "Xi's Davos Speech: Is China the New Champion for the liberal International Order?" *The Diplomat*, January 24, 2017, https://thediplomat.com/2017/01/xis-davos-speech-is-china-the-new-champion-for-the-liberal-international-order/ (accessed March 1, 2022).
56. Jennifer Summers et al., "Potential Lessons from the Taiwan and New Zealand Health Responses to the COVID-19 Pandemic," *Lancet Regional Health Western Pacific* 4 (2020): 100044.

57. Ş. İlgü Özler, "The United Nations at Seventy-Five: Passing the COVID Test?" *Ethics & International Affairs* 34, no. 4 (2020): 445–6.
58. Marco Hafner et al., *COVID-19 and the Cost of Vaccine Nationalism* (Santa Monica, CA, and Cambridge, England: RAND, 2020), available at https://www.rand.org/pubs/research_reports/RRA769-1.html (accessed March 1, 2022).

3

Globalization and Security: A Great Unsettling

Paul James

Introduction

We now live in a world of abiding existential insecurity. Sometimes a particular dimension of human insecurity hits us in the face. Mostly it accumulates behind our backs as an intensifying matrix of nonpalpable threats and risks. Whereas once, people could find sanctuary far from the madding shroud of risk, the risk matrix is becoming increasingly interconnected and globalized. Nuclear winter will not fade off at its edges. Viral pandemics arrive with dramatic virulence, even in ostensibly isolated places. And climate change is globally changing the planet, including in ways that become even more intense at its poles. In short, these threats and risks are representative of ontological changes that are unsettling *all* social and environmental life across the planet.

In previous work, Manfred Steger and I named this globalizing deepening process the Great Unsettling.[1] But without further explanation this short-hand designation too easily gets reduced to either psychological unease or accumulating physical disruption of planetary systems. What we intend this concept to mean includes and goes beyond the sense of deep agitation about climate change, solastalgia, or the general feeling that all is not right in the world.[2] It is more than the physical disruption of the world by ripping, arming, extracting, polluting, cutting down, and commodifying—all dimensions of a longer-term history. More broadly, it describes the objective and subjective unsettling of the human condition in general that has been intensifying over the last half century or so. This ontological unsettling turns on the relativization of basic ontologies of living: embodiment, time, space, epistemology, performativity, objectivity, subjectivity, and so on. Nonrelativizing ways of life continue, as do older forms of exploitation and domination, but they are increasingly drawn into contradictory and disjunctive relations with newer developments.

Disjunctive relations are as true of questions of military and other forms of security as everything else. The increasingly disembodied war fought from the skies over Afghanistan, for example, was nevertheless associated with mortal attacks on the bodies of thousands of combatants and civilians.[3] Similarly, the final outcome of that war was disjunctive as part of a more general trend in which the distinction between winning and losing wars has all but lost its meaning. Even *if* a techno-regime of military control *could have* continued indefinitely (a potential temporal stretching of the meaning of war), a neotraditional movement that did not use remotely piloted vehicles or algorithmic surveillance systems "won" the twenty-year war against an otherwise undefeatable military machine. Concomitantly, despite this win, the trend toward automation, technological mediation, action-at-a-distance, and cyber-engagement both continues apace and has the capacity for increasing military dominance—at least when political will and perceived legitimacy are maintained.[4] From one side of these postmodern-neotraditional wars, semiautomated machines navigate vast extensions of space and diminish time differences between a war room decision in one place and the engagement of a drone-enabled "targeted killing" on the other side of the world. War zones are no longer confined to the nationally bounded territories of the declared combatants. And identification of kill targets is no longer based primarily on eye-to-eye confirmation but is rather "tested" by computerized algorithmic verification. (From the other side—not the subject of this chapter—neotraditionalizing cosmological understandings reframe the meaning of existence and death.)

As will be described in this chapter, the techno-revolution, on the one hand, depends upon incremental political and technological developments—for example, shifting the political meaning of "collateral damage," declaring a war with a nonnational antagonist which acknowledges nothing in return, or defining a combatant by loose categorization as a supporter of an organization defined as hostile. Similarly, the technological changes have been long in the making and not always spectacular—the automation of the machinery of war has an extended and initially staccato history. On the other hand, taken together these developments have become transformative in their contradictory intensification and uncomfortable normalization.

Thinking about the Great Unsettling in relation to questions of security prompts us to step back from the technology for a moment and revisit an old concept—*ontological security*.[5] Anthony Giddens reduced the concept to the disembedding of subjectivites of security, which occurs within what he disparagingly calls "the wasteland of everyday life."[6] This means that modern everyday life is (supposedly) emptied of all its meaning except that afforded by routine and spectacle. Subjective security thus comes to rely on what Giddens calls "trust in abstract systems." This refers to individuals trusting in the systems developed by particular disciplines of intellectual work, for example, the work of engineers, designers, and physicists in providing technical specifications for bridge construction, banking software, or nuclear weapons development. This part of the elaboration of "trust in abstract systems" is important, but in Giddens's writing it remained a one-dimensional concept framed by personal subjective terms. Relevant to the present discussion, we need to ask what happens to trust in abstract systems when their architects now build systems that "secure" one aspect of life while leading to new globalizing meta-insecurities—from the climate emergency to nuclear exterminism. What happens when the basis of our knowledge of these systems is epistemologically unsettled by fake news and posttruths? All of this adds up to ontological *in*security being built into the heart of regimes of security: hence we need a composite term with brackets to capture this shift, "(in) security." It is an ugly term, but it begins to capture an ugly process.

The nuclear (in)security of assured destruction

The development of nuclear weaponry is paradigmatic of the transformation of security that is being argued here. In one sense, I will be going over old ground, but it will involve a very different take on the usual narrative. The atom bomb, I argue, ushered in the existential unsettling of all prior regimes of security. Moreover, it marked the ontological unsettling of nature in general. This accords with the bigger argument that the consequences of the Great Unsettling have become uneven and disjunctive across all social and environmental life,[7] including within and between the domains of ecology, economy, politics, and culture. These domains provide useful and familiar points of focus, even if our "engaged theory" method emphasizes cross-cutting relations.

Ecologically, the science of the bomb required the dismembering of the basic elements of nature as they were conceived at the time. Obviously, atomic philosophy was not new. From the fifth century BCE, when the Greek philosophers Leucippus and Democritus had posited atoms as the ultimate structure of reality, to the late nineteenth century, atoms were treated as irreducible. The notion that humans could take this foundational structure apart was completely unprecedented.[8] The Manhattan Project to split the atom was built upon an emerging general line of intellectual intervention to relativize both the meaning and practice of "nature." Niels Bohr's quantum theory had unsettled modern laws of dynamics and measurement, just as Albert Einstein's theory of temporal-material relativity had signaled an emergent way of rethinking (and unsettling) the nature of modern time itself.[9] This is what might be called the postmodernization of science, the development of an emerging epistemological layer of knowing and acting overlaying the continuing modern emphasis on test tubes, machines, and patterned hypotheses.[10] In these terms, it is not just the new relativization that was causing the Great Unsettling, but also the disjuncture between this relativization and the enhanced (un)certainty that came with intensifying modern measurement and technological application. This point will become clearer as the discussion proceeds.

Culturally, the bomb disrupted centuries-old tropes about light as the source of life and enlightenment. The Hiroshima explosion, described as the light of "a thousand suns," instead brought darkness and fear to both the people of Hiroshima and then to generations of Cold War civilians. The realization of this change took time. Despite the many accounts of J. Robert Oppenheimer using the *Bhagavad Gita* to describe his immediate response to the explosion, it took him years after the Trinity test to find suitable words in the ancient fragments of a Hindu cosmological text: "If the radiance of a thousand suns were to burst into the sky, that would be like the splendour of the Mighty One." And then, metaphorically, supposedly as the cloud rose, he added: "Now, I am become Death, the shatterer of worlds."[11] We now know that even the poetry of a thousand suns was implicitly tested by scientific measurement in the first Los Alamos test in July 1945. A detector placed 10,000 yards (9,100 meters) from the Trinity explosion registered the peak illumination at the equivalent of 80 "suns." This too was finally made public years later.[12] In any case, human impact on the constituents of nature had surpassed our experience of the brightness of nature itself, and modern science now had provided the measure of poetry while postmodern science returned to revel in it.

Politically, postmodern science and its nuclear application breached the limits of human understanding of the relation between means and ends. Long before the MAD doctrine in the 1960s (mutual assured destruction or "assured destruction" as it was formally known) and then, later still, the technical possibility of global extermination through nuclear winter,[13] the proponents of the nuclear age were prepared to risk the end of the world in order to save it.[14] In other words, the technical-political means (instigating the possible end of the world) was in tension with the social ends (the saving of the world from further war). I say this with all the considerable understatement that the key people originally thinking about these questions tended to muster. Oppenheimer as head of the Los Alamos

Laboratory was no exception. Speaking in the early 1960s and reflecting back on the Manhattan Project, he appears to give the question of the possible end of the world less consequence than the logistical question of enriching sufficient U-235 for building the bombs:

> When I came into it my predecessor had the title Co-ordinator of Rapid Rupture. There were really very many questions. Would a bomb work and what sort of a thing would it be, how much material would it need, what kind of energies would it release; would it ignite the atmosphere in nuclear reactions and end us all; could it be used to start fusion reactions? There was also the problem of producing, in industrial processes that had no previous analogue in human history, the very considerable number of pounds of the special materials, uranium and plutonium, of which the first bombs had to be made.[15]

Note here how the possible end of the world disappears into a list of questions after pointing to the title of "rapid rupture." Similarly, James Conant, chair of the National Defense Research Committee, and part of the highly secret Interim Committee, which recommended the use of the bomb on civilians (incidentally, a war crime, as I will discuss later), acknowledged: "I was quite aware of the potentialities for global destruction which were inherent in the project."[16] As his biographer describes, Conant discounted the meaning of this possibility until the moment of the explosion when the sky was turned to white light: "for a split second, Conant believed he was one of the last men" on the earth. To relieve the tension at the Los Alamos test, Enrico Fermi, another of the key physicists, said: "Now, let's make a bet whether the atmosphere will be set on fire by this test"—will the planet be engulfed in fire or just a 35-kilometer radius in New Mexico? The odds of destroying the world by runaway fusion had previously been calculated earlier as slightly less than one in three million. We were "completely certain," Conant said, that the world was not going to end.[17] That certainty (about a haunting uncertainty) was to surface regularly across the subsequent decades in public interviews, magazine articles, and biographies, and finally in 1979 the calculations that suggested *relative* or "near certainty" were released publicly.[18] The small number of people who read that technical paper to the end would have found the following conclusion: "There remains the distant probability that some other less simple mode of burning may maintain itself in the atmosphere . . . catastrophic on a world-wide scale." By inference, the public release signaled that nuclear unsettling had become so generalized, so globalized (and so normalized) that it was now safe to make it public, even revealing the level of (un)certainty.

Other tragic contradictions that came with nuclear (in)security compounded the political unsettling. Defended as bringing peace, the Hiroshima devastation brought about the mass carnage of civilians in an act of unprecedented state terrorism. Certainly, state terrorism was not new. The fire-bombing sorties over German and Japanese cities in World War II were conducted as earlier forms of state terrorism, as were the Nazi sorties over Britain. However, the meaning of the ongoing civilian-targeted carpet bombing was neither made public at the time by the Allies nor defended as a 'legitimate' act of civilian terror. The other side of this is telling. During the war, both the Allied and Axis powers adopted commensurate "civil defense" practices, including what in effect became transnationally standardized practices for instituting civil defense groups and mandating fire response teams.[19] By transitional comparison to the fire-bombing period, a shift occurred in the days after the Hiroshima and Nagasaki bombings. While the cities were similarly presented as military targets, in President Truman's oblique but stark words, mass civilian deaths could now be threatened as concomitant with nuclear devastation:

> It was to spare the Japanese people from utter destruction that the ultimatum of July 26 was issued at Potsdam. Their leaders promptly rejected that ultimatum. If they do not now accept our terms they may expect a rain of ruin from the air, the like of which has never been seen on this earth.[20]

In the ensuing years, the pursuit of nuclear security set in train an (in)security race with consequences which came to be coldly enumerated in tables of civilian megadeaths, collateral damage and survival ratios. This was underpinned by a question that had never been asked before by Cold War warriors or proponents of limited deterrence: "Will survivors envy the dead?"[21] Even as the proponents of the necessity of nuclear deterrence answered that question in the negative, the abstract systems of nuclear engineering and military planning came to engender basic mistrust. We had begun to distrust the entire system. The previous norm of noncombatant immunity had been shaken to its foundations, even as it was still politically voiced *as if* it were pressingly relevant.[22] (We will see a new stage of this voicing with the onset of drone warfare in the next section.)

Again, the other side of this nuclear (in)security race is telling. Both the United States and, to an even greater extent, the Soviet Union devoted massive funds to civilian nuclear (in)security programs and infrastructure such as advertising campaigns and fallout shelters. Across the world, systematically institutionalized "civil defense" programs in the 1950s and early 1960s—including the early US "Duck and Cover" campaign—existentially unsettled a generation of Americans, Europeans, East Asians, and Soviet Bloc citizens.[23] In other words, at least in relation to nuclear war, the objective and subjective distinction between civilian and military deaths was dissolving in all but political voicing. Over time, the escalating end-of-the-world potential of thermonuclear holocaust eventually meant that nuclear "civil defense" became meaningless and, by the mid-1960s, it was transformed without acknowledgement into general disaster preparedness, and then bureaucratized in federal and national bodies.

It was certainly not an even process. For the immediate period after the dropping of the bomb at least, the crisis contributed to a series of international attempts to integrate (not relativize) world politics. However, the globalizing logic of nuclear unsettlement quickly overcame such politics of modern integration and international institution building. Compounding insecurities began to add up: thermonuclear fusion weapons, nuclear proliferation, intercontinental ballistic missiles, multiple independently targetable reentry vehicles, and the "Star Wars" missile shield, as well as "limited" nuclear weapon capabilities and computer-automated nuclear launch systems—one appropriately called "the Dead Hand" (though never operationalized as fully automatic). All contributed to an escalating state of objective unsettlement. For example, the Soviet Perimeter System could be set to relayed automatic global retaliation should a nuclear attack on Russia be detected.

With these developments, the residual narrative of modern certainty made less and less sense, even with precision targeting. But it was not just a contradiction between technological escalation and political-civil reassurance. As Daniel Ellsberg documents, no US president since 1945—not even Barack Obama, the winner of a Nobel Peace Prize—has discounted the possibility of optional first use of nuclear weapons. In Ellsberg's metaphor, it is a gun that, though it has not been fired since 1945, has been often pointed at enemies' heads.[24] This makes it a continuing material reality of global politics. In summary, it may have been the implied (un)certainty of the assured destruction doctrine that confirmed the relativizing of political engagement, but even with the contemporary dissipation of the direct discussion of assured destruction, the first-use/never-to-be-used disjuncture continues to the present day as a profoundly unsettling but background phenomenon. Nuclear (in)security has been normalized in public consciousness, but it has not gone away.

The automated (in)security of drone warfare

Into the twenty-first century, the tension between the first-use option and the never-to-be-used *obiter dictum* was exacerbated by other major doctrinal, political, and technological developments. Most graphically, the emergence of nonstate enemies such as al-Qaeda changed the global field of military engagement. Nuclear weapons were so obviously useless against a nonterritorial enemy that even veiled threats of use became counterproductive. Even before the 2001 terrorist attack on the World Trade Center, organizational and technological changes were in train to make the abstracted killing machine more usable. This was bound up with the doctrine of a "Revolution in Military Affairs." One of the first expressions of this, at least for the United States, was a series of global mobility campaigns characterized by stealth aircraft, super-precision targeting, and an integrated global information system.[25] This was not just a technical issue of extending the disembodied reach of the machines of so-called "conventional" war; it also concerned the legal apparatus that justified the extension of war by machine. Ironically, leading the way was an apparently redemptive American president whose early speeches suggested that he was going to dismantle the war machine. As Samuel Moyn writes:

> In just the first few months of 2009, after Obama took the oath of office, the initial metamorphosis of American war into humane form was achieved. As the worst sins of the prior administration were disowned, Obama's lawyers claimed authority to continue war indefinitely across space and time, devising formal legal frameworks for targeted killings. The rise of the armed drone empire under Obama's watch was merely the symbol of the extension and expansion of endless war.[26]

This process was begun through an apparently innocuous legal brief in March 2009 to clarify considerations of *habeas corpus* in irregular war. After initially issuing executive orders to stop torture and to close Guantanamo Bay (though this has still not happened, and Joe Biden has now made a similar promise to close the Cuban prison), a legal intervention was used to extend the possibility of globalizing "legitimate" force against whoever was deemed by the president to be an enemy. The space, time, and embodiment of the still-unnamed War on Terror were thus relativized. The brief's overt question was to define who could be detained as a prisoner of war in Guantanamo Bay. However, in the process the brief confirmed George Bush's 2001 Authorization for the Use of Military Force (AUMF),[27] which opened the way "to all necessary and appropriate force" to be used against al-Qaeda. Going further than AUMF, the Obama brief then legally rendered two elements as intentionally and "legitimately" undefined (that is, rather than just vague). The first was the meaning of "substantial support" for an act of terror. The second was what it meant to say that a person or group was an "associated force" of a defined terrorist grouping "like al-Qaida."[28] In short, as a number of commentators have suggested, it dissolved most of the limitations on deciding who was the enemy, both across the globe and across time.[29] The spatial, temporal, and corporeal parameters of *this* war were now to be determined by the relative and changing standpoint of the US president.

Across the course of Obama's presidency, by *not* bringing any prisoners to Guantanamo Bay to test *habeas corpus*, and by eschewing in-person torture, a new regime of indefinite killing was imposed.[30] (I could write here, "a new regime of semi-legitimized state terror.") The first drone operation of Obama's presidency was sent to kill someone on the third day of his incumbency. At the end of that first year, Obama had presided over more killer drone strikes than George W. Bush during the entire period of his incumbency, including the first confirmed double-tap strike. Such strikes send a second missile from a drone a short period after the first, thus intending to kill the first responders who are trying the help the victims of the first strike.[31] Later in 2009, two related events occurred: Obama received the Nobel Peace Prize and the first books on killer robots were published.[32] Peace was thus being redefined and automation was in the air.

It needs to be recognized that during Obama's time in office the rhetoric of "humane warfare" was accompanied by increasingly precise targeting technologies and an actual minimization of collateral damage. Fully automated strikes were renounced, and persons were engaged with algorithmic decision making to make the final decision. However, despite these liberal qualifications, as the strikes expanded in number and range, the disjunctures between disembodied engagement and effects on actual people intensified. This effect extended from local people in targeted areas, including Afghanistan, Pakistan, Yemen, and Somalia, to the drone operators themselves in the United States. The effects of the process continued to be exacerbated by the following elements:

- Relativizing knowledge by information overload, or "data crush." The sheer quantity of available surveillance information now far outpaces the analytic capacities of the drone operators, particularly given the temporal compression of decision-making schedules. At the same time, this hides the narrowing perspective of the cameras as a drone moves in for a kill.

- Relativizing what it means to target a person precisely. Despite using precision instruments and increasing surveillance sophistication, the targeting continues to depend upon a relative accumulation of what are called the "signature" characteristics (or social profiling) of the person to be killed. Social profiling is a process that in domestic policing is deeply criticized as full of biases. In war, when it comes to killing people, social profiling is now somehow sufficient to make a life-or-death decision.
- Relativizing the civilian/combatant distinction. "Signature strikes" assume for example that males of fighting age in the immediate vicinity of targets are also threats. While the move to establish "noncombatant cut-off values" minimized the number of "civilians" killed, it also built their legitimate killing into the algorithmic equation. Below the decided threshold of possible civilian deaths for a particular strike it was deemed legitimate to take that risk.
- Relativizing the rules of war. Personality and signature strikes (or assassination kills, as they should be called) presume that a targeted person deserves to be killed rather than be offered the possibility of surrendering, retreating, or proving their innocence—thus instituting globalizing capital punishment and bypassing the centuries-long legal principle of *habeas corpus*.
- Relativizing the ethics of war. The controversy over drones has turned almost exclusively to whether or not a *particular* act in war was ethical or not—that is, how many angels can dance on the head of a missile. This took all attention away from whether or not the war itself was ethical and legitimate in the first place.
- Relativizing the distinction between everyday life and engagement in war. As will be elaborated in a moment, this occurred both in the extended regions beyond immediate war zones where drones might strike and for drone operators as soldiers/workers.

Examined from the side of those communities experiencing drone warfare in western Asia and Africa, it is very hard to find extended deep research on the consequences for ontological insecurity. From the many descriptions of the searing pain of those experiencing the drone wars—particularly during the period when weddings and funerals seemed to be regular targets—the circumstantial evidence suggests that community life and personal subjectivity were and continue to be profoundly affected. That is, without having enough systematic evidence to be more than suggestive here, the mixed research and reporting indicates that the arbitrariness of drone death is unsettling local people's sense of ontological security. Locals talk of death coming unpredictably, seemingly arbitrarily, sometimes by stealth, sometimes from brightly lit skies after an extended period (often hours) of buzzing surveillance circling.[33] The common element is that the violence is wrought arbitrarily and remotely by strangers named as agents of a distant imperial power. It is a significant but defensible step to argue that this unsettling may have sent many people back to the encompassing security of available cosmological worldviews—in this case, including those effected by various forms of Islamic neotraditionalism and distorted fundamentalisms.

My argument here appears to be tempered by the dominant strand of the international security literature, which assesses drone warfare in terms of an old concept that was coined in 1954 by the CIA: "blowback."[34] The concept is used well by Chalmers Johnson to describe the counterproductive effect of covert operations in deepening violent resistance. There has been an ongoing debate about the blowback effects of drone warfare. However, because of the drama of the term, mainstream analysis tends to focus on what James Page and John Williams call "narrowly construed accounts of 'effectiveness.'"[35] Because most security analysts are looking for one-to-one determinative relations between drone activity and people joining terrorist organizations, they conclude that drones do not cause blowback.[36] This misses the point and redefines the original meaning of the concept of "blowback." The 1953 installation of the Shah of Iran organized by the United States and the United Kingdom, and the subsequent reign of the ayatollahs—the original basis of the concept—was a generation-framing process, not a question of who joined what organization in 1954. The fleeing of the Shah in 1979 and the fleeing of President Ashraf Ghani from Afghanistan in 2021 were both the outcomes of fast and slow, structural and predictable, processes. Neither event made the world more secure.

Given the broader framing of the present analysis, President Barack Obama's claim that the threshold for a drone strike is "near certainty that no civilians will be killed or injured—the highest standard we can set"[37] begins to sound like a pious diversion. And it is worth noting that we are beginning to see a pattern to the concept of "near certainty." Here in Obama's words it becomes an expression of postmodern (un)certainty, this time defended by implied modern measurement (covertly counting civilian deaths), while parading modern morality. Donald Trump on assuming office simply dropped the pious legitimation and, since then, President Biden has pledged to continue what he calls "over-the-horizon" counterterrorism. He has already been mired in controversy about misplaced drone killings.

Moving now to examine the other side of drone warfare—that is, the social condition of those who control the machines that bring death—evidence for the ontological unsettling of drone operators is also apparent, even if again not systematically documented. For all of the modern morality about precision and pseudo-ethical assertions about the importance of the continuing human decision-making process, something else is happening. This can be seen, for example, in the subjective-objective tensions involved in the act of killing. The technical process of assassination is mixed with detailed long-term video surveillance of the persons to be killed—that is, the targeted bodies for killing are at once more mediated (objectively) *and* more "present" (subjectively) to the operators than in previous wars. For hours, sometimes days, the operators watch the everyday movements of their targets—washing clothes, playing soccer with their children, building weapons, or laying landmines (the last example actually turned out to be kids pulling sticks out of a culvert).[38] It is what Scott Fitzsimmons and Karina Sangha call "killing in high definition."[39] Then the operators watch live video feed of the smoking outcome of the assassination attack to ascertain its effectiveness (before going home each day). By (ambiguously) returning human judgment to those who press the button, and by providing graphic live feedback of the outcome of "their" decision, as well as by turning the military deployment of drone operators into a daily commute (war moves in and out of everyday life), the pressure is made intense.[40] This becomes a new world, even by comparison to the upheaval experienced by those Americans flying the *Enola Gay* 31,060 feet (9,470 meters) above Hiroshima in order to drop the first atomic bomb.[41]

The introduction of artificial intelligence (AI) to algorithmically supported human decision making further intensifies this tension between technical mediation and human authority. In the case of drone warfare, Aiden Warren and Alek Hillas draw our attention to the way in which the new algorithmic decision-making processes use human trust as a means of dealing with the need for *relative certainty* in a world of (in)security.[42] This returns us to the theme of trust in abstract systems but with a difference. Because trust in abstract systems has over the past few decades been objectively and ethically shaken, the military designers of the war machine systems are now directly confronting this issue and explicitly placing their faith in the emotional intelligence of operators and their capacity for what they call "informed trust" in drone systems. *Informed trust* is based on the highly trained operator knowing about "cognitive congruence and transparency, situation awareness, human-systems integration, and human-system teaming and training."[43] That all sounds fine—impressive even—except for the unsettling factors listed earlier. To those we can now add another. Through informed trust, teamed with the enhanced capacity of artificial intelligence, the neoliberal efficiency imperative is being pushed beyond the market to get more out of the killing machines. It does not fill one with reassurance that the OFFSET program of DARPA (the Defense Advanced Research Projects Agency) has been researching the capacity for an AI-supported operator to manage a drone swarm, upwards of 250 machines.

As a footnote, and lest we forget, nuclear deterrence continues to be a background force in this objective unsettling (even if it has receded subjectively), and this same machine learning process is being considered in the nuclear weapons area, introducing even more insecurity to an already insecure situation of relatively assured global destruction.[44]

The known unknowns of bio (in)security

At the beginning of the twenty-first century, it was the global War on Terror and its continuing impact (now without an official name) that unsettled the world, contributing to the relativizing of time and space. It has since informally and critically been called the "forever war." Now, two decades into this century, a further round of unsettling developments has slowly entered the global imaginary, including the disaster-intensifying effects of climate change and the consequences of the COVID crisis for embodied social interchange. These developments confirm, at least in an inchoate and subjective sense, that we are living through an encompassing unsettling. In this final section, I want to ask some questions about the consequences of COVID for basic human security.

The COVID crisis has certainly exacerbated the *subjective* sense of unsettling. It has been globally disruptive. But in current commentary and policymaking the foundational basis of the crisis has been almost completely ignored.[45] Commentary and policy continue to remain focused on the phenomenal consequences of COVID or its proximate sources, not its social origins. In terms of human security, the search for Patient Zero in Wuhan has been a distraction, at least in its current form. And, perhaps not surprisingly, the vast energy of global attention has been directed toward the vaccine technoscience and distribution governance issues rather than the existential sources of insecurity. The military has been enlisted in various countries to support quarantine or distribution processes, but this has made little difference to the underlying insecurities. The symptomatic securing of biosecurity after COVID has taken a number of forms:

- Curtailing movement of people across regional and national borders. While such quarantining had dissipated by the end of 2021, there has been a more recent discussion of the introduction of vaccine passports. Italy has mandated vaccine passports within the country, and the European Union has instituted a digital COVID certificate which it says, awkwardly, should facilitate free movement without being a precondition to free movement (which is a fundamental right in the EU).
- Enlisting military support for quarantine and vaccination arrangements. In Australia, Lieutenant-General John Frewen was appointed by the prime minister as head of the National COVID Vaccine Taskforce. In the United States, the military assisted civil authorities with medical augmentation, logistics, and administrative support, including with contracting. In South Africa, the National Defence Force was deployed to enforce lockdown regulations.
- Supporting the technoscientific vaccination race. A number of the vaccines rely upon fetal cell lines derived from fetuses aborted in the early 1970s. These cell lines are used as what is called a "vaccine factory" to help the vaccine replicate. In brutal summary, a potential human life aborted by someone is instrumentalized for technoscientific investigation, research, and production of the vaccine. But that is a whole other story.
- Investigating the original source of the virus in Wuhan—Patient Zero.

In short, while nation-states have been doing many things in the name of biosecurity, they have without exception failed to focus, even rhetorically, on the unsettling conditions which provide the basis for zoonotically transferred viral pandemics: deforestation, industrialization of agriculture, increasing global inequality, and intensifying climate change.[46] Here there are many factors. To the list we can add the global intensification of industrial fishing, meaning that locals find themselves turning to other sources of animal protein—wild animals that were not previously food sources (this is thought to be the source of the Ebola virus). Together with other processes such as the pattern of species depletion and transborder trade in exotic species there has been a shift in the natural-social relation.[47]

This broader question of the natural-social relation has not been part of any public COVID debates. The difference here from my previous examples is that, although the COVID crisis contributes to the redoubling of ontological insecurity, it does not itself seem to be caused by the deepening *relativization* of social and natural existence. Rather it comes out of the slower Anthropocenic shift of *reconstructive* human impact on the ecology of the planet—what I described earlier as ripping, arming, extracting, polluting, cutting down, and commodifying. We should also be clear that the existential significance of COVID-19 for human security is not because it introduces a completely new threat. Viral pandemics moving across the globe have been part of the human condition for centuries. Rather, it is because it is part of a long-term pattern of social-natural disruption that has been intensifying over the past couple of decades. This time, by comparison with the splitting of the atom, it is the unintended consequence of *other* human impacts. What all this adds up to is the galloping pattern of Ebola, Zika, MERS-CoV, H1N1, SARS, HIV-AIDS and SARS-CoV-2 (COVID), which have led to a combined death toll of tens of millions of people over the last few decades. COVID thus needs to be understood in global context and not as a single viral outbreak. Here two questions stand out as known unknowns. What has speeded up transmission? What has contributed to the intensification of zoonotic transfer?

In relation to the first question, there is much research to be done on hyperconsumption, commodity exchange, and global hypermobility as a more basic explanation of the speed of transmission of global pandemics than tracing the individuals who left Wuhan in December 2019. In relation to the second question, basic science is needed on the viral hosting (with viral mutation and then zoonotic transfer) that occurs through industrial farming of genetically similar creatures in high population densities.[48] Pigs, sheep, pigeons, cattle, civets, and pangolins are all being intensively farmed in the region where SARS-CoV-2 is thought to have originated. The other side of this is the consequences of reduced numbers and near extinction in some species: "Here, we find broad evidence supporting large-scale mechanisms underlying patterns of zoonotic virus richness across species, by which trends in mammalian abundance and drivers of declines among threatened species reflect animal-human interactions that facilitate virus transmission to people."[49]

All of this means that, for all the emphasis on Chinese wet markets as the proximate source of the emergence of COVID-19, we need to confront the ways in which humans have contributed to the basic disruption of our complex planetary ecology, including the human-animal-ecosystem interface. Technoscientifically remaking the boundaries of life through processes that range from genetic engineering to artificial intelligence and nanotechnology may not this time be the source of the COVID insecurity, but it is not the answer either. If something different is happening, a new intensification of bio(in)security derived from an elaborating disjuncture between the social and the natural, then this needs to be addressed directly in itself.

Conclusion

We can draw out a number of issues from these disjunctures of security and insecurity. First, different expressions of the emerging human condition of planetary unsettling are regularly recognized, but mostly they are not yet part of a generalizing worldview that frames theory and practice.[50] Notwithstanding expressions of climate despair or concern about how the War on Terror extended globally, the concern that unless we act decisively now the planet will very quickly become existentially untenable remains only a subordinate oppositional part of the global imaginary.

Second, the forces generated by technoscientific systems of (in)security are astounding, but their profound effects and unintended consequences are clothed either in illusions about our onward-and-upward steps toward more security or their necessity to compete with others. It is indicative that assured destruction was first proclaimed as the means to end all wars, then became instituted as a basis for the continuing unsettling of international relations, and was quickly built into the military-industrial machine.[51] Now, it continues to be a structuring background feature of global geopolitics even as the nature of war has fundamentally changed, making nuclear weapons "*almost* certainly" unusable, at least as an intentional act.

Third, despite these *objective* consequences, each of the clouds of the gathering storm tends to be accompanied by *subjective* vacillations of hope and despair, and then (almost inevitably) a slow dementia of knowing, forgetting, and semi-remembering. For a couple of decades, the terror of nuclear winter intensified in people's minds—the reduction of the world to a "republic of insects and grass" was conceivable.[52] At the same time, the nuclear winter thesis was (dubiously) contested,[53] and then faded from newspaper coverage, to be added to that panoply of risks that mainstream politics are prepared to "live with."[54] Postholocaust novels and films may have kept its potential horror alive, but for many readers those graphic excursions increasingly became thought experiments in post-human desolation rather than representations of ever-present dangers or a new and existentially dangerous turn in the Anthropocene. Some will say that the risk has lessened, but all the objective indicators suggest that the automaticity of nuclear exchange, the proliferation of nuclear capacity, and the continuing stock of missiles make nuclear winter more likely now than in the 1980s. The *Bulletin of the Atomic Scientists* has currently set the Doomsday Clock at 100 seconds to midnight. When we entered the first phase of global exterminism associated with the MAD nuclear doctrine, the clock was set at seven minutes to midnight.

Fourth, perhaps as a summary of the first three points, there are ongoing and changing disjunctures between the objective processes of unsettling and our subjective response to those challenges. Self-exterminism seems to be a condition that can be described and subjectively felt, but not with the level or focus of sustained and generalized attention that leads to positive objective change.

The Anthropocene is now going through a new stage—humans have impacted upon the planet for centuries in geomorphological and reconstructive ways; but now "we" are remaking the nature of nature in reconstitutive ways. The evidence now suggests that the way in which we currently live on this planet—intensifying industrial bioengineering-based agriculture, massive destruction of habitat for wild animals, and climate change itself—have all been exacerbating the possibility and frequency of viral outbreaks.[55] Yes, trade in exotic species may be one of the proximate causes of the COVID crisis, but the crisis goes much deeper into issues that have not been the center of the COVID debate.

In summary, despite prescient spikes of alarm, humanity seems to vacillate between comfort, anxiety, and unhelpful fascination with the (in)security of the planet. Our consciousness of existential threat waxes and wanes. COVID and climate change are the latest comprehensive examples. A generation earlier, it was nuclear winter. In all these cases, the continuing and real possibility of the negation of flourishing life is enhanced by patterned practices and their intended and unintended consequences. Across the course of the twentieth century and into the present, we for the first time developed the capacity to exterminate ourselves—either directly by military means or indirectly by contributing to the collapse of a sustaining ecology. In E. P. Thompson's words, we entered a condition of "global exterminism."[56] However, as T. S. Eliot put it, deepening insecurity will likely come "not with a bang, but a whimper."[57]

Notes

1. Manfred B. Steger and Paul James, *Globalization Matters: Engaging the Global in Unsettled Times* (Cambridge, England: Cambridge University Press, 2019).

2. For an elaboration of the term "solastalgia" see Glenn Albrecht et al., "Solastalgia: The Distress Caused by Environmental Change," *Australasian Psychiatry* 15, no. 1 supplement (2007): S95–S98.
3. Death in Afghanistan's most recent war occurred on a completely different scale from classical modern wars such as World Wars I and II; nevertheless the Costs of War Project puts the overall death toll in Afghanistan during Operation Enduring Freedom at 176,000. Across the period of 2001 to 2021, 2,455 US combatants were killed, and an estimated 46,000 civilians. "Costs of War," September 2021, Watson Institute, Brown University, https://watson.brown.edu/costsofwar/figures/2021/WarDeathToll (accessed February 16, 2022).
4. Here "dominance" does not mean winning but rather having such a substantial effect that it changes the way in which people live.
5. The term comes from R. D. Laing, *The Divided Self: An Existential Study in Sanity and Madness* (Harmondsworth, England: Penguin, 1965).
6. Anthony Giddens, *A Contemporary Critique of Historical Materialism* (Berkeley: University of California Press, 1981), 13.
7. Steger and James, *Globalization Matters*.
8. Alan Chalmers, *The Scientist's Atom and the Philosopher's Stone: How Science Succeeded and Philosophy Failed to Gain Knowledge of Atoms* (Dordrecht: Springer, 2009). While this book provides evidence for my point here, I should note that I disagree profoundly with its central thesis.
9. See Anthony Burke, "Nuclear Time: Temporal Metaphors of the Nuclear Present," *Critical Studies on Security* 4, no. 1 (2016): 73–90, on more specific effects of the nuclear age on conceptions of time in global politics.
10. It needs to be added that this postmodernization of science was not a purely bad thing; it also made possible the shift to a globalizing sense of the planetary system as nonlinear and dynamic. To be more specific, scientists in tracking the globalization of atomic radiation, for example, learned much about the circulations and flows of the planet, important for understanding the ruptures of climate change.
11. The *Bhagavad Gita*, cited most famously in Robert Jungk, *Brighter than a Thousand Suns: A Personal History of the Atomic Scientists* (New York: Harcourt Brace, [1958] 1986), 201. An interview in 1968 where Oppenheimer only implicitly claimed that the thought was cotemporaneous with the event suggests that it could well have been *post facto* myth making. He concluded the interview with the words, "I suppose we all thought that, one way or another."
12. Bruce Cameron Reed, *The Physics of the Manhattan Project*, 4th edn. (Cham, Switzerland: Springer, 2021), 176.
13. The concept of "nuclear winter" entered the public lexicon through a magazine article by Carl Sagan: Carl Sagan, "Nuclear Winter," *Parade*, October 30, 1983, 4–7.
14. This phrase recalls Robert Jay Lifton's phrase "destroying the world in order to save it," but it has a difference. The new global terrorists that he

documents actually did not want to bring on Armageddon: Robert Jay Lifton, *Destroying the World in Order to Save It: Aum Shinrikyō, Apocalyptic Violence, and the New Terrorism* (New York: Henry Holt, 1999).

15. J. Robert Oppenheimer, *The Flying Trapeze: Three Crises for Physicists* (London: Oxford University Press, 1964), 58.
16. Cited in James G. Hershberg, *James B. Conant: Harvard to Hiroshima and the Making of the Nuclear Age* (New York: Alfred A. Knopf, 1993), 229. Here, in 1968, Conant was writing privately to his editor, two decades after Trinity.
17. Ibid., 234.
18. Emil Konopinski, Cloyd Marvin, and Edward Teller, "Ignition of the Atmosphere with Nuclear Bombs," August 14, 1946, available at https://sgp.fas.org/othergov/doe/lanl/docs1/00329010.pdf (accessed February 16, 2022). For a documentation of various examples, see David Sepkoski, *Catastrophic Thinking: Extinction and the Value of Diversity* (Chicago: University of Chicago Press, 2020). For a more contemporary example of this sporadic public discussion, see John Horgan, "Bethe, Teller, Trinity and the End of Earth," *Scientific American*, August 4, 2015, https://blogs.scientificamerican.com/cross-check/bethe-teller-trinity-and-the-end-of-earth/ (accessed February 16, 2022).
19. Sheldon Garon, "Defending Civilians against Aerial Bombardment: A Comparative/Transnational History of Japanese, German, and British Home Fronts, 1918–1945," *Mass Violence & Resistance*, December 10, 2016, http://bo-k2s.sciences-po.fr/mass-violence-war-massacre-resistance/en/document/defending-civilians-against-aerial-bombardment-comparative-transnational-history-japanese-ge.html (accessed February 17, 2022).
20. Harry S. Truman, "Statement by the President Announcing the Use of the A-Bomb at Hiroshima," August 6, 1945, available at https://millercenter.org/the-presidency/presidential-speeches/august-6-1945-statement-president-announcing-use-bomb (accessed February 17, 2022).
21. Herman Kahn, *On Thermonuclear War* (New Brunswick, NJ: Transaction, [1960] 2007).
22. Sahr Conway-Lanz, *Collateral Damage: Americans, Noncombatant Immunity, and Atrocity after World War II* (New York: Routledge, 2006).
23. Edward M. Geist, *Armageddon Insurance: Civil Defense in the United States and Soviet Union, 1945–1991* (Chapel Hill: University of North Carolina Press, 2019). However, because of censorship, the Soviet Union lacked what some scholars have called an "atomic culture," characteristic of the United States.
24. Daniel Ellsberg, *The Doomsday Machine: Confessions of a Nuclear War Planner* (New York: Bloomsbury, 2017).
25. Christopher G. Warner, *Implementing Joint Vision 2010: A Revolution in Military Affairs for Strategic Air Campaigns* (Montgomery, AL: Air University Press, 1999).
26. Samuel Moyn, "How the US Created a World of Endless War," *The Guardian*, August 31, 2021, https://www.theguardian.com/us-news/

2021/aug/31/how-the-us-created-a-world-of-endless-war (accessed February 17, 2022).

27. Authorization for the Use of Military Force, Pub. L. 107-40, 115 Stat. 224.
28. United States Government, "Respondents' Memorandum Regarding the Government's Detention Authority Relative to Detainees Held at Guantanamo Bay," Misc. No. 08-442 (TFH), www.justice.gov/sites/default/files/opa/legacy/2009/03/13/memo-re-det-auth.pdf (accessed February 17, 2022).
29. Samuel Moyn, *Humane: How the United States Abandoned Peace and Reinvented War* (New York: Farrar, Straus & Giroux, 2021).
30. Curtis A. Bradley and Jack L. Goldsmith, "Obama's AUMF Legacy," *American Journal of International Law* 110, no. 4 (2016): 628–45.
31. Samuel Alexander, "Double-Tap Warfare: Should President Obama Be Investigated for War Crimes?" *Florida Law Review* 69, no. 1 (1997): 262–95.
32. Armin Krishnan, *Killer Robots: Legality and Ethicality of Autonomous Weapons* (Farnham, England: Ashgate, 2009); P. W. Singer, *Wired for War: The Robotics Revolution and War in the Twenty-First Century* (New York: Penguin Press, 2009).
33. Hugh Gusterson, "Drone Warfare in Waziristan and the New Military Humanism," *Current Anthropology* 60, no. S19 (2019): S77–S86; James Michael Page and John Williams, "Drones, Afghanistan, and Beyond: Towards Analysis and Assessment in Context," *European Journal of International Security* (2021), https://doi.org/10.1017/eis.2021.19 (accessed February 17, 2022).
34. Chalmers Johnson, *Blowback: The Costs and Consequences of American Empire* (New York: Henry Holt, 2000).
35. Page and Williams, "Drones, Afghanistan, and Beyond," 4.
36. See for example, Aqil Shah, "Do US Drone Strikes Cause Blowback? Evidence from Pakistan and Beyond," *International Security* 42, no. 4 (2018): 47–84, one of the more convincing essays in this literature.
37. Barack Obama, speech to the Defense University, 2013, cited in Gusterson, "Drone Warfare in Waziristan."
38. Drone operator: "The two people we were watching ended up walking up to two full-grown adults. Once we saw the relative size, we knew the two people we had been watching were kids. They [had been] pulling sticks out of a culvert to get the water to flow. If we hadn't stalled the kill chain, who knows what would have happened?" Cited in Joseph Chapa, "Human Judgment in Remote Warfare," in *Remote Warfare: Interdisciplinary Perspectives*, ed. Alasdair McKay, Abigail Watson, and Megan Karlshøj-Pedersen (Bristol: E-International Relations, 2021), 210. It should be said that in this text the example is used to defend the thoroughness of the kill-chain process; I am using it differently to show the possible distortions of the high-definition camera surveillance process.

39. Scott Fitzsimmons and Karina Sangha, "Killing in High Definition: Combat Stress among Operators of Remotely Piloted Aircraft," *Technology* 12 (2013): 289–92.
40. For drone operators, "entering" the war zone becomes a short commute to shift work at a military office close to home. This means that the exceptional nature of war is annulled and war becomes part of everyday life. At the same time, the support structures associated with exceptional engagement, including the comradery of other soldiers in the same position in space and time, is profoundly diminished.
41. The *Enola Gay* was already 11½ miles (18½ kilometers) away when the bomb exploded. However, neither act was post-human as some commentators have suggested. Colonel Paul Tibbets, the copilot of the *Enola Gay*, "with his back to the explosion, observes a silver blue flash and experiences a strange feeling in his mouth, the same feeling as if he touched the lead and silver fillings in his mouth with a fork." It was morning rush hour in Hiroshima, but nobody in the plane saw the effect on people's bodies. "Hiroshima and Nagasaki Bombing Timeline," Atomic Heritage Foundation, 2019, www.atomicheritage.org/history/hiroshima-and-nagasaki-bombing-timeline (accessed February 17, 2022).
42. Aiden Warren and Alek Hillas, "Friend or Frenemy? The Role of Trust in Human-Machine Teaming and Lethal Autonomous Weapons Systems," *Small Wars & Insurgencies* 31, no. 4 (2020): 822–50.
43. US Air Force Office of the Chief Scientist in Autonomous Horizons, 2019, cited ibid., 827.
44. See S. M. Amadae and Shahar Avin, "Autonomy and Machine Learning at the Interface of Nuclear Weapons, Computers and People," in *The Impact of Artificial Intelligence on Strategic Stability and Nuclear Risk, Vol. 1: Euro-Atlantic Perspectives*, ed. Vincent Boulanin (Stockholm: SIPRI, 2019), 105–18.
45. Paul James and Manfred B. Steger, "On Living in an Already-Unsettled World: COVID as an Expression of Larger Transformations," *Globalizations* 19, no. 3 (2022), 426–38.
46. S. Lakshmi Priyadarsini, M. Suresh, and Donald Huisingh, "What Can We Learn from Previous Pandemics to Reduce the Frequency of Emerging Infectious Diseases like COVID-19?" *Global Transitions* 2 (2020): 202–20.
47. Mike Davis, *The Monster Enters: COVID-19, Avian Flu and the Plagues of Capitalism* (New York: OR Books, 2020); Mark Hongisbaum, *The Pandemic Century: A History of Global Contagion from the Spanish Flu to Covid-19* (New York: Penguin, 2020).
48. Wolfgang Brozek and Christof Falkenberg, "Industrial Animal Farming and Zoonotic Risk: COVID-19 as a Gateway to Sustainable Change? A Scoping Study," *Sustainability* 13, no. 16 (2021): 9251.
49. Christine K. Johnson et al., "Global Shifts in Mammalian Population Trends Reveal Key Predictors of Virus Spillover Risk," *Proceedings of the Royal Society B* 287 (2020): 20192736.

50. See for example, John Leslie, *The End of the World: The Science and Ethics of Human Extinction* (London: Routledge, 1996). And, it should be said that the emerging voices include scientists. See, for example, Martin Rees, *Our Final Hour: A Scientist's Warning—How Terror, Error, and Environmental Disaster Threaten Humankind's Future in This Century* (New York: Basic, 2003), a descriptive account of the threats to human survival.
51. One now-forgotten documenter of this history was James S. Allen, with his *Atomic Imperialism: The State, Monopoly and the Bomb* (New York: International Publishers, 1952).
52. The phrase "republic of insects and grass" comes from Jonathan Schell's *Fate of the Earth* (London: Pan, 1982), first excerpted in the *New Yorker*, causing a public furor.
53. The nuclear winter argument was incredibly controversial, dismissed by the right, and challenged by other scientists. The tempered (in tone at least) dismissal from Russel Seitz in the then-neoconservative journal the *National Interest* is exemplary of the depth of damnation: Russel Seitz, "In from the Cold: 'Nuclear Winter' Melts Down," *National Interest* 5 (1986): 3–17. However, later climate modeling, such as by Alan Robock, Luke Oman, and Georgiy L. Stenchikov ("Nuclear Winter Revisited with a Modern Climate Model and Current Nuclear Arsenals: Still Catastrophic Consequences," *Journal of Geophysical Research: Atmospheres* 112, no. D13 (2007): D13107), confirmed the disastrous consequences of thermonuclear exchange, even suggesting that the blanketing effects would probably be longer term than originally claimed.
54. For example, despite the turn during the COVID crisis to show public policy concern for the dying, the World Health Organization estimates that annually seven million people across the world continue to die of air pollution. "Air Pollution," World Health Organization, 2021, https://www.who.int/health-topics/air-pollution#tab=tab_1 (accessed February 17, 2022). While COVID-19 has brought one set of mortality concerns to the fore, global capitalism ignores others where it could more adequately act to mitigate the consequences.
55. Aaron Bernstein, "Coronavirus, Climate Change and the Environment," Harvard T. H. Chan School of Public Health, www.hsph.harvard.edu/c-change/subtopics/coronavirus-and-climate-change/ (accessed February 17, 2022).
56. The concept of "exterminism" comes from E. P. Thompson et al., *Exterminism and Cold War* (London: Verso, 1982). The authors of that volume were worried that World War III could burst out as something that no-one willed, the result of competing configurations of social forces: ibid., 2.
57. T. S. Eliot, "The Hollow Men" (1925).

4

Great Power Politics and Security: The US-China Balance of Power in Transition

Reuben Steff

Introduction

The United States and China are the world's two most influential nations. The nature and trajectory of their bilateral relationship will determine whether the twenty-first century is one of stability and relative peace or one of instability and tension—and presently their relationship is deteriorating. Washington, under both Republican and Democratic administrations, has replaced the post-1972 policy of engagement toward China with competition across a range of fronts, leading some to charge that a new Cold War is underway.[1] This signals the end of the US's global preeminence and the onset of a more competitive and dangerous multipolar world. To complicate relations further, in early 2020, a systemic "black swan" phenomenon—the COVID-19 global pandemic—emerged, intersecting with, deepening, and intensifying US-China competition as both sought advantage amid the chaos.

The predominant narrative is that China's success in getting COVID-19 under control domestically, relative to the US, has empowered Beijing's rise.[2] Here, a division in the literature exists with some claiming COVID-19 is a "reordering" or "epochal" moment—an inflection point of no return—that confirms China's rise to superpower status.[3] Others view it as an accelerant of existing trend lines that were already swinging against the US.[4] This chapter relates to this debate by considering how COVID-19 has altered the relative US-China balance of power across traditional hard power metrics (economics, technology, military power, and alliances) and soft power metrics (the appeal of a nation's culture, political values, and foreign policies). While the traditional metrics of state power are open to criticism (the penultimate section of the chapter considers how COVID-19 has revealed weaknesses in traditional concepts) in an increasingly complex and multidimensional international system, word count considerations necessitate a manageable focus on this topic. Recent analyses also show US-China competition tracking along material power lines: the nature of their relationship is changing as the balance shifts between them. It has led China (like previous great powers) to expand its core interests and pursue calibrated revisionism. In turn, this is spurring a US response.[5] Additionally, both the US and China are operating as if traditional metrics *are critical* to their security, prosperity, and prospects of "winning" their great power rivalry and shaping the 21st-century world order.[6] External observers cannot simply ignore this fact. Finally, while the core focus of this chapter is on the US-China power dyad, the Russian invasion of Ukraine on February 24, 2022 is a reminder that great power competition—indeed, at times great power conflict—will remain a feature of international relations in the twenty-first century. History is well and truly *not* dead, and research on the balance of power remains essential given that it influences the ambitions of states and how they prosecute their strategies.

This chapter draws upon empirical data from January 2020 (the outbreak of COVID-19 in Wuhan, China) to mid-2021. Firstly, the chapter briefly outlines the breakdown of the US-China relationship during the Trump administration and the trajectory of their relations throughout the first year of the Biden administration.[7] Secondly, four subsections consider how COVID-19 impacted the relative power balance, comprising (1) economic, (2) military, (3) soft power, and (4) technological (5G) metrics. The third section includes a macro consideration of how COVID-19 influenced the balance across the four metrics. The fourth part questions whether traditional approaches to the balance of power are still worthwhile in an interdependent international security landscape.

The breakdown of US-China relations

US-China relations were deteriorating prior to the outbreak of COVID-19, as President Donald J. Trump's administration (2017–2021) took aim at Beijing. It asserted that Beijing was taking advantage of the US policy of engagement (an effort from 1972 to bring China into the global economy and multilateral global governance system) by cheating on international trade and carving out a maritime sphere of influence in the South China Sea based upon flimsy historical claims. As such, Trump launched a trade war, began decoupling from China in high-tech sectors, raised the US military budget, expanded ties with Taiwan and Japan, reenergized the fledgling Quadrilateral Security Initiative (QUAD)—a forum composed of the US, UK, Australia, and Japan that some Trump officials charged should eventually become an Indo-Pacific military alliance[8]—and supported the Pacific Deterrence Initiative. The latter is a plan designed to "maintain a credible balance of military power" vis-à-vis China's military rise by increasing investments to strengthen America's regional military presence. It was passed by the US Congress in December 2020.[9]

Tensions escalated from 2017 to 2019 while a potential breakthrough, the US-China "Phase I" trade deal signed in January 2020, was immediately derailed by the outbreak of COVID-19 in Wuhan the same month.[10] A disinformation war followed as Chinese and American officials sought to shape the global narrative. They blamed one another as being the source of the outbreak,[11] while the Trump administration missed an opportunity to promote Washington's global leadership credentials by disregarding multilateralism; it halted funding to the World Health Organization (WHO) for being too "China-centric" and "a puppet of China," arguing it released misleading information about the virus to please Beijing.[12]

In a marked shift, US officials began to emphasize the ideological aspects of US-China competition.[13] Thus, by the end of Trump's term, a bipartisan consensus had been cemented in Washington that China was a near-peer challenger to US primacy. A policy of whole-of-government competition had replaced the policy of engagement as new US president Joe Biden (2021–present) sustained and endorsed the Trump administration's policies toward China, and the administration announced Washington's intention to "prevail in strategic competition with China."[14] While some tactics shifted, with a greater emphasis on rallying like-minded democracies and allies to the US side, the emphasis on competition remained.[15] Relations did not improve through 2021, with the first attempt at Biden-era diplomacy at Anchorage, Alaska, in March failing spectacularly.[16]

The chapter now turns to consider COVID-19's effects on the US-China balance of power.

The effect of COVID-19 on the US-China balance of power

Economic power

The pandemic dealt a larger blow to the US economy than to China's. The latter swiftly returned to growth in June 2020, reporting 3.2 percent growth in the second quarter, 4.9 percent in the third, and 6.5 percent in the fourth.[17] Overall, it was the *only* major economy to record positive economic growth in 2020, with 2.3 percent.[18] By contrast, the US began to recover only in the third quarter of 2020, posting a quarterly gain of 33.1 percent.[19] This impressive figure is deceptive, as it reflected recovery from a severe decline in economic activity that preceded it. Overall, US GDP decreased by 3.4 percent in 2020.[20] China's economy was expected to grow by 8.5 percent in 2021, before dropping to 5.4 percent in 2022.[21] The US was projected to grow by 5.6 percent in 2021 and 3.7 percent in 2022.[22]

The blow to the US was also revealed through unemployment statistics. The rate of unemployment stood at 3.5 percent in February 2020 and skyrocketed to 14.7 percent in April 2020, before slowly dropping to 6.7 percent by the end of the year. In contrast, unemployment figures in China at the high point of their outbreak reportedly reached 6.2 percent in February 2020, and progressively decreased to 5.2 percent by the end of 2020—they never came near to the high figures of the US.

As a result of COVID-19 and the differential effects it had on the US and China, multiple economic forecasters brought forward their estimates for when they expect the size of China's economy to overtake that of the US. The Oxford Economics Forecast projects China will overtake the US by 2029 instead of 2030; China Renaissance predicts it could be in 2031, down from 2036; the Centre for Economics and Business Research brought its forecast forward by five years, from 2033 to 2028; and Nomura Holdings shortened its forecast from 2030 to 2026.[23] Despite variations, their collective post-COVID-19 adjustments suggest China's GDP will overtake the US by the end of 2029, 3¾ years faster than if there had been no pandemic. In short, the trend in the economic balance of power, which had already been trending toward China prior to the pandemic, has accelerated. A note of caution here is warranted as China's zero-COVID policy, which was very successful in initially restricting the spread of COVID in China and allowing it to rapidly open back up economically, has continued to be sustained as of July 12, 2022.[24] This policy has forced Beijing to, at times, continue to lock down large Chinese cities and tens of millions of Chinese workers, in turn impeding China's economic growth and causing supply-chain distortions. In short, this policy has continued long after much of the rest of the world has become willing to accept the spread of a certain amount of the virus amongst broadly-vaccinated populations in exchange for economically opening up. As such, whether, and to what degree, China's economy will suffer in the coming years as a result of this policy and its effect on the relative US-China economic balance is unknown but it could very well reduce the growth that China would otherwise experience.

China also remains committed to free trade, bolstering its reputation as a supporter of globalization and the multilateral trading system. Notably, it signed the fifteen-nation Regional Comprehensive Economic Partnership on 15 November 2020. This comprises significant developing and developed nations, including Brunei-Darussalam, Cambodia, Indonesia, Laos, Malaysia, Myanmar, the Philippines, Singapore, Thailand, Vietnam, Australia, China, Japan, South Korea, and New Zealand. Once ratified it will be the largest free trade agreement (FTA) in the world—and one that excludes the US.[25] China also applied to join the Comprehensive and Progressive Agreement for Trans-Pacific Partnership (members include Australia, Brunei, Canada, Chile, Japan, Malaysia, Mexico, New Zealand, Peru, Singapore, and Vietnam) in September 2021.[26] This is a successor agreement to the Trans-Pacific Partnership that the Obama administration championed and negotiated to join but that the Trump administration withdrew from on its first day in office.[27] Here, President Biden's rhetoric that "America is back" is found wanting, given that his administration has not elected to try to rejoin this agreement and it gave up its fast-track Trade Promotion Authority (which streamlines the congressional approval process for considering FTAs) on 1 July 2021.[28]

Military power

On defense spending, the available data suggests COVID-19 has not decisively altered the previous trend. Here we see that the percentage annual increase of spending on defense is larger for China than the US, but the total year-to-year increase in spending is larger for the US, given its total defense budget is much higher than China's. China's defense budget was $193.3 billion in 2020, an increase of 5.2 percent (down from a 5.9 percent increase in 2019);[29] its 2021 defense spending was projected to rise by 6.8 percent to $208.47 billion (no estimates exist for its projected level of spending for 2022).[30] These figures are consistent with China's annual percentage increases since 2016. By comparison, in 2020, the US defense budget increased by 2.5 percent from 2019 levels to $717 billion.[31] In 2021, defense spending was projected to increase by 2.8 percent to $738 billion, and the Biden administration's request for 2022 was $753 billion, an increase of 2.0 percent.[32]

The spread of COVID-19 created operational challenges, albeit temporary, for the US military in the Indo-Pacific. It forced the suspension of all overseas deployments for 60 days and the cancellation of the annual US-Philippine Balikatan exercise, as well as the rotational deployment of 2,500 US Marines through Darwin, Australia. The biennial multilateral US-led Rim of the Pacific naval exercises were pushed to August from July and made an "at-sea-only" event.[33] Notably, COVID-19 forced two US aircraft carriers to be confined to port for a month due to an outbreak among the crew, temporarily reducing the number available for operations in the West Pacific.

Meanwhile, Beijing was not dissuaded by the outbreak of COVID-19 or the response by the Trump and Biden administrations to its growing power, electing to exploit the distraction that COVID-19 posed to its proximate region by asserting itself. It reinforced its control over Hong Kong, consolidated its presence in the South China Sea (naming eighty new geographical features in April 2020 and establishing new administrative districts), increased military activity around Taiwan and Japan, and directed naval vessels and coastguard escort ships to enter Vietnamese, Malaysian, and Philippine waters.[34] China also engaged in a border skirmish with India in June 2020 that led to the deaths of twenty Indian soldiers in the worst clash since 1967 and escalated a diplomatic spat with Australia (leading China to reduce its imports from Australia owing to, according to Beijing, Canberra's "rash participation in the US administration's attempts to contain China").[35]

As China took advantage of COVID-19 to ramp up regional military activities, the US responded by boosting the number and intensity of its freedom of navigation operations (FONOPs) throughout the South China Sea near disputed islands and key Chinese military facilities.[36] US surface vessel transits of the Taiwan Strait were thirteen in 2020—the highest number since 2007 and up from nine in 2019 and just three in 2018; US island "reef-trespassing" activities in the South China Seas were nine in 2020, up from eight in 2019 and five in 2018.[37] Additionally, US Indo-Pacific Command requested $18.5 billion in additional funding for 2022–26 to implement the 2018 National Defense Strategy. The plan, Regain the Advantage, calls for improved long-range precision strike capabilities and air defense systems, enhanced forward deployed capabilities, and greater interoperability with allies and partners to deter China from acts of aggression.[38] Washington also reasserted its commitment to Japan, the Philippines (re-signing the Visiting Forces Agreement in July 2021 that Philippine's President Rodrigo Duterte had previously threatened to cancel), deepened defense ties with the QUAD, and on 15 September 2021, signed a trilateral security pact with Australia and the United Kingdom (AUKUS) aimed at containing China's maritime power. AUKUS will see Australia acquire nuclear submarines, increase basing of US and UK military forces on its territory in the coming years and decades, and bolster cyber, hypersonic missile, artificial intelligence and quantum technology sharing.[39] The deepening of these ties augments Washington's power position in the region relative to Beijing.

Soft power

Brand Finance's comprehensive soft power index provides data to evaluate the relative US-China balance in this area.[40] First introduced by Joseph Nye in 1990, "soft power" suggests states can win support from others by means beyond "hard power"; persuasion and conversion can be used, rather than coercion. The index defines soft power as the "strength of a nation in bringing others on-side . . . [it rests] broadly upon its culture, economy, political values, foreign policies, quality of life, robust academic institutions, and rule of law."[41]

The soft power of both Washington and Beijing has been damaged by COVID-19 and their respective responses: the US, prior to COVID-19, placed first in overall soft power, but fell to sixth in 2021, whereas China dropped from fifth to eighth. On the metric of perceived effectiveness of their respective responses to COVID-19, China placed thirtieth, while the US came in *last* at 105th.[42] The US scores on influence, reputation, and governance also declined, from 7.7, 7.1, and 4.3, respectively, in 2020 down to 7.2, 6.6, and 3.8 in 2021. China's scores on these metrics are lower than the US's, while its rate of decline from 2020 to 2021 dropped from 7.1 (influence), 6.5 (reputation), and 3.4 (governance) in 2020 down to 6.8, 5.5, and 3.0 in 2021.

For the US, its decline is likely attributable to Washington's incompetent response to the crisis, its attack on the WHO, President Trump's erratic leadership, and efforts to overthrow the outcome of the 2020 presidential election. As a role model for other nations, the US's influence was undoubtedly damaged. One bright spot for the US in the index was that, irrespective of the president's behavior, the professionalism and expertise of American scientists in successfully working to forge a vaccine led to improved perceptions on education and science.[43] For China, even though the government addressed the crisis effectively in the short term, its scores likely dropped owing to negative media coverage of its initial handling of the outbreak (including questions over its transparency) and negative perceptions of its political system and foreign policy behavior.

An October 2020 Pew Research Center report provided more evidence of US and Chinese soft power decline. It found *unfavorable views* of China reached historic highs in fourteen nations. The largest increase was in Australia, where unfavorable views of China shifted from 54 percent to 81 percent in one year; in the UK they shifted from 55 percent to 74 percent, and from 60 percent to 73 percent in the US. Unfavorable evaluations increased to 71 percent in Germany, 73 percent in the Netherlands, 85 percent in Sweden, 75 percent in South Korea, 63 percent in Spain, 70 percent in France, 73 percent in Canada, 62 percent in Italy, and 86 percent in Japan.[44] A median of 61 percent across these countries said China did a bad job dealing with the outbreak. Notably, the US received a higher negative score (84 percent) on this question. Unsurprisingly, a September 2020 thirteen-nation Pew

Research Center survey found that America's reputation declined significantly among many of its key allies and partners. Favorable views of the US reached just 41 percent in the UK, 31 percent in France, 26 percent in Germany, 41 percent in Japan, 35 percent in Canada, and 33 percent in Australia.[45] Finally, while Xi Jinping was only trusted by 19 percent of respondents to do the right thing regarding world affairs, this was higher than President Trump, who only received 16 percent.[46]

The significant decline in perceptions of China's behavior in many publics worldwide provides more room for maneuver for elites to voice their concerns publicly over China's behavior, including its human rights record and its geopolitical assertion in the South China Sea. They may feel they can run the risk that, even if Beijing retaliates materially against their nation's interests, their public will be willing to accept the costs. Indeed, we have seen this since COVID-19, with many nations voicing publicly, sometimes in coalition, their disapproval of China's behavior and even suffering economic consequences (for example in the case of Australia), but not walking back their criticism.[47] While the US decline seemingly opened a similar window for criticism, there have been no material repercussions—no close partners or allies have significantly altered their defense or political ties with Washington. As explained in the summary section below, many close US allies and partners have maintained or deepened their defense ties with the US.

It is possible that China's global efforts post-outbreak have made inroads in the developing world that the data above does not capture. For example, while its index score on governance declined, Beijing, with some credibility, was able to attribute its success relative to the US on managing the virus to its institutional and governance advantages.[48] It also promoted itself as a "humanitarian" global power concerned with the "shared future of mankind" (a phrase that became commonplace in official Chinese press conferences).[49] In this, Beijing used "mask diplomacy," leveraging its industrial capacities and position as the global market leader (and the fact that much of the global economy had shut down just as its economy was opening back up) in medical supplies (China has 43 percent of global supplies) to provide global public goods—medical and protective equipment, masks, ventilators, testing kits, and a need for knowledge on effective pandemic responses.[50] In the three months between March and June 2020, China delivered medical supplies to 125 countries, including to recipient countries' armed forces, sent medical teams to eleven nations, and held video conferences with foreign ministries and militaries.[51] In an extraordinary show of capacity, in the space of just one month (March to April), China exported 8 billion masks (4 billion to the US), 37.5 million protective suits, 2.8 million testing kits, and 16,000 ventilators among other equipment.[52] And once China produced its own Sinopharm vaccine, it prioritized supplying it to developing countries, with 750 million vaccine doses sent to other nations as of August 2021, and a pledge to distribute two billion by the end of the year.[53] In comparison, the US, as of September 2021, had provided 1.1 billion doses globally, pledging to send another 500 million in January 2022.[54]

Although China's efforts included some developed countries (such as Japan, Germany, Italy, and Spain[55]), it focused on developing countries in Asia, the Middle East, and Africa, as well as some in eastern Europe and Latin America. These states are strategically important for China's long-term ambitions—they include many nations along the Belt and Road Initiative that are sympathetic to Beijing's model of governance and hold many votes in international institutions.[56] Finally, in southeast Asia, officials say China has been a "better neighbor" since COVID-19 and its presence in the region has been judged as "positive."[57]

The 5G race

US decoupling from China in high-tech sectors was already underway prior to COVID-19, but it was accelerated by the pandemic's outbreak. According to Eurasia Group, this "Great Decoupling" in high technologies will be "the single most impactful geopolitical development for globalization since the collapse of the Soviet Union."[58] Although we do not know what the effects of this will be on the future US-China balance of power, it is one area worth speculating on as it could prove significant—not just to their respective national capabilities, but also to their ability to secure technological spheres of influence and, with it, global political influence.

The primary driver behind decoupling is the growing need by Washington and Beijing to access and control data and related sources (cloud computing, social media, and critical infrastructure) beyond their borders, so that they can position themselves to take advantage of critical emerging Fourth Industrial Revolution technologies (artificial intelligence, quantum computing, semiconductors, and robotics). In this struggle, China- or US-backed 5G networks are essential, and they will also set a baseline for how countries interact with technology. The division here is marked by a philosophical disagreement over tech governance and the "politics of the internet," with democracies promoting open systems and the free flow of information, and autocratic states seeking to control the flow of information and create hybrid systems. The rollout of 5G across the world is critical to this equation, given both China and the US seek to internationalize and institutionalize their specific value systems and preferences in international tech standards.[59] The recent global trend toward authoritarianism could deepen, which could give China greater influence over authoritarian nations or nations with mixed regimes that, in turn, strengthens its power relative to the US. Intimately connected to this is the likelihood that 5G will create technological path dependency by giving China or the US immense influence to impede and/or proffer critical technologies, data, and upgrades that lock patrons into the adoption of successor technologies (such as 6G) in the 2030s.

As such, a nascent "virtual Berlin Wall" is emerging between what Biden termed the "techno-democracies" (comprising the US, its allies, and close partners), and the "techno-autocracies" (including China and Russia).[60] In this vein, the US, Australia, New Zealand, Canada, and the UK have blocked Huawei 5G equipment from their core telecommunications infrastructure[61] (a number of other countries have put restrictions in place, including Belgium, Croatia, Finland, France, Greece, India, Italy, Norway, Portugal, Singapore, Spain, and Vietnam). Many of these states already have close political and security ties with the US, and could form the embryo of a US-centric technology bloc "walled off" from a China bloc.[62]

The US, unable to offer its own end-to-end 5G, has sought to bar sales of essential computer chips to Huawei, China's major 5G telecommunications company, which Washington views as an extension of China's intelligence operations.[63] Limiting Huawei's reach and operations will, in turn, bolster US-preferred suppliers (Nokia, Samsung, and Ericsson). Even though Huawei's operations took a significant hit as a result of Washington's 5G pressure campaign, it remains a global telecommunications behemoth[64] and a number of US allies have elected to use it, including Hungary, Iceland, the Netherlands, Saudi Arabia, Turkey, and the United Arab Emirates.[65] These states may prove to be "pivot states," eventually falling into either technological sphere. In Africa, Huawei has 70 percent of the continent's 4G networks, with South Africa, Mozambique, and Namibia using Chinese 5G (and while a lack of data exists for the rest of Africa, Huawei will likely be widely adopted given its cost advantage); much of Latin America is using or planning to use Huawei in their 5G; so are Russia, much of southeast Asia, and central Asia.[66] China also has cloud computing agreements with countries in Africa, the Middle East, and southeast Asia.[67]

Summary

The above statistics suggest that the trend lines prior to COVID-19, in which China was catching up to the US on a number of levels, have accelerated. There was no "reordering" moment as a result of COVID-19's outbreak, although it has brought forward the time we might expect that to occur. Consider the economic front: the size of China's economy will, in all likelihood, albeit dependent on the effects of sustaining its zero-COVID policy, now overtake the US economy approximately 3¾ years ahead of schedule (by the end of 2029). This is reinforced by the fact that China has continued to expand and deepen its trade links via multilateral FTAs at precisely the time the US, under both Trump and Biden, has turned away from free trade. On military power, outside of a temporary halt to some US operations in the Indo-Pacific, neither China nor the US appear to have been significantly affected. Both continued to increase their military budgets in 2020 and 2021, and both increased their military operations in the Pacific (the deepening of the US's defense alliances is discussed below). It is possible that military expenditure by one or both could be reduced in the future to offset the increased domestic expenditure that has occurred to address the effects of COVID-19. On soft power, the US suffered a slightly larger reputational hit than China in much of the world, although it remains ahead overall given that it started at a higher position prior to the pandemic.

In the tech race, the effect of COVID-19 on the 5G balance of power is difficult to ascertain; it did energize US decoupling from China, and China's momentum was damaged by the US pressure campaign on 5G. In that sense, the balance may have shifted slightly away from China but its telecommunications companies still have a global presence. It is plausible (given most US allies and close partners have either banned Huawei or imposed limits on its operations in their countries) that COVID-19 has cemented a trend whereby US-backed 5G companies will secure a foothold in much of the developed world (this might have occurred without the pandemic, but China's increased assertive behavior may have influenced some states' decisions to impose limits on their 5G participation), while China's 5G will dominate in developing countries. This may eventually lead to two separate spheres of technological influence and facilitate whether the Western model of liberal democracy or China's authoritarian system will prevail in these countries. Only time will tell what, precisely, this will mean for the overall technological (and national) balance of power. It bears close monitoring.

Ultimately, if the short-term reverberations of COVID-19 slightly improved China's overall power position relative to the US, and even accelerated the emergence of a bipolar system, the second-order effects may redound in the US's favor. Consider China's behavior after the pandemic, in which it took advantage of the distraction COVID-19 posed to many states (via "wolf warrior" diplomacy, intimidation of its east Asian and southeast Asian neighbors, picking a fight with India over the Himalayas, and a diplomatic and trade clash with Australia), which led all these states to *increase their defense cooperation with the US*. As such, rather than China's assertiveness fracturing the US alliance system throughout the Indo-Pacific, it seemingly reified and deepened it. The latest manifestation of this is the AUKUS trilateral agreement, which might not have come to fruition without COVID-19, given that Australia's incentives to deepen its military alignment with the US were increased by China reducing Australian imports, which in turn was a result of Australia leading calls for an international inquiry into the origins of COVID-19.[68] To add to China's problems in this area, it has no countervailing Indo-Pacific alliances of any significance that it could energize "tit-for-tat," although its relationship with Russia has continued to deepen.[69]

Discussion

A focus on traditional power metrics can be criticized for reflecting a binary state-centric understanding of national power and influence. Military power, especially, is open to criticism as there is the simple fact that the US's formidable military power has not provided victory in 21st-century conflicts (in Afghanistan and Iraq), and it is poorly equipped to counter new hybrid forms of interference. On the technological front, it is not emerging technologies themselves but their *creative uses* that will be able to deliver significant outcomes.[70] We simply do not yet know what new potentialities will emerge out of 5G and the concomitant exponential increase in data; we do not know if the US or China, or some other state, will be best able to harness and utilize it, and thus, how it will affect the balance of power on the military front and in economics and innovation, human well-being, and the ability of states to project soft power and win the war of ideas and ideology.

Nor are traditional metrics seemingly fit for purpose when it comes to the complexities of a globalized international system in which the boundary between the domestic and foreign is increasingly blurred. At present, we are seeing a mounting number of interrelated negative trends and issues involving a weakening rules-based international order, extreme weather events, economic decoupling in high-tech industries, backsliding democracies and ever-growing levels of inequality. Indeed, it is not outside the realm of possibility that the confluence of these intersecting issues and "black swan" events, like the COVID-19 pandemic, could pose existential challenges to modern societies and economies in coming years. This raises a question: Even if the US and China are able to amass formidable amounts of national power in order to try to one-up each other in their great power competition, what if this is unable to satisfy the human security needs of their populations? Should American or Chinese citizens be satisfied that their nations are incredibly powerful if they personally face economic hardship and precarity (and in some cases repression)? Or what about the international community? The mounting international and interdependent security issues necessitate unprecedented levels of international cooperation. The spectacular levels of resources Washington and Beijing direct to ensuring their national power is larger than the other do nothing to address global issues. In fact, they divert from addressing them and cement a fixation on great power competition.

It is worth acknowledging that there is a distinction between state power and state *strength* and *resiliency*.[71] State power includes traditional power measures. State *strength* relates to the factors necessary to ensure the sociopolitical cohesion of a state and the state's ability to improve the human security of their citizens. *Resiliency*, defined by Uri Friedman, is "a country's capacity to absorb systemic shocks, adapt to these disruptions, and quickly bounce back from them."[72] The US's position as the world's most powerful state did not improve its ability to effectively address COVID-19 once it reached its shores—the virus did not care how many aircraft carriers Washington had or how large its tech companies were. Furthermore, precisely at a time when competent leadership was needed, President Trump was found wanting by ignoring scientific evidence and polarizing the nation to bolster his election prospects. Additionally, underfunding of the US healthcare system, poor decision making at the Centers for Disease Control, political polarization, and a lack of trust in government (and indeed in fellow Americans), alongside weak domestic state capacity, all doomed the US response to COVID-19.[73] The statistics are damning: as of July 12, 2022, the US has reported 90.5 million cases of COVID-19 with total deaths reaching 1,046,232—a death toll larger than the lives the US lost in all the wars it was involved in throughout the twentieth and twenty-first centuries.[74] Notwithstanding some concerns around the accuracy of its counting, China has reported 226,811 cases and 5,226 deaths from COVID-19.[75] While this is almost certainly an undercount, it is likely much lower than the US figures. Additionally, a recent study of twenty-nine countries (comprising the twenty-seven nations in the European Union, the US, and Chile) found that the pandemic has caused the largest decrease in life expectancy since World War II. US males experienced the largest decline, with 2.2 years cut off their life expectancy.[76] We do not have figures for China but, given its case numbers, any decline in life expectancy would likely be very small. If national power was all that was necessary, then the US should have been the most successful nation at combatting COVID-19 rather than one of the worst.

It is reasonable to argue that the US, despite its formidable state power, is becoming a weak state in terms of its strength and resiliency. It is like a muscle-bound boxer that is poorly conditioned and trained; it looks powerful, but it cannot deliver on what its primary purpose should be: caring for the well-being of its own people, especially during times of crisis (like the arrival of a pandemic to its shores). It is outside the scope of this chapter, but future research should consider the degree to which a nation's power is ultimately underpinned by its resiliency. This is especially pertinent given that the confluence of negative international trends can be expected to continue and lead to more international shocks of increasing intensity. Furthermore, the quest to ensure the balance of international power remains weighted in Washington's direction may divert resources and attention from the critical need to address the human security of its own people. Indeed, the most successful states in the twenty-first century will be those that invest the most in infrastructure, knowledge, and education, and in relationships that improve their resiliency to shocks.

Conclusion

This chapter has considered how the outbreak of COVID-19 has altered the US-China balance of power across traditional hard power metrics and soft power. China's relative success in managing COVID-19 domestically, and its concomitant swift return to economic growth, made it apparent in early 2020 that it would likely emerge in a better power position relative to the US. Meanwhile, the flawed response in the US to the pandemic, in addition to a fractious international response (except for scientific cooperation on forging a vaccine), created a window of opportunity for Beijing to assert itself even more than it had done pre-pandemic. A reordering moment has not occurred but preexisting trend lines suggesting a shift in the balance toward China were accelerated, albeit to differing degrees across different levels of power. Ultimately, we only have a small timeframe of data upon which to discern the implications of COVID-19 for the US–China balance of power. Many of the second- and third-order consequences have yet to manifest, and they could be unpredictable.

This chapter recognizes, and agrees with, criticisms that focusing on traditional metrics does not tell the full story of a state's strength, especially when it comes to resiliency and the ability to take care of the human security of its people. The penultimate section above discusses this. A counterpoint here is that both Beijing and Washington are acting as if traditional metrics, and the relative balance between them, are critical to their prospects of prevailing over one another in the twenty-first century. This is an unhealthy obsession, perhaps, but it does motivate their behavior, and it affects the nature of the US-China relationship (and how they engage with the rest of the international community) and the prospects for successful global responses to interdependent security challenges. As such, it bears monitoring and should be subjected to continued analysis, while scholars and citizens should push their governments to reconsider what, ultimately, will best contribute to meaningful state power, strength, and resiliency in the twenty-first century.

Notes

1. For articles that make this case, see Robert D. Kaplan, "A New Cold War Has Begun," *Foreign Policy*, January 7, 2019, https://foreignpolicy.com/2019/01/07/a-new-cold-war-has-begun/; Rick Gladstone, "How the Cold War between China and US Is Intensifying," *New York Times*, July 22, 2020, https://www.nytimes.com/2020/07/22/world/asia/us-china-cold-war.html. For articles that reject this view and seek to add nuance to the discussion, see: Thomas J. Christensen, "There Will Not Be a New Cold War: The Limits of US-Chinese Competition," *Foreign Affairs*, March 24, 2001, https://www.foreignaffairs.com/articles/united-states/2021-03-24/there-will-not-be-new-cold-war; Fareed Zakaria, "The New China Scare: Why America Shouldn't Panic About Its Latest Challenger," *Foreign Affairs*, January/February 2020, https://www.foreignaffairs.com/articles/china/2019-12-06/new-china-scare (all accessed February 17, 2022).
2. Carla Norrlöf, "Is COVID-19 the End of US Hegemony? Public Bads, Leadership Failures and Monetary Hegemony," *International Affairs* 96, no. 5 (2020): 1281–1303.
3. For instance, Chinese scholar Cui Liru argued that the world was witnessing a new "period of historic opportunities" due to the "profound changes" in it. Cui Liru, "China's 'Period of Historic Opportunities,'" *China-US Focus*, February 1, 2018, https://www.chinausfocus.com/foreign-policy/chinas-period-of-historic-opportunities. See also Robert D. Blackwill and Thomas Wright, *The End of World Order and American Foreign Policy* (New York: Council on Foreign Relations, 2020). Nicholas Ross Smith and Tracey Fallon asserted that the pandemic was an "epochal" moment—a juncture that disrupted the status quo and that will create new realities in its wake. Nicholas Ross Smith and Tracey Fallon, "An Epochal Moment? The COVID-19 Pandemic and China's

International Order Building," *World Affairs* 183, no. 3 (2020): 235–55. Also, see Benjamin Zala, "Weighing Up the Balance: What Role for the Balance of Power in the Twenty-First Century?" *Cooperation and Conflict* 45, no. 2 (2010): 245–52; Henry A. Kissinger, "The Coronavirus Pandemic Will Forever Alter the World Order," *Wall Street Journal*, April 3, 2020, https://www.wsj.com/articles/the-coronavirus-pandemic-will-forever-alter-the-world-order-11585953005; Jacques deLisle, "When Rivalry Goes Viral: COVID-19, US-China Relations, and East Asia," *Orbis*, Winter 2021, 46–74; Titli Basu, "Sino-US Disorder: Power and Policy in Post-COVID-19 Indo-Pacific," *Journal of Asian Economic Integration* 2, no. 2 (2020): 159–79; Brandon M. Boylan, Jerry McBeath, and Bo Wang, "US-China Relations: Nationalism, the Trade War, and COVID-19," *Fudan Journal of the Humanities and Social Sciences* 14, no. 1 (2021): 23–40; Dali L. Yang, "The COVID-19 Pandemic and the Estrangement of US-China Relations," *Asian Perspective* 45, no. 1 (2021), 7–31; Min Ye, "The COVID-19 Effect: US-China Narratives and Realities," *Washington Quarterly* 44, no. 1 (2021): 89–105; Thomas J. Christensen, "A Modern Tragedy? COVID-19 and US-China Relations," Brookings Institution, May 2020, https://www.brookings.edu/wp-content/uploads/2020/05/FP_20200511_covid_us_china_christensen_v3.pdf; Kevin Rudd, "The Coming Post-COVID-19 Anarchy," *Foreign Affairs*, May 6, 2020, https://www.foreignaffairs.com/articles/united-states/2020-05-06/coming-post-COVID-19-anarchy; Joshua Shifrinson, "The Rise of China, Balance of Power Theory and US National Security: Reasons for Optimism?" *Journal of Strategic Studies* 43, no. 2 (2020): 175–216 (all URLs accessed February 17, 2022).

4. Richard Haass, "The Pandemic Will Accelerate History Rather than Reshape It," *Foreign Affairs*, April 7, 2020, https://www.foreignaffairs.com/articles/united-states/2020-04-07/pandemic-will-accelerate-history-rather-reshape-it; Joseph S. Nye Jr., "No, the Coronavirus Will Not Change the Global Order," *Foreign Policy*, April 6, 2020, https://foreignpolicy.com/2020/04/16/coronavirus-pandemic-china-united-states-power-competition/ (both accessed February 17, 2022).
5. Nicholas Khoo, "The Trump Administration and the United States' China Engagement Policy," *National Security Journal* 3, no. 2 (2021).
6. Furthermore, China has done little to reassure the US, with Xi Jinping saying in 2017 that China will have "the dominant position" in the world by 2049. Zoya Sheftalovich and Stuart Lau, "How Xi Jinping Lost Australia," Politico, September 27, 2021, https://www.politico.eu/article/how-china-xi-jinping-lost-australia-trade-diplomacy/ (accessed April 11, 2022).
7. For those interested, a small literature exists. (There is already a sizable literature on how COVID-19 has affected US-China relations, so this is only covered in brief in this chapter.)
8. Hiroyuki Akita and Eri Sugiura, "Pompeo Aims to 'Institutionalize' Quad Ties to Counter China," Nikkei Asia, October 6, 2020, https://

asia.nikkei.com/Editor-s-Picks/Interview/Pompeo-aims-to-institutionalize-Quad-ties-to-counter-China (accessed February 17, 2022).

9. *National Defense Authorization Act for Fiscal Year 2021*, HR 6395, 116th Congress, 2nd session, December 15, 2020, https://www.govtrack.us/congress/bills/116/hr6395/text; Jim Inhofe and Jack Reed, "The Pacific Deterrence Initiative: Peace through Strength in the Indo-Pacific," *War on the Rocks*, May 28, 2020, https://warontherocks.com/2020/05/the-pacific-deterrence-initiative-peace-through-strength-in-the-indo-pacific/ (both accessed February 17, 2022).
10. Sergei Klebnikov, "The Trade Deal May Be Dead, Trump Says China Relationship 'Severely Damaged,'" *Forbes*, July 10, 2020, https://www.forbes.com/sites/sergeiklebnikov/2020/07/10/the-trade-deal-may-be-dead-trump-says-china-relationship-severely-damaged/ (accessed April 11, 2022).
11. Gareth Davey, "The China-US Blame Game: Claims-Making about the Origin of a New Virus," *Social Anthropology* 28, no. 2 (2020): 250–1.
12. "Coronavirus: Trump Accuses WHO of Being a 'Puppet of China,'" BBC News, May 19, 2020, https://www.bbc.co.uk/news/health-52679329; Steve Holland and Michelle Nichols, " Trump Cutting US Ties with World Health Organization over Virus," Reuters, May 30, 2020, https://www.reuters.com/article/us-health-coronavirus-trump-who-idUSKBN2352YJ (both accessed February 17, 2022).
13. Robert C. O'Brien, "The Chinese Communist Party's Ideology and Global Ambitions," White House, June 26, 2020, https://trumpwhitehouse.archives.gov/briefings-statements/chinese-communist-partys-ideology-global-ambitions/ (accessed April 11, 2022); Michael R. Pompeo, "Communist China and the Free World's Future," US Department of State, July 23, 2020, https://www.state.gov/communist-china-and-the-free-worlds-future/ (accessed April 11, 2022); Gordon G. Chang, "Mike Pompeo Just Declared America's New China Policy: Regime Change," *National Interest*, July 25, 2020, https://nationalinterest.org/feature/mike-pompeo-just-declared-america's-new-china-policy-regime-change-165639 (accessed February 17, 2022).
14. Joseph R. Biden, *Interim National Security Strategic Guidance*, White House, March 2021, 20, https://www.whitehouse.gov/wp-content/uploads/2021/03/NSC-1v2.pdf (accessed February 17, 2022).
15. David Brunnstrom and Humeyra Pamuk, "US Secretary of State Nominee Blinken Sees Strong Foundation for Bipartisan China Policy," Reuters, January 20, 2021, https://www.reuters.com/article/us-usa-biden-state-china-idUSKBN29O2GB (accessed February 17, 2022).
16. David Brunnstrom, Humeyra Pamuk, and Michael Martina, "US, Chinese Diplomats Clash in High-Level Meeting of Biden Administration," Reuters, March 19, 2021, https://www.reuters.com/world/us/us-china-set-broach-icy-relations-alaska-talks-2021-03-18/ (accessed February 17, 2022). The Biden administration's view was summed up in the 2021 report *Annual Threat Assessment of the US Intelligence Community*,

which frames Beijing as Washington's major global competitor, which, through its "whole-of-government efforts," seeks to "spread China's influence, undercut that of the United States, drive wedges between Washington and its allies and partners, and foster new international norms that favor the authoritarian Chinese system." *Annual Threat Assessment of the US Intelligence Community*, Office of the Director of National Intelligence, April 9, 2021, https://www.dni.gov/files/ODNI/documents/assessments/ATA-2021-Unclassified-Report.pdf (accessed February 17, 2022).

17. World Bank, *Pandemic, Recession: The Global Economy in Crisis* (Washington, DC: World Bank Group, 2020), 8–10; Jonathan Cheng, "China's Economy Is Bouncing Back—And Gaining Ground on the US," *Wall Street Journal*, August 24, 2020, https://www.wsj.com/articles/chinas-economy-is-bouncing-backand-gaining-ground-on-the-u-s-11598280917; Philip Bump, "On Metric after Metric, the Coronavirus Pandemic Has Been Worse in the US than Nearly Any Other Country," *Washington Post*, July 21, 2020, https://www.washingtonpost.com/politics/2020/07/21/metric-after-metric-coronavirus-pandemic-has-been-worse-us-than-nearly-any-other-country/; Keith Bradsher, "With COVID-19 under Control, China's Economy Surges Ahead," *New York Times*, October 18, 2020, https://www.nytimes.com/2020/10/18/world/with-covid-19-under-control-chinas-economy-surges-ahead.html (all URLs accessed February 17, 2022).
18. Gabriel Crossley and Kevin Yao, "China's Economy Picks Up Speed in Fourth Quarter, Ends 2020 in Solid Shape after COVID-19 Shock," Reuters, January 18, 2021, https://www.reuters.com/article/us-china-economy-gdp/chinas-economy-picks-up-speed-in-fourth-quarter-ends-2020-in-solid-shape-after-COVID-19-shock-idUSKBN29N04S; Naomi Xu Elegant, "China's 2020 GDP Means It Will Overtake US as World's No. 1 Economy Sooner than Expected," *Fortune*, January 18, 2021, https://fortune.com/2021/01/18/chinas-2020-gdp-world-no-1-economy-us/; Karen M. Sutter and Michael D. Sutherland, "China's Economy: Current Trends and Issues," Congressional Research Service, January 12, 2021, https://crsreports.congress.gov/product/pdf/IF/IF11667 (all accessed February 17, 2022).
19. Jeff Cox, "US GDP Booms at 33.1% Rate in Q3, Better than Expected," CNBC, October 29, 2020, https://www.cnbc.com/2020/10/29/us-gdp-report-third-quarter-2020.html (accessed February 17, 2022).
20. James K. Jackson et al., "Global Economic Effects of COVID-19," Congressional Research Service, November 10, 2021, https://fas.org/sgp/crs/row/R46270.pdf; "Tentative Stabilization, Sluggish Recovery?" *World Economic Outlook*, January 2020, https://www.imf.org/en/Publications/WEO/Issues/2020/01/20/weo-update-january2020 (both accessed February 17, 2022).
21. Amanda Lee, "China's Retail 'Coma' Set to Weigh on Economic Growth amid Increasingly Tight Credit Controls," *South China Morning Post*,

June 29, 2021, https://www.scmp.com/economy/china-economy/article/3139059/chinas-retail-coma-set-weigh-economic-growth-amid (accessed February 17, 2022).

22. "Economic Forecast Summary (December 2021)," OECD, https://www.oecd.org/economy/united-states-economic-snapshot/ (accessed February 17, 2022).

23. Elegant, "China's 2020 GDP"; "Chinese Economy to Overtake US 'by 2028' Due to COVID-19," BBC News, December 26, 2020, https://www.bbc.com/news/world-asia-china-55454146 (accessed February 17, 2022).

24. Helen Davidson, "Alarm in Beijing after announcement zero-Covid policy may last five years," *The Guardian*, June 27, 2022, https://www.theguardian.com/world/2022/jun/27/alarm-in-beijing-after-announcement-zero-covid-policy-may-last-five-years (accessed August, 2022).

25. "Regional Comprehensive Economic Partnership: Overview and Economic Impact," *ADB Briefs* 164 (2020), https://www.adb.org/sites/default/files/publication/664096/adb-brief-164-regional-comprehensive-economic-partnership.pdf (accessed February 17, 2022).

26. Jack Mahony, "China Applies to Join Pacific Trade Agreement Designed to Counter its Growth in the Region, Just Hours after Criticising AUKUS," Sky News (Australia), September 17, 2021, https://www.skynews.com.au/world-news/global-affairs/china-applies-to-join-pacific-trade-agreement-designed-to-counter-its-grown-in-the-region-just-hours-after-criticising-aukus/news-story/3955ccf749109462bb40d2f22611e0fb (accessed February 17, 2022).

27. Mireya Solis, "Trump Withdrawing from the Trans-Pacific Partnership," Brookings, March 24, 2017, https://www.brookings.edu/blog/unpacked/2017/03/24/trump-withdrawing-from-the-trans-pacific-partnership/ (accessed February 17, 2022).

28. Eric Martin, "US Worker-Aid Plan Is Casualty as Trade Deal Fast-Track Ends," Bloomberg, July 7, 2021, https://www.bloomberg.com/news/newsletters/2021-07-07/u-s-worker-aid-plan-is-casualty-as-trade-deal-fast-track-ends (accessed February 17, 2022).

29. "Editor's introduction to *The Military Balance 2021*," International Institute for Strategic Studies, February 25, 2021, https://www.iiss.org/blogs/analysis/2021/02/military-balance-2021-introduction (accessed February 17, 2022).

30. Yew Lun Tian, "China Defence Spending Gets Mild Boost amid Economic Caution," Reuters, March 5, 2021, https://www.reuters.com/article/us-china-parliament-defence-idUSKBN2AX07Z (accessed February 17, 2022).

31. Amanda Macias, "Trump Gives $717 Billion Defense Bill a Green Light. Here's What the Pentagon Is Poised to Get," CNBC, August 14, 2018, https://www.cnbc.com/2018/08/13/trump-signs-717-billion-defense-bill.html (accessed February 17, 2022).

32. Amanda Macias, "Trump Signs $738 Billion Defense Bill. Here's What the Pentagon Is Poised to Get," CNBC, December 20, 2019, https://

www.cnbc.com/2019/12/21/trump-signs-738-billion-defense-bill.html (accessed February 17, 2022).

33. Malcolm Cook and Ian Storey, "Images Reinforced: COVID-19, US-China Rivalry and Southeast Asia," *ISEAS Perspective* no. 2020/34; "US Pacific Fleet Announces Rim of the Pacific 2020", Commander, United States Pacific Fleet, April 29, 2020, https://www.cpf.navy.mil/News/Article/2637794/us-pacific-fleet-announces-rim-of-the-pacific-2020/ (accessed February 17, 2022).
34. Cook and Storey, "Images Reinforced"; "US Pacific Fleet Announces Rim of the Pacific 2020"; Simela Victor Muhammad, "Escalation of Tension in South China Sea and ASEAN Stance," *Info Singkat* 12, no. 10 (2020): 7–12 (allegedly a Chinese warship turned its fire control radar on a Philippine Navy vessel).
35. DeLisle, "When Rivalry Goes Viral"; Helena Legarda, "The PLA's Mask Diplomacy," International Institute for Strategic Studies, August 12, 2020, https://www.iiss.org/blogs/research-paper/2020/08/pla-covid-diplomacy (accessed February 17, 2022); Richard Javad Heydarian, "China Seizes COVID-19 Advantage in South China Sea," *Asia Times*, April 1, 2020, https://asiatimes.com/2020/04/china-seizes-COVID-19-advantage-in-south-china-sea/ (accessed February 17, 2022); Kartik Bommakanti (ed.), *China's Strategic Ambitions in the Age of COVID-19* (New Delhi: Observer Research Foundation, 2020); Erin Handley, "China Warns Australian Economy Could 'Suffer Further Pain' after Reported Export Ban," ABC News (Australia), November 6, 2020, https://www.abc.net.au/news/2020-11-06/china-daily-warns-australia-economic-pain-export-ban/12857988 (accessed February 25, 2022).
36. Guo Yuandan and Liu Xuanzun, "US Military Activities in S. China Sea in 2020 Unprecedented," Global Times, March 12, 2021, https://www.globaltimes.cn/page/202103/1218193.shtml (accessed February 17, 2022).
37. Ibid.
38. Cook and Storey, "Images Reinforced"; "US Pacific Fleet Announces Rim of the Pacific 2020."
39. Scott Morrison, Boris Johnson, and Joseph R. Biden, "Joint Leaders Statement on AUKUS," media release, Prime Minister of Australia, September 16, 2021, https://www.pm.gov.au/media/joint-leaders-statement-aukus (accessed February 17, 2022).
40. They canvassed 75,000 general public respondents and 1,000 experts and data sources from the International Monetary Fund, the International Institute for Management Development, and the World Economic Forum, among others. *Global Soft Power Index 2021*, Brand Finance, 2021, https://brandirectory.com/globalsoftpower/download/brand-finance-global-soft-power-index-2021.pdf (accessed February 17, 2022).
41. Ibid., 17.
42. "Global Soft Power Index: The World's Most Comprehensive Research Study on Perceptions of Nation Brands," Brand Finance, https://

brandirectory.com/globalsoftpower/dashboard. (accessed February 17, 2022).

43. *Global Soft Power Index 2021*.
44. Laura Silver, Kat Devlin, and Christine Huang, "Unfavorable Views of China Reach Historic Highs in Many Countries," Pew Research Center, October 6, 2020, https://www.pewresearch.org/global/2020/10/06/unfavorable-views-of-china-reach-historic-highs-in-many-countries/ (accessed February 17, 2022).
45. Richard Wike, Janell Fetterolf, and Maria Mordecai, "US Image Plummets Internationally as Most Say Country Has Handled Coronavirus Badly," Pew Research Center, September 15, 2020, https://www.pewresearch.org/global/2020/09/15/us-image-plummets-internationally-as-most-say-country-has-handled-coronavirus-badly/ (accessed February 17, 2022).
46. Ibid.
47. Edith M. Lederer, "Nearly 40 Nations Criticize China's Human Rights Policies," AP News, October 6, 2020, https://apnews.com/article/virus-outbreak-race-and-ethnicity-tibet-hong-kong-united-states-a69609b46705f97bdec509e009577cb5; Ye Xue, "China's Economic Sanctions Made Australia More Confident," *The Interpreter*, October 22, 2021, https://www.lowyinstitute.org/the-interpreter/china-s-economic-sanctions-made-australia-more-confident (both accessed February 17, 2022).
48. DeLisle, "When Rivalry Goes Viral"; see also Nourah S. AlTakarli, "China's Response to the COVID-19 Outbreak: A Model for Epidemic Preparedness and Management," *Dubai Medical Journal* 3, no. 2 (2020): 44–9.
49. Smith and Fallon, "An Epochal Moment?"
50. Ibid.
51. Legarda, "The PLA's Mask Diplomacy."
52. Shabana Fayyaz and Salma Malik, "Question of US Hegemony and COVID-19 Pandemic," *Global Political Review* 5, no. 1 (2020): 72–83.
53. Xu Wei, "China's Bigger Role in Offering Vaccine Stressed," *China Daily*, August 9, 2021, https://www.chinadaily.com.cn/a/202108/09/WS61106199a310efa1bd66771d.html (accessed February 17, 2022).
54. "Fact Sheet: President Biden's Global COVID-19 Summit: Ending the Pandemic and Building Back Better," White House, September 22, 2021, https://www.whitehouse.gov/briefing-room/statements-releases/2021/09/22/fact-sheet-president-bidens-global-COVID-19-summit-ending-the-pandemic-and-building-back-better/ (accessed February 17, 2022).
55. "China, Serbia Sign Memorandum on Space Technology," Xinhua, June 6, 2020, http://www.xinhuanet.com/english/2020-06/06/c_139117562.htm (accessed February 17, 2022).
56. Legarda, "The PLA's Mask Diplomacy."
57. For example, see Ole Tangen Jr., "Is China Taking Advantage of COVID-19 to Pursue South China Sea Ambitions?" *DW*, May 25, 2020, https://www.dw.com/en/is-china-taking-advantage-of-COVID-19-to-pursue-

south-china-sea-ambitions/a-53573918; Bill Hayton, "The South China Sea in 2020: Statement before the US-China Economic and Security Review Commission Hearing on 'US-China Relations in 2020: Enduring Problems and Emerging Challenges,'" September 9, 2020, https://www.uscc.gov/sites/default/files/2020-09/Hayton_Testimony.pdf (both accessed February 17, 2022).

58. Ian Bremmer and Cliff Kupchan, *Top Risks 2020*, Eurasia Group, https://www.eurasiagroup.net/files/upload/Top_Risks_2020_Report_1.pdf (accessed February 17, 2022).

59. In the multilateral space, China Standards 2035 seeks to institutionalize authoritarian values and preferences in international tech standards. This includes the Digital Silk Road—cooperation agreements to facilitate Chinese digital infrastructure and technology overseas. This could allow Beijing to carve out its own high-tech sphere of influence. Robert Greene and Paul Triolo, "Will China Control the Global Internet via its Digital Silk Road?" Carnegie Endowment for International Peace, May 8, 2020, https://carnegieendowment.org/2020/05/08/will-china-control-global-internet-via-its-digital-silk-road-pub-81857; Scott Bade, "Is Washington Prepared for a Geopolitical 'Tech Race'?" *TechCrunch*, May 2, 2021, https://techcrunch.com/2021/05/01/is-washington-prepared-for-a-geopolitical-tech-race/ (both accessed February 17, 2022); Andrew B. Kennedy and David L. Dwyer, "The Stakes in Decoupling Discovery: China's Role in Transnational Innovation," *Pacific Review* 35, no. 1 (2022): 147–71.

60. "Biden Putting Tech, Not Troops, at Core of US-China Policy," *Straits Times*, March 2, 2021, https://www.straitstimes.com/asia/east-asia/biden-putting-tech-not-troops-at-core-of-us-china-policy (accessed February 17, 2022).

61. The US has made it clear that its diplomatic and military posts will only use "clean paths"—5G telecom networks free of Chinese gear—for communications. The threat of the loss of intelligence sharing and security partnerships is unlikely to persuade countries that are not formal allies or close security partners with Washington. Scott Kennedy, "Washington's China Policy Has Lost Its Wei," Centre for Strategic and International Studies, July 27, 2020, https://www.csis.org/analysis/washingtons-china-policy-has-lost-its-wei (accessed February 17, 2022).

62. David Sacks, "China's Huawei Is Winning the 5G Race. Here's What the United States Should Do to Respond," Council on Foreign Relations, March 29, 2021, https://www.cfr.org/blog/china-huawei-5g (accessed February 17, 2022). Additionally, the EU is championing a US-EU trans-Atlantic economic model to compete with Beijing; and, to address COVID-19 disruption, the US announced the formation of a "trusted supplier network" (including Australia, India, Japan, New Zealand, South Korea, and Vietnam) that excluded China. David Capie, Natasha Hamilton-Hart, and Jason Young, "The Tech War Is the One to Watch," *Newsroom*, January 7, 2021, https://www.newsroom.co.nz/ideasroom/the-tech-war-is-the-one-to-watch (accessed February 17, 2022).

63. Department of Commerce, "Addition of Entities to the Entity List," *Federal Register* 84, no. 98 (2019), 22961, https://www.govinfo.gov/content/pkg/FR-2019-05-21/pdf/2019-10616.pdf (accessed February 17, 2022).
64. Juan Pedro Tomás, "Huawei Claims to Be Involved in Half of Global 5G Networks," RCR Wireless, February 22, 2021, https://www.rcrwireless.com/20210222/business/huawei-claims-involved-half-global-5g-networks (accessed February 17, 2022).
65. Sacks, "China's Huawei Is Winning the 5G Race."
66. Ibid.
67. Fergus Ryan, Audrey Fritz, and Daria Impiombato, "Mapping China's Tech Giants: Reining In China's Technology Giants," Australian Strategic Policy Institute, June 8, 2021, https://www.aspi.org.au/report/mapping-chinas-technology-giants-reining-chinas-technology-giants (accessed February 17, 2022).
68. Mahalia Dobson, "Australia Embraces US and Pays Price with China as Trade War Hits Bottom Line," NBC News, June 20, 2021, https://www.nbcnews.com/news/world/australia-embraces-u-s-pays-price-china-trade-war-hits-n1270458 (accessed February 17, 2022).
69. Andrew Radin et al., *China-Russia Cooperation: Determining Factors, Future Trajectories, Implications for the United States* (Santa Monica, CA: RAND, 2021); Vladimir Isachenkov, "Putin: Russia-China Military Alliance Can't Be Ruled Out," AP News, October 22, 2020, https://apnews.com/article/beijing-moscow-foreign-policy-russia-vladimir-putin-1d4b112d2fe8cb66192c5225f4d614c4 (accessed February 17, 2022); Emily Young Carr, "China and Russia Cooperate on Rival to GPS," *The Diplomat*, November 18, 2021, https://thediplomat.com/2021/11/china-and-russia-cooperate-on-rival-to-gps/ (accessed February 17, 2022).
70. Michael Horowitz et al., "Artificial Intelligence and International Security," Center for a New American Security, July 10, 2018, https://www.cnas.org/publications/reports/artificial-intelligence-and-international-security (accessed February 17, 2022).
71. *Network Challenge Report: COVID-19*, MINDS, June 2020, https://umanitoba.ca/centres/media/MINDS-Network-Challenge-Report-COVID-19-EN.pdf (accessed February 17, 2022).
72. Uri Friedman, "The Pandemic Is Revealing a New Form of National Power," *The Atlantic*, November, 15, 2021, https://www.theatlantic.com/ideas/archive/2020/11/pandemic-revealing-new-form-national-power/616944/ (accessed February 17, 2022).
73. Ibid.; David Brooks, "America Is Having a Moral Convulsion," *The Atlantic*, October 5, 2020, https://www.theatlantic.com/ideas/archive/2020/10/collapsing-levels-trust-are-devastating-america/616581/ (accessed February 17, 2022); Balzhan Serikbayeva, Kanat Abdulla, and Yessengali Oskenbayev, "State Capacity in Responding to COVID-19," MPRA Paper 101511, University Library of Munich, 2020; Brett Murphy and Letitia Stein, "How the CDC Failed Public Health Officials

Fighting the Coronavirus," *USA Today*, January 26, 2021, https://www.usatoday.com/in-depth/news/investigations/2020/09/16/how-cdc-failed-local-health-officials-desperate-COVID-19-help/3435762001/ (accessed February 17, 2022).

74. Worldometer, "United States. Coronavirus Cases and Deaths", February 17, 2022, https://www.worldometers.info/coronavirus/country/us/; Aaron O'Neill, "Number of Military Fatalities in All Major Wars Involving the United States from 1775 to 2021," Statista, November 22, 2021, https://www.statista.com/statistics/1009819/total-us-military-fatalities-in-american-wars-1775-present/ (both accessed February 17, 2022).
75. Worldometer, "China. Coronavirus Cases and Deaths," February 17, 2022, https://www.worldometers.info/coronavirus/country/china/ (accessed February 17, 2022).
76. Ben Quinn, "Covid Has Wiped Out Years of Progress on Life Expectancy, Finds Study," *The Guardian*, September 27, 2021, https://www.theguardian.com/society/2021/sep/27/COVID-has-wiped-out-years-of-progress-on-life-expectancy-finds-study (accessed February 17, 2022).

5

Gender and Security: Reconceptualizing Risk and Response

Kaye Quek

Introduction

Feminist scholars have long argued that gender "matters"[1] to understanding world politics and issues of global security. In 1989, Cynthia Enloe famously asked the question: "Where are the women?"[2] in studies of global security, highlighting the profound neglect of gender as a framework for analysis in traditional international relations (IR) approaches. Enloe, in her landmark text *Bananas, Beaches and Bases*, showed that, far from being absent from the machinations of international affairs—as the silences in conventional IR would suggest—women are in fact present at all levels of world politics and, moreover, critical to their functioning. Charting the multiple and varied roles performed by women in contexts ranging from backroom diplomacy to military brothels and banana plantations, her analysis pointed to the significance of gender, or the "workings of both femininity and masculinity,"[3] in the structures, behaviors, and norms of international relations.

In the years since Enloe first posed her question, feminist inquiry into the subject of global security has grown exponentially. The quantity of feminist work on security produced over the last three decades is such that it is now recognized as its own academic subfield, known as feminist security studies (FSS). It is important to note that the scholarship generated under the banner of FSS is diverse. As Annick Wibben observes, there is "no singular feminist position on security" amid the "veritable explosion" in feminist theorizing on war, violence, and peace that has taken place.[4] Rather, the FSS literature draws on an array of theoretical approaches, with scholars contributing from numerous disciplinary backgrounds (including, but also from outside, mainstream IR), where the aims, subject matter, implications, and methods of study vary, too. The diversity of approaches apparent in FSS means, as Laura Sjoberg cautions, that "there is no *one* Feminist Security Studies . . . and no *one* on-balance normatively correct way to handle feminist security theorizing around global politics."[5] Yet, even with the differences (and, indeed, tensions) that exist across the field, it is clear that there is a shared commitment to the concept of gender in the work that is constitutive of FSS, which sets it apart from both traditional and more critical security studies research. In FSS, "gender" operates as a *central* category for analyzing "security" (however this may be defined) and as a normative standpoint from which unequal and unjust relations of power can be remade. A key characteristic of feminist work on security is thus its emancipatory objective;[6] feminist scholars interested in studying security study gender as fundamental to shaping the norms and behaviors of world politics, with a view to eradicating oppressive hierarchies and promoting positive social change.

This chapter examines key insights on the relationship between gender and security highlighted by the FSS literature, most notably its core argument that thinking about gender is necessary for "making sense"[7] of international relations and security. It does so in order to apply these insights to the context of the COVID-19 pandemic, and subsequently to illustrate the relevance of feminist work on security to developing a more comprehensive understanding of the security threats that the pandemic presents. The COVID-19 pandemic, in many respects, offers a timely reminder of why an ungendered account of global security is deficient.

The chapter begins by outlining some of the core tenets of feminist theorizing on security, focusing on the significance of "gender" as a concept therein. It then examines two major concerns from the FSS literature: How "security" is defined or what counts as a "security issue," and the way gender is mobilized in global security behaviors and discourse, often with the effect of creating more *in*security. The discussion explicates these concerns in the context of the pandemic via two short case studies: firstly, the increased risk of gendered violence faced by many women as a result of lockdowns and other state measures to curb the virus; and secondly, the gendered values that have come to be attributed to the wearing of face masks. The chapter uses these examples to argue that gender remains, as ever, a critical framework for conceptualizing, and responding to, threats to global security: those that have emerged in the course of the pandemic and those that can be expected to replicate in its wake.

Gender matters: feminist theorizing on global security

Feminist interventions in security studies began with "mapping" women's roles in international politics; however, it is important to recognize that it is "gender," rather than "women," that tends to be the broader concern of FSS scholarship. Much feminist work on security certainly takes women's experiences as its starting point for analysis but, crucially, "gender" is not synonymous with "women" in the FSS literature. While *women* can be understood as referring to the social group or class of women (noting that the stability of this categorization is contested by some scholars[8]), *gender* is conceptualized as the socially learned and constructed norms, expectations, and behaviors associated with masculinity and femininity. Feminist scholars note that the relationship between masculinity and femininity is hierarchical, where the former is perceived as superior to, and privileged over, the latter. Gender is thus inseparable from relations of power; it operates as a system that produces social inequalities due to the valorizing of masculine traits over those deemed feminine. An important insight from much contemporary feminist theorizing has been to demonstrate how gender hierarchies interact with other social relations of power (such as those relating to class, race, sexuality, and so on) to create *intersectional* forms of oppression.[9] The inequalities experienced by a middle-class heterosexual white woman could therefore be expected to be quite different from those of a woman in less privileged circumstances, even though both are subjected to gender dynamics where femininity is subordinated to masculinity. The particular meanings associated with masculinity and femininity are also context specific; time, place, and culture all produce different gendered values and norms.[10] Feminist scholars working on issues of international relations thus note the plurality of gendered experiences that are borne out in this context,[11] while remaining attentive to the ways that gender gives meaning and hierarchy to social relations, especially those relating to security.

Bearing this understanding of gender in mind, the central premise of feminist work in security studies has been to demonstrate the pivotal role of gender in shaping the interactions and structures of world affairs, as well as the inadequacy of perspectives that fail to take gender into account. In asking "Where are the women?" Enloe not only drew into focus the gender norms that designate "high politics" (for example foreign policy, diplomacy, war making) the rightful domain of men—or an appropriately masculine space—to the exclusion of women. Her analysis also pointed to the limitations of an IR that fails to tell this story and to locate the many ways in which women are critical to the workings of international affairs. The global political system would not function, for example, without the wives of career diplomats who create the suitably "comfortable"[12] environment for international negotiations to take place and agreements to be formed. The same system could not operate without the women in military brothels who, through the prostitution transaction, shore up the version of masculinity cultivated by military institutions, one which legitimizes soldiers' use of controlled and deliberate violence against fellow human beings. In relation to banana plantations, a valuable site for unpacking the gendered dynamics underpinning international politics, Enloe noted that "behind every all-male . . . plantation stand scores of women performing unpaid domestic and productive labor."[13] A great many women, whose value is deemed marginal in the international political system, are in fact vital to the workings *of the system*. That their activities are marginalized in the academic discipline that claims to study world affairs (that is, IR) "leaves us," in Enloe's words, "with a political analysis that is incomplete, even naïve."[14] That women's actions are repetitively devalued in the everyday processes of global politics speaks to the gendered relations of power on which the system rests. Across contexts that seemingly could not be more different, "the conduct of international politics has depended on men's control of women,"[15] where specific constructions of gender diminish the roles designated to women in international affairs as secondary to those of men.

The centrality of gender to the processes of international relations extends to the very structures and concepts that constitute the realm of world politics. Where Enloe's analysis focuses on the necessary activities undertaken by women *at the margins* of the international political system, the work of Ann Tickner demonstrates how the entities and ideals *at the heart* of global security are themselves gendered. In contrast to mainstream IR, which presents the key actors (states, military organizations, policymakers) and endeavors (diplomacy, warfare) in international politics in gender-neutral terms, Tickner calls into question assumptions of gender neutrality, observing, quite plainly, that "international politics is a man's world."[16]

Here, the problem is not only that key positions of power and influence are populated by men, but that the processes and institutions of international relations rely on gendered hierarchies of power. Tickner highlights that the traits most prized in international politics are those most aligned with traditional notions of masculinity. She argues: "Strength, power, autonomy, independence, and rationality, all typically associated with men and masculinity, are characteristics we most value in those to whom we entrust the conduct of our foreign policy and the defense of our national interest."[17] In contrast, the domestic context or homeland in need of protection, where women (and children) *are* visible in IR, is feminized. In the theory and practice of international relations, states' and other actors' measure of success lies in their "power capabilities and capacity for self-help and autonomy,"[18] which are treated as conventionally masculine attributes. Soldier-citizens, enacting violence in the name of protecting those at home, are frequently conceptualized as embodying the pinnacle of manhood or the masculine ideal. As Tickner explains, the extent to which masculinity as the norm is embedded in the values that drive the international system is problematic from a feminist perspective due to the inequalities it reproduces and the limitations it places on creating a more secure world. The valorization of masculine behaviors, and consequential *devaluing* of that which is deemed feminine, serves to exclude women (and other oppressed groups) from positions of global influence. As our conceptualization of world politics is restricted to the masculine concepts celebrated in the conduct of international affairs, so too are "the options available to states and their policymakers"[19] for achieving security. Recognizing the gendered foundations of international relations thereby forms a necessary step to envisioning more meaningful and diverse possibilities for addressing threats to global security.

Rethinking security (and insecurity) from a feminist perspective

Yet, how are these threats identified and defined? FSS scholars argue that mainstream conceptualizations of "security," too, are reflective of the masculine bias that pervades international relations, both practically and in the discipline of IR. As Tickner and others show, "security" in the sphere of international politics most often refers to the security of the state, which is construed as seeking to act autonomously in the context of a hostile and competitive environment, in response to external threats. In conventional approaches, Jan Jindy Pettman explains, "security becomes national security . . . hence IR's focus on wars and violence between states, despite the overwhelming experience of violence within states."[20] For feminists, such an approach to security is inadequate because it is born predominantly out of men's perceptions and experiences of insecurity; that is, what men, and most particularly very powerful men, identify as a security threat, while privileging traditionally masculine traits—expressions of autonomy, strategic prowess, and the legitimized use-of-force—as the appropriate responses.

Mainstream conceptions of security, as such, are limited by their neglect of what happens within states and of the experiences of those at the periphery of global power structures, including women. Tickner poses the question: "If we were to include women's experiences in our assumptions about the security-seeking behavior of states, how would it change the way in which we think about national security?"[21] By centering women's experiences, FSS scholars show that the dominant definitions of security in international relations rely on a false gendered distinction between the international and the domestic, one that mirrors the public-private distinction underpinning states' reluctance to address women's oppression in the private sphere of the home. Like the public-private distinction, which positions the home and family life as beyond the proper jurisdiction of the state, the distinction between the international and the domestic renders women's experiences of insecurity invisible, including in apparently stable, secure states.[22] The statist account of security, commonly deployed in mainstream IR, is—at best—incomplete and constrained in its applicability. More problematically, it allows gendered (and other) insecurities to continue unabated by obscuring their occurrence from view.

Consequently, a major concern of FSS scholarship has been to reconceptualize how security is understood and defined in relation to global affairs. In seeking to widen conceptions of security beyond the bounds of state security, feminist scholars have tended to employ a bottom-up approach, rather than the top-down schema characteristic of IR, based on the recognition that "the security of the state is often built on the insecurity of its most vulnerable populations."[23] Enloe's work is again instructive in this respect. In focusing on the roles performed by women at the fringes of global power, her research illustrates how the ordinary and unremarkable everyday workings of gender, tied to insecurity for those subordinated in this hierarchy, come to underpin the broader structures of world politics. Her analysis demonstrates that the "personal" is, at once, "political" *and* "international."[24] That is, the security enjoyed and pursued at the level of the state, in most cases, is dependent on sacrificing, to some extent, the security of those who are marginalized within state borders.

There are, therefore, important connections to be made between the insecurities experienced by women (and others feminized in international politics) at the level of the everyday and those at the more macro levels of global and national security. Feminist scholars make the point, for instance, that a broader conception of *insecurity* is needed in international politics if women's experiences of violence, risk, and vulnerability are to be more meaningfully captured and addressed. In support of their claim, they note that challenges to women's security are often not a consequence of national security events but are a fixture of women's everyday lives in the form of gendered violence perpetrated, most commonly, by men that they know; an endemic insecurity of pandemic proportions[25] but one not easily recognized in conventional IR accounts of security "threats."[26] The failure of IR to identify women's daily insecurity to violence within its conception of security risks does not mean that the two are unrelated. Rather, an important correlation exists between state-sanctioned, militarized violence and the gendered violence women experience even in times of "peace." The relationship can be conceptualized in terms of a two-way continuum: on the one hand, processes of militarization permeate everyday life to normalize male aggression as characteristic of contemporary masculinity; while on the other, the violence against women that is tolerated in everyday life forms the basis for men's legitimized use of violence as soldiers engaged in warfare.[27] That is to say, there is a connection between the masculinized violence that underpins war and that which occurs ordinarily in relatively stable "peaceful" states, yet an ungendered account of "insecurity" is unable to recognize it as such.

Feminist scholars further contend that, in order to be meaningful, "insecurity" cannot be understood to only refer to militarized and physical forms of violence but must take into account structural manifestations of violence, as well. Sjoberg explains: "Feminists have pointed out that threats to women's security come not only from guns, bombs, and fists but also from inadequate access to nutrition, healthcare, and birth control."[28] A gendered analysis of global insecurity reveals the interdependence of the different forms of violence that create challenges to security in women's lives. As a case in point, much FSS research demonstrates how structural inequalities work to produce gendered violence wherein the state is implicated as a source of insecurity. For V. Spike Peterson, the state plays a considerable role in contributing to the ways that women become

> objects of masculinist social control not only through direct violence . . . but also through ideological constructs, such as "women's work" and the cult of motherhood, that justify structural violence—inadequate health care, sexual harassment, and sex-segregated wages, rights and resources.[29]

The state, then, in FSS theorizing, cannot be straightforwardly understood as the primary guarantor of safety for its citizens, but instead exists and operates as a fundamentally masculine construct.[30] At the same time, feminist researchers call attention to the violence that stems from environmental crises such as climate change, economic hardship, and financial crises, as well as war, which produce gendered experiences of displacement, homelessness, disease, and poverty, among other insecurities.[31] To restrict what counts as a security threat to acts of war perpetrated by states (or even by nonstate actors) is to offer an impoverished analysis of how insecurity manifests most immediately and in the day-to-day lives of a great number of people, especially women. It also involves overlooking many of the ways in which gender is mobilized in global security behaviors and discourse, often with the effect of creating more *in*security.

This latter point is demonstrated by feminist security scholars in relation to a number of contexts. The FSS literature calls attention, for instance, to the contradiction that can exist in states' pursuit of security, particularly when these endeavors take the form of militarized action. Armed conflict, as a form of masculine violence sanctioned by states, is shown by feminists to increase women's vulnerability to male violence; both during (and at the site of) conflict (consider, for example, the mass rape of women in wartime) and postconflict, when soldiers return home and enact domestic violence against the women in their homes.[32] State efforts to achieve security instead often produce greater risk for women, when "security" is conceived and sought out in traditionally masculine terms.

Feminist analyses of the rhetoric and discourse of global security are equally revealing of how gender is deployed in international relations in ways that heighten insecurity, rather than diminish it. Carol Cohn's early ethnographic research on the language used by United States defense intellectuals in relation to nuclear weapons is especially telling in this regard. Cohn highlights the gendered discourse—of "erector launchers," "soft laydowns," and "deep penetration"—employed by defense staff to describe nuclear warfare.[33] Her analysis shows how the privileging of masculine tropes constrains actors from engaging other, nonmasculine and nonviolent options for promoting and imagining security. More recently, Susan Faludi has expressed concern about the reemergence of a masculinized state security discourse in the US in the period following the 9/11 attacks, in which "national male strength" is measured commensurate to "female peril."[34] As she and other theorists note, such gendered ways of thinking effectively disable alternative possibilities for dealing with risks to global security beyond the set of responses legitimized by prevailing masculine conceptions of IR.[35] For feminist scholars, "gender" thus forms a necessary category for thinking about global security issues, allowing for a more accurate picture of both security and insecurity to be developed and known, and so too pathways forward for dealing with these threats.

Gendered insecurity and the COVID-19 pandemic

There are any number of ways in which the security challenges presented by the COVID-19 pandemic can be understood as gendered.

While men are more likely to contract the virus and suffer higher rates of mortality, it is widely recognized that women are far more greatly affected by the social and economic repercussions that stem from state responses to reduce the risk of COVID-19 to public health.[36] Already, there is a significant body of research that documents, for instance, the increased *economic* insecurity that vast numbers of women around the world are experiencing (in different ways and to varying degrees) due to the pandemic. The concentration of women, globally, in low-paid, precarious forms of labor means that women are particularly vulnerable to job loss and reductions in income as a result of the economic downturns driven by COVID-19.[37] Women are also overrepresented in major sectors (for example hospitality, tourism, retail) that have been unable to trade for extended periods as a consequence of state lockdowns.[38] These factors are shaped and worsened by gender norms which construct women's paid work as secondary to that of a male breadwinner, and which characterize the unpaid care economy (cleaning, cooking, fetching water or firewood, home schooling, and so on) primarily as the responsibility of women. With more people at home, the gendered burden of unpaid care has dramatically increased. In research from Ireland,[39] Germany,[40] Hungary,[41] Bangladesh,[42] Morocco,[43] South Africa,[44] Australia, and Canada[45] (among others), there is evidence to demonstrate that women are prioritizing the care of their loved ones over their own economic security, with both short- and long-term consequences.

The worsening of gendered health insecurities is another related effect of the pandemic that is identified in the emerging literature. Women's mental health is shown to have suffered greatly in situations where they have assumed a disproportionate responsibility for home schooling when stay-at-home orders have been in place.[46] The pandemic has also contributed to insecurities around women's sexual and reproductive health, where access to family planning services (including abortion) has been limited.[47] There is a concerning trend coming to light where high numbers of women, across several countries, are seeking later than usual abortions for unintended pregnancies.[48] The challenge to women's bodily and health security here is directly linked to the gendered division of household labor exacerbated by the pandemic, as changes to women's bodies signaling pregnancy have gone unnoticed for longer periods as they have absorbed the increased burdens of care.

The patterns of gendered economic and health insecurities that are intensified by COVID-19 underline the argument of feminist security scholars that to conceptualize "security" principally in terms of risk to the state is to overlook the complex web of relationships that inform how security is experienced in the everyday lives of individuals and groups, in particular women. In the brief examples cited here, threats to national security (that is, the spread of the virus) exist alongside gendered security threats, at once direct and indirect, immediate and ongoing. Yet, as Sophie Harman argues, in pandemic responses generally, and in relation to COVID-19 specifically, gender is rarely recognized as a factor that increases risks to women's security. In health emergencies, gender is instead operationalized as a "solution" to the problems that pandemics create, one "that constructs and maintains free or low-paid labour, voluntary care work, social protection and absorption of the crisis—all of which are fundamental to pandemic response."[49] The mobilization of gender norms as a "fix" to the challenges of life under COVID-19 indicates that, as a site for unpacking the relationship between gender and *insecurity*, the pandemic, unfortunately, has plenty to offer.

This section of the chapter focuses on two further instances of global gendered insecurity emanating from the COVID-19 pandemic: women's increased risk to gendered violence, which has occurred around the world, and the gendered values that have come to be associated with the wearing of face masks in many countries. The discussion draws on these examples as case studies which demonstrate the continued relevance of feminist theorizing on security, and its importance for ensuring an inclusive and in-depth understanding of the threats to security that the pandemic entails. Both cases underline the core argument found in the FSS literature that thinking about gender is necessary for making sense of international relations and security. Together, they also illustrate why gender must form a necessary framework in the responses developed to address challenges to global security, now and in the future, if those responses are to be meaningful and effective for those they seek to protect.

The "shadow pandemic" of violence against women

In April 2020, the United Nations recognized the worldwide escalation in women's risk to gendered violence as the "shadow pandemic" to COVID-19.[50] As stay-at-home orders came into force, the early months of the pandemic saw domestic violence (DV) services around the world report significant increases in requests for help. In Singapore and Cyprus, calls to DV helplines surged by 30 percent, and in some parts of Australia they did so by 40 percent.[51] In France and the US, incidents of DV rose by up to 35 percent[52] and in the United Kingdom (where the national DV hotline saw a 25 percent increase in calls), almost three times as many women were killed by a former or current partner in the weeks between late March and early April 2020, compared to the same period in each year over the previous decade.[53] Even in China, where information on gendered violence can be difficult to obtain, higher numbers of incidents were observed; reported cases of DV in February 2020 were three times the figures recorded in the previous year.[54] The growth in women's requests for help were not uniform, however. UN Women notes that, in several countries, reporting was actually down in the initial lockdown period of the pandemic.[55] The trend is attributed to situations where women were so constrained by the social isolation created by stay-at-home orders, and the subsequent heightened control of their abusers, that they were simply unable to access support.

The effect of state responses to COVID-19 has been not only to increase the prevalence of gendered violence but to shape the severity and forms in which it manifests. Of particular concern is the way in which the shelter-in-place mandates, implemented by states to protect the community at large from the virus, effectively generate conditions for perpetrators to expand the means by which to enact harm. Most obviously, women's risk of suffering male violence is heightened by factors such as being unable to leave their house, where the perpetrator may also reside, encountering greater difficulties in accessing frontline services, and having fewer opportunities to seek support from family or wider social contacts, resulting in further isolation.[56] Crises, more broadly, are recognized to sharply exacerbate rates of violence against women (VAW), as economic stress and the more generalized instability related to the crisis intensify preexisting gender inequalities and the associated power dynamics.[57] However, research on VAW in the COVID-19 pandemic identifies novel ways in which offenders seek to terrify and control victims. These include telling women when they must or cannot wash their hands (with some being forced to wash their hands to the point of bleeding), using children to demand cohabitation where previously victims and perpetrators had been living separately, and threatening to bring a COVID-positive person into the house to infect women and their children.[58] The early literature on gendered violence and the pandemic makes clear that these insecurities are particularly heightened for women who experience intersecting forms of marginalization. Older women (especially those who reside in facilities such as aged-care homes), and migrant and disabled women, for example, who are likely to experience greater challenges in accessing help, are more vulnerable to gendered violence as a concurrent security threat in the pandemic.[59]

At the same time, technology-facilitated abuse of women has spiked considerably. In the UK and Australia, incidents of image-based abuse—the sharing and/or creation of intimate images without women's consent (also known as "revenge porn")—more than doubled in periods of lockdown.[60] During these same periods, the consumption of online pornography—much of which normalizes VAW and features in DV survivors' accounts of their abuse[61]—also substantially increased.[62] In some cases, the stay-at-home orders themselves have formed a further source of trauma for victims, who experience being trapped in their houses as a trigger for reliving earlier abuse.[63] Several scholars thus describe gendered violence in the context of the pandemic as a form of domestic "terrorism,"[64] which warrants the same level of concern and response from states as the virus itself.

COVID-19 has additionally raised the visibility of certain groups of women in the public eye, in turn amplifying their vulnerability to gendered violence. In New Zealand, the UK, and Australia, health workers have been verbally and physically targeted for abuse in public, for instance, being spat on while wearing hospital scrubs on the way to work, and aggressively shouted at for "spreading" the virus.[65] The pattern of heightened gendered abuse extends to workplaces, with several international studies documenting increased violence against healthcare staff in the context of their work environments.[66] As two thirds of the health workforce globally are women (a proportion that increases to 90 percent when expanded to include social care workers),[67] the rise in violence against health workers manifests largely as a form of gendered insecurity. Scientists and medical experts who feature in news media coverage of the pandemic, too, have been subject to more frequent threats, particularly online bullying. Anecdotal evidence indicates that gender plays a role in the content of the abuse, with female experts more frequently targeted with threats of a sexualized nature, in contrast to those directed at men.[68] The abuse they encounter can be conceptualized in terms of the patriarchal silencing of women that occurs when women appear "out of place,"[69] not dissimilar to the prevalent and commonly sexualized abuse confronted by female politicians when they seek or obtain high public office.

The global manifestation of greater VAW in the pandemic thus illustrates, most tellingly, the feminist concern that state efforts to achieve "security," where this is conventionally defined, frequently entail new or heightened forms of insecurity for women. In particular, it highlights the need—as outlined by FSS scholars—to conceive of "security" in ways that better capture the synchronicity of multiple gendered security challenges. Sjoberg makes the point that "[a] gender-based analysis . . . questions the unitary nature of state security by arguing that secure states often only achieve security by sacrificing the security of some of their citizens, namely, women."[70] In the brief case study presented here, state efforts to limit the spread of the virus, and to protect the public at large, have direct consequences for the immediate security of many women, for whom the threat of contracting COVID-19 exists parallel to threats to their person (and often that of their children). For women who are threatened with coming into contact with the virus by abusive partners, who use such threats as a method of coercive control, the profound contradiction in state lockdown and associated measures (curfews, travel limits, and so on) designed to keep the community safe is especially acute. Their experiences of violence underline the feminist argument that, in order to be both meaningful and comprehensive, state conceptions of "security" must start with the perspectives of those most at the margins of global power structures,[71] including at-risk women.

This is not to say that governments around the world have been ignorant of the gendered harms to women that have intensified as a consequence of efforts to minimize the threat to public health created by COVID-19. In fact, in response to the "shadow pandemic," many states have significantly increased public funding for specialist counseling services (including for men at risk of committing violence), acquired buildings to be used as additional refuges for women, and promoted public messaging around the heightened risk of gendered violence and the support services available.[72] Yet none have sought to address VAW—itself characterized as a "pandemic" by the World Health Organization long before COVID-19[73]—with the same level of urgency and commitment as that which has been mustered to mitigate the effects of the virus. As Harman contends, gendered insecurity, when it is recognized in health emergencies, only ever amounts to a "secondary"[74] concern in the eyes of states and those in positions of power. The lack of primacy given to VAW in responses to the pandemic demonstrates the work that is still to be done to "de-gender" conventional approaches to security, while also signaling how these approaches might be reimagined to address threats to global security more effectively and systematically in the future.

The gendered politics of mask wearing

The gendered discourse that has emerged on the use of face masks in certain countries further illustrates the relevance of feminist theorizing on global security to more fully understanding the threats posed by the pandemic. While in many states, wearing a mask when unwell or in the midst of a health crisis is the social norm (this is the case, for example, in countries across Asia[75]), in settings such as the US, mask use in relation to COVID-19 has been met with notable resistance by some sections of the community. An analysis of the discourse around mask wearing in the US (as well as elsewhere) points to the significance of gender in explaining this trend. It becomes clear that, for many individuals, wearing a face mask (even in the context of a global pandemic) constitutes a *gendered* activity, specifically one that conveys messages of femininity and weakness, where these traits are conceptualized in binary opposition to the strength and independence associated with traditional masculinity.[76] For adherents to this perspective, public health advice or mandates to wear a mask when out in public are thus construed as an affront to normative manhood, an incursion against the autonomy and freedom enjoyed by those with the most power in society.

In the pandemic, the embedding of gendered values in the uptake of mask wearing has been evident at the highest levels of global power. As president of the United States, Donald Trump continually sought to invoke mask wearing as a way to demean and feminize his opponents. The correlation between mask use and femininity was evident, for instance, in Trump's October 2020 tweet directed at House majority leader Nancy Pelosi, which said: "Wear your mask in the 'beauty' parlor, Nancy!"[77] after Pelosi criticized Trump for removing his mask to be photographed while infected with COVID-19. The association between masks and feminine weakness was also deployed throughout the presidential election campaign the same year, by Trump and several conservative commentators alike. At the September 29 debate, Trump sought to weaponize the gendered discourse on masks to ridicule his opponent, Joe Biden, for Biden's adherence to public health guidelines that identified mask use as one way to limit the spread of the virus. He derided Biden: "I don't wear masks, like him. Every time you see him, he's got a mask. He could be speaking 200 feet away from them and he shows up with the biggest mask I've ever seen."[78] Fox Nation presenter Tomi Lahren similarly employed the gendered connotations around face masks to present Biden as feminized—that is, as vulnerable and not up to the job of president of the United States[79]—tweeting: "Might as well carry a purse with that mask, Joe."[80] More broadly, the invocation of gender norms in Trump's quest for reelection was evident in his urging of Americans not to let the virus "dominate" them,[81] something that, presumably, a "real" man would never allow to happen. This was a message captured symbolically in his dramatic removal of his face mask upon returning from hospital for treatment for COVID-19, while saluting his Marine One helicopter as it flew away.[82]

Feminist work on the performance of masculinity in international politics goes some way to making sense of the gendered values at play in relation to the gendering of face masks and their meaning for global security. As Anne Sisson Runyan and V. Spike Peterson explain, far from being static, masculinity, in the context of international politics, is something that must be continually proven and displayed. They contend: "In societies where masculinity is associated with power-over and violence, men are under constant pressure to prove their manhood by being tough, adversarial, and aggressive."[83] The need to continually reassert one's masculinity is particularly acute in the realm of world politics, given that these are the characteristics most valued in this sphere and, historically, deemed necessary for "success." Trump's efforts to project an infallible masculinity, via the derision and feminization of face masks—themselves, a very public display of recognition of vulnerability (to a disease)—can thus be read as entirely in keeping with the "thoroughly masculinized"[84] norms and behaviors of international relations. However, as feminist research on global security shows, assertions of masculinity in IR are no guarantee of security actually being achieved or restored; in fact, the opposite is more likely to be true. In the case of the gendered discourse surrounding the use of face masks in the pandemic, we can see how gender norms—and specifically, assertions of traditional masculinity—serve to heighten security risks by undermining an effective means by which to reduce transmission of the virus. In this instance, masculinity itself comes to form a threat to state security.

It is important to note that the association between gender hierarchy and the use of face masks is not limited to the rhetoric of Donald Trump nor to the political environment of the United States. Brazilian president Jair Bolsonaro, too, has attempted to link mask wearing to feminized conceptions of vulnerability, including via the characterization of masks as being "for fairies," which is a homophobic slur in Brazil, and in many other countries, too.[85] Beyond formal politics, there are also numerous studies internationally which highlight a connection between individual men's support for traditional gender norms and a reluctance or refusal to use a face mask. The research consistently shows that, across very different settings, men are less likely than women to wear a mask[86] and that their behavior is frequently attributed to the view that to do so is in some way emasculating, that is, "shameful . . . and a sign of weakness,"[87] and "infringing on their independence."[88] Scholars, therefore, largely attribute the gendered perceptions that exist around face masks to the prevalence of gender stereotypes, which socialize men to celebrate risk-taking behaviors as shows of strength, and to fear behaviors that may convey signs of weakness. As Dan Cassino and Yasemin Besen-Cassino observe, *not* wearing a mask for some men can be interpreted as a performance of conventional masculinity: "Signaling that they are unconcerned about the prospect of getting sick may be working as a masculinity display for these men."[89] In the discourse of political leaders *and* at the level of the everyday, gender is necessary to explain the underlying basis of this particular threat to state security.

Where a feminist analysis identifies gender as a source of insecurity, so too does it open up the possibilities for alternative options to be countenanced in state efforts to address security risks. In relation to face masks, Tyler T. Reny points out that understanding the connection between mask wearing and gender can be used to adjust "messaging around public health measures . . . to overcome barriers around the perceived 'masculinity' of behaviors."[90] In this way, feminist work on security proves significant both to thinking about how global security threats manifest, and as a framework that can inform state efforts to develop strategies for dealing with global threats to security, not only now but also beyond the pandemic.

Conclusion

Feminist work on global security has much to offer to analyses of insecurity in the pandemic and beyond. Drawing on the extensive literature on gender and security developed by FSS scholars, this chapter has sought to underline the importance of feminist approaches to understanding the extent and gendered nature of the security risks that have emerged in the pandemic and that will continue long after its immediate impact is felt. There are countless ways in which the insecurities created by COVID-19 can be understood as gendered. The discussion here has focused on the increased incidence of VAW evidenced around the world, and the gendered values attributed to face masks in certain countries, to illustrate the necessity of "gender" as a framework of analysis for "making sense" of global security issues. The hope is that in centering gender in our approach to security threats we can begin to imagine new possibilities for global security in which gender and *insecurity* are more often decoupled.

Notes

1. See Laura J. Shepherd (ed.), *Gender Matters in Global Politics: A Feminist Introduction to International Relations*, 2nd edn. (Abingdon, England: Routledge, 2015).

2. Cynthia Enloe, *Bananas, Beaches and Bases: Making Feminist Sense of International Politics*, updated edn. (Berkeley: University of California Press, 2000), 133. The first edition of Enloe's text was published in 1989.
3. Ibid., 11.
4. Annick T. R. Wibben, "Debates in Feminist Security Studies," in *Routledge Handbook of Security Studies*, ed. Myriam Dunn Cavelty and Thierry Balzacq, 2nd edn. (Abingdon, England: Routledge, 2017), 121–2.
5. Laura Sjoberg, "Feminist Security and Security Studies," in *The Oxford Handbook of International Security*, ed. Alexandra Gheciu and William C. Wohlforth (Oxford: Oxford University Press, 2018), 51 (original emphasis).
6. J. Ann Tickner, "Feminist Responses to International Security Studies," *Peace Review* 16, no. 1 (2004): 45.
7. I borrow here from the full title of Enloe, *Bananas, Beaches and Bases*.
8. See Columba Peoples and Nick Vaughan-Williams, *Critical Security Studies: An Introduction* (Abingdon, England: Routledge, 2010), 41–3.
9. The concept of "intersectionality" originated in the work of Kimberle Crenshaw. See Kimberle Crenshaw, "Mapping the Margins: Intersectionality, Identity Politics, and Violence against Women of Color," *Stanford Law Review* 43, no. 6 (1991): 1241–99. In the context of IR, see Ann Sisson Runyan and V. Spike Peterson, *Global Gender Issues in the New Millennium* (Boulder, CO: Westview Press, 2015), 2.
10. Runyan and Peterson, Global Gender Issues, 3.
11. Laura Sjoberg, "Introduction to *Security Studies*: Feminist Contributions," *Security Studies* 18, no. 2 (2009): 187.
12. Enloe, *Bananas, Beaches and Bases*, 96.
13. Ibid., 137.
14. Ibid., 2.
15. Ibid., 4.
16. J. Ann Tickner, *Gender in International Relations: Feminist Perspectives on Achieving Global Security* (New York: Columbia University Press, 1992), 1.
17. Ibid., 3.
18. Ibid., 7.
19. Ibid., 17.
20. Jan Jindy Pettman, *Worlding Women: A Feminist International Politics* (London: Routledge, 1996), 2.
21. Tickner, *Gender in International Relations*, 30.
22. Sjoberg, "Introduction to *Security Studies*," 196.
23. J. Ann Tickner, "What Is Your Research Program? Some Feminist Answers to International Relations Methodological Questions," *International Studies Quarterly* 49, no. 1 (2005): 11.

24. Enloe, *Bananas, Beaches and Bases*, 196.
25. "Violence against Women: Impact and Scale," World Health Organization, 2021, https://www.who.int/health-topics/violence-against-women#tab=tab_2 (accessed February 18, 2022).
26. See Catharine A. MacKinnon, "State of Emergency," in *September 11, 2001: Feminist Perspectives*, ed. Susan Hawthorne and Bronwyn Winter (North Melbourne: Spinifex, 2002), 426–31; Liz Kelly, "Wars against Women: Sexual Violence, Sexual Politics and the Militarised State," in *States of Conflict: Gender, Violence and Resistance*, ed. Susie Jacobs, Ruth Jacobson, and Jennifer Marchbank (London: Zed, 2000), 45–65.
27. Kelly, "Wars against Women." Also see Cynthia Cockburn, *Antimilitarism: Political and Gender Dynamics of Peace Movements* (Basingstoke, England: Palgrave Macmillan, 2012), 17.
28. Sjoberg, "Feminist Security," 48–9.
29. V. Spike Peterson, "Security and Sovereign States: What Is at Stake in Taking Feminism Seriously?" in *Gendered States: Feminist (Re)visions of International Relations Theory*, ed. V. Spike Peterson (Boulder, CO: Lynne Rienner, 1992), 46.
30. See Pettman, *Worlding Women*, 3; Charlotte Hooper, *Manly States: Masculinities, International Relations, and Gender Politics* (New York: Columbia University Press, 2001); Catharine A. MacKinnon, *Are Women Human? And Other International Dialogues* (Cambridge, MA: Belknap Press, 2006), 190.
31. Runyan and Peterson, *Global Gender Issues*, 83.
32. Kelly, "Wars against Women"; MacKinnon, *Are Women Human?*, 180–91.
33. Carol Cohn, "Sex and Death in the Rational World of Defense Intellectuals," *Signs: Journal of Women and Culture in Society* 12, no. 4 (1987): 693.
34. Susan Faludi, *The Terror Dream: Fear and Fantasy in Post-9/11 America* (Melbourne: Scribe, 2008), 262.
35. Tickner, *Gender in International Relations*, 17.
36. UN Women, *From Insights to Action: Gender Equality in the Wake of COVID-19* (New York: UN Women, 2020), 2. Also see António Guterres, "Put Women and Girls at the Centre of Efforts to Recover from COVID-19," United Nations COVID-19 Response, https://www.un.org/en/un-coronavirus-communications-team/put-women-and-girls-centre-efforts-recover-covid-19 (accessed February 18, 2022).
37. UN Women, *From Insights to Action*, 4. Also see Nikki Fortier, "COVID-19, Gender Inequality, and the Responsibility of the State," *International Journal of Wellbeing* 10, no. 3 (2020): 77–93.
38. UN Women, *From Insights to Action*, 4.
39. Serena Clark et al., "'You're a Teacher, You're a Mother, You're a Worker': Gender Inequality during COVID-19 in Ireland," *Gender, Work & Organization* 28, no. 4 (2021): 1352–62.

40. Christian S. Czymara, Alexander Langenkamp, and Tomás Cano, "Cause for Concerns: Gender Inequality in Experiencing the COVID-19 Lockdown in Germany," *European Societies* 23, no. s1 (2021): s68–s81.
41. Éva Fodor et al., "The Impact of COVID-19 on the Gender Division of Childcare Work in Hungary," *European Societies* 23, no. s1 (2021): s95–s110.
42. Mahi Uddin, "Addressing Work-Life Balance Challenges of Working Women during COVID-19 in Bangladesh," *International Social Science Journal* 71, no. 239–40 (2021): 7–20.
43. Moha Ennaji, "Women and Gender Relations during the Pandemic in Morocco," *Gender and Women's Studies* 4, no. 1 (2021): 3.
44. Odile Mackett, "The Effects of COVID-19 on Women in South Africa: An Analysis Using the Social Provisioning Framework," *Social and Health Sciences* 18, no. 2 (2020): 70–95.
45. Regan M. Johnston, Anwar Mohammed, and Clifton van der Linden, "Evidence of Exacerbated Gender Inequality in Child Care Obligations in Canada and Australia during the COVID-19 Pandemic," *Politics & Gender* 16, no. 4 (2020): 1131–41.
46. Fortier, "COVID-19," 79; Clark et al., "You're a Teacher"; Johnston et al., "Evidence of Exacerbated Gender Inequality," 1132.
47. UN Women, *From Insights to Action*, 2–3.
48. Wendy Tuohy, "Home Schooling, Job Loss, Pandemic Fear Drove Quadrupling of Abortion Calls," *The Age*, October 21, 2021, https://www.theage.com.au/national/home-schooling-job-loss-pandemic-fear-drove-quadrupling-of-abortion-calls-20211020-p591rp.html; Sarah Newey, "Pandemic Could Trigger a 'Baby Boom' as Millions of Women Lose Access to Contraception and Abortion," *The Telegraph*, August 19, 2020, https://www.telegraph.co.uk/news/2020/08/19/millions-women-lose-access-contraceptives-abortions-covid-19 (both accessed February 18, 2022)
49. Sophie Harman, "Threat Not Solution: Gender, Global Health Security and COVID-19," *International Affairs* 97, no. 3 (2021): 616.
50. Phumzile Mlambo-Ngcuka, "Violence against Women and Girls: The Shadow Pandemic," UN Women, April 6, 2020, https://www.unwomen.org/en/news/stories/2020/4/statement-ed-phumzile-violence-against-women-during-pandemic (accessed February 18, 2022).
51. Nobuhle Judy Dlamini, "Gender-Based Violence, Twin Pandemic to COVID-19," *Critical Sociology* 47, no. 4–5 (2021): 585. Also see UN Women, *From Insights to Action*, 10.
52. Kim Usher et al., "Family Violence and COVID-19: Increased Vulnerability and Reduced Options for Support," *International Journal of Mental Health Nursing* 29, no. 4 (2020): 549.
53. UN Women, *From Insights to Action*, 10. Also see Usher et al., "Family Violence and COVID-19," 549.
54. Usher et al, "Family Violence and COVID-19," 549.
55. UN Women, *From Insights to Action*, 10.

56. Usher et al, "Family Violence and COVID-19," 549. Also see UN Women, *From Insights to Action*, 10–11.
57. Shalini Mittal and Tushar Singh, "Gender-Based Violence during COVID-19 Pandemic: A Mini-review," *Frontiers in Global Women's Health* 1 (2020): 4.
58. See Usher et al., "Family Violence and COVID-19," 550; Naomi Pfitzner et al., "A Bubble Set to Burst: Why Urgent Support Must Be Given to Domestic Violence Workers," *Lens*, July 1, 2020, https://lens.monash.edu/@politics-society/2020/07/01/1380770/we-are-in-a-bubble-that-is-set-to-burst-why-urgent-support-must-be-given-to-domestic-violence-workers (accessed February 18, 2022).
59. UN Women, *From Insights to Action*, 10–11. Also see Dlamini, "Gender-Based Violence," 583–90.
60. Anastasia Powell and Asher Flynn, "Reports of 'Revenge Porn' Skyrocketed during Lockdown, We Must Stop Blaming Victims for It," *The Conversation*, June 3, 2020, https://theconversation.com/reports-of-revenge-porn-skyrocketed-during-lockdown-we-must-stop-blaming-victims-for-it-139659 (accessed February 18, 2022).
61. Laura Tarzia and Meagan Tyler, "Recognizing Connections between Intimate Partner Sexual Violence and Pornography," *Violence against Women* 27, no. 14 (2021): 2687–2708. Also see Fiona Vera-Gray et al., "Sexual Violence as a Sexual Script in Mainstream Online Pornography," *British Journal of Criminology* 61, no. 5 (2021): 1243–60.
62. Hashir Ali Awan et al., "Internet and Pornography Use during the COVID-19 Pandemic: Presumed Impact and What Can Be Done," *Frontiers in Psychiatry* 12 (2021): 623508.
63. Kate Fitz-Gibbon, Jacqui True, and Naomi Pfitzner, "More Help Required: The Crisis in Family Violence during the Coronavirus Pandemic," *The Conversation*, August 18, 2020, https://theconversation.com/more-help-required-the-crisis-in-family-violence-during-the-coronavirus-pandemic-144126 (accessed February 18, 2022).
64. For example, see Jeremy Gibson, "Domestic Violence during COVID-19: The GP Role," *British Journal of General Practice* 70, no. 696 (2020): 340; Shari Bloomberg, "Reflections on COVID-19, Domestic Violence, and Shared Trauma," in *Shared Trauma, Shared Resilience during a Pandemic*, ed. Carole Tosone (Cham, Switzerland: Springer, 2021), 69–77.
65. Sophie Roborgh and Larissa Fast, "Healthcare Workers Are Still Coming under Attack during the Coronavirus Pandemic," *The Conversation*, April 28, 2020, https://theconversation.com/healthcare-workers-are-still-coming-under-attack-during-the-coronavirus-pandemic-136573 (accessed February 21, 2022).
66. See Clare Wenham et al., "Gender and Race on the Frontline: Experiences of Health Workers in Brazil during the COVID-19 Pandemic," *Social Politics* (2021), https://doi.org/10.1093/sp/jxab031 (accessed April 20, 2022).
67. Ibid., 4.

68. Anna Salleh, "Scientists Talking about COVID-19 Are Copping Widespread Abuse and Death Threats, Survey Finds," ABC News (Australia), October 14, 2021, https://www.abc.net.au/news/science/2021-10-14/covid-scientists-receiving-death-threats-abuse/100533564 (accessed February 21, 2022).
69. Marysia Zalewski, "Feminist International Relations: Making Sense. . .," in *Gender Matters in Global Politics: A Feminist Introduction to International Relations*, ed. Laura J. Shepherd (Abingdon, England: Routledge, 2015), 7.
70. Sjoberg, "Introduction to *Security Studies*," 196–7.
71. Ibid., 197.
72. Usher et al, "Family Violence and COVID-19," 549; Fitz-Gibbon et al., "More Help Required."
73. "Violence against Women."
74. Harman, "Threat Not Solution," 608.
75. Giovanni Landoni et al., "Why Are Asian Countries Outperforming the Western World in Controlling COVID-19 Pandemic," *Pathogens and Global Health* 115, no. 1 (2021): 70–2.
76. See Dan Cassino and Yasemin Besen-Cassino, "Of Masks and Men? Gender, Sex, and Protective Measures during COVID-19," *Politics & Gender* 16, no. 4 (2020), 1052–62; Carl L. Palmer and Rolfe D. Peterson, "Toxic Mask-ulinity: The Link between Masculine Toughness and Affective Reactions to Mask Wearing in the COVID-19 Era," *Politics & Gender* 16, no. 4 (2020): 1044–51.
77. "Donald Trump Embarks on Twitter Storm after Returning to White House While Still Being Treated for Coronavirus," SBS News, October 7, 2020, https://www.sbs.com.au/news/donald-trump-embarks-on-twitter-storm-after-returning-to-white-house-while-still-being-treated-for-coronavirus/6e7684e0-e79e-44e8-ba2e-05053edcf815 (accessed February 21, 2022).
78. Madison Pauly, "The War on Masks is a Cover-up for Toxic Masculinity," *Mother Jones*, October 8, 2020, https://www.motherjones.com/coronavirus-updates/2020/10/trump-masks-covid-toxic-masculinity/ (accessed February 21, 2022).
79. Tickner, *Gender in International Relations*, 17.
80. Tomi Lahren (@TomiLahren), "Might as well carry a purse with that mask, Joe," Twitter, October 6, 2020, https://twitter.com/TomiLahren/status/1313312828670046208 (accessed February 21, 2022).
81. Pauly, "The War on Masks."
82. Ibid.
83. Runyan and Peterson, *Global Gender Issues*, 96.
84. Tickner, *Gender in International Relations*, 17.
85. Tom Phillips, "Brazil: Bolsonaro Reportedly Uses Homophobic Slur to Mock Masks," *The Guardian*, July 9, 2020, https://www.theguardian.com/world/2020/jul/08/bolsonaro-masks-slur-brazil-coronavirus (accessed February 21, 2022).

86. See Yating Chuang and John Chung-En Liu, "Who Wears a Mask? Gender Differences in Risk Behaviours in the COVID-19 Early Days in Taiwan," *Economics Bulletin* 40, no. 4 (2020): 2619–27; Palmer and Peterson, "Toxic Mask-ulinity."
87. Valerio Capraro and Helene Barcelo, "The Effect of Messaging and Gender on Intentions to Wear a Face Covering to Slow Down COVID-19 Transmission," *Journal of Behavioural Economics for Policy* 4, no. S2 (2020): 45–55.
88. Matt C. Howard, "Gender, Face Mask Perceptions, and Face Mask Wearing: Are Men Being Dangerous during the COVID-19 Pandemic?" *Personality and Individual Differences* 170 (2021): 110417.
89. Cassino and Besen-Cassino, "Of Masks and Men?" 1061.
90. Tyler T. Reny, "Masculine Norms and Infectious Disease: The Case of COVID-19," *Politics & Gender* 16, no. 4 (2020): 1034.

6

Postcolonialism and Security: Fractured Empires

Peter Phipps

Introduction

That we are in an era of compounding crises with the most serious global security implications is an established fact. Less clear is how to make sense of those multiple crises, and the extent to which such complex challenges can be treated as discrete issues or are better understood as wicked problems: interconnected, complex, and demanding diverse multilateral responses.[1] This chapter, like others in this volume taking a critical perspective on security studies, argues for the latter perspective. It is primarily concerned with demonstrating how postcolonial perspectives on contemporary security shift the understanding of security challenges from a focus on "great power politics" to a decentered and subaltern view. Like other critically informed perspectives on security, this argument reflects on the ethical dimensions and purposes of understanding security and acting on those understandings, in this instance for a decolonial security studies practice. Finally, the chapter makes the argument that security studies critically informed by postcolonialism offers a far more clear-eyed perspective on the complexities of a multipolar world in the pandemic age; a view free from nostalgic illusions about the "liberal international order," which is the era of Western domination of world affairs.

As the chapters by Reuben Steff and Adam Bartley in this volume have shown, conventional security studies takes the state as a normative point of reference.[2] Realist and other dominant approaches to security studies think in terms of strong states, and weak and dysfunctional or "failed states," but the high-functioning strong state is rarely considered as a security problem unless it enters into great power rivalry or the much-cited Thucydides trap. While the domestic order of the state is presumed to be lawful and orderly, conflicts between states in the "anarchic" sphere of international relations are the central security concern, so-called "great power" conflict in particular. This chapter adopts insights and methods from postcolonial studies to interrogate the global security challenges and risks presented by states generally considered stable and secure, particularly Western liberal democratic states. It examines the sources of global insecurity created externally by settler-colonial states with belligerent expansionist reflexes. Additionally, it uses the Australian involvement in the American war of occupation in Afghanistan as a detailed case study.

Postcolonialism

At its simplest, "postcolonialism" is a critical perspective on the world from the margins of global power. Postcolonialism is concerned with the experiences and perspectives of the previously colonized world and the ways in which colonial and imperialist legacies linger on, long after the era of formal decolonization. Not merely a description of the postcolonial world, like other critical theories it closely interrogates established truths, intellectual hierarchies, and disciplinary boundaries. Most importantly for security studies, postcolonial analysis of international relations is deeply skeptical of the claims made for the benevolence of global powers and the universality of the state. From its origins in the anti-imperialist intellectual activism of the postwar period of decolonization, postcolonialism had an insurgent energy directed against the normalization of neocolonial relations.[3]

This refusal of established powers extends to the new imperialisms of the post-Cold War era; both its reckless military adventurism and its evangelizing neoliberal globalization. For Robert Young, "'postcolonial theory' involves a conceptual reorientation towards the perspectives of knowledges, as well as needs, developed outside the west."[4] Indeed, he argues elsewhere that the foundations for postcolonial theory were laid at the 1955 Bandung Conference, which was explicitly an act of anti-imperialist international solidarity against the dominant Eurocentric order. Young writes that Bandung represents "a foundational moment for postcolonialism. Bandung in many ways marked the beginning of the production of 'the postcolonial.'"[5]

Postcolonialism is concerned with the effects of history, particularly colonial and imperial history, in determining conditions in the present. This inquiry is not limited to the formerly colonized world, but includes the metropolitan centers of colonial expansion and imperial domination. Postcolonialism considers the disjuncture between the uneven, worldwide tendencies of entire lifeworlds to be modernized, developed, globalized, and dominated, and the plight of specific localisms. It considers how these local differences might continue to exist in conditions where the combined forces of capitalist accumulation and scientific rationality colonize ever-expanding aspects of social, cultural, and biological life. Postcolonialism highlights the plight of marginalized and subaltern peoples in the post-Cold War intensification of hypercapitalism and United States-led military triumphalism that characterized the first two decades of the twenty-first century.

Postcolonial studies emerged from a series of cultural critiques of colonialism unleashed and reinvigorated by the 1978 publication of Edward Said's *Orientalism*.[6] *Orientalism* presented a direct challenge to claims of objectivity by established academic disciplines producing knowledge about the non-West. By linking the practices of academic research, liberal culture, media, and literature with systems of colonial administration and imperial domination, Said identified a system he referred to as "orientalism." He emphasized that colonialism operates not only as a form of military domination, but also as a discourse of cultural domination. Orientalism is a construct that projects cultural power over colonized peoples through the entire assemblage of representations of those colonized peoples and knowledge about them. These cultural representations and knowledges are internalized in particular by the colonized elites upon whose loyalty, or at least cooperation across administration, policing, and commerce, colonial rule depends.[7]

While this critique extended to anthropology, and literary and cultural studies, the area studies disciplines (China studies, Middle East studies, Southeast Asian studies, African studies, etc.) that had grown with the imperatives of the US Cold War security establishment were a particularly sensitive target of *Orientalism*.[8] Said was certainly not the first to point to the intimate intersections of academic knowledge and Cold War operations: for example in 1971 the American Anthropology Association took a stand against CIA covert recruitment of anthropologists and the weaponization of anthropological knowledge during the Vietnam War.[9] Said's innovative contribution was to identify this intersection of scholarly discourse and worldly power as a coherent system, not a mere aberration or temporary corruption of otherwise noble purposes in the pursuit of social science. As a Palestinian exile and activist, Said was acutely aware of the material dimensions of colonialism, the centrality of land in colonial and imperial systems, and the uses of culture to naturalize and support that domination of territory. His work influenced and encouraged postcolonial thinkers across a wide range of disciplines from literary and psychoanalytic cultural studies to political science, anthropology, critical legal theory, indigenous studies, and history.[10]

Gayatri Spivak, the renowned postcolonial scholar and a close associate of the Subaltern Studies collective, refers to Said's *Orientalism* as "the source book in our discipline."[11] The collective, a diaspora of mostly Indian academics cohering around the work of Ranajit Guha, brought a similar skepticism toward state centrality to the practice of history. The conventional narrative of the Indian independence movement was as a national history, an "awakening" of national consciousness and action led by key, British-educated figures such as Gandhi, Nehru, and Jinnah. In contrast to this bourgeois national history, Subaltern Studies were concerned with how to bring the vast majority of Indians—locally rural, illiterate, and variously religious—into the narrative of the anti-imperial national struggle as historical and therefore political actors, not mere ciphers in that history.

The collective's organizing term for this refigured historical agent was borrowed from the modified Marxist language of Antonio Gramsci in his *Prison Notebooks*.[12] They drew out Gramsci's idea of the "subaltern" as a way of thinking and writing hitherto marginalized people into historical agency. Spivak's seminal contribution to this group, rhetorically titled "Can the Subaltern Speak?," challenges and extends this shared project by foregrounding the problem of gender in historical research, using the case study of a young female suicide bomber in colonial Bengal to highlight the complexities of reading into the agency and intentions of marginalized historical actors.[13] It may now be more apparent how this intellectual movement for rethinking historical agency has contemporary significance for security studies. Postcolonial analysis broadens the possibilities of who can be understood as an agent of history and how to understand otherwise opaque, or apparently nihilistic, acts as both political and meaningful in a complex world of security threats, including domestic terrorism and asymmetrical warfare. More importantly, postcolonialism challenges the core assumptions at the heart of the "security" concept.

Another of the significant contributions of postcolonialism has been to investigate the continuing effects of colonialism on the former colonizers. In the case of the European colonizing powers this can range from rereading the cultural canon to make sense of the colonial connections that might be barely mentioned, but constitute a necessary underlying element of works such as the novels of Jane Austen or Charles Dickens, to reassessing the architecture of eighteenth- and nineteenth-century Britain, to rethinking the enormous financial capital generated in the City of London banking system by Caribbean slavery, the opium trade, and systematically stripping wealth from India.[14] These cultural reassessments bring a deeply critical view to the increasingly hollow claims of the superiority of "Western civilization" and its purported "civilizing missions" that are a favorite theme of conservatives and reactionaries in the English-speaking world (and elsewhere). The newer, more liberal iterations of this Western interventionist tradition continue in many forms: covertly in the "responsibility to protect" (R2P) doctrine[15] or the structures of international financial aid, more overtly in the unilateral interventions, invasions, occupations, and peacekeeping missions best exemplified by the US-led invasions of Afghanistan and Iraq.

Postcolonialism has opened new forms of analysis of the peculiar situation of the settler colonies, those nations formed by a European occupation of Indigenous lands that continues with no or few prospects of ever decolonizing. Latin-American, Native American, Aboriginal, and Pacifica scholars[16] have been at the forefront of this reassessment of settler-colonial nations, states, and identities. Patrick Wolfe has identified the underlying logic of settler colonialism as being about the acquisition and control of productive territory through "the elimination of the native" inhabitants—through genocidal practices of direct killing, social marginalization, and cultural elimination.[17] In settler-colonial nations such as the United States, Australia, Israel-Palestine, Canada, and New Zealand, cultural and academic historical narratives have downplayed or romanticized colonial violence in favor of the narratives of pilgrims, pioneers, and peaceful settlers, counterposed with "the last of their tribe" eliminationist colonial nostalgia. These same histories have erased the role of Indigenous peoples, slaves, nonwhite migrants, and women in the formation, development, and defense of these nations. The dominant cultural preference has been celebrating and reinforcing white patriarchal dominance while rejecting, repressing, and denying these disruptive "subaltern" histories.

Postcolonialism has been one of the critically informed approaches that has generated intellectual challenges to this white patriarchal order in the social, cultural, and political histories of both formerly colonized and colonizing societies. Along with the fields of critical indigenous studies and critical race theory, these challenges have become a staple of the so-called "culture wars" generated by right-wing media and populist public figures in the English-speaking world. The intent of the "culture wars" promoters is to generate reactionary, racist movements in defense of patriarchal white domination. This has proven to be both a profitable business model (Fox News, talk radio, etc.) and an effective political recruitment tool, attracting an ideologically motivated far-right base to the established conservative political parties.

While political and most security discourse in these settler-colonial nations is directed at the threats of a “rising China” or “Islamist terrorism,” these reactionary denialist movements have become a major security threat within the settler-colonial states themselves: from regular white supremacist terror attacks and killings, through to the violent Trumpist January 2021 insurrection which sought to overthrow the United States’ constitutional order and established conventions surrounding the peaceful transition of government. Postcolonialism is a powerful paradigm for understanding these white supremacists’ terrorist ideologies in those different polities, and the links between them. It helps explain the open promotion, and relative official indulgence, of these movements and their divisive, violent ideologies in mainstream political, corporate media, security, and military establishments.

Postcolonialism and security studies: The international is not what we think it is

Postcolonial critiques of security studies have been growing in momentum and scope over the past two decades.[18] They have ranged from the simple inclusion of the Third World and non-Western perspectives[19] on security and international relations (IR), to full-blown critiques of the Eurocentric and state-centric foundational concepts of security and international relations,[20] and further to that a critique of the European Enlightenment as a universal truth-seeking enterprise.[21]

Non-Western models of international relations and security

The first of these moves, the inclusion of Third World or Global South perspectives on security and the related development of non-Western models of international relations and security, is conceptually the most straightforward, but by no means easily accepted into the dominant strands of security analysis. This move toward a non-Western international relations has been most strongly advocated through various Asian perspectives on security and IR. Amitav Acharya and Barry Buzan have used this tension between the global significance of regional relations in east Asia (most notably between Japan, China, and the two Koreas) as a critical reflection on the Eurocentrism of most IR theory.[22] Acharya and Buzan advocate a global IR that can travel beyond the West. As they write, “our key concern about any national school is whether it can ‘deprovincialize’—i.e. travel beyond the national or regional context from which it is derived in the first place."[23] As David Kang and others have argued, this leads to security studies "getting Asia wrong."[24]

Immediate nuclear security risks and the rise of China as a great power add far more urgency to this task of thinking beyond Eurocentric models of IR and security. Whether it be in terms of the vastly ambitious Chinese Belt and Road Initiative, understanding the significance of Xi Jinping's "China Dream," or the new military assertiveness of China in the South China Sea and across the Taiwan Strait, security theorists need to at least apprise themselves of Chinese (if not other) models of security and international relations. In a comprehensive review of attempts to develop various Asian models of security and international relations, Yong-Soo Eun concludes that the tension between "nativism" and a properly global international relations remains unresolved in attempts to develop non-Western or post-Westphalian models.[25] He describes three such attempts in some detail, "Qin Yaqing's relational theory, Yan Xuetong's moral realism, and Zhao Tingyang's Tianxia theory," the last being the much-cited Chinese imperial ideal of "universal cooperation and harmony" under implicit Chinese leadership.[26] Critics of these approaches have pointed to the fact that historically, east Asian states have labored under similar struggles of anarchy and survival as states in Europe.[27] Another attempt to construct a global international relations from a Chinese cultural base is by L. H. M. Ling, who critiques the foundational model of Westphalian international relations as a Eurocentric historical allegory. In its place she offers a "worldist" model grounded in Chinese Daoist philosophical and ethical principles of harmony, nonviolence, and compassion.[28]

Critique of state-centrism

The second postcolonial contribution to security studies is to move from the idea of "inclusion" of non-Western perspectives to a more comprehensive critique of key assumptions around security: Eurocentrism, state-centrism, and "great powers." Much like the "subalterns" of Indian historiography, postcolonial states (that is, those states that have been formally decolonized) have been seen as objects of security studies, but generally not as significant international actors in themselves. As Kenneth Waltz infamously argued:

> It would be as ridiculous to construct a theory of international politics based on Malaysia and Costa Rica as it would be to construct an economic theory of oligopolistic competition based on the minor firms in a sector of an economy.[29]

Postcolonial critics of security studies have argued that a postcolonial theoretical lens opens up precisely this kind of possibility: seeing questions of security from the perspectives of the Global South. They have variously argued that an understanding of security and international relations from the margins is no longer ridiculous, but necessary to properly understand the multiple sources of insecurity facing states, nations, peoples, and the relations between them.[30]

Philip Darby argues there are four main "moves" that have normalized this dismissal of a decentered security and IR from a Third World or non-Western perspective.[31] First he argues that the normalization of great power violence as deterrence or preemption, most notably in the United States' chaotic pursuit of the "Global War on Terror," has normalized the destructive impacts this endless war has on the Third World peoples and communities targeted. No stronger evidence of this normalization can be found than the Nobel Committee awarding the 2009 Nobel Peace Prize to President Barack Obama, despite his continuation and extension of the Bush-era campaign of drone-strike remote killings of participants in Islamist insurgencies. Second, Darby cites the liberal and realist narratives imposed on Asia and Africa by Western scholarship through the Cold War era and beyond. Third, and as an extension from this projection, is the systematic undermining and ridiculing of the idea (and reality) of strong Third World or nonaligned states, and instead projecting the image of them as weak or failed states vulnerable to exploitation and in need of "strengthening mechanisms" in the dominant Western mode. This Cold War campaign included the targeted assassinations of prominent nonaligned leaders such as Ben Bella; military coups against Sukarno, Nasser, and others; and the unleashing of campaigns of violent chaos and disruption throughout Asia, Africa, the Arab world, Iran, and Central and South America: "anarchy" indeed! This is not to dismiss the evidence of poor domestic governance, endemic corruption, and elite indifference to the security of the masses (including persecution of minorities) in many of these postcolonial states, but there is also abundant evidence of Western collusion against their success.

Finally, Darby cites the gap between the promises of neoliberal globalism and the realities of persistent global inequalities of wealth, security, and opportunity as the fourth mechanism for "writing off" the non-West in global affairs. This last point emphasizes the grotesque circumstances of extreme global inequality, including the profoundly unequal distribution of human security, described more recently as "necropolitics." Francophone theorist Achille Mbembe draws on the Foucauldian concept of "biopower" to analyze the systems which reinforce the plight of non-Western masses who suffer blighted lives as "the living dead": to die prematurely by violence or deprivation purely because of where they are born. Mbembe describes the West's indifference and contribution to this necropolitics as a normalized set of global economic, health, and security arrangements overseen by states and the international system.[32] Jasbir Puar took a similar turn from biopolitics to argue for an understanding of "queer necropolitics" as central to properly understanding the "terrorist assemblages" of state and nonstate actors in the Global War on Terror. Puar takes up the example of the ways in which certain lives are valued, and others entirely devalued, in the Israeli-Palestinian occupation and conflict. She points to the contradictions in the "progressive" focus on the "tolerance" for queer lives within Israel as a justification for the "necropolitics" practiced against Palestinian lives in the occupied territories, including queer (LGBTQI) Palestinians.[33]

Postcolonialism denaturalizes the established IR view of an anarchic international order of competing state actors.[34] Rather than being natural, Partha Chatterjee argues that this "anarchy" was a product of decolonization and Cold War competition, as described above. Rather than the European national template simply "rolling out" consistently across the decolonizing world, postcolonial nations have variously adapted the national form to their specific contingent circumstances and changed it in the process.[35] As anticolonial movements sought to break away from the empires that dominated them, it was simply that the form of the nation-state was the most useful and adaptable vehicle available for that struggle. The disciplines of international relations and its offshoot security studies have misapprehended the coincidence of culture, territory, and polity in the nation-state as the natural order of things, whereas empirical reality shows these to be more the exception than the rule, even in the West.

Sanjay Seth argues that international relations needs to take a deeper historical perspective beyond the West, to understand that most of the world's peoples have lived under various forms of culturally diverse, hierarchically organized empires until relatively recently.[36] He argues that this postcolonial critique is not just about a "more inclusive" international relations incorporating diverse, non-Western perspectives, but a fundamental challenge to its core presumptions about the state. These same presumptions about the internally coherent nation-state, yet externally anarchic international relations, flow into security studies and the Kantian idea of a liberal, "rules-based" international order developed to counter this anarchic international tendency.

Decentering the West

Going further still, postcolonial theory seeks to decenter Europe and the north Atlantic. This decentering involves a complete rethinking of non-Western states, peoples, and histories beyond Western paradigms. Continuing Partha Chatterjee's critique of the assumption that all nations must follow the nationalist path of Europe, postcolonialism incites further extensions of this argument when it comes to the subjects of those nations, and their conceptions of politics and of history. As Subaltern Studies scholar Dipesh Chakrabarty famously put it, postcolonialism seeks to "provincialize Europe" including in the domain of history.[37]

This intellectual and conceptual decolonization is complex and continuous work in a world space powerfully framed by the history of Western dominance, as not only direct imperial domination, but epistemological domination as well. Foundational categories such as subjectivity, politics, history, and the state are all open to contestation and reconceptualization in order to account for the lived realities of lives beyond Europe. These critiques highlight the intersections of nonsecular, nonmodern, rural, or newly urban ways of being with domestic institutional politics in ways that can violently disrupt the Kantian ideal of evolving domestic constitutional orders as integral to the universal historical evolution of a "world history."[38]

The rules-based order

The "rules-based order" has been a much-used phrase in recent years, primarily by the United States and its NATO and other allies. It has been invoked with increasing shrillness in the context of the global power shifts manifesting as regional tensions and direct challenges: from Iran's growing influence in Iraq and Syria, to China in the South China Sea and Taiwan Strait, to Russia in Ukraine, Crimea, and elsewhere.[39] It has been used interchangeably with the "liberal international order," previously used to describe the economic and political order of the Cold War era with its architecture of institutions dominated by the United States, in contrast with the Soviet Union, Warsaw Pact countries, China, and others. Other states were enticed to join this "liberal order" on the established terms of United States dominance in partnership with Europe and Japan. Developing nations were brought into this unequal regime through a range of measures, from unequal trade to finance and technology dependencies epitomized by IMF and World Bank loans. For postcolonial critics these arrangements were understood through the lens of neocolonialism, that is, the extension of colonial-era relations of domination and dependency between the West and its former colonies through new asymmetrical institutional arrangements.[40]

After the collapse of the Soviet Union, post-Soviet republics and most significantly China were drawn into this system through membership of the World Trade Organization. With the end of the Cold War and a period of apparently uncontested United States supremacy epitomized by Francis Fukuyama's declaration of the "end of history,"[41] and Bush Senior's declaration of a New World Order, postcolonial and other critics turned to a critique of United States dominance as a new imperialism.[42] In this period the (international) "liberal order" quietly morphed into the (global) "rules-based order" so frequently invoked today by the United States and its closest allies. The use of these phrases in Western diplomatic circles was an attempt to reinforce the naturalness of the new international order as an established and cooperative realm of mutually agreed rules and norms between nations, overseen and underwritten by American military and institutional dominance: a Pax Americana.

The invasions of Afghanistan and Iraq were grounded in the hubristic assumption that this order could be extended by military force. It was assumed by the neoconservative architects of the "New American Century" who ran the George W. Bush presidency that local populations across the world were ready to willingly receive the gifts of the liberal international order. These hawkish neocons assumed that these societies—Arab, Afghan, or any other—would become democratic national polities with neoliberal market systems under benevolent Western tutelage. As that international order now visibly frays, both at the edges and closer to the center, postcolonialism offers an insightful critical perspective free from the illusions of Western benevolence or the naturalness of this "rules-based order."

"Security assistance" and war crimes in "the longest war"

The United States' invasion of Afghanistan was a unilateral response to the al-Qaeda-inspired September 11 terror attacks by mostly Saudi nationals[43] using hijacked commercial airliners to attack the New York World Trade Center and the Pentagon. The attacks elicited widespread global sympathy for the many victims of the attacks, for New York City, and for the United States. Less well known to Westerners was a widespread sentiment across the postcolonial world, particularly those places that had been the theater of United States-sponsored Cold War violence, that at some level "they had it coming." At the time the existence of this sentiment was difficult to report, even in academic circles. Yet for many of the peoples who saw themselves as historic victims (or sympathetic allies of those on the receiving end) of US imperialism, their humanitarian response for the victims was tempered with a sense of historical justice or inevitability; that the weak could finally strike back at the strong in the symbolic center of financial and military power. The US targets had been selected for precisely this symbolic reason.[44]

As it became clear that the United States was seeking a military response, the clamor for revenge drowned out advocates for a more tempered diplomatic and legal solution. The argument for treating the attacks as criminal terrorist acts, rather than giving them the elevated status of acts of war, was both principled and strategic. Advocates of international law were concerned that an invasion would be illegal and irrational. While the Taliban government in Afghanistan had provided a sanctuary for al-Qaeda, it was not an Afghan attack on the United States. The United Nations did not endorse an invasion. The liberal, rules-based international order was being shown up as partial and selective in its application once more. There was a degree of resignation at the international level that, in a classic realist mode as the preeminent global power, the United States would respond exactly as it wanted without hindrance from other countries.

The invasion of Afghanistan began in earnest in October 2001 as a US bombing campaign with British support under the presumptuous name "Operation Enduring Freedom." Facing the advancing anti-Taliban Northern Alliance (of Afghan warlords and drug lords from the Tajik and Uzbek minority ethnic groups based in the north) with US air and logistical support, the Taliban Afghan government fled Kabul and by the end of the year appeared to be militarily defeated. Taliban overtures via Hamid Karzai, then khan (hereditary traditional leader) of the Popalzai Pashtuns, for negotiated surrender and amnesty were rejected by US secretary of defense Donald Rumsfeld. Instead, US policy sought both revenge against the Taliban for harboring the planners of the 9/11 attacks and the remaking of Afghanistan without Taliban input, despite their residual support among the majority Pashtuns. Taliban operatives retreated to the mountains and into the urban stronghold of Kandahar in the south, and crossed into Pakistan with tacit support from the Pakistani security establishment.

By 2002 the US and UK had been joined by special operations forces from Australia, Canada, Denmark, France, Germany, and Norway, with thirty-six nations being drawn into the Afghanistan operations over time. With the support of this "International Security Assistance Force" (ISAF) the United States occupation forces embarked on the project of building core institutions of the Afghan state-to-be, with Karzai installed as interim president. The Afghan state came with all the perverse contradictions and compromises of a hastily and incompletely conceived imperial project. The heavily militarized international green zone in Kabul became the focus of the occupation, while the kleptocratic elite around the new government built luxurious villas under international protection.[45] By 2004 a new constitution was endorsed by a *loya jirga* (a gathering of traditional tribal and clan leaders), which created a powerful central government and weaker regional and local authorities, completely at odds with Afghan traditions of decentralized powers. In 2004 the presidential election confirmed Karzai as president, and the next year elections were held for a new Afghan National Assembly (including a proportion of seats reserved for women), which cemented the new arrangements.

With the United States preoccupied by the much more challenging insurgency against its occupation in Iraq, it handed military responsibility for Afghanistan over to NATO command in 2006, just as the Taliban insurgency was gaining traction using improvised explosive devices (IEDs) at roadsides and suicide bombings, with many casualties in crowded locations including the Bagram Air Base. While the occupying forces built a national army, police, and other administrative apparatus, the contradictions between the mission and its practices on the ground became increasingly stark. The corruption and enrichment of the government and their associates, the flourishing opium trade and widespread addiction, and the relatively lavish lifestyles of international NGO staff, private military contractors, and international troops had built a substantial services trade in restaurants, alcohol, and sexual services around the Kabul green zone. The slums that grew all around this opulence provided the labor to service this entirely international "nation-building" enterprise and its pools of foreign exchange. By 2009 the strategies of night raids on remote villages to "root out" Taliban operatives, drone strikes against alleged Taliban in remote areas including Pakistan, and the "Obama surge" in US troop numbers led to sharply increasing civilian casualties and commensurate resentment of the occupation. In 2010 classified US military reports detailing the failures of the occupation strategy including details of civilian deaths and atrocities by occupation forces, known as the *Afghan War Diary*, was published by WikiLeaks.[46]

Postcolonial critics were alert to the insincerity of the new rationales for the international occupation from the start: "nation building" with a strong emphasis on security and "women's rights." This is not to dispute that the previous Taliban regime was deeply misogynist in its

Salafist interpretation and brutal practice of Sharia law, with a heavy-handed repression of many aspects of Afghan social life, from music to education. Postcolonial feminists have consistently cautioned against colonizing uses of "women's rights" as a justification for imperialism.[47] Similarly, claims that the occupying forces needed to learn from the old British imperialists how to conduct an occupation properly were regarded with great skepticism by postcolonial historians familiar with the brutality of that history, not least the 1842 loss of an entire British army in Afghanistan as they attempted to retreat from Kabul back to British India. These imperial nostalgists emphasized "cultural sensitivity" and "engaging traditional leaders" while ignoring the substantive underlying causes of Afghan (particularly Pashtun) resentment: violent foreign occupation in collusion with corrupt collaborating tribal warlords. The British Army attempted this new-old imperialism as part of ISAF, which in the mid-2000s saw them outplayed and ineffective as they made an "accord" with opium-growing Taliban associates in Helmand Province, to the point that the US military effectively replaced them.

Much of this revisionist imperialist thinking came to inform the new counterinsurgency strategy coming out of the much more demanding US war in Iraq. The new US Army and Marine Corps *Counterinsurgency Field Manual*, coauthored by the now-disgraced US general David Petraeus and Australian Army major David Kilcullen (on secondment to the US), was an attempt to rethink US military strategy for a new era of imperial occupations.[48] Released to the military in 2006, then published commercially the following year, it is a remarkable document for its overt attempt to retool the social sciences for military purposes, treating counterinsurgency as a process of constant research and adaptive strategic development. As the University of Chicago Press online publicity puts it: "The manual espouses an approach to combat that emphasizes constant adaptation and learning, the importance of decentralized decision-making, the need to understand local politics and customs, and the key role of intelligence in winning the support of the population."[49] In an academic introduction to the Chicago edition, Sarah Sewall makes the connection to British imperial strategy overt, writing that the manual "is based on principles learned during Britain's early period of imperial policing and relearned during responses to twentieth century independence struggles in Malaya and Kenya."[50] The chapter headings of the *Counterinsurgency Field Manual* are worth noting for the way the manual moves seamlessly from cultural sensitivity and appendices on social science methodology, to the concluding note on aerial bombardment, as if they exist on a logical continuum. These chapter headings include "Unity of Effort: Integrating Civilian and Military Activities" and "Appendix B: Social Network Analysis and Other Analytical Tools," followed finally by "Appendix E: Airpower in Counterinsurgency."[51]

"Legal considerations" and ISAF war crimes

Those responsible for the conduct of the war in Afghanistan suffered from a lack of attention to many aspects of counterinsurgency, but for brevity I will mention, as the *Manual* does, "Appendix D: Legal Considerations." The international publication of details from the WikiLeaks *Afghan War Diary* highlighted the centrality of special operations forces to the conduct of the war, and brought reports and rumors of war crimes by ISAF forces in Afghanistan into the public domain. In the case of the activities of the Australian Special Operations Group, a further leak direct from the Australian Defence Force was followed up by investigative journalist Dan Oakes from the Australian Broadcasting Corporation.[52] The federal government responded furiously by prosecuting the whistleblower and the journalists involved, and making Australian Federal Police raids on the homes of the journalists and their offices looking for evidence of the leak. Possible war crimes having been made public in Australia, the Australian Defence Force had to initiate its own process of internal investigation into allegations of war crimes committed between 2005 and 2016. The Inspector-General of the Australian Defence Force Afghanistan Inquiry Report was finalized (and was publicly released in a highly redacted form) in November 2020.[53] It came to be known for brevity as the Brereton Report, having been headed by Paul Brereton, a New South Wales Supreme Court judge and also a major-general in the army reserve.

In summary, the report found evidence of Australian special forces involvement in thirty-nine unlawful killings (murders) of civilians and prisoners in Afghanistan, with twenty-five Australian servicepeople implicated in these killings and their concealment. The report is a significant and disturbing document for many reasons. It describes in great detail the pattern of deteriorating military discipline and loss of respect for the basic rules of war in a drifting mission with unclear outcomes and no endpoint in sight. The pattern included Australian special forces on repeat rotations to support the ISAF "nation-building" process in Oruzgan Province, where they were neither welcome nor invited. In the classic insurgency scenario, as outlined in the *Manual*, occupying troops could never be sure if a civilian was actually a Taliban combatant, offering support and intelligence to the Taliban, or simply a farmer, and they faced irregular threats from IEDs and only occasional direct combat. The inquiry found that, particularly around 2012, Australian special forces from a particular SAS regiment repeatedly carried out murders of civilians and prisoners, including children, in an "initiation ritual" known as "blooding," that is, instructing new members of the troop to murder a person under their control. The crime was then concealed by using "throw down" enemy weapons or equipment next to the body to justify the killing as "legitimate" combat against an armed adversary. There is also a great deal the Brereton Report elides, including the oral testimony of other killings given to a sociologist embedded within the Australian forces (an embedded social scientist as per the recommendation of the aforementioned *Counterinsurgency Manual*). The report also concludes that senior commanding officers did not know about these crimes or their concealment, despite the extended period of time, repetition, and rumors involved.[54]

From a postcolonial perspective none of this should be a surprise, but is, as Tariq Ali puts it in the subtitle of his book of essays on war in Afghanistan, "a chronicle foretold."[55] In fact, to anyone knowledgeable about insurgency against an occupying force, counterinsurgency, and the histories of British imperialism and settler colonialism in Australia or elsewhere, these war crimes and the broader pattern of failure in Afghanistan are sadly predictable. The Brereton Report has an early and substantial chapter titled "War Crimes in Australian History," beginning with the Boer War in South Africa and continuing with the "Boxer Rebellion" in China and both world wars, in a constant history of conflicts through to the Vietnam War. It provides excellent historical description, with little explanatory insight beyond command structures and troop composition. What the report was unable to include is the longest undeclared Australian war, waged continuously against Indigenous peoples, and the way this has profoundly informed national culture, including ideas about race, religion, national belonging, and security.[56] Media reports revealed that the soldiers committing these crimes in Afghanistan participated in rituals of dehumanization of Afghans through the use of constant racist terminology, that they sometimes wore neo-Nazi insignia while in the field (the Crusader Cross and Iron Cross specifically), and, in a particularly perverse twist, had a ritual of drinking beer from the artificial leg retrieved from a murdered combatant as an illegal "war trophy."[57] Furthermore, the Brereton Report was unable to examine the foundational premise of Australian defense strategy as a slavish adherence to American military adventurism, even in the face of the most egregious lack of strategic clarity or moral purpose.

Postcolonialism is a particularly useful approach for understanding the circumstances of the Australian involvement in the Afghan War. It can offer explanatory analysis of the intersection of imperialist wars, racist fantasies, and the domestic culture wars which include the securitization of Australian foreign policy. Postcolonialism can also analyze the sources of resistance to the experience of Western occupation in Afghanistan, and identify the causal factors without becoming a "handmaiden" to the occupation in the way the *Counterinsurgency Manual* would have the embedded and weaponized social sciences do. Returning to Robert Young's claims about the ethicopolitical commitment of postcolonialism early in this chapter, he writes: "[W]hat makes a politics postcolonial is a broader shared political philosophy that guides its ethics and its practical aims."[58] While he notes that postcolonialism is "morally committed to transforming the conditions of exploitation and poverty in which large sections of the world's population live out their daily lives,"[59] postcolonial analysis makes very clear this is not going to be delivered through imperialist (or "liberal humanitarian") invasion and occupation of Afghanistan by the United States and its allies.

Conclusion

The disastrous retreat of United States forces and the ISAF from Afghanistan in August 2021 stands as a milestone in the annals of American decline. The US-Afghan debacle cedes US influence in the central Asian region (such as it was) to those countries in and bordering it, particularly Pakistan, Iran, China, and Russia. The failed twenty-year occupation and rapid withdrawal from Afghanistan should not just be dismissed as yet another strategic blunder bequeathed by the Bush years, and doubled down on by subsequent administrations. This failure reinforces the rapid decline of US global hegemony, the further loss of any residual US legitimacy in international affairs, and a loss of confidence in American commitments by its allies. By 2022 the effects of this American retreat were already playing out in eastern Europe and the Taiwan Strait.

Additionally, this tale of American decline has been severely compounded by the decadence of US security establishment elites from the Bush-Cheney years (Rumsfeld, Wolfowitz, Rice, and associates), Obama-Clinton foreign policy, and the domestic disruptions and institutional decline brought to the surface by the chaotic Trump years. In the United States a series of profound domestic security risks remain unresolved, and the future of not only US democratic institutions (such as they are) but also the union itself is seriously in jeopardy. Again, postcolonial theory can provide an analysis of the cultural and social elements of this internal division: the combination of deepening economic inequality with powerful and persistent racist narratives that drive white supremacist ideologies, the linkages between imperialism and lawlessness abroad, and a sense of institutional illegitimacy at home.

Postcolonial perspectives on these security challenges highlight threats previously seen as marginal or insignificant, by emphasizing the contradictions and fractures within societies and states. In particular, postcolonial analysis of the dynamics of settler-colonial societies foregrounds security risks less readily identified by state-centric security analysis. These internal fractures and their related security risks of domestic terrorism and perpetual external wars are likely to become more volatile as the larger global power shift plays out. Postcolonialism is an effective lens through which we can better understand domestic and global security in the wake of colonialism and the anticolonial movements that contest colonial domination over much of the developing world. Postcolonial theories have opened up new understandings of both intra- and inter-state dynamics as complex, sometimes contradictory sets of relationships founded in deep historical interconnections between colonizing and colonized polities. Postcolonial theory has necessitated a reexamination of the origins of the established international order, the unequal relations between "the West and the rest," and the origins of the wealth and power those five centuries of imperialism were founded on.[60] The COVID-19 pandemic has brought these dynamics into starker contrast, with sobering implications for how we understand security and risk.

Notes

1. William E. Connolly argues that crises can no longer be properly understood in isolation, but as the interaction of complex, interdependent living systems: William E. Connolly, *The Fragility of Things: Self-Organizing Processes, Neoliberal Fantasies, and Democratic Activism* (Durham, NC: Duke University Press, 2013).
2. Barry Buzan and Lene Hansen, *The Evolution of International Security Studies* (Cambridge, England: Cambridge University Press, 2009).
3. Walter Mignolo, "Epistemic Disobedience, Independent Thought and Decolonial Freedom," *Theory, Culture and Society* 26, no. 7–8 (2009): 159–81.
4. Robert J. C. Young, *Postcolonialism: A Very Short Introduction* (Oxford: Oxford University Press, 2003), 6.
5. Robert J. C. Young, *Postcolonialism: An Historical Introduction* (Oxford: Blackwell, 2001), 191.

6. Edward W. Said, *Orientalism* (Ringwood, VIC: Penguin, 1985).
7. Edward Said, *Culture and Imperialism* (New York: Knopf, 1993).
8. Masao Miyoshi and H. D. Hartoonian (eds.), *Learning Places: The Afterlives of Area Studies* (Durham, NC: Duke University Press, 2002).
9. Hugh Gusterson, "Militarizing Knowledge," in Network of Concerned Anthropologists (eds.), *The Counter-Counterinsurgency Manual: Or, Notes on Demilitarizing American Society* (Chicago: Prickly Paradigm Press, 2009), 48–9. Leading American cultural anthropologist Franz Boas wrote in the letters section of *The Nation* in 1919 criticizing the military uses of anthropologists as spies in Mexico during World War I: Franz Boas, "Scientists as Spies," *The Nation*, December 20, 1919.
10. Sanjay Seth, *Beyond Reason: Postcolonial Theory and the Social Sciences* (New York: Oxford University Press, 2021).
11. Gayatri Chakravorty Spivak, *Outside in the Teaching Machine* (New York: Routledge, 1993), 56.
12. Antonio Gramsci, *Selections from the Prison Notebooks* (London: Lawrence & Wishart, 1971).
13. Gayatri Spivak, "Can the Subaltern Speak?," in *Marxism and the Interpretation of Culture*, ed. Cary Nelson and Lawrence Grossberg (Basingstoke, England: Macmillan, 1988), 271–313.
14. Vijay Prashad, *The Darker Nations: A People's History of the Third World* (New York: New Press, 2007); Mike Davis, *Late Victorian Holocausts: El Niño Famines and the Making of the Third World* (London: Verso, 2001).
15. Mojtaba Mahdavi, "A Postcolonial Critique of Responsibility to Protect in the Middle East," *Perceptions: Journal of International Affairs* 20, no. 1 (2015): 7–36.
16. The Native American and Indigenous Studies Association began holding conferences in 2007, bringing together the growing influence of Indigenous scholars from across the Americas, Australia, and the Pacific.
17. Patrick Wolfe, "Settler Colonialism and the Elimination of the Native," *Journal of Genocide Research* 8, no. 4 (2006): 397; Patrick Wolfe (ed.), *The Settler Complex: Recuperating Binarism in Colonial Studies* (Los Angeles: American Indian Studies Center, 2016).
18. Tarak Barkawi and Mark Laffey, "The Postcolonial Moment in Security Studies," *Review of International Studies* 32, no. 2 (2006): 329–52; Giorgio Shani, "Human Security as Ontological Security: A Postcolonial Approach," *Postcolonial Studies* 20, no. 3 (2017): 275–93; Noureddin Zaamout, "Post-colonialism and Security," in *The Palgrave Encyclopedia of Global Security Studies*, ed. Scott Romaniuk, Manish Thapa, and Péter Marton (Cham, Switzerland: Palgrave Macmillan, 2020), https://doi.org/10.1007/978-3-319-74336-3_569-1 (accessed February 21, 2022); Nivi Manchanda, "Postcolonialism," in *Security Studies*, ed. Paul D. Williams and Matt McDonald, 3rd edn., vol. 1 (Abingdon, England: Routledge, 2018), 114–28.

19. Mohammed Ayoob, *The Third World Security Predicament: State Making, Regional Conflict, and the International System* (Boulder, CO: Lynne Rienner, 1995); Amitav Acharya and Barry Buzan, "Why Is There No Non-Western International Relations Theory? An Introduction," in *Non-Western International Relations Theory: Perspectives on and beyond Asia*, ed. Amitav Acharya and Barry Buzan (Abingdon, England: Routledge, 2010), 1–25.
20. Phillip Darby (ed.), *Postcolonizing the International: Working to Change the Way We Are* (Honolulu: University of Hawai'i Press, 2006).
21. Gayatri Chakravorty Spivak, *A Critique of Postcolonial Reason: Toward a History of the Vanishing Present* (Cambridge, MA: Harvard University Press, 1999); Walter Mignolo, *The Darker Side of Western Modernity: Global Futures, Decolonial Options* (Durham, NC: Duke University Press, 2011); Seth, *Beyond Reason*; Siba Grovogui, "IR as Theology: Reading Kant Badly, and the Incapacity of Western Political Theory to Travel Very Far in Non-Western Contexts," Theory Talks, August 29, 2013, http://www.theory-talks.org/2013/08/theory-talk-57.html (accessed February 21, 2022); Hamid Dabashi, *The Arab Spring: The End of Post-colonialism* (New York: Zed, 2012).
22. Amitav Acharya and Barry Buzan, "Why Is There No Non-Western International Relations Theory? Ten Years On," *International Relations of the Asia-Pacific* 17, no. 3 (2017): 345.
23. Ibid., 361.
24. David Kang, "Getting Asia Wrong: The Need for New Analytical Frameworks," *International Security* 27, no. 4 (2003): 57–85.
25. Yong-Soo Eun, "Non-Western International Relations Theorisation: Reflexive Stocktaking," *E-International Relations*, April 12, 2020, https://www.e-ir.info/2020/04/12/non-western-international-relations-theorisation-reflexive-stocktaking/ (accessed February 21, 2022).
26. Ibid.
27. Yuan-Kang Wang, *Harmony and War: Confucian Culture and Chinese Power Politics* (New York: Columbia University Press, 2011).
28. L. H. M. Ling, *The Dao of World Politics: Towards a Post-Westphalian, Worldist International Relations* (Abingdon, England: Routledge, 2014).
29. Kenneth N. Waltz, "Reductionist and Systemic Theories," in *Theory of International Politics*, ed. Kenneth N. Waltz (Reading, MA: Addison-Wesley, 1979), 72.
30. Farooq Yousaf and Steve Wakhu, "Security in the 'Periphery' of Post-colonial States: Analysing Pakistan's 'Tribal' Pashtuns and Kenyan-Somalis," *Social Identities* 26, no. 4 (2020): 515–32; Sanjay Seth, "Post-colonial Theory and the Critique of International Relations," *Millennium: Journal of International Studies* 40, no. 1 (2011): 167–83.
31. Phillip Darby, "Rethinking the Political," in *Postcolonizing the International: Working to Change the Way We Are*, ed. Phillip Darby (Honolulu: University of Hawai'i Press, 2006), 52–5.

32. Achille Mbembe, *Necropolitics* (Durham, NC: Duke University Press, 2019).
33. Jasbir Puar, *Terrorist Assemblages: Homonationalism in Queer Times* (Durham, NC: Duke University Press, 2007).
34. Hedley Bull, *The Anarchical Society: A Study of Order in World Politics*, 2nd ed. (London: Macmillan, 1995).
35. Partha Chatterjee, *The Nation and Its Fragments: Colonial and Postcolonial Histories* (Princeton, NJ: Princeton University Press, 1993).
36. Sanjay Seth, "International Relations: Plural or Postcolonial?" *International Politics Reviews* 9, no. 2 (2021): 301–5; Sanjay Seth, "Introduction," in *Postcolonial Theory and International Relations: A Critical Introduction*, ed. Sanjay Seth (Abingdon, England: Routledge, 2013), 1–12.
37. Dipesh Chakrabarty, *Provincializing Europe: Postcolonial Thought and Historical Difference*, new edn. (Princeton, NJ: Princeton University Press, 2008).
38. Immanuel Kant, "Idea of a Universal History with a Cosmopolitan Purpose," in *The Cosmopolitanism Reader*, ed. Garrett Wallace Brown and David Held (Cambridge, England: Polity Press, 2010), 17–26.
39. Ben Scott, "Rules-Based Order: What's in a Name?" *The Interpreter*, June 30, 2021, https://www.lowyinstitute.org/the-interpreter/rules-based-order-whats-in-a-name (accessed February 21, 2022).
40. Peter Phipps, "Neocolonialism," in *Encyclopedia of Global Studies*, ed. Helmut Anheier and Mark Juergensmeyer (Thousand Oaks, CA: Sage, 2012).
41. Francis Fukuyama, *The End of History and the Last Man* (New York: Free Press, 1992).
42. Peter Phipps, "Modern Empires," in *Encyclopedia of Global Studies*, ed. Helmut Anheier and Mark Juergensmeyer (Thousand Oaks, CA: Sage, 2012).
43. Fifteen of the nineteen attackers were Saudi Arabian nationals.
44. See Seamus Milne, *The Revenge of History: The Battle for the 21st Century* (London: Verso, 2013).
45. Tariq Ali, *The Forty Year War in Afghanistan: A Chronicle Foretold* (London: Verso, 2021).
46. Wikileaks, *Afghanistan War Diary, 2004–2010*, 2010, archived at https://wikileaks.org/wiki/Afghan_War_Diary,_2004–2010.
47. Chandra Mohanty, "Under Western Eyes: Feminist Scholarship and Colonial Discourses," *Feminist Review* 30, no. 1 (1988): 61–88; Spivak, "Can the Subaltern Speak?"; Christine Delphy, Separate and Dominate: *Feminism and Racism After the War on Terror* (London: Verso, 2015).
48. *The US Army / Marine Corps Counterinsurgency Field Manual* (Chicago: University of Chicago Press, 2007).
49. "The US Army / Marine Corps Counterinsurgency Field Manual," University of Chicago Press website, 2007, https://press.uchicago.edu/ucp/books/book/chicago/U/bo5748917.html (accessed February 21, 2022).

50. Sarah Sewall, "Introduction," in *Counterinsurgency Field Manual*, xxi–xliii.
51. *Counterinsurgency Field Manual*.
52. Dan Oakes and Sam Clark, "The Afghan Files: Defence Leak Exposes Deadly Secrets of Australia's Special Forces," ABC News (Australia), July 11, 2017, https://www.abc.net.au/news/2017-07-11/killings-of-unarmed-afghans-by-australian-special-forces/8466642 (accessed February 21, 2022).
53. IGADF, *Inspector-General of the Australian Defence Force Afghanistan Inquiry Report* (Commonwealth of Australia, 2020) https://afghanistaninquiry.defence.gov.au/sites/default/files/2020-11/IGADF-Afghanistan-Inquiry-Public-Release-Version.pdf
54. Georgia Hitch, "What War Crimes Did Australian Soldiers Commit in Afghanistan and Will Anyone Go to Jail?" ABC News (Australia), November 19, 2020, https://www.abc.net.au/news/2020-11-19/afghan-war-crimes-report-released-what-you-need-to-know/12899880 (accessed February 21, 2022).
55. Ali, *The Forty Year War in Afghanistan*.
56. Aileen Moreton-Robinson, *The White Possessive: Property, Power and Indigenous Sovereignty* (Minneapolis: University of Minnesota Press, 2015); Ghassan Hage, *White Nation: Fantasies of White Supremacy in a Multicultural Nation* (Annandale, NSW: Pluto Press, 1998).
57. Jamie McKinnell, "Ben Roberts-Smith Defamation Trial Told Soldiers Drank Beer from Dead Afghan Man's Prosthetic Leg," ABC News (Australia), June 7, 2021, https://www.abc.net.au/news/2021-06-07/ben-roberts-smith-reputation-destroyed-defamation-trial-told/100194790 (accessed February 21, 2022).
58. Young, *Postcolonialism: A Very Short Introduction*, 113.
59. Ibid., 6.
60. There is a whole subgenre of historical writing pointing to the profound interconnections that underwrote the "European Age of Discovery" and Industrial Revolution in terms of gifted, borrowed, and more commonly stolen knowledge, labor, land, and capital from Africa, the Americas, and Asia. For just two recent examples of this genre see Howard W. French, *Born in Blackness: Africa, Africans, and the Making of the Modern World, 1471 to the Second World War* (New York: Liveright, 2021); William Dalrymple, *The Anarchy: The Relentless Rise of the East India Company* (New York: Bloomsbury, 2019).

7

Human Security: The Domino Effect of Threats to Everyday Survival, Livelihoods, and Dignity

Shahrbanou Tadjbakhsh

Introduction

The human security approach, as an alternative analytical and normative approach to the traditional security lens for identifying threats, to whom and how to address them, is one of those overlooked great ideas that fall victim to their genesis. Although it is a continuation of constructivist attempts to broaden and deepen security studies by moving the referent object from states to people and communities,[1] human security, given its normative agenda and close association with international organizations, has stayed at the fringes of academia. The concept was officially coined in the United Nations Development Programme (UNDP)'s *Human Development Report 1994*.[2] Since then, it has officially served as the umbrella concept for the foreign policy of middle-power countries such as Canada and Japan, and the subject of an international Commission on Human Security co-chaired by Sadako Ogata, the former head of the UN High Commissioner for Refugees, and the academic Amartya Sen. By 2012, after years of lobbying by a coalition of countries under the banner of Friends of Human Security, it became the subject of a United Nations General Assembly resolution.[3]

Despite its noble and logical aim to look at security from the perspective of those for whom it matters, namely people, the human security concept has not been able to gather much political or academic currency. Within academia, an interdisciplinary approach that puts the focus on people has not been able to extensively break into security studies, which continues to be dominated by realism and liberalism. Despite the UN resolution calling it an approach that is defined by freedom from want, freedom from fear, and freedom from indignity, debates still rage about the lack of a precise definition and the virtues of narrow versus broad definitions. Politically, the concept still courts controversy and rejection nearly thirty years after its introduction. Its close association with the notion of the responsibility to protect (R2P) in debates about international interventions has alienated Southern countries that are skeptical about violations of state sovereignty and new conditionalities for receiving aid. No country has adopted it as a goal at the national level, raising skepticism about its utility for domestic policymaking.

Yet the human security concept represents a malleable tool for analyzing the root causes of threats and their multidimensional consequences for different types of insecurities. It can be operationalized through applying specific principles to policymaking. The COVID-19 pandemic, as a case in point, presents an appropriate opportunity to apply the human security approach, both in terms of understanding its causes and consequences for people's lives, and also for developing policy principles to mitigate its long- and short-term impacts.

After all, traditional security thinking and the tools of national security, that is, military force, proved inadequate when it came to protecting the lives and well-being of citizens threatened by the COVID-19 pandemic. Hundreds of thousands of people died from a virus worldwide and a number of heads of state declared "war" followed by a state of public health emergency. Yet there had not been an attack by an enemy using armed forces against any nation. The coronavirus started as a health insecurity that led to loss of life but also "avalanched" into massive economic insecurities as people lost their livelihoods as a result of shutdowns, communities became increasingly isolated and stigmatized, food prices went up, and political security declined as people came to mistrust the state and their politicians. The pandemic had devastating impacts on the economic, food, personal, environmental, and political security of states and people everywhere, in different ways and to different degrees. It showed how threats are linked in a domino effect across nations and across sectors: A shock in one area can ripple in other areas, leading to a multidimensional crisis.

While the traditional national security paradigm cannot capture such complexities, this chapter argues for a broader conception of security which concerns itself not just with the stability of the state, but also with risks to people in their everyday lives. The chapter first introduces the concept of human security, its genesis, critiques, and added value to analyzing threats and how to address them. In the second half, it looks at the different ways that the causes and consequences of the COVID-19 pandemic can be analyzed: first, from a state security perspective; second from a liberal, institutional perspective; and third, from the human security perspective. The chapter ends by looking at how the human security approach can be used to design appropriate policies to mitigate the multiple risks from the fallout of the COVID-19 pandemic.

What is human security and how does it add value to analyzing security threats?

Security, "an essentially contested concept"[4] by itself, is in the eye of the beholder. For Barry Buzan and colleagues, security is a political process, "when an issue is presented as posing an existential threat to a designated referent object."[5] The *Oxford English Dictionary* instead highlights the subjectivity inherent in security as a "feeling" for individuals: "The condition of being protected from or not exposed to danger; safety . . . Freedom from care, anxiety or apprehension; a feeling of safety or freedom from an absence of danger."[6] That feeling of safety from care, anxiety, and apprehension has different connotations in different contexts: for some, it entails a sudden loss of access to jobs, healthcare, social welfare, and so on. For others, it can stem from violence, conflicts, and displacement. From a people-centered perspective, security needs to be defined as a subjective experience at the micro level to gain meaning. This experience may be decidedly different from states' concerns for their national security.

The concepts of "security" and "insecurity" have relative connotations in different contexts. For states, security comes with sheer force, power, and defense (the protection of borders, buildup of armies, and so on). For individuals within states, security can be the assurance that what has been gained today will not be lost tomorrow: insecurity, therefore, can refer to the loss of guaranteed access to jobs, healthcare, social welfare, and education, as much as it can to the fear, objective and subjective, arising from domestic violence, political instability, crime, and displacement. The meanings of "security" for a refugee fleeing war, a farmer losing their crops to drought, an elderly couple losing their assets following a bank crisis, and a woman scared of her violent husband are decisively different from its meaning for a state at the brink of collapse, failure, or invasion. To be meaningful, therefore, human security needs to be recognized at the micro level in terms of people's everyday experiences.

Dominant state-centered security theories rest on the protection of territorial integrity and national sovereignty against existential threats posed by other belligerent states. The human security approach instead proposes that state-focused security can fail to address the gamut of possible insecurities of individuals within a state in a comprehensive manner, and that, by extension, security for the state does not automatically trickle down to that of people.

Human security threats include both objective, tangible elements, such as insufficient income, chronic unemployment, and dismal access to adequate healthcare and quality education, as well as subjective perceptions, such as the inability to control one's destiny, loss of dignity, fear of crime and violent conflict, and so on. They can be both direct (those that are deliberately orchestrated, such as systematic persecutions) and indirect (those that arise inadvertently or structurally, for example, underinvestment in key social and economic sectors such as education and healthcare). Threats can hamper people's *survival* (physical abuse, violence, persecution, or death), their *livelihoods* (unemployment, food insecurity, pandemics), and their *dignity* (violations of human rights, inequality, exclusion, discrimination). By the same token, nontraditional threats can menace states in ways similar to individuals: by hampering states' *existence* (territorial integrity), their *functioning* (whether they have the resources and capacity to function and develop as a state), and their *sovereignty* (legitimacy and recognition).

Genesis and critiques

Long before they were defined as the pillars of a new conception of security which rode on hopes for a peace dividend at the end of the Cold War in the UNDP's *Human Development Report 1994*, "freedom from fear" and "freedom from want" were first introduced by President F. D. Roosevelt in 1941 as part of his vision for a world founded on four essential human freedoms. In 1945, the two freedoms appeared in the speech of the US secretary of state, Edward R. Stettinius Jr., speaking on the results of the conference in San Francisco that established the UN:

> The battle of peace has to be fought on two fronts. The first is the security front where victory spells freedom from fear. The second is the economic and social front where victory means freedom from want. Only victory on both fronts can assure the world of an enduring peace. No provisions that can be written into the Charter will enable the Security Council to make the world secure from war if men and women have no security in their homes and their jobs.[7]

In 1990 the Pakistani economist Mahbub ul Haq summarized the goal of development with a simple yet revolutionary statement in the first UNDP *Human Development Report*: "The obvious is the most difficult to see: the true wealth of a country is its people." By 1994 he had made another key statement:

> Human security is a child that did not die, a disease that did not spread, an ethnic violence that did not explode, a woman who was not raped, a poor person who did not starve, a dissident who was not silenced, a human spirit that was not crushed. Human security is not a concern with weapons. It is a concern with human dignity.[8]

The *Human Development Report 1994* characterized human security as "safety from such chronic threats as hunger, disease and repression [as well as] protection from sudden and hurtful disruptions in the patterns of daily life—whether in homes, in jobs or in communities."[9] It also listed seven interconnected components or seven specific insecurities and vulnerabilities that need to be protected: economic, food, health, environmental, personal, community, and political security.

The approach can be considered an ethical rupture from traditional security paradigms (by making the security of people and communities the ultimate goal), and a methodological one (with the idea that, by securing individuals, the security of the state, the region, and the international system can also be better ensured). For the authors of the UNDP *Human Development Report*, the distinction of the human development approach was and is more than semantics: If human development is about widening people's choices and ensuring growth with equity, human security is about enabling people to exercise these choices safely and freely, and to be relatively confident that the opportunities they have today will not be lost tomorrow.

An independent Commission on Human Security was set up in 2001, funded by Japan and cochaired by Sadako Ogata and Amartya Sen. In 2003, in its report *Human Security Now*, it presented a broader definition:

> [T]o protect the vital core of all human lives in ways that enhance human freedoms and human fulfilment . . . [It] means protecting people from critical (severe) and pervasive (widespread) threats and situations . . . creating political, social, environmental, economic, military and cultural systems that together give people the building blocks of survival, livelihood and dignity.[10]

A Trust Fund for Human Security was initially set up by the Japanese government and now, including other donors, provides the biggest contribution to the UN, run by a dedicated Human Security Unit within the UN. A thirteen-member Human Security Network and a separate Friends of Human Security Network were created as caucuses of interested UN member states. After years of debates and successive reports of the UN secretary-general, a UN General Assembly resolution was adopted in September 2012 that squarely positioned human security in the intersection between peace, development, and human rights. The resolution penned a common understanding of human security as an "approach to assist Member States in identifying and addressing widespread and cross-cutting challenges to the survival, livelihood and dignity of their people."[11] After two decades of definitional debates, the "common understanding" of the human security approach included three pillars:

- freedom from fear, absence of threats to survival, such as physical exploitation, violence, persecution, death, which requires protective measures;
- freedom from want, absence of threats to livelihoods such as unemployment, but also pandemics, food shortages, and so on, which requires provision of adequate development interventions;
- freedom from threats to dignity, such as infringement of human rights, inequality, marginalization, displacement, and discrimination, which requires the expansion of opportunities, empowerment, and ensuring human rights.

Underutilized so far

Since its introduction in 1994, this commonsense idea has nonetheless courted controversy. Critiques have negated its value as an analytical framework, rejected its utility as a policy agenda, and even opposed its very existence as a concept. Within academia, the broad definition that encompasses the three freedoms (fear, want, loss of dignity) is rejected not only by those who altogether deny human security as a valid paradigm shift, but also by those who prefer to limit it to particular types of existential threats to individuals. Three schools of thought have evolved from the debates around human security in academia. A first group argues that human security lacks analytical rigor, and is consequently at best a "rallying cry" and at worst unadulterated "hot air" as a mere political agenda.[12] Among the most adamant critics are realist scholars who warn against the securitization of what is not, essentially, an existential threat. A second school, while accepting the term, insists on limiting the definitions to "freedom from fear" and direct threats to individuals' safety and to their physical integrity: armed conflict, gross violations of human rights that lead to fears such as imprisonment and death, public insecurity, and organized crime. Proponents of the narrower version argue that a useful and workable definition should be restricted to threats falling under the realm of tangible violence,[13] measured, for instance, by the number of battle-related deaths.[14] As their argument goes, broadening the agenda of threats to include poverty or food shortages, for example, would be the equivalent of making a shopping list of all bad things that can happen, making the concept unworkable.[15] A third school, to which this author belongs, argues that a broad definition is essential for understanding contemporary crises, regardless of whether the concept is "workable" or not, even though tools and methods have been developed to take a more comprehensive and strategic approach to interventions.[16]

Instead of lamenting the lack of workable definitions, proponents of the broad version believe that research should be concerned with ways in which definitions insisted on by security studies circumvent political, moral, and ethical concerns in order to concentrate on relations of power.[17] From this perspective, the lack of an agreed-upon definition is not a conceptual weakness but represents a refusal to succumb to the dominant political agenda. Even though adopting the narrow definition facilitates researchers' work, the reality of people's lives means that threats like poverty or disease can have an impact as severe as tangible violence. When agency is returned to people, it is the localized, subjective sense of the security of individuals that in the last analysis is of paramount importance. To critics who lament the normativity and subjectivity of a prescriptive (as opposed to descriptive) concept, one should respond by recalling that all acts of defining or delimiting, even in an academic milieu, cannot be objective exercises dissociated from political considerations in terms of ideology, time, money, and the will to act on behalf of others. Human security is decidedly normative, and belongs—much like the human development concept launched in the early 1990s—to the realm of ethics.

Within the policy world, in the past two decades much lip service has been paid to the concept in international relations, but the road to acceptance has not been smooth. In Haq's original writing, human security was supposed to mend the North-South divide, since, as he put it, it could be applicable to people everywhere.[18] Yet, immediately after its launch, the concept was met with skepticism from G77 countries during the 1995 World Summit for Social Development in Copenhagen for fear it would lead to violations of state sovereignty. Countries of the Global South feared the new concept was a tool for the West to impose its liberal values and order and for big powers to justify their ad hoc interventions abroad. They also feared that human security might be used as a new conditionality for receiving aid.[19]

The skepticism was proven partly right when the debate at the global level increasingly associated two *faux amis*: human security with interventions in the name of responsibility to protect (RTP).

The International Commission on Intervention and State Sovereignty (ICISS), which Canada set up in 2001, determined that, under certain well-defined circumstances, interventions could be legitimized in countries where the state, whether weak or predatory, could not or did not protect the security of individuals. The report of the commission put equal emphasis on the responsibilities to prevent, to protect, and to rebuild, but political events cast the responsibility-to-protect norm into the global limelight. No matter how much the original report of the ICISS sought to put breaks on trigger-happy interventions, it became associated with action on behalf of the needy and, by implication, those whose human security had been violated by states unwilling or unable to protect their citizens. For countries looking for responsibility to "act" in the aftermath of humanitarian emergencies, the concept became a rallying point to justify interventions not out of national interest, but out of concerns for other nations' suffering people. For countries of the South, however, such ethical concerns were often seen as excuses for selective interventions and interference in sovereign states in the name of human rights, all while failing to address ills such as the asymmetrical use-of-force. Perceptions of double standards, excessive moralism, selectivity, and bias that have shrouded debates on international interventions in Kosovo, Iraq, Afghanistan, and Libya have prevented developing countries from warming to the concept thus tainted with RTP. The UN General Assembly, in an attempt to build consensus among its Southern member states, tried to dissociate the two in its 2012 resolution by explicitly stating that the notion of human security does not entail the threat or the use-of-force or coercive actions. It must be

> implemented with full respect for the purposes and principles enshrined in the Charter of the United Nations, including full respect for the sovereignty of States, territorial integrity and non-interference in matters that are essentially within the domestic jurisdiction of States.[20]

A second apprehension about the political currency of the concept is both caused by and manifested in the fact that, while human security has been adapted as a foreign and aid policy tool by a number of countries in the past two decades, no country has adopted it as a national policy agenda. Canada, Japan, briefly Norway, and now Switzerland have at different points based their foreign policy under the human security banner, with the premise that the security of people in other states/regions would trickle out to security at home. Human security relegated to foreign policy as enlightened self-interest became a good that some better-off countries could provide to others through external relations or through aid. Relegation to the domain of foreign or aid policy implies, falsely, that human security is not universally applicable in regard to people's daily concerns—no matter where they live geographically—or that industrialized societies are immune to insecurities. The reality of urban violence, forbidding food prices, pockets of poverty, social exclusion, the crisis of multiculturalism, and even the loneliness and depression of the elderly could, and in fact should, be addressed through a broadened security agenda at the national level.

The potential of human security

A key way in which fears of intervention and breach of sovereignty could be alleviated would be to address a broader range of threats to individuals' security: not only acts of direct violence, but also acts of structural violence, such as those associated with lack of development or inability to mitigate the impact of natural disasters, for example. Adopting the human security agenda to mitigate the impact of the coronavirus pandemic, for example, would be the optimal way for the concept to go beyond the narrow RTP norm associated with controversial military interventions.

The shift in paradigm that human security represents is not only an intellectual critical exercise to debunk the primacy and prerogative of the state. It can also be a principle-based policy tool for comprehensive analysis, policymaking, and evaluation. The concept can be used analytically to recognize widespread threats and their root causes as well as their multidimensional consequences for different insecurities (political, economic, health, food, community, personal, and environmental). From such a multidimensional analysis of the way that threats pile onto each other in a domino effect comes the need for holistic responses.

The human security approach can further be used as a programmatic tool by applying a set of principles to policymaking. As the General Assembly resolution mentioned, the approach should be operationalized through policies and programs that are: (1) *people centered*, in order to ensure that individuals and communities can fulfill their proper role as both actors (agents) and subjects (beneficiaries) of interventions; (2) *interconnected and comprehensive*—given that threats are mutually reinforcing and interlinked, coherence is needed in order to avoid negative harms while promoting the multiplying effects of positive intervention; and (3) *context specific*, because, although insecurities vary considerably across different settings and at different times, the human security framework is universal, in that it is relevant to people everywhere. The response should therefore take the situation into context and not impose cookie cutter approaches in very different settings. Finally, the approach requires preventive measures which avert downside risks and help prevent their impacts from escalating, and this requires an analysis of causes and risk factors, and mature early warning systems, as well as adequate coordination between institutions.

The case of COVID

Applying the human security approach to understanding the causes and consequences of the COVID-19 pandemic, on the one hand, and to seeking solutions that are people centered, comprehensive, targeted, and specific to the given context, on the other, presents an opportunity to bring the concept to the forefront of global security. It would also help alleviate the two main reasons for opposition to the approach in the political world: that the concept advocates military interventions in the name of human rights, which is the fear of the G77 countries, and second, that countries, both North and South, are inclined to adopt the concept as part of international development aid or a foreign policy tool, rather than a national policy to address the concerns of their own populations.

Different approaches can be used to analyze the threats that the pandemic caused and to whom, and how these should be addressed. Here, I will compare the traditional security approach (realism), the institutional approach (liberalism), and the human security approach to analyzing the causes of the insecurity caused by COVID-19, its consequences, and what needs to be done.

The pandemic as a state security problem

In dominant state-centered security theories, the protection of territorial integrity and national sovereignty reigns supreme, and threats are recognized primarily as existential ones posed by other states. From a state security perspective, the causes of the spread of the pandemic had to do with the way other states failed to contain the threat within their borders. Much blame, for example, was put on the country where the virus was first identified, China, for failing to pay attention to the severity of the threat and to raise the alarm, and for proceeding slowly to close borders.

At the national level, countries tightened borders and implemented draconian lockdown measures as COVID-19 was seen as a national security threat. While these measures limited the spread of the virus, they came with economic and social consequences. Governments all struggled to manage the pandemic. Law enforcement agencies were also forced to tackle increased security threats such as domestic violence, political and social unrest, and cybercrime, which spiked during the pandemic. An Interpol assessment of the impact of COVID-19 on cybercrime, for example, found a significant target shift from individuals to major corporations, governments, and critical infrastructure.[21] The pandemic also stirred unrest in many countries[22] of the world as people protested economic hardships, inequalities, injustice, and failures of governments to protect.[23] The Fund for Peace's Fragile States Index, which tracks social, economic, and political trends across 179 countries, found that COVID-19 was the "first domino in a chain of events that ignited more longstanding and deep-seated grievances" such as political polarization.[24] Before the pandemic, countries that were widely believed to have greater capacity to prevent and manage risk, including public health treatment, relied on economic wealth and technical expertise for their power. Yet, many of these wealthy and developed countries were among the ones worst impacted by the pandemic and had their fragilities and fault lines clearly exposed. Fragility can develop in the most powerful countries in the world: the US saw the severest worsening on the fragility scale, and the country saw the largest protest against police violence and efforts to delegitimize the election process, which escalated violently in January 2021 with the takeover of the Capitol.

Mercy Corps, in a year-long research study which involved interviews with 600 individuals, showed that COVID-19 had worsened conflict drivers in Afghanistan, Colombia, and Nigeria. These included, as expected, diminishing trust in government, increasing economic hardships and erosion of social cohesion, an uptick in criminal and gender-based violence, and expanded recruitment by armed opposition groups. These drivers of potential conflict necessitate that conflict prevention and peace-building measures must be included—if not prioritized—by donors and policymakers in COVID-19 recovery schemes.[25]

For the first time in its history NATO had to face an attack against each of its member states at once with the outbreak of the COVID-19 pandemic. NATO's 2010 Strategic Concept had already contemplated "health risks" as a future area of concern for NATO's operations: it had identified key environmental and resource constraints, including health risks, climate change, water scarcity, and increasing energy needs as factors that would further shape the future security environment and which had the potential to significantly affect NATO planning and operations.[26] Despite the warning about such a scenario a decade before, however, the organization did not take sufficient measures to strengthen its crisis management apparatus, according to officials and professionals in international defense.[27] With the pandemic, the Operations Division of NATO headquarters in Brussels admitted that the alliance was ill prepared to handle such a crisis. The alliance lacked its own means and political bandwidth to do more.[28]

All this showed that neither a strong military power nor a strong economy was enough to prevent the risks emanating from a health crisis and to prevent further fragility in the face of shocks. The consequences, from the perspective of international security, were increased aggressive discourse blaming other nations, breakdown of trust between nations, and tit-for-tat policies of border closures between countries, including those of the same regional bloc such as the European Union. While calls were made for increased global cooperation, including through global institutions such as the World Health Organization, mistrust in other countries' abilities to contain their threats led to more isolation and protective policies.

The traditional security paradigm failed to predict the damage that the pandemic brought to states, societies, and economies. It also could not prevent the spread of the virus or protect the lives and livelihoods of people within states. Conventional tools of national security did not guarantee protection for people. No matter how much countries had spent on defending their populations from conventional threats, the global pandemic made people insecure: people died, they became sick, they lost their jobs.

Some of the most "advanced" states, measured by traditional military security capacity, were ill prepared to address COVID-19. States realized that security strategies (military, police, border closures) are not enough to prevent the spread of disease. The disease easily traveled across borders and across communities. The securitization approach led to behaviors that showed that countries did not learn their lessons: the Stockholm International Peace Research Institute (SIPRI) estimates that in 2020, global military expenditure rose by 2.6 percent to $1.98 trillion even as some defense funds were reallocated to fight the COVID-19 pandemic. The five biggest spenders in 2020, which together accounted for 62 percent of military spending worldwide, were the United States, China, India, Russia, and the United Kingdom in that order.[29] Most of these countries were also precisely where most people were affected by the coronavirus. By contrast, countries such as Chile and South Korea redirected part of their planned military spending to their pandemic response, a move that no doubt contributed to their relative success in controlling the virus.

The institutional perspective

A second narrative pertains to putting institutions' security at the center of interest, exemplified by the liberal approach to security. A broadened conception of nontraditional threats (such as pandemics, economic crisis, terrorism) includes those that can menace states' essence in similar ways as that of individuals: they can hamper states' existence (territorial integrity), their functioning (whether they have the resources and capacity to function and develop as a state) and their sovereignty (legitimacy and recognition).

From the perspective of societal security, the crisis was a failure of institutions: the failure to have proper contingency planning for a health emergency, and to have adequate equipment (masks, sanitizers, ventilators, beds), given cutbacks in expenditures on health systems. Medical personnel and health institutions, caught off guard and unprepared, gave contradictory directives in the early stages of the pandemic regarding ways that the disease could spread, the efficacy of masks, and so on.

The consequences for the security of institutions were not negligible: in addition to the costs to severely slowed-down economies, the interruption of trade, and rising prices of commodities, there was a breakdown of social infrastructure that ultimately failed to protect. Trust in national and global institutions eroded as they were unable to help people navigate the crisis and to protect and provide for people. An assessment of the EU, for example, concluded that the pandemic revealed the vulnerabilities of member states' infrastructure and supply chains, and the limited competence of the EU in supporting member states' management of public health emergencies.[30] Institutions were not able to properly protect people either.

The human security perspective

While the realist and liberal perspectives search for causes for the spread of the pandemic in the behavior of states and institutions, the human security perspective recognizes the role that people played in this regard, as well as the consequences in their everyday lives. Traditional security could not protect against the effects of the pandemic. Institutions did not prevent and prepare. And people did not adhere to security precautions.

The COVID-19 virus itself was not caused by people, but people contributed to its spread with actions such as not practicing social distancing, not reporting their medical condition, spreading misinformation, and refusing to believe in the severity of the pandemic. Some people were willing to endanger themselves and others for the sake of more freedoms or for economic choices by failing to take into consideration directives such as quarantines, restrictions on movement, wearing of masks, and so on. Ironically though, countries with authoritarian political systems were best able to contain the spread of COVID-19 by making their populations obey stay-at-home orders, lockdowns, and border closures.[31]

Domino implications

The human security approach to the pandemic is especially helpful in putting a focus on multidimensional consequences in people's everyday lives and recognizing the domino effect of threats spreading into different insecurity areas. The seven areas of insecurity listed in the UNDP's *Human Development Report 1994* present a good framework to examine these multiple consequences. The coronavirus started as a health insecurity that led to loss of lives but soon avalanched into massive economic insecurities as people lost their livelihoods as a result of shutdowns, communities became increasingly isolated, food prices went up, and political security declined as people came to mistrust the state and their politicians.

According to the COVID-19 dashboard set up online by the Center for Systems Science and Engineering at Johns Hopkins University, by the end of February 2022, there had been almost 6 million deaths registered as a result of the global pandemic worldwide, and around 450 million total cases.[32] By the summer of 2021, the Brookings Institution was estimating that the COVID-19 global recession was the deepest since the end of World War II.[33] Every country posted negative growth in 2020. The World Bank estimated that the COVID-19 pandemic would "push an additional 88 million to 115 million people into extreme poverty . . . with the total rising to as many as 150 million by 2021, depending on the severity of the economic contraction."[34]

The slowdown of economies and border closures led to shortages of consumer goods and rising prices for imported products. Where food products were dependent on imports, price hikes meant less availability of certain products. For families living in the most underprivileged areas, rising prices meant they had to spend more of their income on their food basket. Fluctuations and hikes in food prices increased the burden on household budgets. The pandemic may have added between 83 and 132 million people to the total number of undernourished in the world in 2020.[35]

The pandemic also widened the gender inequality gap. Women lost their jobs at a faster rate (19 percent) than men because they tend to work in sectors affected by lockdowns.[36] In France alone, the incidence of violence against women is estimated to have increased by 30 percent during the first round of lockdown, from March to May 2020.[37] The health consequences of the disease are well known, and, depending on the immunity of the person infected, can have devastating consequences. Health impacts also include mental health issues related to stress, isolation, and the need to take care of sick people.

UNESCO estimated that at least 1.5 billion students were out of school at the peak of the pandemic in March 2020.[38] It also estimated that eleven million girls might never return to their studies following the pandemic.[39] Interruptions in the education system will not only have short-term effects on learning, but also diminishing economic opportunities for this generation of students in the long term.

Workers' or migrants' remittances—the transfer of part of their earnings in the form of cash or goods to support their families—were expected to decline by 14 percent by the end of 2021 compared to pre-COVID-19 levels in 2019.[40] The drop in remittances will increase poverty and food insecurity among many poor families, and households risk losing the means to afford services like healthcare. Refugees, migrants, and displaced persons stand to suffer disproportionately both from the pandemic and its aftermath.

The COVID-19 pandemic thus had consequences for the three freedoms (freedom from fear, from want, and freedom from indignity) and the seven insecurity areas identified in the UNDR's *Human Development Report 1994*: it led to health insecurities in terms of death, mobility, and mental health consequences; it provided economic insecurity in terms of loss of incomes and jobs; it had food security consequences in terms of rising prices and food shortages in the supply chain; personal insecurity was exacerbated with the rise of domestic violence and criminal behavior; community security was eroded with rising discrimination against specific ethnic groups, an increase in hate crimes, marginalization and isolation of the elderly, and stigmatization of the sick; and finally, the pandemic had political insecurity consequences when people lost their trust in the state and political systems, and frustrations against the establishment led to riots and political instability in many parts of the world, as discussed above. The pandemic had both positive and negative impacts on environmental security: On the one hand, reduced transport facilities and lockdowns contributed to reductions in greenhouse gas emissions and air pollutants; on the other hand, lifestyle changes (such as reliance on home delivery meals and online shopping) and the production and disposal of surgical masks and gloves led to increases in nonrecyclable waste.

Structural inequalities revealed

Even though people suffered everywhere, the context mattered: the crisis deepened existing structural inequalities between people. The poor became poorer. Some women, children, elderly people, displaced people, and sick people became more vulnerable and more stigmatized, hence with more insecurities.

The pandemic had more negative impacts among already vulnerable populations within countries around the world. These included people working in informal economic activity and working in companies related to services, tourism, travel, import-export, event management, and so on. Women who worked in the informal sector and were not covered by any social protection were more adversely affected. Economic impacts were felt especially by women and girls who were earning less and holding insecure jobs or living close to poverty. The risk of domestic violence went up and added to already existing problems. Social isolation measures exacerbated gender-based violence within families. [41]

Another vulnerable group consisted of young people looking for employment opportunities, newly entering the job market at a time of slowdown in economic growth. They were impacted by the lack of employment opportunities but also the lack of opportunity to travel abroad for education, given the devaluation of currency, and the closure of borders and educational institutions aboard. Students studying abroad could not return to their higher educational establishments due to travel restrictions.

Children became vulnerable as increases in prices negatively affected the quality of their health, nutrition, and education within their families. Rural populations were vulnerable when access to social services was hampered by the decrease in the purchasing power of income. Regional disparities created additional barriers to families and communities realizing their human security. People with disabilities were more vulnerable to the serious consequences of a potential infection, in addition to the secondary consequences: for example, increases in the price of food and other consumer goods due to importation restrictions reduced their availability to vulnerable groups dependent on social benefits, which may have affected not only the quality and quantity of their nutrition, but also their access to health services. The elderly became more vulnerable not only to the grave form of the disease itself but also to a host of other insecurities, starting with the consequences of the possible increase in food prices and reduced purchasing power of income, as their pension earnings were limited. Price increases also affected the availability of medical services and medicines for the elderly.

Finally, migrants who were stranded abroad were affected by travel restrictions and their ability to earn a living. They needed more medical care, financial support, and help to return home. Migrants' families who were dependent on remittances faced financial difficulties. The decline in economic growth rates everywhere also complicated the livelihoods of stateless persons and refugees, who faced challenges of access to health systems and social security schemes.

The human security perspective not only recognizes the impacts of threats on people's lives, but also reveals the degree of vulnerability to risks and shocks that people have according to structural inequalities based on gender, age, geography, race, citizenship, and so on.

Policy solutions

The human security approach is not only an analytical framework to understand causes and consequences; it can also be applied to specific policies in order to find adequate, people-centered responses. Expanding the notion of security from its narrow focus on the national security paradigm requires designing policies that are centered on people and their needs, deal with damages in multiple insecurity domains, target different communities according to their risks, and are designed in a way that prevents future insecurities.

Taking guidance from the 2012 General Assembly resolution, applying the human security approach requires policies and interventions to be developed in ways that are people centered, comprehensive, context specific, and preventive:

1. Solutions should first and foremost be designed to alleviate risks to people, including by taking them into consideration in the design and implementation of interventions. People should be agents of change in their lives, and this requires having sufficient knowledge on how to mitigate risks. In practical terms this means that interventions should start with an assessment of threats, risks, and people's vulnerabilities as well as their capacity to mitigate those risks. All interventions need to involve people and communities in identifying their own insecurities and vulnerabilities on the one hand, and empower them so that they can help secure themselves on the other.

2. Because threats are multidimensional, a comprehensive solution is necessary. For example, a public health response is not enough to tackle the consequences of the COVID-19 pandemic. It is necessary to tackle the multidimensional consequences of the health crisis simultaneously. In practical terms, this would mean involving a variety of stakeholders and service providers to plan a comprehensive multisectoral response. The challenge, however, is to overcome the way institutions are organized, with unitary goals and expertise, and the way in which silo mentalities, turf battles, and the absence of mechanisms for integration hamper possibilities for comprehensive responses. Integrated approaches require broad partnerships so that each brings to the table their own specific knowledge, and it requires cross-sectoral/integrated institutional frameworks that allow cross-fertilization.
3. The context matters. Different communities or regions need different types of interventions according to the risks they are exposed to. All interventions should address findings of assessment of potential threats at the local level as well as existing capacities. Based on in-depth local knowledge, region-specific interventions should be developed that address the given context, including for the more vulnerable parts of society. Baseline studies help the understanding of the impacts of the pandemic at the local levels only when they take into account objective factors of risk (through quantitative indicators) as well as subjective factors that contribute to feelings of insecurity (through perception studies).
4. People and communities should be protected by the state but also empowered so that they can build their resilience to the consequences of the pandemic. Human security policies and interventions should be preventive in the first place and build on people's resilience. These include interventions that help build skills for people so that they can deploy their positive coping mechanisms. The preventive approach can for example be ensured by investing in the potential of youth as a catalyst of resilience in communities. As a population group that has a lot to lose in terms of education and employment opportunities, youth are vulnerable to the impact of the global pandemic. At the same time, they can be mobilized to bring information and change to their community.

Conclusion

After the shock of COVID-19 has abated, states will most likely return to traditional means of upholding their notions of security, continuing to spend on their militaries in a trend that had picked up in 2020. At the same time, the lasting legacy of the pandemic will be a reminder that the health of a nation depends on everyday securities in people's lives. Despite the frequent characterization of the human security approach as too broad or ambitious, its essence is ethical: to prevent threats and mitigate their impacts when they materialize. Human security should not be reduced to lists or to a narrow definition, but remain flexible enough to allow for a deeper understanding of the root of insecurities and capacities and the will to address them.

Despite the existence of a UN General Assembly resolution that has finally concluded the definitional debate by calling human security an "approach," implementing the agenda at the global level will most likely be confronted with political challenges. There is little chance that there will be a consensus to genuinely reconcile the concerns of the North and the South, the East and the West. Critics of the concept include both countries of the North, which would seek an agreement on enforcement mechanisms, and countries from the South or the emerging world, who mistrust the concept out of fear of new conditionality, unwarranted interventions, and violations of state sovereignty. Yet, perhaps more important than a global agenda is the need to develop domestic human security policies, which no country has done so far. It is at the national and local levels that the human security approach can genuinely be used as a blueprint for alternative policies. The way that human security can finally become relevant in international politics is for it to be adopted by all countries for their national domestic policy (not just foreign policy) in order to address not only human rights violations but also pandemics and other massive health insecurities that have widespread impacts on everyday freedoms.

Notes

1. Keith Krause and M. C. Williams, "Broadening the Agenda of Security Studies: Politics and Methods," *Mershon International Studies Review* 40, no. 2 (1996): 229–54.
2. United Nations Development Programme (UNDP), *Human Development Report 1994* (New York: Oxford University Press, 1994).
3. United Nations General Assembly (UNGA), "Resolution 66/290. Follow-Up to Paragraph 143 on Human Security of the 2005 World Summit Outcome," A/RES/66/290, October 25, 2012.
4. Steve Smith, "The Contested Concept of Security," in "The Concept of Security Before and After September 11," Working Paper No. 23, Institute of Defence and Strategic Studies, May 2002, https://www.rsis.edu.sg/wp-content/uploads/rsis-pubs/WP23.pdf (accessed February 21, 2022).
5. Barry Buzan, Ole Wæver, and Jaap de Wilde, *Security: A New Framework for Analysis* (Boulder, CO: Lynne Rienner, 1998), 23–4.

6. Quoted in Gary King and Christopher Murray, "Rethinking Human Security," *Political Science Quarterly* 116, no. 4 (2001): 585–610.
7. UNDP, *Human Development Report 1994*, 24.
8. Ibid., 22.
9. Ibid., 23.
10. *Human Security Now*, Commission on Human Security, 2003, 4, https://reliefweb.int/sites/reliefweb.int/files/resources/91BAEEDBA50C6907C1256D19006A9353-chs-security-may03.pdf (accessed February 21, 2022).
11. UNGA, "Resolution 66/290."
12. Roland Paris, "Human Security—Paradigm Shift or Hot Air?" *International Security* 26, no. 2 (2001), 91.
13. Taylor Owen, "Human Security—Conflict, Critique and Consensus: Colloquium Remarks and a Proposal for a Threshold-Based Definition," *Security Dialogue* 35, no. 3 (2004): 373–87; King and Murray, "Rethinking Human Security."
14. See for example the Human Security Report Project, Simon Fraser University.
15. Keith Krause, "The Key to a Powerful Agenda, if Properly Delimited," *Security Dialogue* 35, no. 3 (2004): 367.
16. See Shahrbanou Tadjbakhsh, "In Defense of the Broad View of Human Security," in Mary Martin and Taylor Owen (eds.), *Routledge Handbook of Human Security* (Abingdon, England: Routledge, 2014).
17. Kyle Grayson, "A Challenge to the Power over Knowledge of Traditional Security Studies," *Security Dialogue* 35, no. 3 (2004): 357.
18. Mahbub ul Haq, *Reflections on Human Development* (New York: Oxford University Press, 1995); UNDP, *Human Development Report 1994*.
19. See discussions in Chapter 1, "Rationale and Political Usage," in Shahrbanou Tadjbakhsh and Anuradha Chenoy, *Human Security: Concepts and Implications* (Abingdon, England: Routledge, 2007).
20. UNGA, "Resolution 66/290."
21. *Cybercrime: COVID-19 Impact*, Interpol, August 2020, https://www.interpol.int/en/content/download/15526/file/COVID-19%20Cybercrime%20Analysis%20Report-%20August%202020.pdf (accessed February 22, 2022).
22. Natalie Fiertz, "A Health Crisis Is More than a Health Crisis," Fragile States Index, May 20, 2021, https://fragilestatesindex.org/2021/05/20/a-health-crisis-is-more-than-a-health-crisis/ (accessed February 22, 2022).
23. Elise Labott, "Get Ready for a Spike in Global Unrest", *Foreign Policy*, July 22, 2011, https://foreignpolicy.com/2021/07/22/covid-global-unrest-political-upheaval/ (accessed February 22, 2022).
24. Fiertz, "A Health Crisis."
25. *A Clash of Contagions: The Impact of COVID-19 on Conflict in Nigeria, Colombia and Afghanistan*, Mercy Corps, June 2021, https://www.mercycorps.org/sites/default/files/2021-06/Clash-of-Contagions-Full-Report-June-2021.pdf (accessed February 22, 2022).

26. *Active Engagement, Modern Defence: Strategic Concept for the Defence and Security of the Members of the North Atlantic Treaty Organization*, NATO, 2010, https://www.nato.int/nato_static_fl2014/assets/pdf/pdf_publications/20120214_strategic-concept-2010-eng.pdf (accessed February 22, 2022).
27. Giovanna di Maio, "NATO's Response to COVID-19: Lessons for Resilience and Readiness," Brookings Institution, October 2020, https://www.brookings.edu/wp-content/uploads/2020/10/FP_20201028_nato_covid_demaio-1.pdf (accessed February 22, 2022).
28. Olivier Rittimann, "NATO and the COVID-19 Emergency: Actions and Lessons," NDC Policy Brief No. 15, NATO Defense College, September 15, 2020, https://www.ndc.nato.int/news/news.php?icode=1463 (accessed February 22, 2022).
29. Diego Lopes da Silva, Nan Tian, and Alexandra Marksteiner, "Trends in World Military Expenditure, 2020," SIPRI, April 2021, https://www.sipri.org/sites/default/files/2021-04/fs_2104_milex_0.pdf (accessed February 22, 2022).
30. Directorate General for External Policies of the Union, *How the COVID-19 Crisis Has Affected Security and Defence-Related Aspects of the EU* (Brussels: European Parliament, 2021).
31. See, for example, the rankings provided by the Lowy Institute, an Australian think tank, which analyzed and compared the performance of 116 countries in managing the COVID-19 pandemic. "Political Systems," in "COVID Performance Index: Deconstructing Pandemic Responses," Lowy Institute, https://interactives.lowyinstitute.org/features/covid-performance/#politics (accessed February 22, 2022).
32. Johns Hopkins Coronavirus Resource Center, "COVID-19 Dashboard," 2021, https://coronavirus.jhu.edu/map.html (accessed February 22, 2022).
33. Eduardo Levy Yeyati and Federico Filippini, "Social and Economic Impact of COVID-19," Brookings Global Working Paper No. 158, Brookings Institution, June 2021, https://www.brookings.edu/wp-content/uploads/2021/06/Social-and-economic-impact-COVID.pdf (accessed February 22, 2022).
34. "COVID-19 to Add as Many as 150 Million Extreme Poor by 2021," press release, World Bank, October 7, 2020, https://www.worldbank.org/en/news/press-release/2020/10/07/covid-19-to-add-as-many-as-150-million-extreme-poor-by-2021 (accessed February 22, 2022).
35. *The State of Food Security and Nutrition in the World 2020: Transforming Food Systems for Affordable Healthy Diets* (Rome: Food and Agriculture Organization, 2020), available at https://www.fao.org/3/ca9692en/online/ca9692en.html (accessed February 22, 2022).
36. "Policy Brief: The Impact of COVID-19 on Women," United Nations, April 9, 2020, https://digitallibrary.un.org/record/3856948?ln=en (accessed February 22, 2022).
37. "Impact of the Covid-19 Pandemic on Domestic Violence," press release, Académie nationale de médecine, December 18, 2020, https://

www.academie-medecine.fr/impact-of-the-covid-19-pandemic-on-domestic-violence/?lang=en (accessed February 22, 2022).

38. "#LearningNeverStops: COVID-19 Education Response," Global Education Coalition, UNESCO, https://en.unesco.org/covid19/education-response/globalcoalition (accessed February 22, 2022).

39. "Keeping Girls in the Picture," Global Education Coalition, UNESCO, https://en.unesco.org/covid19/educationresponse/girlseducation (accessed February 22, 2022).

40. "COVID-19: Remittance Flows to Shrink 14% by 2021," news release, World Bank, October 29, 2020, https://www.worldbank.org/en/news/press-release/2020/10/29/covid-19-remittance-flows-to-shrink-14-by-2021 (accessed February 22, 2022).

41. See John Bluedorn et al., "Gender and Employment in the COVID-19 Recession: Cross-Country Evidence on 'She-cessions,'" *COVID Economics*, no. 75 (2021), as well as other papers documenting the impact of COVID-19 on social and human life published by the Centre for Economic Policy Research at https://cepr.org/content/covid-economics-vetted-and-real-time-papers-0 (accessed February 22, 2022).

8

Humanitarianism and Security: The Amplification of Crises and Threats

Vandra Harris Agisilaou

Introduction

Much humanitarian practice now takes place in complex environments, in which humanitarian need is exacerbated by conflict. Conflict causes civilian injury and death, and destruction of housing, critical infrastructure, trading routes and production. This impact is amplified in places where extreme poverty is already pervasive, infrastructure already poor, and extreme weather and natural hazards already creating stress. As such, the intersection of crises creates urgent human need, and is known as a complex emergency. While identification of complex emergencies invokes broad, cross-sectoral responses, it also makes such responses extremely difficult. The challenge of access that characterizes many humanitarian responses is intensified when conflict places humanitarian actors themselves at risk of injury and death. The core principles of humanitarian action are deeply challenged when humanitarians must balance the fundamental right of every person to humanitarian assistance with the need to engage with conflict actors to secure access to the people in greatest need.

This volume looks beyond the pandemic that characterizes the time of writing, to imagine the security landscape that will face us in decades to come. This chapter centers on humanitarianism, which is an area actively engaged with the "inextricably linked" experiences of poverty and crisis,[1] where the intersection of state fragility and poverty magnifies humanitarian crises and disasters. It is also a field in which the COVID-19 pandemic is both a crisis and an amplifier of other crises—and one in which the disproportionate impact of disease on poor nations and people will see significantly increased challenges for a very long time to come. This chapter therefore argues that the lasting impact of the pandemic will be increasing inequality that creates new crises and exacerbates existing ones. In this light,

COVID-19's impact on fragility, stability, and poverty will be central to humanitarian practice long after offices and schools reopen and transport and travel resume.

Importantly, the COVID-19 pandemic has not encountered a well-structured and well-financed system serving a minority hit by devastating, life-threatening crises. Rather, humanitarian action was already severely underfunded, and humanitarian crises affect millions of people each year—235 million in 2020—in ways that disproportionally impact those already suffering. The last decade has seen increasingly intense political conflicts, in which more than 90 percent of casualties have been civilians; conflict and violence have been key drivers of rising hunger; there have been record levels of internal displacement; and environmental crises have increased in frequency and severity.[2] Close to half of low-income countries were experiencing or at high risk of debt distress even before the pandemic[3] and, while poverty was reducing, progress was already slowing in 2019.[4] Meanwhile, inequality between nations persists despite some impressive gains aligned with the Millennium Development Goals.

Humanitarian concerns do not exist in isolation; they intersect in a very real way with other areas including security and development. The impact of insecurity and instability on those vulnerabile to crisis is significant. Despite the measured success of the Millennium Development Goals project, the world is not on a consistent and comfortable path toward shared growth and prosperity, with key indicators showing rising inequality and humanitarian need.[5] Appeals for humanitarian funds increased by 136 percent between 2011 and 2020 and, while the funding has increased, it has consistently equated to approximately 60 percent of those requirements—with a shortfall of more than US$18.8 billion in 2020.[6] Adding to the difficulty of addressing human need, these funds are not distributed evenly according to need. Rather, funders allocate funds according to a range of their priorities, leading to a reality in which, for example, 100 percent of appeal funds were met for Mozambique in 2020, while just 7 percent were met for the Democratic Republic of Congo.[7]

In this context, the devastating impact of the pandemic is much greater than disease and death alone, with economic impacts of government attempts to control the spread of disease described as triggering "the deepest global recession since the 1930s."[8] As indicated, humanitarian capabilities are already impacted by factors such as insufficient funding and diminished access, and these have been drastically increased by the measures implemented to prevent the spread of COVID-19. In addition to the pandemic itself constituting a humanitarian emergency, COVID-19 joins the ranks of hazard multipliers including climate change and conflict, which create and magnify crisis, exacerbate poverty and inequality, and hamper humanitarian action.

In seeking to unpack these complexities, this chapter begins by setting the context of humanitarian practice, explaining what it is, and pointing to the kinds of crisis it relates to. It introduces the intersection between humanitarianism and conflict, and explains the triple nexus concept as a framework for addressing intersecting global concerns. Turning to insecurity in humanitarian contexts, it considers how human security influences and is impacted by crisis; and how conflict features in humanitarianism. This opens the chapter up to a discussion of the intersection of humanitarianism, development, and security—that is to say, the complexity of working with security challenges in humanitarian practice. It talks about the security challenges faced by humanitarians in conflict environments, using Yemen as an example, and the impact on crisis of insecurity and conflict. On this foundation, it argues that COVID-19 constitutes an important humanitarian crisis (and it is being treated as such globally), and that the ongoing impact will be central to humanitarian practice throughout the coming decade, even if the disease itself is contained. Lastly, this chapter explores the existing challenges to humanitarianism in conflict environments, and contends that these will be exacerbated by the impact of COVID-19, which has already seen the first rise of global poverty in about a quarter of a century. It concludes that the pandemic brings to a head a series of challenges already faced by this sector, and will test the agility, creativity, and flexibility of the sector in reimagining lifesaving action. Thus, the enormous task facing humanitarian actors is to avoid outcomes that further entrench disadvantage in ways that are systemic, bodily, and enduring.

Humanitarianism

This chapter is concerned with humanitarian action by nongovernmental and international organizations, rather than government-driven armed humanitarian intervention, which is described in similar terms and often takes place in the same spaces. Internationally coordinated and regulated armed intervention by individual states or groups of states is a key part of "an international regime focused on the protection of populations from atrocities"[9] and, while important, it is not the central concern here. Rather, this chapter focuses on the kind of humanitarian action Hugo Slim describes as "a compassionate response to extreme and particular forms of suffering arising from organized human violence and natural disaster"[10]—actions broadly summarized as saving lives, alleviating suffering, and maintaining human dignity.[11]

There are many kinds of crisis that cause death and human suffering; however, humanitarian support is sought and offered when the scale of a crisis overwhelms the capacity of a community or nation to respond. This can be triggered by a range of hazards, which may be "natural" (originating in the natural environment, but often with human triggers), technological, or intentional (including civil and political actions).[12] These hazards only become a disaster when they overwhelm the capacity to respond, and that hinges in part on the resilience and vulnerability or exposure of the population.

Often when we think of humanitarian crises, we think of so-called natural disasters, where an extreme weather or geological event leads to an acute crisis with major physical damage and significant loss of life, demanding an immediate, lifesaving rescue mission from the international community. The number of disasters related to climate and weather has increased almost 35 percent in the last three decades, and over 1.7 billion people have been affected by this kind of disaster in the last decade.[13] The *World Disasters Report* states clearly that "climate change is a risk magnifier" that is already interacting with other hazards to create enormous impact on people's lives.[14] As with other crises, climate vulnerability is intricately tied to poverty, such that those with the fewest resources to survive and recover from environmental crisis are generally the hardest hit.

A fuller picture reveals that "crises are increasingly complex and long lasting."[15] Complexity in this context refers to intersecting challenges or crises, very often including conflict. This means humanitarians may be responding to weather-related disasters in severely conflict-affected environments, or hunger and disease among displaced populations. Crises not (necessarily) directly arising from climate and weather-related hazards include disease, displacement, food insecurity, and conflict, and it is increasingly common to experience "intersecting crisis risks and vulnerabilities, often resulting in complex crises with different forms of crisis overlaying one another."[16] Add to this mix protracted crisis, where "a significant proportion of the population is acutely vulnerable to death, disease and disruption of livelihoods over a prolonged period of time," and governments are weak and poorly resourced to respond.[17] Populations in these environments are more likely to be in poverty (over half, compared to one in five in other low- and middle-income countries, LMICs), and significantly more likely to experience extreme poverty (30 percent, as opposed to 6 percent in other LMICs).[18]

Humanitarian crises are diverse, yet an increasingly common characteristic of contemporary crisis is complexity, or the intersection of several challenges. In contrast with conventional conceptions of crisis that emphasize acuteness and deviance, contemporary crises are often protracted and very much part of the lives of those living through them. They are chronic in duration but acute in intensity, with "the average humanitarian crisis" enduring for nine years.[19] They are also decreasingly exceptional, in that countries experiencing protracted crises are home to one in six of the global population, or over one billion people.[20] Protracted crises do not always involve conflict, though it is an important factor in many humanitarian crises; for example eight of the ten countries with the greatest humanitarian need are in conflict, nine are experiencing displacement, and seven have been assessed as high or very high risk for COVID-19.[21]

The impact of disasters is uneven, and politics, wealth, and power all feed into both vulnerability and the responsiveness of the international community. Vulnerability can be understood as that which makes communities and individuals unsafe "not simply because they are exposed to hazard, but as a result of a marginality."[22] Inequality and disadvantage contribute to vulnerability in ways that both stem from and exacerbate people's inability to meet their needs and claim their rights and entitlements.[23] In other words, those with the fewest physical, social, and political resources are more likely to be exposed to hazards, and less likely to be able to withstand them or overcome their impact. Compounding this, vulnerability often corresponds with increased exposure to violence and its effects, including not just interpersonal violence but also destruction of infrastructure, livelihoods, and future prospects.[24] This is reflected on a national level, where states that are institutionally weak are "the most vulnerable to violence and instability and the least able to respond to internal and external stresses."[25]

This is compounded by a lack of political capital needed to attract humanitarian funding, such that "the pattern of humanitarian aid is more closely related to donors' interest than to the needs of the affected communities,"[26] with many crises severely underfunded, forgotten,[27] neglected,[28] and underreported.[29] The twenty countries receiving the most funding per capita in relation to disaster risk and climate change in 2020 did not include any of the twenty most vulnerable countries—two of which received no funding at all.[30] This echoes humanitarian assistance more broadly, in which, of the ten countries most in need of assistance, only four numbered among the top ten recipients of assistance.[31] Not surprisingly, this is extremely problematic since, by definition, it is the ability of people and nations to withstand and respond to hazards that determines whether a hazard becomes a humanitarian crisis.

Pointing to the global trends of importance to humanitarian actors, the UN Office for the Coordination of Humanitarian Affairs lists COVID-19 (including its impact on vulnerable groups, mental health, gender equality, and youth), political conflict, internal displacement due to violence and conflict, rising hunger, severe weather events and natural disasters, and outbreaks of other diseases.[32] This highlights the interdependence of the impacts of humanitarianism, development, and security on whether environments are enabling or limiting. While security and humanitarian practice both draw attention to acute, immediate need, like development they also relate to long-term actions and choices. Indeed, though the idea of a triple nexus implies neat divisions between distinct sectors, the boundaries between these three areas are very blurry and interdependence is strong.

Braithwaite et al. highlight a strong connection between conflict and poverty, but caution that it is quite difficult to identify the direction of causality within this dyad.[33] They conclude that there is evidence of poverty contributing to conflict, but that "international inequalities" are also an important contributing factor. Whether or not causality can be agreed, in the decade from 2010 to 2020, there was an 8 percent rise in extreme poverty within fragile states, in contrast to a 63 percent decline in states not classified as fragile.[34] The extraordinary decline in global poverty was already slowing when the pandemic began, but the globe is now experiencing historic and uneven reversals of that poverty reduction. This renders daily life increasingly difficult for those enduring conflict and rising poverty, as well as making resolution of underlying grievances increasingly difficult.

In this context, current patterns of conflict are important. Patterns of current, protracted conflict are distinct, "characterized by their longevity, intractability and mutability," and their immediate and cumulative consequences are profound.[35] In addition, they are largely urban, they impact civilians much more than previous conflicts, and they require complex responses from a range of actors.[36] These aspects have been examined in the other chapters in this volume. What is of interest here is the evolving understanding of the intersections between humanitarian, development, and security practices and needs.

These intersections have long been recognized and have driven a range of responses within and beyond the humanitarian sector. For example, the label *complex humanitarian emergency* evolved to describe "a humanitarian crisis in a country, region or society where there is a total or considerable breakdown of authority resulting from internal or external conflict," and requiring an integrated response beyond a single agency or UN program.[37] Most recently, the thinking has led to the concept of the humanitarian-development-peace nexus, or *triple nexus*. Applying a label such as this reflects the ongoing desire to improve coherence between diverse sectors and actors, to improve outcomes.[38] It reflects contemporary changes in global experiences and practices, and in particular grows out of Agenda 2030 for Sustainable Development (the Sustainable Development Goals), the 2016 World Humanitarian Summit and the commitments to better collaboration and engagement in its "New Way of Working" and Grand Bargain, and the UN's sustaining peace approach.[39] The uptake of the concept is reflected in the recommendations adopted by the OECD's Development Assistance Commission in 2020.

The idea of the nexus has an important place in humanitarian and development thinking, and at times climate is added to form a quadruple humanitarian-development-peace-environment nexus. All of these are important, and the focus on the ways they intersect drives an intersectional humanitarianism that persistently reorients us to see the diverse factors and actors at play in the humanitarian space. A key example of this is that recent success in poverty reduction has been concentrated in nonfragile states and, while this achievement is transformational for millions of people around the world, it has increased the concentration of poverty in fragile states. Poverty and conflict increase vulnerability to crisis and they are therefore central to humanitarian concerns. As a potent example of this, the UN's Global Humanitarian Response Plan for COVID-19 addresses sixty-three countries needing assistance, more than half of which are experiencing protracted crisis.[40]

Likewise, displacement and conflict increase climate vulnerability, resource scarcity kindled by climatic factors can drive conflict, and food insecurity is exacerbated by conflict.[41] The complex responses that are needed are largely grounded in a human security approach, described in this context as "a more horizontal, demand-driven approach, encouraging the capacity-building of local communities, governments and the international cooperation system to deal with crises as well as enhanced partnership among these actors."[42] This translates into a focus on lives, livelihoods, and dignity as they impact and are impacted by security, with special attention to those most vulnerable.

Security

The way that conflict impacts humanitarian practice is complex and multifaceted. It can constitute a humanitarian crisis in itself, it can exacerbate an existing or unfolding crisis, and it often impedes effective, principled humanitarian action. Conflict can create or increase humanitarian need by posing physical danger, injury, and death, while also damaging livelihoods, redirecting resources, and damaging infrastructure. For humanitarian actors, a key concern is the restriction of access to those in need due to the presence of conflict,[43] as has been the case in Yemen, where in 2020 alone there were over 4,500 incidents causing interruptions or delays to assistance (nearly double the number in 2019).[44] Conflict also poses direct personal danger to humanitarian actors, who are increasingly targeted by parties to conflicts.[45]

In addition to impeding access, conflict poses many challenges for humanitarian organizations, including "providing the highest attainable quality of care and services," "acquisition and management of assets," and "protecting and caring for workers," along with meeting the humanitarian principles.[46] These principles (humanity, neutrality, impartiality, and independence) are agreed "values, principles and standards to guide the conduct of humanitarian operations."[47] They encapsulate the convictions that human suffering demands a response; that need must be the only factor influencing who receives assistance; that humanitarian actors must not take sides; and that action must be driven by these humanitarian values, not political, military, or other motivations.[48]

The particular challenges around neutrality and independence are tied to the importance placed on separation between humanitarian and military or political motivations and action. Distinguishing themselves as separate is seen as critical for the protection of humanitarian actors and access, as well as supporting assertions that distribution is determined by need rather than representing support for particular groups.[49] This means that in environments of active conflict humanitarian actors may experience the paradox of particularly needing to demonstrate separation from military actors, while also needing protection and protected spaces for aid distribution. When active fighting means that they cannot safely access people in extreme need, or specialized and expensive transport or equipment is required to reach isolated communities, commitment to the humanitarian principles may mean that humanitarians face impossible choices. This is addressed in the Oslo Guidelines, which clearly set out the principles for use of military and defense assets in response to disasters, on the basis that this can only be a path of last resort.[50] This is an important interface between traditional security actors and humanitarians, and it is carefully structured on both sides by guidelines and doctrine.

Protracted crisis and enduring conflict are ubiquitous within humanitarian practice, and like all other humanitarian concerns they have been amplified by the pandemic. As such, it is an absurdity to talk of contemporary humanitarian matters without placing the COVID-19 pandemic at the center. This is a matter that fundamentally shapes the delivery of humanitarian assistance, the funding available, and the needs of communities already in crisis and newly thrown into crisis. The existing security landscape is exacerbated by the direct impact of COVID, the impact of attempts to contain it (especially lockdowns and border closures), and the impact of the recession—local and global—arising from the pandemic.

While insecurity and humanitarian crises create complex environments that need multifaceted and adaptive responses,[51] throughout the last decade humanitarian assistance has received only about 60 percent of annual funding requirements. UN appeals are not the sole source of humanitarian funding, however, with approximately one third of these funds coming from other sources. Yet this too is declining.[52] These low levels of funding are unevenly distributed across appeals and Yemen provides a stark example of this. Proclaimed "the world's largest humanitarian crisis" for the last four years, its challenges include not just protracted conflict, but also food insecurity, displacement, institutional failure, economic challenges, and the pandemic and other diseases.[53] With two thirds of its population of nearly thirty million in need of assistance, humanitarian assistance fell 42 percent short of requirements in 2020,[54] and humanitarian access is impaired by the conflict. By late 2021, several sectors had received "less than 15 per cent of the funds needed"—with the critical sector of water, sanitation, and hygiene receiving just 8 percent by the end of August 2021.[55] Crucial actions including addressing the causes of conflict, protection of civilians, and supporting internally displaced persons and minorities are all key to humanitarian, development, and security approaches, yet they are almost impossible under these circumstances.

In Yemen and elsewhere a key challenge that conflict creates for humanitarian actors is access—that is, the ability to bring humanitarian response to people in the greatest need. In 1991 the UN passed a resolution highlighting the importance of humanitarian assistance, and calling on states to facilitate access to people in need through a variety of strategies.[56] Despite uptake of a range of relevant agreements at the UN, humanitarian actors continue to face significant barriers when they attempt to reach those most in need of assistance, whether in the face of armed conflict or disaster. These include physical impediments, bureaucratic restrictions, direct interference or diversion of aid, active conflict, and attacks on humanitarians and their resources.[57] A key humanitarian concern is protection, which is articulated through four principles: promote people's rights, dignity, and safety; ensure their access to assistance; assist in recovery; and help people claim their rights.[58] Protection activity can encounter barriers in disaster contexts where, for example, there are challenges providing emergency shelter that protects people from further direct impacts of the disaster, as well as supporting dignity and meeting needs through physical safety, food supplies, and the capacity to do what is important (for example religious rituals). In conflict and in complex emergencies where conflict and other humanitarian crises coexist, protection and access are even more challenging.

Yemen is one of ten countries with "extreme constraints" on humanitarian access in July 2021. A relatively young state, Yemen has been in civil war since September 2014, and faces multiple humanitarian challenges, including hunger, acute malnutrition in children, disease, internal displacement, and destruction of infrastructure. Three quarters of the population live in poverty. At the beginning of 2020, a UN panel of experts reported protection concerns arising from violations of human rights and international humanitarian law relating to the conflict, while humanitarian action was facing barriers to access including significant delays to aid shipments, increasing threats and incidents against aid workers, denial of access and travel authorization, looting and diversion of aid, and halting of aid due to political transition.[59]

In early 2020, the emergence of the pandemic coincided with major flooding in the country, increasing humanitarian need at a time when the international community was beginning to lose interest. By mid-2021, the combined impact of the pandemic response, conflict and insecurity, bureaucratic hurdles, and increased fuel costs severely impeded humanitarian access. Organizations that were able to overcome cost and physical barriers were faced with requirements incompatible with protection of civilians and ongoing humanitarian operations in the country—as an example, new conditions for travel permits included "sharing aid recipients' lists, vehicle lease contracts, and other sensitive or protected information."[60]

COVID-19 as both crisis and amplifier

A key premise of this volume is that the pandemic is accelerating global processes rather than redefining them and this is certainly the case in the context of humanitarian practice. As shown above, the humanitarian system is "already under strain"[61] and has been hit hard by a pandemic that is both a crisis in itself and a powerful amplifier of other crises. COVID-19 constitutes a significant humanitarian event, challenging all governments' capacity to contain it and to protect their citizens. It has overwhelmed even the wealthiest nations, though the discourse has always been of governments in control of the crisis despite rising rates of infection and death, and social restrictions causing increasing loss of livelihood and stability. For lower-income countries, the impact is profound. Calculations are that the pandemic has seen 270 million people newly experiencing acute food insecurity,[62] and "as many as 150 million" people pushed into extreme poverty by the end of 2021.[63] By mid-2021 it was becoming evident that for most regions there had been a sharp initial increase in poverty followed by a return to the prepandemic poverty reduction trajectory. In other words, poverty reduction has been set back but not derailed in most regions. For low-income countries and the countries of sub-Saharan Africa, however, poverty is increasing at a pace higher than prior to the pandemic.[64]

While the global economic downturn impacts critical income sources for crisis-affected countries—including official development assistance and remittances—"humanitarian needs are currently higher than ever before."[65] In 2020 $US38.8 billion was sought for UN-coordinated appeals (an increase of just over 25 percent on 2019). While this includes $US9.5 billion for pandemic response, funding needs for protracted crises also increased on average by 39 percent. In the face of these increases, total humanitarian funding increased by just 3.4 percent, and just 52 percent of funding requests were met.[66]

This represents a further increase to global and local inequalities, which is significant given that the World Bank and the United Nations were already concerned about rising inequality well before the pandemic.[67] Compounding this matter, the poor have fewer resources with which to withstand crises, and are therefore disproportionately experiencing negative impacts of the pandemic. Furthermore, both poverty and inequality are correlated with conflict, so as they increase it is likely that conflict will too. From a humanitarian perspective this means that we are seeing rising challenges in precisely the places we have been unable to resolve those challenges. In human terms, these impacts mean a massive decrease in food security, 1.4 billion children out of school, and "a tragic increase in gender-based violence."[68] While poverty increases have largely been felt in sub-Saharan Africa, South America has suffered disproportionate rates of COVID-19 infection and death.[69] At the same time as humanitarian need is increasing, funding has stagnated.

The pandemic not only increases challenges for humanitarian actors in the present, but is also creating significant future challenges, especially where the health and education of children and young adults are concerned. While educators around the world have worked extraordinarily hard to keep education going, the effective out-of-school rate ("the best performance that the school system can deliver given the structural conditions") has risen from 26.5 percent to 85.9 percent in low-income countries—and from 9.5 percent to 59.6 percent globally.[70] Even this figure is optimistic, since it rests on the assumption that access to the internet equates with continued learning—which of itself overlooks factors such as the quality of internet access, and the skills, equipment, space, and resources required to study in the home.[71] These young people cannot simply join the workforce, since the economic impact of the pandemic saw two in five youth losing income by mid-2020.[72] Impacts of youth poverty go beyond health risks and the loss of education and work, also delaying the achievement of "social adulthood," through the markers or functions that legitimate the transition to adulthood.[73]

The measures put into place to control the spread of the disease slow humanitarian responses and create further need by significantly disrupting the livelihoods of agricultural workers, but also impacting food security in both urban and rural areas.[74] Brazil, a nation that reduced undernourishment by 80 percent in the decade to 2014, has seen since a steady rise in food insecurity that has been sharply increased by COVID-19. Food insecurity impacted more than half its citizens in 2020.[75] Yet this is not an impact of the pandemic alone—rather it builds on challenges that were already present or emerging. Food security has been drastically impacted by pandemic responses, but it was already being severely eroded by "conflict, natural disaster, climate change, and the arrival of pests and plagues on a transcontinental scale."[76] Thus the pandemic has multiplied the impact of existing hazards and reduced the resilience of communities to withstand those hazards.

Critically, food insecurity is not just intense hunger that can be redressed so that life can continue as before. An important impact of food insecurity is that children may be severely malnourished, or even stunted, thanks to poor diet. For example in Yemen the impact of the pandemic was swift, and by April 2020 there was a marked increase in the number of families "consuming only three or fewer food groups . . . mainly cereals, fats and sugar."[77] One in two Yemeni children under five years old is acutely malnourished.[78] Pandemic-related food insecurity in already insecure areas will likely result in an increase in stunting among children, which is irreversible and is associated with delayed brain development and reduced cognitive function—and thus future prospects. Malnutrition is among the many facets of poverty that impact a child's development in ways that can embed disadvantage before a child turns two.[79] Disadvantage emerges and is consolidated very early in life, and deprivation in a child's early environment will "put the fullest realization of children's development at risk."[80] In this way, systemic disadvantage is literally embodied by children, cementing "the systemic production of inequality across the life course."[81]

It does not stop there, however. With children out of school and parents out of work, there will be more pressure for children to do adult things like work and marry—and with less work available, children and adults will be pushed into more dangerous work, for lower wages. Child labor is driven by a range of factors including poverty, availability of work, inequality, and lack of access to education—all of which are exacerbated by the pandemic.[82] The conflict in Yemen has seen a doubling of the number of children out of school to two million, and two thirds of teachers are not receiving regular pay.[83] Here and in other places, children who struggled to maintain school attendance before the pandemic have now been out of school for so long that they will never return. These compounding impacts of poverty, inequality, insecurity, and crisis have lifelong human security implications. Children's capacity for educational achievement is reduced by acute malnutrition and by access impediments of conflict and disease; therefore their job prospects and capacity to sustain a livelihood are reduced; and therefore their health and well-being are impacted . . . and this is passed on to their future children.

Looking ahead: pandemic inequality

Importantly, conflict, humanitarian crises, and COVID-19 all have a disproportionate impact on those already in poverty. They shoulder most of the burden in these crises, with less capacity to adapt to severe shocks because they are already functioning at crisis levels. Indeed, the World Bank noted in mid-2020 that "people who are already poor and vulnerable are bearing the brunt of the crisis."[84] They also experience the complex intersections of development, security, and humanitarian practice—and hazard multipliers like the pandemic, climate change, and conflict increase the vulnerability of the poor and marginalized, disrupting livelihoods and further increasing poverty and inequality.

The world is yet to realize the early hopes of global cooperation embodied in the United Nations and other global institutions, to sustain an environment in which rights and equality prevail. A strong example of this is the global response to the pandemic. Launched in April 2020, the Access to COVID-19 Tools (ACT) Accelerator brought together "governments, global health organizations, manufacturers, scientists, private sector, civil society and philanthropy" around three pillars (tests, treatments, and vaccines), with a commitment to equal access to each of these. The COVAX program is the third of these pillars, designed as a "lifeline" for lower-income countries (and high-income countries without direct agreements with manufacturers) by ensuring "equal access" to COVID-19 vaccines.[85]

While COVAX aimed to ensure access to vaccines for 20 percent of each low- or middle-income country's population, actual vaccination lags far behind this, reflecting failures of production and distribution. However, the charity-based model of providing vaccines rather than enabling these countries to produce the vaccines themselves[86] has emerged as a significant flaw in the model, as producing nations have prioritized their own populations, and COVAX has repeatedly revised its targets downwards as promised money and vaccine doses have failed to materialize.[87] This has been exacerbated by vaccine hesitancy and poor infrastructure in recipient countries, and by donated vaccines being too close to expiry to be delivered and administered.[88] This is starkly embodied in vaccination figures: while 45 percent of the global population had received at least one dose of a vaccine by the end of September 2021, this was the case for less than 2.5 percent of people in low-income countries—in Yemen just 1 percent of the population has had at least one dose of a vaccine,[89] after the country received 380,000 vaccine doses through COVAX in March 2021.[90] Although reported case numbers are relatively low (under 7,000 by mid-2021), the case fatality rate is high, at almost 20 percent.[91]

Looking ahead: local leadership?

Attempts to control COVID-19 through closure of borders and imposition of lockdowns and restrictions on movement have impacted humanitarian practice significantly. One positive impact is that this has perhaps accelerated the localization of practice, by forcing international actors to remain remote and allowing local first responders to drive the response.[92] After the first six months it became evident that the pandemic must impact global humanitarian practices, at least in the short to medium term. Localization is the current terminology for the idea that development and humanitarian practice must not be externally driven, top-down processes that treat local communities as passive victims of misfortune. It has gained momentum in humanitarian practice thanks to its prominence in the 2016 Grand Bargain, which applies a range of levers to increase transparency, predictability, and effectiveness in humanitarian action, and gives greater power to "local" governments, organizations, and communities.

In many ways, the pandemic has "'forced' a more localized response"[93] by preventing an influx of external actors and allowing greater communication through increased utilization of virtual meeting forums. This has functioned as a control on donors and international actors, and their physical absence has created "new spaces for local leadership," collaboration, and decentralization through on-the-ground networks.[94] Although this has highlighted the strengths of local actors, it has not translated into a systemic shift toward "tailored and flexible humanitarian funding for local actors" that would sustain localization practices and more fully implement Grand Bargain commitments.[95] It is therefore unlikely that the pandemic will in fact create a sustained acceleration of humanitarian localization.

Conclusion

The repeated refrain in this chapter has been that the coronavirus pandemic is both a crisis itself and an amplifier of other crises. As a humanitarian crisis it has disrupted global poverty reduction, pushed many into acute poverty, hampered humanitarian access, and exacerbated existing vulnerabilities. This is to say nothing of the death and illness it has caused. The idealism of humanitarian practice and its aspirational values continues to struggle in the face of expanding demand, shrinking or static budgets, and increasingly unstable environments. Both primary and secondary impacts of COVID-19 are furthering each of these, while also restricting movement, access, and supply, all in the face of a climate crisis that further damages and destabilizes.

Experiences with COVAX, ACT Accelerator, and recent humanitarian funding trends give us some indication of what is to come in the aftermath of this pandemic—and a longer view of history gives us even more insight. The influenza pandemic that followed World War I is "the closest relative and ancestor" of COVID-19[96] and this connection has already been invoked regularly by commentators on the contemporary pandemic. Nina Boberg-Fazlic and colleagues contend that death rates from the 1918–20 influenza pandemic were a "non-trivial" contributor to the degree to which individual countries joined the turn away from globalism following World War I, as exemplified by increased trade tariffs.[97] This suggests a historical precedent for another phase of isolationism and increased attempts to constrain globalization.

Another lesson we may learn from comparing these pandemics centers around what we prioritize as global threats. In the early days of the COVID-19 pandemic Philip Mackowiak concluded that studying previous pandemics reveals that "a time of worldwide social disruption"—such as World War I—would be required to see this aggressive new pathogen evolving to a pandemic.[98] Perhaps this teaches us that we should pay more attention to the disruption experienced by the majority of the world in the forms of growing inequality, increased concentration of extreme poverty, and climate change, all of which had already been flagged as concerning by key global institutions prior to 2020.

The triple nexus approach spotlights the intersections between development, humanitarianism, and security without getting lost in causality—these three areas will continue to influence each other, for better and for worse, but following the pandemic they will do so in the face of increasing and concentrated inequality. While the extreme poverty and disadvantage concentrated in sub-Saharan Africa rightly demands urgent attention, so too will the impact of climate change and slow development progress in extremely poor environments.

It is certainly plausible to argue that this is an acceleration of global trends: that the pandemic is hastening rather than redefining an existing trajectory. Whether this is the case is not entirely important from a humanitarian perspective. What matters more is what we do in the face of rising extreme inequality and the growth of extreme poverty, concentrated in countries already experiencing pronounced disadvantage.

The COVID-19 pandemic highlights the insecurity faced by the global majority and the increasing distance between them and the world's richest nations. For much of the Global South, the argument is moot. They live in the triple nexus, and while we argue about whether increasing inequality will drive them to violence and threaten our safe, stable lives, they focus on feeding their families, taking whatever path they can to stay healthy and survive in a world where others live to excess. While we in the Global North struggle to identify what we should have learned from history and whether this pandemic changes or simply accelerates future security challenges, the daily reality of the majority of the world continues to require urgent attention. Additionally, as the minority build their wealth and their distance from the ubiquitous "rest," the Global South is disproportionately affected by poverty, climate change, and disasters, with fewer resources to withstand and rebuild. If this disrupts the security landscape for the minority, it is because we have chosen to close our eyes to the many alarms that have been raised.

Notes

1. Fran Girling and Angus Urquhart, *Global Humanitarian Assistance Report 2021* (Bristol: Development Initiatives, 2021), 11, available at https://devinit.org/resources/global-humanitarian-assistance-report-2021/ (accessed February 22, 2022).
2. *Global Humanitarian Overview 2021* (Geneva: Office for the Coordination of Humanitarian Affairs, 2021), 8, https://2021.gho.unocha.org/ (accessed February 22, 2022).
3. Ibid., 22.
4. *Reversals of Fortune: Poverty and Shared Prosperity 2020* (Washington, DC: World Bank, 2020), https://openknowledge.worldbank.org/bitstream/handle/10986/34496/9781464816024.pdf; *Human Development Report 2019: Beyond Income, Beyond Averages, Beyond Today— Inequalities in Human Development in the 21st Century* (New York: United Nations Development Programme, 2019), 2, https://hdr.undp.org/sites/default/files/hdr2019.pdf (both accessed February 22, 2022).
5. See *Human Development Report 2019*; *Reversals of Fortune*.
6. Girling and Urquhart, *Global Humanitarian Assistance*, 35.
7. Ibid., 36.
8. *Global Humanitarian Overview 2021*, 20.
9. Alex J. Bellamy and Stephen McLoughlin, *Rethinking Humanitarian Intervention* (London: Palgrave, 2018), xiii.
10. Hugo Slim, *Humanitarian Ethics: A Guide to the Morality of Aid in War and Disaster* (Oxford: Oxford University Press, 2015), 1.
11. See, for example, "24 Principles and Good Practice of Humanitarian Donorship," Good Humanitarian Donorship, https://www.ghdinitiative.org/ghd/gns/principles-good-practice-of-ghd/principles-good-practice-ghd.html (accessed February 22, 2022).
12. Damon P. Coppola, *Introduction to International Disaster Management*, 3rd edn. (Oxford: Butterworth-Heinemann, 2015), 41.
13. Kirsten Hagon (ed.), *World Disasters Report 2020: Come Heat or High Water—Tackling the Humanitarian Impacts of the Climate Crisis Together* (Geneva: International Federation of Red Cross and Red Crescent Societies, 2020), 2.
14. Ibid., 22.
15. Girling and Urquhart, *Global Humanitarian Assistance*, 17.
16. Ibid., 24.
17. The governance of these environments is usually very weak, with the state having a limited capacity to respond to, and mitigate, the threats to the population, or provide adequate levels of protection. Adele Harmer and Joanna Macrae (eds.), *Beyond the Continuum:*

Aid Policy in Protracted Crises, HPG Research Report No. 18, Overseas Development Institute, July 2004, 1, https://cdn.odi.org/media/documents/279_GpS59wf.pdf (accessed February 22, 2022).

18. Girling and Urquhart, *Global Humanitarian Assistance*, 18.
19. *Global Humanitarian Overview 2019* (Geneva: Office for the Coordination of Humanitarian Affairs, 2019), 4, https://www.unocha.org/sites/unocha/files/GHO2019.pdf (accessed February 22, 2022).
20. Girling and Urquhart, *Global Humanitarian Assistance*, 19.
21. Ibid., 24.
22. Gregory Bankoff, "Rendering the World Unsafe: 'Vulnerability' as Western Discourse," *Disasters* 25, no. 1 (2001): 25.
23. Michael J. Watts and Hans G. Bohle, "Hunger, Famine and the Space of Vulnerability," *GeoJournal* 30, no. 2 (1993): 118.
24. *World Development Report 2011: Conflict, Security, and Development* (Washington, DC: World Bank, 2011), 59.
25. Ibid., 9.
26. Tony Vaux, "Humanitarian Trends and Dilemmas," in *Development and Humanitarianism: Practical Issues*, ed. Deborah Eade and Tony Vaux (Bloomfield, CT: Kumarian Press, 2007), 2.
27. "Working with DG ECHO as an NGO Partner: Forgotten Crisis Assessment (FCA)," DG Echo Partners' Website, https://www.dgecho-partners-helpdesk.eu/ngo/financing-decision/dg-echo-strategy/forgotten-crisis (accessed February 22, 2022).
28. Michelle Delaney et al., *The World's Most Neglected Displacement Crises 2020*, Norwegian Refugee Council, May 27, 2021, https://www.nrc.no/globalassets/pdf/reports/neglected-displacement-crises-2020/neglected-crises-list-2020.pdf (accessed February 22, 2022).
29. Zenab Bagha, *The 10 Most Under-reported Humanitarian Crises of 2020*, CARE International, 2020, care-international.org/files/files/Ten_most_underreported_humanitarian_crises_2020.pdf (accessed February 22, 2022).
30. Hagon, *World Disasters Report*, 4.
31. Girling and Urquhart, *Global Humanitarian Assistance*, 24–6.
32. *Global Humanitarian Overview 2021*, 8–9.
33. Alex Braithwaite, Niheer Dasandi, and David Hudson, "Does Poverty Cause Conflict? Isolating the Causal Origins of the Conflict Trap," *Conflict Management and Peace Science* 33, no. 1 (2016): 60–1.
34. Girling and Urquhart, *Global Humanitarian Assistance*, 12.
35. *Protracted Conflict and Humanitarian Action: Some Recent ICRC Experiences* (Geneva: International Committee of the Red Cross, 2016), 5.
36. Sultan Barakat and Sansom Milton, "Localisation across the Humanitarian-Development-Peace Nexus," *Journal of Peacebuilding & Development* 15, no. 2 (2020): 149; *Protracted Conflict and Humanitarian Action*, 5.
37. "Coordination in Complex Emergencies," UNHCR, September 1, 2001, https://www.unhcr.org/en-au/partners/partners/3ba88e7c6/coordination-complex-emergencies.html (accessed February 22, 2022).

38. Barakat and Milton, "Localisation across the Humanitarian-Development-Peace Nexus," 148; Melissa T. Labonte and Anne C. Edgerton, "Towards a Typology of Humanitarian Access Denial," *Third World Quarterly* 34, no. 1 (2013): 39.
39. Paul Howe, "The Triple Nexus: A Potential Approach to Supporting the Achievement of the Sustainable Development Goals?" *World Development* 124 (2019): 104629.
40. Koji Flynn-Do and Dan Walton, *Tracking the Global Humanitarian Response to Covid-19*, Development Initiatives / International Rescue Committee, April 2021, 12, https://www.rescue.org/report/tracking-global-humanitarian-response-covid-19 (accessed February 22, 2022).
41. Katie Peters and Mairi Dupar, "The Humanitarian Impact of Combined Conflict, Climate and Environmental Risks: Highlights and Recommendations from a High-Level Side Event at the 75th United Nations General Assembly," Overseas Development Institute, December 2020, https://cdn.odi.org/media/documents/Briefing_note__The_humanitarian_impact_of_combined_conflict_climate_and_enviro_AC78KvY.pdf (accessed February 22, 2022). See also Santiago Daroca Oller, "Exploring the Pathways from Climate-Related Risks to Conflict and the Humanitarian-Development-Peace Nexus as an Integrated Response," Issue Brief 21/2020, United Nations Development Program, 2020.
42. Oscar A. Gómez, "Protecting Our Human World Order: A Human Security Compass for a New Sustainability Decade," Background Paper No. 4-2020, United Nations Development Program, 2020, 14, https://hdr.undp.org/sites/default/files/hdr2020_backgroundpaper_gomez.pdf (accessed February 22, 2022).
43. Barakat and Milton, "Localisation across the Humanitarian-Development-Peace Nexus," 149.
44. "Yemen: Annual Humanitarian Access Overview, 2020," ReliefWeb, March 14, 2021, https://reliefweb.int/report/yemen/yemen-annual-humanitarian-access-overview-2020 (accessed February 22, 2022).
45. Larissa Fast, *Aid in Danger: The Perils and Promise of Humanitarianism* (Philadelphia: University of Pennsylvania Press, 2014), 1.
46. Grant Broussard et al., "Challenges to Ethical Obligations and Humanitarian Principles in Conflict Settings: A Systematic Review," *Journal of International Humanitarian Action* 4 (2019): 15.
47. Slim, *Humanitarian Ethics*, 5.
48. See "OCHA on Message: Humanitarian Principles," Office for the Coordination of Humanitarian Affairs, June 2012, https://www.unocha.org/sites/dms/Documents/OOM-humanitarianprinciples_eng_June12.pdf (accessed February 22, 2022).
49. See Fast, *Aid in Danger*, and Slim, *Humanitarian Ethics*, for thorough discussions of this.
50. *Oslo Guidelines: Guidelines on the Use of Foreign Military and Civil Defence Assets in Disaster Relief*, Office for the Coordination

of Humanitarian Affairs, November 2007, https://www.unocha.org/sites/unocha/files/OSLO%20Guidelines%20Rev%201.1%20-%20Nov%2007.pdf (accessed February 22, 2022).

51. Broussard et al., "Challenges to Ethical Obligations"; Barakat and Milton, "Localisation across the Humanitarian-Development-Peace Nexus"; Gomez, "Protecting Our Human World Order," 13–14.
52. Girling and Urquhart, *Global Humanitarian Assistance*, 36.
53. "Yemen Situation Report," Office for the Coordination of Humanitarian Affairs, January 2022, https://reports.unocha.org/en/country/yemen (accessed February 22, 2022).
54. Girling and Urquhart, *Global Humanitarian Assistance*, 62.
55. "Yemen Situation Report."
56. United Nations General Assembly, "Resolution 46/182: Strengthening of the Coordination of Humanitarian Emergency Assistance of the United Nations," A/RES/46/182, December 19, 1991.
57. "OCHA on Message: Humanitarian Access," Office for the Coordination of Humanitarian Affairs, April 2010, https://www.unocha.org/sites/unocha/files/dms/Documents/OOM_HumAccess_English.pdf (accessed February 22, 2022).
58. Sphere Association, *The Sphere Handbook: Humanitarian Charter and Minimum Standards in Humanitarian Response*, 4th edn. (Geneva: Sphere Association, 2018), 36.
59. Dakshinie Ruwanthika Gunaratne et al., "Letter Dated 27 January 2020 from the Panel of Experts on Yemen Addressed to the President of the Security Council," United Nations Security Council, January 27, 2020, https://reliefweb.int/sites/reliefweb.int/files/resources/%5BEN%5DLetter%20dated%2027%20January%202020%20from%20the%20Panel%20of%20Experts%20on%20Yemen%20addressed%20to%20the%20President%20of%20the%20Security%20Council%20-%20Final%20report%20of%20the%20Panel%20of%20Experts%20on%20Yemen%20%28S-2020-70%29.pdf (accessed February 22, 2022).
60. *Humanitarian Access Overview*, ACAPS, July 2021, 8, https://www.acaps.org/sites/acaps/files/products/files/20210719_acaps_humanitarian_access_overview_july_2021.pdf (accessed February 22, 2022).
61. Flynn-Do and Walton, *Tracking the Global Humanitarian Response*.
62. Ibid., 7.
63. "Covid-19 to Add as Many as 150 Million Extreme Poor by 2021," press release, World Bank, October 7, 2020, https://www.worldbank.org/en/news/press-release/2020/10/07/covid-19-to-add-as-many-as-150-million-extreme-poor-by-2021 (accessed February 22, 2022).
64. Daniel Gerszon Mahler et al., "Updated Estimates of the Impact of COVID-19 on Global Poverty: Turning the Corner on the Pandemic in 2021?" World Bank Data Blog, June 24, 2021, https://blogs.worldbank.org/opendata/updated-estimates-impact-covid-19-global-poverty-turning-corner-pandemic-2021 (accessed February 22, 2022).
65. Girling and Urquhart, *Global Humanitarian Assistance*, 59.

66. Ibid., 33–36. In fact only seven of the fifty-five appeals received over 70 percent of funding: ibid., 35.
67. *Reversals of Fortune*; *Human Development Report 2019*.
68. Flynn-Do and Walton, *Tracking the Global Humanitarian Response*, 7.
69. Ibid., 7.
70. Human Development Report Office, "Covid-19's Impact on Education," Data Futures Platform, United Nations Development Programme, https://data.undp.org/content/out-of-school-during-covid-19/ (accessed February 22, 2022).
71. *Youth and COVID-19: Impacts on Jobs, Education, Rights and Mental Well-Being* (Geneva: International Labour Organization, 2020), 24.
72. Ibid., 16.
73. Nicola Ansell, *Children, Youth and Development*, 2nd edn. (Abingdon, England: Routledge, 2017), 55.
74. "Policy Brief: The Impact of COVID-19 on Food Security and Nutrition," United Nations, June 2020, 2, https://unsdg.un.org/sites/default/files/2020-06/SG-Policy-Brief-on-COVID-Impact-on-Food-Security.pdf (accessed February 22, 2022).
75. Lise Alves, "Pandemic Puts Brazil Back on the World Hunger Map," *New Humanitarian*, July 19, 2021, https://www.thenewhumanitarian.org/news-feature/2021/7/19/pandemic-puts-brazil-back-on-the-world-hunger-map (accessed February 22, 2022).
76. "Policy Brief," 6.
77. *The State of Food Security and Nutrition in the World 2021: Transforming Food Systems for Food Security, Improved Nutrition and Affordable Healthy Diets for All* (Rome: Food and Agriculture Organization, 2021), 35.
78. Ibid., 90.
79. Jo Boyden et al., *Tracing the Consequences of Child Poverty: Evidence from the Young Lives Study in Ethiopia, India, Peru and Vietnam* (Bristol: Policy Press, 2019); James J. Heckman, "Schools, Skills, and Synapses," NBER Working Paper 14064, National Bureau of Economic Research, June 2008, https://www.nber.org/papers/w14064 (accessed February 22, 2022).
80. Frances Degen Horowitz, "Child Development and the PITS: Simple Questions, Complex Answers, and Developmental Theory," *Child Development* 71, no. 1 (2000): 6.
81. Penny Vera-Sanso, "Population Ageing and Development: Time to Drop Ageist Demographies for a Critical, Decolonial, Sociology of Ageing," in *Routledge Handbook of Global Development: Problems, Possibilities and Pedagogy*, ed. Kearrin Sims et al. (Abingdon, England: Routledge, 2022).
82. *Youth and COVID-19*, 4.
83. *Education Disrupted: Impact of the Conflict on Children's Education in Yemen*, UNICEF, July 2021, https://yemen.un.org/en/135092-education-disrupted-impact-conflict-childrens-education-yemen (accessed February 22, 2022).

84. *Reversals of Fortune*, 7.
85. Seth Berkley, "COVAX Explained," Gavi, September 3, 2020, https://www.gavi.org/vaccineswork/covax-explained (accessed February 23, 2022).
86. Sara Jerving and Jenny Lei Ravelo, "Deep Dive: Is COVID-19 Vaccine Equity a Pipe Dream?" Devex, August 26, 2021, https://www.devex.com/news/deep-dive-is-covid-19-vaccine-equity-a-pipe-dream-100588 (accessed February 23, 2022).
87. Sara Jerving, "COVAX Reduces End-of-Year Forecast Figures," Devex, September 8, 2021, https://www.devex.com/news/covax-reduces-end-of-year-forecast-figures-101576 (accessed February 23, 2022).
88. "Covax: How Many Covid Vaccines Have the US and the Other G7 Countries Pledged?" BBC News, September 24, 2021, https://www.bbc.com/news/world-55795297 (accessed February 23, 2022).
89. Edouard Mathieu et al., "A Global Database of COVID-19 Vaccinations," *Nature Human Behaviour* 5 (2021): 947–53.
90. "Yemen: Complex Crisis," ACAPS, August 26, 2021, https://www.acaps.org/country/yemen/crisis/complex-crisis (accessed February 23, 2022).
91. "Yemen Country Office Humanitarian Situation Report Mid-Year," UNICEF, August 24, 2021, https://reliefweb.int/report/yemen/unicef-yemen-country-office-humanitarian-situation-report-mid-year-reporting-period-1 (accessed February 23, 2022).
92. Australian Red Cross (ARC) et al., "A Window of Opportunity: Learning from Covid-10 to Progress Locally Led Response and Development Think Piece," La Trobe University, November 2020, https://www.latrobe.edu.au/__data/assets/pdf_file/0005/1188779/A-Window-of-Opportunity-COVID-think-piece-December-2020.pdf (accessed February 23, 2022).
93. Veronique Barbelet, John Bryant, and Alexandra Spencer, "Local Humanitarian Action during Covid-19: Findings from a Diary Study," HPG working paper, ODI, July 2021, 8, https://cdn.odi.org/media/documents/C19__localisation_diary_methods_WEB.pdf (accessed February 23, 2022).
94. ARC et al., "A Window of Opportunity."
95. Barbelet et al., "Local Humanitarian Action," 27.
96. John Ashton, "COVID-19 and the 'Spanish' Flu," *Journal of the Royal Society of Medicine* 113, no. 5 (2020): 197.
97. Nina Boberg-Fazlic et al., "Pandemics and Protectionism: Evidence from the 'Spanish' Flu," *Humanities and Social Science Communications* 8 (2021): 145.
98. Philip A. Mackowiak, "Prior Pandemics: Looking to the Past for Insight into the COVID-19 Pandemic," *Journal of Community Hospital Internal Medicine Perspectives* 11, no. 2 (2021): 170.

Part II

Issues and Challenges

9

Pandemics and Health Security: Risks to Global Stability

Erin M. Sorrell

Introduction

COVID-19 showed the world what many in the public health sphere have been counseling for years: that pandemics coupled with weak health systems not only cost lives but pose some of the greatest risks to the contemporary global economy and security. The effects of health security successes and failures can influence foreign policy, society, and security. Pandemics are a truly global threat. Nations cannot shelter in place and avoid an infectious disease. Pandemics have underscored that treating health security as a niche issue for a small number of stakeholders will fail. It takes a global community to prepare and respond. Traditionally, national security has been viewed and defined broadly in a defense context; however, pandemics can disrupt security as destructively as, if not more so than, a traditional intentional enemy. There are clear, inextricable links between global security, pandemics, and health security, and we have in our arsenal existing health frameworks that we can leverage to plan and prepare against future threats. As this chapter will illustrate, health security cannot be treated as the sole responsibility of national ministries of health and international health organizations, nor can it be considered a secondary issue behind transnational threats that claim fewer lives annually. It must be approached from a multisectoral position and given proper attention and political and financial commitment. Pandemics will recur. The drivers of disease emergence are multifaceted and include environmental, geopolitical, and socioeconomic factors. Data gathered over the last century from a myriad of pandemics emphasizes the enduring risks of additional pandemics as well as the risks of our own behaviors. One need look no further than December 2019 for an example of what happens when only one sector is aware and preparing for a pandemic threat.

Global health security

Trends and drivers of disease emergence, including environmental, geopolitical, and socioeconomic factors, are disrupting the equilibrium of the microbial world. Novel disease threats are emerging at unprecedented rates, disrupting people's health and causing social and economic impacts.[1] Climate change, extreme weather events, wildlife biodiversity, and pathogen and vector ecology are just a few of the key environmental drivers that place humans and animals in closer, more frequent contact, providing ample opportunities for animal pathogens to spill over and infect human hosts. This risk, ever-increasing due to human behaviors and land use changes, has resulted in a number of outbreaks, both localized epidemics and global pandemics.[2] The same factors drive human migration and relocation to urban centers and previously uninhabited areas. Disease threats can emerge from humans, animals, and our environment, including agricultural food sources. Geopolitical influences and human-induced disasters from war and conflict and lack of governance present vulnerabilities in civil society, public systems including public health services, and basic infrastructure. They place unstable nations, and neighboring states, at great risk for diseases emerging or reemerging due to lapses in vaccine campaigns, access to clean water and sanitation, available nutritional programs, or preventative health services.[3] Finally, socioeconomic trends including population density and mobility, agricultural practices, land use, and antimicrobial use can impact our access to clean water and healthy food, secure living environments, and safe and effective medicines.[4] The impact of insecurity on public health events, including epidemics and pandemics, may elevate the risk of disease emergence, but we must also consider that insecurity and lack of governance will undermine national and international capacity to control it.

State collapse and civil war can elevate the risk of pandemics in the same way that pandemics can disrupt world order. Novel diseases as well as diseases once contained and managed by public health measures (including vaccine-preventable diseases) are emerging and reemerging at unprecedented rates, causing disruptions to individual, national, and global health, economics, and policy.[5] As the global population becomes more mobile and economically interdependent, disease threats will not be contained by traditional public health measures implemented within national boundaries. These public health measures include capacities for the detection of disease threats (whether it be from an environmental, animal, or human host), including the ability to perform laboratory and clinical diagnostics, the systems in place to communicate, liaise, and report within and among sectors (subnational, national, and international), human resources and systems to manage and control outbreaks, and policies and procedures for containment, response, and recovery. Detection of, prevention of, response to, and recovery from infectious disease threats require strong national health systems with open communication and coordination channels at the regional and national levels. The processes and procedures we have in place for pandemic preparedness at the national and international levels have been tested and have failed. It is important to look to the future of pandemics as a global health and global security priority to develop tools, networks, and plans that meet the challenges across systems of government and health systems. These challenges are not limited to global health security; they are issues that need to be tackled across a variety of global threats including migration, urbanization, and climate change.[6]

Our approaches to health security challenges must be global: we are only as strong as our weakest system. "Health systems strengthening" is a term used in the global health literature that outlines capacities and capabilities to build and/or improve the healthcare system of a country. Health systems include systems for governance (plans, policies), adequate and consistent financing, a trained and motivated workforce, health services delivery, essential medicines and health products (vaccines, medication, infrastructure), and health information systems (internal and external reporting mechanisms).[7] National systems require the capacity to contain and address global health security threats from epidemics to pandemics and must involve sectors outside traditional health roles. Pandemics not only cost lives but pose some of the greatest risks to the global economy and security faced today.[8]

History of pandemics

Infectious diseases with pandemic potential have emerged regularly throughout history from bubonic plague in the fourteenth century to the novel coronavirus in 2019. Many of the pathogens that caused previous pandemics are still circulating today, a reminder that, while modern advances in sanitation, public health practices, epidemiology, and countermeasures including vaccines have greatly mitigated disease threats, completely eradicating infectious diseases remains an immense challenge.

Pandemics are not a problem to be solved; instead they are a constant risk to manage, requiring continuous capacity building, global coordination and scientific cooperation, sustainable financing, and political investment. To date there have only been two successful disease eradication campaigns. The first was smallpox: on May 8, 1980 the World Health Organization (WHO) declared the world free of smallpox, a little over two years after the last naturally occurring case was reported and fourteen years after the World Health Assembly voted on a special budget and program to eliminate the disease globally.[9] Some of the key factors that supported the elimination of smallpox included the fact that this virus did not have an animal reservoir host, that is, it could only infect and transmit between humans; it had a distinctive clinical manifestation (a rash); and it had a single serotype, meaning once you were infected, if you recovered, you had lifelong immunity. In addition, and quite crucial to the campaign, the vaccine was effective and easily administered. Once a community had been vaccinated (or had recovered from infection) there was nowhere for the virus to go. Effective vaccine campaigns required continued education, advocacy, and outreach alongside sustained funding and global political will. The second disease, rinderpest, an extremely debilitating virus to cattle and buffalo, with up to 100 percent case fatality rates and major economic impacts, was last reported in 2001 and declared eradicated in 2011.[10]

While these two eradication programs were successful, they serve as exceptions to the rule as we face an uphill battle today against new and emerging infectious diseases. Four other disease eradication programs (hookworm, yellow fever, yaws—a chronic bacterial skin infection—and malaria) had been undertaken before smallpox was successfully eradicated.[11] The guinea worm eradication program, initiated in 1986 and still ongoing, is an impressive effort to battle a parasitic pathogen without vaccine or medicines. Current challenges include infections in a number of animals and insecurity in particular regions preventing access to vulnerable people.[12]

One of the greatest threats to public health and pandemic preparedness is the risk of zoonotic disease spillover. Zoonotic diseases are pathogens that reside in vertebrate animals and due to a number of factors, including new and consistent interactions with humans, have an opportunity to spill over and infect a human host.[13] Spillover may happen multiple times with no major impact on the infected person. However, when a pathogen is able to establish an effective infection (infection and replication) and transmit efficiently in its new host, a novel disease has emerged. When a zoonotic agent has gained the requirements for efficient infection and transmission in an immunologically naive population a potential pandemic has emerged. Without operational national health systems for detection, surveillance, testing, containment, and response at the source, the global population is at risk. Early detection allows scientists to characterize a pathogen, leading to diagnostic tools, countermeasures, and vaccine development, as well as providing public health professionals opportunities to prepare case definitions and case management strategies, and to train the healthcare workforce on recognition, infection control, and available treatments. Surveillance systems provide a mechanism to collect, analyze, and disseminate data at the local, subnational, and national levels. This data assists epidemiologists in determining where and how diseases are spreading, thus allowing efficient outbreak management and response systems including identification of cases, treatment for those who are ill, education campaigns to prevent onward transmission, and activation of vaccine campaigns (when available) before diseases spread regionally or globally.[14] Emerging infectious disease events are dominated by zoonoses, at roughly 60 percent of all emerging threats; of these the majority, over 70 percent, are found in wildlife.[15] The US Centers for Disease Control and Prevention (CDC) estimate that zoonotic diseases, outside pandemics, are responsible for 2.5 billion cases of illness and 2.7 million human deaths worldwide each year.[16]

Zoonotic diseases have been responsible for a number of pandemics in the last century. At least seven different coronaviruses have caused human illness and death, three of them within the last twenty years (SARS-2002, MERS-2012, COVID-19), due to spillover of animal coronaviruses to humans. Ebola outbreaks have been reported an estimated twenty-five times in the past forty-five years, with almost every epidemic the result of a spillover event.[17] Influenza viruses are zoonotic, constantly undergoing mutations in avian and mammalian hosts that allow them to expand their host range, evade existing immunity, and potentially lead to more transmissible strains. Four major influenza pandemics have been recognized in the twentieth and twenty-first centuries: the 1918 H1N1 Spanish influenza pandemic, the 1957 Asian influenza (H2N2), the 1968 Hong Kong influenza (H3N2), and the 2009 H1N1 pandemic. While each strain originated from avian and/or animal hosts and led to global outbreaks, associated disease, and death, the most severe was the 1918 pandemic, in which 50–100 million people died worldwide in the course of two years.[18] Once a pandemic starts, we often end up living with the disease long term. In regard to influenza, we face annual seasonal influenza epidemics, originating from parental pandemic strains that have evolved and require annual vaccines. These strains are continuously monitored and surveyed by global influenza surveillance and response networks.[19]

Even before the COVID-19 pandemic, the frequency and severity of infectious disease outbreaks was on the rise. Since the turn of the century, the world has seen a number of major epidemics and pandemics that have cost the global population in both lives and livelihood. The severe acute respiratory syndrome (SARS) epidemic of 2002–03 led to roughly 8,000 cases and 774 deaths across 29 countries and an estimated cost of $54 billion.[20] The World Bank also estimates that a "severe flu pandemic" could cost over $3 trillion, nearly 5 percent of global GDP.[21]

Health security as a security issue

Health security addresses measures, policies, and activities across sovereign boundaries to mitigate public health threats and events and to ensure population health. The WHO defines it as "activities required, both proactive and reactive, to minimize the danger and impact of acute public health events that endanger people's health across geographical regions and international boundaries."[22] Health security has been elevated by a number of regional epidemics and pandemics and is addressed by a number of international health and global health security frameworks.[23] Global health security is not separate from or less important than national security. We must consider the scale, range, and complexity of health security, creating new approaches to deal with pandemic threats alongside endemic diseases, epidemics, and risk factors for disease emergence linked to climate change and human mobility.

Traditionally, national security has been broadly defined as protecting citizens, the homeland, and a way of life. This is conventionally thought of in a primarily military context, to protect against an enemy that intends to disrupt a nation-state's way of life or stability.[24] Security systems implemented following World War II, the Cold War, and 9/11 were in response to various tangible threats from armed conflict, nuclear war, and nonstate actor aggressions. COVID-19 has disrupted national and global security enterprises in a manner previously only associated with a sentient, intentional enemy. The loss of life[25] and economic viability during this pandemic demonstrates that naturally occurring biological organisms can pose just as severe risks to all levels of security, and thus must become a central element of national security doctrine and broader global responses. COVID-19 is officially America's deadliest pandemic, overtaking the 1918 influenza pandemic, which killed an estimated 675,000 Americans (1 in every 150 Americans compared to 1 in every 500 to COVID-19), and more than all battle/theater deaths (392,393) from World War I,

World War II, and the Vietnam War combined.[26] As of February 23, 2022 the world has lost over 5,900,000 lives to COVID-19.[27] Public health and security cannot be considered as separate capacities in a world that has become and will remain globalized and interconnected. Disease threats that pose both acute and protracted harm to a nation's health security may begin their chains of transmission thousands of miles away. COVID-19 is not the first epidemic turned pandemic to show that pathogens move faster than governments, international frameworks, or response structures. Surveillance and mitigation that starts and ends within a nation's borders will be predictably inefficient.

Disease threats are no less consequential than traditional security threats. Traditional measures taken in combat, application of sanctions, or establishing Security Council resolutions to counter adversaries are not options. Infectious diseases, and all diseases for that matter, may kill but they take time and do not rally public support or outcries for decisive action against a foe the same way physical attacks on security forces can do and have done. Infectious disease can spread in unpredictable ways, using humans, animals, and fomites (objects) as vectors, reaching corners of the globe in ways traditionally defined security threats never have. Millions have been infected by COVID-19, many have lost their lives, still many more will be affected in indirect ways by other public health threats, including suffering from chronic and acute disease that goes untreated or undiagnosed due to limitations of an overburdened, understaffed healthcare system, as well as those suffering from loss of livelihood and long-term disruptions to mental health and well-being.[28] These issues affect national, regional, and global stability and security. The ramifications may be felt across various sectors for years to come.

It is important to remember in all of this that disease outbreaks do not operate in predictable cycles; they often occur in sequence and they emerge in nations with both weak and strong health systems. They do not consider borders in transmission to a susceptible population. Many emerging disease threats may be underrepresented or absent from national surveillance and preparedness plans due to a lack of consideration of various drivers of emergence including human mobility, climate change, and globalization, meaning nations and regions might not detect initial cases before an epidemic has taken hold. Vector-borne diseases once limited to warmer climates are increasing in incidence across a variety of regions that, due to rising temperatures, can now support mosquito population life cycles.[29] Diseases like dengue, for example, would never have been considered a risk for most locations in the US, but they are now a reality.[30]

Existing health security frameworks

National capacity for the detection and containment of an infectious disease or biological event, regardless of origin and before it becomes a regional or global threat, is the ultimate goal of health systems strengthening and the key objective of a number of existing international health frameworks including the International Health Regulations (IHR), Global Health Security Agenda (GHSA), and Biological Weapons Convention.[31] Effective disease detection and rapid reporting allow for timely responses, saving lives and preventing cross-border impacts. These national capabilities, however, depend on effective global and regional efforts.

In 2005, in the aftermath of the 2003 SARS epidemic, the WHO and its member states adopted the revised IHR. Entering into force in 2007, the IHR confer new responsibilities on the WHO and the global health community to coordinate resources for capacity building and emergency response, and on the now 196 states parties to develop the core capacities required to detect, assess, report, and respond to potential public health emergencies of international concern. The IHR outline standards and core capacities for states parties in addressing national public health threats that have the potential to become global public health threats, also referred to as public health emergencies of international concern (PHEICs).[32] A member state reporting a PHEIC activates an emergency committee to review the data and assess the risk, many times through multiple assessments. The final decision on whether to declare an event a PHEIC rests with the WHO director-general. This declaration is meant to accelerate action across states parties and to limit the public health and societal impacts of emerging and reemerging disease risks. As of August 2021, there have been six PHEICs declared: pandemic H1N1 influenza (April 2009), wildtype polio (May 2014), Ebola (August 2014), Zika (February 2016), Ebola (July 2018), and COVID-19 (January 2020).[33]

The IHR have a two-component Monitoring and Evaluation Framework which aims to ensure accountability of states parties and the secretariat for global public health security through transparent reporting and dialogue. States parties conduct and provide a self-assessment annual report (SPAR) as well as an external evaluation by a board of experts led by the WHO, the Joint External Evaluation (JEE).[34] The JEE is designed to identify the most significant priorities to strengthen preparedness, detection, and response capacity, including setting national priorities through the development of a national action plan for health security and a corresponding budget for implementation. The SPAR is a mandatory annual process; however, the

JEE is voluntary and intended to be conducted every four to five years. While these tools are meant to be complementary, there is no clear system to map indicators.

It is important to note that the IHR take a preventative approach, focusing on strengthening capabilities to confront all potential PHEICs when and where they occur. States parties commit to core public health capacities to achieve compliance, building networks that can prevent local public health crises from becoming international catastrophes. While legally binding, the IHR lack a formal enforcement mechanism for failing to comply with recommendations. As such, despite purported compliance with the IHR, many countries fail to report potential PHEICs, fearing repercussions to their economy, foreign policy, and global standing; while others close borders or restrict travel in an attempt to prevent disease from entering their territory, in complete opposition to the IHR and against WHO recommendations.[35]

The launch of the GHSA in February 2014 by twenty-nine partner nations, the WHO, the Food and Agriculture Organization of the UN, and the World Organisation for Animal Health capped over a decade of global efforts to develop new approaches to emerging and reemerging infectious diseases—part of the growing recognition that disease events, whether natural, accidental, or intentional, threaten not just public health, but national, regional, and global security interests.[36] The GHSA views global health security as a shared responsibility that requires multilateral and multisectoral approaches to strengthen both global capacity and nations' capacity to prevent, detect, and respond to infectious threats.[37] While not legally binding, the GHSA was established to support ongoing efforts of health systems by strengthening and elevating the conversation, fostering responsibility and action beyond health ministries toward whole-of-government approaches by providing a framework with targets, and emphasizing milestones to accelerate progress. The agenda was initially established for a five-year term and in 2019 was extended for an additional five years. The GHSA is currently a network of over seventy countries, international and nongovernment organizations, and private sector companies working together to achieve the vision of a world safe and secure from global health threats posed by infectious diseases.[38] The GHSA 2024 Framework aims to "advance a multisectoral approach, support adherence to international human and animal health standards, collaboratively identify and address gaps and priorities in global health security, and advance sustainable financing for global health security efforts for all relevant sectors."[39]

Both the GHSA and the IHR aim to raise political attention and encourage participation, coordination, and collaboration by multiple stakeholders, while leveraging previously existing commitments and multilateral efforts. The GHSA and the IHR are platforms for action; ensuring that countries use these frameworks and accompanying evaluation tools for assessment remains a challenge. Expertise and experience exist across a number of sectors to fight pandemics. There are numerous examples of after-action reports and lessons learned from epidemics and pandemics on what the health system can do to better prepare. Unfortunately, these lessons are typically reviewed, discussed, and absorbed by the same circles of experts who prepare the reports, and they do not reach the applicable stakeholders who should be considering biological threats in their preparedness planning. A few case studies below highlight the impact of the COVID-19 pandemic and other relevant outbreaks on national security and global supply chain systems.

Case studies

Impact on national defense systems

A pandemic can, in a matter of days, take an entire aircraft carrier offline, creating gaps in critical defense systems. The USS *Theodore Roosevelt* (CVN-71), a Nimitz class, nuclear-powered aircraft carrier 1,092 feet (333 meters) long, weighing more than 100,000 tons (90,000 tonnes) and capable of handling ninety tactical high-performance aircraft and helicopters, is a perfect case study.[40] The crew of roughly 4,800 sailors residing and working in close quarters was deployed from San Diego, California, in January 2020, the same day the US CDC began screening in three major airports (based on air traffic from Wuhan) and one day before the first case of COVID was identified in the US.[41] After conducting joint exercises near Thailand, the carrier received US Pacific Fleet approval to port in Da Nang, Vietnam, following a US CDC risk classification of "low risk," despite confirmation of coronavirus cases there. The stop had been planned for months to mark the twenty-fifth anniversary of diplomatic relations between Vietnam and the United States. It was also meant to serve as a symbolic show of US strength and influence in the region, countering the rising threat from China.

As part of the port stop the US Pacific Fleet hosted a 400-person event at a local hotel and provided a carrier tour to an estimated thirty reporters.[42] The carrier was notified via the US embassy that sailors staying at a particular hotel (a different hotel from where the event was held) had been at risk of close contact with two British citizens who had tested positive. The carrier quickly identified thirty-nine sailors at risk and quarantined them, preventing any returning sailor from disembarking. During this quarantine the carrier absorbed an additional twenty-nine sailors arriving from air force bases in the Philippines, placing additional individuals at risk of exposure. There was no testing capacity on board the carrier, which had a linear air flow system; however, efforts were made to socially distance and disinfect, albeit this was a challenge on a ship.[43]

By March 24, about two weeks later, sailors were reporting symptoms linked to COVID-19, with many of them returning to work because of unclear case definitions. Diagnostic testing and expertise were provided by personnel from the Biological Defense Research Directorate. Three sailors tested positive, none of whom had been a close contact of the thirty-nine individuals categorized as at high risk of exposure. Within a day, cases had quadrupled. Restrictions on personal communications and social media were put in place to avoid exposing the carriers' vulnerabilities to potential adversaries. The USS *Theodore Roosevelt* arrived at Naval Base Guam and was placed in isolation from March 31 until April 15. It was not until June 4 that the carrier left Guam following confirmation of full outbreak containment. The US military now uses premovement sequestration procedures to lower the risk of outbreaks. However, this particular case led to over 1,200 sailors contracting the virus, six hospitalizations, one death, the removal of the commanding officer, and the eventual resignation of former acting secretary of the navy Thomas Modly, and adds to the long list of highly contagious respiratory outbreaks on naval ships.[44]

Pandemics and supply chains

COVID-19 has placed a spotlight on the ability of global supply chains to operate in times of stress. Many companies were left vulnerable because they depended on a single supplier for a crucial component, precursor, or material, especially when that supplier produced an item in a country experiencing a severe outbreak of a pandemic pathogen. These issues ranged across materials for critical personal protective equipment (PPE), components of medical equipment, and precursors for medicines and vaccines, as well as key consumables like electronics and everyday commodities including meat, vegetables, and paper products. Starting as early as February 2020, COVID-19 interrupted the global economy, exposing vulnerabilities across various production and supply lines in China and eventually every corner of the globe.

Past outbreaks have shown economic impacts from trade embargoes, limiting meat products from countries experiencing disease outbreaks that impact livestock. One need look no further than the immediate and unnecessary ban on live pigs, feed, and various pork and livestock products by at least twenty countries in 2009 in response to reports of a novel influenza virus which originated from swine. This influenza strain was not carried in any of the products that were banned and, even with reassurances from the WHO and World Trade Organization, the multibillion-dollar trade was greatly impacted, particularly across the US, Mexico, and Canada where the virus was first isolated and reported.[45] This highlights that pandemics can affect global trade both because of scientifically and medically necessary responses and because of misinformation and poor policy.

Prior to 2020 there was an operational interdependence of trade in and production of medical supplies with some countries, like the US and Germany, specializing in the medical device sector while China and other production hubs across south and southeast Asia were producing PPE materials including face masks, disposable medical gowns, and latex gloves.[46] When COVID-19 hit, global shortages of PPE led countries to impose export controls and redirect and/or increase national production to meet growing needs. Many health security experts expressed their repeated concerns about key items of national security importance being linked to overseas manufacturing and production lines.[47] Multiple reports from previous outbreaks indicated the need to develop national capacities and committed purchases from both the central government and the health system to establish a sustainable supply chain and national stockpile for future public health events.[48]

In the US at the beginning of the pandemic, PPE inventory was low and supplies were disrupted as the country relied on overseas production. Horrific reports of first responders, doctors, and nurses wearing the same mask for days or weeks and/or creating makeshift gowns from plastic bags highlighted both the risk of nosocomial transmission among unprotected healthcare workers, a huge threat to our ability to treat and respond to the surging cases, and the immense reliance on China and other major manufacturers of basic face masks and gloves. China, the main producer of surgical masks in early 2020, accounting for roughly half of the global production, was at the epicenter of the pandemic.[49] Production was insufficient to meet national demand in China let alone the surging global crisis. Even with a tenfold increase in production from January to March 2020, global demand could not be met. It was estimated that global demand could be as high as ten times production capacity prior to the pandemic.[50] The US and every other country faced serious challenges in providing adequate supplies of surgical and N95 masks for healthcare workers, let alone the public demand that arose in the spring of 2020. By March 2020, the US estimated a monthly requirement of 290 million N95 masks to protect healthcare workers compared to the projected domestic production capacity of 80 million.[51]

Face masks were not the first nor were they the only challenge for supply chains in response to the pandemic. Consumables and raw materials included in testing kits and rapid diagnostic tests made large-scale production and procurement constant headaches for many countries attempting to ramp up testing for containment and mitigation measures.[52] Key precursors for developing DNA- and RNA-based vaccines come from a handful of countries and, while the rapid response to the development of crucial safe and effective vaccines is a success story in this pandemic, we must consider challenges for large-scale production and global supply. As a consequence, manufacturers are under greater political and competitive pressures to increase domestic production and reduce their dependence on sources that are perceived as risky. We must consider other disruptors like natural disasters, cyberattacks on key infrastructure and/or inventory management systems, and even blocks or grounded ships at key points like the Suez Canal as major risks to prepare for.

Building national manufacturing and/or supplier infrastructure in a different country or region will take considerable time, money, and political will beyond a single administration. COVID-19 did not reveal new supply chain challenges; it just reinforced them at an exponential level compared to previous pandemics. For example, one of the major take-aways from a 2011 US Government Accountability Office report on lessons from the 2009 H1N1 pandemic influenza was that the supply of medicines and medical supplies intended for a national emergency met the goals but that CDC and state officials identified gaps in planning, including disparities between the materials expected and those delivered, as well as the need for long-term storage plans for stockpiled materials.[53] In addition, a report by the Institute of Medicine of the National Academies (requested by the National Institute for Occupational Safety and Health) on occupational PPE strategic guidance following experiences from the 2009 influenza pandemic stressed the importance of continued research on influenza transmission and PPE use in respiratory outbreaks. The report's findings and recommendations highlighted an urgent need for development in three areas: understanding influenza transmission, commitment to worker safety and appropriate use of PPE, and innovation and strengthening of PPE design and certification.[54]

Conclusion: future approaches and opportunities

Governments and foundations have invested millions into building pandemic preparedness capabilities. Researchers have developed and evaluated plans and implemented outbreak simulations to map out strengths and weaknesses and fill in the gaps in policies and investments in programs. Yet, this pandemic has highlighted the reality of national and global preparedness for high-impact public health events. Frameworks exist for coordination and capacity building, but they are not used to their full potential and need to be elevated and implemented beyond traditional health sectors. The limitations exacerbated by pandemics will not go away once an outbreak is declared over. We face vulnerabilities across domestic and global capacities for detecting, reporting, and responding to disease threats. These vulnerabilities can be addressed through a variety of mechanisms including elevating health security in policies and programs and investment in technology and biological research.

Health security must be part of the dialogue and included as a core element of national security in both statute and policy guidance. Preparing for pandemics within and across sectors is critical. A robust health security system will require investments commensurate with the threat. Budgets have not kept pace with requirements. Global efforts to reduce the impact of disease outbreaks have focused on the postemergence phase; however, investments in preparedness and outbreak response are a fraction of the cost of responding to major epidemics. COVID-19 provides grim evidence in support. One estimate from late 2020 puts the total cost of this pandemic at $16 trillion,[55] equating to more than 1,000 years of health security programming at 2019 levels. Yet health security experts struggle to show the return on investment in prevention and detection because it is intrinsically difficult to prove why or how an outbreak did not happen. That is, if you invest in a strong health system capable of capturing cases before they become clusters, there is no outbreak data to report. In addition, progress and investments made to prevent health security incidents—including capacity building, strengthening health systems, changes in human behavior, and infrastructure changes—can be hard to directly apply to a metrics checklist. Unlike nuclear and conventional weapons, health security threats are nearly impossible to prevent. Health security funding, therefore, should be evaluated on the ability not to prevent an incident but to limit an incident's magnitude. We can prepare for diseases that are known; what we cannot do is develop technical and political approaches to unknown or novel disease threats. As such, we must continue to invest in predictive modeling to elucidate the risk of a particular pathogen spillover and emergence, and to support basic research to develop diagnostic capacity, vaccine platforms, and effective countermeasures while also considering and preventing bottlenecks in supply chains and source materials.

Until recently disease outbreaks relied on traditional epidemiological methods where health officials would investigate outbreaks on site and interview those infected or in close contact. The laboratory was usually excluded or slow (days to weeks) to respond, requiring lengthy processes for culturing pathogens. Innovations to laboratory diagnostics have changed this dynamic, providing opportunities for the international research community to collaborate and investigate an emerging pathogen. COVID-19 represents the first time scientists informed outbreak preparedness and response by sharing and using genomic sequence data in real time through open-source platforms, rather than waiting for live virus isolation and characterization.[56] Why is this relevant? Viral sequences can be clues that help scientists determine the potential origin host and location of the outbreak; they can be used to predict how well the virus will respond to current countermeasures and to develop diagnostic tests that assist in surveillance. Upon publication of the novel coronavirus sequences, assays capable of rapidly detecting SARS-CoV-2 were developed. This is a major win for our fight against emerging and novel diseases. Accurate, fast, and reliable testing is critical not only to identifying and treating cases appropriately, but to understanding and preventing the further transmission of disease. In contrast to the six months it took to develop diagnostic assays for SARS in 2002, diagnostic tests for SARS-CoV-2 were developed and validated in a matter of weeks.[57]

The use of vaccine technology platforms to respond to novel disease threats is no longer a hope for the future. We have seen first-hand the successful development and authorization of two safe and effective mRNA vaccines within a year of the first COVID-19 cases. Moderna, for example, managed within four days of receiving the SARS-CoV-2 genome sequence to create a vaccine. This candidate was then used in proof-of-concept experiments in mice before initiating human testing in a span of just two months.[58] Traditional approaches to vaccine development require tailored, onerous, and expensive, steps for every candidate. These time-consuming processes are why global influenza networks[59] must choose strains for each year's seasonal flu vaccine months ahead of the actual flu season. The selection may miss the mark, and there is no time to go back and test an alternative. As a result, flu vaccines are rarely more than 60 percent effective, compared to the over 90 percent efficacy of the licensed Moderna and Pfizer mRNA vaccines during Phase 3 clinical trials for COVID-19.[60]

COVID-19 has demonstrated that the world was even less prepared than most had imagined. This pandemic is not an anomaly: this has happened before, and it will happen again. We cannot repeat the same conversations and revisit strategies we had in 2019, as they clearly did not work. Instead, we must learn from our lessons instead of just documenting them. We must apply technical capacities in our global health security network to larger communities for implementation, revisiting mindset and methodology. What we do next to recover, regroup, and reprioritize will determine our response to the next big pandemic threat.

Notes

1. Katherine F. Smith et al. "Global Rise in Human Infectious Disease Outbreaks," *Journal of the Royal Society Interface* 11 (2014): 20140950; Kate E. Jones et al., "Global Trends in Emerging Infectious Diseases," *Nature* 451, no. 7181 (2008): 990–3.
2. Juliet Bedford et al., "A New Twenty-First Century Science for Effective Epidemic Response," *Nature* 575, no. 7781 (2019): 130–6; Rory Gibb et al., "Zoonotic Host Diversity Increases in Human-Dominated Ecosystems," *Nature* 584, no. 7821 (2020): 398–402.
3. Krzysztof Goniewicz et al, "The Influence of War and Conflict on Infectious Disease: A Rapid Review of Historical Lessons We Have Yet to Learn," *Sustainability* 13, no, 19 (2021): 10783; Michelle Gayer et al. "Conflict and Emerging Infectious Diseases," *Emerging Infectious Diseases* 13, no. 11 (2007): 1625–31.
4. Paul Farmer, "Social Inequalities and Emerging Infectious Diseases," *Emerging Infectious Diseases* 2, no. 4 (1996): 259–69; Jones et al., "Global Trends."
5. Paul H. Wise and Michele Barry, "Civil War and the Global Threat of Pandemics," *Dædalus* 146, no. 4 (2017): 71–84.
6. Bedford et al., "A New Twenty-First Century Science."
7. "Health Systems Strengthening," Global Health Observatory, World Health Organization, https://www.who.int/data/gho/data/themes/topics/health-systems-strengthening (accessed February 23, 2022).
8. Commission on a Global Health Risk Framework for the Future and National Academy of Medicine, Secretariat, *The Neglected Dimension of Global Security: A Framework to Counter Infectious Disease Crises* (Washington, DC: National Academies Press; 2016). ch. 2.
9. Marc A. Strassburg, "The Global Eradication of Smallpox," *American Journal of Infection Control* 10, no. 2 (1982): 53–9.
10. David M. Morens et al., "Global Rinderpest Eradication: Lessons Learned and Why Humans Should Celebrate Too," *Journal of Infectious*

Diseases 204, no. 4 (2011): 502–5; "Rinderpest," World Organisation for Animal Health, https://www.oie.int/en/disease/rinderpest/ (accessed February 23, 2022).

11. D. A. Henderson and Petra Klepac, "Lessons from the Eradication of Smallpox: An Interview with D. A. Henderson," *Philosophical Transactions of the Royal Society of London B: Biological Sciences* 368, no. 1623 (2013): 20130113.
12. Claire Standley and Jordan Schermerhorn, "Reaching the 'Last Mile': Fresh Approaches Needed for Guinea Worm Eradication," *American Journal of Tropical Medicine and Hygiene* 105, no. 1 (2021): 1–2.
13. Stephen S. Morse et al., "Prediction and Prevention of the Next Pandemic Zoonosis," *The Lancet* 380, no. 9857 (2012): 1956–65; Fredrick A. Murphy, "Emerging Zoonoses," *Emerging Infectious Diseases* 4, no. 3 (1998): 429–35.
14. Celine H. Taboy, "Integrated Disease Investigations and Surveillance Planning: A Systems Approach to Strengthening National Surveillance and Detection of Events of Public Health Importance in Support of the International Health Regulations," *BMC Public Health* 10, Supplement 1 (2010): S6.
15. Jones et al., "Global Trends."
16. "Prioritizing and Preventing Deadly Zoonotic Diseases," Centers for Disease Control and Prevention, February 28, 2018, https://www.cdc.gov/globalhealth/healthprotection/fieldupdates/winter-2017/prevent-zoonotic-diseases.html (accessed February 23, 2022).
17. "History of Ebola Virus Disease (EVD) Outbreaks," Centers for Disease Control and Prevention, https://www.cdc.gov/vhf/ebola/history/chronology.html (accessed February 23, 2022).
18. "1918 Pandemic (H1N1 Virus)," Centers for Disease Control and Prevention, https://www.cdc.gov/flu/pandemic-resources/1918-pandemic-h1n1.html (accessed February 23, 2022); Erin M. Sorrell et al., "Predicting 'Airborne' Influenza Viruses: (Trans-)Mission Impossible?" *Current Opinion in Virology* 1, no. 6 (2011): 635–42.
19. "Global Influenza Surveillance and Response System (GISRS)," World Health Organization, https://www.who.int/initiatives/global-influenza-surveillance-and-response-system; "European Influenza Surveillance Network (EISN)," European Centre for Disease Prevention and Control, https://www.ecdc.europa.eu/en/about-us/partnerships-and-networks/disease-and-laboratory-networks/eisn (both accessed February 23, 2022).
20. Anmar Frangoul, "Counting the Costs of a Global Epidemic," CNBC, February 5, 2014, https://www.cnbc.com/2014/02/05/counting-the-costs-of-a-global-epidemic.html (accessed February 23, 2022).
21. "Flu Outbreaks Reminder of Pandemic Threat," World Bank, March 5, 2013. https://www.worldbank.org/en/news/feature/2013/03/05/flu-outbreaks-reminder-of-pandemic-threat (accessed February 23, 2022).

22. "Health Security," World Health Organization, https://www.who.int/health-topics/health-security#tab=tab_1 (accessed February 23, 2022).
23. David P. Fidler, "Public Health and National Security in the Global Age: Infectious Diseases, Bioterrorism, and Realpolitik," *George Washington International Law Review* 35 (2003): 787–856; David L. Heymann et al., "Global Health Security: The Wider Lessons from the West African Ebola Virus Disease Epidemic," *The Lancet* 385, no. 9980 (2015): 1884–1901; Guénaël Rodier et al., "Global Public Health Security," *Emerging Infectious Diseases* 13, no. 10 (2007): 1447–52; "International Health Regulations," World Health Organization, https://www.who.int/health-topics/international-health-regulations#tab=tab_1 (accessed February 23, 2022); Global Health Security Agenda, https://ghsagenda.org (accessed February 23, 2022).
24. Katie Lange, "What Is the National Defense Strategy?" US Department of Defense, October 8, 2018, https://www.defense.gov/News/Feature-Stories/Story/Article/1656414/what-is-the-national-defense-strategy/ (accessed February 23, 2022).
25. Charlie Giattino et al., "Excess Mortality during the Coronavirus Pandemic (COVID-19)," Our World in Data, https://ourworldindata.org/excess-mortality-covid; Haidong Wang, "Estimation of Total and Excess Mortality Due to COVID-19," Institute for Health Metrics and Evaluation, October 15, 2021, http://www.healthdata.org/special-analysis/estimation-excess-mortality-due-covid-19-and-scalars-reported-covid-19-deaths (both accessed February 23, 2022).
26. Elizabeth Gamillo, "Covid-19 Surpasses 1918 Flu to Become Deadliest Pandemic in American History," *Smithsonian Magazine*, September 24, 2021, https://www.smithsonianmag.com/smart-news/the-covid-19-pandemic-is-considered-the-deadliest-in-american-history-as-death-toll-surpasses-1918-estimates-180978748/; "America's Wars," Department of Veterans Affairs, May 2021, https://www.va.gov/opa/publications/factsheets/fs_americas_wars.pdf (both accessed February 23, 2022).
27. Johns Hopkins Coronavirus Resource Center, https://coronavirus.jhu.edu/ (accessed February 23, 2022).
28. Julio Torales et al., "The Outbreak of COVID-19 Coronavirus and Its Impact on Global Mental Health," *International Journal of Social Psychiatry* 66, no. 4 (2020): 317–20; Steven H. Woolf et al., "Excess Deaths from COVID-19 and Other Causes, March–April 2020," *JAMA* 324, no. 5 (2020): 510–13.
29. Bayissa Chala and Feyissa Hamde, "Emerging and Re-emerging Vector-Borne Infectious Diseases and the Challenges for Control: A Review," *Frontiers in Public Health* 9 (2021): 715759; Sara Savić et al. "Emerging Vector-Borne Diseases—Incidence through Vectors," *Frontiers in Public Health* 2 (2014): 267.
30. Xiao Wei Sylvia Gwee, Pearleen Ee Yong Chua, and Junxiong Pang, "Global Dengue Importation: A Systematic Review," *BMC Infectious Diseases* 21 (2021): 1078.

31. "International Health Regulations"; Global Health Security Agenda, https://ghsagenda.org/ (accessed February 23, 2022); UN Office for Disarmament Affairs, "Biological Weapons Convention," https://www.un.org/disarmament/biological-weapons (accessed April 11, 2022).
32. "International Health Regulations."
33. Annelies Wilder-Smith and Sarah Osman, "Public Health Emergencies of International Concern: A Historic Overview," *Journal of Travel Medicine* 27, no. 8 (2020): taaa227.
34. "IHR Monitoring and Evaluation Framework," World Health Organization, https://extranet.who.int/sph/ihr-monitoring-evaluation (accessed February 23, 2022).
35. Roojin Habibi et al., "Do Not Violate the International Health Regulations during the COVID-19 Outbreak," *The Lancet* 395, no. 10225 (2020): 664–6.
36. Rebecca Katz et al., "Global Health Security Agenda and the International Health Regulations: Moving Forward," *Biosecurity and Bioterrorism: Biodefense Strategy, Practice, and Science* 12, no. 5 (2014): 231–8.
37. Global Health Security Agenda.
38. Ibid.
39. "Global Health Security Agenda (GHSA) 2024 Framework," November 2018, 3, https://ghsagenda.org/wp-content/uploads/2020/06/ghsa2024-framework.pdf (accessed February 23, 2022).
40. Sam LaGrone, "USS Theodore Roosevelt Returns to San Diego Following Deployment Interrupted by Outbreak," USNI News, July 9, 2020, https://news.usni.org/2020/07/09/uss-theodore-roosevelt-returns-to-san-diego-following-deployment-interrupted-by-outbreak (accessed February 23, 2022).
41. AJMC Staff, "A Timeline of COVID-19 Developments in 2020," AJMC, January 1, 2021, https://www.ajmc.com/view/a-timeline-of-covid19-developments-in-2020 (accessed February 23, 2022).
42. "Timeline: Theodore Roosevelt COVID-19 Outbreak Investigation," USNI News, June 23, 2020, https://news.usni.org/2020/06/23/timeline-theodore-roosevelt-covid-19-outbreak-investigation (accessed February 23, 2022).
43. Ibid.
44. John D. Malone, "USS Theodore Roosevelt, COVID-19, and Ships: Lessons Learned,' *JAMA Network Open* 3, no. 10 (2020): e2022095; "Timeline: Theodore Roosevelt COVID-19 Outbreak Investigation."
45. Laura MacInnis, "Flu Fears Prompt New Bans on Pork, Meat Imports," Reuters. May 4, 2009, https://www.reuters.com/article/us-flu-who-trade/flu-fears-prompt-new-bans-on-pork-meat-imports-idUSTRE5434NP20090504 (accessed February 23, 2022).
46. Gary Gereffi, "What Does the COVID-19 Pandemic Teach Us about Global Value Chains? The Case of Medical Supplies," *Journal of International Business Policy* 3 (2020): 287–301, https://doi.org/10.1057/s42214-020-00062-w (accessed April 20, 2022).

47. Ge Bai, Tinglong Dai, and Shivaram Rajgopal, "The PPE Supply Chain Is a Black Box—That Needs to Change," *Fortune*, July 25, 2020, https://fortune.com/2020/07/25/ppe-supply-chain-national-security/ (accessed February 23, 2022).
48. George J. Busenberg, "Policy Lessons from the History of Pandemic Preparedness," White Paper 23, COVID-19 Rapid Response Impact Initiative, Edmond J. Safra Center for Ethics, September 3, 2020, https://ethics.harvard.edu/files/center-for-ethics/files/23pandemicpreparedness.pdf?m=1599224522 (accessed February 23, 2022).
49. "The Face Mask Global Value Chain in the COVID-19 Outbreak: Evidence and Policy Lessons," Organisation for Economic Co-operation and Development, May 4, 2020, https://www.oecd.org/coronavirus/policy-responses/the-face-mask-global-value-chain-in-the-covid-19-outbreak-evidence-and-policy-lessons-a4df866d/ (accessed February 23, 2022).
50. Ibid.
51. Gereffi, "What Does the COVID-19 Pandemic Teach Us?"
52. Ashley Hagen, "Laboratory Supply Shortages Are Impacting COVID-19 and Non-COVID Diagnostic Testing," October 15, 2020, American Society for Microbiology, https://asm.org/Articles/2020/September/Laboratory-Supply-Shortages-Are-Impacting-COVID-19; Amanda K. Sarata and Simi V. Siddalingaiah, "COVID-19 Testing Supply Chain," Congressional Research Service, February 25, 2021, https://crsreports.congress.gov/product/pdf/IF/IF11774 (both accessed February 23, 2022).
53. "Influenza Pandemic: Lessons from the H1N1 Pandemic Should Be Incorporated into Future Planning," Government Accountability Office, Report to Congressional Requesters, June 2011, https://www.gao.gov/assets/gao-11-632.pdf (accessed February 23, 2022).
54. Lewis R. Goldfrank and Catharyn T. Liverman (eds.), *Preparing for an Influenza Pandemic: Personal Protective Equipment for Healthcare Workers* (Washington, DC: National Academies Press, 2008).
55. David M. Cutler and Lawrence H. Summers, "The COVID-19 Pandemic and the $16 Trillion Virus," *JAMA* 324, no. 15 (2020): 1495–6.
56. Erin M. Sorrell, Gigi Kwik Gronvall, and Julie E. Fischer, "Laboratory Diagnostics—Rarely Appreciated Until Something Goes Wrong," *Think Global Health*, March 11, 2020, https://www.thinkglobalhealth.org/article/laboratory-diagnostics-rarely-appreciated-until-something-goes-wrong (accessed February 23, 2022).
57. Victor M. Corman et al., "Detection of 2019 Novel Coronavirus (2019-nCoV) by Real-Time RT-PCR," *Eurosurveillance* 25, no. 3 (2020): 2000045.
58. Elie Dolgin, "How COVID Unlocked the Power of RNA Vaccines," *Nature* 589, no. 7841 (2021): 189–91.
59. "Global Influenza Surveillance and Response System (GISRS)," World Health Ogranization, https://www.who.int/initiatives/global-influenza-surveillance-and-response-system (accessed April 11, 2022).

60. "CDC Seasonal Flu Vaccine Effectiveness Studies", Centers for Disease Control and Protection, https://www.cdc.gov/flu/vaccines-work/effectiveness-studies.htm; Kathy Katella, "Comparing the COVID-19 Vaccines: How Are They Different?" February 18, 2022, https://www.yalemedicine.org/news/covid-19-vaccine-comparison (both accessed February 23, 2022).

10

Environmental Security in the Anthropocene

Maria Julia Trombetta

Introduction: a new old world?

The COVID-19 pandemic has highlighted the vulnerability of contemporary societies and exposed the limitations and paradoxes of existing security provisions. Pandemics are not a new phenomenon and yet states and societies were highly unprepared to handle the latest one. The number of deaths, the pervasiveness of the impacts, and the deep consequences on people's ways of life are prompting a moment of reflection, making evident the links between the personal and the political, between everyday life and geopolitics, between humans and other species, and questioning the very "subject of security."[1]

The pandemic is only one of the many challenges humanity is facing: environmental problems, from climate change to biodiversity loss, can have equally devastating consequences. Even if their impacts have not manifested themselves on a global scale, regional impacts, from wildfires in Australia and America[2] to severe flooding from Germany to China,[3] are becoming more evident. The impacts can be even more dramatic in the Global South.

These challenges suggest that we have entered the Anthropocene, a new geological era in which human actions are shaping the planet and its destiny.[4] Growing concerns for energy, food, and water security coexist with new, potentially catastrophic threats, like global extinction of species or abrupt climate change, while old problems like conflicts remain relevant. Paradoxes appear as efforts to secure existing ways of life contribute to creating more insecurity.[5] As Simon Dalby noted, "security continues to be formulated in terms of the perpetuation of the existing political order, precisely the order that has generated such dramatic ecological disruption in the first place."[6] The Anthropocene, considering human action similar to a geological force, able to change and transform the planet, questions that order and the separation between humans and nature. Nature is no longer a secure, taken-for-granted background against which human actions and history unfold, nor is it the foundation of a positivist epistemology and the security perspectives that rely on it. The debate about environmental security, with different attempts to conceptualize the link between the environment and security, has anticipated much of this debate. As Daniel Deudney warned, back in 1990, environmental degradation is not a threat to national security, but environmentalism is a threat to a specific conceptualization of security focused on the state, on external threats, and on reactive measures, which still characterizes much of the contemporary discourse, and so is the Anthropocene.[7] If positivist assumptions about nature are challenged, so is the objectivity of threats. If state centrism is problematized, so is the national security mindset and institutions. When nature and humans become entangled, securing one from the other becomes a challenge.[8]

These challenges have long been debated in environmental security discourses. As global environmental problems started to emerge and become political, the traditional security discourse that dominated during the Cold War, with its emphasis on states, military threats, and reactive measures against external threats, was challenged. This was part of an attempt to "broaden" and "deepen"[9] the security agenda to include new threats and move beyond the state. For many of its proponents it was not only an analytical move but also a normative one, aimed at refocusing security discourses on the issues that really matter, promoting solidarity, and downplaying "the values traditionally associated with the nation state—identity, territoriality, sovereignty" to prioritize "a different set of values associated with environmental change—ecology, globality and governance."[10] Scholars and practitioners have been divided on the opportunities of considering environmental problems as security issues for different reasons, ranging from realist scholars pointing out that environmental problems do not fit the criteria used to identify security issues and that including them would jeopardize the coherence and relevance of the field, to critical scholars concerned about militarizing the environment rather than greening security. However, one aspect is clear: Talking about environmental security was a challenge to existing security discourses, as Deudney pointed out,[11] and continued to transform them.

The chapter outlines how environmental security emerged as a (contested) discourse. It identifies three main threats discourses: one about threats to global commons; one about threats to global order; and one about threats to the global economy and liberal order. In doing so, it considers how they relate with discourses about national security, human security, and ecological security. It shows that, even if environmental security is often mobilized to include environmental considerations in foreign policy, these interventions remain rather conservative as they do not challenge the assumptions that have contributed to the environmental crisis or the very conceptualization of a state system that eschews the complexity and interconnections that environmental awareness presents. At the same time, however, academic debates about environmental security, and the need to find practical solutions to deal with a variety of emergencies, are contributing to questioning and transforming security practices and logics. In this context, this chapter considers the pandemic as an opportunity to reconsider ideas and arguments that have been developed as part of environmental security debates and in the discussion on reconceptualizing security in the Anthropocene.[12] It is an opportunity not only because it creates a moment of reflection but also because the resources mobilized can contribute to materializing different versions of the future.

Talking about environmental security involves a process of selection of threats, of who needs to be protected, and in turn reflects assumptions about what counts as security and as the environment or nature. The framework to analyze how the link between the environment and security has been conceptualized is provided by critical security studies and securitization theory,[13] even though it integrates elements from science and technology studies. Securitization, broadly understood, provides the tools to consider the social construction of security and the implications of transforming a problem into a security issue due to the resilience of a specific political tradition and understanding of security. At the same time, the chapter argues that the process of construction is not limited to threats, it involves the logic of security, and it is not only linguistic but assembles material and discursive elements.

Security, security discourses, and securitization

This chapter starts from the assumption that there are different discourses about security. These discourses are consequential. Not only do they imply different assumptions about values and who or what needs to be protected, but they also have consequences for the actions they envision or legitimize.[14] Some, however, have dominated the discourse and shaped relevant practices.

In order to provide an account of how environmental security has been invented and how the discourse has evolved, this chapter combines a discourse analysis that traces the environmental security debate with an engagement with securitization theory. The reasoning behind this choice is not only to provide a theoretical framework for the analysis, but also to recognize the role of securitization theory in shaping the debate and pointing at the challenges that conceptualizing environmental security poses for existing security discourses and the theories that analyze them.

Securitization emerged as an attempt to identify the meaning of security from its usage rather than providing a definition of what security is. As such the approach was quite open and allowed a broader security agenda to be accounted for that considered how different problems were transformed into security issues, reflecting emerging concerns and different political priorities and strategies. At the same time, securitization theory has identified a specific security formation, a specific meaning and usage of the term "security," and it has contributed to crystallizing it.[15]

Much of the debate about environmental security was about challenging (or defending and applying) those assumptions that associate security with high politics, the protection of the state against external threats, and exceptional, reactive measures. In this way the evolution of the debate about environmental security and the questioning of securitization went hand in hand. Several attempts to apply securitization theory to the environment pointed at the limitations of the approach, while actually pointing at the limitation of a too narrow security discourse that securitization theory captured, and in turn contributing to transforming it. Debates about different logics of security characterizing the environmental sectors contributed to challenging the reactive, exceptionalist logic the Copenhagen School provided, with an emphasis on risk management, precaution, and resilience that went beyond the environmental security debate. Similarly, the environmental security literature borrowed resources from sociology, science, and technology, and questioned the excessive reliance on language over practices and the downplay of the material aspect. It focused on the constitution of global objects of governance in specific forms, including the environment, the climate, and the Anthropocene.

The remainder of the chapter provides a selective account of the evolution of environmental security discourses. In order to do so, securitization theory is briefly introduced before the narrative proceeds with a discourse analysis. The final part of the chapter provides an account of the challenges of moving beyond environmental security in the Anthropocene and in the post-COVID-19 era.

Securitization and environmental security as an object of knowledge

Securitization theory, and the framework for analysis presented in the 1998 book by Barry Buzan, Ole Wæver, and Jaap de Wilde[16] has provided one of the most dynamic fields of research within security studies.[17] With this also came a popularization and simplification,[18] and attempts to stretch, adapt, and transform this framework.[19] This chapter is interested in both these dynamics because they reflect the attempts to apply securitization to the environmental sector and the tensions they highlight.

Securitization theory argues that security is a specific form of social practice that transforms the way of dealing with an issue. There are not objective threats out there, waiting to be discovered and counteracted. Threats are constructed. A variety of problems can be transformed into a security issue if a political community agrees. A successful speech act, saying that something is a security issue, can do the trick. The transformation has consequences because it changes the way of handling a problem. The word "security" brings about a specific logic or rationality, a specific way of framing social relations and politics according to the rationality of security, independent of the context and the intentions of the speakers. Security, the Copenhagen School suggested, has a long political tradition it cannot escape. In the name of survival, exceptional measures (and sovereign decisions) are legitimized. For the Copenhagen School, while the construction of threats is a social process, open to political debate and contestation, the practices that follow are not. Even if these practices are not necessarily specified and fixed, the rationality they entail is. The Copenhagen School provides a relevant tool to explore how the link with security is established and with what consequences. At the same time, it sets up and crystallizes a specific security logic, or grammar of security. Moreover, by focusing on speech acts, securitizations, as originally formulated by the Copenhagen School, tended to prioritize the linguistic aspects, downplaying other elements like practices or material ones.[20]

In the account of the evolution of the environmental security discourse provided below, these two aspects will be considered as the debate about environmental security questioned them. First, it contributed to questioning the enduring relevance of that specific logic of security as illustrated by the literature on riskification[21] and climatization of security[22] and that on resilience. Second, it contributed to considering the importance of practices and materiality; more specifically, the literature on environmental security showed how referent objects and security discourse assemble material and linguistic aspects and highlighted the impossibility of separating the two.[23]

Inventing environmental security

Incorporating the environment into a security discourse

As environmental problems started to emerge and become political in the 1960s and 1970s, the security implications of environmental degradation were also considered. The debate gained momentum in the 1980s due to global environmental problems, like the depletion of the ozone layer or global warming. "The Earth is one but the world is not," warned the Brundtland Commission, which used the term "environmental security" in the UN context for the first time.[24]

On the academic side, scholars like Richard Falk and Harold and Margaret Sprout have been criticizing the dominant realist state-centric security discourse for failing to acknowledge environmental threats for years.[25] They were calling for collective responses to environmental problems. More generally, scholars were using the security argument to mobilize environmental action, often evoking indirect threats to national security, like the specter of millions of environmental refugees[26] or the possibility of conflict over resources.[27] The overall narrative was that environmental degradation, resource depletion, and pollution were threatening the global commons, from the oceans to the atmosphere, and thus the security of states.[28] In the Cold War context, the argument was also used to promote a more cooperative approach to security, starting with cooperation on low politics issues to build up a basis for cooperation on high ones.

Despite the relevance of national security considerations, the narrative was promoting a more cooperative approach to security and international politics, which became relevant briefly after the end of the Cold War and, on the environmental side, characterized the preparatory works for the 1992 UN Earth Summit in Rio de Janeiro, where three relevant UN conventions to preserve the global commons (biodiversity, climate, and forests) were meant to be signed.[29] In the case of climate change, the construction of the threats went hand in hand with the representation of climate as a stable yet complex system and the assumption that maintaining anthropogenic transformation within limits would provide the possibility of adaptation to climate change and ensured security. Appeals to security were used to call for a more proactive approach attentive to the environment without embracing the more radical transformations that environmentalists were advocating. In this context, critics started to warn about the implications of framing environmental problems in security terms, for the conservative, defensive, and antagonistic mindset it could have prompted.[30]

As the challenges of cooperation on environmental issues became evident and the optimism of the early 1990s faded, a discourse presenting environmental problems as a threat to global order gained relevance. Environmental degradation and depletion of natural resources were considered a cause of instability, prompting conflict and destabilizing fragile states in the Global South. Extensive and well-funded research projects on environmental conflict were carried out in both North America and Europe.[31] Robert Kaplan popularized the threat to global order discourse in an article in the *Atlantic Monthly*.[32] He evoked a grim picture of chaos in the periphery, conflict, and massive migration, and argued that environmental security was going to be the national security issue of the twenty-first century. The argument was quite influential on the Clinton administration,[33] despite the cautious conclusions of the projections of environmental conflict[34] and the critiques of their methodology and assumptions. The emphasis on external threats, conflict, and chaos in the periphery was resonating with traditional national security discourses, often suggesting new roles for the military even when it was promoting environmental and developmental actions. Conventional ideas about what counts as a threat and as security have shaped the way in which environmental conflict has become an object of knowledge.[35]

It is in this context that the concept of human security gained relevance as a normative discourse aimed at rearticulating security, and scholars were arguing for a reconceptualization of environmental security as human security.[36] It broadened the agenda to include issues like natural disasters and advocating "freedom from fear and freedom from want," which was endorsed by several UN agencies as part of the development agenda.[37] It reflected both the concern for reorienting the discourse toward the security of people and the evolution of the debate on environmental conflicts, which showed how such conflicts were likely to be low intensity and subnational and contributed to incorporating environmental considerations into more proactive foreign policy. Moreover, the debate contributed to two developments. First, it has legitimized the role of new actors and instruments as part of security governance. Second, it has contributed to promoting preventive intervention measures justified in the name of human security.

The emphasis on conflict was also a way to marginalize climate change, as the link with conflict was more blurred. Climate change came back only in the mid-2000s after the alarming reports of the Intergovernmental Panel on Climate Change (IPCC).[38] The worrying message was echoed by influential think tanks in both North America and Europe.[39] Hollywood popularized the message with movies like Roland Emmerich's *The Day after Tomorrow*, while the destruction brought by Hurricane Katrina in New Orleans pointed at the fragility of even developed states like the US. While the United Nations Framework Convention on Climate Change was struggling to move the debate forward, in 2007 a British initiative brought climate change to the UN Security Council, and the Nobel Peace Prize was awarded to Al Gore and the IPCC.

Jon Barnett and Geoff Dabelko, mapping the different discourses about environmental security, for didactical purposes identified six main discourses: "common security," "national security," "human security," "environmental violence," "greening defence," and "ecological security."[40] The common security discourse reflects the first debate on environmental security; it highlights the transnational character of most environmental problems that states are facing and argues that collective action is necessary to provide security, mainly understood as national security. Several international organizations have embraced this approach. The national security discourse emphasizes how environmental degradation threatens states, impacting on the quality and quantity of resources, their economy, and their stability. It resonates with two other discourses that focus on environmental conflict and the role of the military both in causing environmental problems and in providing protection, even if the environmental violence discourse has become more and more attentive to the human security aspects involved in preventing conflicts. The human security discourse focuses on the way environmental change affects the lives and welfare of individuals and communities, and it encourages a comprehensive, proactive approach. The ecological security approach emphasizes the importance of moving beyond states to focus on securing ecosystems and ecological processes, maintaining equilibrium. It moves beyond humans and promotes an ethos of care[41] and aims at protecting the most vulnerable.[42] The multiplicity of discourses reflects the attempts to consider new threats and different referent objects, moving away from the state.

Early debates about climate security contributed to broadening the security agenda to include new threats. Securitization was often applied to analyze that transformation.[43] It allowed the capturing of the selective process of threat construction but also how environmental security discourses were pointing at new referent objects, or the entities to be protected, from the global commons to ecosystems. The approach, however, remained conservative. While some scholars consider environmental and ecological security as the terrain for alternative, critical approaches to security, little consideration has been paid to the fact that the "environment" or climate change are already mediated through security discourses that are more difficult to challenge.

Questioning the security logic and the reliance on language

Securitization became a relevant tool to analyze the process of threat construction and warn about its implications. It also provided a matrix for questioning which threats were constructed, whose security was involved, and the means that were legitimated, and it was questioning practices associated with security. Two main critiques, however, emerged in the academic debate. On the one hand, the emphasis on a specific logic, rationality of security, while relevant for pointing at the implications of evoking security, was problematic when applied to the environment; on the other, the focus on language tended to downplay material aspects and perpetuate a dualism that many environmentalists, and more recently discourses on the Anthropocene, are trying to overcome.

Regarding the first aspects, commentators were arguing that many securitizing moves failed to mobilize exceptional measures and transform the handling of the issue according to the security script. While some considered those as failed securitizations, mainly for the difficulties of creating a unified perspective on global issues,[44] others suggested that, by securitizing nontraditional issues like the environment, the very logic of security was being challenged[45] and new practices were emerging. By securitizing the environment, not only was the exceptionalist, antagonistic logic of security that characterized many realist security discourses applied to it, but practices and logic based on resilience and precautionary approaches that characterized the environmental sector were transferred back and influenced the security discourse[46] often beyond the handling of environmental security issues.[47] Moreover, the process of securitization appeared to involve more mundane practices and transformations.[48] This suggests a process of "environmentalization" of security rather than a securitization of the environment. Focusing on climate change, commentators have dubbed the process "climatization" of the security field,[49] showing how practices are transformed below the threshold of exceptionality and issues are rendered governable as, for instance, human security issues, or by managing risks and securing resilience.[50] While securitization pointed at the implications of applying the security logic, climatization considers the extent of the transformation and resonates with attempts to translate security into different contexts.[51]

The possibility that security practices and logics developed within the environmental sector can impact and shape security provisions beyond that sector have contributed to bringing into the debate risk, precautionary approaches, and resilience. Commentators have noticed that, in more and more sectors, the logic of risk is replacing that of emergency and exceptional measures. Olaf Corry, for instance, has identified a process of riskification, complementary to securitization, in which risks instead of threats are evoked, and different practices are brought about in the environmental sector and beyond.[52] However, as complexity and uncertainty question a logic of security based on compensation and on reactive measures, resilience and precautionary approaches have gained relevance over risk management. As Ulrich Beck suggested, in the face of catastrophic risks "the logic of compensation breaks down and is replaced by the principle of precaution through prevention."[53] Moreover, complexity and radical contingency further question the possibility of calculating and minimizing risks.

Resilience, a concept originally developed within ecology, has gained relevance. It emphasizes the capability of systems (and actors) to endure shocks, including unexpected ones, and recover, returning to their original status. It provides stability and considers the ability of systems to respond to multiple, complex socioecological drivers of insecurity. As commentators have noticed, resilience stresses the importance of practices like adaptation to risk and shared responsibility to achieve human security, and as a result, it has been embraced as an empowering strategy[54] and is permeating security discourses and practices. While initially welcoming, however, critics have pointed out how the responsibility for becoming resilient is left to individuals, with little consideration for the most vulnerable who cannot adapt.[55] Moreover, resilience implies the preservation of the status quo, contributing to maintaining the existing order, which has determined the environmental crisis. To some extent the debate on resilience resembles initial debates on environmental security: appeals to security, which were initially welcomed for their ability to mobilize action, were then questioned for their implications. This points at the challenges of redefining security practices and logics, moving beyond existing approaches, and yet suggests that engaging with environmental problems provides an opportunity to constantly question and challenge existing security practices and rationalities.

The debate on environmental security and the new condition of the Anthropocene, in which it is not possible to separate humans from nature, has also prompted discussion on the relevance of material factors. An approach like securitization prioritizes the discursive elements of environmental threats over the material ones. Not only has this been considered a way to downplay environmental problems and their "reality," but the focus on language can be seen as a way to reiterate the nature-society divide and "delink[s] 'discursive' security from the 'objectively determined realm to which nature belongs,'"[56] which, once again, reiterates the distinction between a fixed, stable background which is considered "natural" and the contingent processes that characterize societies. Securitization, however, is not only a linguistic construction but a process that brings together speeches, practices, and material aspects and weaves them together, making them intelligible as security problems. Both poststructuralist and sociological approaches to security and securitization that built on the original contribution of the Copenhagen School have emphasized the point.[57] The main contributions to understanding its implications come from actor network theory, science and technology studies, and new materialism.[58]

Using the concept of assemblage, scholars working within the actor network theory tradition have shown how securitization assembles social, biological, and physical elements to fit specific agendas. Assemblages selectively include and exclude. In the process "entities are continually reconstituted through material-discursive 'intra-actions,' where neither the material, nor the cultural aspect takes precedence."[59] Securitization is not only a social, linguistic process but an interweaving of "social and material elements, political and economic practices,"[60] as well as security discourses and practices. To act on a complex array of social and biophysical elements those elements need to be translated, as Maximilian Mayer and Peer Schouten explain, "into a language that permits intervention, by separating out what matters into economically or politically apprehensible concerns."[61] Translation, they explain, quoting Callon and Latour, refers to "all the negotiations, intrigues, calculations, acts of persuasion and violence, thanks to which an actor or force takes, or causes to be conferred on itself, authority to speak or act on behalf of another actor or force."[62] The process, they persuasively argue, captures the same transformation that a process of securitization brings about.

Questioning and embracing the divide: an open challenge

The very term "environmental security" is problematic in the Anthropocene as the word "environment" suggests a divide between humans and nature, the very distinction that the Anthropocene discourse questions. To some extent, the relevance of the environmental security debate seems to have come full circle, from promoting a critical engagement to becoming part of the very problem it tried to address.

Such a perspective, however, would downplay the way the debate is still framed and the emphasis on providing a stable "safe operating space" for humankind, which suggests the difficulty of embracing the Anthropocene. While discourses of ecological security reveal the enduring anthropocentrism and the quest for boundaries and stability, they acknowledge a greater degree of complexity and interdependence. The point is evident in the planetary boundary approach. Johan Rockström and colleagues describe the planet as an "Earth System" characterized by nine systemic control variables that identify the "planetary boundaries" (including biodiversity, climate change, and other bio-geochemical cycles) which define the earth's safe operating space and warn about the catastrophic consequences of passing these key thresholds.[63] Some of them, like the level of carbon dioxide in the atmosphere and the rate of biodiversity loss, have already been passed. This represents a specific security assemblage that is then securitized.

While providing a very anthropocentric global stewardship framework in order to secure human well-being and avoid catastrophic impacts,[64] the planetary boundaries approach incorporates and weaves together environmental, social, and economic dimensions as part of complex, interconnected systems. It is in this process of assembling social and material aspects that the Anthropocene is translated into security discourses and becomes matter of fact and acted upon. The approach is similar to the "doughnut approach" proposed by Kate Raworth, which sets a number of additional social boundaries within the planetary boundaries (illustrated by the external and internal limits of a doughnut),[65] but also by the UN 2015 Sustainable Development Goals, each of which incorporates economic, social, and environmental objectives. Similarly, approaches that point at the relevance of ecosystems[66] or complex, fragile socioecological systems[67] operate within attempts to secure existing entities, however assembled, from an anthropocentric perspective. The result is a picture "consisting of intricate interwovenness, perpetual feedback loops and the essential embeddedness of the human enterprise in nature,"[68] which remains deeply anthropocentric.

That is quite relevant from a security perspective, and it is a reminder that the Anthropocene is not only a condition but a specific security discourse,[69] which can potentially provide the wording for the normative commitment that environmental security suggested and the contemporary crisis commands. Discourses about the Anthropocene are making ecological security discourses normatively more relevant. The ecological security discourses and their focus on securing ecosystems (rather than states or individuals) are a way to refocus on sustainability, and an appeal to consider the multiple dimensions of contemporary environmental crises. They are pointing at the need for "new ecological assemblages and technologies that are increasingly a matter of human choice."[70] These assemblages may include planetary boundaries, but it is necessary to move beyond that.[71] Considering nature as no longer external to the political suggests an integrated approach that questions modes of production and existing patterns of consumption, lifestyles, and the institutions that support them. It also implies giving nature an intrinsic value. "Humans have speciously separated themselves from other living things and processes on the planet and . . . turned the earth and its many other beings into resources to be used with no moral, intrinsic worth."[72] It involves sustaining an ethics of care for other species.[73] As Matt McDonald explains, ecological security, refocusing on the "resilience of ecosystems themselves," in turn enables "the protection of the most vulnerable across time, space and species" as it "encourages us to consider the rights and needs of others—now and into the future—who rely on the continued functions of these ecosystems."[74] Living in the Anthropocene requires coming back "Down to Earth"[75] as Bruno Latour suggests, and realizing that we have only one planet and that we are part of it, moving from being humans in nature to being terrestrials among terrestrials, part of more than human entanglements.[76]

The extent of the challenges is alarming. As the latest IPCC report states, "it is unequivocal that human influence has warmed the atmosphere, ocean and land. Widespread and rapid changes in the atmosphere, ocean, cryosphere and biosphere have occurred."[77] According to the World Meteorological Organization, 2011–20 was the warmest decade on record, and 2020 was one of the three warmest years since 1880, when recording started, the other two being 2016 and 2019, all in the last decade.[78] According to *World Energy Outlook 2021*,[79] the stated policies scenario, which takes into consideration all climate and energy policies already implemented ahead of COP26 in Glasgow, would lead to an increase in temperature of 2.6 degrees Celsius above preindustrial levels by the end of the century. Exceeding 3 degrees will likely plunge the planet into catastrophic climate scenarios with substantial species extinction and large risks to regional food security, as commentators remind us, depicting the Hothouse Earth and warning about shrinking carbon budgets.[80] Global warming will cause the destruction of the habitat of many species, and a "biological annihilation" is already underway as the earth is facing the sixth mass extinction event in its history.[81] Biodiversity is relevant not only for the symbolic value of species like the white rhino but for the services that working ecosystems provide and for the genetic resources on which the pharmaceutical and food industries rely. As biodiversity sinks so does the resilience of the biosphere. Youth movements are marching under the banners of "extinction rebellion" and "climate emergency."

The consequences of this crisis are going to manifest themselves in different ways in different parts of the planet, with a greater impact on the most vulnerable in the Global South, those that lack the resources and the resilience to adapt, and yet, as the COVID-19 pandemic has shown, developed countries are not immune.

The pandemic

The COVID-19 pandemic has contributed to accelerating existing dynamics. The most evident message has been the fragility of existing societies and how people and species are interconnected as part of global, complex systems.

On the one hand the pandemic has once again presented the power of nature: it has highlighted how a virus can threaten existing societies and economies, even the most advanced ones, which have demonstrated a lack of both preparedness and resilience. It has also highlighted the self-healing capacity of ecosystems. During weeks of lockdown, as most economic activities came to a halt, and people stopped moving and retreated, "nature" bounced back, with blue skies and clear blue waters. Fish returned to rivers, and dolphins to the harbors: a powerful reminder that humans are not alone.[82] It has been a message of both hope and despair. A message that on the one hand has reminded us of the power of nature as the grounding signifier of our modern life and science, and on the other hand has highlighted the importance of governance, political choices, and leadership to navigate the pandemic and its consequences.

It has also been an opportunity, for many, to rethink priorities. The pandemic presented people with the loss of habits and relations that had been taken for granted, questioning their ontological security both in terms of relations and in patterns of consumption. While the results of these reflections are largely to be seen—whether they will prompt a more ethical consumption, oriented to prioritize relations and values over material consumption, or whether consumption will bounce back in a frenzy to catch up—the articulation of different security discourses, including environmental security ones, will be increasingly relevant.

This is especially relevant in consideration of the huge economic stimuli that major economies have provided to recover from the pandemic. They provide opportunities for investment with long-term consequences for the environment and sustainability. Europe has invested heavily in a green plan as a way to promote growth, decarbonize the economy, and project leadership, ensuring a more solidaristic approach within the continent after the deep divisions that emerged with Brexit first and with the first stages of the handling of the pandemic. The US is also reclaiming a global role, and environmental negotiations are providing the opportunity to engage with China in the context of increasingly confrontational politics. China is embracing the environmental card as part of a discourse of environmental civilization aimed at reorienting priorities domestically and gaining legitimacy abroad as a responsible stakeholder, but it is once again reclaiming its status as a developing country and pointing at the greater role that developed nations should take, as the statement at the G20 summit in 2021 shows.[83] China has been extremely successful in developing renewable energies, but the October 2021 energy crisis that hit the country with power shortages and cuts in production cast doubts on its priorities. While the crisis has been blamed for attempts to reach environmental targets,[84] the immediate response was an increase in coal production and use.[85] These developments suggest some considerations about which threats are prioritized, and the extent of transformation of security practices and logics.

Climate change is dominating the discussion, even if other issues such as biodiversity loss and resource depletion are equally urgent and question an economy based on fossil fuels and massive resource extraction. The framing of climate change as a threat multiplier (and the argument that it can make new pandemics more likely) has contributed to a new momentum. Once again this demonstrates the importance of a process of securitization that prioritizes and selects threats. The process, however, involves different practices and assembles different referent objects to be protected, like the climate, but also the carbon budget and planetary boundaries, which suggest different concerns for peoples, places, and species.

The issues of defining or redefining the subject of security or the way we conceptualize security (and the link with the environment) and what security legitimizes run deeper. Parallels have been drawn between the way of handling the pandemic and the way of handling climate change as a security issue. In many Western countries they have been rather similar, with efforts to manage risk, maintain circulation and regulate flows, which reflects the neoliberal approach to security.[86] At the same time, there are attempts to protect territory with authoritarian measures to control movement as part of an exercise of pastoral power. While, in the case of COVID-19, this has been part of a contested narrative, with China and Western countries on opposite sides, it has involved forms of governmentality and command and control on both sides. The tension questions not only the relevance of the liberal model and its ability to secure life, but also the possibility that emergency power and appeals to security lead to greater forms of control, shifting, for instance, in the case of the environment, from authoritarian environmentalism to environmental authoritarianism.[87]

The second consideration is that the pandemic and the discussion about climate change have brought together human and national security dimensions. On the one hand, despite the arguments about the transformation of security and the extent to which resilience, and security provision based on managing risk, have dominated the debate, during the crises national security discourses and strategies bounced back. On the other, geopolitical considerations have shaped actors' actions aimed at promoting human security. The term "ecological diplomacy" is emerging and becoming instrumental in gaining more relevance on the international stage in a time of growing geopolitical confrontations.[88]

This, in turn, suggests two developments. On the one hand, a new securitizing move is emerging. It presents a system based on fossil and massive resource extraction as unsustainable and a threat to economic stability and liberal order. It calls for renewable energy sources, carbon neutrality and a less globalized economy that shortens (protects and differentiates) value chains. Ultimately, it advocates a circular economy, which will require massive investments and create winners and losers, but that will allow the winners to move up on the value chains, depending on technologies rather than resources. This security discourse is gaining relevance, and it incorporates arguments from the normative discourse on ecological security. On the other hand, the security discourse remains conservative, operating within the structures that determined the environmental crisis and environmental security discourses in the first instance. Securing the global economy (and the modern subject) may not be the best way to protect the earth.

Conclusion: environmental security is defining and securing sustainability

Environmental security remains an ambiguous term but despite that, or perhaps because of it, it is used and contested. The link between environment and security has been conceptualized in different ways:

some have suggested a refocus on humans and ecosystems, while others have pointed at conflicts and national security. Yet, as this chapter has tried to emphasize, the point is not only to define what environmental security is about but also what framing the debate in security terms does.

On the one hand, the debate has warned about the risk of applying a specific logic of security to environmental problems and the consequences of doing so. On the other, it has been about questioning and challenging a specific logic of security, contributing to transforming it to promote resilience and more integrated approaches. This attempt is echoed by discourses about ecological security and security in the Anthropocene.

While the Anthropocene is presented as a new condition that challenges existing ontological and epistemological assumptions about the modern subject and the way in which it is possible to meaningfully think about security, it is also a social construct with deep security implications. On the one hand, ecomodernist approaches enthusiastically embrace the Anthropocene and the resulting "politics of possibility."[89] Human ingenuity will be able to solve environmental problems. Geoengineering is considered a way to stop and reverse climate change. In this context appeals to security may suggest a depoliticization through appeals to science and technology. Rather than exceptional measures, what are promoted are technical measures, lifting an issue not above politics but away from politics, in a process of technification[90] that can be equally problematic, especially given the level of uncertainty and the high consequences of these "technical" decisions.

On the other hand, the Anthropocene is seen as a warning about extinction. Unprecedented global warming and massive species extinction pose fundamental issues for survival, as youth movements remind us, marching under the banners of "extinction rebellion" and "climate emergency." In 2019 the Oxford English Dictionary declared "climate emergency" the Word of the Year.[91] At the same time, however, this approach can be a way to legitimize the endurance of the exceptionalist logic of security that allows exceptional measures in the name of survival of existing structures rather than their transformation. Warnings have been presented in the case of environmental conflict, or even migration, in which the consequences rather than the root causes are addressed in a short-term perspective that points at acting now before it is too late.

In between there is an ongoing process of adaptation, and it is within this perspective that much of the rearticulation of security practices and logics is occurring. The rise of resilience reflects a broader material and ideational context as well the actions of practitioners in the environmental and security fields. Despite the rhetoric of emergency, constant efforts to increase resilience and operate within planetary boundaries dominate the debate and point at a process of transformation of the way security is conceptualized and provided. While often conservative and captured by existing security discourse, the debate about environmental security has contributed to this transformation. In describing the quality of security in the environmental sector, Buzan, Wæver and Wilde pointed at sustainability as the key value and the focus of power struggle; it remains central.[92] The framework, however, has largely changed: The environment is framed in terms of growing complexity and interdependence, and the possibility of action depends on how different security discourses are assembled.

Notes

1. R. B. J. Walker, "The Subject of Security," in *Critical Security Studies: Concepts and Cases*, ed. Keith Krause and Michael C. Williams (Minneapolis: Minnesota University Press, 1997), 61–82.
2. Matt McDonald, "After the Fires? Climate Change and Security in Australia," *Australian Journal of Political Science* 56, no. 1 (2021): 1–18.
3. Li Hongyang, "Record-High Floods Leave Regions Ravaged," *China Daily*, October 15, 2021, https://www.chinadaily.com.cn/a/202110/15/WS616938c0a310cdd39bc6f3fa.html; "China Floods: Nearly 2 Million Displaced in Shanxi Province," BBC News, October 11, 2021, https://www.bbc.com/news/world-asia-china-58866854; DW, "Floods in Germany," DW, February 2, 2022, https://p.dw.com/p/3wceK (all accessed February 23, 2022).
4. Donna Haraway, "Anthropocene, Capitalocene, Plantationocene, Chthulucene: Making Kin," *Environmental Humanities* 6, no. 1 (2015): 159–65; Will Steffen, Paul J. Crutzen, and John R. McNeill, "The Anthropocene: Are Humans Now Overwhelming the Great Forces of Nature?" *Ambio* 36, no. 8 (2007): 614–21.
5. Maximilian Mayer and Peer Schouten, "Energy Security and Climate Security under Conditions of the Anthropocene," in *Energy Security in the Era of Climate Change*, ed. Luca Anceschi and Jonathan Symons (London: Palgrave Macmillan, 2012), 13–35; Jonna Nyman, *The Energy Security Paradox: Rethinking Energy (In)security in the United States and China* (Oxford: Oxford University Press, 2018); Maria Julia Trombetta, "Security in the Anthropocene," in *International Relations in the Anthropocene*, ed. David Chandler, Franziska Müller, and Delf Rothe (Cham, Switzerland: Palgrave Macmillan, 2021), 155–72.
6. Simon Dalby, "Anthropocene Formations: Environmental Security, Geopolitics and Disaster," *Theory, Culture and Society* 34, no. 2–3 (2017): 235.

7. Daniel Deudney, "The Case against Linking Environmental Degradation and National Security," *Millennium: Journal of International Studies* 19, no. 3 (1990): 461–76.
8. Trombetta, "Security in the Anthropocene," 158.
9. Emma Rothschild, "What Is Security?" *Dædalus* 124, no. 3 (1995): 53–98.
10. Hugh C. Dyer, "Theoretical Aspects of Environmental Security," in *Responding to Environmental Conflicts: Implications for Theory and Practices*, ed. Eileen Petzold-Bradley, Alexander Carius, and Arpád Vincze (Dordrecht: Kluwer, 2001), 68.
11. Deudney, "The Case against Linking Environmental Degradation and National Security."
12. David Chandler, "Securing the Anthropocene? International Policy Experiments in Digital Hacktivism—A Case Study of Jakarta," *Security Dialogue* 48, no. 2 (2017): 113–30; Cameron Harrington and Clifford D. Shearing, *Security in the Anthropocene: Reflections on Safety and Care* (Bielefeld, Germany: Transcript, 2017); Matt McDonald, *Ecological Security: Climate Change and the Construction of Security* (Cambridge, England: Cambridge University Press, 2021).
13. Barry Buzan, Ole Wæver, and Jaap de Wilde, *Security: A New Framework for Analysis* (Boulder, CO: Lynne Rienner, 1998); Ole Wæver, "Securitisation and Desecuritisation," in *On Security*, ed. Ronnie D. Lipschutz (New York: Columbia University Press, 1995), 46–86.
14. McDonald, *Ecological Security*.
15. Jef Huysmans, "Revisiting Copenhagen: Or, On the Creative Development of a Security Studies Agenda in Europe," *European Journal of International Relations* 4, no. 4 (1998): 479–505; Maria Julia Trombetta, "Environmental Security and Climate Change: Analysing the Discourse," *Cambridge Review of International Affairs* 21, no. 4 (2008): 585–602.
16. Buzan et al., *Security*.
17. Michael C. Williams, "Words, Images, Enemies: Securitization and International Politics," *International Studies Quarterly* 47, no. 4 (2003): 511–31.
18. Stefano Guzzini, "Securitization as a Causal Mechanism," *Security Dialogue* 42, no. 4–5 (2011): 329–41.
19. Thierry Balzacq, Sarah Léonard, and Jan Ruzicka, "'Securitization' Revisited: Theory and Cases," *International Relations* 30, no. 4 (2016): 494–531.
20. This is the case even if the separation between linguistic and material aspects is often a byproduct of the existing literature that opposes an internalist, philosophical version of securitization to an externalist, sociological one. Securitization is neither objective nor subjective but discursive. As Lene Hansen points out, if securitization theory is approached from a poststructuralist perspective the problem of the separation disappears. For the characterizations of the two approaches, see Thierry Balzacq,

"A Theory of Securitization: Origins, Core Assumptions, and Variants," in *Securitization Theory: How Security Problems Emerge and Dissolve*, ed. Thierry Balzacq (Abingdon, England: Routledge, 2010): 15–44, and Holger Stritzel, "Towards a Theory of Securitization: Copenhagen and Beyond," *European Journal of International Relations* 13, no. 3 (2007): 357–83; for a critique, see Lene Hansen, "The Politics of Securitization and the Muhammad Cartoon Crisis: A Post-structuralist Perspective," *Security Dialogue* 42, no. 4–5 (2011): 357–69.

21. Olaf Corry, "Securitisation and 'Riskification': Second-Order Security and the Politics of Climate Change," *Millennium: Journal of International Studies* 40, no. 2 (2012): 235–58; Jonna Nyman, "Energy Security in an Age of Environmental Change," in *Traditions and Trends in Global Environmental Politics: International Relations and the Earth*, ed. Olaf Corry and Hayley Stevenson (Abingdon, England: Routledge, 2017), 171–86.
22. Lucile Maertens, "Climatizing the UN Security Council," *International Politics* 58, no. 4 (2021): 640–60; Angela Oels, "From 'Securitization' of Climate Change to 'Climatization' of the Security Field: Comparing Three Theoretical Perspectives,'" in *Climate Change, Human Security and Violent Conflict: Challenges for Societal Stability*, ed. Jürgen Scheffran et al. (Heidelberg: Springer, 2012), 185–205.
23. Maximilian Mayer, "Chaotic Climate Change and Security," *International Political Sociology* 6, no. 2 (2012): 165–85; Hansen, "The Politics of Securitization."
24. World Commission on Environment and Development, *Our Common Future* (Oxford: Oxford University Press, 1987), 39.
25. Richard A. Falk, *This Endangered Planet: Prospects and Proposals for Human Survival* (New York: Random House, 1971); Harold Sprout and Margaret Sprout, Toward a Politics of the Planet Earth (New York: Van Nostrand Reinhold, 1971).
26. Lester R. Brown, *Redefining National Security* (Washington, DC: Worldwatch Institute, 1977); Norman Myers, "Environmental Refugees," *Population and Environment* 19, no. 2 (1997): 167–82.
27. Richard H. Ullman, "Redefining Security," *International Security* 8, no. 1 (1983): 129–53.
28. Maria Julia Trombetta, "Climate Change and the Environmental Conflict Discourse," in Climate Change, Human Security and Violent Conflict, ed. Jürgen Scheffran et al. (Heidelberg: Springer, 2012), 151–64.
29. Two were signed, while the one on forests was dropped.
30. Simon Dalby, "Ecopolitical Discourse: 'Environmental Security' and Political Geography," *Progress in Human Geography* 16, no. 4 (1992): 503–22; Simon Dalby, "Contesting an Essential Concept: Reading the Dilemmas in Contemporary Security Discourse," in *Critical Security Studies: Concepts and Cases*, ed. Keith Krause and Michael C. Williams (London: Routledge, 1997), 31; Deudney, "The Case against Linking Environmental Degradation and National Security."

31. Günther Bächler, "Why Environmental Transformation Causes Violence: A Synthesis," *Environmental Change and Security Program Report* 4 (1998), 24–44; Thomas F. Homer-Dixon, "Environmental Scarcities and Violent Conflict: Evidence from Cases," *International Security* 19, no. 1 (1994): 5–40.
32. Robert D. Kaplan, "The Coming Anarchy: How Scarcity, Crime, Overpopulation and Disease Are Rapidly Destroying the Social Fabric of Our Planet," *Atlantic Monthly*, February 1994, pp. 44–76.
33. Richard Matthew, "In Defense of Environment and Security Research," *Environmental Change and Security Project Report* 8 (2002): 111.
34. Homer-Dixon, "Environmental Scarcities"; Thomas F. Homer-Dixon, *Environment, Scarcity, and Violence* (Princeton, NJ: Princeton University Press, 1999).
35. Trombetta, "Climate Change," 164.
36. Jon Barnett, *The Meaning of Environmental Security: Ecological Politics and Policy in the New Security Era* (New York: Zed, 2001).
37. United Nations Development Programme, *Human Development Report 1994* (New York: Oxford University Press, 1994).
38. Mayer, "Chaotic Climate Change."
39. "National Security and the Threat of Climate Change," CNA Corporation, 2007, https://www.cna.org/cna_files/pdf/national%20security%20and%20the%20threat%20of%20climate%20change.pdf (accessed February 24, 2022); Nick Mabey, "Delivering Climate Security: International Security Responses to a Climate Changed World," Whitehall Paper 69, RUSI, April 22, 2008; Peter Schwartz and Doug Randall, *An Abrupt Climate Change Scenario and Its Implications for United States National Security* (Pasadena, CA: Jet Propulsion Laboratory, 2003).
40. Jon Barnett and Geoff Dabelko, "Environmental Security," in *Contemporary Security Studies*, 5th edn., ed. Alan Collins (Oxford: Oxford University Press, 2019), 235–52.
41. Harrington and Shearing, *Security in the Anthropocene*.
42. McDonald, *Ecological Security*.
43. Rita Floyd, "The Environmental Security Debate and Its Significance for Climate Change," *International Spectator* 43, no. 3 (2008): 51–65; Trombetta, "Environmental Security"; Jaap H. de Wilde, "Environmental Security Deconstructed," in *Globalization and Environmental Challenges*, ed. Hans-Guenther Brauch et al. (Berlin: Springer, 2008), 595–602.
44. Buzan and Wæver discuss these dynamics, which they label macrosecuritization, and, providing the example of climate change, point at the difficulties of sustaining them. Barry Buzan and Ole Wæver, "Macrosecuritisation and Security Constellations: Reconsidering Scale in Securitisation Theory," *Review of International Studies* 35, no. 2 (2009): 253–76.
45. Trombetta, "Environmental Security."
46. Ibid.

47. Claudia Aradau and Rens Van Munster, "Governing Terrorism through Risk: Taking Precautions, (Un)Knowing the Future," *European Journal of International Relations* 13, no. 1 (2007): 89–115.
48. Thierry Balzacq et al., "Security Practices," *Oxford Research Encyclopedia of International Studies* (Oxford: Oxford University Press, 2010); Didier Bigo, "Security and Immigration: Toward a Critique of the Governmentality of Unease," *Alternatives* 27, no. 1 (Supplement) (2002): 63–92.
49. Maertens, "Climatizing the UN Security Council"; Oels, "From 'Securitization.'" Interestingly, discourses about climatization of the security field reflect the growing relevance of climate change as an example of the challenges that the Anthropocene is posing, as global warming is considered both a threat multiplier and the cause of potentially catastrophic threats. At the same time the climatization of the security field downplays other environmental problems, such as biodiversity loss.
50. Oels, "From 'Securitization,'" 202.
51. Trine Villumsen Berling et al., *Translations of Security: A Framework for the Study of Unwanted Futures* (Abingdon, England: Routledge, 2022); Holger Stritzel, "Security, the Translation," *Security Dialogue* 42, no. 4–5 (2011): 343–55.
52. Corry, "Securitisation and 'Riskification'"; Trombetta, "Security in the Anthropocene."
53. Ulrich Beck, "Living in the World Risk Society," *Economy and Society* 35, no. 3 (2006): 334.
54. Ingrid Boas and Delf Rothe, "From Conflict to Resilience? Explaining Recent Changes in Climate Security Discourse and Practice," *Environmental Politics* 25, no. 4 (2016): 613–32.
55. David Chandler, "Resilience and Human Security: The Post-interventionist Paradigm," *Security Dialogue* 43, no. 3 (2012): 213–29; Myriam Dunn Cavelty, Mareile Kaufmann, and Kristian Søby Kristensen, "Resilience and (In)Security: Practices, Subjects, Temporalities," *Security Dialogue* 46, no. 1 (2015): 3–14.
56. Mayer and Schouten, "Energy Security," 16.
57. Hansen "The Politics of Securitization"; Thierry Balzacq (ed.), *Securitization Theory: How Security Problems Emerge and Dissolve* (Abingdon, England: Routledge, 2010); Oels, "From 'Securitization.'"
58. Claudia Aradau, "Security That Matters: Critical Infrastructure and Objects of Protection," *Security Dialogue* 41, no. 5 (2010): 491–514; Mayer, "Chaotic Climate Change"; Delf Rothe, "Seeing like a Satellite: Remote Sensing and the Ontological Politics of Environmental Security," *Security Dialogue* 48, no. 4 (2017): 334–53.
59. Luigi Pellizzoni, "Emancipation, Capture, and Rescue? On the Ontological Turn and Its Critique," in *Rethinking the Environment for the Anthropocene: Political Theory and Socionatural Relations in the New Geological Epoch*, ed. Manuel Arias-Maldonado and Zev Trachtenberg (Abingdon, England: Routledge, 2019), 38. See also Trombetta, "Security in the Anthropocene."

60. Mayer and Schouten, "Energy Security," 20.
61. Ibid., 20.
62. Ibid., 20.
63. Johan Rockström et al., "Planetary Boundaries: Exploring the Safe Operating Space for Humanity," *Ecology and Society* 14, no. 2 (2009): 32.
64. Will Steffen et al., "The Emergence and Evolution of Earth System Science," *Nature Reviews: Earth and Environment* 1, no. 1 (2020): 54–63.
65. Kate Raworth, "A Doughnut for the Anthropocene: Appendix, " *The Lancet: Planetary Health* 1, no. 2 (2017), e48–e49.
66. McDonald, *Ecological Security*.
67. Aleh Cherp and Jessica Jewell, "The Concept of Energy Security: Beyond the Four As," *Energy Policy* 75 (2014): 415–21.
68. Mayer and Schouten, "Energy Security," 19.
69. Trombetta, "Security in the Anthropocene."
70. Dalby, "Anthropocene Formations," 244.
71. Anthony Burke et al., "Planet Politics: A Manifesto from the End of IR," *Millennium: Journal of International Studies* 44, no. 3 (2016): 499–523.
72. Stefanie Fishel, "Performing the Posthuman: An Essay in Three Acts," in *Reflections on the Posthuman in International Relations: The Anthropocene, Security and Ecology*, eds. Clara Eroukhmanhoff and Matt Harker (Bristol: E-International Relations, 2017), 53.
73. Harrington and Shearing, *Security in the Anthropocene*.
74. Matt McDonald "Ecological Security" *in Reflections on the Posthuman in International Relations: The Anthropocene, Security and Ecology*, eds. Clara Eroukhmanoff and Matt Harker (Bristol: E-International Relations, 2017), 64–8.
75. Bruno Latour, *Down to Earth : Politics in the New Climatic Regime* (Cambridge, England: Polity Press, 2018).
76. Ibid., 86.
77. *Climate Change 2021: The Physical Science Basis—Summary for Policymakers* (Geneva: Intergovernmental Panel on Climate Change, 2021), 4.
78. "State of the Global Climate 2021: WMO Provisional Report," World Meteorological Organization, 2021, https://library.wmo.int/doc_num.php?explnum_id=10859 (accessed February 24, 2022).
79. World Energy Outlook 2021, International Energy Agency, 2021, https://iea.blob.core.windows.net/assets/4ed140c1-c3f3-4fd9-acae-789a4e14a23c/WorldEnergyOutlook2021.pdf (accessed February 24, 2022).
80. Joana Castro Pereira, "Environmental Security in the Anthropocene," in *Security at a Crossroad: New Tools for New Challenges*, ed. Teresa Rodrigues and André Inácio (Hauppauge, NY: Nova Science, 2019), 35–54; Judith Nora Hardt, "Encounters between Security and Earth System Sciences: Planetary Boundaries and Hothouse Earth," in *International Relations in the Anthropocene: New Agendas, New Agencies and New Approaches*, ed. David Chandler, Franziska Müller, and Delf Rothe (Cham, Switzerland: Palgrave Macmillan, 2021), 39–58.

81. Gerardo Ceballos, Paul R. Ehrlich, and Rodolfo Dirzo, "Biological Annihilation via the Ongoing Sixth Mass Extinction Signaled by Vertebrate Population Losses and Declines," *Proceedings of the National Academy of Sciences of the United States of America* 114, no. 30 (2017): E6089–E6096.
82. "Coronavirus: Wild Animals Enjoy Freedom of a Quieter World," BBC News, April 29, 2020, https://www.bbc.com/news/world-52459487 (accessed February 24, 2022).
83. "Remarks by Chinese President Xi Jinping at 15th G20 Leaders' Summit," XinhuaNet, November 21, 2020, http://www.xinhuanet.com/english/2020-11/21/c_139533609.htm (accessed February 24, 2022).
84. Andrew Mullen, "5 Things You Need to Know about China's Power Crisis," *South China Morning Post*, October 29, 2021, https://www.scmp.com/economy/china-economy/article/3153998/5-things-you-need-know-about-chinas-power-crisis (accessed February 24, 2022).
85. Philip Wang, "China Tells Mines to Produce 'as Much Coal as Possible,'" CNN Business, October 20, 2021, https://edition.cnn.com/2021/10/20/business/china-coal-production-intl-hnk/index.html (accessed February 24, 2022).
86. Michael Dillon, "Governing through Contingency: The Security of Biopolitical Governance," *Political Geography* 26, no.1 (2007): 41–7; Julian Reid, "Interrogating the Neoliberal Biopolitics of the Sustainable Development-Resilience Nexus," *International Political Sociology* 7, no. 4 (2013): 353–67.
87. Yifei Li and Judith Shapiro, *China Goes Green: Coercive Environmentalism for a Troubled Planet* (Cambridge, England: Polity Press, 2020).
88. A report by Carnegie Europe suggests: "To fulfil its ambition of becoming an effective geopolitical power, the EU should place ecological security and diplomacy at the heart of its foreign and security policy." Olivia Lazard and Richard Youngs, "The EU and Climate Security: Toward Ecological Diplomacy," Carnegie Europe, July 12, 2021, https://carnegieeurope.eu/2021/07/12/eu-and-climate-security-toward-ecological-diplomacy-pub-84873 (accessed February 24, 2022).
89. Ted Nordhaus and Michael Shellenberger, *Break Through: From the Death of Environmentalism to the Politics of Possibility* (Boston: Houghton Mifflin Harcourt, 2007).
90. Lene Hansen and Helen Nissenbaum, "Digital Disaster, Cyber Security, and the Copenhagen School," *International Studies Quarterly* 53, no. 4 (2009): 1155–75.
91. "Word of the Year 2019," Oxford Languages, https://languages.oup.com/word-of-the-year/2019/ (accessed February 24, 2022).
92. Buzan et al., *Security*, 196.

11

Global Terrorism and Security: Extremist Groups and Exploiting the Pandemic

Mia Bloom

Introduction

In the spring of 2020, there were over 3.9 billion people under some sort of stay-at-home order to contain COVID-19. While most people at the time were focused on the overwhelming spread of the virus and the mounting casualties, extremists from across the political spectrum exploited the pandemic for their own objectives. Violent extremists often capitalize on "black swan" events or crises: events such as war, economic downturn, natural disasters, or even a global pandemic open up the political space for malign actors to fill with misinformation, foster mistrust in legitimate governments, or exacerbate people's fears of "the other."[1] The crisis led to a litany of new grievances, while exacerbating existing ones: "A growing sense of instability [was] inflamed by the proliferation of disinformation designed to sow chaos and confusion, while exploiting emerging rifts in society—driving further polarization."[2] This chapter explains how some groups capitalized on the COVID-19 crisis and what the long-term impact is expected to be on democracy, the role played by civil society groups, and how ethnic politics likely shaped government responses.

Definition of terrorism

According to the literature there are as many as 100 different definitions of terrorism and no agreed-upon definition is used by every government agency, let alone across different countries or traditions, or throughout history. While each organization tends to define terrorism in self-interested ways (military definitions include attacks against people in uniform; industry definitions include attacks against economic targets), the definition that is most frequently used is from the US State Department, in which terrorism is "premeditated, politically motivated violence perpetrated against noncombatant targets by subnational groups or clandestine agents."[3] In more specific terms, global terrorism tends to be violence perpetrated across borders or by nonnationals inside a state.

During the COVID-19 pandemic militant actors intensified their online propaganda, hoping to influence millions of people confined by the lockdown orders to their homes, where they were compelled to spend more time online and on social media. The pandemic induced an interruption of the daily functioning of society. This was interpreted by jihadist and far-right extremist groups as an ideal opportunity for recruitment, to carry out attacks, and spread chaos and confusion intended to topple governments and achieve the terrorists' utopias.[4] Groups from across the spectrum, from violent right-wing extremists to Salafi jihadists, "exploited vulnerabilities in the social media ecosystem to manipulate people and disseminate conspiracy theories,"[5] designed to reinforce existing violent narratives and incite terrorism. From the beginning of the COVID-19 pandemic violent extremists took advantage of this "black swan" event by leveraging the virus into their existing victimhood narratives and increasing exponentially the volume of online propaganda.[6]

The global coronavirus crisis led to new grievances, while exacerbating the existing ones. There was "a growing sense of instability . . . inflamed by the proliferation of disinformation designed to sow chaos and confusion, while exploiting growing rifts in society and driving polarization."[7] This was heightened by former President Trump's threat to suspend immigration to the United States, implying and sometimes stating outright that immigrants were to blame for the spread of COVID-19. As a result, many memes circulating on social media pushed this narrative—capitalizing on the word "corona" (which is also the name of a popular Mexican beer) to link the disease to people from Mexico.

In the months leading up to the pandemic, civil society organizations and government agencies were on high alert because of increased right-wing extremism. The number of anti-Semitic incidents rose to its highest level in 2019 just before the outbreak of the pandemic. The Anti-Defamation League and the FBI warned the public about the potential surge in hate crimes against Asian Americans because of the pandemic. The politicization of the virus, including by the former president, Fox News, and the right-wing media ecosystem, which insisted on using terms like the "Wuhan flu" or "kung flu," led to a significant uptick in hate crimes throughout the United States. These ranged from acid attacks against Asian Americans in Brooklyn, to racist posts on social media, to boycotting Chinese businesses, to street attacks that left older Asian victims battered, bruised, or dead.

"White racially motivated" attacks were found to be the most active and violent domestic terrorism type of all, but we also observed an uptick in emerging incel (involuntary celibate)-related incidents. There was a general increase in misogynist social media content. Digital forums were used to disseminate false rhetoric and hate speech about women, which had the potential to provoke online and offline harm.[8] According to a January 2020 study conducted in Texas, incels constitute a subgenre of the violent extremist right wing: "Once viewed as a criminal threat by many law enforcement authorities, incels are now seen as a growing domestic terrorism concern due to the ideological nature of recent incel attacks internationally, nationwide, and in Texas."[9] What became palpable was that attackers could have multiple incentives at the same time and that it became less productive to pigeonhole an attack as being inspired by one single motivation or another. For example, the mass casualty attack in Atlanta in March 2021, which left six dead, demonstrated a new appreciation of *intersectionality* in which attacks could be motivated by overlapping hatreds, of women, of minorities, of Asians or of nonwhites:

> The crime happened, and they were targeted not only because they were Asian American, but also because they were Asian American women. And, you know, I'm concerned that that the intersectional identity of these women who died so tragically is getting lost when we only talk about the racialized nature of this crime and talking about the history of racism against Asian Americans.[10]

While there is a debate as to whether incels constitute an ideology or whether they can be considered terrorists, the underlying misogyny across these groups is clear. Incels are usually defined as "[i]nvoluntary celibate . . . actors [who] blame women and society for their failures to develop intimate relationships. Many advocate the use of violence against persons, both women and men, they perceive to be successfully engaging in relationships."[11] The mass casualty attack in Atlanta included elements of anti-Asian bias, toxic masculinity, and both racist extremist ideology and incel beliefs.

The origin of the term "incel" dates back to a website in 1997 called "Alana's Involuntary Celibacy Project." Shortened to "invcel," and eventually to "incel," it means "anybody of any gender who was lonely, had never had sex, or who hadn't had a relationship in a long time. But we can't call it that anymore."[12] Alana's Involuntary Celibacy Project—an online community of socially awkward youth—"was [originally] a welcoming place, one where men who didn't know how to talk to women could ask the community's female members for advice (and vice versa)."[13] The incel community constitutes a minor tranche of the internet, but exists across multiple platforms and applications. The so-called "Manosphere" is complex and convoluted. Many of the men's forums are built around memes, gifs, and lolz, inside jokes that become "meta" as they get reposted. Simon Cottee explains the incel worldview is "rooted in a kind of Incel lore—a stock of inherited clichés, wisdoms, and cautionary tales—about the natural order of things."[14] At the core of incel ideology or "worldview" is the belief that they are unable to form sexual relationships with women as a result of their genetic deficiencies (i.e., physical appearance, height, weight, and cognitive abilities), lack of social skills or status,[15] and women's "sexual selectivity."

The extreme incel view is that they are *entitled* to women and to sex. This leads to resentment and the dehumanization of women, some of which has resulted in violence like the attacks in Atlanta in 2021. Caron Gentry explains that different varieties of misogynist violence (including mass casualty attacks) constitute terrorism—given the political and ideological nature of perpetrator motivations.[16] The stereotypical incel is usually assumed to be male, white, and underachieving. It is no surprise that intersectionality exists across the groups and that many incels might also harbor right-wing extremist ideology. Right-wing groups individually sought to capitalize on the coronavirus. According to security analysts, "[f]ederal law enforcement warned that white supremacist terrorists had considered weaponising coronavirus through saliva-filled spray bottles and contaminating non-white neighborhoods" and "targeting law enforcement by leaving 'saliva on door handles' and elevator buttons at government offices."[17] Right-wing extremists discussed COVID-19 in their semi-encrypted Telegram chats and mused about the ways to employ the virus as a bioweapon.

In some respects, the pandemic limited the scope of terrorist attacks. People were not congregating in public places (often the preferred soft targets for terrorist attacks might include markets, restaurants, and dance clubs) and the travel restrictions, stay-at-home orders, and imposition of strict quarantines may have made it more difficult for terrorists to identify a target to carry out an attack.[18] But "[a]s States proceeded to impose limits on in-person gatherings (such as markets and places of worship), there were concerns that terrorists would shift their attention to critical infrastructure (e.g., hospitals or clinics)."[19]

There were three primary mechanisms by which violent extremists from across the political spectrum capitalized on the global pandemic health crisis. First, groups exploited the pandemic to undermine people's trust in government institutions and to shore up their popular support (to recruit new members). Second, they used the ineptitude of government leaders to promote their own messages about inequalities, corruption, and failed secular states by confirming state failure and demonstrating their apocalyptic prophecies were coming true. Third, extremists used the distraction of the crisis to expand their bases of operations (territorially and virtually), including targeting the most "at risk" populations, comprising the poor, prisoners, and refugees in internally displaced persons camps. Their strategy was to present themselves as service providers—inculcating the appreciation and gratitude of the population. ISIS also used the crisis as cover for several jailbreaks in Iraq and Syria. The BBC suggested that more children and youth might have accessed extremist content because they were spending more time online for school or other activities.[20] In some parts of the Global South, the increased time online offered jihadist groups opportunities to add functionality to their online platforms and their websites.

Undermining trust

The urge to capitalize on people's misery and suffering is consistent among extremist groups across the ideological spectrum, from the far right to violent jihadists. As the world reeled from the spread of COVID-19 we witnessed an explosion of malign disinformation campaigns orchestrated by Russia or within the US by extreme right-wing movements. Violent extremists had overlapping incentives to undermine the existing political order and shift blame onto states which bungled their response to the public health crisis. They blamed the coronavirus on the usual and predictable bogeymen—Jews, George Soros, Bill Gates—or they disseminated conspiracy theories about the virus's origin in a Chinese laboratory instead of a wet market in Wuhan.

The conspiracy was exacerbated when it was repeated by the Trump administration or its proxies on national media and at Trump rallies. Tracking with the administration's conspiracy theories, white supremacist groups touted accelerationist, siege, and Great Replacement theories (all of which posit the superiority of the white race and the inferiority of minorities seeking to replace them) in hopes of attracting new followers and motivating individuals to take action against their enemies, including the New World Order, Agenda 21, Soros, the Chinese government, or anyone else they perceive as working to eliminate the "white race."[21] One of the effects of this was a massive uptick in anti-Asian attacks and racism because the previous administration insisted on emphasizing that it was a *Chinese* virus despite evidence that much of the spread on the east coast had arrived from Italy and not China.

FBI director Christopher Wray testified to the House Homeland Security Committee that the threat of far-right domestic violent extremism was a "national threat priority" for 2020 and posed a "steady threat of violence and economic harm."[22] The factors that Director Wray identified as the underlying drivers for white right-wing extremists, "perceptions of government or law enforcement overreach, socio-political conditions, racism, anti-Semitism, Islamophobia, and reactions to legislative actions,"[23] have all been accentuated and intensified by the pandemic and requirements for social distancing. While Director Wray understood that conspiracy theories offer a potential for terrorism (such as the attack against the Hoover Dam in 2018), more QAnon followers suffer from mental illness than are potential radicalized violent extremists.[24]

Violent extremists use the very real history of corruption to highlight that the government cannot be trusted and does not have the population's best interest at heart. In countries with recent experiences of terrorism and state counterterrorism campaigns, such as Iraq, there is already a trust deficit. It is likely that people view any information or policies emanating from the central government in the capital with suspicion. This lack of trust is just as evident in Zimbabwe, where the government criminalized the circulation of disinformation, carrying a possible jail sentence of up to twenty years. So, while terrorists took advantage of the pandemic situation, so did totalitarian regimes, to attack their enemies and accumulate power and resources, and curb criticism of their authoritarian policies. In Zimbabwe

> [t]he government [took] advantage of the COVID-19 situation to introduce a law that shuts down freedom of speech. This new law [was] used beyond the pandemic period to threaten and convict those who speak truth to power and those who speak truth about power.[25]

There are important distinctions between central authority (in the capital) and local governance. During the pandemic, it is likely that there was greater confidence in local institutions—when they existed—than national governments. This made it especially important for civil society to step in where governments failed.

The situation in conflict zones was exacerbated by preexisting weaknesses of state institutions—because many countries had preexisting health problems concurrent with the coronavirus, such as Ebola, cholera, or other outbreaks of disease. The health response in Syria was complicated by an existing collapsed medical system operating at an already decreased capacity in which, even prior to the pandemic, fewer than 50 percent of hospitals were functioning. This dire situation was the direct result of aerial bombardments by Assad and his allies Russia and Turkey of many medical facilities before the pandemic.[26]

In countries like Egypt, where over two million people do not have water to wash their hands, the distribution of aid fell victim to age-old problems of corruption and a lack of transparency. There were problems in Egypt with transparency, but also with competency. Egyptian journalists were harassed for reporting on the spread of the coronavirus and disclosing the number of fatalities. In Iraq, there was no information about the number of people who had contracted COVID-19. Many of the local governorates consistently reported a zero infection rate despite the growing number of people afflicted with the virus and seeking medical care. Any information emanating from the region was suspect and unreliable. There was also a perception that politicians would likely abuse access to international aid from nongovernment and international organizations. Corrupt leaders were perceived to have embezzled resources as they saw fit and subsequently shared a portion of the riches with their most docile supporters as a form of patronage, while simultaneously punishing their opposition and squashing potential dissent.[27]

Other governments resorted to emergency legislation to allow the police to enforce lockdowns and social isolation. Public distrust of government and the existence of fragmented authority was a key impediment to successfully combatting COVID-19. In countries with preexisting ethnic, factional, or sectarian divisions, benefits were distributed unequally. This certainly exacerbated perceptions of government corruption. In Nigeria, where 70 percent of the population reside outside of the main cities, they rely on water vendors. Most homes do not have indoor plumbing and only select regions are offered free water.[28] In Sri Lanka Sinhalese politicians used access to international aid as a form of patronage available only to their most loyal supporters. In both countries this patronage tended to exclude the local Muslim population. This further empowered radical preachers to make the claim that the government refused to protect Muslim citizens—allowing the jihadi narrative to further resonate and adding validity to a theme of victimhood.[29]

In some places the military took an active role in distributing personal protective equipment (PPE) or vaccines. This might be viewed with distrust as militaries and security forces took a front-facing role in combatting COVID-19. The involvement of the military might be normal behavior in autocratic regimes, but this was an unprecedented step in liberal democracies, at least during peacetime. "Repressive legislation allows intrusive surveillance, detention, and prevents freedom of assembly and movement."[30] Although research has shown that there is no direct link between poverty and terrorism, the pandemic severely exacerbated socio-economic discrepancies.[31]

Government repression can turn aggrieved citizens into violent extremists. Around the world, the pandemic effected a shift in state militaries' and security forces' missions from securing the homeland to providing healthcare, producing and distributing medical supplies (PPE), and even distributing basic needs like food and water. This occurred in democracies as well as authoritarian regimes. In South Korea, the army housed coronavirus patients when the hospitals were overrun; in China and Iran, the state militaries enforced the government-mandated quarantines and have spearheaded clean-up operations. Militaries were forced to provide logistical support in Europe. For example, the German air force transported patients to and from neighboring EU allies when hospitals in Italy faced severe overcrowding in March 2020 at the beginning of the pandemic.[32] Finally, security and intelligence agencies assisted with contact tracing and managing the global crisis—especially in the countries that were the most unprepared.

Providing service, currying support, and justifying their own vision

From Afghanistan to Lebanon to Colombia, terrorist organizations provided mobile healthcare and other essential items to combat the COVID-19 pandemic. In Lebanon, Hezbollah provided medical facilities and access to their hospitals regardless of which sectarian group the patient belonged to, and they rented hotels for doctors to access during long shifts and distributed soap and hand sanitizer.[33] The Taliban demonstrated surprising flexibility and pragmatism—cooperating with the Afghan ministry of health to distribute medical supplies and initiating a sensible information campaign in the areas under their control.[34] Even though the group were notorious for their opposition to international health workers, and had targeted (that is, killed) sixty-three polio inoculators in Pakistan in the Khyber tribal region and Baluchistan[35] (partly as a result of anti-vaccination positions and also because polio vaccination was how Osama bin Laden had been identified in Abbottabad), they switched from their customary opposition and allowed international health workers into their territories:

> On April 2, 2020, the Taliban spokesman tweeted: "God forbid, if there is an outbreak of coronavirus in areas under our control, we will have control over the situation, then we will not fight in that particular area so that health workers [can] deliver assistance to that area."[36]

The Taliban introduced information campaigns about hand washing and social distancing and even donned full protective gear to explain to Afghans how the coronavirus spread while they distributed gloves, masks, and soap.[37] They used the crisis to portray themselves as responsible stakeholders delivering basic services to citizens: "In its quest to acquire more widespread political legitimacy, the group is working to highlight its ability to execute and manage public administration and civic works, proving that it can be a functioning entity in a future Afghan government."[38]

Nonstate criminal actors were also at the forefront of distributing basic goods and enforcing social distancing campaigns at the outset of the pandemic: In Italy, the Mafia delivered food and essential items to families in Sicily, Puglia, Campania, and Calabria, and enforced government regulations regarding sheltering in place,[39] while quarantine regulations were enforced by drug gangs in the Brazilian favelas (slums), and street gangs in El Salvador. Their actions were far from altruistic; they were designed to foster allegiance and benefit the criminal networks in the long term—having demonstrated themselves to be an alternative to the flailing Italian or Salvadoran states. The Mafia

> are providing everyday necessities in poor neighborhoods, offering credit to businesses on the verge of bankruptcy and planning to siphon off a chunk of the billions of euros being lined up in stimulus funds . . . Lending money to distressed companies and then gradually taking control of them is a well-oiled mafia tactic.[40]

According to Jürgen Stock, the Interpol secretary-general, "terrorists—like all criminals—have sought to profit from COVID-19, to make money, strengthen their base and to fuel division."[41]

Prescient prophecies and exploiting the situation

There were three primary indicators of jihadi reactions to the pandemic: motivation, ideology, and capability. The intersection of economic disruption and injustice experienced by the poor was exacerbated by the pandemic, and jihadi groups used the pandemic to demonstrate the salience of their prophecies about the apocalypse. Moreover, the fact that the "end was nigh" translated to every

Muslim that he (or she) must join the jihadis immediately, if only to secure their place in paradise.

The virus has been a source of renewed inspiration for jihadi groups, who have regarded it as a sign from God and a repudiation of secular states, who have mismanaged the crisis. Al-Qaeda released a statement on March 31, 2020, in which they accused Western governments of ignoring their citizens' health: "[I]nstead of ensuring the provision of health facilities and medical supplies they [remain] obsessed with the tools of war and human eradication." Several jihadist groups, such as the Taliban, declared that coronavirus "was a disease ordained by the Almighty Allah which has perhaps been sent by Allah because of the disobedience and sins of mankind or other reasons."[42] In a press release distributed by its propaganda arm, as-Sahab, al-Qaeda stated:

> Allah, the Creator, has revealed the brittleness and vulnerability of your material strength. It is now clear for all to see that it was but a deception that could not stand the test of the smallest soldier of God on the face of the earth.[43]

In the six-page communiqué, al-Qaeda drilled down into the economic impact of COVID-19, which brought America's booming economy to a dead end, caused the filing of millions of unemployment claims (6 percent unemployment), and forced Congress to adopt multiple emergency stimulus plans. Bleeding the US economy has always been a goal of the terrorist group, and the financial cost was something bin Laden considered to be one of the great successes of 9/11.[44]

These groups misused the crisis as evidence that their apocalyptic prophecies were coming to fruition, in order to create additional inducements to carry out attacks. For example, in Yemen jihadis promoted the idea that it is better to die a martyr's death than to die alone at home. In Malaysia, a similar message by jihadis contended that it was better to die a martyr than to die at home of COVID-19. By making this a choice between dying alone versus dying a *shahid*, they exploited the certainty of death to encourage their followers to take a few of the nonbelievers (*kuffar*) along with them. In Somalia, the jihadis did not believe in the virus's lethality; they nevertheless attributed COVID-19 to the crusaders (outside actors) who had been providing humanitarian assistance. They have also insisted that "Allah will protect the population"—echoing similar statements made by the former president of the United States, they insisted that coronavirus would miraculously disappear in April 2020. In Nigeria people did not believe the virus was real and religious leaders perpetuated myths about who was vulnerable (nonbelievers) and who was immune. Jihadi groups pushed back against state messaging campaigns in Algeria: For example, when the government used the hashtag #wewilldefeatcorona, religious authorities balked that the secular government was usurping the power and will of God.[45]

Jihadi groups insisted that the pandemic was *divine* retribution. The virus was God's revenge against "infidels." Their list of alleged infidels began with the Chinese for their discrimination against and mistreatment of the Muslim Uyghur population and extended to the allegation that the spread of COVID-19 was revenge against the United States for the attacks against the final ISIS stronghold in Baghouz, when the Syrian Democratic Forces declared they had ended 100 percent of ISIS's territorial control—formally bringing an end to the Caliphate.[46] (These statements were issued on ISIS encrypted networks on the first anniversary of the attack.)

ISIS propaganda has called on God "to increase their [nonbelievers'] torment and save the believers from all that. Indeed, he metes out harsh punishment against the one who rebels against Him, and merciful to the one who obeys Him and stands with Him."[47] As early as January 2020, ISIS described a "new virus spreading death and terror in China," adding that the epidemic was a "punishment from God Almighty" for China's abuse of Uyghurs.

At the outset of the global pandemic, ISIS warned its supporters to stay away from Europe, exhorting healthy members not to enter "the land of the epidemic" to avoid becoming infected. ISIS disseminated information about safety and health measures well before many countries in the West did. It created an infographic in its magazine *al-Naba* for its followers, warning them to maintain proper cleanliness. It even cited a religious hadith about germs and contamination so as to provide a religious precedent for the group's guidance:

> Cover the vessels and tie up the water skins, for there is one night in the year when pestilence descends, and it does not pass by any vessel that is not covered or any water skin that is not tied up, but some of that pestilence descends into it.[48]

ISIS's main message was that the virus was God's will but, nevertheless, it was crucial to take precautions against catching or transmitting it. Moreover, the virus was portrayed as a punishment against Iran and the Shia, with ISIS insisting that God "has imposed something of His painful torment on the nations of His creation" and claiming that this is God's response to idolatrous nations.[49]

On March 19, 2020, ISIS shifted its narrative to claim that the spread of the virus was actually an opportunity for militants and their supporters to step up attacks in the West and elsewhere. In an article in *al-Naba* entitled "Nightmare of the Crusaders," ISIS highlighted that, given the structural conditions of the United States, the country would be the source of spreading the infection and encouraged followers to exploit this opportunity by undertaking attacks against the West.[50] This was reproduced across all the ISIS-affiliated local groups from the Maldives, to Indonesia, to Yemen. Rather than suggesting ISIS followers avoid the areas of infection, the new tactic was to suggest that infected members be deployed strategically to infect others (although, with successful social distancing, the efficacy of such attacks would likely be limited).

ISIS sought to take advantage of the pandemic by launching attacks where there were fewer security measures, such as areas where security personnel were preoccupied with maintaining social distancing and trying to preserve socioeconomic order, especially where Western countries' armed forces might be "stretched to the maximum" to contain the pandemic and restricted in their deployments abroad. In spring 2020 we saw attacks in Afghanistan, Egypt, Iraq, Kenya, Niger, the Philippines, Somalia, and Yemen, which have all been claimed by either ISIS or al-Qaeda's affiliate al-Shabaab.[51]

While many countries commenced programs for early prisoner release (such as France, Indonesia, Iran, Turkey, and the UK), in Iraq and Syria unguarded prisons became especially attractive targets for ISIS to mount prison breaks during the crisis. The conditions made it "a duty" for ISIS members and supporters to strike even harder and raid prisons and free prisoners, especially in camps in eastern Syria, where the residents driven out of Baghouz had relocated. ISIS said that Muslims should "not pity the disbelievers and apostates but should use the current opportunities to continue working to free Muslim prisoners from the camps in which they face subjugation and disease and should intensify the pressure on them however they can."[52]

In southeast Asia, jihadi groups capitalized on the fact that youth were at home, frustrated, and online for hours at a time. In Malaysia, the population was vulnerable given that as much as 90 percent of recruitment was online, and during the lockdowns people spent additional time online. This exposed people to the extremist narrative, mobilized people against the government, and highlighted the Malaysian government's failure to protect its own citizens from the COVID-19 virus. In Thailand, social disobedience by members of the Jama'Ah Tabligh (JAT), a Salafi group, challenged the government's shelter-in-place regulations, and group members insisted on continuing to congregate, despite the government's strict regulations during lockdown. Their gatherings led to increased transmissions within the group, with 16,500 people infected in Thailand, who then spread the epidemic to Malaysia, Brunei, Cambodia, Singapore, and the Philippines when they attended a meeting held in Kuala Lumpur.[53]

In India on March 19, 2020 on JAT's YouTube channel, its chief Maulana Saad called coronavirus an *azaab* (a punishment from God) and asked followers to flock to the mosques. He asserted it to be a "*baatil khayal*" (falsehood) that people gathering in the mosque might cause more infections. One third of New Delhi's coronavirus infections were allegedly traced back to a single meeting at the Markaz (Center) in March 2020. This exacerbated anti-Muslim and antiforeigner sentiment in India. The government blacklisted 960 foreign nationals in violation of their visas. The Delhi police threatened to arrest Maulana Saad under the British-era Epidemic Diseases Act, charging him and the Markaz with defying government regulations about social distancing.[54] The reaction from Hindutva and other anti-Muslim groups was the circulation of the hashtag #CoronaJihad, which appeared in hundreds of thousands of tweets on social media.

The backlash against Muslim communities and the allocation of government assistance based on sectarian divides created fertile ground for the groups to recruit. The pandemic also afforded the jihadis a novel opportunity to recruit followers online. ISIS platforms provided a virtual Netflix of jihadi propaganda, from older ISIS videos from their glory days of the Caliphate to sermons by a gamut of fiery preachers in multiple languages. All the while new materials were added daily. Rather than reflect a decrease in the quantity and quality of propaganda, all of this time spent isolated gave the groups the chance to enhance their online functionality and technical skills, as young members were at home online perfecting their propaganda messages and increasing the amount of propaganda instead of decreasing the narratives. Academic research on jihadi online messaging found a fivefold increase in the number of messages being posted daily throughout April 2020, reverting to the heyday of ISIS propaganda in 2015.

All told, jihadi groups sought to capitalize on the pandemic, the general public's increased fears, and the lack of trust and confidence in governments by engaging in targeted attacks. In March 2020, ISIS claimed responsibility for the attack on a Sikh temple in Kabul that killed twenty-five people. During the first few weeks of the pandemic, ISIS claimed over half a dozen attacks around the globe. After twenty-four months, it has become less clear whether jihadi groups have benefited. There has been a resurgence of jihadi violence in places like Iraq, Afghanistan, and especially in Africa. It is clear, however, that the groups that benefited the most from the pandemic were far-right groups in North America and Europe, especially conspiracy theorists. Once-fringe conspiracies became mainstream largely as a result of the pandemic coupled with the extended hours people spent online. QAnon posts and content increased by 174 percent after March 2020 when many of the stay-at-home orders were issued and the pandemic raged through the United States and across the globe.[55]

One of the underlying reasons why conspiracy theories have metastasized is that the people who believe in them tend to believe in more than one at any given time. People who are vulnerable to one conspiracy are significantly more likely to believe in other related, adjacent, or overlapping conspiracy theories. Many women who believe in QAnon might also be antivaxxers or oppose 5G technologies.[56] The pandemic and ensuing stay-at-home orders for most of the world offered an intersection of beliefs from QAnon, COVID-19 denial, and vaccine skepticism. Parenting and antivaccine groups on Facebook posited that dark forces were to blame for the COVID-19 crisis and expanded into antimask, antilockdown sentiments, while "QAnon eagerly folded all of these conspiracies into its own master narrative."[57]

Part of the reason that the pandemic saw the transformation of social media and the typically left-wing essential-oil-and-yoga crowd was the video "Plandemic." "Plandemic" was a fake documentary fueling disinformation about the coronavirus. The social media companies took down the video, but not before eight million people had watched it.[58] The 26-minute video featured a discredited scientist, Judy Mikovits, describing a secret plot by global elites like Bill Gates and Dr. Anthony Fauci to use the pandemic to profit and seize political power.[59] Mikovits soon became a regular guest on far-right media channels and she became the darling of far-right publications like the *Epoch Times* and the *Gateway Pundit*.[60]

The role of women-led civil society

During the pandemic, many governments dropped the ball and failed to address the basic needs of their citizens. Criminal gangs and networks often filled the lacunas left by weak states rife with corruption. In countries where the governments allocated benefits, PPE, or funding to cronies and allies, women peace builders filled the void. In countries with a history of violent extremism, there was an uptick in xenophobia against minority communities, increased reports of domestic violence against women, and the exacerbation of preexisting conditions of poverty. Women-led civil society organizations reported increased government interference with their ability to engage in society. An unexpected consequence of the virus was that authoritarian governments used the pandemic as an excuse to clamp down on opposition—under the veil of lockdowns or public safety.

Studies in 2020 and 2021 provided evidence that countries led by female leaders fared better during the COVID-19 crisis than countries led by men.[61] Similarly, women peace builders were at the forefront of combatting the virus while successfully holding off the extremists in their midst. They devised innovative ways to fight the crisis and simultaneously address the economic challenges of the lockdown. In Pakistan, women's organizations spearheaded the distribution of food to address basic needs. This offered a better alternative to extremist organizations, which were attempting to replace the central government by offering food and water. In Qilis, on the Turkish border with Syria, a women-led nongovernment organization activated local merchants to provide the necessary food and act as intermediaries who could deliver the food while maintaining a revenue stream from sales. As many as 7,000 families are being fed in this border area as a result of this innovative approach that feeds people and helps keep the merchants in business.

Women took to their sewing machines to provide masks from Mexico to the Maldives when governments ran out of protective equipment and leveraged their existing distribution networks to provide people with their most basic needs. Women's groups had to respond to increasing rates of domestic violence as couples were forced to stay under one roof during quarantine, and they had to accomplish this task while also socially distancing.[62]

Militant organizations tried to fill the void and offered varying benefits with the long-term goal of replacing the state by addressing people's needs (for food, medicine, or pandemic-related supplies). Female-led civil society organizations also filled the gap left by weak states and provided basic needs to the population. This worked despite a forty-year period during which international aid and development policies have focused on building legal frameworks and institutions in the developing world, which translated into the provision of basic needs being relegated to civil society. Many women's groups and civil society organizations were hobbled by a lack of infrastructure, but they nevertheless managed to spearhead the fight as the first line of defense against the virus and against the extremists who tried to capitalize on COVID-19 for their advantage.

Conclusion

Terrorist organizations used the pandemic to disseminate hateful propaganda and undermine the public's trust in public institutions. This was true for jihadi groups around the globe but also for right-wing extremist groups and conspiracy theorists (like QAnon).[63] According to a 2021 report from the European Union, "[e]xpressions of social dissatisfaction increased, both online and offline, with social media playing a facilitating and mobilizing role, as well as the proliferation of disinformation and conspiracy theories."[64]

The number of European terrorist incidents in 2020 included fifty-seven "completed, failed and foiled" attacks in Austria, Belgium, France, Germany, Italy, and Spain. Outside the EU, the UK had the largest number of incidents (62) and there were two jihadi terror attacks in Switzerland. As this chapter has detailed, the COVID-19 pandemic exacerbated a number of structural conditions that increased the likelihood of mental health problems leading to radicalization, including making people more vulnerable to terrorist messages online that leveraged the stress caused by the pandemic and encouraged vulnerable individuals to turn to violence as an expression of their fear, frustration, and anger.

In addition to declining mental health (with a 400 percent increase in those reporting depression), "many government pandemic policies and emergency measures might have resulted in human rights overreach, the suppression of dissent, and possible government abuses that created root causes for exploitable grievances."[65] For many terrorism analysts, the pandemic appeared to offer the perfect storm to exacerbate existing grievances and create new ones. The ways in which government assistance, PPE, and, after January 2021, vaccines were distributed revealed significant inconsistencies and inequities. According to Michael King and Sam Mullins, the "perfect storm" theory of the pandemic's impact on terrorism is logical but might be flawed. For them, despite the challenging conditions of the COVID-19 pandemic, there was no way to anticipate the extent of individual vulnerability to violent extremism. King and Mullins argued:

> People are spending more time on the internet, but this does not necessarily increase their chances of engaging with extremist content, even if they are bored and lonely. Among those who have encountered such

> content online, the risk of radicalization is generally low and as our data show, there has so far been no spike in terrorism.[66]

They predicted that the vast majority of people radicalized online by emerging groups like QAnon and Boogaloo Bois were far more likely to engage in criminality than acts of terror. Despite Europol's statistics, the United Nations Counter-Terrorism Committee Executive Directorate suggested that there is no clear evidence to draw comprehensive conclusions regarding the impact of the pandemic on terrorism or counterterrorism:

> Several pandemic-related policies and emergency measures have also faced criticism for human rights overreach, suppression of dissent, and possible abuses. This situation must be addressed. Moreover, counter-terrorism resources continue to be diverted to aid public health responses. This can be detrimental for fragile States requiring security assistance and capacity-building to combat terrorism.[67]

Securitization in the health sector has given space for implementing measures to deal with the COVID-19 outbreak that is not managed symmetrically.[68] As we saw regarding PPE and other state benefits, the vaccines were not distributed equally between Western countries and the Global South. Despite progress in vaccinations, outbreaks continue and new variants appear, and inequalities in vaccination coverage may emerge as a potential challenge.

We know that terrorist groups exploit state weakness. When there is a global pandemic terrorist groups are able to demonstrate how states fail to protect their populations, how corrupt they are when they distribute benefits, and how minority populations will always be an afterthought. Such weaknesses within the state create opportunities, but they also create the chance for the states to respond coherently and with foresight. The extent to which terrorist groups will continue to exploit the coronavirus hinges on state and societal responses. We are dealing with multiple and overlapping crises, and the "infodemic" is almost as dangerous as the pandemic.

Notes

1. This work was supported by the Minerva research initiative FY 21-024 "Weaponized Conspiracies: Mapping the Social Ecology of Misinformation, Radicalization and Violence," N00014-21-1-2339, under the auspices of the Office of Naval Research. The views and conclusions contained in this document are those of the author and should not be interpreted as representing the official policies, either expressed or

implied, of the Department of Defense, the Office of Naval Research, or the US Government.

2. "IntelBrief: Coronavirus Will Increase Extremisms across the Ideological Spectrum," Soufan Center, April 13, 2020, https://thesoufancenter.org/intelbrief-the-coronavirus-will-increase-extremism-across-the-ideological-spectrum/ (accessed February 24, 2022).
3. "Glossary," US Department of State, https://2001-2009.state.gov/s/ct/info/c16718.htm (accessed April 20, 2022).
4. Alexa Lardieri, "Homeland Security Warns Terrorists Could Exploit Coronavirus Pandemic," *US News*, March 24, 2020, https://www.usnews.com/news/politics/articles/2020-03-24/homeland-security-warns-that-terrorists-could-exploit-coronavirus-pandemic (accessed February 24, 2022).
5. Michael King and Sam Mullins, "Covid-19 and Terrorism in the West: Has Radicalization Really Gone Viral?" *Just Security*, March 4, 2021, https://www.justsecurity.org/75064/covid-19-and-terrorism-in-the-west-has-radicalization-really-gone-viral/ (accessed February 24, 2022).
6. Ibid.
7. "Coronavirus Will Increase Extremisms."
8. "Update on the Impact of the COVID-19 Pandemic on Terrorism, Counter-terrorism and Countering Violent Extremism," Counter-terrorism Committee Executive Directorate, June 2021, 6, https://www.un.org/securitycouncil/ctc/sites/www.un.org.securitycouncil.ctc/files/files/documents/2021/Jun/cted_covid_paper_15june2021_1.pdf (accessed February 24, 2022).
9. "Texas Domestic Terrorism Threat Assessment," Texas Department of Public Safety, January 2020, 3, https://www.dps.texas.gov/sites/default/files/documents/director_staff/media_and_communications/2020/txterrorthreatassessment.pdf (accessed February 24, 2022).
10. Jonathan Chang and Meghna Chakrabarti, "What the Georgia Shootings Reveal about Anti-Asian Racism in the US," WBUR, March 22, 2021, https://www.wbur.org/onpoint/2021/03/22/what-the-georgia-shootings-reveal-about-anti-asian-racism-in-the-u-s (accessed February 24, 2022).
11. "Texas Domestic Terrorism Threat Assessment," 29.
12. Jim Taylor, "The Woman Who Founded the 'Incel' Movement," BBC News, August 30, 2018, https://www.bbc.com/news/world-us-canada-45284455 (accessed February 24, 2022).
13. Zack Beauchamp, "Our Incel Problem," *Vox*, April 23, 2019, https://www.vox.com/the-highlight/2019/4/16/18287446/incel-definition-reddit (accessed April 21, 2022).
14. Simon Cottee, "Incel (E)motives: Resentment, Shame and Revenge," *Studies in Conflict and Terrorism* 44, no. 2 (2021): 96.
15. Some incels recognize that women will select non-Chad (ideal type men who are deemed attractive by society) men if they are exceptionally high status or wealthy. They point to Mark Zuckerberg or Bill Gates as examples of comparable men overcoming physical deficiencies.

16. Caron E. Gentry, *Disordered Violence: How Gender, Race and Heteronormativity Structure Terrorism* (Edinburgh: Edinburgh University Press, 2020).
17. Alex Woodward, "Coronavirus: White Supremacists Planned to Use the Virus as a Bioweapon," *The Independent*, March 22, 2020, https://www.independent.co.uk/news/world/americas/coronavirus-terrorist-white-supremacy-fbi-bioterrorism-a9417296.html (accessed February 24, 2022).
18. Nadine L. Salman and Paul Gill, "Terrorism during the COVID-19 Pandemic," Special Series on COVID-19 No. 13, UCL Jill Dando Institute, May 2020, https://www.ucl.ac.uk/jill-dando-institute/sites/jill-dando-institute/files/terrrosim_covid19_final_no_13.pdf (accessed February 24, 2022).
19. "Update on the Impact of the COVID-19 Pandemic," 2.
20. Caleb Spencer, "Coronavirus: 'Children May Have Been Radicalised during Lockdown,'" BBC News, June 30, 2020, https://www.bbc.com/news/uk-wales-53082476 (accessed April 21, 2022).
21. "IntelBrief: White Supremacists and the Weaponization of the Coronavirus," Soufan Center, March 25, 2020, https://thesoufancenter.org/intelbrief-white-supremacists-and-the-weaponization-of-the-coronavirus-covid-19/ (accessed February 24, 2022).
22. Woodward, "Coronavirus."
23. Ibid.
24. Sophia Moskalenko, "Many QAnon Followers Report Having Mental Health Diagnoses," *The Conversation*, March 25, 2021, https://theconversation.com/many-qanon-followers-report-having-mental-health-diagnoses-157299 (accessed February 24, 2022).
25. Farida Nabourema, "Dictators Love Lockdowns," *African Arguments*, April 21, 2020, https://africanarguments.org/2020/04/21/dictatorships-love-lockdown-coronavirus-togo/ (accessed February 24, 2022).
26. Amany Qaddour, speech at "Coronavirus and Conflict: The Security Sector Response," United States Peace Institute virtual conference, April 15, 2020, https://www.usip.org/events/coronavirus-and-conflict-security-sector-response (accessed February 24, 2022).
27. Nabourema, "Dictators Love Lockdowns."
28. Author interviews with female civil society organization (CSO) leaders working in Nigeria, April 2020.
29. Author interviews with female CSO leaders working in Sri Lanka, April 2020.
30. James Wither and Richard Mašek, "The COVID-19 Pandemic: Counterterrorism Practitioners' Assessments," George C. Marshall Center, October 2020, https://www.marshallcenter.org/en/publications/perspectives/covid-19-pandemic-counterterrorism-practitioners-assessments (accessed February 24, 2022).
31. Ibid.
32. "Coronavirus and Conflict."

33. Tom Perry and Laila Bassam, "Hezbollah Deploys Medics, Hospitals against Coronavirus in Lebanon," Reuters, March 25, 2020, https://www.reuters.com/article/us-health-coronavirus-hezbollah/hezbollah-deploys-medics-hospitals-against-coronavirus-in-lebanon-idUSKBN21C3R7 (accessed February 25, 2022).
34. "IntelBrief: How Will Coronavirus Impact Afghanistan?" Soufan Center, April 16, 2020, https://thesoufancenter.org/intelbrief-how-will-the-coronavirus-impact-afghanistan/ (accessed February 25, 2022).
35. Tim McGirk, "Taliban Assassins Target Pakistan's Polio Vaccinators," *National Geographic*, March 3, 2015, https://www.nationalgeographic.com/news/2015/03/150303-polio-pakistan-islamic-state-refugees-vaccination-health/ (accessed February 25, 2022).
36. Roudabeh Kishi, "Taliban in Afghanistan," ACLED, April 16, 2020, https://acleddata.com/2020/04/16/cdt-spotlight-taliban-in-afghanistan/ (accessed February 25, 2022).
37. Ibid.
38. "IntelBrief: How Will Coronavirus Impact Afghanistan?"
39. Zachary Keyser, "Coronavirus: Mafia Delivers Food, Essentials to Italy's Worst Affected," *Jerusalem Post*, April 12, 2020, https://www.jpost.com/international/coronavirus-mafia-delivers-food-essentials-to-italys-worst-affected-624401 (accessed February 25, 2022).
40. Valentina Di Donato and Tim Lister, "The Mafia Is Poised to Exploit Coronavirus, and Not Just in Italy," CNN, April 19, 2020, https://www.cnn.com/2020/04/19/europe/italy-mafia-exploiting-coronavirus-crisis-aid-intl/index.html (accessed February 25, 2022).
41. "Interpol—Terrorist Groups Using COVID-19 to Reinforce Power and Influence," Interpol, December 22, 2020, https://www.interpol.int/en/News-and-Events/News/2020/INTERPOL-Terrorist-groups-using-COVID-19-to-reinforce-power-and-influence (accessed February 25, 2022).
42. Mia Bloom, "How Terrorists Will Try to Capitalize on the Coronavirus Crisis," *Just Security*, April 3, 2020, https://www.justsecurity.org/69508/how-terrorist-groups-will-try-to-capitalize-on-the-coronavirus-crisis/ (accessed February 25, 2022).
43. James Gordon Meek, "Terrorist Groups Spin Covid-19 as God's 'Smallest Soldier' Attacking West," ABC News (USA), April 2, 2020, https://abcnews.go.com/International/terrorist-groups-spin-covid-19-gods-smallest-soldier/story?id=69930563 (accessed February 25, 2022).
44. Ibid.
45. Zoom interviews with the members of WASL, the Women Alliance and Security Leadership network, March–April 2020. The group includes women from forty-seven countries in the Global South who run CSOs.
46. Ben Wedeman and Lauren Said-Moorhouse, "ISIS Has Lost Its Final Stronghold in Syria, the Syrian Democratic Forces Says," CNN, March 23, 2019, https://www.cnn.com/2019/03/23/middleeast/isis-caliphate-end-intl/index.html (accessed February 25, 2022).

47. Semi-encrypted Telegram messages posted by ISIS supporters. This material is part of the author's sponsored research supported by the Minerva Research Initiative and the Office of Naval Research, https://minerva.defense.gov/Media/Images/igphoto/2001693605/ (accessed February 25, 2022).
48. Bridget Johnson, "Notable and Quotable: ISIS on the Coronavirus," *Wall Street Journal*, March 15, 2020, https://www.wsj.com/articles/notable-quotable-isis-on-the-coronavirus-11584314005 (accessed February 25, 2022).
49. Aymenn Jawad Al-Tamimi, "Islamic State Editorial on the Coronavirus Pandemic," Aymenn Jawad Al-Tamimi (blog), March 19, 2020, http://www.aymennjawad.org/2020/03/islamic-state-editorial-on-the-coronavirus (accessed February 25, 2022).
50. Valerio Mazzoni, "Coronavirus: How Islamist Militants Are Reacting to the Outbreak," *European Eye on Radicalization*, March 30, 2020, https://eeradicalization.com/coronavirus-how-islamist-militants-are-reacting-to-the-outbreak/ (accessed April 21, 2022).
51. Bloom, "How Terrorists Will Try."
52. Ibid.
53. "COVID-19 Crisis Response in ASEAN Member States," Organisation for Economic Co-operation and Development, May 4, 2020, https://www.oecd.org/coronavirus/policy-responses/covid-19-crisis-response-in-asean-member-states-02f828a2/ (accessed February 25, 2022).
54. Akash Bisht and Sadiq Nakvi, "How Tablighi Jemaat Event Became India's Worst Coronavirus Vector," Al Jazeera, April 7, 2020, https://www.aljazeera.com/news/2020/04/tablighi-jamaat-event-india-worst-coronavirus-vector-200407052957511.html (accessed February 25, 2022).
55. Mia Bloom and Sophia Moskalenko, *Pastels and Pedophiles: Inside the Mind of QAnon* (Stanford, CA: Redwood Press, 2021).
56. Ibid.
57. Anne Kelly, "Mothers for QAnon," *New York Times*, September 10, 2020, https://www.nytimes.com./2020/09/10/opinion/qanon-women-conspiracy.html (accessed February 25, 2022).
58. Casey Newton, "How the 'Plandemic' Video Hoax Went Viral," *The Verge*, May 12, 2020, https://www.theverge.com/2020/5/12/21254184/how-plandemic-went-viral-facebook-youtube (accessed April 21, 2022).
59. Davey Alba, "Virus Conspiracy Theorists Elevate a New Champion," *New York Times*, May 9, 2020, https://www.nytimes.com/2020/05/09/technology/plandemic-judy-mikovitz-coronavirus-disinformation.html (accessed February 25, 2022).
60. Ibid.
61. Leah Windsor et al. "Gender in the Time of Covid-19: Evaluating National Leadership and COVID Fatalities," *PLOS One* 15, no. 12 (2020): e0244531; Allyson Bear and Roselle Agner, "Why More Countries Need Female Leaders," *US News and World Report*, March 8, 2021,

https://www.usnews.com/news/best-countries/articles/2021-03-08/why-countries-with-female-leaders-have-responded-well-to-the-pandemic (accessed April 11, 2022).

62. Author interviews with female CSO leaders, March–April 2020.
63. Bloom and Moskalenko, *Pastels and Pedophiles*.
64. Europol, *European Union Terrorism Situation and Trend Report 2021* (Luxembourg: European Union, 2021), 28, https://www.europol.europa.eu/activities-services/main-reports/european-union-terrorism-situation-and-trend-report-2021-tesat (accessed February 25, 2022).
65. "COVID-19: States Should Not Abuse Emergency Measures to Suppress Human Rights – UN Experts," United Nations Human Rights Office of the High Commissioner, March 16, 2020, https://www.ohchr.org/en/NewsEvents/Pages/DisplayNews.aspx?NewsID=25722&LangID=E (accessed February 25, 2022).
66. King and Mullins, "Covid-19 and Terrorism."
67. "Impacts of the Covid-19 Pandemic on Terrorism, Counter-Terrorism, and Countering Violent Extremism," side event, 2021 United Nations Counter-Terrorism Week, June 25, 2021, concept note, https://www.un.org/securitycouncil/ctc/sites/www.un.org.securitycouncil.ctc/files/un_ct_week_2021_covid-19_side_event_concept_note_-_edited_1_1.pdf (accessed February 25, 2022).
68. Helda Risma, Pujo Widodo, and Resmanto Widodo Putro, "Covid-19 Securitization and Terrorism: National Security Change Management Dilemma," *Jurnal Pertahanan* 6, no. 3 (2020): 496–506.

12

Emerging Technologies and Security: The Abstraction of Conflict

Aiden Warren and Alek Hillas

Introduction

Emerging technologies play a pervasive role across many aspects of everyday life, including in the manufacture of goods and services, global navigation systems, user interface software, and self-driving vehicles (to name a few).[1] In the context of war, the abstraction of violence, and global security more broadly, devices such as unmanned aerial vehicles (UAVs) are used extensively in counterterrorist operations, while lethal autonomous weapons systems (LAWS) continue to pose ethical and reliability questions about the use (and potential for misuse) of military power. Unsurprisingly, the compounding aspects deriving from cybersecurity, artificial intelligence (AI), and the transition from 4G to 5G (and 6G) all have the capacity to engender multiple complexities and disruptions across the state, nonstate, global governance, and security domains.

Other emerging technologies are also developing, such as advanced manufacturing techniques (3D printing), nanotechnology (including miniaturization of military technology), bioengineering (including biological weapons agents and human-machine symbiosis), quantum computing (including the potential decryption of classical information systems), and digitization technologies (including military tools and applications to manage "big data"). Further, it is evident that the most powerful state actors and multinational corporations are investing extensively in the range of such emerging disruptive technologies.[2] While the dangers and security complications of the above-mentioned weapons and devices are not yet fully realized, policymakers will be compelled to address the threats presented by advanced weapons technologies and formulate international provisions to regulate or mitigate their use.

In providing a substantive examination across the emerging technologies "suite"—with specific focus on uninhabited vehicles (drones),

LAWS, AI and cyber—this chapter seeks to elucidate the security challenges emanating from their development and at times aberrant advancement. Indeed, just as emerging technologies are disrupting many sectors of domestic economies, they are also transforming the global security arena. The power and pace of modern technologies call for new approaches to preventing a catastrophic conflict or mitigating a devastating miscalculation. However, diplomacy, deterrence, arms control, and direct military action, tools that have long been utilized to safeguard the national interest, are being challenged by precipitously evolving technologies that are presenting new problems with no clearly defined solutions.

As the chapter conveys, while some efforts have been undertaken in the direction of regulating the usage and application of such technologies, coherency and agreement on pathways forward across the domains of states, nonstate actors, global governance, and security have been hard to attain.[3] In the current era of omnipresent, near-instant communication, today's rapid technological changes have greatly shortened the time for governmental consideration, decision, and action, even as these changes hasten the complexity and difficulty of new problems, which this analysis seeks to unpack. Of course, as this chapter will also discuss, the tumultuous reaction to the COVID-19 pandemic has tested the confidence of even the most fervent global optimists. Many states, including some of the world's most formidable, turned inward, initially implementing travel bans, executing export controls, stockpiling, or controlling information, and sidelining the World Health Organization and other multilateral institutions. Aside from exposing the fragilities in the international community and governance architecture, faltering global cooperation has left the security dimensions of emerging technologies either on pause or incompletely addressed via makeshift and insubstantial avenues.[4]

Artificial intelligence (AI)

Of all the emerging technologies, it is AI that has come to the fore in the international public's imagination. While its meaning has changed over time, AI can be defined as the use of algorithms to undertake actions. One of the major shifts in the understanding of AI pertains to the transition from humans *informing* computers how to act, to a new phase in which computers *learn* how to act. This of course is dependent on the incorporation of machine learning techniques, referred to as "deep learning" and neural networks.[5] At present, most AI tasks still fall into the "narrow" category in which an exact task is undertaken, as opposed to those tasks that would entail the replication of human-level intelligence. Given the numerous conceivable applications of AI, it is perhaps misleading at this stage in time to describe it as a stand-alone capability or one application of technology. In this regard, it is more plausible to look at AI as an "enabler" and refer to systems as being, for example, "AI-enabled financial trading" or "AI-enabled cyber defenses."[6]

In building on this above definition, Michael Klare defines AI as a generic term used to describe an assortment of techniques that provide machines with the capacity to "monitor their surroundings in the physical world or cyberspace and to take independent action in response to various stimuli."[7] Heather Roff sees artificial intelligence as a collection of computational and information-processing techniques that are goal oriented. As stated:

> Maybe it's a physical task and it needs robotic manipulation, or maybe it's a cognitive task and it needs planning capabilities or classification capabilities. Whatever the means that it needs to pursue that task, it also has. So, the intelligence [is] how well it appropriately functions and undertakes its goal-directed task. If it doesn't function so well, it's not that intelligent.[8]

As such, when considered in the context of emerging technologies, the pace at which such devices continue to evolve and incorporate AI applications into their "performance" will have a marked impact on broader global security, particularly in complicated conflict scenarios.

To provide emerging technologies with the requisite capacity to make autonomous decisions, engineers have developed multifaceted algorithms, or computer-based sets of rules, to oversee their execution. For instance, AI aerial drones could be armed with sensors that differentiate and separate adversary tanks from other vehicles in a zone of armed conflict and, when the adversary is identified, can delineate on their own accord whether to engage with it utilizing onboard missiles. Additionally, AI can also be used in a cyberspace context in which an applicable device can watch and wait for enemy cyberattacks, and counter them with a fusillade of counterstrikes. In the future, AI-invested machines may be authorized to ascertain whether a nuclear attack is underway and, if so, execute a retaliatory response.[9] As one of many future scenarios, AI can be considered an "omni-use" technology with manifold implications for war-fighting and arms control applications.[10] Already, intelligent systems are being sought after for the rapidity with which they can identify an approaching threat and their aptitude for estimating the applicable response so as to defuse that threat. As tensions between powerful states become increasingly multidimensional—including competition in the cyberspace and outer space domains—commanders and policymakers may choose to place ever-greater dependence on intelligent machines to monitor and track an adversary's activities, and even to initiate apposite counterresponses. That said, while this could engender an advantage on the battlefield, it also poses numerous concerns, particularly regarding nuclear "crisis stability."[11]

Clearly, AI is a rapidly growing field of technology with significant implications that will, according to some analysts, "revolutionize warfare by allowing military commanders to bolster or, in some cases, replace their personnel with a wide variety of 'smart' machines."[12] An important distinction to make is that, while AI can blend with traditional technologies and devices can become "smart" (such as self-driving vehicles), cyber operations can also be conducted simultaneously with kinetic operations. One example of the latter is found in the US Defense Intelligence Agency's assessment of "Iranian cyberactors" who targeted Israel Defense Forces infrastructure with a distributed denial of service attack during the Israel-Gaza conflict of 2014.[13] AI research continues to be undertaken in the areas of logistics, cyber operations, information operations, data collection and machine analysis, and command and control, and in an assortment of semiautonomous and autonomous vehicles, thereby further intensifying the intersection and crossover in a variety of sectors.[14] While AI technology could simplify autonomous operations, lead to more informed military decision making, and increase the speed and scale of military action, it may also be unpredictable or susceptible to manipulation.

Despite some policymakers and analysts arguing that the technology will have only nominal impact, others believe that AI will have at least an evolutionary—or, as indicated above, revolutionary—effect in the execution of war and violence.[15] The challenges emanating from AI development present concerns for policymakers about governance, including the role of government to implement effective oversight of AI development and the ability to attain a workable equilibrium between research and development related to AI and autonomous systems, and ethical considerations. As AI becomes more sophisticated, the role of the state in defense acquisition initiatives that enable military AI development, while balancing commercial and government funding for other-purpose AI development, will need to be considered. Moreover, the extent to which legislative or regulatory changes are necessary for the integration of military AI applications nationally, and to which global governance measures can manage AI competition globally, may require some further harmonization of measures to militate against AI technologies with lethal applications falling into the hands of nonstate actors.[16] Aside from the above points and more broadly speaking, the use of fully autonomous weapons in combat raises questions about the military's ability to comply with the laws of war and international humanitarian law (IHL), which require belligerents to distinguish between enemy combatants and protected persons and ensure military actions are necessary and proportionate. It is on this basis that opponents of such systems are seeking to negotiate a binding international ban on their deployment.

Drones: from basic infancy to broader complex roles

If AI can be perceived as the accelerating ingredient in the development of other forms of technology, then it is the increasing availability and use of drones that illustrates how technologies once considered to be limited to well-trained and well-funded militaries have gradually become cheaper and more accessible over time, and indeed are considered to be a security threat if obtained by nonstate actors.[17] Referred to by various names including remotely piloted vehicles, unmanned military systems (UMS), and by various categories of unmanned or uninhabited vehicles (UVs) such as their aerial (UAVs), surface (USVs) or underwater (UUVs) varieties,[18] or simply, drones, these applications of technology illustrate that "we are in the midst of an epochal transformation" of violence.[19] Controlled remotely from virtually anywhere on the planet, drones became weaponized devices in the military suite in the early 2000s, and since the early 2010s in particular have contributed significantly to what has been termed the further "dehumanization of death."[20]

However, practically all the "robotic" weapon systems developed and deployed at present necessitate a human operative to make strategic judgments; simply put, they are remotely operated systems or UMS rather than actual autonomous systems. The latter devices comprise UAVs such as the Predator, Reaper, and Global Hawk, which have been used widely in Afghanistan and Iraq. They are robots insofar as they do not have a pilot onboard, they typically possess the capacity to undertake autonomous movements (for example, the Reaper is capable of flying between waypoints without a human operator), and the prevalent view of robots often does not differentiate clearly between autonomous systems and remote-control machines.[21] Furthermore, in comparing high-profile drone strikes, it is evident that national legislation providing the authority for the use-of-force on a target is case by case. For example, the January 2020 US drone strike against Major-General Qasem Soleimani, commander of Iran's Islamic Revolutionary Guard Corps—Qods Force, was conducted pursuant to Congress's Authorization for Use of Military Force against Iraq Resolution of 2002. In 2019, the State Department determined this legislation could apply to Iran "as may be necessary to protect US and partner forces engaged in counterterrorism operations or operations to establish a stable, democratic Iraq," where Soleimani was ultimately targeted.[22] In contrast, an August 2021 drone strike that killed civilians, following the Taliban's takeover of Kabul and amid the US withdrawal, highlighted the difficulties associated with counterterrorism activities with limited military presence.[23] In this light, unpiloted systems widen the scope of how states may conduct military campaigns; however, the associated technologies cannot compensate for human decisions to use force, including their compliance with the principles of distinction and military necessity under IHL.

Aside from the debates surrounding the ethical and "easier" threshold in using drones in conflict, arguments pertaining to their development and increased autonomy, as advanced AI comes into the fray, have also expanded. In particular, as such innovations provide devices with the capacity to "discern" their own specific mission actions and, specifically, make lethal decisions on their own accord, so too have debates become more prevalent.[24] In fact, according to the US delegation's opening statement at a Convention on Certain Conventional Weapons (CCW) meeting,

> too often, the phrase "lethal autonomous weapons system" appears still to evoke the idea of a humanoid machine independently selecting targets for engagement and operating in a dynamic and complex urban environment. But that is a far cry from what we should be focusing on, which is the likely trajectory of technological development, not images from popular culture.[25]

Indeed, much of the extensive discourse has focused on the projections for—and ethics of—fully autonomous weapons systems, which, as the name signifies, are systems that are proficient in undertaking a role in combat with minimal, if any, human control. To clarify, it should be noted that the spectrum of human-machine autonomy has three levels. A human-controlled system that can operate on autopilot for simple tasks but requires a human to make major decisions is often referred to as having a "human in the loop." A human-supervised system that can perform all tasks autonomously but is subject to human override is said to have a "human on the loop." Finally, an unsupervised system capable of full autonomy acts with a "human out of the loop."[26]

Notwithstanding the varying delineations, it is evident that as such weapons continue to evolve out of present-day uninhabited systems to the truly autonomous kind, debates relating to the morals and ethics of war fighting and interventions will become increasingly complex.[27] Certainly, the advent and deployment of autonomous weapons systems that have the capacity to wield deadly force without the involvement of a human actor engenders a distinguishing set of ethical concerns. Particularly the extent to which they may further lower the threshold for military action, the accountability for deaths produced by these devices,[28] and the prospect that autonomous weapons could—as far fetched as this may sound now—turn against those who have designed them. An array of contemporary security theaters signifies that such weapons will continue to play an increasingly important role in future conflicts, particularly in the context of international interventions where state leaders are concerned by casualties and subsequent political fallout.

Lethal autonomous weapons systems (LAWS)

In understanding emerging technologies in the military/security domain, drones can be considered in many ways as the precursor to LAWS. As touched on above, as technology continues to expand and as the human role moves from being "in the loop" of the decision-making process (with such devices not making all the key calls) to being "on the loop" (where the human's role is overseeing operations rather than actually directing), complexities and debate will continue to emerge as the human role ultimately becomes "out of the loop."[29] As cyberconflict, AI, and software algorithms that increasingly make most of the decisions at digital speed continue to expand, the debate will remain ongoing as to where such emerging, disruptive technologies will fit in the context of current and future conflicts, interventions, international law, and considerations regarding the further "abstraction of conflict." The issue has drawn the attention of the international community, underlined by expert meetings on LAWS held by states parties to the CCW in the UN office at Geneva since 2014. While IHL mandates that the use-of-force must be proportional and circumvent indiscriminate casualties and damage to property, some have argued that "killer robots will be unable to adequately assess proportionality and precision"; that is, humane discerning decisions of proportionality of force are needed to evaluate "dynamic environments" and "require highly qualitative and subjective knowledge—just the things that robots could lack."[30] Given that international law is seemingly ill equipped to deal with the myriad of advances in such weapons technology—by the time law is adjusted for one set of technologies, a new set has emerged—the regulation of drones, let alone so-called "killer robots" in the context of complex security scenarios and warfare, as it stands, is by no means in a position to be conclusively addressed.[31]

As technology incorporating AI continues to advance, LAWS, as weapons designed to make decisions about using lethal force without manual human control or override, will present ethical, legal, diplomatic, and strategic complexities. A robot may have "autonomy" over the categories of observing, planning, and task execution (such as manipulating tools, navigating dynamic courses, and collaborating with others). The main focus when fusing AI and robotics is the attempt to maximize and operationalize its level of autonomy through learning. The degree of intelligence can be measured as the capability to "foresee the future," through planning a task, or interacting (either by manipulating or navigating) with the physical environment. While the development of a system displaying human-like intelligence is not expected in the near future, robots that can complete specific autonomous tasks, such as driving a vehicle, flying in natural and human-made environments, swimming, and carrying materials in different terrains, already exist today.[32] Not surprisingly, given the pace with which autonomy is being incorporated into research and development for robotics, international forums have intensified their calls for forms of regulation to address the future security scenarios envisaged from the proliferation of LAWS.[33]

As indicated, the international community has begun to examine the implications of LAWS via discussions held principally under the auspices of the CCW, a multilateral arms control agreement that aims to protect noncombatants from inhumane weapons of war.[34] When the CCW entered into force in December 1983, the treaty applied to combustible weapons, mines and booby traps, and weapons intended to wound through the distribution of small fragments. In more recent times, treaty states parties have proceeded to add provisions on blinding laser weapons and unexploded armaments left over after conflicts end, and more recently,[35] the CCW has been used as a platform for discussing new weapons technologies.[36] How states will react to this new area of weapons technology is still unclear, as is how states may eventually treat international law regulating such force.[37]

Cybersecurity

There continues to be a lack of international consensus on what constitutes cyberterrorism. While the term does not have a universally agreed-upon definition, it generally pertains to an attack which utilizes an electronic component (such as a computer worm, virus, or malware) to infiltrate and seriously destabilize critical infrastructure. This could encompass an attack specifically on amenities, services, and systems which, if taken offline over a protracted timeframe, would spur a serious security risk across the domains of public health, the environment, the economy, or national security. There are of course other definitions that are much wider. For example, a handbook from the US Army attributes the following definition to Kevin Coleman: "The premeditated use of disruptive activities, or the threat thereof, against computers and/or networks, with the intention to cause harm or further social, ideological, religious, political or similar objectives. Or to intimidate any person in furtherance of such objectives."[38]

Across the nonstate spectrum is a range of actors who are reliant on cyber-based technologies to support their organizational objectives. Periodically referred to as "cyber-aggressors," these actors are prepared to utilize technology as a means to wreak havoc in various domains.[39] For instance, cyberterrorists can be defined as state-sponsored or nonstate actors who participate in cyberattacks to pursue their ideology. Global terrorist organizations, insurgents, and violent extremists have utilized the web for planning attacks, radicalization and recruitment, an instrument of propaganda delivery, an avenue to convey their broader message, and overall for disruptive purposes.[40] In Australia, a cyberattack does not necessarily have to undermine or impair critical infrastructure or engender serious harm for it to be perceived as an act of terrorism. Instead, the view also includes extreme intrusive activities to any electronic system for political purposes, and the intimidation of a government or the general public. This of course diverges from other states' legal classifications of terrorism, which necessitates an attack to be executed on an *indispensable* service, facility, or system.[41]

So-called "cyberwarriors" are actors or subactors of states who develop technology and execute cyberattacks in accordance with state objectives.[42] These individuals or groups may or may not be acting on behalf of the regime regarding their target choice, time of attack, and variations of cyberattack, and in many instances are blamed by the host state when allegations are charged by the state that has been attacked.[43] The most overtly political cyberactor is the "hacktivist." These individuals undertake cyberattacks for ideological or nonmonetary reasons. Their actions can range from service-impeding or denying attacks and website vandalism, through to undermining government and commercial sector activities.[44] In contrast, "cyberthieves" engage in cyberattacks for financial gain. This is evident when an organization or individual accesses information technology systems to steal, use, or sell account information or private data, or gain access to a financial account.[45]

Overall, when unpacking the categories of cyberactors, the interconnections in intent and approaches add complexities to response options.[46] For example, a hacker could steal confidential or proprietary data used by governments or commercial entities to leverage both economic and political advantages.[47] Another cyber category is "cyberwar," which can be defined as a state-on-state action, and encompass an armed attack or use-of-force that utilizes cyberactivities that "may trigger a military response with a proportional kinetic use-of-force."[48] Further, a cyberterrorist and cyberwarrior may employ different technological capabilities in upholding a client state's security and political objectives. Some analysts even suggest that "cybercrime" has now overtaken the illicit drug trade as a source of backing for terrorist actors, "although there is some confusion as to whether a particular action should be categorized as cybercrime."[49]

Obtaining the requisite data pertaining to an actor and their capabilities and intent will continue to be a difficult task as other aberrant variables come into the mix. That, coupled with the inclination of nonstate actors to be early users of emerging technologies, which are often interdependent and contain vulnerabilities, makes for a multifaceted environment when attempting to devise and orchestrate applicable "operational responses, policies, and legislation designed to safeguard the nation's strategic economic and security interests."[50] Clearly, secure operations in networked cyberspaces—as well as the information arteries that may be connected to the internet—have become crucial for sustained global economic growth, international security, and broader stability. As an indispensable technology, the internet is susceptible to usurpation by subterranean actors, whether to spread misinformation, disrupt core infrastructure, or steal important data. Many of those malevolent activities are undertaken by actors or groups of individuals to shape public viewpoints. It is also apparent, however, that states could be leading some of the aforementioned categories of actors to undermine their adversaries. Such objectives may include employing cyber techniques for propagating distrust, incapacitating key organizations, and/or strengthening their own defenses.[51]

While encounters in the cyber domain are often viewed to sit below the level of armed conflict, it is not difficult to envisage future skirmishes in cyberspace escalating into fully-fledged war. Such scenarios cannot be considered far fetched, particularly as a cyberattack could destabilize critical infrastructure, such as an energy or financial network, or even an electoral campaign. Further, in the context of a worsening political crisis, preemptive cyberattacks against an enemy's "early-warning, communications, and command and control systems" would "significantly damag[e] its response capabilities,"[52] and may incentivize greater investments in offensively oriented (as opposed to defensive) nuclear weapons capabilities.[53] In all of these scenarios, cybersecurity, or the protection of cyberspace from clandestine attacks, has become a significant state security focus.[54] In this light, cyberspace can be considered as an area where regulatory measures that bear a resemblance to arms control mechanisms could be introduced—although explicitly referring to cyberweapons rather than nuclear or conventional munitions. This could lead, for example, to the imposition of formal legal (and cyber equivalent) mechanisms of disarming a first strike (that is, a digital attack that would impair an adversary's key information systems). This challenge has become a major concern for international policymakers, as technology continues to advance and the spillover effect from cyber to conventional or even nuclear conflict becomes a definite prospect.[55]

In 2012, US secretary of defense Leon Panetta delivered a stern caution pertaining to the perils of a "cyber-Pearl Harbor"—a digital strike that would trigger real-world death and destruction.[56] While the ensuing years have, on one level, made that warning appear to be somewhat embellished, in another sense, the caution appears in some ways insubstantial. Indeed, governments, commercial entities, and citizens alike are now confronting widespread and unyielding cyberthreats that would have been difficult to conceive a decade ago. Today, there are increased levels of risk to the already fraught challenges of security, politics, and governance. As the costs have increased, policymakers have struggled to react. One of the limitations on responding to these increased cyberthreats lies in the sheer fact that the realm of cyberspace is defined not by a binary between war and peace but by a spectrum between those two points—and most cyberattacks are situated someplace in that ambiguous zone. Additionally, approaches to counteract them have not kept pace with this evolving reality, leaving the benefit to assailants even after years of endeavor. A significant concern is the extent to which cyberattacks target the trust that underpins functioning economies, efficient governments, and steady international relations. In this regard, if trust is what is at risk, then the measures states and institutions must adopt to survive and function in this new world are distinct from anything governments have faced in the past. Clearly, policymakers have erred in failing to keep pace with cyberthreats, not having truly understood that such new forms are profoundly dissimilar from other security threats. Aside from having the potential to impact all referent objects across the security spectrum, such threats are now an intrinsic extension of the broader geopolitical arena, which necessitate, in turn, geopolitical resolutions, not narrow technical ones.[57]

Emerging technologies in the pandemic era

Unlike the more visible aspects of the pandemic such as citywide lockdowns, the COVID-related impacts to global security are only beginning to be felt. Nevertheless, two broad trends may be observed. Firstly, states have reprioritized their resources away from long-term goals into emergency response management of the respective public health and economic crises. The second trend is at the international level and concerns the relative decline of diplomacy, due in part to the cancellation of summits and informal dialogue. A common element between these trends is the greater willingness of leaders to target their engagements where they will have the greatest influence, for example, delivering an outcome in close partnerships at greater speed, outside of globally coordinated and administered programs. The specific impact on efforts to address the proliferation of emerging technologies has been inaction on enacting timely regulations, while the risks associated with such technologies continue to advance apace.

The reprioritization of national resources to address the economic impacts of the COVID-19 pandemic will constrain the fiscal policy options of governments for a generation and is likely to flow through to reduced resourcing for global disarmament efforts. As the International Labour Organization estimates, the number of working hours lost in 2020 was four times greater than during the 2009 global financial crisis; half of these working-hour losses were due to reductions within employment, while shifts to unemployment or inactive employment accounted for the other half.[58] Central banks, unable to stimulate further economic activity due to already low interest rates, turned to unconventional monetary policies such as government and corporate bond purchases. Despite these unprecedented conditions, worldwide economic growth fell only by 3.2 percent in 2020, less than some initial forecasts. This is partially because governments adopted fiscal policies to stimulate their economic recoveries.[59] The International Monetary Fund estimates that most of these measures, costing $16.9 trillion, expired at the end of 2021. For government debt to return to prepandemic levels by 2045, the average primary surplus (achieved when governmental income is greater than spending, excluding interest paid on debt) needs to be higher than the prepandemic decade by 0.5 percent of GDP for advanced economies and 1 percent of GDP for emerging markets.[60] Although these figures are cautious forecasts, an implication is that government borrowing and spending could be constrained for at least another generation, which in some cases may lead to austerity or fewer contributions toward global cooperation and security efforts.

The waning appetite for investing in multilateral initiatives not connected with the health or economic emergencies is already observable in budget cuts to the core programs of the United Nations. In October 2020, Secretary-General António Guterres proposed a 2.8 percent reduction in the proposed annual budget for the UN Secretariat in 2021, compared to 2020. Guterres advised the General Assembly: "We are being forced to operate not on the basis of strategic direction, but rather on the availability of cash, which undermines mandate implementation."[61] In his address, Guterres also referred to specific impacts to diplomacy from the COVID-19 pandemic, such as limitations on technology which prevented interpretation for official meetings held online. Indeed, some issues not connected with pandemic response were even put on hold. According to the nongovernmental organization Reaching Critical Will, in a stocktake in February 2021 of certain meetings related to disarmament and arms control, around one year into the pandemic four international meetings had been held, four events had been canceled, six postponed indefinitely, and six deferred.[62] As a consequence of such disruptions, governments will need to invest further resources to mitigate the insecurities that have emerged or increased during the pandemic period.

Many diplomatic efforts ceased or were reduced in scale, as highlighted by the UN's *Disarmament Yearbook* for the year 2020. Unfortunately, some work was not conducted: due to the cancellation of thematic debate, states did not issue a joint statement to the General Assembly on the humanitarian impacts of explosive weapons in populated areas, "marking a departure from the previous two years."[63] Furthermore, a high-profile event on gender dimensions, due to be held on the margins during the review conference of the Nuclear Non-Proliferation Treaty, was canceled.[64] The participating states of the Wassenaar Arrangement on Export Controls for Conventional Arms and Dual-Use Goods and Technologies agreed the existing export control lists would remain unchanged, with "no opportunity" to "undertake their in-depth technical review" of additional technologies with the potential to be subjected to transfer restrictions.[65] In contrast, some forums moved to an online format. For example, the plenary meeting of the Australia Group, which comprises forty-two states and the European Union and seeks to harmonize export controls on chemical and biological weapons, was canceled with discussions held via virtual meetings of its technical subgroups.[66] In addition, the 1540 Committee, established pursuant to UN Security Council Resolution 1540 on the proliferation of nuclear, chemical, and biological weapons and their delivery, postponed events for its next comprehensive review, moving to an online format instead.[67] Also, the Nuclear Suppliers Group, which includes forty-nine states and the European Commission, canceled its annual meeting, and moved to remote consultation.[68] Moreover, the sixth conference of states parties to the Arms Trade Treaty was conducted through written procedure on an exceptional basis.[69]

These examples pertain to some of the international arms control groupings which delivered outcomes at a reduced capacity in the first year of the pandemic, with further cumulative and legacy impacts likely to be forthcoming. While the responses to canceling or deferring these activities or holding them in an alternative format were varied, it is evident that progress on addressing these issues was impacted by public health restrictions in response to COVID-19, including travel restrictions. While the timeframe is currently unknown, the above groupings will foreseeably continue to collaborate with a reduced output until the end of the pandemic. In late 2021, less than half of the world's population had completed their primary vaccination series,[70] and national authorizations for vaccine booster programs were only starting to commence.[71] Until the severity of the coronavirus disease is mitigated, such disruptions may persist—perhaps for years. This presents challenges related to protocols for diplomatic and security-focused engagements, where it is evident states have had different approaches to how they should be represented at meetings that cannot be held under ordinary circumstances.

As indicated above, from the onset of the pandemic, various arms control and disarmament efforts were canceled or worked around via online formats, with participants unable to meet in person. These changes are a timely reminder that "diplomacy"—defined as "the management of relations between independent states by the process of negotiations"[72]—requires state actors to consent to certain conditions before they engage in dialogue with their counterparts. In other words, if a state contests the viability of protocols for conducting diplomacy, discussions may not proceed on substantive matters. As an example, Russia's advance copy letter "The Position on the Status of Meetings in 2020" exemplifies how states have sought to block discussions on conventional weapons, including LAWS. In its letter, Russia lamented the "absence of common understanding" on arrangements for meetings not held in person or "hybrid" format, asserting that its right to representation was governed by the CCW Rules of Procedure. Moscow reiterated its "persistent objections" to the "strong restrictions upon the work of the delegations including upon their presence in the meeting room." Here, the primary consideration of the Russian Federation pertained to abrogation of a decade-long precedent, namely, the "violation of the principle of consensus which is fundamental to the work within the CCW including the [Group of Governmental Experts] on LAWS."[73] Because Russia did not participate in the September 2020 meeting on LAWS, it asserted the meeting would have "no official status," and "no procedural or legal implications whatsoever," and considered that the allocation of funding to hold the meeting was "unjustified" and "impossible" without unanimous approval,[74] which arguably invalidated the outcome.

Through this weaponization of the diplomatic rules of procedure, provocative tone and use of rhetoric, Moscow's paper on the status of CCW meetings served as a warning to other states that, when protocols are no longer reciprocal, the consensus-making approach to multilateral diplomacy loses viability. Human Rights Watch (HRW), a nongovernmental organization that cofounded the Campaign to Stop Killer Robots, assessed that Russia's objections ultimately led to the last-minute postponement of further discussions that had been scheduled to be held in November 2020, thereby compressing the timeframe between the next meetings in April and August 2021, and the milestone Sixth Review Conference scheduled for December 2021, considered to be "the deadline for action on this urgent issue."[75] Following the review conference, HRW asserted that the consensus model of the CCW had prevented negotiation on regulatory proposals and called for an "independent process, as was used for the treaties banning antipersonnel landmines and cluster munitions,"[76] to work toward a treaty on LAWS outside of the CCW's consensus-based approach.

While certainly not the first international conference to end in disappointment for civil society and activist groups, this recent experience with the CCW may offer lessons for the new age of digital diplomacy, which extends to the various groupings on arms control and disarmament noted above such as those concerning weapons of mass destruction or export controls. Throughout the duration of the COVID pandemic, facilitators of international conferences may benefit from standardizing their protocols for online or hybrid meeting formats. While specific bodies may require a tailored format to fulfil their mandate, the harmonization of digital diplomatic arrangements during the COVID-19 period should allow states to focus greater attention on the content of their deliberations, instead of the arrangements for how such discussions ought to be conducted. Moreover, states will likely have fewer resources to invest in holding these activities due to long-term budgetary impacts from their fiscal policies of the early 2020s, meaning that greater coordination on multipurpose applications could provide savings over the long term. While policymakers were already behind the rapid pace of development of emerging technologies before the onset of the pandemic, the reduction of activities since then has placed further strain on the international community's capacity to regulate the proliferation of such technologies.

Conclusion

During World War I, developments in chemical processing were employed to create lethal gases for war-fighting use, producing enormous fatalities and horrific injuries. In the war's wake, appalled societies pressed representatives to sign the Geneva Protocol of 1925, banning the use in war of asphyxiating, toxic, and other deadly gases. World War II saw the catastrophic application of nuclear weapons to conflict, and many postwar diplomatic forums concentrated on attempts to thwart the spread and use of atomic armaments. As this chapter has illustrated, an emerging suite of technologies—artificial intelligence (AI), lethal autonomous weapons, uninhabited vehicles, and cybertechnology, among others—are being cultivated for military use, with potentially wideranging and devastating outcomes.[77] The underpinnings of global security and power are different today, as the capacity to construct and use new proprietary technologies has become the contested source of economic strength and military security. Access to technology and the capability to transform and redefine new technologies have become the foundation of information age power.

It would be remiss not to briefly discuss the extent to which the fifth generation of mobile network technologies, known as "5G"—promising superior speed, security, and capacity—underlies the global economy and supports the pillars for the next generation of digital technologies. As such, it is hardly surprising that there is an intense global race among corporations and states for 5G positioning, as it will decide the route the internet will take and where states will encounter new risks and greater susceptibilities. Who creates and controls the 5G technological space will markedly redefine a progressively competitive technological world, as choices made today will have national security and economic performance ramifications in the short to distant future. While this is a contest among corporations (and groupings of corporations), it is also a battle between market-based and state-directed policymaking and strategy. Specifically, in the great power political domain, the United States remains inextricably linked to the former and China to the latter. As the recent experience of the United Kingdom has illustrated, it takes years to untangle internet infrastructure.[78] Meanwhile, vendors are already establishing tech coalitions to begin research on 6G, indicating that the polarization of internet architecture may continue into the 2030s.[79]

More concerning is that global governance efforts and applicable diplomatic mechanisms to curb the proliferation of emerging technologies for weapons use are evidently not keeping pace with the advent of such new, possibly equally destructive, technologies—particularly in this pandemic "threat multiplying" age. As discussed above, the last several years have seen the swift expansion of discussions on lethal autonomous weapons systems (LAWS). Given their envisaged capacity to intensify conflicts and perpetrate substantial collateral destruction, debates pertaining to restricting the application of autonomy in weapons systems, or even banning fully autonomous systems, have come to the fore.[80] Evidently it has been difficult to come up with a coherent and balanced set of solutions to the problems posed by emerging technologies. While export controls, as an example, are not faultless mechanisms for regulating the propagation of dual-use technologies, they nonetheless provide some level of mitigation. In this regard, controls and regulations to thwart the spread of emerging technologies should more astutely be viewed as "intersecting filters." That is, by assembling adequate filters, as well as sufficient limitations on procurement, states can increase the "cost of entry" to malevolent actors. Applying controls on certain emerging technologies will necessitate cautious deliberation and discussion, but effective controls can assist with decreasing the near-term risk that adversarial actors could use such technology for nefarious ends,[81] while laying groundwork for more comprehensive regulations to become adopted.

Fully comprehending the implications of the emerging technologies for warfare and arms control and formulating efficient processes for their management is a massive mission that will entail the ongoing efforts of many analysts and policymakers around the globe. In more frank terms, the need to provide guardrails for disruptive emerging technologies and their war-fighting and arms control applications—AI, autonomous weaponry, uninhabited vehicles, and cyberwarfare—as they transition into military systems, presents urgent challenges for global security.[82] As the weaponization of critical technologies continues, it will be important to reconsider how current protocols and models may be utilized as the foundation for additional methods envisioned to regulate entirely novel types of armaments. Addressing the weaponization of AI, for example, will prove extraordinarily complicated because regulating something as fundamentally insubstantial as algorithms will resist the exact classification and stockpile oversight elements of most current control procedures. Many of the other emerging technologies discussed above traverse the gap between conventional and nuclear armaments and will present an entirely different type of regulatory difficulty. Responding to these challenges will be complex, especially when considering the insecurities that have arisen since the outbreak of the COVID-19 pandemic and the relative decline of multilateral institutions. But just as preceding representatives, policymakers, and civil society defined ways of regulating technologies in years gone by, so too will current and future actors be required to design innovative solutions[83] to new threats emanating from today's emerging and disruptive technologies.

Notes

1. "Forging a Vision for Security in a New Age of Disruptive Technopolitics," University of Waikato, September 21, 2018, https://www.waikato.ac.nz/news-opinion/media/2018/forging-a-vision-for-security-in-a-new-age-of-disruptive-techno-politics (accessed February 25, 2022). See also Reuben Steff, Joe Burton, and Simona R. Soare, "Introduction: Machines, the State, and War," in *Emerging Technologies and International Security: Machines, the State, and War*, ed. Reuben Steff, Joe Burton, and Simona R. Soare (Abingdon, England: Routledge, 2021), 1.
2. "Forging a Vision"; Steff et al., "Introduction."
3. Michael T. Klare, "The Challenges of Emerging Technologies," *Arms Control Today*, December 2018, http://web.archive.org/web/20211016053559/https://www.armscontrol.org/act/2018-12/features/challenges-emerging-technologies (accessed April 13, 2022).
4. Stewart Patrick, "When the System Fails: COVID-19 and the Costs of Global Dysfunction," *Foreign Affairs*, July/August 2020, https://www.foreignaffairs.com/articles/world/2020-06-09/when-system-fails (accessed February 25, 2022).
5. Ulrike Franke and Paola Sartori, "Machine Politics: Europe and the AI Revolution," Policy Brief, European Council on Foreign Relations, 2019, 4, http://web.archive.org/web/20211016054134/https://ecfr.eu/wp-content/uploads/machine_politics_europe_and_the_ai_revolution.pdf (accessed April 13, 2022).
6. Ibid.

7. Klare, “The Challenges of Emerging Technologies.”
8. Heather M. Roff and Alex Woodson, “Making AI Work, Ethically & Responsibly, with Heather M. Roff,” Carnegie Council for Ethics in International Affairs, October 7, 2019, http://web.archive.org/web/20211016055159/https://www.carnegiecouncil.org/studio/multimedia/20191007-making-ai-work-ethically-responsibly-heather-roff (accessed April 13, 2022).
9. For discussion of such scenarios, see Edward Geist and Andrew J. Lohn, *How Might Artificial Intelligence Affect the Risk of Nuclear War?* (Santa Monica, CA: RAND, 2018).
10. Klare, “The Challenges of Emerging Technologies.”
11. Ibid. See also James Johnson, “Inadvertent Escalation in the Age of Intelligence Machines: A New Model for Nuclear Risk in the Digital Age,” *European Journal of International Security* (2021), https://doi.org/10.1017/eis.2021.23 (accessed February 25, 2022).
12. Klare, “The Challenges of Emerging Technologies.”
13. Defense Intelligence Agency, *Iran Military Power: Ensuring Regime Survival and Securing Regional Dominance* (Washington, DC: US Government Publishing Office, 2019), 36, http://web.archive.org/web/20211016061759/https://www.dia.mil/Portals/27/Documents/News/Military%20Power%20Publications/Iran_Military_Power_LR.pdf (accessed April 13, 2022).
14. Kelley M. Sayler, “Artificial Intelligence and National Security,” Congressional Research Service, November 10, 2020, http://web.archive.org/web/20211222091026/https://crsreports.congress.gov/product/pdf/R/R45178 (accessed April 13, 2022).
15. Ibid.
16. Ibid.
17. Aiden Warren and Alek Hillas, “Lethal Autonomous Robotics: Rethinking the Dehumanization of Warfare,” *UCLA Journal of International Law and Foreign Affairs* 22, no. 2 (2018): 226.
18. The names of other varieties of UVs can refer to their size. For example, “extra-large unmanned undersea vehicles” (XLUUVs) are defined as having a diameter of more than 84 inches (213 centimeters), which exceeds the size of large-diameter vertical launch tubes; XLUUVs are too large to be launched from human-occupied navy submarines. Ronald O’Rourke, “Navy Large Unmanned Surface and Undersea Vehicles: Background and Issues for Congress,” Congressional Research Service, October 20, 2021, 1, 15, http://web.archive.org/web/20211026062620/https://crsreports.congress.gov/product/pdf/R/R45757/43 (accessed April 13, 2022).
19. Andrew A. Latham and James Christenson, “Historicizing the ‘New Wars’: The Case of *Jihad* in the Early Years of Islam,” *European Journal of International Relations* 20, no. 3 (2014): 767.
20. Bradley Jay Strawser, “Introduction: The Moral Landscape of Unmanned Weapons,” in *Killing by Remote Control: The Ethics of an Unmanned*

Military, ed. Bradley Jay Strawser (New York: Oxford University Press, 2013), 3.

21. David Whetham, "Drones and Targeted Killing: Angels or Assassins?" in *Killing by Remote Control: The Ethics of an Unmanned Military*, ed. Bradley Jay Strawser (New York: Oxford University Press, 2013), 69–83.
22. State Department, quoted in Clayton Thomas et al., "US Killing of Qasem Soleimani: Frequently Asked Questions," Congressional Research Service, January 13, 2020, 14, http://web.archive.org/web/20211026072435/https://crsreports.congress.gov/product/pdf/R/R46148/3 (accessed April 13, 2022).
23. Clayton Thomas, "Taliban Government in Afghanistan: Background and Issues for Congress," Congressional Research Service, November 2, 2021, 18, http://web.archive.org/web/20211222103338/https://crsreports.congress.gov/product/pdf/R/R46955; Clayton Thomas et al., "US Military Withdrawal and Taliban Takeover in Afghanistan: Frequently Asked Questions," Congressional Research Service, September 17, 2021, 27, http://web.archive.org/web/20211222103536/https://crsreports.congress.gov/product/pdf/R/R46879 (both accessed April 13, 2022).
24. Strawser, "Introduction," 16.
25. US Mission Geneva, "US Delegation Opening Statement at CCW Informal Experts Meeting on Lethal Autonomous Weapons Systems," US Mission to International Organizations in Geneva, May 13, 2014, http://web.archive.org/web/20211221093159/https://geneva.usmission.gov/2014/05/13/u-s-delegation-opening-statement-at-ccw-informal-experts-meeting-on-lethal-autonomous-weapons-systems/ (accessed April 13, 2022).
26. Nils Melzer, *Human Rights Implications of the Usage of Drones and Unmanned Robots in Warfare* (Brussels: European Parliament, 2013), 6, http://web.archive.org/web/20211221092605/https://www.europarl.europa.eu/RegData/etudes/etudes/join/2013/410220/EXPO-DROI_ET%282013%29410220_EN.pdf (accessed April 13, 2022).
27. Strawser, "Introduction," 16.
28. Robert Sparrow, "Killer Robots," *Journal of Applied Philosophy* 24, no. 1 (2007): 62–77; Gary E. Marchant et al., "International Governance of Autonomous Military Robots," *Columbia Science and Technology Law Review* 12 (2011): 272–315; Noel Sharkey, "Cassandra or False Prophet of Doom: AI Robots and War," *IEEE Intelligent Systems* 23, no. 4 (2008): 14–17; Peter M. Asaro, "How Just Could a Robot War Be?" in *Current Issues in Computing and Philosophy*, ed. Adam Briggle, Katrina Waelbers, and Philip A. E. Brey (Amsterdam: IOS Press, 2008), 50–64.
29. Melzer, *Human Rights Implications*, 6.
30. Denise Garcia, "The Case against Killer Robots: Why the United States Should Ban Them," *Foreign Affairs*, May 10, 2014, http://www.foreignaffairs.com/articles/141407/denise-garcia/the-case-against-killer-robots (accessed February 25, 2022).

31. Aiden Warren, "Regulating the Abstraction of Violence: Interventions and the Deployment of New Technologies Globally," in *Rethinking Humanitarian Intervention in the 21st Century*, ed. Aiden Warren and Damian Grenfell (Edinburgh: Edinburgh University Press, 2017), 216–44.
32. Javier Andreu-Perez et al., *Artificial Intelligence and Robotics* (London: UK-RAS Network, 2018), 24.
33. Aiden Warren and Ingvild Bode, "Altering the Playing Field: The US Redefinition of the Use-of-Force," *Contemporary Security Policy* 36, no. 2 (2015): 174–99.
34. Kelley M. Sayler, "International Discussions Concerning Lethal Autonomous Weapon Systems," Congressional Research Service, April 19, 2021, http://web.archive.org/web/20211221101534/https://crsreports.congress.gov/product/pdf/IF/IF11294/4 (accessed April 13, 2022).
35. "Convention on Certain Conventional Weapons (CCW) at a Glance," Arms Control Association, September 2017, http://web.archive.org/web/20211221101926/https://www.armscontrol.org/factsheets/CCW (accessed April 13, 2022).
36. Sayler, "International Discussions."
37. Warren and Bode, "Altering the Playing Field."
38. *Cyber Operations and Cyber Terrorism*, DCSINT Handbook No. 1.02, US Army Training & Doctrine Command, August 15, 2005, II-2, http://web.archive.org/web/20211221105116/https://apps.dtic.mil/sti/pdfs/ADA439217.pdf; see also Catherine A. Theohary and John W. Rollins, "Cyberwarfare and Cyberterrorism: In Brief," Congressional Research Service, March 27, 2015, http://web.archive.org/web/20211222074425/https://crsreports.congress.gov/product/pdf/R/R43955 (both accessed April 13, 2022).
39. Keiran Hardy, "Is Cyberterrorism a Threat?" *Australian Outlook*, February 20, 2017, http://web.archive.org/web/20211222071856/https://www.internationalaffairs.org.au/australianoutlook/is-cyber-terrorism-a-threat/ (accessed April 13, 2022).
40. For additional information, see John Rollins and Clay Wilson, "Terrorist Capabilities for Cyberattack: Overview and Policy Issues," Congressional Research Service, January 22, 2007, http://web.archive.org/web/20211222072626/https://crsreports.congress.gov/product/pdf/RL/RL33123 (accessed April 13, 2022).
41. Hardy, "Is Cyberterrorism a Threat?"
42. For additional information, see Catherine A. Theohary, "Cyber Operations in DOD Policy and Plans: Issues for Congress," Congressional Research Service, January 5, 2015, http://web.archive.org/web/20211222072848/https://crsreports.congress.gov/product/pdf/R/R43848 (accessed April 13, 2022).
43. Theohary and Rollins, "Cyberwarfare and Cyberterrorism," 3.
44. Ibid.
45. For discussions of federal US law and issues relating to cybercrime, see Charles Doyle, "Cybercrime: An Overview of the Federal Computer

Fraud and Abuse Statute and Related Federal Criminal Laws," Congressional Research Service, October 15, 2014, http://web.archive.org/web/20211222074553/https://crsreports.congress.gov/product/pdf/RL/97-1025; Kristin M. Finklea, "The Interplay of Borders, Turf, Cyberspace, and Jurisdiction: Issues Confronting US Law Enforcement," Congressional Research Service, January 17, 2013, http://web.archive.org/web/20211222074843/https://crsreports.congress.gov/product/pdf/R/R41927 (both accessed April 13, 2022).

46. Theohary and Rollins, "Cyberwarfare and Cyberterrorism."
47. Shawn Henry, "Responding to the Cyber Threat," speech given at the Information Systems Security Association International Conference, Baltimore, MD, October 20, 2011, transcript available at http://web.archive.org/web/20211222085654/https://archives.fbi.gov/archives/news/speeches/responding-to-the-cyber-threat (accessed April 13, 2022).
48. Theohary and Rollins, "Cyberwarfare and Cyberterrorism," 1.
49. Ibid., 3; see also Lillian Ablon, Martin C. Libicki, and Andrea A. Golay, *Markets for Cybercrime Tools and Stolen Data: Hackers' Bazaar* (Santa Monica, CA: RAND, 2014). For more information on cybercrime definitions, see Kristin Finklea and Catherine A. Theohary, "Cybercrime: Conceptual Issues for Congress and US Law Enforcement," Congressional Research Service, January 15, 2015, http://web.archive.org/web/20211222090222/https://crsreports.congress.gov/product/pdf/R/R42547 (accessed April 13, 2022).
50. Hardy, "Is Cyberterrorism a Threat?"
51. Klare, "The Challenges of Emerging Technologies."
52. Ibid.
53. Andrew Futter, "The Dangers of Using Cyberattacks to Counter Nuclear Threats," *Arms Control Today* July/August 2016, http://web.archive.org/web/20211222091743/https://www.armscontrol.org/act/2016-07/features/dangers-using-cyberattacks-counter-nuclear-threats (accessed April 13, 2022).
54. For more on cyberwarfare and cybersecurity, see Chris Jaikaran et al., "Cybersecurity: Selected Issues for the 115th Congress," Congressional Research Service, March 9, 2018, http://web.archive.org/web/20211222092022/https://crsreports.congress.gov/product/pdf/R/R45127 (accessed April 13, 2022).
55. David Elliott, "Weighing the Case for a Convention to Limit Cyberwarfare," *Arms Control Today*, November 2009, http://web.archive.org/web/20211222092445/https://www.armscontrol.org/act/2009-11/weighing-case-convention-limit-cyberwarfare (accessed April 13, 2022).
56. Elisabeth Bumiller and Thom Shanker, "Panetta Warns of Dire Threat of Cyberattack on US," *New York Times*, October 11, 2012, https://www.nytimes.com/2012/10/12/world/panetta-warns-of-dire-threat-of-cyberattack.html (accessed February 25, 2022).

57. Daniel Kurtz-Phelan, “War and Peace in the Cyber Age: Governments, Businesses, and Citizens Alike Now Face Pervasive and Unrelenting Cyberthreats,” *Foreign Affairs*, January/February 2022, http://web.archive.org/web/20220110080133/https://www.foreignaffairs.com/issue-packages/2021-12-14/digital-disorder (accessed April 13, 2022).
58. “ILO Monitor: COVID-19 and the World of Work,” 7th edn., International Labour Organization, January 25, 2021, http://web.archive.org/web/20211215091611/https://www.ilo.org/wcmsp5/groups/public/@dgreports/@dcomm/documents/briefingnote/wcms_767028.pdf (accessed April 13, 2022).
59. James K. Jackson et al., “Global Economic Effects of COVID-19,” Congressional Research Service, November 10, 2021), i, 36–7, 63, http://web.archive.org/web/20211214093530/https://crsreports.congress.gov/product/pdf/R/R46270 (accessed April 13, 2022).
60. International Monetary Fund, *Fiscal Monitor: Strengthening the Credibility of Public Finances* (Washington, DC: International Monetary Fund, 2021), 1, 19, https://www.imf.org/-/media/Files/Publications/fiscal-monitor/2021/October/English/text.ashx (accessed February 28, 2022).
61. António Guterres, “Secretary-General’s Remarks to the Fifth Committee: Introduction of the Proposed Programme Budget for 2021 [as delivered],” United Nations Secretary-General, October 12, 2020, http://web.archive.org/web/20211214085503/https://www.un.org/sg/en/content/sg/statement/2020-10-12/secretary-generals-remarks-the-fifth-committee-introduction-of-the-proposed-programme-budget-for-2021-delivered (accessed April 13, 2022).
62. “COVID-19: Up-to-Date List of Postponed or Cancelled Disarmament and Arms Control Meetings,” Reaching Critical Will, February 1, 2021, http://web.archive.org/web/20211107015057/https://www.reachingcriticalwill.org/news/latest-news/14666-covid-19-up-to-date-list-of-postponed-or-cancelled-disarmament-and-arms-control-meetings (accessed April 13, 2022).
63. *United Nations Disarmament Yearbook*, Vol. 45, Part II: 2020 (New York: United Nations, 2021), 101, http://web.archive.org/web/20211209074016/https://front.un-arm.org/wp-content/uploads/2021/10/en-yb-vol-45-2020-part2_rev-1.pdf (accessed April 13, 2022).
64. Ibid., 225.
65. Ibid., 105.
66. Ibid., 71.
67. Ibid., 195.
68. Ibid., 41.
69. Ibid., 77–8.
70. World Health Organization, “WHO Coronavirus (COVID-19) Dashboard: Data Table,” December 19, 2021, http://web.archive.org/web/20211219003041/https://covid19.who.int/table/ (accessed February 28, 2022).

71. Claire Parker and Bryan Pietsch, "Countries around the World are Debating Coronavirus Booster Shots. Here's Where They've Been Approved," *Washington Post*, November 16, 2021, https://www.washingtonpost.com/world/2021/11/12/coronavirus-vaccine-boosters-global/ (accessed February 28, 2022).
72. Harold Nicolson, cited in Joseph M. Siracusa, *Diplomacy: A Very Short Introduction* (New York: Oxford University Press, 2010), xiii.
73. Russian Federation, "The Position on the Status of Meetings in 2020," Convention on Certain Conventional Weapons—Meeting of High Contracting Parties, CCW/2020/2, April 13, 2021, 1, http://web.archive.org/web/20211107012815/https://documents.unoda.org/wp-content/uploads/2021/04/CCW-2020-2-Advance-copy.pdf (accessed April 13, 2022).
74. Ibid., 1–3.
75. "Areas of Alignment: Common Visions for a Killer Robots Treaty," Human Rights Watch and Harvard Law School International Human Rights Clinic, July 2021, 1–2, http://web.archive.org/web/20211220081812/https://www.hrw.org/sites/default/files/media_2021/07/07.2021%20Areas%20of%20Alignment.pdf (accessed April 13, 2022).
76. "Killer Robots: Military Powers Stymie Ban," Human Rights Watch, December 20, 2021, http://web.archive.org/web/20211220090749/https://www.hrw.org/news/2021/12/19/killer-robots-military-powers-stymie-ban (accessed April 13, 2022).
77. Klare, "The Challenges of Emerging Technologies."
78. Leo Kelion, "Huawei 5G Kit Must Be Removed from UK by 2027," BBC News, July 14, 2020, http://web.archive.org/web/20220105050109/https://www.bbc.com/news/technology-53403793 (accessed April 13, 2022).
79. Samuel Yang, "China Claims It's Leading the Way in 6G Mobile Tech Research, But the Reality Is Still Years Away," ABC News (Australia), June 22, 2021, http://web.archive.org/web/20220105051653/https://www.abc.net.au/news/2021-06-22/china-claims-its-lead-in-the-global-5g-rollout-and-6g-research/100165362 (accessed April 13, 2022).
80. Philip Chertoff, "Perils of Lethal Autonomous Weapons Systems Proliferation: Preventing Non-State Acquisition," Geneva Centre for Security Policy, October 2018, http://web.archive.org/web/20200103221102/https://dam.gcsp.ch/files/2y10RR5E5mmEpZE4rnkLPZwUleGsxaWXTH3aoibziMaV0JJrWCxFyxXGS (accessed April 13, 2022).
81. Ibid.
82. Klare, "The Challenges of Emerging Technologies."
83. Ibid.

13

Cybersecurity: Emerging Threats

Jennifer S. Hunt

Introduction

Cyber has become the connective tissue through critical state, economic, and social systems. As the newest domain, cyberspace encompasses a vast threat landscape and is characterized by a rapid evolution of tactics and techniques. Cyber incidents, involving both state and nonstate actors with differing motivations, have become "more expensive, more disruptive and in many cases more political and strategic."[1] The disruption of the information technology that underpins modern systems—whether through malicious intrusion or through data manipulation—constitutes an evolving security challenge. In 2021, a water treatment plant in Florida was hacked through remote access and the sodium hydroxide mix remotely changed to dangerous levels before being caught and reversed in real time by the plant operator.[2] It follows high-profile attacks against state agencies, industries, and critical infrastructure such as hospitals and electoral systems, with the increasing sophistication and severity of cyberattacks elevating cybersecurity on the national security and popular agenda.[3] While cybersecurity was once considered a technical issue focusing on CIA (confidentiality, integrity, and availability) of information systems, the field now encompasses social scientists, national security strategists and other professionals who approach cybersecurity from multiple directions.

What does the threat landscape look like in the immediate post-pandemic era? This chapter examines the role of COVID-19 in accelerating two cybersecurity trends. The first is the targeting of critical infrastructure. While critical infrastructure has traditionally been conceived as comprising public utilities, government agencies, and strategic industries, the pandemic has expanded the list of valuable targets to encompass public health infrastructure. This follows the previous expansion of critical infrastructure to include electoral systems in the wake of cyberattacks in 2016. During COVID-19, hospitals, research centers, and related industries were targeted by ransomware demands, exfiltration of sensitive data, and cyberscam operations. As businesses rapidly shifted to online operations, state and nonstate actors took advantage of weaker security protocols and the proliferation of remote work-from-home devices to infiltrate systems.

The second cybersecurity trend is the use of cyber-enabled disinformation, the latest evolution of cyberattacks in the information ecosystem. Malicious actors leveraging the connectivity of modern communication systems use deliberately false or misleading information to undermine collective action, undercut state response, and damage social cohesion. These tactics, referred to as active measures, seek to create general distrust or confusion over information sources by blurring the lines between fact and fiction, to exacerbate divisive political fissures, to undermine citizen confidence in democratic governance, and to erode trust between citizens and elected officials and their institutions. In information warfare for the digital age, active measures peddled pandemic disinformation designed to undermine collective mitigation efforts against a virus that contributed to excess deaths of more than twenty million worldwide as of February 2022.[4]

These two trends represent two different types: attacks that exploit the *technical vulnerabilities* of the systems, and attacks that leverage its *technical virtues.*[5] While vulnerabilities include loopholes to gain unauthorized access, virtues include the connectivity, speed, and reach of social media, which now constitutes the global information commons. These online mediums, operating as designed to boost connection and virality, constitute a potent weapon in information warfare, as hostile foreign actors seek to weaken adversaries from within through social fracturing, disorder, and a breakdown in trust between government and citizens. The pandemic both facilitated and demonstrated the immediate impacts of both types of cyberattacks. These trends, whether for great power, competition or profit, represent a strategic challenge to democracies. This chapter examines the state of cybersecurity during the COVID-19 pandemic, including the evolution of cyberattacks and implications for national security.

The newest domain

Cyberspace is the newest domain in the security realm. Alongside land, sea, and air, cyberspace is an arena of conflict as well as commerce and connection. Unlike other domains, it is "man-made" and thus encompasses both physical and virtual spaces. Cyberspace is also characterized by asymmetric power dynamics that disrupt traditional levers of influence. The technological innovation and capital investment that served as prerequisites for great power superiority in traditional domains are upended in cyberspace. Individuals or small groups with relevant skills and a few rubles can disrupt critical infrastructure thousands of kilometers away. With lowered barriers to entry, cyber is characterized by the ability to cross vast distances remotely and at relatively low cost, creating both opportunities and risks. These vulnerabilities can be traced to cyber's very inception, starting with ARPANET in the 1960s. Myriam Dunn Cavelty argues that these systems were not designed with security in mind, and that this legacy, combined with rapid growth of the network and its commercialization, makes computer networks "inherently insecure."[6]

Cybersecurity discourse has mainly focused on technical controls and defense-in-depth measures, a law enforcement discourse around cybercrime, an intelligence focus on cyberespionage, and a broader strategic narrative around critical infrastructure and state power. Paramount is the protection of assets from unauthorized access, disclosure or manipulation. However, the referent object to be protected has steadily expanded: from the corporate entity, to the consumer (particularly from a privacy lens), to a state or society as a whole. Security protocols have expanded to recognize classified networks, utilities, supply chains, electoral systems, and research infrastructure. The newest iteration of cyberattacks threatens the integrity of the global information commons itself. Cyber-enabled disinformation constitutes a form of information warfare as it seeks to influence decision making by hacking minds as well as machines.

Security in cyberspace thus encompasses a vast threat landscape, involving both state and nonstate actors with differing motivations and tactics. The COVID-19 pandemic has expanded the list of vulnerable and valuable targets for financially and politically motivated malicious agents. At the same time, the rapid proliferation of remote work, access devices, and online information spaces has multiplied the potential vectors of attack against both states and communities. This chapter focuses on the twin challenges of cyberattacks against critical infrastructure and cyber-enabled disinformation, and the overlaps between them as demonstrated by the pandemic. The United States constitutes the main case study, both as an early global hotspot of the pandemic, and a target of both types of attacks. Moreover, as the United States is the home of technological platforms through which cyber-enabled disinformation travels, the impacts are global. The challenges examined are thus not limited to the United States and will likely manifest in various countries to varying degrees. Several dynamics detailed herein will likely outlive the virus itself, such as weakened democratic resilience, politicized institutions, and diminished trust in scientific communities. Thus, these challenges are explored with a view toward their durability and endurance both temporally and geographically.

Exploiting technical vulnerabilities

Cyberattacks leverage opportunities and crises, and the pandemic was no exception. Existing tools such as malware, ransomware, and spear phishing campaigns were adapted with COVID-19 lures for financial gain, while politically motivated cyberespionage and data exfiltration efforts targeted critical infrastructure including medical and research facilities. This section reviews the categories of cyberattacks during the pandemic, their implications, and possibilities for future exploitation.

Within the first two months of the pandemic in 2020, more than 4,000 new coronavirus-related domains were registered and these new sites were twice as likely to be malicious than other sites.[7] By May 2020, this number had ballooned to almost 20,000 new coronavirus-related domains.[8] In an example of the reach and scale of these new sites, Microsoft would later seek legal action against some of these COVID-19-themed domains on behalf of victims in sixty-two countries.[9] Scammers created spoof websites posing as health authorities or financial institutions advertising COVID-19 relief programs, gained access through fake mobile contact tracing apps, and took advantage of shortages to sell PPE and testing kits, and peddle fake cures. Entire states were the target of scams and wire fraud.[10] In April 2020, a US man tried to "sell" fifty million N95 respirator masks to a state government in Australia. The New South Wales authorities wired nearly USD$317 million in funds to complete the purchase when US authorities intercepted the transaction.[11]

Ransomware demands targeted a variety of industries including healthcare and pharmaceuticals, as well as finance, manufacturing, technology, telecommunications, and research institutions. In June 2020, hackers infiltrated servers in the epidemiology and biostatistics department of the University of California San Francisco. The university paid $1 million ransom for the decryption key. Conducting sequencing research from cells of recovered COVID-19 patients, US firm 10x Genomics was also the target of a ransomware attack. In the UK, a British research company preparing to conduct trials of a COVID-19 vaccine was infiltrated. The hackers published personal and medical details of thousands of former patients after failed attempts to disable the system.[12]

With the inherently economic and political implications of COVID-19 recovery, state-linked "advanced persistent threat" groups pivoted to exfiltrating vaccine research. As the director of the US National Counterintelligence and Security Center warned, "there is nothing more valuable or worth stealing than any kind of biomedical research that is going to help with a coronavirus vaccine."[13] Britain's National Cyber Security Centre and Canada's Communications Security Establishment publicly accused Russian cyberespionage group APT29, a group "almost certainly linked" to Russian intelligence, of spearheading online attacks to steal COVID-19 vaccine development.[14] When the US Department of Justice announced the indictment of two Chinese nationals in mid-2020 on hacking charges against hundreds of organizations worldwide including tech manufacturing, medical devices, civil engineering, business, education and gaming software, defense, energy, and pharmaceuticals, the indictment detailed operations in which the defendants probed the servers of US biotechnology and medical companies for vulnerabilities, seeking to obtain sensitive COVID-19-related research.[15]

These tactics were not novel, merely adapting or redirecting existing techniques to an emerging crisis. Spear phishing, for instance, targeted workers in key industries using established methods of social engineering. Social engineering is used to trick victims into circumventing their organization's own security protocols. This process is documented in the film *Kill Chain: The Cyber War on America's Elections*, in which Harri Hursti, an ethical "white hat" hacker, demonstrates the ease of social engineering to gain access to credentials by piecing together information found on publicly available sites like LinkedIn.[16] As the HHS Cybersecurity Program noted in its August 2020 update, "[t]he majority of cyber espionage, information operations and financially motivated activity leveraging COVID-19 lures and campaigns remains consistent with established objectives, targeting patterns, tactics, techniques and procedures."[17] The pandemic merely enlarged the list of vulnerable and valuable targets.

Medical facilities offered rich targets for cyberattacks including ransomware and extortion. Of an estimated 239 million cyberattacks attempted in 2020, there were an average of 816 attempted attacks per healthcare endpoint, representing more than a 9,000 percent increase from 2019.[18] Hospital data networks hold sensitive health information that can be exploited for financial and political gain, while the increasing proliferation of personal devices, remote work, and the internet of things broadens the landscape of potential access.

The first known death from a cyberattack at a hospital was investigated in September 2020 after cybercriminals hit a hospital in Germany demanding ransomware. The patient died when being rerouted to another healthcare facility during the ransomware attack, though local investigators later concluded that this did not rise to the level of a homicide charge.[19] Ransom attacks blocked access to patient records, hobbled treatment services, and forced mass cancellations. In other examples of ransomware attacks, ambulances were rerouted, and treatments were delayed when medical records were rendered inaccessible or in some cases permanently lost. Interpol warned that "[a]s hospitals and medical organizations around the world are working non-stop to preserve the well-being of individuals stricken with the coronavirus, they have become targets for ruthless cybercriminals who are looking to make a profit at the expense of sick patients."[20] The security company Ransome estimates 560 healthcare organizations were impacted across 80 major incidents. In the US, 250 hospitals lost the use of their systems for an average of three weeks, with an estimated cost of at least $1.5 million per day.

The attacks continued more than a year into the pandemic. In May 2021, the Irish health system was targeted with ransomware that disabled access to patient records. Physicians were forced to rely on written descriptions rather than diagnostic imagery, communicate via insecure messaging apps, and improvise new systems, all contributing to treatment delays. Radiation therapy for cancer patients was largely suspended because computers are needed for precise dosing control. As one of the local doctors told ABC News, "[t]he opportunity for error is massive . . . things like people getting the wrong blood transfusions, samples being sent under the wrong patient's name."[21] Even using backups, the system took several weeks to get back online.

For the healthcare community, the assaults were on multiple fronts: from cyberattacks at their place of work, to cyber-enabled disinformation that incited personal threats at home. Disinformation promulgated by malicious actors portrayed the pandemic as a hoax, mitigation efforts such as masks and lockdowns as tyranny, and healthcare workers and researchers as complicit in both. The impact on vaccination acceptance and mitigation efforts means that disinformation has potentially costs tens of thousands of lives. The next section of the chapter deals with cyberattacks that exploit the technical virtues of the system rather than technical vulnerabilities.

Exploiting technical virtues: cyber-enabled disinformation

Security scholars and public health researchers have documented ongoing cyber-enabled disinformation campaigns around public health issues. A 2018 study examined the role of hostile foreign actors on social media platforms in undermining trust in vaccines, with Russian bots and trolls promoting confusion and discord. David Broniatowski and colleagues concluded that Russian "accounts masquerading as legitimate users create false equivalency, eroding public consensus on vaccination."[22] In 2020, reports by the European Commission and the US State Department found that foreign actors led by Beijing, Moscow, and Tehran had carried out campaigns through social media aimed at stoking confusion about the COVID-19 pandemic and undermining state responses. Kremlin-linked sites boosted conspiracy theories that allege COVID-19 is a bioweapon, that billionaire Bill Gates is plotting to use the pandemic as an excuse to microchip people, and that plans for the vaccine are a well-orchestrated money grab by pharmaceutical companies.[23] As some of these efforts predate COVID-19, they are likely to continue beyond it. But why?

Scholars such as Kate Starbird and colleagues argue that disinformation is best understood as a campaign, a suite of information actions, deployed to mislead for a strategic political purpose.[24] A former Soviet disinformation officer defines disinformation as "a carefully constructed false message leaked to an opponent's communication system in order to deceive the decision-making elite or the public."[25] One of those tactics is to erode trust and credibility. The purpose is to create doubt about facts and their sources, and thus the threshold of success is not necessarily to convince but to confuse. Together these activities are known in security circles as Russian active measures.[26] Active measures

- create general distrust or confusion over information sources by blurring the lines between fact and fiction
- foment and exacerbate divisive political fissures
- undermine citizen confidence in democratic governance
- erode trust between citizens and elected officials and their institutions.

As counterterrorism expert Clint Watts noted in his Congressional testimony, these active measures have been upgraded to the cyber age, and used to weaken adversaries in a form of information warfare. The most comprehensive report on the tactics, methods, and goals of disinformation campaigns was released by the US Senate Intelligence Committee. Over four volumes on its investigation of Russian interference in the US 2016 election, these reports confirmed that the cyber tools used by Russia included intrusion into voter rolls and electoral systems, email hacking of candidates, and algorithmically targeted propaganda and disinformation campaigns launched over social media designed to rupture civil society. The documents detail the Kremlin's strategic disinformation narratives around voter fraud in order to erode trust in electoral infrastructure and democratic processes, a narrative that started in 2012, when Kremlin-aligned *Russia Today* ran regular segments alleging US election fraud, contending that US election results cannot be trusted and do not reflect the popular will.[27] This narrative, combined with a Supreme Court decision dismantling antidiscrimination provisions of the Voting Rights Act 1965 in 2013,[28] later formed the foundation for "stolen election" narratives which emboldened more than 1,000 people to convene at the US Capitol building in January 2021, threatening to kill lawmakers who certified the election.[29] With calls of "fraud" and "rigged elections" continuing, federal legislation has been introduced to protect the safety of election workers, who have been subject to intimidation and threats of violence.[30] As Richard Hornik argued in the *Harvard Business Review*:

> Social media platforms in particular have been manipulated in ways that interfere with elections, fuel conspiracy theories that deepen ethnic and sectarian divisions and generally erode the ability of communities to have rational, fact-based discussions on topics of public interest.[31]

The United States has been particularly hard hit by the pandemic, with 1 million fatalities (as of June 2022), and at its height, more than forty million unemployed, and several million of those losing their employer-provided health insurance. In the midst of health, financial, emotional, and mental strain, popular platforms such as Facebook, YouTube, and Twitter housed pockets of conspiracy theorists ready with both answers (clarity) and community in a time of fear and isolation. Conspiracy theories are inherently adaptive, and the COVID-19 crisis has provided a captive audience to recruit from preexisting narratives. For instance, QAnon, a large online conspiracy theory community, has leveraged concern about government malfeasance and child trafficking to label COVID-19 a hoax and a cover.

The allure of conspiracy theories as a form of inside knowledge providing certainty and community in a time of great chaos makes them valuable political weapons. For instance, Ilya Yablokov argued that the conspiratorial component of *Russia Today*'s broadcasts appears to be a political instrument designed to attract a wide global audience with different political views.[32] These broadcasts are not limited to television viewing audiences. A US Director of National Intelligence report from 2017 revealed that *Russia Today*'s YouTube channel was one of the most highly watched by American audiences, even beating out the BBC.[33] Conspiratorial assertions can be disseminated for the interlocking purposes of politics, profit, and entertainment, all while successfully degrading authoritative sources of information as they become more powerful. These tactics were leveraged during the pandemic to drive extremist recruitment.

Driving extremism

From recruitment to radicalization, technology is the conduit to access new audiences. The weaponization of social media and the promulgation of extremist groups on Facebook has exacerbated challenges in nearly every policy area, from aiding terrorist recruitment, to being a state tool of great power competition, to damaging the vitality of democracy.[34] In 2019, the FBI warned against "conspiracy-driven domestic terrorism."[35] One group identified in the report, QAnon, adapted its core message of child sex trafficking by political enemies (heir to the Pizzagate conspiracy theory) to COVID-related antigovernment narratives. For instance, the QAnon #SaveTheChildren mantra was redirected to fight mitigation efforts in schools, including mask mandates and vaccination. When Facebook attempted to shut down QAnon groups, membership surpassed one million members across fifteen countries.[36] The global reach of these groups is accelerated by technological connectivity, their influence expanded by elite cues.

Allied nations report similar phenomena. In Australia, the head of the Australian Secret Intelligence Organization (ASIO) warned in a rare public briefing that far-right extremists were exploiting coronavirus to gather new members. The ABC reported:

> "COVID-19 restrictions are being exploited by extreme right-wing narratives that paint the state as oppressive, and globalization and democracy as flawed and failing," the intelligence agency warned. "We assess the COVID-19 pandemic has reinforced an extreme right-wing belief in the inevitability of societal collapse and a 'race war.'"[37]

ASIO's director-general had earlier in the year identified the far right as the fastest growing extremist group in Australia:

> In Australia, the extreme right-wing threat is real and it is growing. In suburbs around Australia, small cells regularly meet to salute Nazi flags, inspect weapons, train in combat and share their hateful ideology. These groups are more organized than they were in previous years.[38]

Cyber-enabled disinformation has been the nexus of conspiracy-driven extremism. During COVID-19, conspiracy theories blaming technology, religious minorities, immigrants, secret cabals, and political adversaries spread from the dark corners of the internet to Facebook group pages, to traditional media and public officials. These narratives implicitly rationalized violence. Narratives around 5G technology were coopted to rationalize destruction of critical infrastructure across the United Kingdom, Australia, and the Netherlands. According to Mobile UK, there were more than ninety arson attacks in the UK against mobile infrastructure, and more than 200 documented instances of abuse toward engineers sent to repair them in the first two months of the pandemic.[39] According to the Asian Americans Advancing Justice organization, which tracks hate crimes, more than 2,000 cases of assault were reported between March and June 2020, with perpetrators mirroring the rhetoric of "kung flu" or "China virus" used by elected officials and influencers.[40] Similar tactics targeted public health officials, state governors, scholars, researchers, philanthropists, and other public figures on the frontline of the COVID-19 response. Later they would target local school boards and university leadership. These conspiracy theories helped to derail public health mitigation mandates as well as hinder vaccination efforts, and endangered scientific communities and educational practitioners. In an article entitled "I Hope You Die" a *Nature* survey of 300 scientists revealed the growing prevalence of threats against researchers in Germany, Australia, and the US.[41] As extremist groups leverage disinformation to build their popularity to run for electoral office, they have come to directly influence policymaking and public funding. The next subsection briefly examines these consequences and their potential longevity.

Undermining the pandemic response

By 2021, the US had lost 1 percent of its total population to COVID-19, a grim record surpassing even World War II and the 1918 influenza pandemic. Despite a relatively small portion of the global population (5 percent), the US was a global hotspot with more than 25 percent of global cases. The consequences of cyber-enabled disinformation in undermining mitigation efforts and vaccine acceptance will be long-lasting. *The Lancet* identified the US as having the fourth highest number in the world of COVID-19 orphans, despite having more highly advanced medical care comparatively.[42] These numbers demonstrate the toll of disinformation in politicizing the pandemic response, undermining public trust in scientific institutions, practitioners, and researchers, and boosting the electoral success of conspiracy theorists, which has further threatened the funding of public goods such as health and education.

During the pandemic and its aftermath, conspiracy theories regarding the virus's origin and severity, the need for and efficacy of public health responses and mitigation efforts, and the role of officials and global institutions were spread through social media to traditional outlets and even political actors. The most vivid demonstration of the reach and impact of cyber-enabled disinformation campaigns was armed demonstrators invading legislative buildings to stop elected officials from passing pandemic response measures. When the demonstrators defied state-issued stay-at-home orders by gathering illegally in front of court houses and state legislatures, then-president Donald Trump encouraged their actions. In April 2020, Trump tweeted to his eighty million followers, "Liberate Michigan! Liberate Virginia! Liberate Minnesota! They are trying to take your Second Amendment!"[43] Demonstrators carrying tactical weapons and wearing military-style gear also convened at the houses of policymakers. Outside the Kentucky governor's mansion, one such group gathered for the "Patriot Day 2nd Amendment Rally" strung up an effigy of the governor with the sign "*Sic semper tyrannis*" or "Thus always to tyrants" around his neck. In Illinois, antilockdown demonstrators used Nazi slogans to intimidate the governor, who was Jewish, a tactic which drew the rebuke of the Auschwitz Museum, whose verified Twitter account posted on May 2:

> "Arbeit macht frei" was a false, cynical illusion the SS gave to prisoners of #Auschwitz. Those words became one of the icons of human hatred. It's painful to see this symbol instrumentalized & used again to spread hate. It's a symptom of moral & intellectual degeneration.[44]

In Michigan, the governor was targeted for kidnapping, trial, and potential execution by a militia group. A total of fourteen participants were charged with federal- and state-level domestic terrorism offenses.[45] In what would become known as the "Night of the Long Terms of Service," Trump lost his Twitter account following the January 6 insurrection in which he incited violence, in violation of Twitter's terms of service.

Disinformation narratives around the pandemic called into question the integrity and independence of key public health institutions such as the World Health Organization (WHO) as well as health practitioners, scientists, and researchers. Trump subsequently ordered a halt to WHO funding, claiming a virus "cover-up," and formally withdrew the United States from the organization (though the US was reinstated by President Biden the following year). These narratives have driven harassment campaigns and protests against healthcare institutions and personnel. During the first wave of COVID-19 more than thirty senior health officials across thirteen US states resigned, retired, or were dismissed from their post, due to violent harassment, strain, or political clashes.[46] The most significant and frequently reported attacks on healthcare related to COVID-19 included denial of services, cyberattacks, psychological threats, physical assaults, and heavy weapon attacks at hospitals and health centers.[47] Though applauded as heroes at the start of the pandemic, frontline nurses have been the target of abuse and intimidation leading to retention problems in the profession. Nurses have noted:

> [P]eople accuse us of giving their loved one something else so that they would die and we could report it as Covid. We heard it more than once that we were fudging the numbers, or we were killing people on purpose to make Covid look like it was worse than it was, or to make it look real when it wasn't.[48]

Together with higher risk of infection to frontline health workers, such developments could result in a hollowing out of expertise and practitioners for a generation, not only from attrition but by driving down recruitment.

One challenge of disinformation is that it not only stops others from acting collectively but actively attempts to thwart others from doing so. As I noted in "The COVID-19 Pandemic vs Post-truth," this will manifest not only in personal refusal to take part in mitigation measures and vaccination programs, but in efforts to prevent others from doing so.[49] Protestors have blocked mass vaccination sites, burned vaccination infrastructure, and threatened the healthcare workers who staff them. In an early incident, one of the largest vaccination sites in the US, Dodger Stadium in Los Angeles, was shut down in January 2021. The protest organizers, coordinating on social media, noted that "[t]his is a march against everything COVID, Vaccine, PCR Tests, Lockdowns, Masks, Fauci, Gates, Newsom, China, digital tracking, etc.," and in a nod to the political overtones implored protestors to "[p]lease refrain from wearing Trump/MAGA attire as we want our statement to resonate with the sheeple."[50] Security guards were hired to protect health workers "for the foreseeable future" at three mobile COVID vaccination sites in Colorado following harassment and vandalism including protestors throwing lit fireworks into the work site.[51] In one incident a woman rammed her car into an outdoor drive-through COVID testing site shouting, "No vaccine," endangering seven healthcare workers.[52]

These demonstrations are not limited to the United States. In Australia a drive-through COVID testing site in the west of Sydney was the target of an arson attack in which the burned-out shell was graffitied with "take back the power" and "COVID equals lies."[53] This followed on from lockdown protests in Melbourne where protestors chanted, "Arrest Bill Gates!"[54] By late 2021, protests included gallows, nooses, and other symbols of violence against elected officials.[55]

The concomitant attacks on research institutes and public health institutions such as the Centers for Disease Control and Prevention, the WHO, and educational institutions point to long-term problems of politicization and funding. The span of institutions under fire has expanded from public health agencies to courts, school boards, and local governments. Town hall and school board meetings broadcast live have documented concerted efforts to undermine COVID-19 mitigation strategies such as masks and vaccines. Meanwhile public health officials and practitioners are increasingly subject to threats of violence. German virologist Christian Drosten received a parcel with a vial of liquid labelled "positive" and a letter telling him to drink it. In Belgium, another virologist, Marc Van Ranst, and his family were placed in a safe house when a military sniper outlined his intentions to target virologists.[56] In Maryland, USA, a pharmacist was murdered for distributing the COVID-19 vaccine.[57]

Disinformation is even more dangerous when spread by groups with a high degree of social trust such as the military, law enforcement, and officers of the court. Research demonstrates that cyber-enabled disinformation has been microtargeted to these groups, sometimes successfully. A New York court officer was suspended after he revealed personal information about a chief judge who upheld a vaccine or testing mandate for court officers, directing the public to target her at her home.[58] The previous year, the same judge's information had been found in the car of the suspect alleged to have shot a New Jersey judge's son and husband. Similarly in 2020, COVID-19 was the main cause of death for law enforcement in the United States, but police unions in New York, Chicago, and Seattle fiercely opposed vaccine mandates despite their interaction with vulnerable members of the community.[59]

The weakening of these institutions and the fracturing of social trust provides opportunities for charlatans and conspiracy theorists to fill the vacuum, mounting their own electoral campaigns for power over decision making. School board members detail intimidation and harassment efforts to force them from office. In Florida, local school board member Jennifer Jenkins described intimidation and credible threats of violence including armed men showing up at her home, being followed in her car, and being reported as making bogus allegations to social services in an attempt to rob her of custody of her children.[60] In the same state, Governor DeSantis withheld pay from school board members who enacted mask mandates,[61] and later referred to countries that maintained COVID-19 restrictions like Australia as "authoritarian." Conspiracy-driven extremists are running for local, state, and federal office to overturn mask mandates and vaccination efforts. Two Republican candidates backed by President Trump won high office in the 2020 election on the back of QAnon narratives, and have consistently conflated mitigation efforts and Nazism. These include federal representative Lauren Boebert (R-CO), who tweeted that Biden "has deployed his Needle Nazis,"[62] and fellow Congresswoman Marjorie Taylor Greene (R-GA), who compared vaccination workers to "Nazi Brown shirts" and vaccine mandates to "segregation."[63] During her electoral run, Greene said of her candidacy, "There's a once-in-a-lifetime opportunity to take this global cabal of Satan-worshiping pedophiles out." By smearing political opponents as pedophiles, Satanists, and Nazis, little cooperation or compromise is possible. This type of rhetoric undermines democratic functioning.

These tactics have trickled down to state-level government. A member of the Alaska legislature attempted to invoke the 1947 Nuremberg Code to harass doctors who distribute COVID-19 vaccines.[64] In Kansas, county officials mandating indoor public masks to protect 2–12-year-olds, who are too young to be vaccinated, were met with an angry, mostly maskless crowd. Journalists noted that "during four hours of public comment, opponents invoked the Holocaust, the Taliban, and Japanese internment camps."[65] Language about "medical tyranny" is used by far-right politicians from Australia to the UK. While stoked by hostile foreign actors, these narratives become more potent when picked up by domestic political actors, against whom there are fewer avenues for redress.

Defense against the dark arts

Cyberattacks and cyber-enabled disinformation have significant and potentially long-lasting impacts. While attacks on infrastructure disrupt daily life, conspiracy theories and alternative facts circulating in the information commons poison debate, erode consensus, and paralyze policymaking.[66] By undermining trust in institutions and creating confusion over facts, they also stymie collective action and cooperation both domestically and with international partners. The deputy secretary of NATO, Rose Gottemoeller, called "alternative facts a threat to the alliance" as they undermine a sense of shared reality and a will to fight together against common challenges.[67] The implications for national security are considerable. From climate to COVID, disinformation hampers policy responses. Over the last few years, cyber-enabled disinformation campaigns, both foreign and domestic, have altered what people read, share, believe, and act upon. Trust in those who proffer facts—educational institutions, researchers, public health officials, and health practitioners—has suffered a decline and undermined their influence. In an early indicator, a sudden and partisan shift, a 2019 Pew Research Center report on higher education found that the majority of Republicans surveyed identified universities as a threat to the nation's well-being: 58 percent in 2017, up from 37 percent in 2015, said "universities have a negative effect on the way things are going in the country."[68] Throughout the COVID-19 pandemic, President Trump and Republican governors threatened to withhold federal funds from universities and public schools. These trends are not limited to the United States. In Australia, universities, suffering from AUS$1 billion in government funding cuts over the last five years,[69] were systematically excluded from COVID-19 financial recovery packages, leading to layoffs of more than 40,000 researchers and teachers in higher education.[70] With funding cuts to universities and schools, and research and development cuts in the private sector, job opportunities for researchers will likely shrink, and with them the scientific and technological innovation that drives modern economies. While the economic impacts of lockdowns are frequently cited by critics of mitigation efforts, the largest enduring economic consequence could be the loss of key expertise and the industries on which it depends.

In the competition for influence, the COVID-19 pandemic has demonstrated fruitful avenues for hostile foreign powers and domestic partisans to exploit to reshape power and decision making. To combat both traditional cyberattacks and cyber-enabled disinformation warfare, democracies have turned to individual and collective responses. Sanctions provide one tool. In the wake of the SolarWinds hack, the US 2021 executive order under President Biden utilized targeted financial sanctions against key individuals and agencies, in order to undermine Russian financing of activities

> undermining the conduct of free and fair elections and democratic institutions in the United States and its allies and partners; engaging in and facilitating malicious cyber activities against the United States and its allies and partners that threaten the free flow of information.[71]

Democracies have steadily begun to bolster their collective defenses. Estonia, the target of one of the earliest state-based cyber-attacks, has developed a model for cyber education including civil cyber defense. It has also helped develop cyber norms beneath the threshold of war embodied in the *Tallinn Manual 2.0* as part of its NATO Cooperative Cyber Defense Centre of Excellence. At the time of publication, these lessons have most recently been applied by Ukraine in its fight against Russian-backed cyber-enabled disinformation amid the invasion.[72]

Stanford Professor of Cybersecurity Herb Lin notes the difficulties of defense securing the information global commons—while traditional cybersecurity threats exploit the vulnerabilities of the system, these evolving attacks exploit its virtues, harnessing the openness and virality of social media.[73] Countries like Finland have demonstrated that defenses are cross-disciplinary, including the social sciences and humanities. Finland has consistently topped the annual Media Literacy Index, which measures resistance to fake news and disinformation among thirty-five countries.[74] Social sciences research in psychology, political science, and communication studies can also help support the design of countermessaging strategies to fight disinformation in cyberspace.[75]

Meanwhile, automated tools used to identify extremist and illegal content, such as Islamic State recruitment and child pornography rings, have been adapted to current challengers. Artificial intelligence tools help identify public health misinformation, disinformation, and conspiracy theories, as multinational information corporations such as Alphabet (Google) and Meta (Facebook, Instagram) navigate enforcement. regulation, and education. Similar to twentieth-century pollution, a few main actors appear to comprise the majority of the problem. A report from the Centre for Countering Digital Hate showed a mere twelve anti-vaccine accounts spread nearly two thirds of the anti-vaccine misinformation online.[76] The scale and the reach of a small number of influential actors cannot be overestimated. When a minor celebrity tweeted an anecdote conflating sexually transmitted infection symptoms with a COVID-19 vaccine response, the impacts were felt as far apart as the UK and Trinidad and Tobago, which directed substantial resources to squashing the misinformation.[77] Similarly, trucker convoys in Canada, spurred by vaccine disinformation spread online, caused millions of dollars of economic damage when they blockaded the capital city and shut down a major US-Canada border crossing for weeks.[78] Eventually the prime minister declared a state of emergency.[79] The political, social, and economic consequences of disinformation around the pandemic have yet to be fully quantified. But it is no surprise that when the developers of the AstraZeneca vaccine wrote about their journey from design to manufacturing and noted the deleterious effects of disinformation, they agreed that "[c]ertainly next time—and there will be a next time—we should include some political scientists on the team."[80]

Conclusion

Cyber incidents have rocketed upwards in the political agenda and expanded sideways into a multitude of policy areas. As a result, cybersecurity, once considered an exclusively technical issue, now requires wide interdisciplinary knowledge. The pandemic highlighted two cybersecurity trends, namely the expansion of targets and the means to access them. These targets are both mind and machine. From attacks on medical facilities to the viral promulgation of cyber-enabled disinformation, the COVID-19 pandemic demonstrated the deadly consequences of the expansion of targets now reachable in real time through technical systems. The implications of social cyber-attacks such as cyber-enabled disinformation, which undermines democratic discourse, decision making, and collective responses to crises, will likely linger far longer than one-off data breaches and ransomware attacks. At the state and society level, these challenges require technical, political, and civil responses. At the international level, cybersecurity also requires statecraft responses, sanctions, and collective defense. In the postpandemic world, defense against these cyberattacks should include hardening targets, regulatory responses, and educational campaigns. Through technical and nontechnical initiatives, countries and allies can strengthen their own cyber capability and resilience while contributing to emerging norms and practices to counter cyber challenges in all their diverse forms.

Notes

1. Myriam Dunn Cavelty and Andreas Wenger, "Cyber Security Meets Security Politics: Complex Technology, Fragmented Politics, and Networked Science," *Contemporary Security Policy* 41, no. 1 (2020): 5.
2. Jenni Bergal, "Florida Hack Exposes Danger to Water Systems," *Stateline*, March 10, 2021, https://www.pewtrusts.org/en/research-and-analysis/blogs/stateline/2021/03/10/florida-hack-exposes-danger-to-water-systems (accessed February 28, 2022).
3. Jacob Poushter and Christine Huang, "Despite Pandemic, Many Europeans See Climate Change as Greatest Threat to Their Countries," Pew

Research Center, September 9, 2020, https://www.pewresearch.org/global/2020/09/09/despite-pandemic-many-europeans-still-see-climate-change-as-greatest-threat-to-their-countries/ (accessed February 28, 2022).

4. "The Pandemic's True Death Toll", *The Economist*, February 17, 2022, http://web.archive.org/web/20220217184437/https://www.economist.com/graphic-detail/coronavirus-excess-deaths-estimates (accessed April 13, 2022)
5. "Cyber Operations vs Information Operations: CyCon 2019 Twilight Talk," natoccdcoe/YouTube, August 12, 2019, https://www.youtu.be/KyCDvEzq25s (accessed February 28, 2022).
6. Myriam Dunn Cavelty, "Cyber-security," in *Contemporary Security Studies*, ed. Alan Collins, 4th edn. (Oxford: Oxford University Press, 2016), 400–16.
7. "Update: Coronavirus-Themed Domains 50% More Likely to Be Malicious than Other Domains," Check Point Blog, March 5, 2020, https://blog.checkpoint.com/2020/03/05/update-coronavirus-themed-domains-50-more-likely-to-be-malicious-than-other-domains/ (accessed February 28, 2022).
8. "2020: A Retrospective Look at Healthcare Cybersecurity," US Department of Health and Human Services, February 18, 2021, https://www.hhs.gov/sites/default/files/2020-hph-cybersecurty-retrospective-tlpwhite.pdf (accessed February 28, 2022).
9. Tom Burt, "Microsoft Takes Legal Action against COVID-19-Related Cybercrime," Microsoft On the Issues blog, July 7, 2020, https://blogs.microsoft.com/on-the-issues/2020/07/07/digital-crimes-unit-covid-19-cybercrime/ (accessed February 28, 2022).
10. "COVID-19 Cyber Threats (Update)," August 13, 2020, US Department of Health and Human Services, https://www.hhs.gov/sites/default/files/covid-19-cyber-threats-update.pdf (accessed February 28, 2022).
11. "Two Houston Men Charged with Attempting to Fraudulently Sell 50 Million Masks," press release, United States Attorney's Office, Southern District of Texas, November 24, 2020, https://www.justice.gov/usao-sdtx/pr/two-houston-men-charged-attempting-fraudulently-sell-50-million-masks (accessed February 28, 2022).
12. Jessica Davis, "Another COVID-19 Research Firm Targeted by Ransomware Attack," HealthIT Security, April 8, 2020, https://healthitsecurity.com/news/another-covid-19-research-firm-targeted-by-ransomware-attack (accessed February 28, 2022).
13. Gordon Corera, "Coronavirus: Cyber-Spies Hunt COVID-19 Research, US and UK Warn." BBC News, May 5, 2020, https://www.bbc.com/news/technology-52551023 (accessed February 28, 2022).
14. "Advisory: APT29 Targets COVID-19 Vaccine Development," National Cyber Security Centre, July 16, 2020, https://www.ncsc.gov.uk/files/Advisory-APT29-targets-COVID-19-vaccine-development.pdf (accessed February 28, 2022).

15. "Two Chinese Hackers Working with the Ministry of State Security Charged with Global Computer Intrusion Campaign Targeting Intellectual Property and Confidential Business Information, Including COVID-19 Research," press release, US Department of Justice, July 21, 2020, https://www.justice.gov/opa/pr/two-chinese-hackers-working-ministry-state-security-charged-global-computer-intrusion (accessed February 28, 2022).
16. *Kill Chain: The Cyber War on America's Election*, directed by Simon Ardizzone, Russell Michaels, and Sarah Teale (HBO, 2020).
17. "COVID-19 Cyber Threats."
18. Steve Alder, "VMWare Carbon Black Explores the State of Healthcare Cybersecurity in 2020," *HIPAA Journal*, February 8, 2020, https://www.hipaajournal.com/vmware-carbon-black-explores-the-state-of-healthcare-cybersecurity-in-2020/ (accessed February 28, 2022).
19. Patrick Howell O'Neil, "Ransomware Did Not Kill a German Hospital Patient," *MIT Technology Review*, November 12, 2020, https://www.technologyreview.com/2020/11/12/1012015/ransomware-did-not-kill-a-german-hospital-patient/ (accessed February 28, 2022).
20. "Cybercriminals Targeting Critical Healthcare Institutions with Ransomware," Interpol, April 4, 2020, https://www.interpol.int/en/News-and-Events/News/2020/Cybercriminals-targeting-critical-healthcare-institutions-with-ransomware (accessed February 28, 2022).
21. Alice Chambers and Patrick Reevell, "10 Days after Ransomware Attack, Irish Health System Struggling," ABC News (USA), May 25, 2021, https://abcnews.go.com/International/10-days-ransomware-attack-irish-health-system-struggling/story?id=77876092 (accessed February 28, 2022).
22. David Broniatowski et al., "Weaponised Health Communication: Twitter Bots and Russian Trolls Amplify the Vaccine Debate," *American Journal of Public Health* 108, no. 10 (2018): 1378.
23. *GEC Special Report: Russia's Pillars of Disinformation and Propaganda*, US Department of State, August 2020, https://www.state.gov/wp-content/uploads/2020/08/Pillars-of-Russia%E2%80%99s-Disinformation-and-Propaganda-Ecosystem_08-04-20.pdf (accessed February 28, 2022).
24. Kate Starbird, Ahmer Arif, and Tom Wilson, "Disinformation as Collaborative Work: Surfacing the Participatory Nature of Strategic Information Operations," *Proceedings of the ACM on Human Centred Interaction* 3, issue CSCW (2019), 127.
25. Ladislav Bittman, *The KGB and Soviet Disinformation: An Insider's View* (Washington, DC: Pergamon-Brasseys, 1985), 49.
26. Clint Watts, "Disinformation: A Primer in Russian Active Measures and Influence Campaigns," Statement Prepared for the US Senate Committee on Intelligence Hearing, March 30, 2017, https://www.intelligence.senate.gov/sites/default/files/documents/os-cwatts-033017.pdf (accessed February 28, 2022).

27. "Background to 'Assessing Russian Activities and Intentions in Recent US Elections': The Analytic Process and Cyber Incident Attribution," Office of the Director of National Intelligence, January 6, 2017, available at https://www.dni.gov/files/documents/ICA_2017_01.pdf (accessed April 13, 2022).
28. Stephanie Condon, "Supreme Court Strikes Down Section of Voting Rights Act," CBS News, June 25, 2013, https://www.cbsnews.com/news/supreme-court-strikes-down-section-of-voting-rights-act/ (accessed February 28, 2022).
29. Jennifer S. Hunt, "As Joe Biden Prepares to Become President, the US Still Reels from the Deadly Consequences of Alternative Facts," *The Conversation*, January 19, 2021, https://theconversation.com/as-joe-biden-prepares-to-become-president-the-us-still-reels-from-the-deadly-consequences-of-alternative-facts-153449 (accessed February 28, 2022).
30. Kristal Dixon, "Federal Law Seeks to Protect Election Workers from Threats," *Axios Atlanta*, October 7, 2021, https://www.axios.com/local/atlanta/2021/10/07/federal-law-protect-threats-election-poll-workers (accessed February 28, 2022).
31. Richard Hornik, "We Get the News We Demand," *Harvard Business Review*, August 2, 2018, https://hbr.org/2018/08/we-get-the-news-we-demand (accessed February 28, 2022).
32. Ilya Yablokov, "Conspiracy Theories as a Russian Public Diplomacy Tool: The Case of *Russia Today* (*RT*)," *Politics* 35, no. 3–4 (2015): 301–15.
33. "Assessing Russian Activities."
34. P. W. Singer and Emerson T. Brooking, *Likewar: The Weaponization of Social Media* (Boston: Eamon Dolan, 2018).
35. Jana Winter, "Exclusive: FBI Document Warns Conspiracy Theories Are a New Domestic Terrorism Threat," Yahoo! News, August 2, 2019, https://news.yahoo.com/fbi-documents-conspiracy-theories-terrorism-160000507.html (accessed February 28, 2022).
36. Julia Carrie Wong, "Revealed: QAnon Facebook Groups Are Growing at a Rapid Pace around the World," *The Guardian*, August 11, 2020, https://www.theguardian.com/us-news/2020/aug/11/qanon-facebook-groups-growing-conspiracy-theory (accessed February 28, 2022).
37. Mario Christodoulou, "ASIO Briefing Warns that the Far-Right Is Exploiting Coronavirus to Recruit New Members," ABC News (Australia), June 11, 2020, https://www.abc.net.au/news/2020-06-12/asio-briefing-warns-far-right-is-exploiting-coronavirus/12344472 (accessed February 28, 2022).
38. ASIO director-general, "1st Annual Threat Assessment," speech, Canberra, Australia, February 4, 2020.
39. James Vincent, "Something in the Air," *The Verge*, June 3, 2020, https://www.theverge.com/2020/6/3/21276912/5g-conspiracy-theories-coronavirus-uk-telecoms-engineers-attacks-abuse (accessed February 28, 2022).

40. Erin Donaghue, “2,120 Hate Incidents against Asian Americans Reported during Coronavirus Pandemic,” CBS News, July 2, 2020, https://www.cbsnews.com/news/anti-asian-american-hate-incidents-up-racism/ (accessed February 28, 2022).
41. Bianca Nogrady, “‘I Hope You Die’: How the Covid Pandemic Unleased Attacks on Scientists,” *Nature*, October 14, 2021, https://www.nature.com/articles/d41586-021-02741-x (accessed February 28, 2022).
42. Susan D. Hillis et al., “Global Minimum Estimates of Children Affected by COVID-19-Associated Orphanhood and Deaths of Caregivers: A Modelling Study,” *The Lancet* 398, no. 10298 (2021): 391–402.
43. Donald Trump (@realDonaldTrump), “Liberate Michigan,” Twitter, April 17, 2020, https://twitter.com/realDonaldTrump/status/1251169217531056130.
44. Auschwitz Memorial (@AuschwitzMuseum), “‘Arbeit macht frei` was a false, cynical illusion the SS gave to prisoners of #Auschwitz,” Twitter, May 2, 2020, https://twitter.com/AuschwitzMuseum/status/1256446016510930945?s=20 (accessed February 28, 2022).
45. Tyler Clifford, “Man Sentenced to 6 Years in Plot to Kidnap Michigan Governor,” Reuters, August 25, 2021, https://www.reuters.com/world/us/man-sentenced-6-years-plot-kidnap-michigan-governor-2021-08-25/ (accessed February 28, 2022).
46. Cheri Mossburg, Theresa Waldrop, and Naomi Thomas, “Some Public Health Officials Are Resigning amid Threats during the COVID-19 Pandemic,” CNN, June 23, 2020, https://edition.cnn.com/2020/06/22/us/health-officials-threats-coronavirus/index.html (accessed February 28, 2022).
47. “Attacks on Health Care in the Context of COVID-19,” World Health Organization, July 30, 2020, https://www.who.int/news-room/feature-stories/detail/attacks-on-health-care-in-the-context-of-covid-19 (accessed February 28, 2022).
48. Elle Reeve, Samantha Guff, and Deborah Brunswick, “The Surreal Lives of Arkansas Nurses Fighting Covid-19 Inside the Hospital and Denial on the Outside,” CNN, July 23, 2021, https://edition.cnn.com/2021/07/22/us/arkansas-covid-nurse-vaccine/index.html (accessed February 28, 2022).
49. Jennifer S. Hunt, “The COVID-19 Pandemic vs Post-Truth,” Global Health Security Network, August 2020, https://www.ghsn.org/resources/Documents/GHSN%20Policy%20Report%201.pdf (accessed February 28, 2022).
50. Marisa Gerber and Irfan Khan, “Dodger Stadium’s COVID-19 Vaccination Site Temporarily Shut Down after Protesters Gather at Entrance,” *Los Angeles Times*, January 30, 2021, https://www.latimes.com/california/story/2021-01-30/dodger-stadiums-covid-19-vaccination-site-shutdown-after-dozens-of-protesters-gather-at-entrance (accessed February 28, 2022).
51. Thomas Kika, “Security Guards to Accompany Mobile Vaccination Unites after Harassment by Anti-Vaxxers,” *Newsweek*, September 11,

2021, https://www.newsweek.com/security-guards-accompany-mobile-vaccination-units-after-harassment-anti-vaxxers-1628202 (accessed February 28, 2022).

52. Timothy Bella, "'No Vaccine!' Woman Arrested for Allegedly Driving through Vaccination Site, Nearly Hitting Workers," *Washington Post*, May 27, 2021, https://www.washingtonpost.com/nation/2021/05/27/covid-vaccine-car-protest-tennessee/ (accessed February 28, 2022).
53. Jessica Riga, "Drive Through Testing Site in Sydney's West Target of Possible Arson Attack," ABC News Blog (Australia), August 29, 2021, https://www.abc.net.au/news/2021-08-29/covid-live-blog-nsw-press-conference-vic-lockdown/100415572 (accessed February 28, 2022).
54. Cameron Wilson, "Why Are Australians Chanting 'Arrest Bill Gates' at Protests? This Wild Facebook Group Has the Answers," *Buzzfeed News*, May 11, 2020, https://www.buzzfeed.com/cameronwilson/lockdown-protest-australia-bill-gates-conspiracy-theories (accessed February 28, 2022).
55. Mostafa Rachwani, "Melbourne Protests: Prop Gallows Seen as Thousands March against Victoria's Covid Powers," *The Guardian*, November 13, 2021, https://www.theguardian.com/australia-news/2021/nov/13/melbourne-protests-prop-gallows-seen-as-thousands-march-against-victorias-covid-powers (accessed February 28, 2022).
56. Nogrady, "'I Hope You Die.'"
57. Jessica Anderson, "Maryland Man Allegedly Fatally Shot His Pharmacist Brother for 'Killing People' with the COVID Vaccine, Court Records Show," *Baltimore Sun*, October 7, 2021, https://www.baltimoresun.com/news/crime/bs-md-cr-burnham-follow-20211006-srubyenoujenvkd5igalidruwm-story.html.
58. Molly Craine Newman, "NY Court Officers Suspended for Doxxing State's Chief Judge Janet DiFiore," *New York Daily News*, August 27, 2021, https://www.nydailynews.com/new-york/manhattan/ny-court-officers-dennis-quirk-suspended-30-days-doxxing-chief-judge-20210827-acctvxwspvacnjiebqekzylfyy-story.html.
59. Janelle Griffith, "'My Dad Didn't Have a Fighting Chance': Covid Is Leading Cause of Death among Law Enforcement," NBC News, September 17, 2021, https://www.nbcnews.com/news/us-news/it-doesn-t-have-happen-covid-leading-cause-death-among-n1279289 (accessed February 28, 2022).
60. Bailey Gallion, "School Board Member Jenkins' Comments about Threats, Harassment Grab National Attention," *Florida Today*, October 14, 2021, https://www.floridatoday.com/story/news/education/2021/10/14/jennifer-jenkins-details-threats-harassment-over-mask-vote/8450501002/ (accessed February 28, 2022).
61. Wilson Wong, "Despite Court's Decision, Florida Withholds School Board Salaries over Mask Mandates," NBC News, August 31, 2021, https://www.nbcnews.com/news/us-news/despite-court-s-decision-

florida-withholds-school-board-salaries-over-n1278107 (accessed February 28, 2022).

62. Lauren Boebert (@laurenboebert), "Biden has deployed his Needle Nazis to Mesa County," Twitter, June 8, 2021, https://twitter.com/laurenboebert/status/1413103995967746051 (accessed February 28, 2022).
63. Marjorie Taylor Green (@mtgreenee), Twitter, July 26, 2021, https://twitter.com/mtgreenee/status/1419489724985643008.
64. James Brooks, "Alaska House Rejects Vote on Nuremberg Code Pushed by COVID Vaccine Skeptics," *Anchorage Daily News*, September 13, 2021, https://www.adn.com/politics/alaska-legislature/2021/09/12/alaska-house-rejects-vote-on-nuremberg-code-a-topic-cited-by-covid-vaccine-skeptics/ (accessed February 28, 2022).
65. Jennifer Sinco Kelleher, Terry Tang, and Olga R. Rodriguez, "Mask, Vaccine Conflicts Descend into Violence and Harassment," Associated Press, August 22, 2021, https://apnews.com/article/health-coronavirus-pandemic-2eba81ebe3bd54b3bcde890b8cf11c70 (accessed February 28, 2022).
66. Hunt, "The COVID-19 Pandemic."
67. Rose Gottemoeller, speech, Shangri-La Dialogue, Singapore, June 2, 2018.
68. Kim Parker, "The Growing Partisan Divide in Views of Higher Education," Pew Research Center, August 19, https://www.pewresearch.org/social-trends/2019/08/19/the-growing-partisan-divide-in-views-of-higher-education-2/ (accessed February 28, 2022).
69. Bianca Nogrady, "Australia Cuts Research Funding to Universities," *Nature*, December 19, 2018, https://www.nature.com/articles/d41586-018-07840-w (accessed February 28, 2022).
70. Gavin Moodie, "Why Is the Australian Government Letting Universities Suffer?" *The Conversation*, May 19, 2020, https://theconversation.com/why-is-the-australian-government-letting-universities-suffer-138514 (accessed February 28, 2022).
71. "Treasury Sanctions Russia with Sweeping New Sanctions Authority," press release, US Department of the Treasury, April 15, 2021, https://home.treasury.gov/news/press-releases/jy0127 (accessed February 28, 2022).
72. Peter W. Singer, "How Ukraine Won the #LikeWar," *Politico*, March 13, 2022, https://www.politico.com/news/magazine/2022/03/12/ukraine-russia-information-warfare-likewar-00016562 (accessed April 13, 2022).
73. "Cyber Operations v Information Operations."
74. Marin Lessenski, "Just Think About It: Findings of the Media Literacy Index," Policy Brief 55, Open Society Institute Sofia, November 2019, https://osis.bg/wp-content/uploads/2019/11/MediaLiteracyIndex2019_-ENG.pdf (accessed February 28, 2022).
75. National Academies of Sciences, Engineering, and Medicine, *A Decadal Survey of the Social and Behavioral Sciences: A Research Agenda for*

Advancing Intelligence Analysis (Washington, DC: National Academies Press, 2019).

76. "The Disinformation Dozen: The Sequel," Center for Countering Digital Hate, July 2021, https://www.counterhate.com/disinfosequel (accessed February 28, 2022).
77. Rich Mendez, "UK and Trinidad Health Officials Refute Nicki Minaj's 'False Claim' COVID Shots Cause Swollen Testicles," CNBC, September 15, 2021, https://www.cnbc.com/2021/09/15/nicki-minaj-health-officials-in-uk-and-trinidad-refute-false-claim-covid-shots-cause-swollen-testicles-.html (accessed February 28, 2022).
78. Priscilla Ki Sun Hwang, "'Freedom Convoy' Cost Downtown Ottawa Millions per Day, Experts Estimate," CBC, March 11, 2022, https://www.cbc.ca/news/canada/ottawa/economic-impact-freedom-convoy-downtown-ottawa-1.6376248 (accessed April 13, 2022).
79. Steve Scherer and Ismail Shakil, "Canada's Trudeau Ends Emergency Powers Invoked to Clear Protests," Reuters, February 23, 2022, https://www.reuters.com/world/americas/canada-ends-emergency-powers-invoked-tackle-truckers-protests-pm-trudeau-2022-02-23/ (accessed April 13, 2022).
80. Sarah Gilbert and Catherine Green, *Vaxxers: The Inside Story of the Oxford AstraZeneca Vaccine and the Race against the Virus* (London: Hodder & Stoughton, 2021), 27.

14

Nuclear Weapons and Security: Nonproliferation and Arms Control under Stress

Aiden Warren

Introduction

The specter of nuclear weapons and their associated material continue to pose a significant threat to global security deep into the twenty-first century.[1] While many in the international community indolently regard such devices as being remnants of the Cold War with a limited impact on global stability, this assessment could not be further from the truth. Notwithstanding the substantial reductions in nuclear arsenals since the early 1990s, there is sufficient evidence to suggest that the risks emanating from nuclear (in)security have actually expanded: more states in more unstable regions have attained such weapons, nonstate actors continue to pursue them, and the command-and-control systems in even the most sophisticated nuclear-armed states remain susceptible not only to system and human error but, increasingly, to cyberattack. Even a limited regional nuclear war would have calamitous global consequences.[2] Moreover, the failure of *existing* nuclear-armed states to disarm, the inability to impede *new* states from obtaining nuclear weapons, the potential of terrorists gaining access to such weapons and their concomitant material, and the potential "gaps" presented by the construction and expansion of nuclear energy plants all present serious security challenges in the twenty-first century.[3]

There is a positive. The number of nuclear weapons has declined markedly since the Cold War's demise: down from a peak of approximately 70,300 in 1986 to an estimated 12,700 warheads as of mid-2022.[4] However, their very presence remains a global strategic/political driver, evident in their storage and possession across ninety-eight sites in fourteen nation-states. Some 9,500 of these weapons are in military arsenals, while the others are either in the process of being retired or awaiting dismantlement. Roughly 3,650 are operationally available, and some 2,000 are on high alert and gauged toward potential use within a very short timeframe. The largest possessors of nuclear weapons are Russia and the United States, which together hold 91 percent of the total global suite. Significantly, the United States "houses" its nuclear weapons on eighteen sites, including twelve sites in eleven states within the United States, and a further six sites in five European countries.[5] Given the recent deterioration of US-Russian bilateral relations and the position of NATO in the US-EU security calculi, the placement and strategic consideration of such weapons remains a source of ongoing consternation.

In unpacking where nuclear weapons are situated in the context of broader global security, this chapter will begin by briefly conveying the four categories of nuclear threats. It will then assess the extent to which arms control agreements and the Non-Proliferation Treaty (NPT) regime are under stress given the actions (or lack of them) from nuclear weapon states. This will be illustrated further by the apparent penchant of such states, particularly UN Security Council states (notably China, Russia, and the US), for modernizing their respective nuclear suites and the intensification of great power politics to this end. Lastly, the chapter will consider the degree to which the COVID-19 threat has impacted nuclear security in the context of hampering arms control efforts and broader nuclear diplomacy, as well as the applicable forums. While the pandemic has focused attention on the susceptibility of human security in the context of infectious disease, it has also highlighted the calamitous impact nuclear weapons would have on society should they ever be used again. The overwhelming stress the pandemic has placed on health services and its interference with "normal" life has evidently complicated decisions regarding the regulation of civil liberties and protection of key workers, among other considerations. As such, and in more frank terms, if the COVID-19 era has illustrated that safeguarding the ongoing functioning of society has been challenging, the chaos experienced in the aftermath of a nuclear detonation would make social "functioning" near impossible. Therefore, in addition to rethinking how to prevent and mitigate global pandemics, the analysis of the experiences of the existing crisis needs to be much more extensive, and should engender a revitalization of global community education, concern, and political action to decrease nuclear danger.[6]

Nuclear threats

Before assessing contemporary nuclear weapons security challenges, it is important to delineate the four categories of nuclear threats.

Firstly, the sheer fact that there are *existing nuclear-armed states* that possess these devastating devices is in itself a source of concern. Indeed, some thirty years after the end of the Cold War there are at least 12,700 nuclear warheads still in existence, with a collective explosion capacity comparable to 80,000 Hiroshima bombs. Approximately 30–40 percent of all warheads are still operationally deployed, and the US and Russia both have a substantial portion on perilously high alert, prepared to be unleashed instantly—within a decision window of just 4–8 minutes for each leader—on the occasion of a seeming attack. The command-and-control systems of the Cold War years were frequently hindered and undermined by errors and false alarms. With more nuclear-armed states today, and more potential system susceptibilities, including those relating to cyberattacks, there is no guarantee that we can continue to avoid nuclear conflict.

The second category of threat is *new nuclear-armed states*, none of which are party to the NPT. In recent years, the advent of such states has put the NPT system under immense pressure, with the International Atomic Energy Agency (IAEA) struggling with verification, compliance, and enforcement, and regular clandestine activities occurring in the world's most unstable regions. India and Pakistan joined the undeclared Israel as fully fledged nuclear-armed states in 1998; North Korea now has approximately 40–50 nuclear explosive devices;[7] and Iran is again potentially moving toward a weapon-making capability (in response to US violations and departure from the 2015 Iran nuclear deal), with the capacity to spur a regional proliferation drive should it decide to cross the weaponization threshold.[8]

The third category is *nuclear terrorism*. It cannot be denied that certain terrorist groups exist with the objective and potential capability to wield massive nuclear devastation. We can no longer be under any illusions about the intent of certain messianic groups to cause destruction on a massive scale. And although the probability is small, and most likely lower than some analysts' accounts have suggested, a nonstate attack only has to succeed once to have devastating consequences. With the applicable technology very much in the public sphere, and subterranean black-market sourcing becoming more prominent in a globalized world of porous borders, a Hiroshima-sized nuclear device could conceivably be discharged from a truck inside any main city. A "dirty bomb," blending conventional explosives with radioactive substances such as medical isotopes, would be a much simpler alternative. Although not producing anything on the scale of a fission or fusion bomb, it would have a massive psychological impact on a city and state. While not necessarily exclusive to nuclear terrorists or nonstate actors, it is also evident that clandestine cyberattacks on the command-and-control centers of nuclear-armed states can now be considered a major threat. These could involve faking a nuclear attack, faking a command signal to launch an attack, positing untrue claims of responsibility on state websites where possible, confusing or debasing with untrue data emergency response networks within and between governments (including channels created between states to deal with volatile, intense, or uncertain scenarios), and, in the occurrence of a nuclear warhead actually being released, massively interrupting disaster support operations.

The fourth and last category is the *peaceful uses of nuclear energy*. As the precipitous development of civil nuclear energy continues apace, not least in reaction to the climate change security issue, there will be complexities associated with proliferation and security risks. Aside from accidents as seen in the Fukushima or Chernobyl examples, building new plants for enrichment at the front end of the fuel cycle and reprocessing at the back end could mean that a substantial amount of fissile material becomes susceptible to incremental theft and, ultimately, future nefarious activities.[9]

Controlling nuclear threats

In order to regulate or control such nuclear threats, there is a patchwork quilt, or "regime," of formal and nonformal, binding and nonbinding, multilateral, regional, and bilateral instruments in the form of treaties, protocols, and agreements. The Non-Proliferation Treaty (NPT) is positioned as the defining, overarching pillar of what is regularly referred to as the "NPT regime." Despite many forebodings, not to mention the nonparticipation of France and China until 1992, the regime held together moderately well for the first thirty years of its existence. However, with India and Pakistan, who had never signed the NPT, joining the undeclared Israel as nuclear-armed states in 1998, North Korea's ongoing nuclear and missiles tests and withdrawal from the NPT, and Iran's uranium enrichment program, the regime has been well and truly under strain. With such developments taking place in some of the most unpredictable regions, a diminishing confidence in weapons security and the command systems of the longer-established nuclear powers, and the continuance of proliferation in new nuclear weapon states, there is much to be concerned about. Additionally, as the United States, Russia, and China[10] continue their modernization drives, the adherence to the NPT's core principle of pursuing "negotiations in good faith on effective measures relating to cessation of the nuclear arms race at an early date and to nuclear disarmament" seems a long way off. Simply put, in the context of meeting the obligations of Article VI of the NPT, there appears to be a stalling, if not breaking down, of the nonproliferation regime based on state ambivalence at the very least, or perhaps more accurately state recalcitrance.

Despite the immense challenges the nuclear nonproliferation regime has encountered over the years, there have been instances in which the impetus for change has been notable. In 2007, for instance, a seminal opinion piece put together by four US statesmen, Secretaries George Shultz, William Perry, and Henry Kissinger, and Senator Sam Nunn, garnered much international traction and spurred a small period of global action.[11] Published in *The Wall Street Journal*, they argued that while nuclear weapons were central to maintaining international security during the Cold War, the doctrine of mutual Soviet-American deterrence was now obsolescent. Although deterrence would continue to be a pertinent consideration for many states with regard to threats from other states, the dependence on nuclear weapons for this purpose was becoming increasingly perilous and ineffective. As a means to revitalize the nonproliferation regime for the twenty-first century and to work toward the ultimate goal of "global zero," a joint initiative encompassing a series of steps would need to be undertaken. The steps, they argued, would entail changing the Cold War posture of deployed nuclear weapons to one that encompassed an increase in warning time, therefore markedly reducing the danger of an accidental or unauthorized use of a nuclear weapon. Naturally, the steps should also include the continued and substantial reduction in the size of nuclear forces in all states that possess them, and the elimination of short-range nuclear weapons designed to be forward deployed.[12]

Additionally, Shultz, Perry, Kissinger, and Nunn argued, the pursuit of the highest possible standards of security worldwide for all stocks of weapons, weapons-usable plutonium, and highly enriched uranium should be an imperative. Similarly, attaining control of the uranium enrichment process combined with the guarantee that uranium for nuclear power reactors could be obtained at a reasonable price, via the Nuclear Suppliers Group and then from the IAEA, was also flagged.[13] Further steps pertaining to halting the global production of fissile material for weapons were canvassed, involving phasing out the use of highly enriched uranium in civil commerce and removing weapons-usable uranium from research facilities around the world. Realizing the goal of a world free of nuclear weapons, they continued, would also require proficient actions to thwart or counter any nuclear-related conduct that was potentially threatening to the security of any state or people. In alluding to the potential impact that US leadership could have in this context, Shultz, Perry, Kissinger, and Nunn maintained that reasserting the vision of a world free of nuclear weapons and implementing practical measures toward achieving that goal required a "bold initiative" that could ultimately "have a profoundly positive impact on the security of future generations."[14]

In extending on such nuclear ambitions, Barack Obama attempted to redefine the pathway ahead in various speeches and interviews in the lead-up to his presidential victory and inauguration, culminating with his landmark speech at Hradčany Square, Prague, on April 5, 2009. He pledged to "set a new direction in US nuclear weapons policy and show the world that America believes in its existing commitment under the Nuclear Non-Proliferation Treaty to work to ultimately eliminate all nuclear weapons."[15] In this push for nuclear disarmament, Obama argued that a leadership role for the United States was needed not only because of its global standing or the size of the US nuclear arsenal, but as a matter of "moral responsibility." Having set up the imperative for action, which itself was a remarkable change in the presidential "lexicon for international security policy," Obama made a dual pledge.[16] On the one hand, his administration would "take concrete steps towards a world without nuclear weapons" and to "put an end to Cold War thinking" by reducing "the role of nuclear weapons in our national security strategy, and [urging] others to do the same." On the other, Obama pledged to "maintain a safe, secure and effective arsenal to deter any adversary, and guarantee that defense to our allies."[17]

In simpler terms, Obama's vision called for a stronger global effort to curb the spread of nuclear weapons, greater progress on long-overdue disarmament measures, more unified efforts in mitigating nuclear terrorism, and in due course, the abolition of nuclear weapons.[18] According to Daryl Kimball, "the US nuclear-weapons policy can and must change and the United States must lead by example, or else the global effort to reduce the risk of nuclear war, curb proliferation, and prevent catastrophic terrorism will falter."[19] There is no doubt that the political impetus forged via the election of Barack Obama as president of the United States in November 2008 spurred a series of diplomatic initiatives seeking nuclear nonproliferation and disarmament. He negotiated a START follow-on treaty with Russia, pressed for the US ratification of the Comprehensive Test Ban Treaty (CTBT), and changed the US stance on fissile material cut-off treaty negotiations, arguing that the treaty should be verifiable. Additionally, he presided over a meeting of the UN Security Council in September 2009 which fashioned the important consensus Resolution 1887, and he was responsible for the US hosting a world summit on nuclear security issues early in 2010. As a result of these efforts, a wave of optimism was evident at the 2010 NPT Review Conference.[20]

Of course, the reality is that by the end of Obama's tenure in office, notwithstanding the ratification of the New Strategic Arms Reduction Treaty (New START) and the Iran nuclear deal of 2015, many of these efforts had fallen short. Not surprisingly, it is evident that in recent times the United States has been moving *away* from Obama's initial pronouncements, especially under President Donald J. Trump. Aside from slowing down its nuclear stockpile reductions during its second term in office, the Obama administration embarked on an overhaul of its entire nuclear weapons enterprise, encompassing the development of new weapons delivery systems and modernizing its enduring nuclear warhead types and nuclear weapons production facilities in a program that analysts estimated could cost more than a trillion dollars.[21] Additionally, recent substantial investments by other nuclear weapon states in the upkeep and modernization of their nuclear postures indicate a return of the nuclear factor in international politics—where deterrence is clearly taking precedence over nuclear arms control and disarmament, and the ultimate global goal of nuclear abolition.[22] Moreover, the nuclear reductions of Russia and the United States are slowing; France seems determined to retain its capability for the long term; India and Pakistan continue to upgrade their delivery and weapons capabilities; and China is also adding to its arsenal apace. In short, there has been a decisive global shift toward modernizing, proliferating, and sustaining nuclear arsenals for the indefinite future.

At present, it is unclear whether the global nuclear nonproliferation regime will survive the fractures that are opening up as a result of these developments. If nuclear force modernization programs continue without a renewed focus on arms control and disarmament, the future prospects of the NPT—which is almost universally acknowledged to be the cornerstone of the nuclear nonproliferation regime and one of the most important pillars of global security—look increasingly bleak. While some delegates and policymakers earnestly attempt to keep the NPT buoyant and alive, there appears to be a broader disdain and very little understanding of the stresses the NPT is under. The silent atmosphere in the Assembly Hall at the UN complex during a Preparatory Committee meeting in 2018 was described by one representative as "the quiet in a crowded room into which a hand grenade has just been tossed."[23] This somewhat embellished comparison of course was alluding to the significant issues that have in recent times come to the fore in the international discourse and which constitute a major challenge to the continued legitimacy of the treaty. The deterioration of the strategic relationship between the United States and Russia over the last several years, in conjunction with increasingly truculent statements and accusations of treaty violations, continues to pose significant challenges. Further, the division within the NPT membership over the appropriate pathway to address the nuclear disarmament commitments under Article VI of the NPT—two thirds support the 2017 Treaty on the Prohibition of Nuclear Weapons (TPNW), while a dissenting minority of the nuclear armed states and their allies reject it—has also exacerbated tensions. As Paul Meyer lamented, "The NPT was to celebrate the 50th anniversary of its entry into force at the 2020 Review Conference," but based on the state of the current geopolitical environment, COVID-19, and the broader lack of political will, "it is an open question whether the Review Conference when it convenes in 2022" will be an "occasion for celebration or mourning."[24]

Nuclear modernization

As indicated, one of the most concerning trends challenging the nuclear domain in the context of security is the substantial investments being undertaken by nuclear weapon states to maintain and modernize their nuclear arsenals. As a reflection of the deterioration in global power politics, it is clear that deterrence options have taken priority over nuclear arms control and disarmament endeavors, with nuclear weapons states seemingly placing the goal of nuclear abolition on the backburner.[25] In unambiguous terms, "all nations with nuclear weapons are modernizing their arsenals, delivery systems, and related infrastructure"[26] and appear to be in the nuclear game for the long haul.

Given the various disagreements among analysts, academics, and policymakers in the nuclear modernization debate, it is imperative to conceptualize and specify what is meant by the term "modernization." To start with, it is evident that many of the land-, air-, and sea-based systems which comprise the so-called nuclear triad came into service during the Cold War and will be approaching the end of their life cycle across the next two decades. In both the United States and Russia, this process will see the phasing out and replacement of ballistic missiles, submarines, bombers, fighters, and air-launched cruise missiles with newer operating systems, new nuclear warheads, and improved facilities that produce and uphold nuclear weapons.[27] In other more structured terms, "modernization" consists of three elements of nuclear weapon capabilities. The first is the goal of retiring or supplementing existing aging stockpiles and subsequent efforts to construct new but approximately similar weapons. Related, the second pillar consists of the modernization and expansion of the size of nuclear arsenals. Finally, modernization includes the development of new types of nuclear weapons or delivery platforms, or the integration of new technologies to supplement the nuclear arsenal.[28]

It should be noted, however, that to limit the assessment of modernization to only one segment would miss or discount the applicable linkages and security implications. For example, if the modernization discussion is restricted to notions of merely swapping old weapons for more up-to-date ones, then the developments in arsenal expansion, technology advancement, and technology integration would be left unexamined. Along the same line, if the discussion was to touch only on proposed technological advancements or integration with other weapon platforms, the examination would not address the salient issue of arsenal fatigue. With this in mind, a wide-lens approach to understanding and defining modernization is necessary in order to address the shifts in nuclear weapon arsenals in the United States, China, and Russia. Finally, a working definition of modernization should extend beyond the nuclear warheads themselves. Modernization efforts apply to all elements of strategic weapons, including various delivery systems. For instance, while pit production and warhead fabrication capabilities are important to the discussion, how a state chooses to invest to deploy its nuclear weapons is equally important as this can determine its deterrent strategy and strategic objectives.[29]

Clearly such nuclear modernization undertakings, particularly by the United States, Russia, and China, present new challenges to the existing arms control and nonproliferation regimes. As states seek to develop new weapons and ensure their viability, norms against testing will be under duress. Arms racing based on perceived vulnerability stemming from new nuclear capabilities will also put pressure on the ability of nuclear weapon states to negotiate further arms reductions, as well as further ostracizing states without nuclear weapons who view the lack of movement on disarmament as weakening the arguments for continued adherence to the nonproliferation regime. As current nuclear weapon states rearm and introduce new weapon systems, non-nuclear weapon states will continue to question the commitments within the NPT by the recognized weapon states to disarm.[30]

Given the variations in nuclear weapon states' interest and participation in tangible disarmament initiatives, coupled with the rapidly approaching development of technologies for the nuclear weapon enterprise, scenarios can be envisaged in which greater instability arises as states attempt to adjust their deterrence strategies to cope with the perceived vulnerabilities. These technologies are not limited to new nuclear weapons or an increase in the number of nuclear weapons. Highly accurate targeting capabilities of nuclear weapons, it is argued, allow for smaller and thus more "usable" weapons, which seems to have perpetuated a similar need, as well as a need for nonnuclear weapons of similar capabilities. Technologies that allow for striking command-and-control capabilities through cyberattacks coupled, potentially, with artificial intelligence could motivate preemptive action. However, while best practices can be established in cyberspace and defenses bolstered to the greatest extent possible, arms controls are significantly limited in their capacity to regulate these types of capabilities.[31]

The return of great power politics in the nuclear domain

Of course, the modernization drive is illustrative of the fact that great power conflict has once again become a nascent issue for international security, with stark nuclear security ramifications. The concern over the return to a period of great power conflict has sharply risen over the last few years. While many would point to a resurgent Russia and its renewed quest for stature and regional influence, as reflected in its invasion of Ukraine, a significant worry for many Western policymakers, strategists, and analysts continues to be the rapid and monolithic rise of China. How nuclear weapon proliferation and modernization efforts will impact these great power dynamics and the prospects for conflict will remain a pertinent question in the coming decades. The twentieth century was characterized by two broad periods: a multipolar international system marked by great power conventional war, and a bipolar power structure characterized by arms racing and proxy conflicts. The prospect of a tripolar system, with the United States, China, and Russia in competitive and relatively equal positions, or a multipolar system with various spheres of competing influence, introduces new and potentially dangerous scenarios. As states seek out security, either through the promotion of their own forces in anticipation of future conflict or in response to an adversary's development of new technologies or military assets, arms racing and greater uncertainty in intentions is likely to build. Until recent times, scholarship and broader discourse have seemingly struggled to assess great power competition and the extent to which emerging technologies will impact particular power dynamics and perceptions of shifting power. While nuclear weapons have been fully integrated into this thinking about great power competition, the processes of modernization and new technologies associated with their deployment are less understood.[32]

Nuclear modernization in the sense of the refurbishment of older weapons may not necessarily escalate tensions, but other dynamics may. In particular, the advancement of technologies to expand the capabilities or mission set of nuclear forces would introduce greater uncertainty. Additionally, linkages between nuclear forces and other weapon platforms could also present unique escalatory challenges between great powers, for example, cyberattacks against nuclear command-and-control facilities or the further development, deployment, and usage of hypersonic glide weapons. Many have argued that the US and China are on a collision course of great power competition. The cause has been attributed to the contrasting political systems, China's perceived desire for greater power, the desire of the US to limit China's trajectory in the Indo-Pacific, a view of a weakening US vis-à-vis China, the rapid economic advancement of China, and so forth.[33] These perceptions of tensions are exacerbated by Chinese investment and rapid advancement in bolstering its military capabilities, in particular its maritime capacity, information sectors, and nuclear forces.[34] In the context of the last category, the Pentagon's 2021 report to Congress significantly increased the projection for Chinese nuclear weapons, asserting that China "may . . . have up to 700 deliverable nuclear warheads by 2027" and "at least 1,000 warheads by 2030."[35] The projection appears to be dependent principally on China's construction of missile silos and assumptions about imminent plutonium production.[36]

It is plausible to envisage a scenario in which perceptions of an ongoing power transition motivate actors to take actions either to further the shift in power dynamics or to maintain the status quo. With investments by the US, China, and Russia (which sees itself as once again warranting a sphere of influence as a great power) into military assets and nuclear forces in particular, the potential for risk taking grows as perceptions of an ongoing transitory period increase. Such risk-taking behavior could include meeting an opponent's moves with matching or asymmetric capabilities meant to maintain its status or to offset any gains by an opponent, with the latter being more likely to result in conflict. The renewed discussions regarding great power competition provide a unique lens through which to assess modernization programs. In one regard, nuclear modernization can be thought of as merely the process by which a state ensures its current arsenal is safe and well maintained. However, it is evident that current modernization efforts appear to be more focused on strengthening capabilities, introducing new agile tools in nuclear arsenals, and meeting perceived rising challenges. While one could look to diplomatic engagement, broader military activities, political posturing, or other indicators for signs of fraying relations and greater consternation between great powers, the urgency and size of the undertaking in modernizing and "improving" nuclear forces provides evidence that certain states see great power competition not as a relic of the past, but rather a forthcoming period.[37]

A transitioning international system introduces interesting dynamics for existing strategic stability frameworks. The existing framework evolved in a bipolar international system during the Cold War, and centered on deterring large-scale conventional and nuclear conflict between the USA and the USSR. The arms treaties signed near the end of the Cold War locked into this framework for the proceeding unipolar period of US dominance.[38] While the present power structure and its trajectory are extensively debated, it is plausible to postulate that a shift away from unipolarity will actually engender the rise of new strategic stability challenges. Clearly, if the United States seeks to maintain the present security framework and its primacy (albeit this is debated), the management of multiple emerging challengers to its influence will need to be adjusted. At present, most strategists see China as the most worrisome potential challenger to US hegemony, particularly given its size and rapid rise. Similarly, India's power is likely to increase over the next few decades. And while it has a less contentious relationship with the US, it has its own strategic stability concerns emanating from its relationship with Pakistan and China. Meanwhile, Russia sees itself as a reemerging powerful state that has sought to reassert itself and its sphere of influence over the last decade. In addition to continued vertical proliferation by other states not discussed in this chapter, it is evident that nuclear modernization efforts and the emergence of new technologies will present further stress and complexities to the existing strategic paradigms—exacerbated even more if they exist in potentially contentious state relationships.[39]

Indeed, emerging technologies and their integration with previous nuclear weapons missions introduce new challenges for existing structures of strategic stability. As mentioned above, acceptance of the fact that substantive force posture changes would be a futile endeavor is a key element of strategic stability. However, as states seek the integration of new military technologies to bolster their forces and expand their deterrent capabilities, the logic that emerging technologies are distinct from nuclear forces (or other deterrents) and thus do not affect strategic stability is significantly flawed. An example of this would be the development of hypersonic weapons, which, given their capacity for a rapid, long-distance response with conventional armaments, can be viewed as a more usable weapon system than the nuclear arsenal.[40]

As new technologies become available and the domains for potential conflict expand, the rethinking of strategic stability paradigms will need to incorporate not only new actors, such as states with lower nuclear weapon counts, but also states that could potentially upset existing stable relations by asymmetric means. In this regard, a reassessment and rethinking of how new technologies when coupled will impact threat perceptions is imperative. Adding additional nuclear weapons to large stockpiles is not so debilitating to strategic stability when compared to classes of weapons that introduce capabilities. Here, an opponent is put in a perceived (and potentially severely) disadvantaged position which it cannot easily overcome by bolstering its own capabilities, even if more rudimentary. Technologies which could be introduced to the nuclear weapons programs of states over the next few decades could have this impact, and as such, careful consideration of the effects of such new elements on existing strategic outlooks and potential scenarios is critical.[41]

The COVID threat multiplier

Despite a January 2022 joint statement by the permanent members of the United Nations Security Council—China, Russia, the United Kingdom, the United States, and France—that the further spread of nuclear arms and a nuclear war "should be avoided," relations between the three biggest possessors of nuclear weapons remain fractious. Indeed, if avoiding war between the nuclear states and reducing strategic risks was the main emphasis of the declaration, the contrasting proliferation and modernization drives suggest the parties' true intent is otherwise. To varying degrees, the nuclear-armed states are involved in a qualitative arms race. In February 2021, five days before its expiration, US president Joe Biden and Russian president Vladimir Putin extended New START through to 2025. And while in July 2021 they relaunched a "platform dialogue" that could advance toward a more decisive set of discussions on nuclear disarmament, they failed to hastily conclude new agreements that would limit offensive nuclear weapons and strategic missile interceptors. In the meantime, China, France, and the UK are not part of any significant nuclear disarmament discussion, and there is ample indication that China is planning to double or triple its long-range, nuclear-armed ballistic missile force.

Amid the ongoing COVID-19 pandemic and the growing nuclear disarmament deficit, the NPT regime has appeared stymied and/or precariously moribund at the negotiating table. Clearly the pandemic has limited parties' resolve, sense of urgency, spirit of cooperation, and determination to produce meaningful results at the NPT Review Conference, postponed until 2022. Some NPT nuclear-armed states lamented the fact that disarmament progress was "challenging," and claimed that many previous NPT pledges on disarmament have been superseded by global events. According to the Arms Control Association, regardless of the pandemic, the nuclear-armed NPT states should accept their past disarmament obligations, collaborate with other states parties on a practical action strategy that stipulates new targets and deadlines, and undertake to act with the determination that the nuclear weapons threat necessitates. In this regard, the five UN Security Council states must desist from further spurious assaults against the 2017 Treaty on the Prohibition of Nuclear Weapons (TPNW) and its many advocates, and recognize that the TPNW actually exists and contributes to meeting NPT Article VI obligations.[42] Additionally, and notwithstanding the complications deriving from COVID-19, the United States and Russia should aim to resolve negotiations on New START follow-on agreements to include further cuts in nuclear warheads and delivery systems no later than 2025; NPT states should aim to begin disarmament talks in a bilateral or a multilateral format no later than 2025; the five NPT nuclear-armed states (and permanent members of the Security Council) should pledge to suspend the size of their nuclear arsenals and all states should halt the production of fissile material for military purposes; holdout states should ignite their respective procedures to ratify the 1996 CTBT by 2025; and lastly, all states should endeavor to renounce the introduction of nuclear-armed cruise and hypersonic missiles.[43]

While the above recommendations may seem optimistic, and to some analysts unrealistic, the COVID-19 crisis, in addition to being an appropriate reminder of the nature of calamitous global risks, is also illustrative of the enduring nuclear threat the world continues to face. As the recommendations suggest, the first objective when dealing with global security threat risks, such as those presented by nuclear weapons, is recognition of the significance of prevention. It is easy to perceive that nuclear prevention is different from pandemic prevention in the sense that pandemics evolve from the "natural sphere" while nuclear incidents are completely human induced. However, pandemics encompass human activities at all stages, from the way the environment is handled,[44] through to "cordoning off" in facilities that conduct research of and with viral organisms, and through the states and international organizations that attempt to mitigate evolving threats. In this regard, both viral and nuclear risks can be addressed via global cooperation. But as indicated, robust dialogue and communication in the nuclear domain, including bilateral and multilateral agreements, are being treated with inertia and periodical disdain. Ensuring that the current global arms control regime—including the NPT and other multilateral, regional, and bilateral agreements/instruments—continues into a new era is crucial. Similarly, renewed global efforts to decrease the risks posed by nuclear terrorism through safeguarding nuclear facilities and accounting for all fissile materials are also critical. Legitimate political will regarding nuclear disarmament would of course be the definitive prevention mechanism, but when states seem unable to comprehensively meet the arms control "level," notions of disarmament are seemingly unattainable, if not futile.[45]

Aside from the broader global pandemic-related nuclear security considerations and intersections, the COVID-19 crisis also offers insight into the human security challenges citizens would encounter in the event of a nuclear assault or miscalculation (whether minor or substantial in magnitude, or indeed just threatened). A nuclear catastrophe is likely to produce anxiety, stockpiling, and scarcities of medical resources to a more extensive degree than the COVID-19 pandemic. Most likely, there would be a desperate scramble to supply iodine, for example, to counteract the impacts of radiation on the thyroid, but also to attain the requisite equipment to treat injuries or access to clean water. A nuclear assault would also undoubtedly see the restriction of civil freedoms, encompassing lockdowns, curfews, rations, and constraints on travel (both domestically and overseas). So instead of just merely averting the propagation of infection as seen in the COVID-19 era, the response in a postnuclear context would be to implement such measures as a means to enable emergency or police agencies clearer routes to deal with the crisis while impeding potential domestic chaos. A response in some extreme cases could even go as far as implementing martial law or limiting citizens' ability to gain access to dependable information. As seen across the social media and information age of the last decade, access to dependable information is already precariously balanced. While access to news reporting and a plethora of virtual resources keeps the general populace "informed," the obvious question has always been the degree to which this information is plausible, believable, and based on fact.[46] No doubt, governments' ability to convey dependable, transparent, and unambiguous messaging would be truly tested in a post-nuclear assault/catastrophe context, as underscored by the politicized and skewed reactions to COVID-19.[47]

Conclusion

Although coming precariously close to nuclear conflict, the "clarity" of the Cold War era gave way to the ambiguities and uncertainties of a world where global security is now threatened by nuclear terrorism, new nuclear weapon states, regional conflict, and preexisting nuclear arsenals. The dangers inherent in such a mix are in themselves greatly magnified by easier access to nuclear technology, inadequately protected stockpiles of plutonium and highly enriched uranium, the growing availability of missiles worldwide, black market nuclear supply networks, and a trend toward acquisition of "latent" nuclear weapons capabilities through the possession of the entire nuclear fuel cycle. The results are clear: of all the potential threats to the global community today (including global warming and climate change), nuclear weapons—the deadliest weapon ever invented, and really the only true weapon of mass destruction—continue to pose the greatest risk.

Notwithstanding the marked reductions in the overall number of nuclear weapons since the Cold War's demise, all of the world's nine nuclear-armed states are busily modernizing their remaining nuclear forces and appear to be in it for the long haul. As frankly stated by Hans Kristensen:

> None of the nuclear-armed states appears to be planning to eliminate its nuclear weapons anytime soon. Instead, all speak of the continued importance of nuclear weapons . . . Perpetual nuclear modernization appears to undercut the promises made by the five NPT nuclear-weapon states.[48]

Under the terms of that treaty, they are required to "pursue negotiations in good faith on effective measures relating to cessation of the nuclear arms race at an early date and to nuclear disarmament."[49] The nuclear modernization reality only reemphasizes the fact that nuclear weapons remain a threat to global security, even thirty-plus years on from the end of the Cold War. Additionally, actions such as the departure of both the United States and Russia from the landmark INF Treaty, the near breakdown of New START, and the unbridled disdain Donald J. Trump had toward any substantive guardrails, for instance, clearly illustrate the stress the arms control/nonproliferation regime is under. Moreover, President Putin's reckless, veiled yet threatening statements during the earlier stages of the invasion of Ukraine—emphasizing Russia's status as a "nuclear power" that would not be "hindered"—brought the once unthinkable specter of a "modern" nuclear war precariously close to a distinct realization.[50] It is hardly surprising amid such developments that some fifty-plus years after the NPT promise was made, the non-nuclear weapon states, who in return for that commitment renounced nuclear weapons for themselves, can rightly challenge whether the overall actions of nuclear weapons states in perpetuity adhere to the core principles of the NPT.[51]

As signified at various stages of this chapter, there are certainly substantially fewer nuclear weapons today than during the Cold War era, but the overall dangers of nuclear security have in many ways expanded: nonstate actors continue to pursue them, more states in more volatile parts of the world have attained such weapons, and the command-and-control systems in even the most erudite nuclear-armed states remain vulnerable not only to system and human error but, increasingly, to cyberattack.[52] However, it is the failure of *existing* nuclear-armed states to disarm (while busily modernizing) and the inability to inhibit *new* states from obtaining nuclear weapons that pose immense challenges to meeting NPT obligations and attaining some semblance of global security. Indeed, without a definitive set of restrictions on the pace and scope of nuclear weapons, the goals of deep cuts in, and eventual elimination of, such destructive devices remain intangible and increasingly improbable. In this regard, the unremitting reassertion of the significance of nuclear weapons, sustained by an amplified global nuclear rivalry, threatens to extend the nuclear era indefinitely into the twenty-first century.[53]

Not surprisingly, the pervasive and elongated crisis ignited by the spread of COVID-19 will have an ongoing and far-reaching impact on nuclear weapons and security. While the wider effects of the pandemic cannot yet be categorically evaluated, it is evidently plausible to argue that it adds to an already overstretched global security agenda. Even before the coronavirus pandemic entered the global community's perception, there were two concurrent existential threats—climate change and the prospect of nuclear conflict—that put humankind closer to tragedy than at any point since the end of World War II. With the international community and state leaders having demonstrated a distinct inertia in addressing such an existential state of affairs, they have failed to address what can be regarded as the two challenges that could ultimately impact our capacity to survive. The tendency toward national isolationism and insufficient global cooperation has exacerbated the horrendous effects of the COVID-19 pandemic, while seemingly marginalizing some of the core security challenges that have been in play, in some instances, for decades.[54]

Notes

1. "Nuclear Proliferation," Global Governance Monitor, August 17, 2017, http://www.cfr.org/global-governance/global-governance-monitor/

p18985#!/nuclear-proliferation?cid=soc-facebook-in-ggm_nuclear_prolif-082916 (accessed March 1, 2022).

2. Gareth Evans and Yoriko Kawaguchi, *Eliminating Nuclear Threats: A Practical Agenda for Global Policymakers,* (Canberra: International Commission on Nuclear Non-Proliferation and Disarmament, 2009), 3–6; Brian Martin, "Nuclear Winter: Science and Politics," *Science and Public Policy* 15, no. 5 (1988): 321–34; Peter King, "Undermining Proliferation: Nuclear Winter and Nuclear Renunciation," Working Paper No. 09/1, Centre for Peace and Conflict Studies, 2009.
3. Evans and Kawaguchi, *Eliminating Nuclear Threats*, 3–6.
4. Hans M. Kristensen and Robert S. Norris, "Status of World Nuclear Forces," Federation of American Scientists, February 23, 2022, https://fas.org/issues/nuclear-weapons/status-world-nuclear-forces/ (accessed April 13, 2022).
5. Ibid.
6. Andrew Futter et al., "Nuclear War, Public Health, the COVID-19 Epidemic: Lessons for Prevention, Preparation, Mitigation, and Education," *Bulletin of the Atomic Scientists* 76, no. 5 (2020): 271–6.
7. "Nuclear Weapons: Who Has What at a Glance," Arms Control Association, January 2022, https://www.armscontrol.org/factsheets/Nuclearweaponswhohaswhat (accessed March 1, 2022).
8. Evans and Kawaguchi, *Eliminating Nuclear Threats*, 3–6.
9. Ibid.
10. Ibid.
11. George P. Shultz, William J. Perry, Henry A. Kissinger, and Sam Nunn, "A World Free of Nuclear Weapons," *Wall Street Journal*, January 4, 2007, http://online.wsj.com/article/SB116787515251566636.html (accessed March 1, 2022).
12. See Aiden Warren, *The Obama Administration's Nuclear Weapon Strategy: The Promises of Prague* (Abingdon, England: Routledge, 2014).
13. Shultz et al., "A World Free of Nuclear Weapons."
14. Ibid.
15. "Arms Control Today 2008 Presidential Q&A: President-elect Barack Obama," Arms Control Association, https://www.armscontrol.org/act/2008-12/interviews/arms-control-today-2008-presidential-qa-president-elect-barack-obama (accessed March 1, 2022).
16. Paul Meyer, "Prague One Year Later: From Words to Deeds?," *Arms Control Today*, May 2010, http://www.armscontrol.org/act/2010_05/LookingBack (accessed March 1, 2022).
17. "Remarks by President Barack Obama in Prague as Delivered," press release, White House, April 5, 2009, https://obamawhitehouse.archives.gov/the-press-office/remarks-president-barack-obama-prague-delivered (accessed March 1, 2022).
18. Ibid.
19. "Arms Control Association Praises Obama's Commitment to a Nuclear Weapons Free World," news release, Arms Control Association, April 5,

2009, https://www.armscontrol.org/pressroom/2009-04/arms-control-association-praises-obamas-commitment-nuclear-weapons-free-world (accessed March 1, 2022).

20. Evans and Kawaguchi, *Eliminating Nuclear Threats*, 7.
21. Jon B. Wolfsthal, Jeffrey Lewis, and Marc Quint, *The Trillion Dollar Nuclear Triad* (Monterey, CA: James Martin Center for Nonproliferation Studies, 2014); "US Nuclear Modernization Programs," Arms Control Association, October 2016, https://www.armscontrol.org/factsheets/USNuclearModernization (accessed March 1, 2022); William J. Broad and David E. Sanger, "US Ramping Up Major Renewal in Nuclear Arms," *New York Times*, September 22, 2014, https://www.nytimes.com/2014/09/22/us/us-ramping-up-major-renewal-in-nuclear-arms.html (accessed March 1, 2022).
22. "US Nuclear Modernization Programs."
23. Paul Meyer, "Sleepwalking towards the 2020 Review of the Nuclear Non-Proliferation Treaty," *Open Canada*, May 8, 2020, https://www.opencanada.org/features/sleepwalking-towards-2020-review-nuclear-non-proliferation-treaty/ (accessed March 1, 2022).
24. Ibid.
25. "US Nuclear Modernization Programs."
26. Ray Acheson (ed.), *Assuring Destruction Forever: Nuclear Weapon Modernization around the World* (New York: Reaching Critical Will, 2012), 88.
27. Ankit Panda, "US Nuclear Weapons Modernization," Council on Foreign Relations, February 7, 2018, https://www.cfr.org/backgrounder/us-nuclear-weapons-modernization (accessed March 1, 2022).
28. Aiden Warren and Phillip Baxter, *Nuclear Modernization in the 21st Century* (Abingdon, England: Routledge, 2020), 5.
29. Ibid., 195.
30. Ibid.; "Nuclear Weapon Modernization Continues but the Outlook for Arms Control is Bleak," news release, Stockholm International Peace Research Institute, June 15, 2020, https://www.sipri.org/media/press-release/2020/nuclear-weapon-modernization-continues-outlook-arms-control-bleak-new-sipri-yearbook-out-now (accessed March 1, 2022).
31. Warren and Baxter, *Nuclear Modernization*.
32. Ibid., 193.
33. See Aiden Warren and Adam Bartley, *US Foreign Policy and China: Security Challenges during the Bush, Obama, and Trump Administrations* (Edinburgh: Edinburgh University Press, 2020).
34. Warren and Baxter, *Nuclear Modernization*, 194.
35. Office of the Secretary of Defense, *Military and Security Developments Involving the People's Republic of China 2021*, US Department of Defense, 2021, viii, https://media.defense.gov/2021/Nov/03/2002885874/-1/-1/0/2021-CMPR-FINAL.PDF (accessed March 1, 2022).
36. Hans Kristensen and Matt Korda, "Nuclear Notebook: Chinese Nuclear Forces, 2021," *Bulletin of the Atomic Scientists*, November

15, 2021, https://thebulletin.org/premium/2021-11/nuclear-notebook-chinese-nuclear-forces-2021/ (accessed March 1, 2022).

37. Warren and Baxter, *Nuclear Modernization*, 194.
38. See Aiden Warren and Joseph M. Siracusa, *US Presidents and Cold War Nuclear Diplomacy* (Cham, Switzerland: Palgrave Macmillan, 2021).
39. Warren and Baxter, *Nuclear Modernization*, 194.
40. Ibid., 192.
41. Ibid., 193.
42. Daryl G. Kimball, "Toward a Successful NPT Review," *Arms Control Today*, November 2021, https://www.armscontrol.org/act/2021-11/focus/toward-successful-npt-review (accessed March 1, 2022).
43. Ibid.
44. Karin Brulliard, "The Next Pandemic Is Already Coming, Unless Humans Change How We Interact with Wildlife, Scientists Say," *Washington Post*, April 3, 2020, https://www.washingtonpost.com/science/2020/04/03/coronavirus-wildlife-environment/ (accessed March 1, 2022).
45. Futter et al., "Nuclear War."
46. David M. J. Lazer et al., "The Science of Fake News," *Science* 359, no. 6380 (2018): 1094–6.
47. Futter et al., "Nuclear War."
48. Hans Kristensen, "Nuclear Weapons Modernization: A Threat to the NPT?," *Arms Control Today*, May 2014, https://www.armscontrol.org/act/2014-05/nuclear-weapons-modernization-threat-npt (accessed March 1, 2022).
49. "Treaty on the Non-Proliferation of Nuclear Weapons (NPT)," United Nations Office for Disarmament Affairs, https://www.un.org/disarmament/wmd/nuclear/npt/text/ (accessed March 1, 2022).
50. Emma Pinedo, Nathan Allen, and Andrei Khalip, "EU Says Putin's Ominous Threat to Those Who Hinder Him Marks 'Critical Moment,'" Reuters, February 25, 2022, https://www.reuters.com/world/europe/eu-says-putins-ominous-threat-those-who-hinder-him-marks-critical-moment-2022-02-24/ (accessed April 13, 2022).
51. John Mecklin, "Disarm and Modernize," *Foreign Policy*, March/April 2015, https://foreignpolicy.com/2015/03/24/disarm-and-modernize-nuclear-weapons-warheads/ (accessed March 1, 2022).
52. Evans and Kawaguchi, *Eliminating Nuclear Threats*; Martin, "Nuclear Winter"; King, "Undermining Proliferation."
53. Kristensen, "Nuclear Weapons Modernization."
54. Rüdiger Lüdeking, "Nuclear Disarmament and Nonproliferation in Times of the Coronavirus Pandemic," *Arms Control Today*, June 2020, https://www.armscontrol.org/act/2020-06/features/nuclear-disarmament-nonproliferation-times-coronavirus-pandemic (accessed March 1, 2022).

15

Security in the Middle East: Enduring and Emerging Challenges

Ash Rossiter and Brendon J. Cannon

Introduction

The Middle East occupies the minds of policymakers, security experts, and geopolitical pundits arguably far beyond what the region's territorial scope and economic heft appear to warrant. Notwithstanding the significance of hydrocarbon production from the region to the functioning of the global economy, the Middle East's economic output (even when including North Africa, as this chapter does) makes up a small percentage of global gross domestic product (GDP).[1] The region straddles important waterways, not least the Suez Canal, through which an estimated 12 percent of global trade traverses. Yet territorially the Middle East does not hold anything like the same importance to global affairs as the Atlantic zone or, increasingly, the Indo-Pacific, which can now be considered the world's geopolitical center of gravity.[2]

Why the Middle East seems to grab outsized attention can perhaps be pinned to the seemingly imponderable array of security problems occurring in the region. To the casual observer and area specialist alike, the scale of violence can seem bewildering. Stories about the Middle East over the past decade all too often have had conflict at the center. Political violence appears to be on the decline in every region of the world except for the Middle East and North Africa. Indeed, it would be hard to disagree with James L. Gelvin, who characterizes the hallmarks of the "new Middle East" as "rebellion and repression, proxy wars, sectarian strife, the rise of the Islamic State, and intraregional polarization."[3]

It is also a region, perhaps more than any other, where traditional security challenges intersect with emerging, nontraditional ones. The ongoing civil war in Syria is apposite in this regard. Some of the early demonstrations that triggered the heavy government crackdown were protests at the diminishing livelihoods in agricultural areas plagued by climate change-exacerbated drought. Likewise, the COVID-19 global pandemic has placed added stress on fragile states in the region, exposing poor governance structures and broken healthcare systems. The wealthier hydrocarbon producers in the Gulf have been able to weather these challenges, buoyed as they are by rebounding oil prices. As a consequence, the gap between the "haves" and the "have nots" in the Middle East has become increasingly pronounced. Indeed, the region is more heavily characterized today by high wealth inequality between states than possibly at any point in its modern history.

A resurgence in external power involvement in the region sits among these above-mentioned trends. A militarily emboldened Russia and an energy-hungry economic juggernaut, China, are now jostling with the United States (US) for influence across the region. Concurrently, Turkey has firmly enmeshed itself in the politics and security of the Middle East region after a hiatus of nearly seven decades. To be sure, one of the hallmarks of the region's security environment today is the interplay between endogenous and exogenous sources of insecurity.[4] Yet, the extent to which external power involvement and competition become sources of instability remains to be seen.[5] If events in Syria are anything to go by, the future looks inauspicious.

This chapter seeks to bring some analytical clarity to the endless array of seemingly primordial conflicts, geopolitical maneuverings, and freshly imported security challenges that define the region's character. A central theme that emerges is that the sources of insecurity are a combination of longstanding issues as well as new, emerging challenges. In what is necessarily no more than a summary of the most significant factors shaping the regional security environment, this chapter also broaches the important role played by technology. While we in no way posit a technologically deterministic account of security trends in the region, there is little doubt that rapid technological developments are having an important shaping effect, creating new vectors for rivals to target one another, and spurring profound social, political, and economic change.

Moving pieces on the board

Sectarian divisions—primarily those between the Sunni and Shia sects of Islam—continue to shape societal interactions within many Middle Eastern states and relations between those that purport to represent and protect the interests of their coreligionists. The shifting distribution of power within the region frequently overlaps with this ideational factor. An enduring feature of the Middle East in recent decades has been the tension between the would-be regional hegemon, Iran, which is also the major Shia state in the region, and resistance by those states—principally the anti-Tehran Sunni Arab Gulf monarchies, namely Saudi Arabia, the United Arab Emirates (UAE), and Bahrain, but joined by Israel—fearful of its ambitions in the region.[6] The latter grouping is also supported by the US, which views the Iranian regime as malevolent and bent on harming American national interests. All believe Iran's successful pursuit of a nuclear weapon would pose a grave and perhaps—especially for Israel—existential threat. Iran, in turn, works with varying degrees of intensity through an array of substate actors in the region, including Hezbollah in Lebanon, militias and political groupings in Iraq, and the Houthis in Yemen.[7] Moreover, Tehran has formed a de facto alliance with the Syrian regime of Bashir al-Assad and has provided Damascus considerable succor over the course of the civil war there.[8]

The tussle between these opposing sides has set the agenda for the region, and the strategic posture of the countries within it, for several decades. In this competitive interaction, Iran can claim no small victories. Lebanon and Syria were essentially lost to the Iranians in the 1980s; the Syrian civil war has served to move Damascus even further out of the Saudi orbit. The American invasion of Iraq and subsequent elections all but guaranteed Iranian penetration of the Iraqi political scene. The situation in Yemen is less clear cut, given the localized issues at the heart of the conflict, but with Saudi Arabia and the UAE spending billions of dollars and the Iranians spending a fraction of this to keep their allies from collapsing, the cost exchange clearly favors Tehran.[9]

Several developments, however, have served to transform these longstanding and, some would say, immutable features of the region. First, there are concerns that the US's willingness and ability to underpin the security of its friends and allies in the region and its commitment to opposing its adversaries—militarily, if necessary—is eroding. To be sure, Washington's announced reorientation—or pivot, to use a previous US administration's terminology—to the Asia-Pacific leaves many pondering what the Middle East security architecture might look like with a reduced or fast-vanishing US commitment.

Second, the region has seen the establishment of relations between Israel and some previously hostile Arab states, most notably the UAE. This resulted in the August 2020 signing of the Abraham Accords, which led the UAE and Bahrain to establish full diplomatic relations with Israel. They were followed by Morocco and Sudan, which both normalized ties with the Jewish state. To be sure, the Israeli, Bahraini, and Emirati governments share a wide range of security concerns:

they see Iran as a long-term security problem and are hostile to political Islam. Indeed, the Emirati and Israeli governments have been quietly cooperating across a range of security-related initiatives for some years.[10] Although other regional heavyweights such as the Iraqis and the Saudis have not normalized their relations with Israel, new forms of alignment have emerged, bringing together the so-called quartet of Saudi Arabia, Egypt, the UAE, and Bahrain.

Third, the struggle that runs generally along ethnic and sectarian lines (Sunni Arab versus Shia Iranian) has become more complex with the rise of a politically and militarily powerful Turkey. Ankara's renewed interest in the Arab Middle East has led it to weigh in significantly in regional conflicts from Syria to Libya to Egypt. This has pitted Turkey, at times, against not only Iran, but also the Saudis, Emiratis, and Egyptians, and led to a tripolarity of sorts, with polarization manifesting as a divergence in political outlooks and agendas of the regional units, that is, the states and their leaders.[11]

Finally, events in the Middle East are increasingly shaped by the policies and actions of the states that line the Gulf as well as Turkey. In the past, when attempting to understand what was driving events in the Arab world and the Middle East region, analysts would certainly consider the actions taken by the regimes in Damascus, Cairo, and Baghdad, and what their leaders thought, and speculate on what they might to do next. Today area specialists and security experts no longer consider those Arab capitals as Middle Eastern power centers. This is not to say these countries are inconsequential; rather, it serves to highlight the shift in the region's center of gravity from the Levant to both sides of the Gulf—and northward toward Ankara. These structural changes are defining much of the regional security architecture in terms of which states take the lead in confronting regional adversaries, define the ideological fault lines, and are the foci of diplomatic tête-à-têtes.

Great power competition

The Middle East has long been a place extraregional powers have acted upon, whether this was European colonial powers of the nineteenth or twentieth centuries or the great powers today, that is, the US, a militarily resurgent Russia, and, of course, a rising China.[12] External power involvement continues to be a major factor in the security dynamics of the region—a point that is clearly evident in the Syrian civil war, for example, with Washington and Moscow backing competing factions. Yet it is the rise of China as an economic and political heavyweight—and the increasingly common assumption that the US will abandon the region—that may be highly influential to the region's security dynamics in the next decade.

Unveiled in 2013, the Belt and Road Initiative (BRI) is a mammoth infrastructure funding and building scheme whereby

> China is projecting its power in a multi-pronged way as it strives to reshape Eurasia as a terrestrial "Belt" (Silk Road Economic Belt, or SREB) and its periphery as a maritime "Road" (or Maritime Silk Road), each having a web of routes and corridors.[13]

China's economic power coupled with its financing and building of connective infrastructure such as ports and railroads has led most Middle East states to sign up to the BRI in some form or another. Yet common interests in what Beijing has to offer should not be misread as common policies vis-à-vis China. Even among Arab Gulf states the propensity has been to engage China bilaterally in an effort to make their own state a BRI hub and, correspondingly, to downgrade the importance of their neighbors in China's eyes.[14] That Iran, Egypt, the Gulf states, and increasingly Turkey all participate in BRI-linked projects means that China is increasingly enmeshed in the adversarial politics of the region. While it has attempted to maintain cordial relations with everyone, its large footprint is deeply concerning to Washington, and the Arab Gulf states, in particular, face a looming conundrum. This is because they all, to a very large degree, rely on the US to guarantee the security of their respective regimes, currently against Iran but previously against Iraq.

With economic relations booming, to include Chinese investment and technology in sensitive sectors such as telecommunications, artificial intelligence, and defense, the Gulf states have attempted to strategically hedge their bets. That is, they are growing their economic ties with China and maintaining their security ties with the US. This is becoming increasingly untenable for the Arab Gulf states as the US-China competition heats up across the Indo-Pacific and polarizes the region. Hedging is an increasingly nonviable option for Gulf states, with the US publicly voicing its concerns over Chinese influence as well as military and intelligence-gathering infrastructure in places like the UAE.[15] As Jean-Loup Samaan has noted,

> given the extent of the US military footprint in the Gulf, and the current inability as well as a reluctance on the part of China to compete with that footprint coupled with the inability of Gulf militaries to replace their American counterparts, Gulf kingdoms may soon reach the limits of their hedging calculus and face no other choice than to align with the US.[16]

Interventionist tendencies

A newer dynamic is the ambition of a number of states in the Middle East to shape events militarily both inside and outside the region. For more than half a century, the hydrocarbon-rich Arab Gulf states have benefited from staggering sums of money on account of their geological endowments. They have not only created wealthy welfare states but have used this fortune—to various degrees of effectiveness—to shape events within the region and beyond.[17] After the breakdown in the regional order following the 2011 Arab Spring uprisings, Saudi Arabia and the UAE, and to some degree Qatar, adopted more assertive and interventionist foreign policies.[18] Consequentially for the region, this Arab Gulf interventionism has not been pursued along a unified front. Deep divisions emerged between Qatar, backed by Turkey, on the one side and Saudi Arabia, the UAE, and Bahrain on the other, in 2014 and again in 2017.[19] The so-called Gulf Cooperation Council (GCC) crisis, which lasted from June 2017 to December 2020, led the UAE and Saudi Arabia to blockade Qatar and demand, among other things, that Doha shut a small Turkish military base and close Al Jazeera media channels. Instead, the size of the Turkish military base and contingent of soldiers grew, Al Jazeera remained active, and Iran stepped in to assist Qatar in overcoming the blockade. The division, which has only been swept under the carpet to date, came to exert a pernicious influence over many of the region's conflicts, particularly the civil wars in Libya and Syria.

Libya has been riven by fighting, with forces in the east under the banner of the Libyan National Army (LNA) pitted against those in the west aligned with the Government of National Accord (GNA). The former was backed by a combination of external states, with notable support in the form of arms and money coming from Abu Dhabi. With Chinese-made Wing Loong II armed unmanned aerial vehicles (UAVs), Russian-made Pantsir surface-to-air missile systems, and Russian mercenaries, the LNA looked likely to unite Libya. The GNA, however, began to receive arms from Turkey—including Bayraktar TB2 armed UAVs—and financing from Qatar. By 2020, Turkish drones had destroyed much of the LNA's arsenal, and it was forced to sue for peace.[20] As a quid pro quo for its assistance, Turkey signed a maritime agreement with the GNA that established an exclusive economic zone linking the two states across the eastern Mediterranean Sea, the location of massive gas deposits which Turkey was keen to exploit (and to keep others from doing so). This move, in turn, saw a scramble by states as disparate as Egypt, Greece, and the UAE to sign defense agreements, conduct naval exercises, and issue joint statements against Turkish actions in Libya and the Mediterranean.[21]

On the Middle East's periphery, the Horn of Africa has increasingly become a zone of contestation by Middle East states, as they flex their political, economic, and military muscles to the west of the Red Sea.[22] This has been most pronounced since the war in Yemen started in 2015 after the Houthis and their allies seized the capital, Sanaa, and looked poised to march on Aden in the south.[23] The subsequent intervention by a Saudi-led coalition saw the need for military bases in the Horn. The UAE, with no contiguous border with Yemen, needed bases to supply its troops and allies. Abu Dhabi approached Eritrea and the diplomatically isolated Isaias Afwerki regime, which agreed to lease its Hanish Islands and facilities at the port city of Assab to the UAE for thirty years.[24] In February 2017, the government of Somaliland, a de facto independent but internationally unrecognized state with a lengthy Gulf of Aden coastline, agreed to the establishment of a military installation and naval dock near its port at Berbera, which Dubai's DP World was in the process of expanding.[25] That the UAE never stationed troops or built a naval dock in Somaliland is beside the point. Multiple Middle East states saw evidence of a geopolitical scramble for dual-use infrastructure such as ports and airports and pointed to what they perceived as Emirati power projection beachheads in Bosaso (Somalia), Aden, and the Yemeni island of Socotra. Turkey's military base in Mogadishu[26] and its plans to build a naval dock (reportedly financed by Qatar) on the coast of Sudan added more evidence to the "new scramble for Africa" theory.[27]

Turkey has shown a growing proclivity for military intervention. It is currently a middle power experiencing—albeit in fits and starts—significant economic, political, and military growth. Turkey's sense of its own resurgent power has been behind its seemingly sudden interest in its near abroad and beyond, to include Libya, the Caucasus, and the Horn of Africa. Its development of an indigenous arms industry during an era of intensely personal and confrontational relations with its neighbors occurred just as technological advances in relation to hydrocarbon resources made the extraction of significant (and contested) gas reserves in the eastern Mediterranean economically feasible.[28] The UAE, Saudi Arabia, and Iran have all stepped up their own efforts to produce arms indigenously, thus mirroring Turkey's recent—and Israel's decades-old—successes. In this complicated tussle, it is Turkey's armed UAVs that have been the game changer, making striking and lightning-fast impressions.[29] Turkey's new-found assertiveness—with Turkish-made and operated drones at the forefront—has the wider region reeling, and best frames its power to challenge other would-be hegemons in the Middle East. With constantly shifting alignments that have seen a warming of relations between the UAE and Turkey, a cooling between the UAE and Saudi Arabia, and a more stable Iraq reasserting its centrality to the region, the title of hegemon remains up for grabs.

Terrorism threat in the Middle East

The Middle East is indelibly coupled with terrorism. Between 2002 and 2018, the Middle East and North Africa, along with south Asia and sub-Saharan Africa, accounted for 93 per cent of all deaths from terrorism. By far the largest number, however, was recorded in the Middle East and North Africa, at more than 93,700 fatalities.[30] From Palestinian plane hijackers to state sponsors of terrorist groups like Muammar Gaddafi's Libya to the emergence of al-Qaeda, the region has had a long association with terrorism. The Middle East has been both an ideological wellspring for nonstate actors espousing terrorist tactics and the location of major terrorist attacks. Although robust counterterrorism efforts in Yemen, Saudi Arabia, and elsewhere in the region have greatly diminished the threat posed by al-Qaeda and its affiliates, transnational jihadi groups remain a serious challenge, especially in states such as Iraq, Syria, and Egypt that are undergoing political turmoil and social upheaval. Jihadists and other antigovernment fighters in Egypt's Northern Sinai, for example, have targeted security forces and Coptic Christians, as well as foreign tourists.[31] These terrorists, formerly affiliated with al-Qaeda, have shifted their allegiance to the Islamic State in Iraq and al-Sham (ISIS), which came to prominence during the Syrian civil war but whose immediate origins—as opposed to its ideological roots—can be traced to Sunni jihadist groups in Iraq.[32] By January 2014, it had seized Fallujah in Iraq's Anbar Province, followed dramatically by its seizure of Iraq's second city, Mosul, in June of that same year. ISIS's rise was largely a consequence of the policies and weaknesses of its state adversaries.[33] It was able to carve out a so-called caliphate in parts of war-torn Syria and Sunni areas of Iraq hostile to the Shia-dominated government in Iraq. Indeed, parts of Mosul had already been under de facto control of the Islamic State in Iraq (ISIS's earlier incarnation) for several years prior to the capture of the city.[34]

ISIS's ideology was powerful, which enhanced the terrorist group's legitimacy and recruiting appeal. It created offshoots in other parts of the Middle East and far beyond as well as adherents among Muslim communities in Western countries and elsewhere. With adherents and franchises far and wide, ISIS, as a transregional movement, became known more simply as the Islamic State. Between 2014 and 2016, for example, the Islamic State in Libya emerged as a powerful actor in that North African country, already mired by years of violence and internecine fighting between various heavily armed militias.[35]

The Islamic State's substantial territorial gains combined with its brutality in the areas it governed led to international combined efforts to roll back the group. Western and regional militaries worked with local forces and—funded by some Arab Gulf states—dealt the Islamic State a strategic defeat. Air power devastated Islamic State forces on the ground when they massed out in the open. By 2017, the violent group had lost most of its earlier territorial gains and, with the Islamic State's eclipse, the number of terrorist attacks in the Middle East and North Africa declined significantly after 2018.[36] Yet even as the core caliphate contracted, the Islamic State still established affiliates in Asia and sub-Saharan Africa and continued to be a source of inspiration for attacks.[37] Despite its diminished status, the threat it poses remains most severe at the local and regional levels in the Middle East and North Africa.

Compounding this situation, the 2011 Arab uprisings that saw the rise of ISIS also raised the prospects of political Islamist movements coming to power through elections. Most significantly, the 2012 presidential election in Egypt, following the fall of Hosni Mubarak, saw Mohamed Morsi of the Muslim Brotherhood–linked Freedom and Justice Party secure victory. Morsi was the first Muslim Brotherhood–affiliated leader of the Arab world but his victory at the ballot box was followed by others for Muslim Brotherhood candidates in Tunisia, Morocco, and Jordan. The ascendance of the Muslim Brotherhood as a potent political force in the Middle East was already on display, however, in the early 2000s when Turkey's Justice and Development Party, led by Recep Tayyip Erdoğan, was catapulted to power. This led Turkey, along with Qatar, to support Morsi and other political Islamists, much to the chagrin of the more conservative Gulf Arab monarchies. Morsi's subsequent ousting by the army in 2013, and the ascendance of military strongman Abdel Fattah el-Sisi, was supported by Saudi Arabia and the UAE, which bankrolled much of Egypt's transition back to authoritarian rule.[38] The ensuing political crisis not only resulted in an uptick in terrorism across the Sinai, but widened the political and ideological chasm yawning between Turkey and Qatar, on the one hand, and Saudi Arabia, the UAE, and Egypt's new rulers, on the other during the aforementioned GCC crisis.

Technological change: expanding attack vectors

While fears of a conventional attack by the armed forces of an aggressor power do not occupy the minds of leaders in the region in the same way they did in decades past, other methods of sabotage, retribution, and use of violence are flourishing. Technological change has, in no small way, been behind the expansion of the methods available to states and nonstate actors for causing mischief.

First, to a considerable degree many aspects of the ongoing conflicts are now playing out in the cyber domain. Because no state in the region can be considered a top-tier cyberpower, several governments, including Israel and Iran, have acquired significant offensive capabilities, allowing them a degree of deniability and/or anonymity as well as the ability to produce significant—and costly—damage to another state's critical infrastructure and thus its national security.[39] Iran, for example, has allegedly carried out several successful cyberattacks on Saudi Arabia's oil sector. In 2012, hackers—later identified by the US intelligence community as being Iranian—attacked an estimated 35,000 computers belonging to state-owned oil and gas giant Saudi Aramco. A malware called Shamoon wiped data, stole passwords, and prevented computers from rebooting. This offensive action signaled Iran's growing cyber capabilities and Tehran's willingness to use them.[40] Indeed, it was followed by a new variant, Shamoon 2, which first emerged in November 2016 and again targeted energy companies in Saudi Arabia.

Alongside high-profile tit-for-tat cyberattacks between Iran and its regional rivals has been an increasingly prevalent use of drones in the region's simmering conflicts. Nonstate actors, in particular, have taken advantage of new possibilities produced by the availability of this equalizing technology. The use of a variety of systems by militant groups in Syria and Iraq, and especially by the Islamic State during its defense of Mosul, has attracted considerable attention from the public, policymakers, and war fighters alike.[41] Iranian-backed proxy forces have increasingly relied on drones to expand their attack repertoires.[42] In January 2019, the Houthis in Yemen used a bomb-laden drone to attack Yemeni military officials during a military parade at the al-Anad air base, near Aden. In the months that followed Saudi oil infrastructure, airports, and urban areas were struck in southwest Saudi Arabia by explosive-laden Houthi drones.[43] The most prominent Houthi-claimed kamikaze drone attack occurred on September 14, 2019, against oil infrastructure at Saudi Arabia's vast Abqaiq complex. The effectiveness of the strike and the distance between the target and Houthi-controlled territories in Yemen make it likely that the

Iranian regime was responsible for the strike rather than the Houthis.[44] In Iraq, in late 2021, Iranian-backed paramilitary groups attempted to assassinate Prime Minister Mustafa al-Kadhimi with explosive-laden drones. Finally, in January 2022, armed drones attacked oil facilities in the UAE's capital, Abu Dhabi, resulting in the deaths of three people. The UAE, Saudi Arabia, and others quickly condemned the attacks and blamed the Houthis and, by extension, Iran.

Technological change has certainly created more options among an array of attackers for actualizing contestation, harming enemies, and perpetrating violence. The introduction of new technologies can disturb the power relation between state parties and nonstate actors.[45] The introduction of social media at first empowered populations by allowing information to spread without gatekeepers and serving as a platform for organizing protests, as evidenced most clearly in the Arab Spring uprisings.[46] The Houthis' use of explosive-laden kamikaze drones also seems to portend the "democratization" of precision strike capabilities.[47] In turn, countries like Saudi Arabia, which attempt to defend against relatively cheap drones and missiles, must spend billions on air defense systems such as the US's MIM-104 Patriot. Nevertheless, it is far from certain that recent technological innovations overwhelmingly tilt the advantage to the Middle East's nonstate actors. For one thing, accelerating advances in artificial intelligence and a range of sensors make it easier than ever before for regional governments to monitor their citizens.[48]

Maritime dimensions of regional security

The three most prominent maritime security challenges in the region have had very different sources and resulted in dissimilar responses. The first, piracy from the Somali coast, threatened international shipping traversing the Red Sea and western Indian Ocean. The second major security threat is more latent than real: the Iranian ability to disrupt maritime activity in and around the Strait of Hormuz or perhaps even to block this key communication chokepoint.[49] A third potential source of maritime instability comes from the aforementioned eastern Mediterranean dispute over the exploration and exporting of offshore gas reserves.

Although much reduced, piracy is still seen by many as a dormant threat rather than a fully suppressed one. It is true that the presence of international navies off the Horn of Africa has greatly contributed to repressing it. However, this has had little impact on other aspects of maritime security, such as people-trafficking and arms-smuggling operations, which remain enduring issues in the Horn of Africa and Gulf of Aden area.

In terms of the second threat, Iran has steadily increased its naval capabilities in the Gulf area, routinely displaying its prowess in frequent exercises by the maritime wing of the Iranian Revolutionary Guard Corps. At the same time, Arab Gulf states have enhanced their own naval capabilities, albeit these remain inconsequential in terms of deterrence. A flareup in the Gulf would have negative global repercussions. East Asian net energy importers such as South Korea and Japan are especially vulnerable to aggressive action that disrupts the flow of hydrocarbons from the region.[50] For now, the US Navy continues to underpin the security of the Gulf waters. Without this security presence it is hard to see how states in the region would not be subject to intense coercion from Tehran. With Gulf states now questioning the American security commitment, China's role in the region and what its military power may eventually come to mean are thought provoking.

Mounting nontraditional security challenges

The Middle East and its burgeoning population confront a highly complex and fragile security system. Plentiful deposits of natural resources, such as oil and gas, suffer from a strained renewable resource base that includes water and arable land. This, in turn, has contributed to water scarcity, desertification, and land degradation.[51] Consequentially, less and less of the food consumed in much of the region originates from it. Moreover, increasing populations, industrialization in countries such as Egypt, and urbanization have put even more pressure on the food supply. Energy insecurity may not be generally associated with the Middle East, but the countries in the Levant have traditionally been vulnerable to it as their fossil fuel endowments have been low. Another issue is large-scale temporary labor migration and the large number of forced migrants, refugees, and internally displaced persons. But it is water scarcity, engendered by a combination of climate change, the damming of rivers, and increased consumption, that is likely to wreak the greatest havoc on the region. Climate change has resulted in soaring temperatures across the region, with temperatures in the Gulf regularly reaching above 50 degrees Celsius in the summer. Rainfall, in turn, has been increasingly sparse as seasonal trends such as monsoons are either curtailed or amplified, resulting in drought on the one hand, and flooding on the other. Dams on rivers such as the Tigris, Euphrates, and Nile now mean that Iraq, Syria, Jordan, and Egypt all face the prospect of desertification, famine, and the resulting political, social, and economic upheavals associated therewith. This damming by Turkey (at the headwaters of the great Mesopotamian rivers) and Ethiopia (on the Blue Nile) adds another layer—potentially an existential threat—to the adversarial international relations of Middle Eastern and North African states.

Beginning in late 2019, the COVID-19 pandemic placed further strain on these structural pressures. Indeed, it created unique challenges in the conflict-prone region.[52] The human security dimension was clearly in evidence in refugee camps and makeshift detention centers in northern Syria.[53] Studies from Iraq, for example, showed that three overlapping segments of the Iraqi population—the forcibly displaced, women, and children—were hit especially hard by the public health and socioeconomic impacts of COVID-19.[54] The pandemic also laid bare the primacy of the state in the international system, with each country taking a go-it-alone approach to tackling it. This, in turn, showed the weaknesses and strengths of various Middle East and North African states, with the rich Gulf states of the UAE, Qatar, and Bahrain instituting consistent and effective, but prohibitively expensive, policies to bring down infections and death rates. Poorer states like Egypt and Tunisia have fared far worse. In conflict-riven states like Libya and Syria, COVID-19 has largely been downplayed as the perception is that bullets continue to pose a greater threat to safety than the virus.

A final but little-discussed facet of the pandemic was the effect that vaccine partners and vaccine diplomacy had on the region. In short, some states such as Iran and Turkey quickly moved to access Chinese-made vaccines like Sinopharm while others such as Israel and Saudi Arabia opted for British or American vaccines like Pfizer-BioNTech. In the UAE, the emirate of Abu Dhabi opted for Sinopharm while Dubai purchased and distributed stocks of Pfizer-BioNTech. Yet Abu Dhabi went a step further when it began commercial production of Sinopharm, shipping supplies to Egypt shortly thereafter. The UAE's flagship air carriers, Emirates and Etihad, also worked with pharmaceutical companies from Russia to China to India to the US, overcoming significant logistical hurdles in order to deliver vaccines.[55]

Choices in vaccine types and producers again served to demonstrate the gravitational pull of China and further underscore the increasingly common perception in the Middle East and North Africa of an American retreat. Yet, rather than stepping into the vaccine breach, Washington went so far as to publicly direct its embassy and military personnel stationed in the UAE not to be tested or vaccinated because both the kits and the vaccines freely offered by the Emirates were Chinese made.[56]

Conclusion

The structural and systemic factors that influence security in the Middle East are dynamic. The pandemic is a case in point. It had an outsized influence on the political economy of relations between rival blocs and between neighboring states. Nevertheless, even as coalitions of states shift over time, the region's structures and systems—dating back to the demise of the Ottoman Empire and the creation of Middle Eastern states—endure and continue to drive (in)security. They include the type of government (monarchy versus revolutionary), sectarian and ethnic composition (Sunni versus Shia, homogeneous or heterogeneous), and the lack of a natural hegemon. Yet, we should not, for example, expect natural enmity from Sunni Arab states to Turkey's growing power and interests in the region. The tense years during the GCC crisis may have been an aberration as Turkey, on one side, and Egypt, Saudi Arabia, and the UAE, on the other, have patched up relations with one another. Neither should there be an expectation, however, that a state like Egypt would welcome Turkish hegemony. Just as states like Saudi Arabia and the UAE felt more comfortable with a monarchial Iran than a revolutionary Iraq before 1979, so too they felt acute discomfort with Egypt and its attempts at hegemony in the 1960s. Egypt, Iraq, and Iran were all clients, to one degree or another, of outside powers such as the US and the Soviet Union. Great powers will continue to exert a gravitational pull on the region, which means that the brewing Sino-American competition may result in the development of yet another pole in the region, particularly in the Gulf on account of its hydrocarbon reserves and, relatedly, its financial and political clout.

Despite the primacy of the state, laid bare during the pandemic, state ideologies, regime types, or attempts at hegemony may be supplanted by nontraditional security threats as the major drivers of instability and conflict. Climate change has already made what is a dry and hot region even more so. Always scarce water resources are now severely depleted, adding another layer to the "haves" and "have nots" across the Middle East and North Africa. Gulf states with deep pockets can desalinate water using hydrocarbon fuels. Upstream states like Turkey can turn off the tap—either to pressure downstream states to act in a particular way, or to keep water for their own thirsty citizens and economy. The existential threats may still come from other states, but the nature of the threats is no longer just guns, bombs, or drones. They are increasingly about the sources of life itself.

Notes

1. Middle East states' combined GDP hovers somewhere between US$3.1 and $3.4 trillion. Global GDP currently stands at approximately US$84 trillion. "GDP (Current US$)," World Bank, 2021, https://data.worldbank.org/indicator/NY.GDP.MKTP.CD (accessed March 1, 2022).
2. See, in particular, Ash Rossiter and Brendon J. Cannon (eds.), *Conflict and Cooperation in the Indo-Pacific: New Geopolitical Realities* (Abingdon, England: Routledge, 2020).
3. James L. Gelvin, "The New Middle East: What Everyone Needs to Know," book talk delivered at UCLA, Los Angeles, November 9, 2017, recording and transcript available at https://www.international.ucla.edu/cnes/article/185543 (accessed March 1, 2022).
4. See, in particular, Ash Rossiter and Christopher Bolan, "The Middle East: Strategic and Military Balance of Power," in *The Routledge Handbook of Diplomacy and Statecraft*, ed. B. J. C. McKercher (Abingdon, England: Routledge, 2022), pp. 367–78.
5. Samuel F. Wells, Jr., and Mark Bruzonsky, *Security in the Middle East: Regional Change and Great Power Strategies* (New York: Routledge, [1987] 2019).
6. Jon B. Alterman, "The Normalization of UAE-Israel Relations," Center for Strategic and International Studies, August 14, 2020, https://www.csis.org/analysis/normalization-uae-israel-relations (accessed March 1, 2022).
7. Marc R. DeVore, "Exploring the Iran-Hezbollah Relationship: A Case Study of How State Sponsorship Affects Terrorist Group Decision-Making," *Perspectives on Terrorism* 6, no. 4/5 (2012): 85–107.
8. Although the Assad family are from a minority sect of Shiism called Alawites, Iran's support to the regime is grounded on a broader agenda than support to fellow Shias.
9. Thomas Juneau, "How War in Yemen Transformed the Iran-Houthi Partnership," *Studies in Conflict & Terrorism* (2021), https://doi.org/10.1080/1057610X.2021.1954353 (accessed March 1, 2022).
10. Emily Sorkin, "The Abraham Accords: The Culmination of a Decades-Long Normalization Process between Israel and the UAE," PhD dissertation, Boston University, 2021.
11. Federico Donelli and Brendon J. Cannon, "Power Projection of Middle East States in the Horn of Africa: Linking Security Burdens with Capabilities," *Small Wars & Insurgencies* (2021), https://doi.org/10.1080/09592318.2021.1976573 (accessed March 1, 2022).
12. Yoram Evron, "China's Diplomatic Initiatives in the Middle East: The Quest for a Great-Power Role in the Region," *International Relations* 31, no. 2 (2017): 125–44.
13. Kei Hakata and Brendon J. Cannon, "The Indo-Pacific as an Emerging Geography of Strategies," in *Indo-Pacific Strategies: Navigating Geopolitics at the Dawn of a New Age*, ed. Brendon J. Cannon and Kei Hakata (Abingdon, England: Routledge, 2021), 14.

14. Jean-Loup Samaan, "Arab Gulf States in the Indo-Pacific: The Limits of Ambiguous Hedging Strategies," in *Indo-Pacific Strategies: Navigating Geopolitics at the Dawn of a New Age*, ed. Brendon J. Cannon and Kei Hakata (Abingdon, England: Routledge, 2021), p. 204.
15. Alexander Cornwell, "US Flags Huawei 5G Network Security Concerns to Gulf Allies," Reuters, September 12, 2019, https://www.reuters.com/article/us-huawei-security-usa-gulf-idUSKCN1VX241; Gordon Lubold and Warren P. Strobel, "Secret Chinese Port Project in Persian Gulf Rattles US Relations with UAE," *Wall Street Journal*, November 19, 2021, https://www.wsj.com/articles/us-china-uae-military-11637274224 (both accessed March 1, 2022).
16. Samaan, "Arab Gulf States," p. 212.
17. Rory Miller, *Desert Kingdoms to Global Powers: The Rise of the Arab Gulf* (New Haven, CT: Yale University Press, 2016).
18. Karen E. Young, "The Emerging Interventionists of the GCC," LSE Middle East Centre, December 2013, http://eprints.lse.ac.uk/55079/1/__libfile_REPOSITORY_Content_LSE%20Middle%20East%20Centre%20Papers_The%20Emerging%20Interventionists%20of%20the%20GCC.pdf (accessed March 1, 2022).
19. Kuwait and Oman, the two remaining members of the GCC, adopted a more neutral position.
20. Ash Rossiter and Brendon J. Cannon, "Turkey's rise as a drone power: trial by fire," *Defense & Security Analysis* (2022), pp. 216–17, https://doi.org/10.1080/14751798.2022.2068562 (accessed July 12, 2022).
21. In Syria's complex civil war, Turkey supported rebel factions fighting against the Russian- and Iranian-backed regime in Damascus. Saudi Arabia, the UAE, and Qatar all provided, at times, funding to various rebel groups, some of which were supplied by Turkey. In the late-2020 Caucasus conflict, Armenia was supported by the UAE and Iran (along with Russia), while Turkey overtly supported Azerbaijan, which was also helped covertly by Israel. Brendon J. Cannon, "The Arab States and the Karabakh War," in *The Nagorno-Karabakh Conflict: Historical and Political Perspectives*, ed. M. Hakan Yavuz and Michael Gunter (Abingdon, England: Routledge, 2022), pp. 402–19.
22. Brendon J. Cannon and Ash Rossiter, "Patterns of External Involvement in the Modern Political History of the Horn of Africa States," in *The Gulf States and the Horn of Africa: Interests, Influence and Instability*, ed. Robert Mason and Simon Mabon (Manchester: Manchester University Press, 2022).
23. For background to the conflict, see Ash Rossiter, "The Yemeni-Saudi Border: From Boundary to Frontline," in *Yemen and the Gulf States: The Making of a Crisis*, ed. Helen Lackner and Daniel Martin Varisco (Berlin: Gerlach Press, 2018), pp. 29–44.
24. Emile Hokayem and David B. Roberts, "The War in Yemen," *Survival* 58, no. 6 (2016): 157–86.

25. Brendon J. Cannon and Ash Rossiter, "Ethiopia, Berbera Port and the Shifting Balance of Power in the Horn of Africa," *Rising Powers Quarterly* 2, no. 4 (2017): 18.
26. Brendon J. Cannon and Ash Rossiter, "Re-examining the 'Base': The Political and Security Dimensions of Turkey's Military Presence in Somalia," *Insight Turkey* 21, no. 1 (2018): 167–88.
27. For a critical appraisal of the limits of power projection by Middle East states in the Horn of Africa, see Donelli and Cannon, "Power Projection." See also Brendon J. Cannon and Federico Donelli, "Asymmetric Alliances and High Polarity: Evaluating Regional Security Complexes in the Middle East and Horn of Africa," *Third World Quarterly* 41, no. 3 (2020): 505–24.
28. Brendon J. Cannon, "Turkey's Military Strategy in Africa," in *Turkey in Africa: A New Emerging Power?*, ed. Elem Eyrice Tepecikliоğlu and Ali Onur Tepeciklioğlu (Abingdon, England: Routledge, 2021), 127–43.
29. Rossiter and Cannon, "Turkey's rise."
30. For annual figures on terrorist attacks by casualties and location, see Global Terrorism Database, https://www.start.umd.edu/gtd/.
31. Omar Ashour, "Sinai's Insurgency: Implications of Enhanced Guerilla [*sic*] Warfare," *Studies in Conflict & Terrorism* 42, no. 6 (2019): 541–58.
32. See Carter Malkasian, *Illusions of Victory: The Anbar Awakening and the Rise of the Islamic State* (New York: Oxford University Press, 2017).
33. Daniel Byman, "Understanding the Islamic State—A Review Essay," *International Security* 40, no. 4 (2016): 127–65.
34. Author's own observation in 2010–11 while based in Mosul.
35. Christopher S. Chivvis, "Countering the Islamic State in Libya," *Survival* 58, no. 4 (2016): 113–30.
36. Truls Hallberg Tønnessen, "The Islamic State after the Caliphate," *Perspectives on Terrorism* 13, no. 1 (2019): 2–11.
37. Seth G. Jones et al., *Rolling Back the Islamic State* (Santa Barbara, CA: RAND, 2017).
38. Oliver Housden, "Egypt: Coup d'Etat or a Revolution Protected?" *RUSI Journal* 158, no. 5 (2013): 72–8.
39. See for example Julia Voo et al., *National Cyber Power Index 2020: Methodology and Analytical Considerations*, Belfer Center for Science and International Affairs, Harvard University, September 2020, https://www.belfercenter.org/sites/default/files/2020-09/NCPI_2020.pdf (accessed March 2, 2022). No Middle East state falls within the top ten of this ranking system.
40. Christopher Bronk and Eneken Tikk-Ringas, "The Cyber Attack on Saudi Aramco," *Survival* 55, no. 2 (2013): 81–96.
41. Ash Rossiter, "Drone Usage by Militant Groups: Exploring Variation in Adoption," *Defense & Security Analysis* 34, no. 2 (2018): 113–26.

42. "Iranian Technology Transfers to Yemen," Conflict Armament Research, March 2017, https://www.conflictarm.com/perspectives/iranian-technology-transfers-to-yemen/ (accessed March 2, 2022).
43. Jean-Loup C. Samaan, "Missiles, Drones, and the Houthis in Yemen," *Parameters* 50, no. 1 (2020): 51–64.
44. This is certainly the opinion of the US intelligence community. See Summer Said, Jared Malsin, and Jessica Donati, "US Blames Iran for Attack on Saudi Oil Facilities," *Wall Street Journal*, September 14, 2019, https://www.wsj.com/articles/drone-strikes-spark-fires-at-saudi-oil-facilities-11568443375 (accessed March 2, 2022).
45. See, for example, Ash Rossiter, "The Impact of Robotics and Autonomous Systems (RAS) across the Conflict Spectrum," *Small Wars & Insurgencies* 31, no. 4 (2020): 691–700.
46. Gadi Wolfsfeld, Elad Segev, and Tamir Sheafer, "Social Media and the Arab Spring: Politics Comes First," *International Journal of Press/Politics* 18, no. 2 (2013): 115–37; Theodor Tudoroiu, "Social Media and Revolutionary Waves: The Case of the Arab Spring," *New Political Science* 36, no. 3 (2014): 346–65.
47. On how nonstate actors adopt technology for violence, see Audrey Kurth Cronin, *Power to the People: How Open Technological Innovation Is Arming Tomorrow's Terrorists* (New York: Oxford University Press, 2020).
48. H. Akın Ünver, "Artificial Intelligence, Authoritarianism and the Future of Political Systems," EDAM, July 2018, https://edam.org.tr/wp-content/uploads/2018/07/AKIN-Artificial-Intelligence_Bosch-3.pdf (accessed March 2, 2022).
49. Caitlin Talmadge, "Closing Time: Assessing the Iranian Threat to the Strait of Hormuz," *International Security* 33, no. 1 (2008): 82–117.
50. Jeongmin Seo, "South Korea–Gulf Relations and the Iran Factor," in *External Powers and the Gulf Monarchies*, ed. Jonathan Fulton and Li-Chen Sim (Abingdon, England: Routledge, 2018), 159–75.
51. Ashok Swain and Anders Jägerskog, *Emerging Security Threats in the Middle East: The Impact of Climate Change and Globalization* (Lanham, MD: Rowman and Littlefield, 2016).
52. Mohammad Karamouzian and Navid Madani, "COVID-19 Response in the Middle East and North Africa: Challenges and Paths Forward," *Lancet Global Health* 8, no. 7 (2020): e886–e887.
53. Audrey Alexander, "The Security Threat COVID-19 Poses to the Northern Syria Detention Camps Holding Islamic State Members," *CTC Sentinel* 13, no. 6 (2020): 16–25.
54. Jane Arraf, "A Spike in Coronavirus Cases Causes Outrage in Iraq," NPR, June 30, 2020, https://www.npr.org/2020/06/30/885758165/a-spike-in-coronavirus-cases-causes-outrage-in-iraq (accessed March 2, 2022).

55. Mona Ali, "Vaccine Diplomacy: In 2021, the UAE Will Become the New Vaccine Hub of the Middle East," Observer Research Foundation, December 29, 2020, https://www.orfonline.org/expert-speak/uae-will-become-new-vaccine-hub-middle-east/ (accessed March 2, 2022).
56. Samaan, "Arab Gulf States," p. 211.

16

The Indo-Pacific and Security: A New Fault Line

Nick Bisley

Introduction

"The United States is a proud part of the Indo-Pacific. And this region is critically important to our nation's security and prosperity," declared Vice-President Kamala Harris at a speech in Singapore on August 24, 2021.[1] Intended to lay out US strategic resolve in Asia in the wake of the disastrous withdrawal from Afghanistan, Harris continued the American practice, established in 2017 by President Donald Trump, of describing the region as the "Indo-Pacific."[2] Since the end of World War II the US has been the dominant military power in what used to be described as East Asia or the Asia-Pacific. The move by the 46th president's administration to adopt this newer and much more expansive concept—referring to the perceived integrated nature of the Pacific and Indian Ocean regions—is notable and not only because any time the world's preeminent military power adopts a new strategic concept it is inherently significant. That the US and many of its allies and partners have chosen to move away from Asia-centered regional conceptions and toward the bigger Indo-Pacific idea reflects a number of important developments that are key to understanding the security dynamics of this vital part of the globe.

This chapter sets out to provide a survey of the key security issues and dynamics in the Indo-Pacific. It will show that security issues have been the driving force in creating the idea of a new megaregion but also that the security dynamics of the region have become one of the principal fault lines in world politics. While the analogy should not be taken too far, the security matters at the heart of the Indo-Pacific are akin to the military division of Europe in the Cold War: a regional strategic divide of immense global consequence. The chapter is organized in two main parts. The first examines the new strategic concept of the Indo-Pacific, charting its emergence and the role played by security concerns in driving the adoption of this way of imagining Asia's strategic landscape. The second section will discuss the central security concerns within the region. While it has a myriad of issues that acutely threaten the lives and interests of states and societies, this section will focus on the three that are most significant: (1) great power competition between the US and China, (2) transnational security threats and the securitization of economic matters, and (3) the region's longstanding flashpoints, such as the Korean Peninsula and the South China Sea. The chapter will conclude with some reflections on the region's likely future security trajectory.

Security and the idea of the Indo-Pacific

While "the Indo-Pacific" has become the dominant way the US and its principal allies and partners refer to the region, it is a relatively new development and, notably, the US was among the last to make the shift of strategic constructs. The labels scholars, analysts, and policymakers use to refer to regions are not neutral or geographically natural divisions of the map. They reflect the complex mix of interests, values, norms, and culture that create the idea that a region is a natural focus of state power and effort.[3] The idea of the North Atlantic as a region of strategic significance, which has been central to the defense and security policy of the NATO member states, was created by the particular circumstances of World War II and its immediate aftermath. The idea had little salience to policymakers in Washington or elsewhere prior to 1939. It was the destruction of the existing power balance created by the Nazi blitzkrieg that catalyzed the shift in thinking. So, what was it that led the US and its allies to believe things had changed sufficiently that a new strategic construct was deemed to be an appropriate response?

Asia's vast size, diverse cultures and polities, and, crucially, its distinct security complexes and economic patterns meant that it had made more political and economic sense to scholars, policymakers, and businesspeople to refer to the continent's subregions. Southeast Asia was the first of these to coalesce, in the strategic planning among the Allies during the war with Imperial Japan in the 1940s. It was then grasped by the elites of the postcolonial polities to carve out a distinct geopolitical space for the mostly newly independent countries looking to nation-build and seeking to keep the Cold War contest at bay.[4] The first inkling of the idea that has become the Indo-Pacific was seen in a concept advocated by Japan's prime minister Abe Shinzo during his short-lived first term. In 2006 he argued for an "arc of freedom and prosperity" that would link the region's democracies to see off the incipient challenge of authoritarian China.[5] The idea was striking as it was the first time that a major power in the region had argued that India should be conceived of as inhabiting the same strategic context as the countries of the Asia-Pacific. It was followed by the establishment of the Quadrilateral Security Dialogue between the US, Australia, Japan, and India in 2007.[6] But with Abe's fall in 2007 and a new Japanese government showing little interest in this way of thinking about the region, along with some misgivings in Canberra and Washington about four-way security cooperation at the time, the idea faded from view.

The idea of an Indo-Pacific began to appear in the writings of think tank scholars in the region from around 2012, with Australian and Indian writers in particular being early and strong advocates.[7] Australia was the first government to use the term in official documents, with the concept being tentatively endorsed in the 2012 *Australia in the Asian Century* White Paper issued by then-prime minister Julia Gillard.[8] By the publication of the 2016 Defence White Paper, which signaled the beginning of the biggest expansion of defense spending outside of wartime, the Indo-Pacific had not simply become Australia's region; a 'stable Indo-Pacific region' had become one of the country's three core strategic defense interests.[9] From the many reasons put forward by advocates for adopting this new and larger strategic concept can be identified three main arguments. The first was a simple empirical observation. The globalization-fueled economic boom in the region had created much greater levels of connectivity between the states of the western Pacific and those of the Indian Ocean region. Flows of energy, commodities, and finished goods were moving across the vital sea lanes, not simply binding the fates of huge swathes of humanity but expanding the scope of the region's states' vital interests. Where in the past, so the argument went, East Asia and the Indian Ocean region operated according to very different perceptions of security challenge and vital strategic interests, the expanded economic ties were binding those interests together. At its most obvious, a China that depends more on energy and commodity inputs from the Middle East, Africa, and Australia and which also relies on finished goods getting to global markets through the same Indian Ocean sea lanes is more likely to take a strategic interest in those lanes than before.

A second reason relates to the strategic position of key states in the region and how an Indo-Pacific conception provides a clearer sense of the shape of strategic policy during a time of power transition. Asia is moving from a stable, US-dominated power balance to a period of uncertainty and fluidity prompted by China's rise and the US's relative decline. This context is amenable to advocates of a new strategic framework that can help decision makers make sense of a less familiar landscape. The most obvious example of how this works is the way in which it makes India a much more prominent part of the region. This has a number of implications ranging from prompting improvement in bilateral ties through to trying to better include India in the region's multilateral institutions—some of which, such as Asia-Pacific Economic Cooperation (APEC), have a distinctly Asia-Pacific configuration.

The third reason is more normatively laden and relates to the way in which the region is understood not just as a more integrated geographically expansive zone but as a particular configuration of states and values. In some cases this is made quite explicit: In the words of one of Australia's more prominent advocates of the concept, the adoption of the Indo-Pacific also serves the larger purpose of organizing a collective response to China "without resorting to capitulation or conflict."[10] Rethinking how one describes the region is about retaining a particular configuration of power, interests, and ultimately values. In this case it is about bringing India in to help see off the China challenge. While this example is at the more explicit end of the spectrum, nonetheless the label "Indo-Pacific" is used to articulate a preferred way of thinking about a shared geographic and social space. And as the region has begun to enter a phase of overt geostrategic competition, there is contestation about the term.

The most significant component of the Obama administration's foreign policy was what it described as its "pivot" to Asia.[11] Intended to signal the reprioritization of the world's most dynamic region following a decade of overemphasis on the Middle East, it was also supposed to expand the US perspective on the region, leading some to argue that it reflected an "Indo-Pacific" outlook. At various points US leaders flirted with the term: in 2013 the commander of US forces in the Pacific referred to the Indo-Asia-Pacific, but Obama's team largely stuck to the Asia-Pacific framework. In 2017, the Trump administration dispensed with the term and fully embraced the Indo-Pacific concept, which was used by the president for the first time at an APEC summit for business leaders in Vietnam that year.[12] Although it was a little later to adopt the idea than many of its allies and partners, Washington did so wholeheartedly, even going so far as to rename its Pacific Command (PACOM) "Indo-Pacific Command." PACOM already had a remit from Hawaii to the borders of Pakistan, very clearly across both the Pacific and Indian oceans, but the symbolism of the reorientation as well as some reconfiguring of internal mechanics are notable.

Reasonably swiftly the US moved from the geographic to the normative in its regional ambitions. "The Indo-Pacific" is used to describe the region in which the US has been the dominant military power for many decades, and its strategic ambitions for that region are for it to be "free and open."[13] With the frequently used but unlovely acronym FOIP, the Free and Open Indo-Pacific is essentially a formulation to argue for the continuation of the regional order overseen by US military power and economic might. It is clearly intended to see off the threat to US interests in the region posed by the rise of Chinese power and the more assertive prosecution of its interests undertaken by Xi Jinping's leadership. Given the way the term has been used by the US and many others, it is not surprising that the People's Republic of China (PRC) does not use the label. Indeed, in 2018 during a press conference Foreign Minister Wang Yi described it as a headline-grabbing idea that was "like the sea foam in the Pacific or Indian Ocean: they may get some attention, but soon will dissipate."[14]

Following Washington's adoption of the moniker, "the Indo-Pacific" has become the norm for US allies and partners, although others in the region are uneasy with the way in which it has swiftly become caught up in geopolitical jostling. Indonesia, with its dual-ocean geography, has unsurprisingly been attracted to the idea of a concept that links the western Pacific with the Indian Ocean, but is the country most uncomfortable with the idea's competitive resonance. It was thus instrumental in leading the diplomatic maneuvering that led to the adoption of the "ASEAN Outlook on the Indo-Pacific" in June 2019.[15] The Association of Southeast Asian Nations' (ASEAN's) move was as much about trying to retain relevance for the Southeast Asian club as it was trying to create a more open and inclusive conception of the region. ASEAN had, not unreasonably, recognized that the US-led idea not only had a normative dimension that sat uneasily with the many decidedly unfree polities of Southeast Asia, but that it was building contestation and potentially conflict into the mental map of the region.

In marine biology the Indo-Pacific is a well-known ecosystem, its name reflecting the fundamentally interconnected nature of the oceans. At first glance "the Indo-Pacific" appears to be a geographic label reflecting in human terms the connectivity of the maritime domains—much as in marine biology—created by the increased links between the states and societies of the western Pacific and the Indian Ocean region. But as in all human creations there is a good deal more going on and at the center of the forces that have led to the idea's promulgation are questions of security and strategy. The emergence of the idea reflects the destabilization of the old security order in the region and the jostling for influence as power is reconfigured and as Asia's states attempt to create a new regional dispensation.

Security challenges in the Indo-Pacific

In this section I survey the three principal issues that are the most significant challenges faced by the states and peoples of the region and how they relate to the emergence of the Indo-Pacific construct. The three issues are: great power competition; nontraditional threats and geoeconomics; and the six key regional flashpoints.

Great power competition

The rise and decline of great powers and the competition for power and influence is thought by many scholars to be the master narrative of world politics.[16] As states develop power at different rates and places, at any given moment some are rising, some are at their apex, while others are in decline. And it is these differences in levels of power, trajectories, and momentum that makes international relations, from this point of view, such a dangerous environment. Yet for most of the past four and a half decades or so Asia has been a remarkable counterexample to this broader trend. Unlike the years after World War II, which were marked by significant conflict and strife, from the late 1970s until relatively recently the region enjoyed a remarkable period of peace and prosperity.[17] This stability rested on an agreement between the US and China struck initially by Nixon and Mao in which the US would recognize the PRC, giving it full standing in international society, while in return China would stop destabilizing the region and accept Washington's preferred geopolitical order. This deal, formalized in 1979 with ambassadors from each country being posted to the other's capital and followed a decade later by the end of the Cold War, created a period of great power comity in stark contrast with the many decades that had come before.[18]

The unraveling of the Sino-American grand bargain is at the heart of this first and perhaps greatest challenge, the return of great power competition. Many have argued that the contest between the US and China should be seen as a new Cold War.[19] Like the confrontation that dominated the second half of the twentieth century, this vision pits a communist power against a liberal capitalist state and, like its predecessor, is highly militarized but likely to avoid high-intensity warfare between the protagonists. However appealing the analogy, it is misplaced, as China is much more integrated into the global economy than the USSR ever was, its ideology lacks the expansionary internationalism of the Communist Party of the Soviet Union, and, above all, the relationship between the US and the PRC is not a global contest for the fate of humanity. In part this is because the overtly competitive phase of the relationship is relatively recent. Until Xi Jinping's accession to power, China maintained a cautious and deliberately low-profile approach to its regional and global interests.[20] Equally, the US did not really take the PRC seriously as a power capable of challenging its interests and influence in Asia, or globally, until the 2017 National Security Statement issued by the Trump administration.[21] Here, Washington explicitly placed great power competition at the center of its global strategy and China as one of the principal protagonists. Yet precisely what the competition is about, beyond a generalized challenge to US power and interests, remains unclear, due in part to the nebulous nature of competition and the lack of a distinct set of interests which conflicted or ideological ambitions that clashed in a substantive way.

Viewed from the perspective of global strategy US-China competition clearly lacks the coherence and intensity of the post-war Soviet-American rivalry. Within the region, however, things are somewhat more clear cut, even if they are not always recognized as such. There are three principal vectors of competition between the two, operating on different geographic and time scales. The first, and most visible, relates to the clashes of interest and the competition for influence among the states and peoples of the region. The US and China have few direct conflicts of interest; there are no disputes over sovereignty or territory between them of the kind that exist between China and Japan or China and India. But each has key interests which they perceive to be either threatened or thwarted by the other. The most obvious example of the latter is Taiwan, in which the PRC sees it as a national interest of the highest order to bring the island into its direct sovereign control. But this ambition is prevented by the explicit security guarantee provided by Washington.

The US has enjoyed freedom of maneuver in the western Pacific since the 1940s and views that as vital to the success of its regional strategy. The PRC is infringing on this through its South China Sea island-building programs and the development of its military capacity, particularly its missile fleet, which is increasingly placing limits on what the US Navy can do. More recently, the US has seen the advantages that China's firms have in 5G telecommunications, artificial intelligence, and other advanced technologies as an acute threat to its long-term interests and launched what is effectively an industrial attack on their capacities—not only banning them from participating in networks developed in the US but pushing back on their capacity to operate commercially through bans on firms who do business with them. The US clearly wants to reduce the PRC's advantage in these domains.

On their own the clashes of interests of major powers are the standard fare of international relations and indeed these have been common between the two countries for many decades. The Taiwan Strait crisis of 1996—when the PRC tried to intimidate the Taiwanese prior to a presidential election—did not get in the way of the development of a long-term and mutually beneficial relationship between the two powers. It is the two other dimensions that give the competitive relations between Asia's two most important powers particular salience.

The second dimension of competition relates to the longer-run distribution of power in the region. For many decades the US has been the region's preeminent military power in both conventional and nuclear terms. Its scale, technological sophistication, and war-fighting experience was not just an empirical fact, but also intended to make others effectively not even try to keep up with American power. China's economic capacity, when paired with the advantages of its geography and the ambitions of its leadership, has meant that the gap between it and the US is being meaningfully bridged, with some scholars arguing that American military primacy in the region has already gone.[22] Chinese military modernization has been underway for many years,[23] but what began as an effort to move a largely conscript force into a professional one and the development of some basic capacity to protect PRC interests beyond its physical territory has given the PRC a level of military capacity it has hitherto never enjoyed.[24] While the competition between the two has not yet developed the more worrying aspects of arms races and the like, it is clear that each side is committed to its current strategy. The PRC plainly aspires to a military whose capabilities are commensurate with its demographic scale and economic influence. Meanwhile, for its part, the US is strongly committed to retaining its regional influence and the strategy of military primacy on which it is based.

An international order describes the configuration of a range of material and social practices that creates a stable and predictable set of relations between members of the system. The existence of an order creates, as famously described by Hedley Bull, a society of states.[25] While much of the theoretical work about international orders focuses on the global level,[26] regional orders—that is, arrangements among a set of states that perceive that they inhabit a shared circumscribed geopolitical space—have distinct qualities and, in the eyes of some scholars, a greater significance in the security domain than global arrangements.[27] And it is the competition for the future of the Indo-Pacific region's international order that constitutes the third and most challenging aspect of US-China rivalry.

In the half-century since Sino-American rapprochement in the 1970s, the region's international order has been centered around US military primacy and a broadly liberal international economic setting also centered on the US as the primary export market and principal source of foreign direct investment. The great power comity of this period rested on acceptance of this order by the PRC, from which China benefited very greatly, possibly more than any other country. The US wants to try to sustain this setting of a geopolitically stable region, with accepted and broadly liberal "rules of the road" governing international conduct, both economic and political. The order comprises a particular configuration of power—in this case a setting that favors the US—a stable cartography, and a commitment to the UN-centered system of international law and norms as understood by Washington and its allies. For most of the period after the normalization of the Sino-American relationship this order was, in public diplomacy, invisible. There was no need to name it as it functioned so well and, given that it helped manage a shared endeavor of regional stability among states with very diverse values, cultures, and political systems, many of whom did not wish to publicly acknowledge their acceptance of the US-centered system, this invisibility suited all parties. As a marker of the contestation, Washington and its allies and partners have taken to describing those arrangements as "the rules-based order" and many of them, such as Australia, have formally adopted the preservation of this order as a core security interest.

For its part Beijing sees the old order as built to serve Washington and its allies' interests and to keep the PRC from achieving its potential. It now has the capacity and, under Xi Jinping, the will to turn its wealth and power into an international order more aligned to its interests and values. The opacity of the Chinese political system makes it difficult to identify just what it is that the PRC wants to change about the prevailing order; also the view is evolving and subject to significant intra-elite contestation. Nonetheless, as Nadège Rolland shows, the PRC is seeking to establish a loose and malleable system of political primacy, both regionally and at the international level.[28] This is most visible in the region in three places. First, as noted above, it is intent on reducing American military power advantages in its region and, while it is difficult to discern a clear plan, many have reached the conclusion that the ultimate ambition is to replace American military primacy with Chinese might.[29] Second, it is establishing or reconfiguring a set of multilateral institutions and processes to advance its regional ambitions. This includes the creation and leadership of the Shanghai Cooperation Organization, the Asian Infrastructure Investment Bank, the

Conference on Interaction and Confidence Building Measures in Asia, the Xiangshan Forum, and aspects of its expansive Belt and Road Initiative (BRI). The BRI, a massive infrastructure program that seeks to better connect the PRC to global markets and to advance economic development—and, through this, improve China's geopolitical and diplomatic standing—is perhaps the most novel form that great power competition is taking. Not only do the US and China tussle over power and influence through the traditional means of missiles, frigates and ambassadors, China's efforts to enhance connectivity also come with the aim of making Chinese standards in these areas the global norm. When paired with PRC advances in digital payments and other novel forms of digital infrastructure, great power politics in the Indo-Pacific has a decidedly twenty-first-century dimension.

The speed of the return of great power politics to a region from which it had been banished for four decades is matched only by the breadth and reach of the contestation. While it has not yet attained the Cold War's capacity to suffuse almost all local and regional conflicts, it is increasingly bound up in many dimensions of political and economic life in the region. From the development needs of the small states of the South Pacific to domestic politics in Australia, from South Korea's defense policy to the port of Gwadar in Pakistan, the rivalry between the US and China over the shape of the region's order is visible in all corners. The COVID pandemic has significantly increased the sense of rivalry and made more evident the scale of competition. While attitudes within Washington toward China had been hardening for some time, the pandemic's impact on the US came to represent viscerally the threat China posed, and cemented the view across both parties that the PRC was a long-term and major threat to US interests. Meanwhile, for Beijing the pandemic has seemed to confirm the view among party elites that the US is in decline, and incapable of grappling effectively with the major challenges of the day, thus further building PRC confidence for pushing forward its ambitions to change the international environment.

Nontraditional threats and geoeconomics

While the drama of great power competition, with aircraft carrier battle groups, diplomatic encounters, and high politics, is considerable, and indeed given the nuclear arsenals of both the US and the PRC these security risks are extreme, for the vast bulk of the peoples of the region the most immediate threats to their well-being come not from missile fleets or fifth-generation fighter jets, but from diseases, crime, and natural disasters. As other chapters in this volume attest, questions of security used to focus primarily on the military or economic threat that states posed to one another. In recent decades, however, the aperture has begun to widen, driven by the realization that existential challenges to states and societies come from a broader range of sources than had hitherto been considered as well as the recognition that the growing connectivity driven by globalization has opened up new societal vulnerabilities.[30]

The Indo-Pacific is a region of the world in which these nontraditional security challenges are especially prominent. Its geography means that natural disasters, such as typhoons, earthquakes, volcanoes, and tsunamis, regularly disrupt life, while its dramatic economic growth has prompted a surge in the connectivity that brings with it new risks from the spread of infectious diseases, most vividly shown by the COVID-19 pandemic, to transnational crime preying on the flows that move across the region's dense networks, whether of goods, capital, or people. Among the broad range of threats one can identify two overarching categories. The first is best described as transnational harms and includes the damages inflicted on people, societies, and polities by actors taking advantage of the vulnerabilities created by the connections of trade, investment, and the like, which have been at the heart of the growing economic prosperity of the region. These can include pirates using the jurisdictional complexity of the sea lanes of communication in and around the Strait of Malacca, or people smugglers or cybercriminals taking advantage of growing internet connectivity. These are challenges that are the direct result of actors making choices, whereas the second category constitutes threats that derive from human interaction with the natural environment. This includes the threats and damage caused by climatic or seismic conditions in which societal or governmental capacities to cope are limited or inadequate to the task. And some of these threats have been or will soon be badly exacerbated by climate change. Southeast Asia, for example, has long known of the destructive power of the typhoons that regularly appear in late summer and early autumn. As the climate changes the season has become longer and both the frequency and intensity of typhoon activity has increased.

Beyond the fact that nontraditional security challenges, whether emanating from malign actors or the forces of the natural environment, are of particular salience to a region housing around one third of the human population, they have two broader consequences for the dynamics of the regional security setting. One of the central attributes of these kinds of transnational nonstate-based security threats is that no state on its own can manage the challenge or see off the threat. In this sense some see in their emergence something that can bind states together, and their collaborative action to stop piracy, or tackle climate change, can be a platform on which they can work to reduce mistrust and the risks of conflict. This has been one of the central motives behind the creation of a wide range of multilateral institutions in the region.[31] Yet, progress on addressing these significant issues at the international level has been uneven, reflecting the structural limitations of multilateralism in the region. The demands of nontraditional security are almost diametrically opposed to those placed on states by the return of an unsettled geopolitical environment. The region has experienced significant growth in military expenditure during the past decade, which has been prompted by the growing sense of traditional insecurity. The evidence to date based on state choices in relation to this trade-off is that traditional conceptions prevail, that national priorities trump transnational concerns, and that short-term needs will be addressed ahead of long-term demands.

The regional response to the COVID pandemic is perhaps the most depressing example of this. The sudden emergence of a highly contagious and deadly virus in China was precisely the kind of nontraditional security threat that the region's many multilateral security mechanisms had been established to help tackle. Yet, as the SARS-COV-2 virus spread, inter-state cooperation collapsed as countries prioritized their own needs and responses over all else, multilateral institutions could barely issue a media statement, and the region's two great powers added the virus to their growing list of mutual recriminations. The pandemic's lesson, at least as it pertains to the balance states are likely to strike between traditional and nontraditional matters, is clear: great power rivalry and the conventional military security risks that it brings will crowd out the capacity of regional powers to address nontraditional concerns.

A key reason for the heightened awareness of nontraditional security threats has been the increase in connectivity across the region, which has led many to enjoy significant improvements in their lives. Engagement with the global economy has been central to the economic success of Asia's states and societies. And while all have managed this process carefully, following the model established by Japan in the postwar period, until relatively recently economic matters and security concerns were each largely allowed to follow their own logic, and efforts were made to keep them quite separate. Japan and China's economic ties were a case in point. The two have a fraught political relationship and in the East China Sea they each claim sovereignty over a set of strategically well-placed small islands and rocks. Yet their economic relationship has flourished, with the two complementary in terms of capital allocation, labor costs, and technological sophistication. But the days of economic matters being able to operate essentially according to market rules are coming to an end as geoeconomics has become an increasingly visible part of the Indo-Pacific's security landscape. "Geoeconomics" is used to mean not simply that there is a basic link between economic dynamics and security concerns, but something much more deliberate and unsettling: the explicit use of economic instruments to advance geopolitical ends.[32] This can range from blocking access to markets with technical barriers to overt coercion in the form of sanctions, and it is distinguished from ordinary economic interactions by entailing the state deliberately subordinating economic activity to its security and strategic ambitions.

The heightened politicization of economic relations has been most visible with regard to trade and infrastructure. While many assume it was the Trump administration's mercantilist instincts that brought this trend to the surface, it was the US efforts to forge a regionwide preferential trade agreement, the Trans-Pacific Partnership (TPP), from 2010 as part of the Obama administration's "pivot to Asia" that ushered in this new phase. The government was unabashed about its intentions: "[W]e can't let countries like China write the rules of the global economy. We should write those rules, opening new markets to American products while setting high standards for protecting workers and preserving our environment."[33] With the concern that the TPP would be too US dominated, other countries in the region launched an alternate program, the Regional Comprehensive Economic Partnership (RCEP) in 2011. The RCEP was concluded in 2020 and came into force in late 2021, while the US withdrawal from the TPP in 2017 led to a hasty reconfiguration of that agreement, which eventually became the Comprehensive and Progressive Agreement for Trans-Pacific Partnership. The infrastructure supported by Beijing's BRI has, since its launch in 2013, led to concerns that its massive development program would buy influence across the region and also provide geopolitical advantages such as port access or the establishment of intelligence facilities.[34] This prompted the US and others to devise alternative infrastructure programs and protocols to try to dilute Chinese influence. The very real need for significant investment in infrastructure across the region is now overlaid with geopolitical considerations that will lead to inefficient economic decisions and exacerbate cycles of rivalry. Geoeconomic dynamics are also visible in disputes that have emerged in the region relating to cybersecurity and 5G telecommunications technology, foreign interference, and in the national responses to the COVID-19 pandemic.[35]

The return of geoeconomics is disconcerting for several reasons. Most immediately, the logic of security is prevailing over economic and market logics, and this has had and will continue to have a negative consequence for economic growth in the region. It is also confirmation that the competition between the great powers is beginning to change economic patterns that had remained relatively constant for decades. Asia's long boom relied on a clear separation of the political and economic. The diversity of political forms, the complex colonial histories, and many territorial disputes meant that the region had numerous issues which could inflame relations between them. To overcome these obstacles the region's powers forged a consensus about the priority of economic relations to provide advantage for their peoples. The achievements over the past four decades or so have been remarkable, yet this is now at some risk due to the way security issues in general and great power rivalry in particular are distorting the way international economic relations in the region are being conducted.

Flashpoints and futures

The Indo-Pacific has a number of places where disputes have simmered for decades which not only continue to provide complexity to the management of regional security concerns, but have been heightened by changes to the region's strategic dynamics.[36] These places are flashpoints in the sense that they have a particular configuration of interests among key states, as well as military assets, such that they can be very volatile and there is a risk of significant military escalation in a compressed time period. The Korean Peninsula has been a geopolitical risk since the mid-1950s. It is one of the most militarized parts of the planet, the two Koreas technically remain at war, and its location draws in the interests of all the region's key powers—China, Japan, Russia, and the USA. The East China Sea, and in particular the disputed islands and rocks which the Chinese call the Diaoyutai and the Japanese the Senkakus, is the second of the region's risk points.[37] Since 2012, when the Japanese government acquired the islands from a private owner, which in the eyes of Beijing changed a settled status quo, they have been the site of frequent friction as the PRC has sovereignty claims over islands that Japan administers in a strategically crucial part of the western Pacific.

Taiwan's standing, like the division of Korea, is a legacy of the early Cold War period when the nationalist forces retreated after the Chinese Communist Party's (CCP's) victory in China's civil war. Beijing views the island as a rogue province, while the US has guaranteed its security since recognizing the PRC in the late 1970s. The South China Sea is the fourth flashpoint.[38] Across the sea are a range of islands, atolls, reefs, and other features which are the subject of a complex array of competing claims among six parties. Since 2013, the PRC has reclaimed about 3,000 acres (1,200 hectares) of land to create a number of artificial islands and has installed military equipment on them. Given the strategic importance of the waterway, the hydrocarbon reserves, and fishing rights, as well as its symbolism, the sea's disputes are of high significance and tensions have flared over the competing claims for many decades. The last two of the Indo-Pacific's flashpoints relate to border disputes in south Asia. India and Pakistan's unresolved border has been the subject of frequent tension and periodic military conflict since 1948, while the border between India and China has likewise waxed and waned in its temperature including a short war in the 1960s.

The number of points at which the interests of key regional powers clash, the height of the stakes, and their geographic span makes the Indo-Pacific an especially risky region. There are few parts of the world that have so many places at which conflict could ignite among such significant powers. As this chapter has sought to show, the sense of security risk that has prompted the reimagining of the region's strategic geography on the grand Indo-Pacific scale has given these flashpoints added volatility. And it has done so in a number of specific ways. Beyond the basic point that the region's countries are all now richer than they were and are thus more capable of advancing their interests, none more so than the PRC, the disputes also have a specific resonance as parts of the growing competition between China and the US. The standing of the South China Sea disputes was always of interest to the US and its allies but now how those disputes are resolved (or not) reflects the broader dynamics of the competition between Beijing and Washington. If China prevails then it has significant consequences, not just for who is able to extract hydrocarbon resources from the seabed or what navies may do in the sea, but also for how the region's order will function in the future.

A second and related reason for the increased temperature of these flashpoints has been the resurgence of nationalism across the region and the ways in which these disputes relate to the dynamics of nationalist politics within key regional players. It is striking that as Asia has become more economically integrated, and consequently more prosperous, the region has not witnessed the erosion of nationalist sensibility that that some liberals had anticipated; instead, the increased wealth and power has fueled a sense that these states have a capacity to make good on their ambitions. Of course the particular dynamics of nationalism vary across the region. For example, the CCP has placed national redemption at the heart of its legitimation strategy, arguing that it and only it can hold China together and ensure the country is able to attain power and wealth commensurate with its scale and civilizational legacy. This means disputes about sovereignty in the East China Sea have a vector in domestic politics that may increase the risks the elite are willing to bear to resolve the dispute.

The six flashpoints in different ways carry significant risks of escalating into conflict. Of these Taiwan is, at the time of publication, the place where the possibilities of war are at their highest. In January 2019, Xi Jinping publicly stated that he did not want to pass the Taiwan situation on for another generation to resolve.[39] This theme had first surfaced in 2013; however, in the context of how Chinese foreign policy had developed in the intervening six years, it had an added dimension. So while Xi did not and has not set a deadline, it is clear that he has moved from the more cautious approach that was based on the belief that the long-term power imbalance between China and Taiwan would eventually drive matters in Beijing's direction. This has been matched with increased military activity near the island and an increase in public discussion within China about the need for forceful takeover of Taiwan. Some scholars have observed that there is a growing perception within Beijing that the PRC could succeed at an acceptable cost, prompted by the People's Liberation Army's growing military advantages and the particular distribution of US forces in the region, which provides incentives for preemption.[40] Given how important Taiwan is to the nationalist discourse on which the CCP has staked its future and to the broader sense, one that the COVID pandemic has reinforced, that history is on China's side, as well as the perceived need within Washington to defend its alliance promises and its broader vision for the region, the risks of this flashpoint igniting and tipping the region into conflict are very real indeed.

Conclusion

The Indo-Pacific is now at the center of global affairs. It is the most populous zone of the planet, home to its biggest and most dynamic economies, and it is a place that is beset with security risks that are of consequence not only to the billions who live there but to global politics more broadly. If the twentieth century's geopolitics was defined by the tensions created by the post-1945 ideological division of Europe, the twenty-first century's global security environment will be determined by the success or otherwise of the countries of the region in managing their many fault lines and fissures.

While it is impossible to discern precisely how the region's security environment may develop in the future, there are a number of main paths down which it is likely to travel. The first of these is a future of managed competition in which the major powers work out a kind of "rules of the road" to ensure the many areas in which they compete for influence are contained and escalation risks minimized. Under this scenario uncontained contestation is avoided, states are able to maintain a degree of proportion about clashes of interest, and the worst excesses of arms races and the like are avoided. Nonetheless the region, and consequently the world, would be dominated by geopolitical considerations, leading to significant allocation of resources on defense and security spending, while friction caused by these tensions would be the norm across the region. A second path entails the US and China recreating the rapprochement of the 1970s and working out a way in which each can live with the other's vision of the region and their respective roles within it. This would be by some margins the best-case scenario for the Indo-Pacific's future; however, it would require at least one if not both great powers moving very considerably from their current trajectory. For example, it would need China to adopt a much more moderate foreign policy than Xi Jinping has established or it would require the US to accept a significantly reduced military and political role in the region. Both of these remain unlikely outcomes for the foreseeable future. A third scenario is one of unmanaged competition in which the current very unstable situation persists for decades. That is, each has a vision of the region and its place within it that is incompatible with the other, but they are not prepared to fight a full-scale conflict to achieve ultimate resolution and they are also unable or unwilling to establish the kinds of diplomatic structures or processes to compete within an agreed framework. This is a highly risky environment in which the logic of geopolitical competition becomes almost all consuming, creating significant distortions of economic, political, and cultural interactions across the region and greatly increasing the risks of large-scale warfare.

Since the mid-1970s the region now known as the Indo-Pacific has been responsible for the greatest increase in human welfare in history. This was made possible by a remarkably stable security environment. Sadly, the success of that period has made the continuation of that benign security setting increasingly difficult. As the three stylized paths show, the region's future will be more insecure than the recent past. The fragility that the COVID pandemic exposed has not just exacerbated the trends discussed in this chapter; it has led to a decisive ramping up of great power competition. Just how dangerous and risky the decades ahead will be is yet to be determined, but however the elites of the region chart their course, the peoples of the Indo-Pacific, and the world, face a much more dangerous future.

Notes

1. "Remarks by Vice President Harris on the Indo-Pacific Region," White House, August 24, 2021, https://www.whitehouse.gov/briefing-room/speeches-remarks/2021/08/24/remarks-by-vice-president-harris-on-the-indo-pacific-region/ (accessed March 2, 2022).
2. "Remarks by President Trump at APEC CEO Summit," US Embassy and Consulate in Vietnam, November 10, 2017, https://vn.usembassy.gov/20171110-remarks-president-trump-apec-ceo-summit/ (accessed March 2, 2022).
3. Paul J. Kohlenberg and Nadine Godehardt (eds.), *The Multidimensionality of Regions in World Politics* (Abingdon, England: Routledge, 2021).
4. Donald K. Emerson, "'Southeast Asia': What's in a Name?" *Journal of Southeast Asian Studies* 15, no. 1 (1984): 1–21.
5. Shinzo Abe, "Confluence of the Two Seas," Ministry of Foreign Affairs of Japan, August 22, 2007, https://www.mofa.go.jp/region/asia-paci/pmv0708/speech-2.html; Taro Aso, "On the 'Arc of Freedom and Prosperity,'" Ministry of Foreign Affairs of Japan, March 12, 2007, https://www.mofa.go.jp/policy/pillar/address0703.html (both accessed March 2, 2022).
6. Ashok Sharma, "The Quadrilateral Initiative: An Evaluation," *South Asian Survey* 17, no. 2 (2010): 237–53.
7. See for example, Rory Medcalf, "Pivoting the Map: Australia's Indo-Pacific System," Centre of Gravity Series No. 1, Australian National University, November 2012, http://sdsc.bellschool.anu.edu.au/sites/default/files/publications/attachments/2020-10/cog_1_2018_soft-proof_v4.pdf (accessed March 2, 2022); C. Raja Mohan, *Samudra Manthan: Sino-Indian Rivalry in the Indo-Pacific* (Washington, DC: Carnegie Endowment for International Peace, 2012).
8. *Australia in the Asian Century*, White Paper, Australian Government, October 2021, available at https://www.murdoch.edu.au/ALTC-Fellowship/_document/Resources/australia-in-the-asian-century-white-paper.pdf (accessed March 2, 2022).
9. *2016 Defence White Paper*, Department of Defence, Australian Government, 2016, https://www.defence.gov.au/whitepaper/Docs/2016-Defence-White-Paper.pdf (accessed March 2, 2022).

10. Rory Medcalf, *Contest for the Indo-Pacific: Why China Won't Map the Future* (Collingwood, VIC: La Trobe University Press, 2020), 3.
11. Kurt M. Campbell, *The Pivot: The Future of American Statecraft in Asia* (New York: Twelve, 2016).
12. "Remarks by President Trump."
13. "A Free and Open Indo-Pacific: Advancing a Shared Vision," US Department of State, November 4, 2019, https://www.state.gov/wp-content/uploads/2019/11/Free-and-Open-Indo-Pacific-4Nov2019.pdf (accessed March 2, 2022).
14. Bill Birtles, "China Mocks Australia over 'Indo-Pacific' Concept It Says Will 'Dissipate,' ABC News (Australia), March 8, 2018, https://www.abc.net.au/news/2018-03-08/china-mocks-australia-over-indo-pacific-concept/9529548 (accessed April 14, 2022).
15. "ASEAN Outlook on the Indo-Pacific," ASEAN Thailand 2019, June 23, 2019, https://asean2019.go.th/en/news/asean-outlook-on-the-indo-pacific/ (accessed March 2, 2022).
16. John J. Mearsheimer, *The Tragedy of Great Power Politics* (New York: W. W. Norton, 2001).
17. Timo Kivimaki, *The Long Peace of East Asia* (Farnham, England: Ashgate, 2014).
18. Nick Bisley, "Asia's Regional Security Order: Rules, Power and Status," *Australian Journal of Politics & History* 65, no. 3 (2019): 361–76.
19. See, for example, "A New Kind of Cold War," *The Economist*, May 18, 2019, https://www.economist.com/leaders/2019/05/16/a-new-kind-of-cold-war (accessed April 21, 2022).
20. David M. Lampton (ed.), *The Making of Chinese Foreign and Security Policy in the Era of Reform, 1978–2000* (Stanford, CA: Stanford University Press, 2001).
21. *National Security Strategy of the United States of America*, White House, December 2017, https://trumpwhitehouse.archives.gov/wp-content/uploads/2017/12/NSS-Final-12-18-2017-0905.pdf (accessed March 2, 2022).
22. Ashley Townshend, Brendan Thomas-Noone, and Matilda Steward, "Averting Crisis: American Strategy, Military Spending and Collective Defence in the Indo-Pacific," United States Study Centre, August 19, 2019, https://www.ussc.edu.au/analysis/averting-crisis-american-strategy-military-spending-and-collective-defence-in-the-indo-pacific; see also Office of the Secretary of Defense, *Military and Security Developments Involving the People's Republic of China 2021*, US Department of Defense, 2021, viii, https://media.defense.gov/2021/Nov/03/2002885874/-1/-1/0/2021-CMPR-FINAL.PDF (both accessed March 2, 2022).
23. See Anthony H. Cordesman, Ashley Hess, and Nicholas S. Yarosh, *Chinese Military Modernization and Force Development*, CSIS, August 23, 2013, https://csis-website-prod.s3.amazonaws.com/s3fs-public/legacy_files/files/publication/130725_chinesemilmodern.pdf (accessed March 2, 2022).

24. Office of the Secretary of Defense, *Military and Security Developments Involving the People's Republic of China 2020: Annual Report to Congress*, US Department of Defense, 2020, https://media.defense.gov/2020/Sep/01/2002488689/-1/-1/1/2020-DOD-CHINA-MILITARY-POWER-REPORT-FINAL.PDF (accessed March 2, 2022).
25. Hedley Bull, *The Anarchical Society: A Study of Order in World Politics*, 2nd ed. (London: Macmillan, 1995).
26. See, for example, Andrew Hurrell, *On Global Order: Power, Values, and the Constitution of International Society* (Oxford: Oxford University Press, 2007).
27. Barry Buzan and Ole Wæver, *Regions and Powers: The Structure of International Security* (Cambridge, England: Cambridge University Press, 2003).
28. Nadège Rolland, "China's Vision for a New World Order: Implications for the United States," National Bureau of Asian Research, October 2020, https://www.nbr.org/wp-content/uploads/pdfs/publications/china_vision_brief_100220.pdf (accessed March 2, 2022).
29. Thomas Shugart, "Australia and the Growing Reach of China's Military," Lowy Institute, August 9, 2021, https://www.lowyinstitute.org/publications/australia-and-growing-reach-china-s-military (accessed March 2, 2022).
30. Shahar Hameiri and Lee Jones, *Governing Borderless Threats: Non-traditional Security and the Politics of State Transformation* (Cambridge, England: Cambridge University Press, 2015).
31. Nick Bisley, "Building Asia's Security," *Adelphi Papers* 49, no. 408 (2009); Kai He (ed.), *Contested Multilateralism 2.0 and Asian Security Dynamics* (Abingdon, England: Routledge, 2020).
32. Robert D. Blackwill and Jennifer M. Harris, *War by Other Means: Geoeconomics and Statecraft* (Cambridge, MA: Belknap Press, 2016).
33. "Statement by the President on the Trans-Pacific Partnership," White House, October 5, 2015, https://obamawhitehouse.archives.gov/the-press-office/2015/10/05/statement-president-trans-pacific-partnership (accessed March 2, 2022).
34. Mingjiang Li, "The Belt and Road Initiative: Geo-economics and Indo-Pacific Security Competition," *International Affairs* 96, no. 1 (2020): 169–87.
35. See Jeffrey Wilson, "Adapting Australia to an Era of Geoeconomic Competition," Perth USAsia Centre, January 2021, https://perthusasia.edu.au/getattachment/Our-Work/Geoeconomics-Report/PU-184-Geoecon-210526-WEB.pdf.aspx?lang=en-AU (accessed March 2, 2022).
36. Brendan Taylor, *The Four Flashpoints: How Asia Goes to War* (Carlton, VIC: La Trobe University Press, 2018).
37. James Manicom, *Bridging Troubled Waters: China, Japan, and Maritime Order in the East China Sea* (Washington, DC: Georgetown University Press, 2014).

38. Bill Hayton, *The South China Sea: The Struggle for Power in Asia* (New Haven, CT: Yale University Press, 2015).
39. Lily Kuo, "'All Necessary Means': Xi Jinping Reserves Right to Use Force against Taiwan," *The Guardian*, January 2, 2019, https://www.theguardian.com/world/2019/jan/02/all-necessary-means-xi-jinping-reserves-right-to-use-force-against-taiwan (accessed April 21, 2022).
40. Oriana Skylar Mastro, "The Taiwan Temptation: Why Beijing Might Resort to Force," *Foreign Affairs* 100, no. 4 (2021): 58–67.

17

The UN Security Council and Climate Security: Responding to a Multifaceted Threat

Shirley V. Scott and Ngoc Nguyen

Introduction

The subject of the United Nations Security Council (UNSC) and climate change can be viewed from two perspectives: the security implications arising out of humanity's failure to adequately mitigate climate change, and the council's law and practice to date. Viewed from the first of these perspectives, the council has done amazingly little relative to the magnitude of the dangers we are facing, but viewed from the second perspective—and what the founders of the UN envisaged the council would be addressing—it is arguably surprising that the council has even considered what the United Nations Framework Convention on Climate Change (UNFCCC) regime has treated as an issue primarily of sustainable development. This chapter reviews what the council has done to date before considering what the global COVID-19 pandemic might mean for any future response by the council to increasing climate insecurity. The pandemic is possibly yet another major world crisis that was made more likely by climate change. Should there come to be widespread acceptance that the pandemic can be attributed to climate change, it may yet trigger a more far-reaching response by the council to the growing security risks posed by humanity's inadequate response to climate change.

The framing of climate change in global governance

There is a politics to how an issue is framed in global governance. Framing may impact the institutional home within which the issue is addressed, the experts and knowledge brought to bear on policy, and, potentially, the degree of seriousness and urgency associated with the response. The Copenhagen School of security studies has raised awareness that the "securitization" of an issue, through a process by which it comes to be accepted as a security issue as opposed to "only" a political, environmental, or economic one, serves to heighten awareness of and garner support for the issue, to lend a sense of urgency to the need to address it, and then to move the policy response beyond "ordinary" politics to be dealt with in emergency mode. In order for securitization to occur, the relevant "audience" needs to accept the "securitizing move" by which the issue is presented as an existential threat to a valued referent object.[1] There is also a normative dimension to the theory; Ole Wæver preferred that a trend toward full securitization be reversed because of the risk that acceptance of more extreme action would heighten the likelihood of armed conflict.[2]

Climate change is a multifaceted issue, with environmental, economic, societal, political, and security dimensions. Interestingly, the security dimension of the issue was recognized as early as the first major international conference on the subject. The final statement of the 1998 conference in Canada was entitled "The Changing Atmosphere: Implications for Global Security." The participants recognized that "unanticipated and unplanned change" to the atmospheric commons "may well become the major non-military threat to international security and the future of the global economy."[3] And yet, interestingly, neither the 1992 UNFCCC, which entered into force on March 21, 1994, nor the Kyoto Protocol, which entered into force in 2005, even referred to "security." Both treaties were premised on climate change being primarily an environmental issue, to be tackled in such a way as to prioritize economic and social considerations, and in particular the needs of developing countries. The principle of common but differentiated responsibilities and respective capabilities, which underpinned the policy response, was unusual in the world of multilateral treaties insofar as it legitimized a solution to the problem that would serve to challenge, as opposed to reinforce, the geopolitical status quo. This meant that it would function to help rising powers at the expense of developed states and potentially to do so more as time went on:

> [I]f damage to the climate were linked to economic activity and the regime as a whole was to prevent dangerous change to the climate, the cost to Annex I [developed] States would become exponentially higher as the economies of major developing countries continued to grow.[4]

It was little wonder that the United States and certain other developed states were disinclined to accept such a negotiating outcome.

In 2007, two years after the Kyoto Protocol entered into force, the UNSC conducted its first debate on the interrelationship of energy, climate, and security. Nongovernmental organizations had provided much of the impetus for this "securitizing move" on the part of the United Kingdom, which led the debate. As securitization theorists might have anticipated, there was considerable contention around whether climate security was an appropriate subject to be addressed by the council. The most obvious reason for the consternation was the potential ramifications: the Security Council has not only recommendatory but compulsory powers. It can make decisions, including even authorizing the use-of-force, with which member states are required to comply, and it is dominated by its five permanent members.

Although, in legal terms, the compulsory powers of the council can be drawn on only once it has identified a "threat to the peace, breach of the peace, or act of aggression" as per Article 39 of the Charter of the United Nations, the primary limitation on the scope of the powers wielded by the council is the political possibility of securing the requisite number of votes. Developing countries did not have a unanimous position: China preferred that the issue be addressed solely within the UNFCCC process, while over succeeding years small island developing states became increasingly alarmed at this existential threat to their existence, including through changing coastlines, destruction of crops, damage to fish stocks, and loss of territory.[5] And yet just what would constitute a decisive response on the part of the council was unclear; because this was a new issue for the council, it was yet to be determined which of its existing policy tools it might most usefully bring to bear or whether new tools might be devised, just as the council had, for example, introduced peacekeeping and established international criminal tribunals, neither of which had been provided for in the initial design of this UN organ.

Mapping the range of possible council responses

Eight years after the council first considered the security implications of climate change, Shirley Scott developed a framework within which to chart the evolving response of the council.[6] At that stage, much of the debate in the council remained couched in binary terms: either it should or could embrace climate change as an appropriate part of its remit, or else it could or should not do so. Rather than framing the council's involvement in climate change in these simple dichotomous terms of action or inaction, Scott mapped in four categories the range of potential UNSC responses, from outright rejection of a role for the council in climate change governance to doing everything within its powers, including potentially assuming the role of peak body in the global governance response to climate change and its effects. The framework is based on four key variables: whether the council would be using its recommendatory or compulsory powers, which policy tools it would bring to bear, whether these would address mitigation or adaption, and the conceptualization of climate change on which that response was premised. A modified version of the original framework is found in Table 17.1.

The first category was included largely for completeness, and is anticipated to be self-explanatory. A "nonresponse" refers to a situation in which the council does not explicitly acknowledge the impact of climate change on international security, but does respond to crises, whether they be civil war or natural disasters, in which climate change and variability are key drivers or risk multipliers. The linkage between a specific situation or event and climate change is often difficult to establish conclusively, and if the causal link *is* established that may well be some time after the event. In these scenarios, the council has in effect responded to climate change, even though not by name, and possibly not even with awareness or agreement among council members that they were in fact doing so.[7]

Table 17.1 Categories of UN Security Council responses to climate change[i]

Category of response	Conceptualization of climate change and/ or of the appropriate institutional role on which the response is logically premised	Explicitly refers to climate change?	Would the council likely address mitigation or adaptation?	What would the council do? Would it most likely adapt existing tools or develop new ones?
1. Rejection of any involvement with this issue	Climate change is unrelated to international peace and security and/ or the UNSC is an inappropriate forum in which to address climate change	Yes	Neither	Neither
2. Climate change "nonresponse"	Climate change is unrelated to international peace and security and/ or the UNSC is an inappropriate forum in which to address climate change	No	Almost certainly adaptation	Either or both. The council does not explicitly articulate that it is responding to climate change but does so by default by responding to an issue or situation likely exacerbated by climate change

Table 17.1 *continued*

Category of response	Conceptualization of climate change and/ or of the appropriate institutional role on which the response is logically premised	Explicitly refers to climate change?	Would the council likely address mitigation or adaptation?	What would the council do? Would it most likely adapt existing tools or develop new ones?
3. Conscious but measured response to the security risks/ situations made worse by climate change	There are multiple pathways by which climate change can impact international security. The impacts are greatest for those who lack the resilience that development affords. The council should act to the extent that the consequences of climate change intersect with what it would in any case be addressing	Yes (climate change is now partially securitized)	Primarily adaptation; potential for some mitigation	Most likely to explicitly mainstream climate change considerations into use of existing tools; may adapt existing tools to climate change. Likely to be a Chapter VI response
4. Climate change writ large	Climate change is a "wicked problem" posing a far-reaching threat to international security, and even calling into question the long-term viability of human survival. In order to fulfil its Charter mandate, the UNSC cannot avoid taking correspondingly far-reaching measures to do all within its capacity to address the threat at its source and to minimize its harmful impacts	Yes (climate change has been fully securitized)	Both—plus "loss and damage"	Draw on existing tools where applicable and potentially develop new tools. Likely to use both Chapter VI and Chapter VII powers

[i] Adapted from Shirley V. Scott, "Implications of Climate Change for the UN Security Council: Mapping the Range of Potential Policy Responses," *International Affairs* 91, no. 6 (2015): 1317–33, https://doi.org/10.1111/1468-2346.12455.

The third and fourth categories of response are premised upon the council's overt acceptance of the multiple pathways by which climate change can impact international peace and security, such as increasing the chance of conflict, complicating the stabilization of societies after conflict, or intensifying the frequency and severity of extreme weather events that directly threaten human security. The two categories are distinguishable by the degree of seriousness with which the threat is perceived and by the magnitude of the response. The third category would likely involve the use of policy tools under Chapter VI of the Charter of the United Nations, which include noncoercive measures aimed at preventing the outbreak or escalation of conflict, whereas the fourth category of response is the most extreme. This would reflect acceptance of climate change as an existential threat to the very survival of humanity, necessitating far-reaching measures, and the council could even conceivably take on a role as peak body coordinating the work of all international institutions whose work has a climate dimension.

Scott's framework helps us to track the gradual evolution of the council's responses since the first formal discussion of climate change as well as the position of an individual state. It can also help illuminate any discrepancy between the position a state adopts at a national level and that which it takes in the council, or any apparent mismatch between the collective view of the degree of the perceived threat and the council's response. It was not intended to preclude variations on these categories but to provide a benchmark against which to identify those variations. The framework does not mean to imply that the response will move inextricably down through the categories. AIDS/HIV, for example, was an issue that was becoming increasingly securitized before the process reversed.[8] On the other hand, in proposing these four levels of possible response it was also recognized that a dramatic shift in the perceived seriousness of the issue, such as might be prompted by multiple synchronous dramatic weather events or disasters around the world, could result in the council moving through these categories very quickly or even jumping straight to the most extreme category of response. It is not inconceivable that a tipping point in the natural world could translate into a governance tipping point.[9]

The response of the council prior to 2015

By the time the UNSC held its first debate on climate change, it was arguably already operating in the second category of a nonresponse, responding to both traditional and nontraditional situations and security threats that had been exacerbated by climate change. Examples of this include Darfur and Ebola. Although scholars vary in their assessments, many analysts considered the situation in Darfur to have been worsened by climate-induced desertification and its impacts on pastoralist societies.[10] Ebola affords a clear example of the council responding to a nontraditional security concern that had likely been exacerbated by climate change but without explicitly acknowledging that connection. The UNSC in Resolution 2177 of September 18, 2014 identified the "unprecedented extent of the Ebola outbreak in West Africa" as "a threat to international peace and security." This was the first time that it had recognized a disease outbreak as such.[11] The following day the General Assembly by Resolution 69/1 "*welcome[d]* the intention of the Secretary-General to establish the United Nations Mission for Ebola Emergency Response" to stop the outbreak, treat the infected, ensure essential services, preserve stability, and prevent further outbreaks. In terms of the framework, the council's response to Ebola constitutes a nonresponse because scientists consider it highly likely that climate change contributed to the severity and rapid spread of the outbreak,[12] and the council responded to the situation but did so without reference to climate change.

It is worth noting that, at that point in time, a category 2 response seemed all that we might ever realistically see from the council. Individual countries and nongovernment organizations may have been leading a debate on a future (explicit) role for the council in this area, but it would be fair to say that the mainstream position was probably that the possibility of the council ever explicitly addressing climate change was rather far fetched. Certain states, including notably permanent members Russia and China, were firmly positioned within category 1. China perceived the issue as one of sustainable development to be addressed through the UNFCCC process. The representative of China stated in 2013:

> The Group of 77 and China reiterates its position that the United Nations Security Council is not the appropriate forum for this discussion. The Group will repeat that the primary responsibility of the United Nations Security Council is the maintenance of international peace and security, as set out in the Charter of the United Nations.[13]

Russia implied that the council had no legitimate role to play in this area when it emphasized that the council "should only deal with the consideration of questions that directly relate to its mandate."[14] The United States had largely evaded the issue at the first council debate in 2007, but in the 2011 open debate Ambassador Susan Rice stated very clearly that the council had an essential responsibility to address the security implications of climate change.[15]

And yet, particularly when viewed in combination with the actions of the secretary-general and the General Assembly, not only was the council already responding to climate change by default, the very fact that it held two debates on the subject could be interpreted as specific members endeavoring to lay the groundwork for a transition to category 3, in which the council explicitly references climate change in its decisions. This includes the first thematic meeting in open debate format, in 2007, on the interlinkages between energy, climate, and security and the second thematic meeting, held on 20 July 2011, again in open debate format, on the impact of climate change. The secretary-general produced a report in 2009 which highlighted climate change as "a threat multiplier" with the potential to exacerbate existing threats to international peace and security,[16] and the council in its 2011 presidential statement expressed concern over the "possible adverse effects of climate change" that "may, in the long run, aggravate certain existing threats to international peace and security."[17] An informal, consciousness-raising "Arria formula" meeting, in the sense of an informal, confidential, gathering of council and nongovernment representatives, was organized by the UK and Pakistan in 2013 on the security dimensions of climate change, which could be interpreted as another attempt to garner acceptance for the securitization of climate change.

The possibility that pandemics should fall within the purview of the council was also considered, both as another nontraditional security threat, and notably also with reference to their likely becoming more common as the climate changes. On November 23, 2011 Portugal organized a council briefing on "New Challenges to International Peace and Security and Conflict Prevention," including pandemics, climate change, and transnational organized crime. In his opening statement, UN Secretary-General Ban Ki-moon referred to each separately but also to linkages among them. "We are all aware of the risk that a warming world will facilitate the spread of deadly diseases."[18] Margaret Chan, director-general of the World Health Organization, noted that health

> nearly everywhere is being shaped by the same powerful, almost universal, forces—such as ageing populations, the movement of people within and between countries, rapid urbanization and the globalization of unhealthy lifestyles, including substance abuse, and, of course, climate change.[19]

Council members expressed quite divergent views regarding how, or even if, the council should address these interrelated challenges.

Meanwhile, the argument that the council was an inappropriate forum in which to consider climate change had already been weakened by General Assembly Resolution 63/281 (2009), which "invited the relevant organs of the United Nations, as appropriate and within their respective mandates, to intensify their efforts in considering and addressing climate change, including its possible security implications."[20] This could be interpreted as the General Assembly legitimizing a role for the council while at the same time demarcating the respective roles of the two bodies as set out in the relevant provisions of the Charter of the United Nations. In this respect it is worth noting, however, that the General Assembly recognizing the legitimacy of the council considering and addressing climate change, does not exclude the assembly also considering climate security. The responsibility of the council for international peace and security is not exclusive; Chapter IV of the Charter also grants the assembly functions and powers in relation to international security. Resolution 63/281 can nevertheless be interpreted as another important development that contributed to laying the groundwork for a transition to the council consciously responding to climate change and its effects.

The response of the council from 2015 to the start of the pandemic

Notably, this period saw the council transition to the third category, that of a "conscious but measured response" as heralded by operative paragraph 26 of Resolution 2349 (2017) on the Lake Chad basin region, by which the council

> [r]ecognises the adverse effects of climate change and ecological changes among other factors on the stability of the Region, including through water scarcity, drought, desertification, land degradation, and food insecurity, and emphasises the need for adequate risk assessments and risk management strategies by governments and the United Nations relating to these factors.[21]

Similar language was applied to the situation in Somalia in Resolution 2408 (2018), and the council appeared to increase in confidence.[22] Operative paragraph 21 of Resolution 2461 of March 27, 2019, for example, requested "the United Nations and the Federal Government of Somalia and the Federal Member States to consider the adverse implications of climate change . . . in their programmes," and further requested "the Secretary-General to provide information of such assessments in mandated reporting as appropriate."[23]

A presidential statement of August 7, 2019 on the issue of consolidating peace in west Africa stressed "the need for long-term strategies, based on risk assessments, by governments and the United Nations, to support stabilisation and build resilience and encourages UNOWAS [the United Nations Office for West Africa and the Sahel] to continue to integrate this information in its activities."[24] This language became a model text for many of the council's resolutions and presidential statements including those in relation to Mali, Sudan, South Sudan, the Democratic Republic of Congo, and the Central African Republic, as well as those on thematic issues such as women, peace and security, and counterterrorism.[25] By explicitly recommending that governments, the UN, and respective missions incorporate risk assessment on climate change into their activities, the council was addressing climate adaptation.

On December 20, 2017, Japan organized an open debate on "complex challenges to international peace and security," which included discussion of both climate change and pandemics. Japan explained that the pandemics in 2014 and 2015 had been direct causes of instability in the countries affected. It urged the council to take an integrated approach to the mutually reinforcing multidimensional factors that are closely interlinked with peace and security.[26] In words reminiscent of category 4, although it would also support a deeper category 3 response, the representative of Japan urged the council to enhance cooperation with other organs within and outside the United Nations. It also advocated adopting a human security approach; this would mean conceptualizing the subject to be protected as being the individual rather than the state. During debate, speakers referenced both pandemics and climate change, but there was no emphasis on a causal role for climate change in the emergence of pandemics.

Another notable development during this period was the establishment of new institutional mechanisms designed to assist the council to assess the risk of climate change and to develop an appropriate response in its missions. While these mechanisms were not founded by the council per se, they represent an effort to grapple with understanding the varying nature of the climate security challenge and the precise role of the council in this regard, and one is a UN initiative. The Climate Security Mechanism (CSM) was established in 2018 as a joint initiative of the UN Department of Political and Peacebuilding Affairs, the UN Development Programme, and the UN Environment Programme to "leverage existing expertise and strengthen UN capacities for a systematic response to climate-related security risks."[27]

Also in 2018, Germany and Nauru cofounded and cochaired the Group of Friends on Climate and Security (GFCS), which initially consisted of twenty-seven member states. The group is tasked with informing policy with climate change effects, raising awareness of these effects and strengthening UN efforts to counter these threats. Germany also played an active role in the establishment in 2019 of the independent Climate Security Expert Network (CSEN) to provide assessments of climate-related security risks and risk management strategies to help inform UN responses. The Berlin-based think tank Adelphi serves as the secretariat for the network, which when established comprised thirty experts from around the globe. The CSEN supports both the CSM and the GFCS by producing reports and accompanying fact sheets on climate security risks in various countries and regions, including Afghanistan, Ethiopia, the Caribbean, Mali, Nepal, North Africa and the Sahel, northern Central America, the Pacific Islands region, south Asia, and Sudan.[28]

The response of the council since March 2020

Since the outbreak of the pandemic, the council has more frequently discussed climate change at a formal level. There had been four council debates relevant to climate security in the period 2007–19, but the next four took place in a period of only fourteen months, between July 2020 and September 2021. There have been other signals of an apparent greater acceptance of climate securitization. Between its founding in 2018 and 2021, the GFCS doubled in size, and now includes ten current council members and member states from all five UN regions.[29] Also indicative was the establishment by ten members of the council (Belgium, the Dominican Republic, Estonia, France, Germany, Niger, Tunisia, St. Vincent and the Grenadines, the United Kingdom, and Vietnam) of the Informal Expert Group of Members of the Security Council on Climate and Security in 2020.[30] Meetings of the group facilitate exchanging ideas on operational challenges arising from climate-related security risks for UN missions including those to Somalia, west Africa and the Sahel, and South Sudan.

Consciousness-raising efforts, including Arria formula meetings, have continued, as has debate on how the council might best respond, including ascertaining the scope to mainstream climate change into the existing work of the council. Increasing attention has been directed to the implications of climate change for peace operations. A 2020 study by the Stockholm International Peace Research Institute found that six of the ten biggest UN peace operations (by total international personnel) were in countries ranked most exposed to climate change, but called for additional work to be undertaken to identify additional measures, authorities, or partnerships through which to address climate-related security risks in mission contexts.[31]

Following unsuccessful proposals to incorporate climate security language in outcomes on cases including Haiti in 2019 and Iraq in 2020,[32] climate change language was in 2021, for the first time, incorporated in outcomes beyond Africa. These include Resolution 2561, renewing the mandate of the UN Peacekeeping Force in Cyprus; and Resolution 2576, renewing the mandate of the UN Assistance Mission for Iraq.

In the lead-up to an open debate held on July 14, 2020, Germany sought to develop the text of a thematic resolution on "climate change and security." The draft, cosponsored with Belgium, the Dominican Republic, Estonia, France, Niger, St Vincent and the Grenadines, Tunisia, the UK, and Vietnam, invited the secretary-general to consider the security implications of the effects of climate change across a wide range of the council's activities and to prepare regular reports on the security implications of the negative effects of climate change. Significantly, it also requested the secretary-general to appoint a special representative to be responsible for coordinating the UN's efforts to address climate-related security threats and liaising with external actors. China, Russia, and the US were opposed to the resolution, which was therefore abandoned well ahead of the meeting.[33]

In November 2020 the council held an open debate on "contemporary drivers of conflict and instability and insecurity." Speakers frequently juxtaposed climate change and the pandemic as nontraditional security challenges that are exacerbating well-known drivers of conflict and instability, although without drawing any direct connection between the two. The representative of El Salvador highlighted that the pandemic was not only a health crisis but one with social, economic, and political consequences. Speakers referred to the way in which the pandemic had forced us all to recognize our vulnerabilities and many of them referenced collective security. The representative of Denmark highlighted the need for coherent and integrated solutions across the United Nations to complex transnational challenges, Italy referred to "developing a whole-of-system response," and Japan to closer collaboration among the United Nations bodies.[34]

A key point made by securitization theorists is that securitization results in extraordinary measures, such as policy moving out of ordinary politics to an emergency response, as per the fourth category in the framework. This would suggest that the groundwork for moving to category 4 in respect of climate security could be laid by increasing support for actions on the part of the council of a far-reaching order of magnitude, and/or through greater acceptance of a conceptualization of climate change as an existential threat to the very survival of humankind.

It is informative to review the briefing by the secretary-general to the council on March 1, 2021 in this light. Some remarks were reflective of a category 3 conceptualization of climate insecurity and a category 3 response on the part of the council: "Climate disruption is a crisis amplifier and multiplier. Where climate change dries up rivers, reduces harvests, destroys critical infrastructure, and displaces communities, it exacerbates the risks of instability and conflict."[35] Others, however, were more reflective of a conceptualization of the most extreme, category 4, role for the council. The secretary-general referred to the "climate emergency as the defining issue of our time" and the "climate crisis [as the] multilateral challenge of our age . . . It is already impacting every area of human activity." Notably, emphasis on the need for greater coordination among institutions and UN bodies continued the theme of the CSM and is potentially compatible with the idea of the council becoming the peak body in respect of climate change. The secretary-general continued: "Solving it requires coordination and cooperation on a scale that we have never seen before. The engagement of all multilateral bodies, including the Security Council, can play an important role in dealing with the challenge."[36]

Although China and Russia retain strong reservations about a climate change role for the council,[37] the election of President Biden heralded the United States resuming its earlier support for a council response to climate change. During the February 23, 2021 open debate, Special Presidential Envoy for Climate John Kerry announced the intention of the US to work closely with like-minded colleagues "to focus the Council's attention on the climate crisis and its consequences for international peace and security."[38] The United States joined the GFCS and announced its intention to join the Informal Expert Group on Climate and Security.[39]

How might the pandemic influence the council's future responses to climate insecurity?

The analysis has so far traced growing acceptance of a role for the council in respect of climate security. A category 4 conceptualization of the security threat posed by climate change has arguably from a scientific perspective been appropriate and proportionate to the risk for some time. It was noted that, at the time the framework was developed, the variety of positions held, including on the part of the permanent members of the council, meant that any move even into the third category seemed unlikely. In the intervening period we have seen the council step into category 3. The permanent members that did not support securitization did not block the council taking this important step, and we have now seen some developments that, even if not intended in these terms, could be viewed as helping prepare the way for a far broader and deeper category 3 response, or even for the previously unthinkable step into the most extreme category of response. Category 4 would involve a far-reaching response on the part of the council not just to situations made worse by climate change but to climate change itself. It might involve strong measures as for example a Chapter VII resolution requiring all states to become parties to the Paris Agreement or to assist the least developed countries to adapt, or indeed to prohibit, deforestation, or to limit population growth.

The council may have moved as rapidly as it has because of growing awareness of climate security risks and mounting evidence of the inadequacy of the Paris Agreement. One possible trigger for the council adopting a Chapter VII resolution in response to climate change might be multiple synchronous disasters that prompt acceptance of more authoritarian governance of climate impacts at a global level.[40] In future we can anticipate multiple overlapping crises and disasters made worse by climate change and variability. COVID-19 complicated the management of extreme weather events such as hurricanes in the United States.[41] During the timeframe of the pandemic there has been ongoing elevation of the impacts of climate change and variability, and the prospects for human security for all people have continued to deteriorate. This has been documented in information released during the sixth assessment cycle of the Intergovernmental Panel on Climate Change,[42] and highlighted in commentary surrounding the 26th UN Climate Change Conference of the Parties (COP26), which was held from October 31 to November 12, 2021.

Such awareness could be expected to heighten were there to be widespread acceptance of scientific attribution of the pandemic to climate change. The council was made cognizant of the impact of climate change on the frequency of pandemics as far back as 2011, and scientists have already determined that climate change "may have played a key role in the evolution or transmission of the two SARS-CoVs."[43] Climate change has been impacting infectious disease transmission patterns and many of the root causes of climate change also elevate the risk of pandemics;[44] scientists have attributed intensifying pathogen emergence to climate change,[45] and warn that we have entered a "pandemic era."[46] At the very minimum, these crises have been unfolding in parallel, adding to a sense of uncertainty and unpredictability about our future. The under-secretary-general of the United Nations has referred to the pandemic and to "shocks of all kinds," or multifaceted challenges.[47] Viewed in this way, the COVID-19 pandemic is merely indicative of a trend that is underway and that will continue for some time no matter what mitigation is undertaken, but which, absent far more rapid and effective mitigation, is projected to become far worse.

The council has taken steps to link the pandemic and security in its resolutions, but without reference to climate change. On March 23, 2020, Secretary-General António Guterres called for a global ceasefire in response to COVID-19.[48] The Security Council subsequently adopted Resolution 2532 (2020) on July 1, a preambular paragraph of which recognized that "conditions of violence and instability in conflict situations can exacerbate the pandemic, and that inversely the pandemic can exacerbate the adverse humanitarian impact of conflict situations," and went on to demand a general and immediate cessation of hostilities in all situations on its agenda.[49] Resolution 2565 (2021), adopted by the council on February 26, 2021 and focused particularly on equitable and affordable access to vaccines, similarly pointed to the interconnection between the pandemic and security but without reference to causes of the pandemic. Some of the remarks about the COVID-19 pandemic nevertheless echo language increasingly being used in relation to climate change.[50] During the high-level open debate on contemporary drivers of conflict and insecurity on November 12, 2020, the representative of Nigeria referred to the pandemic as "a specific and immediate threat to the very survival of the world population."[51] Singapore noted that modern threats are multifaceted and interconnected; that environmental challenges and pandemics pose an "existential threat to all humankind."[52] This suggests that if the council recognizes the pandemic-climate change-security nexus, it could give impetus to the trend toward securitizing climate change.

Critical for the council to take dramatic action is positive support on the part of all permanent members. The United States, France, and Russia had not suffered to any great extent the effects of Ebola or SARS, and hence this pandemic may have come as more of a shock to them. Notably, democratic nations responded to the pandemic with measures that might previously have been considered an unthinkable negation of civil liberties. Australia even prevented its citizens from leaving the country and the Victoria state premier, Daniel Andrews, (unsuccessfully) proposed letting ordinary residents arrest other citizens suspected of breaching public health orders.[53] The measures are suggestive of the extraordinary powers associated with securitization. Daniel Wild of the Institute of Public Affairs challenged Australian governments to "commit to fully restoring the freedoms of all Australians and to return to the normal operation of parliament and democracy."[54]

Notably, the military has in many countries been integral to the authoritarian response. Fawzia Gibson-Fall identifies three emerging trends of military engagement in domestic health responses, ranging from (1) minimal technical military support through (2) blended civil-military responses to (3) military-led responses.[55] Authoritarian states including China and Vietnam adopted a blended model, in which national militaries took part in population-facing activities in parallel to, or embedded within, the civilian-led response. In these contexts, the military was deployed to assist with enforcing lockdown, providing food for the local population, and contributing medical staff and equipment for the treatment of patients.[56] Meanwhile, in other countries including Indonesia, Sri Lanka, Myanmar, Thailand, and the Philippines, the military took the leadership of the entire COVID-19 response.[57] While the role of the military may reflect a country's historical legacy so far as civil-military relations are concerned, it also aligns with a perception that the crisis necessitates emergency measures.

Conclusion

This chapter has reviewed what the UN Security Council has done regarding climate change since its first formal thematic debate in 2007, and particularly whether there was a discernible shift after the COVID-19 pandemic began in early 2020. By reviewing the council's responses in relation to a four-category framework of possible action, this study has identified a transition from a climate change "non-response"—that is, the council reacting to crises in which climate change was a contributing factor without overtly acknowledging the climate-security nexus—to a "conscious but measured" response. The council's step into such a category 3 response was underpinned by greater acceptance of climate securitization at the council level, the mainstreaming of climate security language into council outcomes even beyond Africa, and a heightened sense of the need to incorporate risk assessment and risk management strategies into its missions. China and Russia still hold strong views against a climate change role for the council, but the COVID-19 pandemic may yet contribute to the council adopting an even more far-reaching response to climate insecurity. The above analysis suggests that this could be the case especially if and when there is broad scientific consensus linking the pandemic to climate change and if, as would seem likely, we experience multiple synchronous natural disasters and emergencies. As US secretary of state Antony Blinken commented, "we have to stop debating whether the climate crisis belongs in the Security Council and instead ask how the Council can leverage its unique powers to tackle the negative impacts of climate on peace and security."[58]

Notes

1. Barry Buzan, Ole Wæver, and Jaap de Wilde, *Security: A New Framework for Analysis* (Boulder, CO: Lynne Rienner, 1998); Ole Wæver, "Securitization and Desecuritization," in *On Security*, ed. Ronnie D. Lipschutz (New York: Columbia University Press, 1995), 46–86.
2. Wæver, "Securitization and Desecuritization," 69; Buzan et al., *Security*, 29.
3. "The Changing atmosphere: Implications for global security" (Conference Statement), Toronto, June 27–30, 1988, https://www.academia.edu/4043227/The_Changing_Atmosphere_Implications_for_Global_Security_Conference_Statement_1988 (accessed August 2022).
4. Shirley V. Scott, "Does the UNFCCC Fulfil the Functions Required of a Framework Convention? Why Abandoning the United Nations Framework Convention on Climate Change Might Constitute a Long Overdue Step Forward," *Journal of Environmental Law* 27, no. 1 (2015): 85.
5. United Nations Security Council, 5,663rd meeting, April 17, 2007, UN Doc. S/PV.5663 (Resumption 1).
6. Shirley V. Scott, "Implications of Climate Change for the UN Security Council: Mapping the Range of Potential Policy Responses," *International Affairs* 91, no. 6 (2015): 1317–33.
7. Ibid., 1325.
8. Colin McInnes and Simon Rushton, "HIV, AIDS and Security: Where Are We Now?," *International Affairs* 86, no. 1 (2010): 225–45.
9. Shirley V. Scott and Charlotte Ku, "The UN Security Council and Global Action on Climate Change," in *Climate Change and the UN Security Council*, ed. Shirley V. Scott and Charlotte Ku (Cheltenham, England: Edward Elgar, 2018), 1–24.
10. *Sudan: Post-conflict Environmental Assessment*, United Nations Environment Program, 2007, 58.
11. Elijah Wolfson, "Ebola and Climate Change: Are Humans Responsible for the Severity of the Current Outbreak?" *Newsweek*, December 8, 2014, https://www.newsweek.com/climate-change-ebola-outbreak-globalization-infectious-disease-264163 (accessed March 2, 2022).
12. Ibid.
13. Peter Thomson, "Statement on Behalf of the Group of 77 by Ambassador Peter Thomson, Permanent Representative of Fiji to the United Nations and Chairman of the Group of 77, and China at the Arria-Formula Meeting on the Security Dimensions of Climate Change," February

15, 2013, http://www.g77.org/statement/getstatement.php?id=130215a (accessed March 2, 2022).

14. United Nations Security Council, 5,663rd meeting.
15. Shirley V. Scott, "The Attitude of the P5 towards a Climate Change Role for the Council," in *Climate Change and the UN Security Council*, ed. Shirley V. Scott and Charlotte Ku (Cheltenham, England: Edward Elgar, 2018), 209–28.
16. "Climate Change and Its Possible Security Implications: Report of the Secretary-General," United Nations General Assembly, September 11, 2009, UN Doc. A/64/350.
17. United Nations Security Council, Statement by the President of the Security Council, July 20, 2011, UN Doc. S/PRST/2011/15, 2.
18. United Nations Security Council, 6,668th meeting, November 23, 2011, UN Doc. S/PV.6668, 3.
19. Ibid., 7.
20. United Nations General Assembly, Resolution 63/281, "Climate Change and its Possible Security Implications," June 11, 2009, UN Doc. A/RES/63/281, 2.
21. United Nations Security Council, Resolution 2349, "Peace and Security in Africa," March 31, 2017, UN Doc. S/RES/2349 (2017), 1.
22. United Nations Security Council, Resolution 2408, "The Situation in Somalia," March 27, 2018, UN Doc. S/RES/2408 (2018).
23. United Nations Security Council, Resolution 2461, "The Situation in Somalia," March 27, 2019, UN Doc S/RES/2461 (2019), 7.
24. United Nations Security Council, Statement by the President of the Security Council, August 7, 2019, UN Doc. S/PRST/2019/7.
25. "The UN Security Council and Climate Change," Security Council Report, June 2021, 21–6, https://www.securitycouncilreport.org/atf/cf/%7B65BFCF9B-6D27-4E9C-8CD3-CF6E4FF96FF9%7D/climate_security_2021.pdf (accessed March 2, 2022). See Annex IV for a detailed description of climate change language in the UNSC's outcomes.
26. United Nations Security Council, 8,144th meeting, December 20, 2017, UN Doc. S/PV.8144, 4.
27. "Toolbox Briefing Note," United Nations Climate Security Mechanism, 2020, 10, https://dppa.un.org/sites/default/files/csm_toolbox-1-briefing_note.pdf (accessed March 2, 2022).
28. Climate Security Expert Network, https://climate-security-expert-network.org/.
29. "The UN Security Council and Climate Change."
30. United Nations, letter dated August 27, 2020 from the chargé d'affaires A.I. of the permanent mission of Germany to the United Nations addressed to the secretary-general, August 27, 2020, UN Doc. S/2020/849.
31. Florian Krampe, "Why United Nations Peace Operations Cannot Ignore Climate Change," Stockholm International Peace Research Institute, February 22, 2021, https://www.sipri.org/commentary/

topical-backgrounder/2021/why-united-nations-peace-operations-cannot-ignore-climate-change (accessed March 3, 2022).

32. "The UN Security Council and Climate Change," 8.
33. Ibid., 6.
34. United Nations, letter dated November 5, 2020 from the president of the Security Council to the secretary-general and the permanent representatives of the members of the Security Council, November 12, 2020, UN Doc. S/2020/1090.
35. United Nations, letter dated February 25, 2021 from the president of the Security Council to the secretary-general and the permanent representatives of the members of the Security Council, March 1, 2021, UN Doc. S/2021/198, 3.
36. Ibid., 5.
37. As evidenced by China abstaining on, and Russia using its veto on, an attempt on December 13, 2021, to pass a chapter VII resolution on integrating climate-related security risk in UN conflict prevention strategies. "Security Council Fails to Adopt Resolution Integrating Climate-Related Security Risk into Conflict-Prevention Strategies," SC/14732, December 13, 2021, https://press.un.org/en/2021/sc14732.doc.htm (accessed August 2022).
38. Ibid., 37.
39. "The UN Security Council and Climate Change," 13.
40. Shirley V. Scott and Christopher Kaindi, "The Responsibility of the UN Security Council for Climate Security," in *Ethiopian Yearbook of International Law 2019: Towards a Global Order Based on Principles of Fairness, Solidarity, and Humanity*, ed. Zeray Yihdego, Melaku Geboye Desta, and Martha Belete Hailu (Cham, Switzerland: Springer, 2020), 211–19.
41. Renee N. Salas, James M. Shultz, and Caren. G. Solomon, "The Climate Crisis and Covid-19—A Major Threat to the Pandemic Response," *New England Journal of Medicine* 383, no. 11 (2020): e70.
42. "Synthesis Report of the Sixth Assessment Report," IPCC, https://www.ipcc.ch/ar6-syr/ (accessed March 3, 2022).
43. Robert M. Beyer, Andrea Manica, and Camilo Mora, "Shifts in Global Bat Diversity Suggest a Possible Role of Climate Change in the Emergence of SARS-CoV-1 and SARS-CoV-2," *Science of The Total Environment* 767 (2021): 145413.
44. "Coronavirus, Climate Change, and the Environment: A Conversation on COVID-19 with Dr. Aaron Bernstein, Director of Harvard Chan C-CHANGE," Harvard T. H. Chan School of Public Health, https://www.hsph.harvard.edu/c-change/subtopics/coronavirus-and-climate-change (accessed March 3, 2022).
45. Dirk S. Schmeller, Franck Courchamp, and Gerry Killeen, "Biodiversity Loss, Emerging Pathogens and Human Health Risks," *Biodiversity and Conservation* 29, no. 11 (2020): 3095–3102.
46. "A Pandemic Era," *Lancet Planetary Health* 5, no. 1 (2021): e1.

47. United Nations, letter dated November 5, 2020, 4.
48. "Secretary-General's Appeal for Global Ceasefire," United Nations Secretary-General, March 23, 2020, https://www.un.org/sg/en/content/sg/statement/2020-03-23/secretary-generals-appeal-for-global-ceasefire (accessed March 3, 2022).
49. United Nations Security Council, Resolution 2532, July 1, 2020, UN Doc. S/RES/2532 (2020).
50. United Nations Security Council, Resolution 2565, February 26, 2021, UN Doc. S/RES/2565 (2021).
51. United Nations, letter dated November 5, 2020, 90.
52. Ibid., 102.
53. Charlie Moore, "The Freedoms We May NEVER Get Back: How Our Privacy, Social Life and Travel Will Be Restricted 'for the Next TWO YEARS'—as Leaders Continue to Use Extraordinary Powers They Gained during the Pandemic Even after Vaccination Targets Are Hit," *Daily Mail*, October 1, 2021, https://www.dailymail.co.uk/news/article-10039985/Pubs-travel-masks-freedoms-NEVER-Covid-19.html (accessed March 3, 2022).
54. Ibid.
55. Fawzia Gibson-Fall, "Military Responses to COVID-19, Emerging Trends in Global Civil-Military Engagements," *Review of International Studies* 47, no. 2 (2021): 155–70.
56. Euan Graham, "The Armed Forces and COVID-19," IISS, April 8, 2020, https://www.iiss.org/blogs/analysis/2020/04/easia-armed-forces-and-covid-19 (accessed March 3, 2022).
57. Gibson-Fall, "Military Responses."
58. Antony J. Blinken, "Secretary Antony J. Blinken at UN Security Council Meeting on Climate and Security," US Department of State, September 23, 2021, https://www.state.gov/secretary-antony-j-blinken-at-un-security-council-meeting-on-climate-and-security/ (accessed March 3, 2022).

Bibliography

Abe, Shinzo, "Confluence of the Two Seas," Ministry of Foreign Affairs of Japan, August 22, 2007, https://www.mofa.go.jp/region/asia-paci/pmv0708/speech-2.html

Abboud, Samer, et al., "Towards a Beirut School of Critical Security Studies," *Critical Studies on Security* 6, no. 3 (2018): 273–95.

Ablon, Lillian, Martin C. Libicki, and Andrea A. Golay, *Markets for Cybercrime Tools and Stolen Data: Hackers' Bazaar* (Santa Monica, CA: RAND, 2014).

Académie nationale de médecine, "Impact of the Covid-19 Pandemic on Domestic Violence," press release, December 18, 2020, https://www.academie-medecine.fr/impact-of-the-covid-19-pandemic-on-domestic-violence/?lang=en

ACAPS, *Humanitarian Access Overview*, July 2021, 8, https://www.acaps.org/sites/acaps/files/products/files/20210719_acaps_humanitarian_access_overview_july_2021.pdf

ACAPS, "Yemen: Complex Crisis," August 26, 2021, https://www.acaps.org/country/yemen/crisis/complex-crisis

Acharya, Amitav, and Barry Buzan, "Why Is There No Non-Western International Relations Theory? An Introduction," in *Non-Western International Relations Theory: Perspectives on and beyond Asia*, ed. Amitav Acharya and Barry Buzan (Abingdon, England: Routledge, 2010).

Acharya, Amitav, and Barry Buzan, "Why Is There No Non-Western International Relations Theory? Ten Years On," *International Relations of the Asia-Pacific* 17, no. 3 (2017): 341–70.

Acheson, Ray (ed.), *Assuring Destruction Forever: Nuclear Weapon Modernization around the World* (New York: Reaching Critical Will, 2012).

ADB, "Regional Comprehensive Economic Partnership: Overview and Economic Impact," *ADB Briefs* 164 (2020), https://www.adb.org/sites/default/files/publication/664096/adb-brief-164-regional-comprehensive-economic-partnership.pdf

Agamben, Giorgio, "The State of Exception Provoked by an Unmotivated Emergency," *Positions Politics* (blog), February 26, 2020, https://positionspolitics.org/giorgio-agamben-the-state-of-exception-provoked-by-an-unmotivated-emergency/

Agius, Christine, Annika Bergman Rosamond, and Catarina Kinnvall, "Populism, Ontological Insecurity and Gendered Nationalism: Masculinity, Climate Denial and Covid-19," *Politics, Religion & Ideology* 21, no. 4 (2020): 432–50.

AJMC Staff, "A Timeline of COVID-19 Developments in 2020," AJMC, January 1, 2021, https://www.ajmc.com/view/a-timeline-of-covid19-developments-in-2020

Akita, Hiroyuki, and Eri Sugiura, "Pompeo Aims to 'Institutionalize' Quad Ties to Counter China," Nikkei Asia, October 6, 2020, https://asia.nikkei.com/Editor-s-Picks/Interview/Pompeo-aims-to-institutionalize-Quad-ties-to-counter-China

Al Jazeera, "COVID Has Worsened Inequality Even as the Rich Thrive: Oxfam," January 25, 2021, https://www.aljazeera.com/economy/2021/1/25/covid-19-worsened-global-inequality-even-as-the-rich-bounced-back

Alba, Davey, "Virus Conspiracy Theorists Elevate a New Champion," *New York Times*, May 9, 2020, https://www.nytimes.com/2020/05/09/technology/plandemic-judy-mikovitz-coronavirus-disinformation.html

Albrecht, Glenn, et al., "Solastalgia: The Distress Caused by Environmental Change," *Australasian Psychiatry* 15, no. 1 supplement (2007): S95–S98.

Alder, Steve, "VMWare Carbon Black Explores the State of Healthcare Cybersecurity in 2020," *HIPAA Journal*, February 8, 2020, https://www.hipaajournal.com/vmware-carbon-black-explores-the-state-of-healthcare-cybersecurity-in-2020/

Alexander, Audrey, "The Security Threat COVID-19 Poses to the Northern Syria Detention Camps Holding Islamic State Members," *CTC Sentinel* 13, no. 6 (2020): 16–25.

Alexander, Samuel, "Double-Tap Warfare: Should President Obama Be Investigated for War Crimes?" *Florida Law Review* 69, no. 1 (1997): 262–95.

Ali, Mona, "Vaccine Diplomacy: In 2021, the UAE Will Become the New Vaccine Hub of the Middle East," Observer Research Foundation, December 29, 2020, https://www.orfonline.org/expert-speak/uae-will-become-new-vaccine-hub-middle-east/

Ali, Tariq, *The Forty Year War in Afghanistan: A Chronicle Foretold* (London: Verso, 2021).

Allen, James S., *Atomic Imperialism: The State, Monopoly and the Bomb* (New York: International Publishers, 1952).

AlTakarli, Nourah S., "China's Response to the COVID-19 Outbreak: A Model for Epidemic Preparedness and Management," *Dubai Medical Journal* 3, no. 2 (2020): 44–9.

Alterman, Jon B., "The Normalization of UAE-Israel Relations," Center for Strategic and International Studies, August 14, 2020, https://www.csis.org/analysis/normalization-uae-israel-relations

Alves, Lise, "Pandemic Puts Brazil Back on the World Hunger Map," *New Humanitarian*, July 19, 2021, https://www.thenewhumanitarian.org/news-feature/2021/7/19/pandemic-puts-brazil-back-on-the-world-hunger-map

Amadae, S. M., and Shahar Avin, "Autonomy and Machine Learning at the Interface of Nuclear Weapons, Computers and People," in *The Impact of Artificial Intelligence on Strategic Stability and Nuclear Risk, Vol. 1: Euro-Atlantic Perspectives*, ed. Vincent Boulanin (Stockholm: SIPRI, 2019).

Anderson, Jessica, "Maryland Man Allegedly Fatally Shot His Pharmacist Brother for 'Killing People' with the COVID Vaccine, Court Records Show," *Baltimore Sun*, October 7, 2021, https://www.baltimoresun.com/news/crime/bs-md-cr-burnham-follow-20211006-srubyenoujenvkd5igalidruwm-story.html

Andreu-Perez, Javier, et al., *Artificial Intelligence and Robotics* (London: UK-RAS Network, 2018).

Ansell, Nicola, *Children, Youth and Development*, 2nd edn. (Abingdon, England: Routledge, 2017).

Aradau, Claudia, "Security That Matters: Critical Infrastructure and Objects of Protection," *Security Dialogue* 41, no. 5 (2010): 491–514.

Aradau, Claudia, and Rens Van Munster, "Governing Terrorism through Risk: Taking Precautions, (Un)Knowing the Future," *European Journal of International Relations* 13, no. 1 (2007): 89–115.

"Areas of Alignment: Common Visions for a Killer Robots Treaty," Human Rights Watch and Harvard Law School International Human Rights Clinic, July 2021, http://web.archive.org/web/20211220081812/https://www.hrw.org/sites/default/files/media_2021/07/07.2021%20Areas%20of%20Alignment.pdf

Arms Control Association, "Arms Control Association Praises Obama's Commitment to a Nuclear Weapons Free World," news release, April 5, 2009, https://www.armscontrol.org/pressroom/2009-04/arms-control-association-praises-obamas-commitment-nuclear-weapons-free-world

Arms Control Association, "Arms Control Today 2008 Presidential Q&A: President-elect Barack Obama," https://www.armscontrol.org/act/2008-12/interviews/arms-control-today-2008-presidential-qa-president-elect-barack-obama

Arms Control Association, "Convention on Certain Conventional Weapons (CCW) at a Glance," September 2017, http://web.archive.org/web/20211221101926/https://www.armscontrol.org/factsheets/CCW

Arms Control Association, "Nuclear Weapons: Who Has What at a Glance," January 2022, https://www.armscontrol.org/factsheets/Nuclearweaponswhohaswhat

Arms Control Association, "US Nuclear Modernization Programs," October 2016, https://www.armscontrol.org/factsheets/USNuclearModernization

Arraf, Jane, "A Spike in Coronavirus Cases Causes Outrage in Iraq," NPR, June 30, 2020, https://www.npr.org/2020/06/30/885758165/a-spike-in-coronavirus-cases-causes-outrage-in-iraq

Asaro, Peter M., "How Just Could a Robot War Be?" in *Current Issues in Computing and Philosophy*, ed. Adam Briggle, Katrina Waelbers, and Philip A. E. Brey (Amsterdam: IOS Press, 2008).

"ASEAN Outlook on the Indo-Pacific," ASEAN Thailand 2019, June 23, 2019, https://asean2019.go.th/en/news/asean-outlook-on-the-indo-pacific/

Ashour, Omar, "Sinai's Insurgency: Implications of Enhanced Guerilla [*sic*] Warfare," *Studies in Conflict & Terrorism* 42, no. 6 (2019): 541–58.

Ashton, John, "COVID-19 and the 'Spanish' Flu," *Journal of the Royal Society of Medicine* 113, no. 5 (2020): 197–8.

ASIO director-general, "1st Annual Threat Assessment," speech, Canberra, Australia, February 4, 2020.

Aso, Taro, "On the 'Arc of Freedom and Prosperity,'" Ministry of Foreign Affairs of Japan, March 12, 2007, https://www.mofa.go.jp/policy/pillar/address0703.html

Atomic Heritage Foundation, "Hiroshima and Nagasaki Bombing Timeline," 2019, www.atomicheritage.org/history/hiroshima-and-nagasaki-bombing-timeline

Auschwitz Memorial (@AuschwitzMuseum), "'Arbeit macht frei' was a false, cynical illusion the SS gave to prisoners of #Auschwitz," Twitter, May 2, 2020, https://twitter.com/AuschwitzMuseum/status/1256446016510930945?s=20

Australian Government, *Australia in the Asian Century*, White Paper, October 2021, available at https://www.murdoch.edu.au/ALTC-Fellowship/_document/Resources/australia-in-the-asian-century-white-paper.pdf

Australian Red Cross et al., "A Window of Opportunity: Learning from Covid-10 to Progress Locally Led Response and Development Think Piece," La Trobe University, November 2020, https://www.latrobe.edu.au/__data/assets/pdf_file/0005/1188779/A-Window-of-Opportunity-COVID-think-piece-December-2020.pdf

Authorization for the Use of Military Force, Pub. L. 107-40, 115 Stat. 224.

Awan, Hashir Ali, et al., "Internet and Pornography Use during the COVID-19 Pandemic: Presumed Impact and What Can Be Done," *Frontiers in Psychiatry* 12 (2021): 623508.

Axe, David, "Turkey Is the Middle East's Newest Drone Super Power," *National Interest*, April 9, 2020, https://nationalinterest.org/blog/buzz/turkey-middle-easts-newest-drone-super-power-142242

Axelrod, Robert, *The Evolution of Cooperation* (New York: Basic, 1984).

Axelrod, Robert, and Robert O. Keohane, "Achieving Cooperation under Anarchy: Strategies and Institutions," *World Politics* 38, no. 1 (1985): 226–54.

Ayoob, Mohammed, "Defining Security: A Subaltern Realist Perspective," in *Critical Security Studies: Concepts and Cases*, ed. Keith Krause and Michael C. Williams (Minneapolis: University of Minnesota Press, 1997).

Ayoob, Mohammed, *The Third World Security Predicament: State Making, Regional Conflict, and the International System* (Boulder, CO: Lynne Rienner, 1995).

Bächler, Günther, "Why Environmental Transformation Causes Violence: A Synthesis," *Environmental Change and Security Program Report* 4 (1998), 24–44.

Bade, Scott, "Is Washington Prepared for a Geopolitical 'Tech Race'?" *TechCrunch*, May 2, 2021, https://techcrunch.com/2021/05/01/is-washington-prepared-for-a-geopolitical-tech-race/

Bagha, Zenab, *The 10 Most Under-reported Humanitarian Crises of 2020*, CARE International, 2020, care-international.org/files/files/Ten_most_underreported_humanitarian_crises_2020.pdf

Bai, Ge, Tinglong Dai, and Shivaram Rajgopal, "The PPE Supply Chain Is a Black Box—That Needs to Change," *Fortune*, July 25, 2020, https://fortune.com/2020/07/25/ppe-supply-chain-national-security/

Baldwin, David A. (ed.), *Neorealism and Neoliberalism: The Contemporary Debate* (New York: Columbia University Press, 1993).

Balzacq, Thierry, "A Theory of Securitization: Origins, Core Assumptions, and Variants," in *Securitization Theory: How Security Problems Emerge and Dissolve*, ed. Thierry Balzacq (Abingdon, England: Routledge, 2010).

Balzacq, Thierry (ed.), *Securitization Theory: How Security Problems Emerge and Dissolve* (Abingdon, England: Routledge, 2010).

Balzacq, Thierry, Sarah Léonard, and Jan Ruzicka, "'Securitization' Revisited: Theory and Cases," *International Relations* 30, no. 4 (2016): 494–531.

Balzacq, Thierry, et al., "Security Practices," *Oxford Research Encyclopedia of International Studies* (Oxford: Oxford University Press, 2010).

Bankoff, Gregory, "Rendering the World Unsafe: 'Vulnerability' as Western Discourse," *Disasters* 25, no. 1 (2001): 19–35.

Barakat, Sultan, and Sansom Milton, "Localisation across the Humanitarian-Development-Peace Nexus," *Journal of Peacebuilding & Development* 15, no. 2 (2020): 147–63.

Barbelet, Veronique, John Bryant, and Alexandra Spencer, "Local Humanitarian Action during Covid-19: Findings from a Diary Study," HPG working paper, ODI, July 2021, https://cdn.odi.org/media/documents/C19__localisation_diary_methods_WEB.pdf

Barkawi, Tarak, and Mark Laffey, "The Postcolonial Moment in Security Studies," *Review of International Studies* 32, no. 2 (2006): 329–52.

Barkin, J. Samuel, "Realist Constructivism," *International Studies Review* 5, no. 3 (2003): 325–42.

Barnett, Jon, *The Meaning of Environmental Security: Ecological Politics and Policy in the New Security Era* (New York: Zed, 2001).

Barnett, Jon, and Geoff Dabelko, "Environmental Security," in *Contemporary Security Studies*, 5th edn., ed. Alan Collins (Oxford: Oxford University Press, 2019).

Barnett, Michael, and Raymond Duvall, "Power in International Politics," *International Organization* 59, no. 1 (2005): 39–75.

Basu, Titli, "Sino-US Disorder: Power and Policy in Post-COVID-19 Indo-Pacific," *Journal of Asian Economic Integration* 2, no. 2 (2020): 159–79.

BBC News, "Australia's India Ban Criticised as 'Racist' Rights Breach," May 3, 2021, https://www.bbc.com/news/world-australia-56967520

BBC News,"China Floods: Nearly 2 Million Displaced in Shanxi Province," October 11, 2021, https://www.bbc.com/news/world-asia-china-58866854

BBC News, "Chinese Economy to Overtake US 'by 2028' Due to COVID-19," December 26, 2020, https://www.bbc.com/news/world-asia-china-55454146

BBC News, "Coronavirus: Australia Sends 1,000 Army Personnel to Victoria to Fight Outbreak," June 25, 2020, https://www.bbc.com/news/world-australia-53174827

BBC News, "Coronavirus: Trump Accuses WHO of Being a 'Puppet of China,'" May 19, 2020, https://www.bbc.co.uk/news/health-52679329

BBC News, "Coronavirus: Wild Animals Enjoy Freedom of a Quieter World," April 29, 2020, https://www.bbc.com/news/world-52459487

BBC News, "Covax: How Many Covid Vaccines Have the US and the Other G7 Countries Pledged?" September 24, 2021, https://www.bbc.com/news/world-55795297

Bear, Allyson, and Roselle Agner, "Why More Countries Need Female Leaders," *US News and World Report*, March 8, 2021, https://www.usnews.com/news/best-countries/articles/2021-03-08/why-countries-with-female-leaders-have-responded-well-to-the-pandemic

Beauchamp, Zack, "Our Incel Problem," *Vox*, April 23, 2019, https://www.vox.com/the-highlight/2019/4/16/18287446/incel-definition-reddit.

Beck, Ulrich, "Living in the World Risk Society," *Economy and Society* 35, no. 3 (2006): 329–45.

Beck, Ulrich, *World Risk Society* (Cambridge, England: Polity Press, 1998).

Beckley, Michael, "The Power of Nations: Measuring What Matters," *International Security* 43, no. 2 (2018): 7–44.

Bedford, Juliet, et al., "A New Twenty-First Century Science for Effective Epidemic Response," *Nature* 575, no. 7781 (2019): 130–6.

Bella, Timothy, "'No Vaccine!' Woman Arrested for Allegedly Driving through Vaccination Site, Nearly Hitting Workers," *Washington Post*, May 27, 2021, https://www.washingtonpost.com/nation/2021/05/27/covid-vaccine-car-protest-tennessee/

Bellamy, Alex J., and Stephen McLoughlin, *Rethinking Humanitarian Intervention* (London: Palgrave, 2018).

Berkley, Seth, "COVAX Explained," Gavi, September 3, 2020, https://www.gavi.org/vaccineswork/covax-explained

Bergal, Jenni, "Florida Hack Exposes Danger to Water Systems," *Stateline*, March 10, 2021, https://www.pewtrusts.org/en/research-and-analysis/blogs/stateline/2021/03/10/florida-hack-exposes-danger-to-water-systems

Berling, Trine Villumsen, et al., *Translations of Security: A Framework for the Study of Unwanted Futures* (Abingdon, England: Routledge, 2022).

Bernstein, Aaron, "Coronavirus, Climate Change and the Environment," Harvard T. H. Chan School of Public Health, www.hsph.harvard.edu/c-change/subtopics/coronavirus-and-climate-change/

Beyer, Robert M., Andrea Manica, and Camilo Mora, "Shifts in Global Bat Diversity Suggest a Possible Role of Climate Change in the Emergence of SARS-CoV-1 and SARS-CoV-2," *Science of The Total Environment* 767 (2021): 145413.

Biden, Joseph R., *Interim National Security Strategic Guidance*, White House, March 2021, https://www.whitehouse.gov/wp-content/uploads/2021/03/NSC-1v2.pdf

"Biden Putting Tech, Not Troops, at Core of US-China Policy," *Straits Times*, March 2, 2021, https://www.straitstimes.com/asia/east-asia/biden-putting-tech-not-troops-at-core-of-us-china-policy

Bigo, Didier, "Security and Immigration: Toward a Critique of the Governmentality of Unease," *Alternatives* 27, no. 1 (Supplement) (2002): 63–92.

Bilgin, Pinar, "The Continuing Appeal of Critical Security Studies," in *Critical Theory in International Relations and Security Studies: Interviews and Reflections*, ed. Shannon Brincat, Laura Lima, and João Nunes (Abingdon, England: Routledge, 2012).

Birtles, Bill, "China Mocks Australia over 'Indo-Pacific' Concept It Says Will 'Dissipate,' ABC News (Australia), March 8, 2018, https://www.abc.net.au/news/2018-03-08/china-mocks-australia-over-indo-pacific-concept/9529548

Bisht, Akash, and Sadiq Nakvi, "How Tablighi Jemaat Event Became India's Worst Coronavirus Vector," Al Jazeera, April 7, 2020, https://www.aljazeera.com/news/2020/04/tablighi-jamaat-event-india-worst-coronavirus-vector-200407052957511.html

Bisley, Nick, "Asia's Regional Security Order: Rules, Power and Status," *Australian Journal of Politics & History* 65, no. 3 (2019): 361–76.

Bisley, Nick, "Building Asia's Security," *Adelphi Papers* 49, no. 408 (2009).

Bittman, Ladislav, *The KGB and Soviet Disinformation: An Insider's View* (Washington, DC: Pergamon-Brasseys, 1985).

Blackwill, Robert D., and Jennifer M. Harris, *War by Other Means: Geoeconomics and Statecraft* (Cambridge, MA: Belknap Press, 2016).

Blackwill, Robert D., and Thomas Wright, *The End of World Order and American Foreign Policy* (New York: Council on Foreign Relations, 2020).

Blinken, Antony J., "Secretary Antony J. Blinken at UN Security Council Meeting on Climate and Security," US Department of State, September 23, 2021, https://www.state.gov/secretary-antony-j-blinken-at-un-security-council-meeting-on-climate-and-security/

Bloom, Mia, "How Terrorists Will Try to Capitalize on the Coronavirus Crisis," *Just Security*, April 3, 2020, https://www.justsecurity.org/69508/how-terrorist-groups-will-try-to-capitalize-on-the-coronavirus-crisis/

Bloom, Mia, and Sophia Moskalenko, *Pastels and Pedophiles: Inside the Mind of QAnon* (Stanford, CA: Redwood Press, 2021).

Bloomberg, Shari, "Reflections on COVID-19, Domestic Violence, and Shared Trauma," in *Shared Trauma, Shared Resilience during a Pandemic*, ed. Carole Tosone (Cham, Switzerland: Springer, 2021).

Bluedorn, John, et al., "Gender and Employment in the COVID-19 Recession: Cross-Country Evidence on 'She-cessions,'" *COVID Economics*, no. 75 (2021).

Boas, Franz, "Scientists as Spies," *The Nation*, December 20, 1919.

Boas, Ingrid, and Delf Rothe, "From Conflict to Resilience? Explaining Recent Changes in Climate Security Discourse and Practice," *Environmental Politics* 25, no. 4 (2016): 613–32.

Boberg-Fazlic, Nina, et al., "Pandemics and Protectionism: Evidence from the 'Spanish' Flu," *Humanities and Social Science Communications* 8 (2021): 145.

Boebert, Lauren (@laurenboebert), "Biden has deployed his Needle Nazis to Mesa County," Twitter, June 8, 2021, https://twitter.com/laurenboebert/status/1413103995967746051

Bommakanti, Kartik (ed.), *China's Strategic Ambitions in the Age of COVID-19* (New Delhi: Observer Research Foundation, 2020).

Booth, Ken, "Security and Emancipation," *Review of International Studies* 17, no. 4 (1991): 313–26.

Booth, Ken, *Theory of World Security* (Cambridge, England: Cambridge University Press, 2007).

Boseley, Sarah, "US Secures World Stock of Key Covid-19 Drug Remdesivir," *The Guardian*, June 30, 2020, https://www.theguardian.com/us-news/2020/jun/30/us-buys-up-world-stock-of-key-covid-19-drug

Boyden, Jo, et al., *Tracing the Consequences of Child Poverty: Evidence from the Young Lives Study in Ethiopia, India, Peru and Vietnam* (Bristol: Policy Press, 2019).

Boylan, Brandon M., Jerry McBeath, and Bo Wang, "US-China Relations: Nationalism, the Trade War, and COVID-19," *Fudan Journal of the Humanities and Social Sciences* 14, no. 1 (2021): 23–40.

Bradley, Curtis A., and Jack L. Goldsmith, "Obama's AUMF Legacy," *American Journal of International Law* 110, no. 4 (2016): 628–45.

Bradsher, Keith, "With COVID-19 under Control, China's Economy Surges Ahead," *New York Times*, October 18, 2020, https://www.nytimes.com/2020/10/18/world/with-covid-19-under-control-chinas-economy-surges-ahead.html

Braithwaite, Alex, Niheer Dasandi, and David Hudson, "Does Poverty Cause Conflict? Isolating the Causal Origins of the Conflict Trap," *Conflict Management and Peace Science* 33, no. 1 (2016): 45–66.

Brand Finance, "Global Soft Power Index: The World's Most Comprehensive Research Study on Perceptions of Nation Brands," https://brandirectory.com/globalsoftpower/dashboard

Brand Finance, *Global Soft Power Index 2021*, 2021, https://brandirectory.com/globalsoftpower/download/brand-finance-global-soft-power-index-2021.pdf

Bremmer, Ian, and Cliff Kupchan, *Top Risks 2020*, Eurasia Group, https://www.eurasiagroup.net/files/upload/Top_Risks_2020_Report_1.pdf

Broad, William J., and David E. Sanger, "US Ramping Up Major Renewal in Nuclear Arms," *New York Times*, September 22, 2014, https://www.nytimes.com/2014/09/22/us/us-ramping-up-major-renewal-in-nuclear-arms.html

Broniatowski, David, et al., "Weaponised Health Communication: Twitter Bots and Russian Trolls Amplify the Vaccine Debate," *American Journal of Public Health* 108, no. 10 (2018): 1378–84.

Bronk, Christopher, and Eneken Tikk-Ringas, "The Cyber Attack on Saudi Aramco," *Survival* 55, no. 2 (2013): 81–96.

Brooks, David, "America Is Having a Moral Convulsion," *The Atlantic*, October 5, 2020, https://www.theatlantic.com/ideas/archive/2020/10/collapsing-levels-trust-are-devastating-america/616581/

Brooks, James, "Alaska House Rejects Vote on Nuremberg Code Pushed by COVID Vaccine Skeptics," *Anchorage Daily News*, September 13, 2021, https://www.adn.com/politics/alaska-legislature/2021/09/12/alaska-house-rejects-vote-on-nuremberg-code-a-topic-cited-by-covid-vaccine-skeptics/

Broussard, Grant, et al., "Challenges to Ethical Obligations and Humanitarian Principles in Conflict Settings: A Systematic Review," *Journal of International Humanitarian Action* 4 (2019): 15.

Brown, Lester R., *Redefining National Security* (Washington, DC: Worldwatch Institute, 1977).

Browning, Christopher S., and Matt McDonald, "The Future of Critical Security Studies: Ethics and the Politics of Security," *European Journal of International Relations* 19, no. 2 (2013): 235–55.

Brozek, Wolfgang, and Christof Falkenberg, "Industrial Animal Farming and Zoonotic Risk: COVID-19 as a Gateway to Sustainable Change? A Scoping Study," *Sustainability* 13, no. 16 (2021): 9251.

Brulliard, Karin, "The Next Pandemic Is Already Coming, Unless Humans Change How We Interact with Wildlife, Scientists Say," *Washington Post*, April 3, 2020, https://www.washingtonpost.com/science/2020/04/03/coronavirus-wildlife-environment/

Brunnstrom, David, and Humeyra Pamuk, "US Secretary of State Nominee Blinken Sees Strong Foundation for Bipartisan China Policy," Reuters, January 20, 2021, https://www.reuters.com/article/us-usa-biden-state-china-idUSKBN29O2GB

Brunnstrom, David, Humeyra Pamuk, and Michael Martina, "US, Chinese Diplomats Clash in High-Level Meeting of Biden Administration," Reuters, March 19, 2021, https://www.reuters.com/world/us/us-china-set-broach-icy-relations-alaska-talks-2021-03-18/

Bull, Hedley, *The Anarchical Society: A Study of Order in World Politics*, 2nd ed. (London: Macmillan, 1995).

Bumiller, Elisabeth, and Thom Shanker, "Panetta Warns of Dire Threat of Cyberattack on US," *New York Times*, October 11, 2012, https://www.nytimes.com/2012/10/12/world/panetta-warns-of-dire-threat-of-cyberattack.html

Bump, Philip, "On Metric after Metric, the Coronavirus Pandemic Has Been Worse in the US than Nearly Any Other Country," *Washington Post*, July 21, 2020, https://www.washingtonpost.com/politics/2020/07/21/metric-after-metric-coronavirus-pandemic-has-been-worse-us-than-nearly-any-other-country/

Burke, Anthony, "Nuclear Time: Temporal Metaphors of the Nuclear Present," *Critical Studies on Security* 4, no. 1 (2016): 73–90.

Burke, Anthony, et al., "Planet Politics: A Manifesto from the End of IR," *Millennium: Journal of International Studies* 44, no. 3 (2016): 499–523.

Burt, Tom, "Microsoft Takes Legal Action against COVID-19-Related Cybercrime," Microsoft On the Issues blog, July 7, 2020, https://blogs.microsoft.com/on-the-issues/2020/07/07/digital-crimes-unit-covid-19-cybercrime/

Busenberg, George J., "Policy Lessons from the History of Pandemic Preparedness," White Paper 23, COVID-19 Rapid Response Impact Initiative, Edmond J. Safra Center for Ethics, September 3, 2020, https://ethics.harvard.edu/files/center-for-ethics/files/23pandemicpreparedness.pdf?m=1599224522

Buzan, Barry, "Peace, Power, and Security: Contending Concepts in the Study of International Relations," *Journal of Peace Research* 21, no. 2 (1984): 109–25.

Buzan, Barry, *People, States and Fear: An Agenda for International Security Studies in the Post-Cold War Era*, 2nd edn. (Boulder, CO: Lynne Rienner, 1991).

Buzan, Barry, and Lene Hansen, *The Evolution of International Security Studies* (Cambridge, England: Cambridge University Press, 2009).

Buzan, Barry, and Ole Wæver, "Macrosecuritisation and Security Constellations: Reconsidering Scale in Securitisation Theory," *Review of International Studies* 35, no. 2 (2009): 253–76.

Buzan, Barry, and Ole Wæver, *Regions and Powers: The Structure of International Security* (Cambridge, England: Cambridge University Press, 2003).

Buzan, Barry, Ole Wæver, and Jaap de Wilde, *Security: A New Framework for Analysis* (Boulder, CO: Lynne Rienner, 1998).

Byman, Daniel, "Understanding the Islamic State—A Review Essay," *International Security* 40, no. 4 (2016): 127–65.

Callaway, Ewen, "The Unequal Scramble for Coronavirus Vaccines—by the Numbers," *Nature* 584, no. 7822 (2020): 506–7.

Campbell, Kurt M., *The Pivot: The Future of American Statecraft in Asia* (New York: Twelve, 2016).

Cannon, Brendon J., "The Arab States and the Karabakh War," in *The Nagorno-Karabakh Conflict: Historical and Political Perspectives*, ed. M. Hakan Yavuz and Michael Gunter (Abingdon, England: Routledge, 2022).

Cannon, Brendon J., "Turkey's Military Strategy in Africa," in *Turkey in Africa: A New Emerging Power?*, ed. Elem Eyrice Tepeciklioğlu and Ali Onur Tepeciklioğlu (Abingdon, England: Routledge, 2021).

Cannon, Brendon J., and Federico Donelli, "Asymmetric Alliances and High Polarity: Evaluating Regional Security Complexes in the Middle East and Horn of Africa," *Third World Quarterly* 41, no. 3 (2020): 505–24.

Cannon, Brendon J., and Ash Rossiter, “Ethiopia, Berbera Port and the Shifting Balance of Power in the Horn of Africa,” *Rising Powers Quarterly* 2, no. 4 (2017): 7–29.

Cannon, Brendon J., and Ash Rossiter, “Patterns of External Involvement in the Modern Political History of the Horn of Africa States,” in *The Gulf States and the Horn of Africa: Interests, Influence and Instability*, ed. Robert Mason and Simon Mabon (Manchester: Manchester University Press, 2022).

Cannon, Brendon J., and Ash Rossiter, “Re-examining the ‘Base’: The Political and Security Dimensions of Turkey’s Military Presence in Somalia,” *Insight Turkey* 21, no. 1 (2018): 167–88.

Capie, David, Natasha Hamilton-Hart, and Jason Young, “The Tech War Is the One to Watch,” *Newsroom*, January 7, 2021, https://www.newsroom.co.nz/ideasroom/the-tech-war-is-the-one-to-watch

Capraro, Valerio, and Helene Barcelo, “The Effect of Messaging and Gender on Intentions to Wear a Face Covering to Slow Down COVID-19 Transmission,” *Journal of Behavioural Economics for Policy* 4, no. S2 (2020): 45–55.

Carr, E. H., *The Twenty Years Crisis, 1919–1939* (Basingstoke, England: Palgrave, [1939] 2001).

Carr, Emily Young, “China and Russia Cooperate on Rival to GPS,” *The Diplomat*, November 18, 2021, https://thediplomat.com/2021/11/china-and-russia-cooperate-on-rival-to-gps/

CASE Collective, “Critical Approaches to Security in Europe: A Networked Manifesto,” *Security Dialogue* 37, no. 4 (2006): 443–87.

Caso, Federica, “Are We at War? The Rhetoric of War in the Coronavirus Pandemic,” *The Disorder of Things* (blog), April 10, 2020, https://thedisorderofthings.com/2020/04/10/are-we-at-war-the-rhetoric-of-war-in-the-coronavirus-pandemic/

Cassidy, Caitlin, “Australia Has Delivered Just 8% of Covid Vaccinations Promised to Developing Nations,” *The Guardian*, October 22, 2021, https://www.theguardian.com/australia-news/2021/oct/22/australia-has-delivered-just-8-of-covid-vaccinations-promised-to-developing-nations

Cassino, Dan, and Yasemin Besen-Cassino, “Of Masks and Men? Gender, Sex, and Protective Measures during COVID-19,” *Politics & Gender* 16, no. 4 (2020), 1052–62.

Cavelty, Myriam Dunn, “Cyber-security,” in *Contemporary Security Studies*, ed. Alan Collins, 4th edn. (Oxford: Oxford University Press, 2016).

Cavelty, Myriam Dunn, and Thierry Balzacq (eds.), *Routledge Handbook of Security Studies*, 2nd edn. (Abingdon, England: Routledge, 2017).

Cavelty, Myriam Dunn, and Andreas Wenger, “Cyber Security Meets Security Politics: Complex Technology, Fragmented Politics, and Networked Science,” *Contemporary Security Policy* 41, no. 1 (2020): 5–32.

Cavelty, Myriam Dunn, Mareile Kaufmann, and Kristian Søby Kristensen, “Resilience and (In)Security: Practices, Subjects, Temporalities,” *Security Dialogue* 46, no. 1 (2015): 3–14.

Ceballos, Gerardo, Paul R. Ehrlich, and Rodolfo Dirzo, "Biological Annihilation via the Ongoing Sixth Mass Extinction Signaled by Vertebrate Population Losses and Declines," *Proceedings of the National Academy of Sciences of the United States of America* 114, no. 30 (2017): E6089–E6096.

Center for Countering Digital Hate, "The Disinformation Dozen: The Sequel," July 2021, https://www.counterhate.com/disinfosequel

Centers for Disease Control and Prevention, "1918 Pandemic (H1N1 Virus)," https://www.cdc.gov/flu/pandemic-resources/1918-pandemic-h1n1.html

Centers for Disease Control and Protection, "CDC Seasonal Flu Vaccine Effectiveness Studies", https://www.cdc.gov/flu/vaccines-work/effectiveness-studies.htm

Centers for Disease Control and Prevention, "History of Ebola Virus Disease (EVD) Outbreaks," https://www.cdc.gov/vhf/ebola/history/chronology.html

Centers for Disease Control and Prevention, "Prioritizing and Preventing Deadly Zoonotic Diseases," February 28, 2018, https://www.cdc.gov/globalhealth/healthprotection/fieldupdates/winter-2017/prevent-zoonotic-diseases.html

Chakrabarty, Dipesh, *Provincializing Europe: Postcolonial Thought and Historical Difference*, new edn. (Princeton, NJ: Princeton University Press, 2008).

Chala, Bayissa, and Feyissa Hamde, "Emerging and Re-emerging Vector-Borne Infectious Diseases and the Challenges for Control: A Review," *Frontiers in Public Health* 9 (2021): 715759.

Chalmers, Alan, *The Scientist's Atom and the Philosopher's Stone: How Science Succeeded and Philosophy Failed to Gain Knowledge of Atoms* (Dordrecht: Springer, 2009).

Chambers, Alice, and Patrick Reevell, "10 Days after Ransomware Attack, Irish Health System Struggling," ABC News (USA), May 25, 2021, https://abcnews.go.com/International/10-days-ransomware-attack-irish-health-system-struggling/story?id=77876092

Chandler, David, "Coronavirus and the End of Resilience," *E-International Relations*, March 25, 2020, https://www.e-ir.info/2020/03/25/opinion-coronavirus-and-the-end-of-resilience/

Chandler, David, "Resilience and Human Security: The Post-interventionist Paradigm," *Security Dialogue* 43, no. 3 (2012): 213–29.

Chandler, David, "Securing the Anthropocene? International Policy Experiments in Digital Hacktivism—A Case Study of Jakarta," *Security Dialogue* 48, no. 2 (2017): 113–30.

Chang, Gordon G., "Mike Pompeo Just Declared America's New China Policy: Regime Change," *National Interest*, July 25, 2020, https://nationalinterest.org/feature/mike-pompeo-just-declared-america's-new-china-policy-regime-change-165639.

Chang, Jonathan, and Meghna Chakrabarti, "What the Georgia Shootings Reveal about Anti-Asian Racism in the US," WBUR, March 22, 2021, https://www.wbur.org/onpoint/2021/03/22/what-the-georgia-shootings-reveal-about-anti-asian-racism-in-the-u-s

Chapa, Joseph, "Human Judgment in Remote Warfare," in *Remote Warfare: Interdisciplinary Perspectives*, ed. Alasdair McKay, Abigail Watson, and Megan Karlshøj-Pedersen (Bristol: E-International Relations, 2021).

Chatterjee, Partha, *The Nation and Its Fragments: Colonial and Postcolonial Histories* (Princeton, NJ: Princeton University Press, 1993).

Check Point Blog, "Update: Coronavirus-Themed Domains 50% More Likely to Be Malicious than Other Domains," March 5, 2020, https://blog.checkpoint.com/2020/03/05/update-coronavirus-themed-domains-50-more-likely-to-be-malicious-than-other-domains/

Cheng, Jonathan, "China's Economy Is Bouncing Back—And Gaining Ground on the US," *Wall Street Journal*, August 24, 2020, https://www.wsj.com/articles/chinas-economy-is-bouncing-backand-gaining-ground-on-the-u-s-11598280917

Cherp, Aleh, and Jessica Jewell, "The Concept of Energy Security: Beyond the Four As," *Energy Policy* 75 (2014): 415–21.

Chertoff, Philip, "Perils of Lethal Autonomous Weapons Systems Proliferation: Preventing Non-State Acquisition," Geneva Centre for Security Policy, October 2018, http://web.archive.org/web/20200103221102/https://dam.gcsp.ch/files/2y10RR5E5mmEpZE4rnkLPZwUleGsxaWXTH3aoibziMaV0JJrWCxFyxXGS

Chivvis, Christopher S., "Countering the Islamic State in Libya," *Survival* 58, no. 4 (2016): 113–30.

Christensen, Thomas J., "A Modern Tragedy? COVID-19 and US-China Relations," Brookings Institution, May 2020, https://www.brookings.edu/wp-content/uploads/2020/05/FP_20200511_covid_us_china_christensen_v3.pdf

Christensen, Thomas J., "There Will Not Be a New Cold War: The Limits of US-Chinese Competition," *Foreign Affairs*, March 24, 2001, https://www.foreignaffairs.com/articles/united-states/2021-03-24/there-will-not-be-new-cold-war

Christodoulou, Mario, "ASIO Briefing Warns that the Far-Right Is Exploiting Coronavirus to Recruit New Members," ABC News (Australia), June 11, 2020, https://www.abc.net.au/news/2020-06-12/asio-briefing-warns-far-right-is-exploiting-coronavirus/12344472

Chuang, Yating, and John Chung-En Liu, "Who Wears a Mask? Gender Differences in Risk Behaviours in the COVID-19 Early Days in Taiwan," *Economics Bulletin* 40, no. 4 (2020): 2619–27.

Clare, Angela, "Australia's Foreign Aid Budget 2020–21," Parliament of Australia, https://www.aph.gov.au/About_Parliament/Parliamentary_Departments/Parliamentary_Library/pubs/rp/BudgetReview202021/AustraliasForeignAidBudget

Clark, Serena, et al., "'You're a Teacher, You're a Mother, You're a Worker': Gender Inequality during COVID-19 in Ireland," *Gender, Work & Organization* 28, no. 4 (2021): 1352–62.

Clifford, Tyler, "Man Sentenced to 6 Years in Plot to Kidnap Michigan Governor," Reuters, August 25, 2021, https://www.reuters.com/world/us/man-sentenced-6-years-plot-kidnap-michigan-governor-2021-08-25/

CNA Corporation, "National Security and the Threat of Climate Change," 2007, https://www.cna.org/cna_files/pdf/national%20security%20and%20the%20threat%20of%20climate%20change.pdf

Coade, Melissa, "Questions as to Whether COVAX Is Benefiting Wealthy Countries like Australia over Developing Nations," *The Mandarin*, August 17, 2021, https://www.themandarin.com.au/166058-questions-as-to-whether-covax-is-benefiting-wealthy-countries-like-australia-over-developing-nations/

Cockburn, Cynthia, *Antimilitarism: Political and Gender Dynamics of Peace Movements* (Basingstoke, England: Palgrave Macmillan, 2012).

Cohn, Carol, "Sex and Death in the Rational World of Defense Intellectuals," *Signs: Journal of Women and Culture in Society* 12, no. 4 (1987): 687–718.

Colby, Elbridge A., *The Strategy of Denial: American Defense in an Age of Great Power Conflict* (New Haven, CT: Yale University Press, 2021).

Colby, Elbridge A., and A. Wess Mitchell, "The Age of Great-Power Competition: How the Trump Administration Refashioned American Strategy," *Foreign Affairs*, January/February 2020, https://www.foreignaffairs.com/articles/2019-12-10/age-great-power-competition

Commander, United States Pacific Fleet, "US Pacific Fleet Announces Rim of the Pacific 2020", April 29, 2020, https://www.cpf.navy.mil/News/Article/2637794/us-pacific-fleet-announces-rim-of-the-pacific-2020/

Commission on a Global Health Risk Framework for the Future and National Academy of Medicine, Secretariat, *The Neglected Dimension of Global Security: A Framework to Counter Infectious Disease Crises* (Washington, DC: National Academies Press; 2016).

Commission on Human Security, *Human Security Now*, 2003, https://reliefweb.int/sites/reliefweb.int/files/resources/91BAEEDBA50C6907C1256D19006A9353-chs-security-may03.pdf

Condon, Stephanie, "Supreme Court Strikes Down Section of Voting Rights Act," CBS News, June 25, 2013, https://www.cbsnews.com/news/supreme-court-strikes-down-section-of-voting-rights-act/

Conflict Armament Research, "Iranian Technology Transfers to Yemen," March 2017, https://www.conflictarm.com/perspectives/iranian-technology-transfers-to-yemen/

Connolly, William E., *The Fragility of Things: Self-Organizing Processes, Neoliberal Fantasies, and Democratic Activism* (Durham, NC: Duke University Press, 2013).

Conway-Lanz, Sahr, *Collateral Damage: Americans, Noncombatant Immunity, and Atrocity after World War II* (New York: Routledge, 2006).

Cook, Malcolm, and Ian Storey, "Images Reinforced: COVID-19, US-China Rivalry and Southeast Asia," *ISEAS Perspective* no. 2020/34

Copeland, Dale C., *Economic Interdependence and War* (Princeton, NJ: Princeton University Press, 2015).

Coppola, Damon P., *Introduction to International Disaster Management*, 3rd edn. (Oxford: Butterworth-Heinemann, 2015).

Cordesman, Anthony H., Ashley Hess, and Nicholas S. Yarosh, *Chinese Military Modernization and Force Development*, CSIS, August 23, 2013, https://csis-website-prod.s3.amazonaws.com/s3fs-public/legacy_files/files/publication/130725_chinesemilmodern.pdf

Corera, Gordon, "Coronavirus: Cyber-Spies Hunt COVID-19 Research, US and UK Warn." BBC News, May 5, 2020, https://www.bbc.com/news/technology-52551023

Corman, Victor M., et al., "Detection of 2019 Novel Coronavirus (2019-nCoV) by Real-Time RT-PCR," *Eurosurveillance* 25, no. 3 (2020): 2000045.

Cornwell, Alexander, "US Flags Huawei 5G Network Security Concerns to Gulf Allies," Reuters, September 12, 2019, https://www.reuters.com/article/us-huawei-security-usa-gulf-idUSKCN1VX241

"Coronavirus, Climate Change, and the Environment: A Conversation on COVID-19 with Dr. Aaron Bernstein, Director of Harvard Chan C-CHANGE," Harvard T. H. Chan School of Public Health, https://www.hsph.harvard.edu/c-change/subtopics/coronavirus-and-climate-change

Correia, Tiago, and Karen Willis, "Applying Critical Realism to the COVID-19 Pandemic to Improve Management of Future Public Health Crises," *International Journal of Health Planning and Management* 37, no. 2 (2022), 599–603.

Corry, Olaf, "Securitisation and 'Riskification': Second-Order Security and the Politics of Climate Change," *Millennium: Journal of International Studies* 40, no. 2 (2012): 235–58.

Corry, Olaf, "Securitization and 'Riskization': Two Grammars of Security," *International Relations* 44 (2010): 1–32.

Cottee, Simon, "Incel (E)motives: Resentment, Shame and Revenge," *Studies in Conflict and Terrorism* 44, no. 2 (2021): 93–114.

Counter-terrorism Committee Executive Directorate, "Update on the Impact of the COVID-19 Pandemic on Terrorism, Counter-terrorism and Countering Violent Extremism," June 2021, https://www.un.org/securitycouncil/ctc/sites/www.un.org.securitycouncil.ctc/files/files/documents/2021/Jun/cted_covid_paper_15june2021_1.pdf

Cox, Jeff, "US GDP Booms at 33.1% Rate in Q3, Better than Expected," CNBC, October 29, 2020, https://www.cnbc.com/2020/10/29/us-gdp-report-third-quarter-2020.html

Cox, Robert W., "Social Forces, States and World Orders: Beyond International Relations Theory," *Millennium* 10, no. 2 (1981): 126–55.

Crenshaw, Kimberle, "Mapping the Margins: Intersectionality, Identity Politics, and Violence against Women of Color," *Stanford Law Review* 43, no. 6 (1991): 1241–99.

Crewe, Ivor, and David Sanders (eds.), *Authoritarian Populism and Liberal Democracy* (Cham, Switzerland: Palgrave Macmillan, 2020).

Cronin, Audrey Kurth, *Power to the People: How Open Technological Innovation Is Arming Tomorrow's Terrorists* (New York: Oxford University Press, 2020).

Crossley, Gabriel, and Kevin Yao, "China's Economy Picks Up Speed in Fourth Quarter, Ends 2020 in Solid Shape after COVID-19 Shock," Reuters, January 18, 2021, https://www.reuters.com/article/us-china-economy-gdp/chinas-economy-picks-up-speed-in-fourth-quarter-ends-2020-in-solid-shape-after-COVID-19-shock-idUSKBN29N04S

Cui Liru, "China's 'Period of Historic Opportunities,'" *China-US Focus*, February 1, 2018, https://www.chinausfocus.com/foreign-policy/chinas-period-of-historic-opportunities

Cutler, David M., and Lawrence H. Summers, "The COVID-19 Pandemic and the $16 Trillion Virus," *JAMA* 324, no. 15 (2020): 1495–6.

"Cyber Operations vs Information Operations: CyCon 2019 Twilight Talk," natoccdcoe/YouTube, August 12, 2019, https://www.youtu.be/KyCDvEzq25s

Czymara, Christian S., Alexander Langenkamp, and Tomás Cano, "Cause for Concerns: Gender Inequality in Experiencing the COVID-19 Lockdown in Germany," *European Societies* 23, no. s1 (2021): s68–s81.

Dabashi, Hamid, *The Arab Spring: The End of Post-colonialism* (New York: Zed, 2012).

Dalby, Simon, "Anthropocene Formations: Environmental Security, Geopolitics and Disaster," *Theory, Culture and Society* 34, no. 2–3 (2017): 233–52.

Dalby, Simon, "Contesting an Essential Concept: Reading the Dilemmas in Contemporary Security Discourse," in *Critical Security Studies: Concepts and Cases*, ed. Keith Krause and Michael C. Williams (London: Routledge, 1997).

Dalby, Simon, "Ecopolitical Discourse: 'Environmental Security' and Political Geography," *Progress in Human Geography* 16, no. 4 (1992): 503–22.

Dalrymple, William, *The Anarchy: The Relentless Rise of the East India Company* (New York: Bloomsbury, 2019).

Darby, Phillip, "Rethinking the Political," in *Postcolonizing the International: Working to Change the Way We Are*, ed. Phillip Darby (Honolulu: University of Hawai'i Press, 2006).

Darby, Phillip (ed.), *Postcolonizing the International: Working to Change the Way We Are* (Honolulu: University of Hawai'i Press, 2006).

Daroca Oller, Santiago, "Exploring the Pathways from Climate-Related Risks to Conflict and the Humanitarian-Development-Peace Nexus as an Integrated Response," Issue Brief 21/2020, United Nations Development Program, 2020.

Davey, Gareth, "The China-US Blame Game: Claims-Making about the Origin of a New Virus," *Social Anthropology* 28, no. 2 (2020): 250–1.

Davidson, Helen, "Alarm in Beijing after announcement zero-Covid policy may last five years," *The Guardian*, June 27, 2022, https://www.

theguardian.com/world/2022/jun/27/alarm-in-beijing-after-announce-ment-zero-covid-policy-may-last-five-years

Davis, Jessica, "Another COVID-19 Research Firm Targeted by Ransomware Attack," Health IT Security, April 8, 2020, https://healthitsecurity.com/news/another-covid-19-research-firm-targeted-by-ransomware-attack

Davis, Mike, *Late Victorian Holocausts: El Niño Famines and the Making of the Third World* (London: Verso, 2001).

Davis, Mike, *The Monster Enters: COVID-19, Avian Flu and the Plagues of Capitalism* (New York: OR Books, 2020)

Defense Intelligence Agency, *Iran Military Power: Ensuring Regime Survival and Securing Regional Dominance* (Washington, DC: US Government Publishing Office, 2019), http://web.archive.org/web/20211016061759/https://www.dia.mil/Portals/27/Documents/News/Military%20Power%20Publications/Iran_Military_Power_LR.pdf

Delaney, Michelle, et al., *The World's Most Neglected Displacement Crises 2020*, Norwegian Refugee Council, May 27, 2021, https://www.nrc.no/globalassets/pdf/reports/neglected-displacement-crises-2020/neglected-crises-list-2020.pdf

DeLisle, Jacques, "When Rivalry Goes Viral: COVID-19, US-China Relations, and East Asia," *Orbis*, Winter 2021, 46–74.

Department of Commerce, "Addition of Entities to the Entity List," *Federal Register* 84, no. 98 (2019), 22961, https://www.govinfo.gov/content/pkg/FR-2019-05-21/pdf/2019-10616.pdf

Department of Defence, Australian Government, *2016 Defence White Paper*, 2016, https://www.defence.gov.au/whitepaper/Docs/2016-Defence-White-Paper.pdf

Department of Veterans Affairs, "America's Wars," May 2021, https://www.va.gov/opa/publications/factsheets/fs_americas_wars.pdf

Deudney, Daniel, "The Case against Linking Environmental Degradation and National Security," *Millennium: Journal of International Studies* 19, no. 3 (1990): 461–76.

DeVore, Marc R., "Exploring the Iran-Hezbollah Relationship: A Case Study of How State Sponsorship Affects Terrorist Group Decision-Making," *Perspectives on Terrorism* 6, no. 4/5 (2012): 85–107.

Di Donato, Valentina, and Tim Lister, "The Mafia Is Poised to Exploit Coronavirus, and Not Just in Italy," CNN, April 19, 2020, https://www.cnn.com/2020/04/19/europe/italy-mafia-exploiting-coronavirus-crisis-aid-intl/index.html

Dillon, Michael, "Governing through Contingency: The Security of Biopolitical Governance," *Political Geography* 26, no.1 (2007): 41–7.

Directorate General for External Policies of the Union, *How the COVID-19 Crisis Has Affected Security and Defence-Related Aspects of the EU* (Brussels: European Parliament, 2021).

Dixon, Kristal, "Federal Law Seeks to Protect Election Workers from Threats," *Axios Atlanta*, October 7, 2021, https://www.axios.com/local/atlanta/2021/10/07/federal-law-protect-threats-election-poll-workers

Dlamini, Nobuhle Judy, "Gender-Based Violence, Twin Pandemic to COVID-19," *Critical Sociology* 47, no. 4–5 (2021): 583–90.

Dobson, Mahalia, "Australia Embraces US and Pays Price with China as Trade War Hits Bottom Line," NBC News, June 20, 2021, https://www.nbcnews.com/news/world/australia-embraces-u-s-pays-price-china-trade-war-hits-n1270458

Dolgin, Elie, "How COVID Unlocked the Power of RNA Vaccines," *Nature* 589, no. 7841 (2021): 189–91.

Donaghue, Erin, "2,120 Hate Incidents against Asian Americans Reported during Coronavirus Pandemic," CBS News, July 2, 2020, https://www.cbsnews.com/news/anti-asian-american-hate-incidents-up-racism/

Donelli, Federico, and Brendon J. Cannon, "Power Projection of Middle East States in the Horn of Africa: Linking Security Burdens with Capabilities," *Small Wars & Insurgencies* (2021), https://doi.org/10.1080/09592318.2021.1976573

Doshi, Rush, *The Long Game: China's Grand Strategy to Displace American Order* (New York: Oxford University Press, 2021), 21–2.

Doyle, Charles, "Cybercrime: An Overview of the Federal Computer Fraud and Abuse Statute and Related Federal Criminal Laws," Congressional Research Service, October 15, 2014, http://web.archive.org/web/20211222074553/https://crsreports.congress.gov/product/pdf/RL/97-1025

Doyle, Michael W., "Kant, Liberal Legacies, and Foreign Affairs," part 1, *Philosophy and Public Affairs* 12, no. 3 (1983): 205–35.

DW, "Floods in Germany," February 2, 2022, https://p.dw.com/p/3wceK

Dyer, Hugh C., "Theoretical Aspects of Environmental Security," in *Responding to Environmental Conflicts: Implications for Theory and Practices*, ed. Eileen Petzold-Bradley, Alexander Carius, and Arpád Vincze (Dordrecht: Kluwer, 2001).

The Economist, "A New Kind of Cold War," May 18, 2019, https://www.economist.com/leaders/2019/05/16/a-new-kind-of-cold-war.

The Economist, "The Pandemic's True Death Toll", February 17, 2022, http://web.archive.org/web/20220217184437/https://www.economist.com/graphic-detail/coronavirus-excess-deaths-estimates

Economist Intelligence Unit, "Limited Covid Vaccines for Poor Countries until 2023," January 27, 2021, https://www.eiu.com/n/85-poor-countries-will-not-have-access-to-coronavirus-vaccines/

Elbe, Stefan, *Security and Global Health* (Cambridge, England: Polity, 2010)

Elegant, Naomi Xu, "China's 2020 GDP Means It Will Overtake US as World's No. 1 Economy Sooner than Expected," *Fortune*, January 18, 2021, https://fortune.com/2021/01/18/chinas-2020-gdp-world-no-1-economy-us/

Eliot, T. S., "The Hollow Men" (1925).

Elliott, David, "Weighing the Case for a Convention to Limit Cyberwarfare," *Arms Control Today*, November 2009, http://web.archive.org/web/20211222092445/https://www.armscontrol.org/act/2009-11/weighing-case-convention-limit-cyberwarfare

Ellsberg, Daniel, *The Doomsday Machine: Confessions of a Nuclear War Planner* (New York: Bloomsbury, 2017).

Emerson, Donald K., "'Southeast Asia': What's in a Name?" *Journal of Southeast Asian Studies* 15, no. 1 (1984): 1–21.

Enloe, Cynthia, *Bananas, Beaches and Bases: Making Feminist Sense of International Politics* (Berkeley: University of California Press, 1989).

Enloe, Cynthia, *Bananas, Beaches and Bases: Making Feminist Sense of International Politics*, updated edn. (Berkeley: University of California Press, 2000).

Ennaji, Moha, "Women and Gender Relations during the Pandemic in Morocco," *Gender and Women's Studies* 4, no. 1 (2021): 3.

Eun, Yong-Soo, "Non-Western International Relations Theorisation: Reflexive Stocktaking," *E-International Relations*, April 12, 2020, https://www.e-ir.info/2020/04/12/non-western-international-relations-theorisation-reflexive-stocktaking/

European Centre for Disease Prevention and Control, "European Influenza Surveillance Network (EISN)," https://www.ecdc.europa.eu/en/about-us/partnerships-and-networks/disease-and-laboratory-networks/eisn

Europol, *European Union Terrorism Situation and Trend Report 2021* (Luxembourg: European Union, 2021), 28, https://www.europol.europa.eu/activities-services/main-reports/european-union-terrorism-situation-and-trend-report-2021-tesa

Evans, Gareth, and Yoriko Kawaguchi, *Eliminating Nuclear Threats: A Practical Agenda for Global Policymakers,* (Canberra: International Commission on Nuclear Non-Proliferation and Disarmament, 2009).

Evron, Yoram, "China's Diplomatic Initiatives in the Middle East: The Quest for a Great-Power Role in the Region," *International Relations* 31, no. 2 (2017): 125–44.

Fahim, Kareem, "Turkey's Military Campaign beyond Its Borders Is Powered by Homemade Armed Drones," *Washington Post*, November 29, 2020, https://www.washingtonpost.com/world/middle_east/turkey-drones-libya-nagorno-karabakh/2020/11/29/d8c98b96-29de-11eb-9c21-3cc501d0981f_story.html

Falk, Richard A., *This Endangered Planet: Prospects and Proposals for Human Survival* (New York: Random House, 1971).

Faludi, Susan, *The Terror Dream: Fear and Fantasy in Post-9/11 America* (Melbourne: Scribe, 2008).

Farmer, Paul, "Social Inequalities and Emerging Infectious Diseases," *Emerging Infectious Diseases* 2, no. 4 (1996): 259–69.

Fast, Larissa, *Aid in Danger: The Perils and Promise of Humanitarianism* (Philadelphia: University of Pennsylvania Press, 2014).

Fayyaz, Shabana, and Salma Malik, "Question of US Hegemony and COVID-19 Pandemic," *Global Political Review* 5, no. 1 (2020): 72–83.

Feigenbaum, Evan A., "Reluctant Stakeholder: Why China's Highly Strategic Brand of Revisionism is More Challenging than Washington Thinks," Macro Polo, April 27, 2018, https://macropolo.org/analysis/reluctant-stakeholder-why-chinas-highly-strategic-brand-of-revisionism-is-more-challenging-than-washington-thinks/

Ferhani, Adam, and Simon Rushton, "The International Health Regulations, COVID-19, and Bordering Practices: Who Gets In, What Gets Out, and Who Gets Rescued?" *Contemporary Security Policy* 41, no. 3 (2020): 458–77.

Fidler, David P., "Public Health and National Security in the Global Age: Infectious Diseases, Bioterrorism, and Realpolitik," *George Washington International Law Review* 35 (2003): 787–856.

Fiertz, Natalie, "A Health Crisis Is More than a Health Crisis," Fragile States Index, May 20, 2021, https://fragilestatesindex.org/2021/05/20/a-health-crisis-is-more-than-a-health-crisis/

Finklea, Kristin M., "The Interplay of Borders, Turf, Cyberspace, and Jurisdiction: Issues Confronting US Law Enforcement," Congressional Research Service, January 17, 2013, http://web.archive.org/web/20211222074843/https://crsreports.congress.gov/product/pdf/R/R41927

Finklea, Kristin, and Catherine A. Theohary, "Cybercrime: Conceptual Issues for Congress and US Law Enforcement," Congressional Research Service, January 15, 2015, http://web.archive.org/web/20211222090222/https://crsreports.congress.gov/product/pdf/R/R42547

Fishel, Stefanie, "Performing the Posthuman: An Essay in Three Acts," in *Reflections on the Posthuman in International Relations: The Anthropocene, Security and Ecology*, ed. Clara Eroukhmanhoff and Matt Harker (Bristol: E-International Relations, 2017).

Fitz-Gibbon, Kate, Jacqui True, and Naomi Pfitzner, "More Help Required: The Crisis in Family Violence during the Coronavirus Pandemic," *The Conversation*, August 18, 2020, https://theconversation.com/more-help-required-the-crisis-in-family-violence-during-the-coronavirus-pandemic-144126

Fitzsimmons, Scott, and Karina Sangha, "Killing in High Definition: Combat Stress among Operators of Remotely Piloted Aircraft," *Technology* 12 (2013): 289–92.

Flinders, Matthew, "Democracy and the Politics of Coronavirus: Trust, Blame and Understanding," *Parliamentary Affairs* 74, no. 2 (2021): 483–502.

Floyd, Rita, "The Environmental Security Debate and Its Significance for Climate Change," *International Spectator* 43, no. 3 (2008): 51–65.

Flynn-Do, Koji, and Dan Walton, *Tracking the Global Humanitarian Response to Covid-19*, Development Initiatives / International Rescue Committee, April 2021, https://www.rescue.org/report/tracking-global-humanitarian-response-covid-19

Fodor, Éva, et al., "The Impact of COVID-19 on the Gender Division of Childcare Work in Hungary," *European Societies* 23, no. s1 (2021): s95–s110.

Food and Agriculture Organization, *The State of Food Security and Nutrition in the World 2020: Transforming Food Systems for Affordable*

Healthy Diets (Rome: Food and Agriculture Organization, 2020), available at https://www.fao.org/3/ca9692en/online/ca9692en.html

Food and Agriculture Organization, *The State of Food Security and Nutrition in the World 2021: Transforming Food Systems for Food Security, Improved Nutrition and Affordable Healthy Diets for All* (Rome: Food and Agriculture Organization, 2021).

"Forging a Vision for Security in a New Age of Disruptive Techno-politics," University of Waikato, September 21, 2018, https://www.waikato.ac.nz/news-opinion/media/2018/forging-a-vision-for-security-in-a-new-age-of-disruptive-techno-politics

Forsberg, Tuomas, "Power in International Relations: An Interdisciplinary Perspective," in *International Studies: Interdisciplinary Approaches*, ed. Pami Aalto, Viho Harle, and Sami Moisio (Basingstoke, England: Palgrave Macmillan, 2011).

Fortier, Nikki, "COVID-19, Gender Inequality, and the Responsibility of the State," *International Journal of Wellbeing* 10, no. 3 (2020): 77–93.

Frangoul, Anmar, "Counting the Costs of a Global Epidemic," CNBC, February 5, 2014, https://www.cnbc.com/2014/02/05/counting-the-costs-of-a-global-epidemic.html

Franke, Ulrike, and Paola Sartori, "Machine Politics: Europe and the AI Revolution," Policy Brief, European Council on Foreign Relations, 2019, http://web.archive.org/web/20211016054134/https://ecfr.eu/wp-content/uploads/machine_politics_europe_and_the_ai_revolution.pdf

French, Howard W., *Born in Blackness: Africa, Africans, and the Making of the Modern World, 1471 to the Second World War* (New York: Liveright, 2021).

Friedman, Uri, "The Pandemic Is Revealing a New Form of National Power," *The Atlantic*, November, 15, 2021, https://www.theatlantic.com/ideas/archive/2020/11/pandemic-revealing-new-form-national-power/616944/

Fukuyama, Francis, *The End of History and the Last Man* (New York: Free Press, 1992).

Futter, Andrew, "The Dangers of Using Cyberattacks to Counter Nuclear Threats," *Arms Control Today* July/August 2016, http://web.archive.org/web/20211222091743/https://www.armscontrol.org/act/2016-07/features/dangers-using-cyberattacks-counter-nuclear-threats

Futter, Andrew, et al., "Nuclear War, Public Health, the COVID-19 Epidemic: Lessons for Prevention, Preparation, Mitigation, and Education," *Bulletin of the Atomic Scientists* 76, no. 5 (2020): 271–6.

Gallie, Walter Bryce, "Essentially Contested Concepts," *Proceedings of the Aristotelian Society* 56 (1956): 167–98.

Gallion, Bailey, "School Board Member Jenkins' Comments about Threats, Harassment Grab National Attention," *Florida Today*, October 14, 2021, https://www.floridatoday.com/story/news/education/2021/10/14/jennifer-jenkins-details-threats-harassment-over-mask-vote/8450501002/

Gamillo, Elizabeth, “Covid-19 Surpasses 1918 Flu to Become Deadliest Pandemic in American History,” *Smithsonian Magazine*, September 24, 2021, https://www.smithsonianmag.com/smart-news/the-covid-19-pandemic-is-considered-the-deadliest-in-american-history-as-death-toll-surpasses-1918-estimates-180978748/

Garcia, Denise, “The Case against Killer Robots: Why the United States Should Ban Them,” *Foreign Affairs*, May 10, 2014, http://www.foreignaffairs.com/articles/141407/denise-garcia/the-case-against-killer-robots

Garon, Sheldon, “Defending Civilians against Aerial Bombardment: A Comparative/Transnational History of Japanese, German, and British Home Fronts, 1918–1945,” *Mass Violence & Resistance*, December 10, 2016, http://bo-k2s.sciences-po.fr/mass-violence-war-massacre-resistance/en/document/defending-civilians-against-aerial-bombardment-comparativetransnational-history-japanese-ge.html

Gayer, Michelle, et al. “Conflict and Emerging Infectious Diseases,” *Emerging Infectious Diseases* 13, no. 11 (2007): 1625–31.

Geist, Edward M., *Armageddon Insurance: Civil Defense in the United States and Soviet Union, 1945–1991* (Chapel Hill: University of North Carolina Press, 2019).

Geist, Edward, and Andrew J. Lohn, *How Might Artificial Intelligence Affect the Risk of Nuclear War?* (Santa Monica, CA: RAND, 2018).

Gelvin, James L., “The New Middle East: What Everyone Needs to Know,” book talk delivered at UCLA, Los Angeles, November 9, 2017, recording and transcript available at https://www.international.ucla.edu/cnes/article/185543

Gentry, Caron E., *Disordered Violence: How Gender, Race and Heteronormativity Structure Terrorism* (Edinburgh: Edinburgh University Press, 2020).

Gerber, Marisa, and Irfan Khan, “Dodger Stadium’s COVID-19 Vaccination Site Temporarily Shut Down after Protesters Gather at Entrance,” *Los Angeles Times*, January 30, 2021, https://www.latimes.com/california/story/2021-01-30/dodger-stadiums-covid-19-vaccination-site-shut-down-after-dozens-of-protesters-gather-at-entrance

Gereffi, Gary, “What Does the COVID-19 Pandemic Teach Us about Global Value Chains? The Case of Medical Supplies,” *Journal of International Business Policy* 3 (2020): 287–301.

Giattino, Charlie, et al., “Excess Mortality during the Coronavirus Pandemic (COVID-19),” Our World in Data, https://ourworldindata.org/excess-mortality-covid

Gibb, Rory, et al., “Zoonotic Host Diversity Increases in Human-Dominated Ecosystems,” *Nature* 584, no. 7821 (2020): 398–402.

Gibson, Jeremy, “Domestic Violence during COVID-19: The GP Role,” *British Journal of General Practice* 70, no. 696 (2020): 340.

Gibson-Fall, Fawzia, “Military Responses to COVID-19, Emerging Trends in Global Civil-Military Engagements,” *Review of International Studies* 47, no. 2 (2021): 155–70.

Giddens, Anthony, *A Contemporary Critique of Historical Materialism* (Berkeley: University of California Press, 1981).

Gilbert, Sarah, and Catherine Green, *Vaxxers: The Inside Story of the Oxford AstraZeneca Vaccine and the Race against the Virus* (London: Hodder & Stoughton, 2021).

Gilpin, Robert, "The Richness of the Tradition of Political Realism," *International Organization* 38, no. 2 (1984): 287–304.

Girling, Fran, and Angus Urquhart, *Global Humanitarian Assistance Report 2021* (Bristol: Development Initiatives, 2021), available at https://devinit.org/resources/global-humanitarian-assistance-report-2021/

Gladstone, Rick, "How the Cold War between China and US Is Intensifying," *New York Times*, July 22, 2020, https://www.nytimes.com/2020/07/22/world/asia/us-china-cold-war.html

Glasner, Charles L., "Realism," in *Contemporary Security Studies*, ed. Alan Collins, 2nd edn. (Oxford: Oxford University Press, 2010).

Global Education Coalition, "Keeping Girls in the Picture," UNESCO, https://en.unesco.org/covid19/educationresponse/girlseducation

Global Education Coalition, "#LearningNeverStops: COVID-19 Education Response," UNESCO, https://en.unesco.org/covid19/educationresponse/globalcoalition

Global Governance Monitor, "Nuclear Proliferation," August 17, 2017, http://www.cfr.org/global-governance/global-governance-monitor/p18985#!/nuclear-proliferation?cid=soc-facebook-in-ggm_nuclear_prolif-082916

Global Health Observatory, "Health Systems Strengthening," World Health Organization, https://www.who.int/data/gho/data/themes/topics/health-systems-strengthening

Global Health Security Agenda, https://ghsagenda.org

"Global Health Security Agenda (GHSA) 2024 Framework," November 2018, https://ghsagenda.org/wp-content/uploads/2020/06/ghsa2024-framework.pdf

Goldfrank, Lewis R., and Catharyn T. Liverman (eds.), *Preparing for an Influenza Pandemic: Personal Protective Equipment for Healthcare Workers* (Washington, DC: National Academies Press, 2008).

Gómez, Oscar A., "Protecting Our Human World Order: A Human Security Compass for a New Sustainability Decade," Background Paper No. 4-2020, United Nations Development Program, 2020, https://hdr.undp.org/sites/default/files/hdr2020_backgroundpaper_gomez.pdf

Goniewicz, Krzysztof, et al, "The Influence of War and Conflict on Infectious Disease: A Rapid Review of Historical Lessons We Have Yet to Learn," *Sustainability* 13, no, 19 (2021): 10783.

Good Humanitarian Donorship, "24 Principles and Good Practice of Humanitarian Donorship," https://www.ghdinitiative.org/ghd/gns/principles-good-practice-of-ghd/principles-good-practice-ghd.html

Gottemoeller, Rose, speech, Shangri-La Dialogue, Singapore, June 2, 2018.

Government Accountability Office, "Influenza Pandemic: Lessons from the H1N1 Pandemic Should Be Incorporated into Future Planning," Report to Congressional Requesters, June 2011, https://www.gao.gov/assets/gao-11-632.pdf

Graham, Euan, "The Armed Forces and COVID-19," IISS, April 8, 2020, https://www.iiss.org/blogs/analysis/2020/04/easia-armed-forces-and-covid-19

Gramsci, Antonio, *Selections from the Prison Notebooks* (London: Lawrence & Wishart, 1971).

Grayson, Kyle, "A Challenge to the Power over Knowledge of Traditional Security Studies," *Security Dialogue* 35, no. 3 (2004): 357.

Green, Marjorie Taylor (@mtgreenee), Twitter, July 26, 2021, https://twitter.com/mtgreenee/status/1419489724985643008.

Greene, Robert, and Paul Triolo, "Will China Control the Global Internet via its Digital Silk Road?" Carnegie Endowment for International Peace, May 8, 2020, https://carnegieendowment.org/2020/05/08/will-china-control-global-internet-via-its-digital-silk-road-pub-81857

Greitens, Sheena Chestnut, "Surveillance, Security, and Liberal Democracy in the Post-COVID World," *International Organization* 74, no. S1 (2020): E169–E190.

Griffith, Janelle, "'My Dad Didn't Have a Fighting Chance': Covid Is Leading Cause of Death among Law Enforcement," NBC News, September 17, 2021, https://www.nbcnews.com/news/us-news/it-doesn-t-have-happen-covid-leading-cause-death-among-n1279289

Grove, Kevin, at al., "The Uneven Distribution of Futurity: Slow Emergencies and the Event of COVID-19," *Geographical Research* 60, no. 1 (2022): 6–17.

Grovogui, Siba, "IR as Theology: Reading Kant Badly, and the Incapacity of Western Political Theory to Travel Very Far in Non-Western Contexts," Theory Talks, August 29, 2013, http://www.theory-talks.org/2013/08/theory-talk-57.html

Gunaratne, Dakshinie Ruwanthika, et al., "Letter Dated 27 January 2020 from the Panel of Experts on Yemen Addressed to the President of the Security Council," United Nations Security Council, January 27, 2020, https://reliefweb.int/sites/reliefweb.int/files/resources/%5BEN%5DLetter%20dated%2027%20January%202020%20from%20the%20Panel%20of%20Experts%20on%20Yemen%20addressed%20to%20the%20President%20of%20the%20Security%20Council%20-%20Final%20report%20of%20the%20Panel%20of%20Experts%20on%20Yemen%20%28S-2020-70%29.pdf

Guo Yuandan and Liu Xuanzun, "US Military Activities in S. China Sea in 2020 Unprecedented," Global Times, March 12, 2021, https://www.globaltimes.cn/page/202103/1218193.shtml

Gusterson, Hugh, "Drone Warfare in Waziristan and the New Military Humanism," *Current Anthropology* 60, no. S19 (2019): S77–S86.

Gusterson, Hugh, "Militarizing Knowledge," in Network of Concerned Anthropologists (eds.), *The Counter-Counterinsurgency Manual: Or,*

Notes on Demilitarizing American Society (Chicago: Prickly Paradigm Press, 2009).

Guterres, António, "Put Women and Girls at the Centre of Efforts to Recover from COVID-19," United Nations COVID-19 Response, https://www.un.org/en/un-coronavirus-communications-team/put-women-and-girls-centre-efforts-recover-covid-19

Guterres, António, "Secretary-General's Remarks to the Fifth Committee: Introduction of the Proposed Programme Budget for 2021 [as delivered]," United Nations Secretary-General, October 12, 2020, http://web.archive.org/web/20211214085503/https://www.un.org/sg/en/content/sg/statement/2020-10-12/secretary-generals-remarks-the-fifth-committee-introduction-of-the-proposed-programme-budget-for-2021-delivered

Guzzini, Stefano, "A Reconstruction of Constructivism in International Relations," *European Journal of International Relations* 6, no. 2 (2000): 147–82.

Guzzini, Stefano, "Securitization as a Causal Mechanism," *Security Dialogue* 42, no. 4–5 (2011): 329–41.

Gwee, Xiao Wei Sylvia, Pearleen Ee Yong Chua, and Junxiong Pang, "Global Dengue Importation: A Systematic Review," *BMC Infectious Diseases* 21 (2021): 1078.

Haass, Richard, "The Pandemic Will Accelerate History Rather than Reshape It," *Foreign Affairs*, April 7, 2020, https://www.foreignaffairs.com/articles/united-states/2020-04-07/pandemic-will-accelerate-history-rather-reshape-it

Habibi, Roojin, et al., "Do Not Violate the International Health Regulations during the COVID-19 Outbreak," *The Lancet* 395, no. 10225 (2020): 664–6.

Haddad, Amy, "Metaphorical Militarisation: Covid-19 and the Language of War," *The Strategist*, May 13, 2020, https://www.aspistrategist.org.au/metaphorical-militarisation-covid-19-and-the-language-of-war/

Hafner, Marco, et al., *COVID-19 and the Cost of Vaccine Nationalism* (Santa Monica, CA, and Cambridge, England: RAND, 2020), available at https://www.rand.org/pubs/research_reports/RRA769-1.html

Hage, Ghassan, *White Nation: Fantasies of White Supremacy in a Multicultural Nation* (Annandale, NSW: Pluto Press, 1998).

Hagen, Ashley, "Laboratory Supply Shortages Are Impacting COVID-19 and Non-COVID Diagnostic Testing," October 15, 2020, American Society for Microbiology, https://asm.org/Articles/2020/September/Laboratory-Supply-Shortages-Are-Impacting-COVID-19

Hagon, Kirsten (ed.), *World Disasters Report 2020: Come Heat or High Water—Tackling the Humanitarian Impacts of the Climate Crisis Together* (Geneva: International Federation of Red Cross and Red Crescent Societies, 2020).

Hakata, Kei, and Brendon J. Cannon, "The Indo-Pacific as an Emerging Geography of Strategies," in *Indo-Pacific Strategies: Navigating Geopolitics at the Dawn of a New Age*, ed. Brendon J. Cannon and Kei Hakata (Abingdon, England: Routledge, 2021).

Hale, Thomas, and David Held (eds.), *Beyond Gridlock* (Cambridge, England: Polity, 2017).

Hameiri, Shahar, "COVID-19: Time to Bring Back the State," *Progress in Political Economy* (blog), March 19, 2020, https://www.ppesydney.net/covid-19-time-to-bring-back-the-state/

Hameiri, Shahar, and Lee Jones, *Governing Borderless Threats: Non-traditional Security and the Politics of State Transformation* (Cambridge, England: Cambridge University Press, 2015).

Handley, Erin, "China Warns Australian Economy Could 'Suffer Further Pain' after Reported Export Ban," ABC News (Australia), November 6, 2020, https://www.abc.net.au/news/2020-11-06/china-daily-warns-australia-economic-pain-export-ban/12857988

Hansen, Lene, "The Politics of Securitization and the Muhammad Cartoon Crisis: A Post-structuralist Perspective," *Security Dialogue* 42, no. 4–5 (2011): 357–69.

Hansen, Lene, and Helen Nissenbaum, "Digital Disaster, Cyber Security, and the Copenhagen School," *International Studies Quarterly* 53, no. 4 (2009): 1155–75.

ul Haq, Mahbub, *Reflections on Human Development* (New York: Oxford University Press, 1995).

Haraway, Donna, "Anthropocene, Capitalocene, Plantationocene, Chthulucene: Making Kin," *Environmental Humanities* 6, no. 1 (2015): 159–65

Hardt, Judith Nora, "Encounters between Security and Earth System Sciences: Planetary Boundaries and Hothouse Earth," in *International Relations in the Anthropocene: New Agendas, New Agencies and New Approaches*, ed. David Chandler, Franziska Müller, and Delf Rothe (Cham, Switzerland: Palgrave Macmillan, 2021).

Hardy, Keiran, "Is Cyberterrorism a Threat?" *Australian Outlook*, February 20, 2017, http://web.archive.org/web/20211222071856/https://www.internationalaffairs.org.au/australianoutlook/is-cyberterrorism-a-threat/

Harman, Sophie, "Threat Not Solution: Gender, Global Health Security and COVID-19," *International Affairs* 97, no. 3 (2021): 601–23.

Harmer, Adele, and Joanna Macrae (eds.), *Beyond the Continuum: Aid Policy in Protracted Crises*, HPG Research Report No. 18, Overseas Development Institute, July 2004, https://cdn.odi.org/media/documents/279_GpS59wf.pdf

Harrington, Cameron, and Clifford D. Shearing, *Security in the Anthropocene: Reflections on Safety and Care* (Bielefeld, Germany: Transcript, 2017).

Hayton, Bill, *The South China Sea: The Struggle for Power in Asia* (New Haven, CT: Yale University Press, 2015).

Hayton, Bill, "The South China Sea in 2020: Statement before the US-China Economic and Security Review Commission Hearing on 'US-China Relations in 2020: Enduring Problems and Emerging Challenges,'" September 9, 2020, https://www.uscc.gov/sites/default/files/2020-09/Hayton_Testimony.pdf

He, Kai (ed.), *Contested Multilateralism 2.0 and Asian Security Dynamics* (Abingdon, England: Routledge, 2020).

Heckman, James J., "Schools, Skills, and Synapses," NBER Working Paper 14064, National Bureau of Economic Research, June 2008, https://www.nber.org/papers/w14064

Held, David, "Elements of a Theory of Global Governance," *Philosophy and Social Criticism* 42, no. 9 (2016): 837–46.

Henderson, D. A., and Petra Klepac, "Lessons from the Eradication of Smallpox: An Interview with D. A. Henderson," *Philosophical Transactions of the Royal Society of London B: Biological Sciences* 368, no. 1623 (2013): 20130113.

Henry, Shawn, "Responding to the Cyber Threat," speech given at the Information Systems Security Association International Conference, Baltimore, MD, October 20, 2011, transcript available at http://web.archive.org/web/20211222085654/https://archives.fbi.gov/archives/news/speeches/responding-to-the-cyber-threat

Hernández, Javier C., "Trump Slammed the WHO over Coronavirus. He's Not Alone," *New York Times*, April 8, 2020, https://www.nytimes.com/2020/04/08/world/asia/trump-who-coronavirus-china.html

Hershberg, James G., *James B. Conant: Harvard to Hiroshima and the Making of the Nuclear Age* (New York: Alfred A. Knopf, 1993).

Heydarian, Richard Javad, "China Seizes COVID-19 Advantage in South China Sea," *Asia Times*, April 1, 2020, https://asiatimes.com/2020/04/china-seizes-COVID-19-advantage-in-south-china-sea/

Heymann, David L., et al., "Global Health Security: The Wider Lessons from the West African Ebola Virus Disease Epidemic," *The Lancet* 385, no. 9980 (2015): 1884–1901.

Hillis, Susan D., et al., "Global Minimum Estimates of Children Affected by COVID-19-Associated Orphanhood and Deaths of Caregivers: A Modelling Study," *The Lancet* 398, no. 10298 (2021): 391–402.

Hitch, Georgia, "What War Crimes Did Australian Soldiers Commit in Afghanistan and Will Anyone Go to Jail?" ABC News (Australia), November 19, 2020, https://www.abc.net.au/news/2020-11-19/afghan-war-crimes-report-released-what-you-need-to-know/12899880

Hoffman, Stanley, "Obstinate or Obsolete? The Fate of the Nation-State and the Case of Western Europe," *Dædalus* 95, no. 3 (1966): 862–915.

Hokayem, Emile, and David B. Roberts, "The War in Yemen," *Survival* 58, no. 6 (2016): 157–86.

Holland, Steve, and Michelle Nichols, " Trump Cutting US Ties with World Health Organization over Virus," Reuters, May 30, 2020, https://www.reuters.com/article/us-health-coronavirus-trump-who-idUSKBN2352YJ

Holsti, K. J., "The Concept of Power in the Study of international Relations," *Background* 7, no. 4 (1964): 179–94.

Holsti, Kalevi, "Change in International Politics: The View from High Altitude," *International Studies Review* 20, no. 2 (2018): 186–94.

Homer-Dixon, Thomas F., *Environment, Scarcity, and Violence* (Princeton, NJ: Princeton University Press, 1999).

Homer-Dixon, Thomas F., "Environmental Scarcities and Violent Conflict: Evidence from Cases," *International Security* 19, no. 1 (1994): 5–40.

Hongisbaum, Mark, *The Pandemic Century: A History of Global Contagion from the Spanish Flu to Covid-19* (New York: Penguin, 2020).

Hooper, Charlotte, *Manly States: Masculinities, International Relations, and Gender Politics* (New York: Columbia University Press, 2001).

Horgan, John, "Bethe, Teller, Trinity and the End of Earth," *Scientific American*, August 4, 2015, https://blogs.scientificamerican.com/cross-check/bethe-teller-trinity-and-the-end-of-earth/

Hornik, Richard, "We Get the News We Demand," *Harvard Business Review*, August 2, 2018, https://hbr.org/2018/08/we-get-the-news-we-demand

Horowitz, Frances Degen, "Child Development and the PITS: Simple Questions, Complex Answers, and Developmental Theory," *Child Development* 71, no. 1 (2000): 1–10.

Horowitz, Michael, et al., "Artificial Intelligence and International Security," Center for a New American Security, July 10, 2018, https://www.cnas.org/publications/reports/artificial-intelligence-and-international-security

Horton, Richard, "Offline: COVID-19 Is Not a Pandemic," *The Lancet* 396, no. 10255 (2020): 874.

Housden, Oliver, "Egypt: Coup d'Etat or a Revolution Protected?" *RUSI Journal* 158, no. 5 (2013): 72–8.

Howard, Matt C., "Gender, Face Mask Perceptions, and Face Mask Wearing: Are Men Being Dangerous during the COVID-19 Pandemic?" *Personality and Individual Differences* 170 (2021): 110417.

Howe, Paul, "The Triple Nexus: A Potential Approach to Supporting the Achievement of the Sustainable Development Goals?" *World Development* 124 (2019): 104629.

Howell, Alison, and Melanie Richter-Montpetit, "Is Securitization Theory Racist? Civilizationism, Methodological Whiteness, and Antiblack Thought in the Copenhagen School," *Security Dialogue* 51, no. 1 (2020): 3–22.

Human Development Report Office, "Covid-19's Impact on Education," Data Futures Platform, United Nations Development Programme, https://data.undp.org/content/out-of-school-during-covid-19/

Human Rights Watch, "Killer Robots: Military Powers Stymie Ban," December 20, 2021, http://web.archive.org/web/20211220090749/https://www.hrw.org/news/2021/12/19/killer-robots-military-powers-stymie-ban

Hunt, Jennifer S., "As Joe Biden Prepares to Become President, the US Still Reels from the Deadly Consequences of Alternative Facts," *The Conversation*, January 19, 2021, https://theconversation.com/as-joe-biden-prepares-to-become-president-the-us-still-reels-from-the-deadly-consequences-of-alternative-facts-153449

Hunt, Jennifer S., "The COVID-19 Pandemic vs Post-Truth," Global Health Security Network, August 2020, https://www.ghsn.org/resources/Documents/GHSN%20Policy%20Report%201.pdf

Hurrell, Andrew, *On Global Order: Power, Values, and the Constitution of International Society* (Oxford: Oxford University Press, 2007).

Huysmans, Jef, "Revisiting Copenhagen: Or, On the Creative Development of a Security Studies Agenda in Europe," *European Journal of International Relations* 4, no. 4 (1998): 479–505.

Hwang, Priscilla Ki Sun, "'Freedom Convoy' Cost Downtown Ottawa Millions per Day, Experts Estimate," CBC, March 11, 2022, https://www.cbc.ca/news/canada/ottawa/economic-impact-freedom-convoy-downtown-ottawa-1.6376248

Hynek, Nik, and David Chandler, "No Emancipatory Alternative, No Critical Security Studies," *Critical Studies on Security* 1, no. 1 (2013): 46–63.

IGADF, *Inspector-General of the Australian Defence Force Afghanistan Inquiry Report* (Commonwealth of Australia, 2020) https://afghanistan-inquiry.defence.gov.au/sites/default/files/2020-11/IGADF-Afghanistan-Inquiry-Public-Release-Version.pdf

"Impacts of the Covid-19 Pandemic on Terrorism, Counter-Terrorism, and Countering Violent Extremism," side event, 2021 United Nations Counter-Terrorism Week, June 25, 2021, concept note, https://www.un.org/securitycouncil/ctc/sites/www.un.org.securitycouncil.ctc/files/un_ct_week_2021_covid-19_side_event_concept_note_-_edited_1_1.pdf

Inhofe, Jim, and Jack Reed, "The Pacific Deterrence Initiative: Peace through Strength in the Indo-Pacific," *War on the Rocks*, May 28, 2020, https://warontherocks.com/2020/05/the-pacific-deterrence-initiative-peace-through-strength-in-the-indo-pacific/

Intergovernmental Panel on Climate Change, *Climate Change 2021: The Physical Science Basis—Summary for Policymakers* (Geneva: Intergovernmental Panel on Climate Change, 2021).

International Committee of the Red Cross, *Protracted Conflict and Humanitarian Action: Some Recent ICRC Experiences* (Geneva: International Committee of the Red Cross, 2016).

International Energy Agency, World Energy Outlook 2021, 2021, https://iea.blob.core.windows.net/assets/4ed140c1-c3f3-4fd9-acae-789a4e14a23c/WorldEnergyOutlook2021.pdf

International Institute for Strategic Studies, "Editor's introduction to *The Military Balance 2021*," February 25, 2021, https://www.iiss.org/blogs/analysis/2021/02/military-balance-2021-introduction

International Labour Organization, "ILO Monitor: COVID-19 and the World of Work," 7th edn., January 25, 2021, http://web.archive.org/web/20211215091611/https://www.ilo.org/wcmsp5/groups/public/@dgreports/@dcomm/documents/briefingnote/wcms_767028.pdf

International Labour Organization, *Youth and COVID-19: Impacts on Jobs, Education, Rights and Mental Well-Being* (Geneva: International Labour Organization, 2020).

International Monetary Fund, *Fiscal Monitor: Strengthening the Credibility of Public Finances* (Washington, DC: International Monetary Fund, 2021), https://www.imf.org/-/media/Files/Publications/fiscal-monitor/2021/October/English/text.ashx

Interpol, *Cybercrime: COVID-19 Impact*, August 2020, https://www.interpol.int/en/content/download/15526/file/COVID-19%20Cybercrime%20Analysis%20Report-%20August%202020.pdf

Interpol, "Cybercriminals Targeting Critical Healthcare Institutions with Ransomware," April 4, 2020, https://www.interpol.int/en/News-and-Events/News/2020/Cybercriminals-targeting-critical-healthcare-institutions-with-ransomware

Interpol, "Interpol—Terrorist Groups Using COVID-19 to Reinforce Power and Influence," December 22, 2020, https://www.interpol.int/en/News-and-Events/News/2020/INTERPOL-Terrorist-groups-using-COVID-19-to-reinforce-power-and-influence

IPCC, "Synthesis Report of the Sixth Assessment Report," https://www.ipcc.ch/ar6-syr/

Isachenkov, Vladimir, "Putin: Russia-China Military Alliance Can't Be Ruled Out," AP News, October 22, 2020, https://apnews.com/article/beijing-moscow-foreign-policy-russia-vladimir-putin-1d4b112d2fe8cb66192c5225f4d614c4

Jackson, James K., et al., "Global Economic Effects of COVID-19," Congressional Research Service, November 10, 2021, https://fas.org/sgp/crs/row/R46270.pdf

Jahn, Beate, "Critical Theory in Crisis? A Reconsideration," *European Journal of International Relations* 27, no. 4 (2021): 1274–99.

Jaikaran, Chris, et al., "Cybersecurity: Selected Issues for the 115th Congress," Congressional Research Service, March 9, 2018, http://web.archive.org/web/20211222092022/https://crsreports.congress.gov/product/pdf/R/R45127

James, Paul, and Manfred B. Steger, "On Living in an Already-Unsettled World: COVID as an Expression of Larger Transformations," *Globalizations* 19, no. 3 (2022), 426–38.

Jerving, Sara, "COVAX Reduces End-of-Year Forecast Figures," Devex, September 8, 2021, https://www.devex.com/news/covax-reduces-end-of-year-forecast-figures-101576

Jerving, Sara, and Jenny Lei Ravelo, "Deep Dive: Is COVID-19 Vaccine Equity a Pipe Dream?" Devex, August 26, 2021, https://www.devex.com/news/deep-dive-is-covid-19-vaccine-equity-a-pipe-dream-100588

Jervis, Robert, "Realism in the Study of World Politics," *International Organization* 52, no. 4 (1998): 971–91.

Jervis, Robert, "Theories of War in an Era of Leading-Power Peace: Presidential Address, American Political Science Association," *American Political Science Review* 96, no. 1 (2002): 1–14.

Johns Hopkins Coronavirus Resource Center, https://coronavirus.jhu.edu/

Johns Hopkins Coronavirus Resource Center, "COVID-19 Dashboard," 2021, https://coronavirus.jhu.edu/map.html

Johnson, Bridget, "Notable and Quotable: ISIS on the Coronavirus," *Wall Street Journal*, March 15, 2020, https://www.wsj.com/articles/notable-quotable-isis-on-the-coronavirus-11584314005

Johnson, Chalmers, *Blowback: The Costs and Consequences of American Empire* (New York: Henry Holt, 2000).

Johnson, Christine K., et al., "Global Shifts in Mammalian Population Trends Reveal Key Predictors of Virus Spillover Risk," *Proceedings of the Royal Society B* 287 (2020): 20192736.

Johnson, James, "Inadvertent Escalation in the Age of Intelligence Machines: A New Model for Nuclear Risk in the Digital Age," *European Journal of International Security* (2021), https://doi.org/10.1017/eis.2021.23

Johnston, Regan M., Anwar Mohammed, and Clifton van der Linden, "Evidence of Exacerbated Gender Inequality in Child Care Obligations in Canada and Australia during the COVID-19 Pandemic," *Politics & Gender* 16, no. 4 (2020): 1131–41.

Jones, Kate E., et al., "Global Trends in Emerging Infectious Diseases," *Nature* 451, no. 7181 (2008): 990–3.

Jones, Seth G., et al., *Rolling Back the Islamic State* (Santa Barbara, CA: RAND, 2017).

Juneau, Thomas, "How War in Yemen Transformed the Iran-Houthi Partnership," *Studies in Conflict & Terrorism* (2021), https://doi.org/10.1080/1057610X.2021.1954353

Jungk, Robert, *Brighter than a Thousand Suns: A Personal History of the Atomic Scientists* (New York: Harcourt Brace, [1958] 1986).

Kahn, Herman, *On Thermonuclear War* (New Brunswick, NJ: Transaction, [1960] 2007).

Kang, David, "Getting Asia Wrong: The Need for New Analytical Frameworks," *International Security* 27, no. 4 (2003): 57–85.

Kant, Immanuel, "Idea of a Universal History with a Cosmopolitan Purpose," in *The Cosmopolitanism Reader*, ed. Garrett Wallace Brown and David Held (Cambridge, England: Polity Press, 2010).

Kaplan, Robert D., "The Coming Anarchy: How Scarcity, Crime, Overpopulation and Disease Are Rapidly Destroying the Social Fabric of Our Planet," *Atlantic Monthly*, February 1994, pp. 44–76.

Kaplan, Robert D., "A New Cold War Has Begun," *Foreign Policy*, January 7, 2019, https://foreignpolicy.com/2019/01/07/a-new-cold-war-has-begun/

Karamouzian, Mohammad, and Navid Madani, "COVID-19 Response in the Middle East and North Africa: Challenges and Paths Forward," *Lancet Global Health* 8, no. 7 (2020): e886–e887.

Katella, Kathy, "Comparing the COVID-19 Vaccines: How Are They Different?" February 18, 2022, https://www.yalemedicine.org/news/covid-19-vaccine-comparison

Katz, Rebecca, et al., "Global Health Security Agenda and the International Health Regulations: Moving Forward," *Biosecurity and Bioterrorism: Biodefense Strategy, Practice, and Science* 12, no. 5 (2014): 231–8.

Katzenstein, Peter J., and Lucea A. Seybert (eds.), *Protean Power: Exploring the Uncertain and Unexpected in World Politics* (Cambridge, England: Cambridge University Press, 2018).

Kelion, Leo, "Huawei 5G Kit Must Be Removed from UK by 2027," BBC News, July 14, 2020, http://web.archive.org/web/20220105050109/https://www.bbc.com/news/technology-53403793

Kelleher, Jennifer Sinco, Terry Tang, and Olga R. Rodriguez, "Mask, Vaccine Conflicts Descend into Violence and Harassment," Associated Press, August 22, 2021, https://apnews.com/article/health-coronavirus-pandemic-2eba81ebe3bd54b3bcde890b8cf11c70

Kellogg, Thomas E., "Xi's Davos Speech: Is China the New Champion for the liberal International Order?" *The Diplomat*, January 24, 2017, https://thediplomat.com/2017/01/xis-davos-speech-is-china-the-new-champion-for-the-liberal-international-order/

Kelly, Anne, "Mothers for QAnon," *New York Times*, September 10, 2020, https://www.nytimes.com./2020/09/10/opinion/qanon-women-conspiracy.html

Kelly, Liz, "Wars against Women: Sexual Violence, Sexual Politics and the Militarised State," in *States of Conflict: Gender, Violence and Resistance*, ed. Susie Jacobs, Ruth Jacobson, and Jennifer Marchbank (London: Zed, 2000).

Kennedy, Andrew B., and David L. Dwyer, "The Stakes in Decoupling Discovery: China's Role in Transnational Innovation," *Pacific Review* 35, no. 1 (2022): 147–71.

Kennedy, Scott, "Washington's China Policy Has Lost Its Wei," Centre for Strategic and International Studies, July 27, 2020, https://www.csis.org/analysis/washingtons-china-policy-has-lost-its-wei

Keohane, Robert O., *After Hegemony: Cooperation and Discord in the World Political Economy* (Princeton, NJ: Princeton University Press, 1984).

Keohane, Robert O., "The Global Politics Paradigm: Guide to the Future or Only the Recent Past?" *International Theory* 13, no. 1 (2021): 112–21.

Keohane, Robert O., "Ideas Part-Way Down," *Review of International Studies* 26, no. 1 (2000): 125–30.

Keohane, Robert O., and Lisa Martin, "Institutional Theory as a Research Program," in Colin Elman and Miriam Fendius Elman (eds.), *Progress in International Relations Theory: Appraising the Field* (Cambridge, MA: MIT Press, 2003).

Kessler, Oliver, and Christopher Daase, "From Insecurity to Uncertainty: Risk and the Paradox of Security Politics," *Alternatives* 33, no. 2 (2008): 211–32.

Keyser, Zachary, "Coronavirus: Mafia Delivers Food, Essentials to Italy's Worst Affected," *Jerusalem Post*, April 12, 2020, https://www.jpost.com/international/coronavirus-mafia-delivers-food-essentials-to-italys-worst-affected-62440

Khoo, Nicholas, "The Trump Administration and the United States' China Engagement Policy," *National Security Journal* 3, no. 2 (2021).

Kika, Thomas, "Security Guards to Accompany Mobile Vaccination Unites after Harassment by Anti-Vaxxers," *Newsweek*, September 11, 2021, https://www.newsweek.com/security-guards-accompany-mobile-vaccination-units-after-harassment-anti-vaxxers-1628202

Kill Chain: The Cyber War on America's Election, directed by Simon Ardizzone, Russell Michaels, and Sarah Teale (HBO, 2020).

Kimball, Daryl G., "Toward a Successful NPT Review," *Arms Control Today*, November 2021, https://www.armscontrol.org/act/2021-11/focus/toward-successful-npt-review

King, Gary, and Christopher Murray, "Rethinking Human Security," *Political Science Quarterly* 116, no. 4 (2001): 585–610.

King, Michael, and Sam Mullins, "Covid-19 and Terrorism in the West: Has Radicalization Really Gone Viral?" *Just Security*, March 4, 2021, https://www.justsecurity.org/75064/covid-19-and-terrorism-in-the-west-has-radicalization-really-gone-viral/

King, Peter, "Undermining Proliferation: Nuclear Winter and Nuclear Renunciation," Working Paper No. 09/1, Centre for Peace and Conflict Studies, 2009.

Kirk, Jessica, and Matt McDonald, "The Politics of Exceptionalism: Securitization and COVID-19," *Global Studies Quarterly* 1, no. 3 (2021): ksab024.

Kishi, Roudabeh, "Taliban in Afghanistan," ACLED, April 16, 2020, https://acleddata.com/2020/04/16/cdt-spotlight-taliban-in-afghanistan

Kissinger, Henry A., "The Coronavirus Pandemic Will Forever Alter the World Order," *Wall Street Journal*, April 3, 2020, https://www.wsj.com/articles/the-coronavirus-pandemic-will-forever-alter-the-world-order-11585953005

Kivimaki, Timo, *The Long Peace of East Asia* (Farnham, England: Ashgate, 2014).

Klare, Michael T., "The Challenges of Emerging Technologies," *Arms Control Today*, December 2018, http://web.archive.org/web/20211016053559/https://www.armscontrol.org/act/2018-12/features/challenges-emerging-technologies

Klebnikov, Sergei, "The Trade Deal May Be Dead, Trump Says China Relationship 'Severely Damaged,'" *Forbes*, July 10, 2020, https://www.forbes.com/sites/sergeiklebnikov/2020/07/10/the-trade-deal-may-be-dead-trump-says-china-relationship-severely-damaged/.

Kohlenberg, Paul J., and Nadine Godehardt (eds.), *The Multidimensionality of Regions in World Politics* (Abingdon, England: Routledge, 2021).

Kolodziej, Edward A., *Security and International Relations* (Cambridge, England: Cambridge University Press, 2005).

Konopinski, Emil, Cloyd Marvin, and Edward Teller, "Ignition of the Atmosphere with Nuclear Bombs," August 14, 1946, available at https://sgp.fas.org/othergov/doe/lanl/docs1/00329010.pdf

Krampe, Florian, "Why United Nations Peace Operations Cannot Ignore Climate Change," Stockholm International Peace Research Institute, February 22, 2021, https://www.sipri.org/commentary/topical-backgrounder/2021/why-united-nations-peace-operations-cannot-ignore-climate-change

Krause, Keith, "The Key to a Powerful Agenda, if Properly Delimited," *Security Dialogue* 35, no. 3 (2004): 367.

Krause, Keith, and M. C. Williams, "Broadening the Agenda of Security Studies: Politics and Methods," *Mershon International Studies Review* 40, no. 2 (1996): 229–54.

Krishnan, Armin, *Killer Robots: Legality and Ethicality of Autonomous Weapons* (Farnham, England: Ashgate, 2009).

Kristensen, Hans, "Nuclear Weapons Modernization: A Threat to the NPT?," *Arms Control Today*, May 2014, https://www.armscontrol.org/act/2014-05/nuclear-weapons-modernization-threat-npt

Kristensen, Hans, and Matt Korda, "Nuclear Notebook: Chinese Nuclear Forces, 2021," *Bulletin of the Atomic Scientists*, November 15, 2021, https://thebulletin.org/premium/2021-11/nuclear-notebook-chinese-nuclear-forces-2021/

Kristensen, Hans M., and Robert S. Norris, "Status of World Nuclear Forces," Federation of American Scientists, February 23, 2022, https://fas.org/issues/nuclear-weapons/status-world-nuclear-forces/

Krnjevic Miskovic, Damjan, "Back with a Vengeance: The Return of Rough and Tumble Geopolitics," *Orbis* 65, no.1 (2020): 118–35.

Kuo, Lily, "'All Necessary Means': Xi Jinping Reserves Right to Use Force against Taiwan," *The Guardian*, January 2, 2019, https://www.theguardian.com/world/2019/jan/02/all-necessary-means-xi-jinping-reserves-right-to-use-force-against-taiwan.

Kurtz-Phelan, Daniel, "War and Peace in the Cyber Age: Governments, Businesses, and Citizens Alike Now Face Pervasive and Unrelenting Cyberthreats," *Foreign Affairs*, January/February 2022, http://web.archive.org/web/20220110080133/https://www.foreignaffairs.com/issue-packages/2021-12-14/digital-disorder

Labonte, Melissa T., and Anne C. Edgerton, "Towards a Typology of Humanitarian Access Denial," *Third World Quarterly* 34, no. 1 (2013): 39–57.

Labott, Elise, "Get Ready for a Spike in Global Unrest", *Foreign Policy*, July 22, 2011, https://foreignpolicy.com/2021/07/22/covid-global-unrest-political-upheaval/

LaGrone, Sam, "USS Theodore Roosevelt Returns to San Diego Following Deployment Interrupted by Outbreak," USNI News, July 9, 2020, https://news.usni.org/2020/07/09/uss-theodore-roosevelt-returns-to-san-diego-following-deployment-interrupted-by-outbreak

Lahren, Tomi (@TomiLahren), "Might as well carry a purse with that mask, Joe," Twitter, October 6, 2020, https://twitter.com/TomiLahren/status/1313312828670046208

Laing, R. D., *The Divided Self: An Existential Study in Sanity and Madness* (Harmondsworth, England: Penguin, 1965).

Lampton, David M. (ed.), *The Making of Chinese Foreign and Security Policy in the Era of Reform, 1978–2000* (Stanford, CA: Stanford University Press, 2001).

Landoni, Giovanni, et al., "Why Are Asian Countries Outperforming the Western World in Controlling COVID-19 Pandemic," *Pathogens and Global Health* 115, no. 1 (2021): 70–2.

Lange, Katie, "What Is the National Defense Strategy?" US Department of Defense, October 8, 2018, https://www.defense.gov/News/Feature-Stories/Story/Article/1656414/what-is-the-national-defense-strategy/

Lardieri, Alexa, "Homeland Security Warns Terrorists Could Exploit Coronavirus Pandemic," *US News*, March 24, 2020, https://www.usnews.com/news/politics/articles/2020-03-24/homeland-security-warns-that-terrorists-could-exploit-coronavirus-pandemic

Latham, Andrew A., and James Christenson, "Historicizing the 'New Wars': The Case of *Jihad* in the Early Years of Islam," *European Journal of International Relations* 20, no. 3 (2014): 766–86.

Latour, Bruno, *Down to Earth : Politics in the New Climatic Regime* (Cambridge, England: Polity Press, 2018).

Lazard, Olivia, and Richard Youngs, "The EU and Climate Security: Toward Ecological Diplomacy," Carnegie Europe, July 12, 2021, https://carnegieeurope.eu/2021/07/12/eu-and-climate-security-toward-ecological-diplomacy-pub-84873

Lazer, David M. J., et al., "The Science of Fake News," *Science* 359, no. 6380 (2018): 1094–6.

Lederer, Edith M., "Nearly 40 Nations Criticize China's Human Rights Policies," AP News, October 6, 2020, https://apnews.com/article/virus-outbreak-race-and-ethnicity-tibet-hong-kong-united-states-a69609b46705f97bdec509e009577cb5

Lee, Amanda, "China's Retail 'Coma' Set to Weigh on Economic Growth amid Increasingly Tight Credit Controls," *South China Morning Post*, June 29, 2021, https://www.scmp.com/economy/china-economy/article/3139059/chinas-retail-coma-set-weigh-economic-growth-amid

Legarda, Helena, "The PLA's Mask Diplomacy," International Institute for Strategic Studies, August 12, 2020, https://www.iiss.org/blogs/research-paper/2020/08/pla-covid-diplomacy

Leslie, John, *The End of the World: The Science and Ethics of Human Extinction* (London: Routledge, 1996).

Lessenski, Marin, "Just Think About It: Findings of the Media Literacy Index," Policy Brief 55, Open Society Institute Sofia, November 2019, https://osis.bg/wp-content/uploads/2019/11/MediaLiteracyIndex2019_-ENG.pdf

Levy Yeyati, Eduardo, and Federico Filippini, "Social and Economic Impact of COVID-19," Brookings Global Working Paper No. 158, Brookings Institution, June 2021, https://www.brookings.edu/wp-content/uploads/2021/06/Social-and-economic-impact-COVID.pdf

Li Hongyang, "Record-High Floods Leave Regions Ravaged," *China Daily*, October 15, 2021, https://www.chinadaily.com.cn/a/202110/15/WS616938c0a310cdd39bc6f3fa.html

Li, Mingjiang, "The Belt and Road Initiative: Geo-economics and Indo-Pacific Security Competition," *International Affairs* 96, no. 1 (2020): 169–87.

Li, Yifei, and Judith Shapiro, *China Goes Green: Coercive Environmentalism for a Troubled Planet* (Cambridge, England: Polity Press, 2020).

Lifton, Robert Jay, *Destroying the World in Order to Save It: Aum Shinrikyō, Apocalyptic Violence, and the New Terrorism* (New York: Henry Holt, 1999).

Ling, L. H. M., *The Dao of World Politics: Towards a Post-Westphalian, Worldist International Relations* (Abingdon, England: Routledge, 2014).

Lopes da Silva, Diego, Nan Tian, and Alexandra Marksteiner, "Trends in World Military Expenditure, 2020," SIPRI, April 2021, https://www.sipri.org/sites/default/files/2021-04/fs_2104_milex_0.pdf

Lowy Institute, "Political Systems," in "COVID Performance Index: Deconstructing Pandemic Responses," https://interactives.lowyinstitute.org/features/covid-performance/#politics

Lubold, Gordon, and Warren P. Strobel, "Secret Chinese Port Project in Persian Gulf Rattles US Relations with UAE," *Wall Street Journal*, November 19, 2021, https://www.wsj.com/articles/us-china-uae-military-11637274224

Lüdeking, Rüdiger, "Nuclear Disarmament and Nonproliferation in Times of the Coronavirus Pandemic," *Arms Control Today*, June 2020, https://www.armscontrol.org/act/2020-06/features/nuclear-disarmament-nonproliferation-times-coronavirus-pandemic

Mabey, Nick, "Delivering Climate Security: International Security Responses to a Climate Changed World," Whitehall Paper 69, RUSI, April 22, 2008.

McDonald, Matt, "Ecological Security" *in Reflections on the Posthuman in International Relations: The Anthropocene, Security and Ecology*, eds. Clara Eroukhmanoff and Matt Harker (Bristol: E-International Relations, 2017), 64–8.

McDonald, Matt, "After the Fires? Climate Change and Security in Australia," *Australian Journal of Political Science* 56, no. 1 (2021): 1–18.

McDonald, Matt, *Ecological Security: Climate Change and the Construction of Security* (Cambridge, England: Cambridge University Press, 2021).

McGirk, Tim, "Taliban Assassins Target Pakistan's Polio Vaccinators," *National Geographic*, March 3, 2015, https://www.nationalgeographic.com/news/2015/03/150303-polio-pakistan-islamic-state-refugees-vaccination-health/

Macias, Amanda, "Trump Gives $717 Billion Defense Bill a Green Light. Here's What the Pentagon Is Poised to Get," CNBC, August 14, 2018, https://www.cnbc.com/2018/08/13/trump-signs-717-billion-defense-bill.html

Macias, Amanda, "Trump Signs $738 Billion Defense Bill. Here's What the Pentagon Is Poised to Get," CNBC, December 20, 2019, https://www.cnbc.com/2019/12/21/trump-signs-738-billion-defense-bill.html

McInnes, Colin, "The Many Meanings of Health Security," in *Routledge Handbook of Global Health Security*, ed. Simon Rushton and Jeremy Youde (Abingdon, England: Routledge, 2014).

McInnes, Colin, and Simon Rushton, "HIV, AIDS and Security: Where Are We Now?," *International Affairs* 86, no. 1 (2010): 225–45.

MacInnis, Laura, "Flu Fears Prompt New Bans on Pork, Meat Imports," Reuters. May 4, 2009, https://www.reuters.com/article/us-flu-who-trade/flu-fears-prompt-new-bans-on-pork-meat-imports-idUS-TRE5434NP20090504

Mackett, Odile, "The Effects of COVID-19 on Women in South Africa: An Analysis Using the Social Provisioning Framework," *Social and Health Sciences* 18, no. 2 (2020): 70–95.

McKinnell, Jamie, "Ben Roberts-Smith Defamation Trial Told Soldiers Drank Beer from Dead Afghan Man's Prosthetic Leg," ABC News (Australia), June 7, 2021, https://www.abc.net.au/news/2021-06-07/ben-roberts-smith-reputation-destroyed-defamation-trial-told/100194790

MacKinnon, Catharine A., *Are Women Human? And Other International Dialogues* (Cambridge, MA: Belknap Press, 2006).

MacKinnon, Catharine A., "State of Emergency," in *September 11, 2001: Feminist Perspectives*, ed. Susan Hawthorne and Bronwyn Winter (North Melbourne: Spinifex, 2002).

Mackowiak, Philip A., "Prior Pandemics: Looking to the Past for Insight into the COVID-19 Pandemic," *Journal of Community Hospital Internal Medicine Perspectives* 11, no. 2 (2021): 163–70.

Maertens, Lucile, "Climatizing the UN Security Council," *International Politics* 58, no. 4 (2021): 640–60.

Mahdavi, Mojtaba, "A Postcolonial Critique of Responsibility to Protect in the Middle East," *Perceptions: Journal of International Affairs 20, no.* 1 (2015): 7–36.

Mahler, Daniel Gerszon, et al., "Updated Estimates of the Impact of COVID-19 on Global Poverty: Turning the Corner on the Pandemic in 2021?" World Bank Data Blog, June 24, 2021, https://blogs.worldbank.org/opendata/updated-estimates-impact-covid-19-global-poverty-turning-corner-pandemic-2021

Mahony, Jack, "China Applies to Join Pacific Trade Agreement Designed to Counter its Growth in the Region, Just Hours after Criticising AUKUS," Sky News (Australia), September 17, 2021, https://www.skynews.com.au/world-news/global-affairs/china-applies-to-join-pacific-trade-agreement-designed-to-counter-its-grown-in-the-region-just-hours-after-criticising-aukus/news-story/3955ccf749109462bb40d2f22611e0fb

Maio, Giovanna di, "NATO's Response to COVID-19: Lessons for Resilience and Readiness," Brookings Institution, October 2020, https://www.brookings.edu/wp-content/uploads/2020/10/FP_20201028_nato_covid_demaio-1.pdf

Malkasian, Carter, *Illusions of Victory: The Anbar Awakening and the Rise of the Islamic State* (New York: Oxford University Press, 2017).

Malone, John D., "USS Theodore Roosevelt, COVID-19, and Ships: Lessons Learned,' *JAMA Network Open* 3, no. 10 (2020): e2022095.

Manchanda, Nivi, "Postcolonialism," in *Security Studies*, ed. Paul D. Williams and Matt McDonald, 3rd edn., vol. 1 (Abingdon, England: Routledge, 2018).

Manicom, James, *Bridging Troubled Waters: China, Japan, and Maritime Order in the East China Sea* (Washington, DC: Georgetown University Press, 2014).

Maoz, Zeev, *Paradoxes of War: On the Art of National Self-Entrapment* (Boston: Unwin Hyman, 1989).

Marchant, Gary E., et al., "International Governance of Autonomous Military Robots," *Columbia Science and Technology Law Review* 12 (2011): 272–315.

Martin, Brian, "Nuclear Winter: Science and Politics," *Science and Public Policy* 15, no. 5 (1988): 321–34.

Martin, Eric, "US Worker-Aid Plan Is Casualty as Trade Deal Fast-Track Ends," Bloomberg, July 7, 2021, https://www.bloomberg.com/news/newsletters/2021-07-07/u-s-worker-aid-plan-is-casualty-as-trade-deal-fast-track-ends

Mastro, Oriana Skylar, "The Taiwan Temptation: Why Beijing Might Resort to Force," *Foreign Affairs* 100, no. 4 (2021): 58–67.

Mathieu, Edouard, et al., "A Global Database of COVID-19 Vaccinations," *Nature Human Behaviour* 5 (2021): 947–53.

Matthew, Richard, "In Defense of Environment and Security Research," *Environmental Change and Security Project Report* 8 (2002): 109–24.

Mayer, Maximilian, "Chaotic Climate Change and Security," *International Political Sociology* 6, no. 2 (2012): 165–85.

Mayer, Maximilian, and Peer Schouten, "Energy Security and Climate Security under Conditions of the Anthropocene," in *Energy Security in the Era of Climate Change*, ed. Luca Anceschi and Jonathan Symons (London: Palgrave Macmillan, 2012).

Mazzoni, Valerio, "Coronavirus: How Islamist Militants Are Reacting to the Outbreak," *European Eye on Radicalization*, March 30, 2020, https://eeradicalization.com/coronavirus-how-islamist-militants-are-reacting-to-the-outbreak/

Mbembe, Achille, *Necropolitics* (Durham, NC: Duke University Press, 2019).

Mearsheimer, John J., "The False Promise of International Institutions," *International Security* 19, no. 3 (1994): 5–49.

Mearsheimer, John, *The Great Delusion: Liberal Dreams and International Realities* (New Haven, CT: Yale University Press, 2018).

Mearsheimer, John J., *The Tragedy of Great Power Politics* (New York: W. W. Norton, 2001).

Mecklin, John, "Disarm and Modernize," *Foreign Policy*, March/April 2015, https://foreignpolicy.com/2015/03/24/disarm-and-modernize-nuclear-weapons-warheads/

Medcalf, Rory, *Contest for the Indo-Pacific: Why China Won't Map the Future* (Collingwood, VIC: La Trobe University Press, 2020).

Medcalf, Rory, "Pivoting the Map: Australia's Indo-Pacific System," Centre of Gravity Series No. 1, Australian National University, November 2012, http://sdsc.bellschool.anu.edu.au/sites/default/files/publications/attachments/2020-10/cog_1_2018_softproof_v4.pdf

Médecins Sans Frontières, "Countries Obstructing COVID-19 Patent Waiver Must Allow Negotiations," press release, March 9, 2021, https://

www.msf.org/countries-obstructing-covid-19-patent-waiver-must-allow-negotiations

Meek, James Gordon, "Terrorist Groups Spin Covid-19 as God's 'Smallest Soldier' Attacking West," ABC News (USA), April 2, 2020, https://abcnews.go.com/International/terrorist-groups-spin-covid-19-gods-smallest-soldier/story?id=69930563

Meibauer, Gustav, "Interests, Ideas, and the Study of State Behaviour in Neoclassical Realism," *Review of International Studies* 46, no. 1 (2020): 20–36.

Melzer, Nils, *Human Rights Implications of the Usage of Drones and Unmanned Robots in Warfare* (Brussels: European Parliament, 2013), http://web.archive.org/web/20211221092605/https://www.europarl.europa.eu/RegData/etudes/etudes/join/2013/410220/EXPO-DROI_ET%282013%29410220_EN.pdf

Mendez, Rich, "UK and Trinidad Health Officials Refute Nicki Minaj's 'False Claim' COVID Shots Cause Swollen Testicles," CNBC, September 15, 2021, https://www.cnbc.com/2021/09/15/nicki-minaj-health-officials-in-uk-and-trinidad-refute-false-claim-covid-shots-cause-swollen-testicles-.html

Mercy Corps, *A Clash of Contagions: The Impact of COVID-19 on Conflict in Nigeria, Colombia and Afghanistan*, June 2021, https://www.mercycorps.org/sites/default/files/2021-06/Clash-of-Contagions-Full-Report-June-2021.pdf.

Meredith, Sam, "Rich Countries Are Refusing to Waive the Rights on Covid Vaccines as Global Cases Hit Record Levels," CNBC, April 22, 2021, https://www.cnbc.com/2021/04/22/covid-rich-countries-are-refusing-to-waive-ip-rights-on-vaccines.html

Meyer, Christoph, Martin Bricknell, and Ramon Pacheco Pardo, *How the COVID-19 Crisis Has Affected Security and Defence-Related Aspects of the EU: In Depth Analysis* (Brussels: European Parliament, 2021).

Meyer, Paul, "Prague One Year Later: From Words to Deeds?," *Arms Control Today*, May 2010, http://www.armscontrol.org/act/2010_05/LookingBack

Meyer, Paul, "Sleepwalking towards the 2020 Review of the Nuclear Non-Proliferation Treaty," *Open Canada*, May 8, 2020, https://www.opencanada.org/features/sleepwalking-towards-2020-review-nuclear-non-proliferation-treaty/

Mignolo, Walter, *The Darker Side of Western Modernity: Global Futures, Decolonial Options* (Durham, NC: Duke University Press, 2011).

Mignolo, Walter, "Epistemic Disobedience, Independent Thought and Decolonial Freedom," *Theory, Culture and Society* 26, no. 7–8 (2009): 159–81.

Miller, Rory, *Desert Kingdoms to Global Powers: The Rise of the Arab Gulf* (New Haven, CT: Yale University Press, 2016).

Milne, Seamus, *The Revenge of History: The Battle for the 21st Century* (London: Verso, 2013).

MINDS, *Network Challenge Report: COVID-19*, June 2020, https://umanitoba.ca/centres/media/MINDS-Network-Challenge-Report-COVID-19-EN.pdf

Mittal, Shalini, and Tushar Singh, "Gender-Based Violence during COVID-19 Pandemic: A Mini-review," *Frontiers in Global Women's Health* 1 (2020): 4.

Miyoshi, Masao, and H. D. Hartoonian (eds.), *Learning Places: The Afterlives of Area Studies* (Durham, NC: Duke University Press, 2002).

Mlambo-Ngcuka, Phumzile, "Violence against Women and Girls: The Shadow Pandemic," UN Women, April 6, 2020, https://www.unwomen.org/en/news/stories/2020/4/statement-ed-phumzile-violence-against-women-during-pandemic

Mohan, C. Raja, *Samudra Manthan: Sino-Indian Rivalry in the Indo-Pacific* (Washington, DC: Carnegie Endowment for International Peace, 2012).

Mohanty, Chandra, "Under Western Eyes: Feminist Scholarship and Colonial Discourses," *Feminist Review 30*, no. 1 (1988): 61–88.

Mohdin, Aamna, "Pots, Pans, Passion: Britons Clap Their Support for NHS Workers Again," *The Guardian*, April 2, 2020, https://www.theguardian.com/world/2020/apr/02/pots-pans-passion-britons-clap-their-support-for-nhs-workers-again

Moodie, Gavin, "Why Is the Australian Government Letting Universities Suffer?" *The Conversation*, May 19, 2020, https://theconversation.com/why-is-the-australian-government-letting-universities-suffer-138514

Moore, Charlie, "The Freedoms We May NEVER Get Back: How Our Privacy, Social Life and Travel Will Be Restricted 'for the Next TWO YEARS'—as Leaders Continue to Use Extraordinary Powers They Gained during the Pandemic Even after Vaccination Targets Are Hit," *Daily Mail*, October 1, 2021, https://www.dailymail.co.uk/news/article-10039985/Pubs-travel-masks-freedoms-NEVER-Covid-19.html

Morens, David M., et al., "Global Rinderpest Eradication: Lessons Learned and Why Humans Should Celebrate Too," *Journal of Infectious Diseases* 204, no. 4 (2011): 502–5.

Moreton-Robinson, Aileen, *The White Possessive: Property, Power and Indigenous Sovereignty* (Minneapolis: University of Minnesota Press, 2015).

Morgan, Patrick M., "Liberalist and Realist Security Studies at 2000: Two Decades of Progress?" in *Critical Reflections on Security and Change*, ed. Stuart Croft and Terry Terriff (London: Frank Cass, 2000).

Morgenthau, Hans, *Politics among Nations: The Struggle for Power and Peace*, 5th edn. (New York: Alfred A. Knopf, 1978).

Morrison, Scott, Boris Johnson, and Joseph R. Biden, "Joint Leaders Statement on AUKUS," media release, Prime Minister of Australia, September 16, 2021, https://www.pm.gov.au/media/joint-leaders-statement-aukus

Morse, Stephen S., et al., "Prediction and Prevention of the Next Pandemic Zoonosis," *The Lancet* 380, no. 9857 (2012): 1956–65.

Moskalenko, Sophia, "Many QAnon Followers Report Having Mental Health Diagnoses," *The Conversation*, March 25, 2021, https://theconversation.com/many-qanon-followers-report-having-mental-health-diagnoses-157299

Mossburg, Cheri, Theresa Waldrop, and Naomi Thomas, "Some Public Health Officials Are Resigning amid Threats during the COVID-19 Pandemic," CNN, June 23, 2020, https://edition.cnn.com/2020/06/22/us/health-officials-threats-coronavirus/index.html

Moyn, Samuel, "How the US Created a World of Endless War," *The Guardian*, August 31, 2021, https://www.theguardian.com/us-news/2021/aug/31/how-the-us-created-a-world-of-endless-war.

Moyn, Samuel, *Humane: How the United States Abandoned Peace and Reinvented War* (New York: Farrar, Straus & Giroux, 2021).

Mueller, Benjamin, and Rebecca Robbins, "'COVAX Hasn't Failed but It Is Failing': Global Vaccine Drive Struggles to Compete," *Sydney Morning Herald*, August 3, 2021, https://www.smh.com.au/world/africa/covax-hasn-t-failed-but-it-is-failing-global-vaccine-drive-struggles-to-compete-20210803-p58fc8.html.

Muhammad, Simela Victor, "Escalation of Tension in South China Sea and ASEAN Stance," *Info Singkat* 12, no. 10 (2020): 7–12.

Mullen, Andrew, "5 Things You Need to Know about China's Power Crisis," *South China Morning Post*, October 29, 2021, https://www.scmp.com/economy/china-economy/article/3153998/5-things-you-need-know-about-chinas-power-crisis

Munster, Rens van, "Book Reviews," *Cambridge Review of International Affairs* 21, no. 3 (2008): 437–50.

Murphy, Brett, and Letitia Stein, "How the CDC Failed Public Health Officials Fighting the Coronavirus," *USA Today*, January 26, 2021, https://www.usatoday.com/in-depth/news/investigations/2020/09/16/how-cdc-failed-local-health-officials-desperate-COVID-19-help/3435762001/

Murphy, Fredrick A., "Emerging Zoonoses," *Emerging Infectious Diseases* 4, no. 3 (1998): 429–35.

Mutimer, David, Kyle Grayson, and J. Marshall Beier, "*Critical Studies on Security*: An Introduction," *Critical Studies on Security* 1, no. 1 (2013): 1–12.

Myers, Norman, "Environmental Refugees," *Population and Environment* 19, no. 2 (1997): 167–82.

Nabourema, Farida, "Dictators Love Lockdowns," *African Arguments*, April 21, 2020, https://africanarguments.org/2020/04/21/dictatorships-love-lockdown-coronavirus-togo/

National Academies of Sciences, Engineering, and Medicine, *A Decadal Survey of the Social and Behavioral Sciences: A Research Agenda for Advancing Intelligence Analysis* (Washington, DC: National Academies Press, 2019).

National Cyber Security Centre, "Advisory: APT29 Targets COVID-19 Vaccine Development," July 16, 2020, https://www.ncsc.gov.uk/files/Advisory-APT29-targets-COVID-19-vaccine-development.pdf

National Defense Authorization Act for Fiscal Year 2021, HR 6395, 116th Congress, 2nd session, December 15, 2020, https://www.govtrack.us/congress/bills/116/hr6395/text

NATO, *Active Engagement, Modern Defence: Strategic Concept for the Defence and Security of the Members of the North Atlantic Treaty Organization*, 2010, https://www.nato.int/nato_static_fl2014/assets/pdf/pdf_publications/20120214_strategic-concept-2010-eng.pdf

Newey, Sarah, "Pandemic Could Trigger a 'Baby Boom' as Millions of Women Lose Access to Contraception and Abortion," *The Telegraph*, August 19, 2020, https://www.telegraph.co.uk/news/2020/08/19/millions-women-lose-access-contraceptives-abortions-covid-19

Newman, Edward, "Covid-19: A Human Security Analysis," *Global Society*, December 2021, https://www.tandfonline.com/doi/full/10.1080/13600826.2021.2010034.

Newman, Edward, "Critical Human Security Studies," *Review of International Studies* 36, no. 1 (2010): 77–94.

Newman, Edward, "Human Security: Reconciling Critical Aspirations with Political 'Realities,'" *British Journal of Criminology* 56, no. 6 (2016): 1165–83.

Newman, Molly Craine, "NY Court Officers Suspended for Doxxing State's Chief Judge Janet DiFiore," *New York Daily News*, August 27, 2021, https://www.nydailynews.com/new-york/manhattan/ny-court-officers-dennis-quirk-suspended-30-days-doxxing-chief-judge-20210827-acct-vxwspvacnjiebqekzylfyy-story.html

Newton, Casey, "How the 'Plandemic' Video Hoax Went Viral," *The Verge*, May 12, 2020, https://www.theverge.com/2020/5/12/21254184/how-plandemic-went-viral-facebook-youtube

Nogrady, Bianca, "Australia Cuts Research Funding to Universities," *Nature*, December 19, 2018, https://www.nature.com/articles/d41586-018-07840-w

Nogrady, Bianca, "'I Hope You Die': How the Covid Pandemic Unleased Attacks on Scientists," *Nature*, October 14, 2021, https://www.nature.com/articles/d41586-021-02741-x

Nordhaus, Ted, and Michael Shellenberger, *Break Through: From the Death of Environmentalism to the Politics of Possibility* (Boston: Houghton Mifflin Harcourt, 2007).

Norrlöf, Carla, "Is COVID-19 the End of US Hegemony? Public Bads, Leadership Failures and Monetary Hegemony," *International Affairs* 96, no. 5 (2020): 1281–1303.

Nunes, João, "The COVID-19 Pandemic: Securitization, Neoliberal Crisis, and Global Vulnerabilization," *Cadernos de Saúde Pública* 36, no. 5 (2020): e00063120.

Nye, Joseph S., Jr., "No, the Coronavirus Will Not Change the Global Order," *Foreign Policy*, April 6, 2020, https://foreignpolicy.com/2020/04/16/coronavirus-pandemic-china-united-states-power-competition/

Nye, Joseph S., Jr., *The Paradox of American Power: Why the World's Only Superpower Can't Go It Alone* (New York: Oxford University Press, 2002).

Nye, Joseph S., "Soft Power," *Foreign Policy* 80 (1990): 153–71.

Nyman, Jonna, "Energy Security in an Age of Environmental Change," in *Traditions and Trends in Global Environmental Politics: International Relations and the Earth*, ed. Olaf Corry and Hayley Stevenson (Abingdon, England: Routledge, 2017).

Nyman, Jonna, *The Energy Security Paradox: Rethinking Energy (In)security in the United States and China* (Oxford: Oxford University Press, 2018).

Oakes, Dan, and Sam Clark, "The Afghan Files: Defence Leak Exposes Deadly Secrets of Australia's Special Forces," ABC News (Australia), July 11, 2017, https://www.abc.net.au/news/2017-07-11/killings-of-unarmed-afghans-by-australian-special-forces/8466642

O'Brien, Robert C., "The Chinese Communist Party's Ideology and Global Ambitions," The White House, June 26, 2020, https://trumpwhitehouse.archives.gov/briefings-statements/chinese-communist-partys-ideology-global-ambitions/

OECD, "Economic Forecast Summary (December 2021)," https://www.oecd.org/economy/united-states-economic-snapshot/

Oels, Angela, "From 'Securitization' of Climate Change to 'Climatization' of the Security Field: Comparing Three Theoretical Perspectives,'" in *Climate Change, Human Security and Violent Conflict: Challenges for Societal Stability*, ed. Jürgen Scheffran et al. (Heidelberg: Springer, 2012).

Office for the Coordination of Humanitarian Affairs, *Global Humanitarian Overview 2019* (Geneva: Office for the Coordination of Humanitarian Affairs, 2019), https://www.unocha.org/sites/unocha/files/GHO2019.pdf.

Office for the Coordination of Humanitarian Affairs, *Global Humanitarian Overview 2021* (Geneva: Office for the Coordination of Humanitarian Affairs, 2021), https://2021.gho.unocha.org/

Office for the Coordination of Humanitarian Affairs, "OCHA on Message: Humanitarian Access," April 2010, https://www.unocha.org/sites/unocha/files/dms/Documents/OOM_HumAccess_English.pdf

Office for the Coordination of Humanitarian Affairs, "OCHA on Message: Humanitarian Principles," June 2012, https://www.unocha.org/sites/dms/Documents/OOM-humanitarianprinciples_eng_June12.pdf

Office for the Coordination of Humanitarian Affairs, *Oslo Guidelines: Guidelines on the Use of Foreign Military and Civil Defence Assets in Disaster Relief*, November 2007, https://www.unocha.org/sites/unocha/files/OSLO%20Guidelines%20Rev%201.1%20-%20Nov%2007.pdf

Office for the Coordination of Humanitarian Affairs, "Yemen Situation Report," January 2022, https://reports.unocha.org/en/country/yemen

Office of the Director of National Intelligence, *Annual Threat Assessment of the US Intelligence Community*, April 9, 2021, https://www.dni.gov/files/ODNI/documents/assessments/ATA-2021-Unclassified-Report.pdf

Office of the Director of National Intelligence, "Background to 'Assessing Russian Activities and Intentions in Recent US Elections': The Analytic Process and Cyber Incident Attribution," January 6, 2017, available at https://www.dni.gov/files/documents/ICA_2017_01.pdf

Office of the Secretary of Defense, *Military and Security Developments Involving the People's Republic of China 2020: Annual Report to Congress*, US Department of Defense, 2020, https://media.defense.gov/2020/Sep/01/2002488689/-1/-1/1/2020-DOD-CHINA-MILITARY-POWER-REPORT-FINAL.PDF

Office of the Secretary of Defense, *Military and Security Developments Involving the People's Republic of China 2021*, US Department of Defense, 2021, https://media.defense.gov/2021/Nov/03/2002885874/-1/-1/0/2021-CMPR-FINAL.PDF

Ogden, Chris, "Beyond Succession: China's Internal Security Challenges," *Strategic Analysis* 37, no. 2 (2013): 193–202.

OHCHR, "In Defence of a Renewed Multilateralism to Address the COVID-19 Pandemic and Other Global Challenges: Report" (Geneva: OHCHR, 2021), https://www.ohchr.org/EN/Issues/IntOrder/Pages/covid19-multilateralism.aspx

O'Neil, Patrick Howell, "Ransomware Did Not Kill a German Hospital Patient," *MIT Technology Review*, November 12, 2020, https://www.technologyreview.com/2020/11/12/1012015/ransomware-did-not-kill-a-german-hospital-patient/

O'Neill, Aaron, "Number of Military Fatalities in All Major Wars Involving the United States from 1775 to 2021," Statista, November 22, 2021, https://www.statista.com/statistics/1009819/total-us-military-fatalities-in-american-wars-1775-present/

Oppenheimer, J. Robert, *The Flying Trapeze: Three Crises for Physicists* (London: Oxford University Press, 1964).

Oprysko, Cailtin, and Susannah Luthi, "Trump Labels Himself 'a Wartime President' Combating Coronavirus," *Politico*, March 18, 2020, https://www.politico.com/news/2020/03/18/trump-administration-self-swab-coronavirus-tests-135590

Organisation for Economic Co-operation and Development, "COVID-19 Crisis Response in ASEAN Member States," May 4, 2020, https://www.oecd.org/coronavirus/policy-responses/covid-19-crisis-response-in-asean-member-states-02f828a2/

Organisation for Economic Co-operation and Development, "The Face Mask Global Value Chain in the COVID-19 Outbreak: Evidence and Policy Lessons," May 4, 2020, https://www.oecd.org/coronavirus/policy-responses/the-face-mask-global-value-chain-in-the-covid-19-outbreak-evidence-and-policy-lessons-a4df866d/

O'Rourke, Ronald, "Navy Large Unmanned Surface and Undersea Vehicles: Background and Issues for Congress," Congressional Research Service, October 20, 2021, http://web.archive.org/web/20211026062620/https://crsreports.congress.gov/product/pdf/R/R45757/43

Otieno Sumba, Eric, "Necropolitics at Large: Pandemic Politics and the Coloniality of the Global Access Gap," *Critical Studies on Security* 9, no. 1 (2021): 48–52.

Owen, Taylor, "Human Security—Conflict, Critique and Consensus: Colloquium Remarks and a Proposal for a Threshold-Based Definition," *Security Dialogue* 35, no. 3 (2004): 373–87.

Oxford Languages, "Word of the Year 2019," https://languages.oup.com/word-of-the-year/2019/

Ozguc, Umut, "Three Lines of Pandemic Borders: From Necropolitics to Hope as a Method of Living," *Critical Studies on Security* 9, no. 1 (2021): 63–6.

Özler, Ş. İlgü, "The United Nations at Seventy-Five: Passing the COVID Test?" *Ethics & International Affairs* 34, no. 4 (2020): 445–6.

Page, James Michael, and John Williams, "Drones, Afghanistan, and Beyond: Towards Analysis and Assessment in Context," *European Journal of International Security* (2021), https://doi.org/10.1017/eis.2021.19

Palmer, Carl L., and Rolfe D. Peterson, "Toxic Mask-ulinity: The Link between Masculine Toughness and Affective Reactions to Mask Wearing in the COVID-19 Era," *Politics & Gender* 16, no. 4 (2020): 1044–51.

Pan, Chengxin, "Racialised Politics of (In)Security and the COVID-19 Westfailure," *Critical Studies on Security* 9, no. 1 (2021): 40–5.

Panda, Ankit, "US Nuclear Weapons Modernization," Council on Foreign Relations, February 7, 2018, https://www.cfr.org/backgrounder/us-nuclear-weapons-modernization

"A Pandemic Era," *Lancet Planetary Health* 5, no. 1 (2021): e1.

Papamichail, Andreas, "COVID-19 and the Limits of the Health-Security Nexus," in Giovanni Agostinis et al., "Forum: COVID-19 and IR Scholarship: One Profession, Many Voices," *International Studies Review* 23, no. 2 (2021): 304–7.

Paris, Roland, "Human Security—Paradigm Shift or Hot Air?" *International Security* 26, no. 2 (2001), 87–102.

Parker, Claire, and Bryan Pietsch, "Countries around the World are Debating Coronavirus Booster Shots. Here's Where They've Been Approved," *Washington Post*, November 16, 2021, https://www.washingtonpost.com/world/2021/11/12/coronavirus-vaccine-boosters-global/

Parker, Kim, "The Growing Partisan Divide in Views of Higher Education," Pew Research Center, August 19, https://www.pewresearch.org/social-trends/2019/08/19/the-growing-partisan-divide-in-views-of-higher-education-2/

Patrick, Stewart, "'Failed' States and Global Security: Empirical Questions and Policy Dilemmas," *International Studies Review* 9, no. 4 (2007): 644–62.

Patrick, Stewart, "When the System Fails: COVID-19 and the Costs of Global Dysfunction," *Foreign Affairs*, July/August 2020, https://www.foreignaffairs.com/articles/world/2020-06-09/when-system-fails

Pauly, Madison, "The War on Masks is a Cover-up for Toxic Masculinity," *Mother Jones*, October 8, 2020, https://www.motherjones.com/coronavirus-updates/2020/10/trump-masks-covid-toxic-masculinity/

Payne, Marise, and Alex Hawke, "Partnering with Our Neighbours to Respond to COVID-19," joint media release, 29 May 2020, https://www.foreignminister.gov.au/minister/marise-payne/media-release/partnering-our-neighbours-respond-covid-19

Pellizzoni, Luigi, "Emancipation, Capture, and Rescue? On the Ontological Turn and Its Critique," in *Rethinking the Environment for the Anthropocene: Political Theory and Socionatural Relations in the New Geological Epoch*, ed. Manuel Arias-Maldonado and Zev Trachtenberg (Abingdon, England: Routledge, 2019).

Peoples, Columba, and Nick Vaughan-Williams, *Critical Security Studies: An Introduction* (Abingdon, England: Routledge, 2010).

Peoples, Columba, and Nick Vaughan-Williams, *Critical Security Studies: An Introduction*, 2nd edn. (Abingdon, England: Routledge, 2015).

Pereira, Joana Castro, "Environmental Security in the Anthropocene," in *Security at a Crossroad: New Tools for New Challenges*, ed. Teresa Rodrigues and André Inácio (Hauppauge, NY: Nova Science, 2019).

Perry, Tom, and Laila Bassam, "Hezbollah Deploys Medics, Hospitals against Coronavirus in Lebanon," Reuters, March 25, 2020, https://www.reuters.com/article/us-health-coronavirus-hezbollah/hezbollah-deploys-medics-hospitals-against-coronavirus-in-lebanon-idUSKBN21C3R7

Peters, Katie, and Mairi Dupar, "The Humanitarian Impact of Combined Conflict, Climate and Environmental Risks: Highlights and Recommendations from a High-Level Side Event at the 75th United Nations General Assembly," Overseas Development Institute, December 2020, https://cdn.odi.org/media/documents/Briefing_note__The_humanitarian_impact_of_combined_conflict_climate_and_enviro_AC78KvY.pdf

Peterson, V. Spike, "Security and Sovereign States: What Is at Stake in Taking Feminism Seriously?" in *Gendered States: Feminist (Re)visions of International Relations Theory*, ed. V. Spike Peterson (Boulder, CO: Lynne Rienner, 1992).

Pettman, Jan Jindy, *Worlding Women: A Feminist International Politics* (London: Routledge, 1996).

Pfitzner, Naomi, et al., "A Bubble Set to Burst: Why Urgent Support Must Be Given to Domestic Violence Workers," *Lens*, July 1, 2020, https://lens.monash.edu/@politics-society/2020/07/01/1380770/we-are-in-a-bubble-that-is-set-to-burst-why-urgent-support-must-be-given-to-domestic-violence-workers

Phillips, Tom, "Brazil: Bolsonaro Reportedly Uses Homophobic Slur to Mock Masks," *The Guardian*, July 9, 2020, https://www.theguardian.com/world/2020/jul/08/bolsonaro-masks-slur-brazil-coronavirus

Phipps, Peter, "Modern Empires," in *Encyclopedia of Global Studies*, ed. Helmut Anheier and Mark Juergensmeyer (Thousand Oaks, CA: Sage, 2012).

Phipps, Peter, "Neocolonialism," in *Encyclopedia of Global Studies*, ed. Helmut Anheier and Mark Juergensmeyer (Thousand Oaks, CA: Sage, 2012).

Pinedo, Emma, Nathan Allen, and Andrei Khalip, "EU Says Putin's Ominous Threat to Those Who Hinder Him Marks 'Critical Moment,'" Reuters, February 25, 2022, https://www.reuters.com/world/europe/eu-says-putins-ominous-threat-those-who-hinder-him-marks-critical-moment-2022-02-24/

Pompeo, Michael R., "Communist China and the Free World's Future," US Department of State, July 23, 2020, https://www.state.gov/communist-china-and-the-free-worlds-future/

Poushter, Jacob, and Christine Huang, "Despite Pandemic, Many Europeans See Climate Change as Greatest Threat to Their Countries," Pew Research Center, September 9, 2020, https://www.pewresearch.org/global/2020/09/09/despite-pandemic-many-europeans-still-see-climate-change-as-greatest-threat-to-their-countries/

Powell, Anastasia, and Asher Flynn, "Reports of 'Revenge Porn' Skyrocketed during Lockdown, We Must Stop Blaming Victims for It," *The Conversation*, June 3, 2020, https://theconversation.com/reports-of-revenge-porn-skyrocketed-during-lockdown-we-must-stop-blaming-victims-for-it-139659

Prashad, Vijay, *The Darker Nations: A People's History of the Third World* (New York: New Press, 2007).

Priyadarsini, S. Lakshmi, M. Suresh, and Donald Huisingh, "What Can We Learn from Previous Pandemics to Reduce the Frequency of Emerging Infectious Diseases like COVID-19?" *Global Transitions* 2 (2020): 202–20.

Puar, Jasbir, *Terrorist Assemblages: Homonationalism in Queer Times* (Durham, NC: Duke University Press, 2007).

Qaddour, Amany, speech at "Coronavirus and Conflict: The Security Sector Response," United States Peace Institute virtual conference, April 15, 2020, https://www.usip.org/events/coronavirus-and-conflict-security-sector-response

Quinn, Ben, "Covid Has Wiped Out Years of Progress on Life Expectancy, Finds Study," *The Guardian*, September 27, 2021, https://www.theguardian.com/society/2021/sep/27/COVID-has-wiped-out-years-of-progress-on-life-expectancy-finds-study

Rachwani, Mostafa, "Melbourne Protests: Prop Gallows Seen as Thousands March against Victoria's Covid Powers," *The Guardian*, November 13, 2021, https://www.theguardian.com/australia-news/2021/nov/13/melbourne-protests-prop-gallows-seen-as-thousands-march-against-victorias-covid-powers

Radin, Andrew, et al., *China-Russia Cooperation: Determining Factors, Future Trajectories, Implications for the United States* (Santa Monica, CA: RAND, 2021).

Ralph, Stuart, and Mark Stoové, "Using Military Language and Presence Might Not Be the Best Approach to COVID and Public Health," *The Conversation*, August 17, 2021, http://theconversation.com/using-military-language-and-presence-might-not-be-the-best-approach-to-covid-and-public-health-166019

Rathbun, Brian C., “Uncertain about Uncertainty: Understanding the Multiple Meanings of a Crucial Concept in International Relations Theory,” *International Studies Quarterly* 51, no. 3 (2007): 533–57.

Raworth, Kate, “A Doughnut for the Anthropocene: Appendix, ” *The Lancet: Planetary Health* 1, no. 2 (2017), e48–e49.

Reaching Critical Will, “COVID-19: Up-to-Date List of Postponed or Cancelled Disarmament and Arms Control Meetings,” February 1, 2021, http://web.archive.org/web/20211107015057/https://www.reachingcriticalwill.org/news/latest-news/14666-covid-19-up-to-date-list-of-postponed-or-cancelled-disarmament-and-arms-control-meetings

Reed, Bruce Cameron, *The Physics of the Manhattan Project*, 4th edn. (Cham, Switzerland: Springer, 2021).

Rees, Martin, *Our Final Hour: A Scientist's Warning—How Terror, Error, and Environmental Disaster Threaten Humankind's Future in This Century* (New York: Basic, 2003).

Reeve, Elle, Samantha Guff, and Deborah Brunswick, “The Surreal Lives of Arkansas Nurses Fighting Covid-19 Inside the Hospital and Denial on the Outside,” CNN, July 23, 2021, https://edition.cnn.com/2021/07/22/us/arkansas-covid-nurse-vaccine/index.html

Reid, Julian, “Interrogating the Neoliberal Biopolitics of the Sustainable Development-Resilience Nexus,” *International Political Sociology* 7, no. 4 (2013): 353–67.

ReliefWeb, “Yemen: Annual Humanitarian Access Overview, 2020,” March 14, 2021, https://reliefweb.int/report/yemen/yemen-annual-humanitarian-access-overview-2020

“Remarks by Chinese President Xi Jinping at 15th G20 Leaders' Summit,” XinhuaNet, November 21, 2020, http://www.xinhuanet.com/english/2020-11/21/c_139533609.htm

Reny, Tyler T., “Masculine Norms and Infectious Disease: The Case of COVID-19,” *Politics & Gender* 16, no. 4 (2020): 1028–35.

Reuters, “World Has Entered Stage of ‘Vaccine Apartheid’—WHO Head,” May 17, 2021, https://www.reuters.com/business/healthcare-pharmaceuticals/world-has-entered-stage-vaccine-apartheid-who-head-2021-05-17/

Riga, Jessica, “Drive Through Testing Site in Sydney's West Target of Possible Arson Attack,” ABC News Blog (Australia), August 29, 2021, https://www.abc.net.au/news/2021-08-29/covid-live-blog-nsw-press-conference-vic-lockdown/100415572

Risma, Helda, Pujo Widodo, and Resmanto Widodo Putro, “Covid-19 Securitization and Terrorism: National Security Change Management Dilemma,” *Jurnal Pertahanan* 6, no. 3 (2020): 496–506.

Rittimann, Olivier, “NATO and the COVID-19 Emergency: Actions and Lessons,” NDC Policy Brief No. 15, NATO Defense College, September 15, 2020, https://www.ndc.nato.int/news/news.php?icode=1463

Roberts, Alasdair, “‘Whatever It Takes': Danger, Necessity, and Realism in American Public Policy,” *Administration & Society* 52, no. 7 (2020): 1131–44.

Robock, Alan, Luke Oman, and Georgiy L. Stenchikov, "Nuclear Winter Revisited with a Modern Climate Model and Current Nuclear Arsenals: Still Catastrophic Consequences," *Journal of Geophysical Research: Atmospheres* 112, no. D13 (2007): D13107.

Roborgh, Sophie, and Larissa Fast, "Healthcare Workers Are Still Coming under Attack during the Coronavirus Pandemic," *The Conversation*, April 28, 2020, https://theconversation.com/healthcare-workers-are-still-coming-under-attack-during-the-coronavirus-pandemic-136573

Rockström, Johan, et al., "Planetary Boundaries: Exploring the Safe Operating Space for Humanity," *Ecology and Society* 14, no. 2 (2009): 32.

Rodier, Guénaël, et al., "Global Public Health Security," *Emerging Infectious Diseases* 13, no. 10 (2007): 1447–52.

Rodó, Xavier, et al., "Changing Climate and the COVID-19 Pandemic: More than Just Heads or Tails," *Nature Medicine* 27, no. 4 (2021): 576–9.

Roff, Heather M., and Alex Woodson, "Making AI Work, Ethically & Responsibly, with Heather M. Roff," Carnegie Council for Ethics in International Affairs, October 7, 2019, http://web.archive.org/web/20211016055159/https://www.carnegiecouncil.org/studio/multimedia/20191007-making-ai-work-ethically-responsibly-heather-roff

Rolland, Nadège, "China's Vision for a New World Order: Implications for the United States," National Bureau of Asian Research, October 2020, https://www.nbr.org/wp-content/uploads/pdfs/publications/china_vision_brief_100220.pdf

Rollins, John, and Clay Wilson, "Terrorist Capabilities for Cyberattack: Overview and Policy Issues," Congressional Research Service, January 22, 2007, http://web.archive.org/web/20211222072626/https://crsreports.congress.gov/product/pdf/RL/RL33123

Rose, Gideon, "What Is Killing Us Is Not Connection; It Is Connection without Cooperation," *Foreign Affairs*, July/August 2020, https://www.foreignaffairs.com/issue-packages/2020-06-03/world-after-pandemic.

Ross, Robert S., "Engagement in US China Policy," in *Engaging China: The Management of an Emerging Power*, ed. Alastair Iain Johnston and Robert S. Ross (Abingdon, England: Routledge, 1999).

Rossiter, Ash, "Drone Usage by Militant Groups: Exploring Variation in Adoption," *Defense & Security Analysis* 34, no. 2 (2018): 113–26.

Rossiter, Ash, "The Impact of Robotics and Autonomous Systems (RAS) across the Conflict Spectrum," *Small Wars & Insurgencies* 31, no. 4 (2020): 691–700.

Rossiter, Ash, "Turkey's Path to Drone Power," Trends, December 8, 2021, https://trendsresearch.org/insight/turkeys-path-to-drone-power/

Rossiter, Ash, "The Yemeni-Saudi Border: From Boundary to Frontline," in *Yemen and the Gulf States: The Making of a Crisis*, ed. Helen Lackner and Daniel Martin Varisco (Berlin: Gerlach Press, 2018).

Rossiter, Ash, and Christopher Bolan, "The Middle East: Strategic and Military Balance of Power," in *The Routledge Handbook of Diplomacy and Statecraft*, ed. B. J. C. McKercher (Abingdon, England: Routledge, 2022).

Rossiter, Ash, and Brendon J. Cannon (eds.), *Conflict and Cooperation in the Indo-Pacific: New Geopolitical Realities* (Abingdon, England: Routledge, 2020).

Rossiter, Ash, and Brendon J. Cannon, "Turkey's rise as a drone power: trial by fire," *Defense & Security Analysis* (2022), pp. 216–17, https://doi.org/10.1080/14751798.2022.2068562 (accessed July 12, 2022).

Rothe, Delf, "Seeing like a Satellite: Remote Sensing and the Ontological Politics of Environmental Security," *Security Dialogue* 48, no. 4 (2017): 334–53.

Rothschild, Emma, "What Is Security?" *Dædalus* 124, no. 3 (1995): 53–98.

Rudd, Kevin, "The Coming Post-COVID-19 Anarchy," *Foreign Affairs*, May 6, 2020, https://www.foreignaffairs.com/articles/united-states/2020-05-06/coming-post-COVID-19-anarchy

Runyan, Ann Sisson, and V. Spike Peterson, *Global Gender Issues in the New Millennium* (Boulder, CO: Westview Press, 2015).

Russett, Bruce, and John R. Oneal, *Triangulating Peace: Democracy, Interdependence, and International Organizations* (New York: W. W. Norton, 2000).

Russian Federation, "The Position on the Status of Meetings in 2020," Convention on Certain Conventional Weapons—Meeting of High Contracting Parties, CCW/2020/2, April 13, 2021, http://web.archive.org/web/20211107012815/https://documents.unoda.org/wp-content/uploads/2021/04/CCW-2020-2-Advance-copy.pdf

Ryan, Fergus, Audrey Fritz, and Daria Impiombato, "Mapping China's Tech Giants: Reining In China's Technology Giants," Australian Strategic Policy Institute, June 8, 2021, https://www.aspi.org.au/report/mapping-chinas-technology-giants-reining-chinas-technology-giants

Sacks, David, "China's Huawei Is Winning the 5G Race. Here's What the United States Should Do to Respond," Council on Foreign Relations, March 29, 2021, https://www.cfr.org/blog/china-huawei-5g

Sagan, Carl, "Nuclear Winter," *Parade*, October 30, 1983, 4–7.

Said, Edward, *Culture and Imperialism* (New York: Knopf, 1993).

Said, Edward W., *Orientalism* (Ringwood, VIC: Penguin, 1985).

Said, Summer, Jared Malsin, and Jessica Donati, "US Blames Iran for Attack on Saudi Oil Facilities," *Wall Street Journal*, September 14, 2019, https://www.wsj.com/articles/drone-strikes-spark-fires-at-saudi-oil-facilities-11568443375

Salas, Renee N., James M. Shultz, and Caren. G. Solomon, "The Climate Crisis and Covid-19—A Major Threat to the Pandemic Response," *New England Journal of Medicine* 383, no. 11 (2020): e70.

Salleh, Anna, "Scientists Talking about COVID-19 Are Copping Widespread Abuse and Death Threats, Survey Finds," ABC News (Australia), October 14, 2021, https://www.abc.net.au/news/science/2021-10-14/covid-scientists-receiving-death-threats-abuse/100533564

Salman, Nadine L., and Paul Gill, "Terrorism during the COVID-19 Pandemic," Special Series on COVID-19 No. 13, UCL Jill Dando Institute,

May 2020, https://www.ucl.ac.uk/jill-dando-institute/sites/jill-dando-institute/files/terrosim_covid19_final_no_13.pdf

Salter, Mark B. (ed.), et al., "Horizon Scan: Critical Security Studies for the Next 50 Years," *Security Dialogue* 50, no. 4 supplement (2019): 9–37.

Samaan, Jean-Loup, "Arab Gulf States in the Indo-Pacific: The Limits of Ambiguous Hedging Strategies," in *Indo-Pacific Strategies: Navigating Geopolitics at the Dawn of a New Age*, ed. Brendon J. Cannon and Kei Hakata (Abingdon, England: Routledge, 2021).

Samaan, Jean-Loup C., "Missiles, Drones, and the Houthis in Yemen," *Parameters* 50, no. 1 (2020): 51–64.

Sarata, Amanda K., and Simi V. Siddalingaiah, "COVID-19 Testing Supply Chain," Congressional Research Service, February 25, 2021, https://crsreports.congress.gov/product/pdf/IF/IF11774

Savić, Sara, et al. "Emerging Vector-Borne Diseases—Incidence through Vectors," *Frontiers in Public Health* 2 (2014): 267.

Sayler, Kelley M., "Artificial Intelligence and National Security," Congressional Research Service, November 10, 2020, http://web.archive.org/web/20211222091026/https://crsreports.congress.gov/product/pdf/R/R45178

Sayler, Kelley M., "International Discussions Concerning Lethal Autonomous Weapon Systems," Congressional Research Service, April 19, 2021, http://web.archive.org/web/20211221101534/https://crsreports.congress.gov/product/pdf/IF/IF11294/4

SBS News, "Donald Trump Embarks on Twitter Storm after Returning to White House While Still Being Treated for Coronavirus," October 7, 2020, https://www.sbs.com.au/news/donald-trump-embarks-on-twitter-storm-after-returning-to-white-house-while-still-being-treated-for-coronavirus/6e7684e0-e79e-44e8-ba2e-05053edcf815

Schell, Jonathan, *Fate of the Earth* (London: Pan, 1982).

Scherer, Steve, and Ismail Shakil, "Canada's Trudeau Ends Emergency Powers Invoked to Clear Protests," Reuters, February 23, 2022, https://www.reuters.com/world/americas/canada-ends-emergency-powers-invoked-tackle-truckers-protests-pm-trudeau-2022-02-23/

Schmeller, Dirk S., Franck Courchamp, and Gerry Killeen, "Biodiversity Loss, Emerging Pathogens and Human Health Risks," *Biodiversity and Conservation* 29, no. 11 (2020): 3095–3102.

Schwartz, Peter, and Doug Randall, *An Abrupt Climate Change Scenario and Its Implications for United States National Security* (Pasadena, CA: Jet Propulsion Laboratory, 2003).

Scott, Ben, "Rules-Based Order: What's in a Name?" *The Interpreter*, June 30, 2021, https://www.lowyinstitute.org/the-interpreter/rules-based-order-whats-in-a-name

Scott, Shirley V., "The Attitude of the P5 towards a Climate Change Role for the Council," in *Climate Change and the UN Security Council*, ed. Shirley V. Scott and Charlotte Ku (Cheltenham, England: Edward Elgar, 2018).

Scott, Shirley V., "Does the UNFCCC Fulfil the Functions Required of a Framework Convention? Why Abandoning the United Nations

Framework Convention on Climate Change Might Constitute a Long Overdue Step Forward," *Journal of Environmental Law* 27, no. 1 (2015): 69–89.

Scott, Shirley V., "Implications of Climate Change for the UN Security Council: Mapping the Range of Potential Policy Responses," *International Affairs* 91, no. 6 (2015): 1317–33.

Scott, Shirley V., and Charlotte Ku, "The UN Security Council and Global Action on Climate Change," in *Climate Change and the UN Security Council*, ed. Shirley V. Scott and Charlotte Ku (Cheltenham, England: Edward Elgar, 2018).

Scott, Shirley V., and Christopher Kaindi, "The Responsibility of the UN Security Council for Climate Security," in *Ethiopian Yearbook of International Law 2019: Towards a Global Order Based on Principles of Fairness, Solidarity, and Humanity*, ed. Zeray Yihdego, Melaku Geboye Desta, and Martha Belete Hailu (Cham, Switzerland: Springer, 2020).

Seitz, Russel, "In from the Cold: 'Nuclear Winter' Melts Down," *National Interest* 5 (1986): 3–17.

Seo, Jeongmin, "South Korea–Gulf Relations and the Iran Factor," in *External Powers and the Gulf Monarchies*, ed. Jonathan Fulton and Li-Chen Sim (Abingdon, England: Routledge, 2018).

Sepkoski, David, *Catastrophic Thinking: Extinction and the Value of Diversity* (Chicago: University of Chicago Press, 2020).

Serikbayeva, Balzhan, Kanat Abdulla, and Yessengali Oskenbayev, "State Capacity in Responding to COVID-19," MPRA Paper 101511, University Library of Munich, 2020.

Seth, Sanjay, *Beyond Reason: Postcolonial Theory and the Social Sciences* (New York: Oxford University Press, 2021).

Seth, Sanjay, "International Relations: Plural or Postcolonial?" *International Politics Reviews* 9, no. 2 (2021): 301–5.

Seth, Sanjay, "Introduction," in *Postcolonial Theory and International Relations: A Critical Introduction*, ed. Sanjay Seth (Abingdon, England: Routledge, 2013).

Seth, Sanjay, "Postcolonial Theory and the Critique of International Relations," *Millennium: Journal of International Studies* 40, no. 1 (2011): 167–83.

Sewall, Sarah, "Introduction," in *The US Army / Marine Corps Counterinsurgency Field Manual* (Chicago: University of Chicago Press, 2007).

Shah, Aqil, "Do US Drone Strikes Cause Blowback? Evidence from Pakistan and Beyond," *International Security* 42, no. 4 (2018): 47–84.

Shambaugh, David, *China Goes Global: The Partial Power* (New York: Oxford University Press, 2013).

Shani, Giorgio, "Human Security as Ontological Security: A Post-colonial Approach," *Postcolonial Studies* 20, no. 3 (2017): 275–93.

Sharkey, Noel, "Cassandra or False Prophet of Doom: AI Robots and War," *IEEE Intelligent Systems* 23, no. 4 (2008): 14–17.

Sharma, Ashok, "The Quadrilateral Initiative: An Evaluation," *South Asian Survey* 17, no. 2 (2010): 237–53.

Sheftalovich, Zoya, and Stuart Lau, "How Xi Jinping Lost Australia," Politico, September 27, 2021, https://www.politico.eu/article/how-china-xi-jinping-lost-australia-trade-diplomacy/

Shepherd, Laura J. (ed.), *Gender Matters in Global Politics: A Feminist Introduction to International Relations*, 2nd edn. (Abingdon, England: Routledge, 2015).

Shifrinson, Joshua, "The Rise of China, Balance of Power Theory and US National Security: Reasons for Optimism?" *Journal of Strategic Studies* 43, no. 2 (2020): 175–216.

Shugart, Thomas, "Australia and the Growing Reach of China's Military," Lowy Institute, August 9, 2021, https://www.lowyinstitute.org/publications/australia-and-growing-reach-china-s-military

Shultz, George P., William J. Perry, Henry A. Kissinger, and Sam Nunn, "A World Free of Nuclear Weapons," *Wall Street Journal*, January 4, 2007, http://online.wsj.com/article/SB116787515251566636.html

Silver, Laura, Kat Devlin, and Christine Huang, "Unfavorable Views of China Reach Historic Highs in Many Countries," Pew Research Center, October 6, 2020, https://www.pewresearch.org/global/2020/10/06/unfavorable-views-of-china-reach-historic-highs-in-many-countries/

Singer, Peter W., "How Ukraine Won the #LikeWar," *Politico*, March 13, 2022, https://www.politico.com/news/magazine/2022/03/12/ukraine-russia-information-warfare-likewar-00016562

Singer, P. W., *Wired for War: The Robotics Revolution and War in the Twenty-First Century* (New York: Penguin Press, 2009).

Singer, P. W., and Emerson T. Brooking, *Likewar: The Weaponization of Social Media* (Boston: Eamon Dolan, 2018).

Siracusa, Joseph M., *Diplomacy: A Very Short Introduction* (New York: Oxford University Press, 2010).

Sjoberg, Laura, "Feminist Security and Security Studies," in *The Oxford Handbook of International Security*, ed. Alexandra Gheciu and William C. Wohlforth (Oxford: Oxford University Press, 2018).

Sjoberg, Laura, "Introduction to *Security Studies*: Feminist Contributions," *Security Studies* 18, no. 2 (2009): 183–213.

Slim, Hugo, *Humanitarian Ethics: A Guide to the Morality of Aid in War and Disaster* (Oxford: Oxford University Press, 2015).

Smith, Katherine F., et al. "Global Rise in Human Infectious Disease Outbreaks," *Journal of the Royal Society Interface* 11 (2014): 20140950

Smith, Nicholas Ross, and Tracey Fallon, "An Epochal Moment? The COVID-19 Pandemic and China's International Order Building," *World Affairs* 183, no. 3 (2020): 235–55.

Smith, Steve, "The Contested Concept of Security," in "The Concept of Security Before and After September 11," Working Paper No. 23, Institute of Defence and Strategic Studies, May 2002, https://www.rsis.edu.sg/wp-content/uploads/rsis-pubs/WP23.pdf

Solis, Mireya, "Trump Withdrawing from the Trans-Pacific Partnership," Brookings, March 24, 2017, https://www.brookings.edu/blog/unpacked/2017/03/24/trump-withdrawing-from-the-trans-pacific-partnership/

Sorkin, Emily, "The Abraham Accords: The Culmination of a Decades-Long Normalization Process between Israel and the UAE," PhD dissertation, Boston University, 2021.

Sorrell, Erin M., Gigi Kwik Gronvall, and Julie E. Fischer, "Laboratory Diagnostics—Rarely Appreciated Until Something Goes Wrong," *Think Global Health*, March 11, 2020, https://www.thinkglobalhealth.org/article/laboratory-diagnostics-rarely-appreciated-until-something-goes-wrong

Sorrell, Erin M., et al., "Predicting 'Airborne' Influenza Viruses: (Trans-) Mission Impossible?" *Current Opinion in Virology* 1, no. 6 (2011): 635–42.

Sotiris, Panagiotis, "Against Agamben: Is a Democratic Biopolitics Possible?" *Critical Legal Thinking* (blog), March 14, 2020, https://criticallegalthinking.com/2020/03/14/against-agamben-is-a-democratic-biopolitics-possible/

Soufan Center, "IntelBrief: Coronavirus Will Increase Extremisms across the Ideological Spectrum," April 13, 2020, https://thesoufancenter.org/intelbrief-the-coronavirus-will-increase-extremism-across-the-ideological-spectrum/

Soufan Center, "IntelBrief: How Will Coronavirus Impact Afghanistan?" April 16, 2020, https://thesoufancenter.org/intelbrief-how-will-the-coronavirus-impact-afghanistan/

Soufan Center,"IntelBrief: White Supremacists and the Weaponization of the Coronavirus," March 25, 2020, https://thesoufancenter.org/intelbrief-white-supremacists-and-the-weaponization-of-the-coronavirus-covid-19/

Sparke, Matthew, and Owain David Williams, "Neoliberal Disease: COVID-19, Co-pathogenesis and Global Health Insecurities," *Environment and Planning A: Economy and Space* 54, no. 1 (2022): 15–32.

Sparrow, Robert, "Killer Robots," *Journal of Applied Philosophy* 24, no. 1 (2007): 62–77.

Spencer, Caleb, "Coronavirus: 'Children May Have Been Radicalised during Lockdown,'" BBC News, June 30, 2020, https://www.bbc.com/news/uk-wales-53082476.

Sphere Association, *The Sphere Handbook: Humanitarian Charter and Minimum Standards in Humanitarian Response*, 4th edn. (Geneva: Sphere Association, 2018).

Spivak, Gayatri, "Can the Subaltern Speak?," in *Marxism and the Interpretation of Culture*, ed. Cary Nelson and Lawrence Grossberg (Basingstoke, England: Macmillan, 1988).

Spivak, Gayatri Chakravorty, *A Critique of Postcolonial Reason: Toward a History of the Vanishing Present* (Cambridge, MA: Harvard University Press, 1999).

Spivak, Gayatri Chakravorty, *Outside in the Teaching Machine* (New York: Routledge, 1993).

Sprout, Harold, and Margaret Sprout, *Toward a Politics of the Planet Earth* (New York: Van Nostrand Reinhold, 1971).

Standley, Claire, and Jordan Schermerhorn, "Reaching the 'Last Mile': Fresh Approaches Needed for Guinea Worm Eradication," *American Journal of Tropical Medicine and Hygiene* 105, no. 1 (2021): 1–2.

Starbird, Kate, Ahmer Arif, and Tom Wilson, "Disinformation as Collaborative Work: Surfacing the Participatory Nature of Strategic Information Operations," *Proceedings of the ACM on Human Centred Interaction* 3, issue CSCW (2019).

Steele, Brent J., "Nowhere to Run To, Nowhere to Hide: Inescapable Dread in the 2020s," *Journal of International Relations and Development* 24, 1037–43 (2021)

Steff, Reuben, Joe Burton, and Simona R. Soare, "Introduction: Machines, the State, and War," in *Emerging Technologies and International Security: Machines, the State, and War*, ed. Reuben Steff, Joe Burton, and Simona R. Soare (Abingdon, England: Routledge, 2021).

Steffen, Will, Paul J. Crutzen, and John R. McNeill, "The Anthropocene: Are Humans Now Overwhelming the Great Forces of Nature?" *Ambio* 36, no. 8 (2007): 614–21.

Steffen, Will, et al., "The Emergence and Evolution of Earth System Science," *Nature Reviews: Earth and Environment* 1, no. 1 (2020): 54–63.

Steger, Manfred B., and Paul James, *Globalization Matters: Engaging the Global in Unsettled Times* (Cambridge, England: Cambridge University Press, 2019).

Strassburg, Marc A., "The Global Eradication of Smallpox," *American Journal of Infection Control* 10, no. 2 (1982): 53–9.

Strawser, Bradley Jay, "Introduction: The Moral Landscape of Unmanned Weapons," in *Killing by Remote Control: The Ethics of an Unmanned Military*, ed. Bradley Jay Strawser (New York: Oxford University Press, 2013).

Stockholm International Peace Research Institute, "Nuclear Weapon Modernization Continues but the Outlook for Arms Control is Bleak," news release, June 15, 2020, https://www.sipri.org/media/press-release/2020/nuclear-weapon-modernization-continues-outlook-arms-control-bleak-new-sipri-yearbook-out-now

Stritzel, Holger, "Security, the Translation," *Security Dialogue* 42, no. 4–5 (2011): 343–55.

Stritzel, Holger, "Towards a Theory of Securitization: Copenhagen and Beyond," *European Journal of International Relations* 13, no. 3 (2007): 357–83.

Summers, Jennifer, et al., "Potential Lessons from the Taiwan and New Zealand Health Responses to the COVID-19 Pandemic," *Lancet Regional Health Western Pacific* 4 (2020): 100044.

Šumonja, Miloš, "Neoliberalism Is Not Dead—On Political Implications of Covid-19," *Capital & Class* 45, no. 2 (2021): 215–27.

Sutter, Karen M., and Michael D. Sutherland, "China's Economy: Current Trends and Issues," Congressional Research Service, January 12, 2021, https://crsreports.congress.gov/product/pdf/IF/IF11667

Swain, Ashok, and Anders Jägerskog, *Emerging Security Threats in the Middle East: The Impact of Climate Change and Globalization* (Lanham, MD: Rowman and Littlefield, 2016).

Taboy, Celine H., "Integrated Disease Investigations and Surveillance Planning: A Systems Approach to Strengthening National Surveillance and Detection of Events of Public Health Importance in Support of the International Health Regulations," *BMC Public Health* 10, Supplement 1 (2010): S6.

Tadjbakhsh, Shahrbanou, "In Defense of the Broad View of Human Security," in Mary Martin and Taylor Owen (eds.), *Routledge Handbook of Human Security* (Abingdon, England: Routledge, 2014).

Tadjbakhsh, Shahrbanou, and Anuradha Chenoy, *Human Security: Concepts and Implications* (Abingdon, England: Routledge, 2007).

Talmadge, Caitlin, "Closing Time: Assessing the Iranian Threat to the Strait of Hormuz," *International Security* 33, no. 1 (2008): 82–117.

Al-Tamimi, Aymenn Jawad, "Islamic State Editorial on the Coronavirus Pandemic," Aymenn Jawad Al-Tamimi (blog), March 19, 2020, http://www.aymennjawad.org/2020/03/islamic-state-editorial-on-the-coronavirus

Tangen, Ole, Jr., "Is China Taking Advantage of COVID-19 to Pursue South China Sea Ambitions?" *DW*, May 25, 2020, https://www.dw.com/en/is-china-taking-advantage-of-COVID-19-to-pursue-south-china-sea-ambitions/a-53573918

Tarzia, Laura, and Meagan Tyler, "Recognizing Connections between Intimate Partner Sexual Violence and Pornography," *Violence against Women* 27, no. 14 (2021): 2687–2708.

Taylor, Brendan, *The Four Flashpoints: How Asia Goes to War* (Carlton, VIC: La Trobe University Press, 2018).

Taylor, Jim, "The Woman Who Founded the 'Incel' Movement," BBC News, August 30, 2018, https://www.bbc.com/news/world-us-canada-45284455

Tazzioli, Martina, "'Stay Safe, Stay Away, and Put Face Masks On'—The Hygienic-Sanitary Borders of Covid-19," Political Economy Research Centre blog, September 21, 2020, https://www.perc.org.uk/project_posts/stay-safe-stay-away-and-put-face-masks-on-the-hygienic-sanitary-borders-of-covid-19/

Tedros Adhanom Ghebreyesus, "WHO Director-General's Opening Remarks at the Media Briefing on COVID-19—18 August 2020," WHO, August 18, 2020, https://www.who.int/director-general/speeches/detail/who-director-general-s-opening-remarks-at-the-media-briefing-on-covid-19---18-august-2020.

"Tentative Stabilization, Sluggish Recovery?" *World Economic Outlook*, January 2020, https://www.imf.org/en/Publications/WEO/Issues/2020/01/20/weo-update-january2020.

Texas Department of Public Safety, "Texas Domestic Terrorism Threat Assessment," January 2020, https://www.dps.texas.gov/sites/default/

files/documents/director_staff/media_and_communications/2020/txterrorthreatassessment.pdf

"The Changing atmosphere: Implications for global security" (Conference Statement), Toronto, June 27–30, 1988, https://www.academia.edu/4043227/The_Changing_Atmosphere_Implications_for_Global_Security_Conference_Statement_1988 (accessed August 2022).

Theohary, Catherine A., "Cyber Operations in DOD Policy and Plans: Issues for Congress," Congressional Research Service, January 5, 2015, http://web.archive.org/web/20211222072848/https://crsreports.congress.gov/product/pdf/R/R43848

Theohary, Catherine A., and John W. Rollins, "Cyberwarfare and Cyberterrorism: In Brief," Congressional Research Service, March 27, 2015, http://web.archive.org/web/20211222074425/https://crsreports.congress.gov/product/pdf/R/R43955

Thomas, Caroline, *Global Governance, Development and Human Security: The Challenge of Poverty and Inequality* (London: Pluto Press, 2000).

Thomas, Clayton, "Taliban Government in Afghanistan: Background and Issues for Congress," Congressional Research Service, November 2, 2021, http://web.archive.org/web/20211222103338/https://crsreports.congress.gov/product/pdf/R/R46955

Thomas, Clayton, et al., "US Killing of Qasem Soleimani: Frequently Asked Questions," Congressional Research Service, January 13, 2020, http://web.archive.org/web/20211026072435/https://crsreports.congress.gov/product/pdf/R/R46148/3

Thomas, Clayton, et al., "US Military Withdrawal and Taliban Takeover in Afghanistan: Frequently Asked Questions," Congressional Research Service, September 17, 2021, http://web.archive.org/web/20211222103536/https://crsreports.congress.gov/product/pdf/R/R46879

Thompson, E. P., et al., *Exterminism and Cold War* (London: Verso, 1982).

Thomson, Peter, "Statement on Behalf of the Group of 77 by Ambassador Peter Thomson, Permanent Representative of Fiji to the United Nations and Chairman of the Group of 77, and China at the Arria-Formula Meeting on the Security Dimensions of Climate Change," February 15, 2013, http://www.g77.org/statement/getstatement.php?id=130215a

Tickner, J. Ann, "Feminist Responses to International Security Studies," *Peace Review* 16, no. 1 (2004): 43–8.

Tickner, J. Ann, *Gender in International Relations: Feminist Perspectives on Achieving Global Security* (New York: Columbia University Press, 1992).

Tickner, J. Ann, "What Is Your Research Program? Some Feminist Answers to International Relations Methodological Questions," *International Studies Quarterly* 49, no. 1 (2005): 1–21.

Tomás, Juan Pedro, "Huawei Claims to Be Involved in Half of Global 5G Networks," RCR Wireless, February 22, 2021, https://www.rcrwireless.com/20210222/business/huawei-claims-involved-half-global-5g-networks

Tønnessen, Truls Hallberg, "The Islamic State after the Caliphate," *Perspectives on Terrorism* 13, no. 1 (2019): 2–11.

Torales, Julio, et al., "The Outbreak of COVID-19 Coronavirus and Its Impact on Global Mental Health," *International Journal of Social Psychiatry* 66, no. 4 (2020): 317–20.

Townshend, Ashley, Brendan Thomas-Noone, and Matilda Steward, "Averting Crisis: American Strategy, Military Spending and Collective Defence in the Indo-Pacific," United States Study Centre, August 19, 2019, https://www.ussc.edu.au/analysis/averting-crisis-american-strategy-military-spending-and-collective-defence-in-the-indo-pacific

Trombetta, Maria Julia, "Climate Change and the Environmental Conflict Discourse," in *Climate Change, Human Security and Violent Conflict*, ed. Jürgen Scheffran et al. (Heidelberg: Springer, 2012).

Trombetta, Maria Julia, "Environmental Security and Climate Change: Analysing the Discourse," *Cambridge Review of International Affairs* 21, no. 4 (2008): 585–602.

Trombetta, Maria Julia, "Security in the Anthropocene," in *International Relations in the Anthropocene*, ed. David Chandler, Franziska Müller, and Delf Rothe (Cham, Switzerland: Palgrave Macmillan, 2021).

Trubowitz, Peter, and Peter Harris, "The End of the American Century? Slow Erosion of the Domestic Sources of Usable Power," *International Affairs* 95, no. 3 (2019): 619–39.

Truman, Harry S., "Statement by the President Announcing the Use of the A-Bomb at Hiroshima," August 6, 1945, available at https://millercenter.org/the-presidency/presidential-speeches/august-6-1945-statement-president-announcing-use-bomb

Trump, Donald (@realDonaldTrump), "Liberate Michigan," Twitter, April 17, 2020, https://twitter.com/realDonaldTrump/status/1251169217531056130

Tudoroiu, Theodor, "Social Media and Revolutionary Waves: The Case of the Arab Spring," *New Political Science* 36, no. 3 (2014): 346–65.

Tuohy, Wendy, "Home Schooling, Job Loss, Pandemic Fear Drove Quadrupling of Abortion Calls," *The Age*, October 21, 2021, https://www.theage.com.au/national/home-schooling-job-loss-pandemic-fear-drove-quadrupling-of-abortion-calls-20211020-p591rp.html

Uddin, Mahi, "Addressing Work-Life Balance Challenges of Working Women during COVID-19 in Bangladesh," *International Social Science Journal* 71, no. 239–40 (2021): 7–20.

Ullman, Richard H., "Redefining Security," *International Security* 8, no. 1 (1983): 129–53.

UN News, "COVID-19 Vaccination 'Wildly Uneven and Unfair': UN Secretary-General," February 17, 2021, https://news.un.org/en/story/2021/02/1084962.

UN News, "UN Chief Calls for Action to Put Out '5-Alarm Global Fire,'" January 11, 2022, https://news.un.org/en/story/2022/01/1110292.

UN Office for Disarmament Affairs, "Biological Weapons Convention," https://www.un.org/disarmament/biological-weapons

UN Women, *From Insights to Action: Gender Equality in the Wake of COVID-19* (New York: UN Women, 2020).

UNHCR, "Coordination in Complex Emergencies," September 1, 2001, https://www.unhcr.org/en-au/partners/partners/3ba88e7c6/coordination-complex-emergencies.html

UNICEF, *Education Disrupted: Impact of the Conflict on Children's Education in Yemen*, July 2021, https://yemen.un.org/en/135092-education-disrupted-impact-conflict-childrens-education-yemen

UNICEF, "Yemen Country Office Humanitarian Situation Report Mid-Year," August 24, 2021, https://reliefweb.int/report/yemen/unicef-yemen-country-office-humanitarian-situation-report-mid-year-reporting-period-1

United Nations, "As COVID-19 Fuels Conflict, Threatens International Security, Global Unity to Fight Terrorism Needed More than Ever, Secretary-General Tells Aqaba Process Meeting," press release, September 2, 2020, https://www.un.org/press/en/2020/sgsm20227.doc.htm

United Nations, "Security Council Fails to Adopt Resolution Integrating Climate-Related Security Risk into Conflict-Prevention Strategies," UN Doc. SC/14732, December 13, 2021, https://press.un.org/en/2021/sc14732.doc.htm

United Nations, letter dated August 27, 2020 from the chargé d'affaires A.I. of the permanent mission of Germany to the United Nations addressed to the secretary-general, August 27, 2020, UN Doc. S/2020/849.

United Nations, letter dated November 5, 2020 from the president of the Security Council to the secretary-general and the permanent representatives of the members of the Security Council, November 12, 2020, UN Doc. S/2020/1090.

United Nations, letter dated February 25, 2021 from the president of the Security Council to the secretary-general and the permanent representatives of the members of the Security Council, March 1, 2021, UN Doc. S/2021/198.

United Nations, "Policy Brief: The Impact of COVID-19 on Food Security and Nutrition," June 2020, 2, https://unsdg.un.org/sites/default/files/2020-06/SG-Policy-Brief-on-COVID-Impact-on-Food-Security.pdf

United Nations, "Policy Brief: The Impact of COVID-19 on Women," April 9, 2020, https://digitallibrary.un.org/record/3856948?ln=en

United Nations Climate Security Mechanism, "Toolbox Briefing Note," 2020, https://dppa.un.org/sites/default/files/csm_toolbox-1-briefing_note.pdf

United Nations Development Programme, *Human Development Report 1994* (New York: Oxford University Press, 1994).

United Nations Development Programme, *Human Development Report 2019: Beyond Income, Beyond Averages, Beyond Today— Inequalities in Human Development in the 21st Century* (New York: United Nations Development Programme, 2019), https://hdr.undp.org/sites/default/files/hdr2019.pdf

United Nations Disarmament Yearbook, Vol. 45, Part II: 2020 (New York: United Nations, 2021), http://web.archive.org/web/20211209074016/https://front.un-arm.org/wp-content/uploads/2021/10/en-yb-vol-45-2020-part2_rev-1.pdf

United Nations Environment Program, *Sudan: Post-conflict Environmental Assessment*, 2007.

United Nations General Assembly, "Climate Change and Its Possible Security Implications: Report of the Secretary-General," September 11, 2009, UN Doc. A/64/350.

United Nations General Assembly, "Resolution 46/182: Strengthening of the Coordination of Humanitarian Emergency Assistance of the United Nations," A/RES/46/182, December 19, 1991.

United Nations General Assembly, Resolution 63/281, "Climate Change and its Possible Security Implications," June 11, 2009, UN Doc. A/RES/63/281.

United Nations General Assembly, "Resolution 66/290. Follow-Up to Paragraph 143 on Human Security of the 2005 World Summit Outcome," A/RES/66/290, October 25, 2012.

United Nations Human Rights Office of the High Commissioner, "COVID-19: States Should Not Abuse Emergency Measures to Suppress Human Rights – UN Experts," March 16, 2020, https://www.ohchr.org/en/NewsEvents/Pages/DisplayNews.aspx?NewsID=25722&LangID=E

United Nations Office for Disarmament Affairs, "Treaty on the Non-Proliferation of Nuclear Weapons (NPT)," https://www.un.org/disarmament/wmd/nuclear/npt/text/

United Nations Secretary-General, "Secretary-General's Appeal for Global Ceasefire," March 23, 2020, https://www.un.org/sg/en/content/sg/statement/2020-03-23/secretary-generals-appeal-for-global-ceasefire

United Nations Security Council, 5,663rd meeting, April 17, 2007, UN Doc. S/PV.5663 (Resumption 1).

United Nations Security Council, 6,668th meeting, November 23, 2011, UN Doc. S/PV.6668.

United Nations Security Council, 8,144th meeting, December 20, 2017, UN Doc. S/PV.8144, 4.

United Nations Security Council, Resolution 2349, "Peace and Security in Africa," March 31, 2017, UN Doc. S/RES/2349 (2017).

United Nations Security Council, Resolution 2408, "The Situation in Somalia," March 27, 2018, UN Doc. S/RES/2408 (2018).

United Nations Security Council, Resolution 2461, "The Situation in Somalia," March 27, 2019, UN Doc S/RES/2461 (2019).

United Nations Security Council, Resolution 2532, July 1, 2020, UN Doc. S/RES/2532 (2020).

United Nations Security Council, Resolution 2565, February 26, 2021, UN Doc. S/RES/2565 (2021).

United Nations Security Council, Statement by the President of the Security Council, July 20, 2011, UN Doc. S/PRST/2011/15.

United Nations Security Council, Statement by the President of the Security Council, August 7, 2019, UN Doc. S/PRST/2019/7.

United Nations Security Council, "The UN Security Council and Climate Change," Security Council Report, June 2021, 21–6, https://www.securitycouncilreport.org/atf/cf/%7B65BFCF9B-6D27-4E9C-8CD3-CF6E4FF96FF9%7D/climate_security_2021.pdf

United States Attorney's Office, Southern District of Texas, "Two Houston Men Charged with Attempting to Fraudulently Sell 50 Million Masks," press release, November 24, 2020, https://www.justice.gov/usao-sdtx/pr/two-houston-men-charged-attempting-fraudulently-sell-50-million-masks

United States Government, "Respondents' Memorandum Regarding the Government's Detention Authority Relative to Detainees Held at Guantanamo Bay," Misc. No. 08-442 (TFH), www.justice.gov/sites/default/files/opa/legacy/2009/03/13/memo-re-det-auth.pdf.

Ünver, H. Akın, "Artificial Intelligence, Authoritarianism and the Future of Political Systems," EDAM, July 2018, https://edam.org.tr/wp-content/uploads/2018/07/AKIN-Artificial-Intelligence_Bosch-3.pdf

The US Army / Marine Corps Counterinsurgency Field Manual (Chicago: University of Chicago Press, 2007).

"The US Army / Marine Corps Counterinsurgency Field Manual," University of Chicago Press website, 2007, https://press.uchicago.edu/ucp/books/book/chicago/U/bo5748917.html

US Army Training & Doctrine Command, *Cyber Operations and Cyber Terrorism*, DCSINT Handbook No. 1.02, August 15, 2005, II-2, http://web.archive.org/web/20211221105116/https://apps.dtic.mil/sti/pdfs/ADA439217.pdf

US Department of Defense, *Indo-Pacific Strategy Report: Preparedness, Partnerships, and Promoting a Networked Region*, June 1, 2019, https://media.defense.gov/2019/Jul/01/2002152311/-1/-1/1/DEPARTMENT-OF-DEFENSE-INDO-PACIFIC-STRATEGY-REPORT-2019.PDF

US Department of Health and Human Services, "2020: A Retrospective Look at Healthcare Cybersecurity," February 18, 2021, https://www.hhs.gov/sites/default/files/2020-hph-cybersecurty-retrospective-tlpwhite.pdf

US Department of Health and Human Services, "COVID-19 Cyber Threats (Update)," August 13, 2020, https://www.hhs.gov/sites/default/files/covid-19-cyber-threats-update.pdf

US Department of Justice, "Two Chinese Hackers Working with the Ministry of State Security Charged with Global Computer Intrusion Campaign Targeting Intellectual Property and Confidential Business Information, Including COVID-19 Research," press release, July 21, 2020, https://www.justice.gov/opa/pr/two-chinese-hackers-working-ministry-state-security-charged-global-computer-intrusion

US Department of State, "A Free and Open Indo-Pacific: Advancing a Shared Vision," November 4, 2019, https://www.state.gov/wp-content/uploads/2019/11/Free-and-Open-Indo-Pacific-4Nov2019.pdf

US Department of State, *GEC Special Report: Russia's Pillars of Disinformation and Propaganda*, August 2020, https://www.state.gov/wp-content/uploads/2020/08/Pillars-of-Russia%E2%80%99s-Disinformation-and-Propaganda-Ecosystem_08-04-20.pdf

US Department of State, "Glossary," https://2001-2009.state.gov/s/ct/info/c16718.htm.

US Department of the Treasury, "Treasury Sanctions Russia with Sweeping New Sanctions Authority," press release, April 15, 2021, https://home.treasury.gov/news/press-releases/jy0127

US Embassy and Consulate in Vietnam, "Remarks by President Trump at APEC CEO Summit," November 10, 2017, https://vn.usembassy.gov/20171110-remarks-president-trump-apec-ceo-summit/

US Mission Geneva, "US Delegation Opening Statement at CCW Informal Experts Meeting on Lethal Autonomous Weapons Systems," US Mission to International Organizations in Geneva, May 13, 2014, http://web.archive.org/web/20211221093159/https://geneva.usmission.gov/2014/05/13/u-s-delegation-opening-statement-at-ccw-informal-experts-meeting-on-lethal-autonomous-weapons-systems/

Usher, Kim, et al., "Family Violence and COVID-19: Increased Vulnerability and Reduced Options for Support," *International Journal of Mental Health Nursing* 29, no. 4 (2020): 549–52.

USNI News, "Timeline: Theodore Roosevelt COVID-19 Outbreak Investigation," June 23, 2020, https://news.usni.org/2020/06/23/timeline-theodore-roosevelt-covid-19-outbreak-investigation

Vaux, Tony, "Humanitarian Trends and Dilemmas," in *Development and Humanitarianism: Practical Issues*, ed. Deborah Eade and Tony Vaux (Bloomfield, CT: Kumarian Press, 2007).

Vera-Gray, Fiona, et al., "Sexual Violence as a Sexual Script in Mainstream Online Pornography," *British Journal of Criminology* 61, no. 5 (2021): 1243–60.

Vera-Sanso, Penny, "Population Ageing and Development: Time to Drop Ageist Demographies for a Critical, Decolonial, Sociology of Ageing," in *Routledge Handbook of Global Development: Problems, Possibilities and Pedagogy*, ed. Kearrin Sims et al. (Abingdon, England: Routledge, 2022).

Vincent, James, "Something in the Air," *The Verge*, June 3, 2020, https://www.theverge.com/2020/6/3/21276912/5g-conspiracy-theories-coronavirus-uk-telecoms-engineers-attacks-abuse

Vollmer, Bastian A., *Borders Revisited: Discourses on the UK Border* (Cham, Switzerland: Palgrave Macmillan, 2021).

Voo, Julia, et al., *National Cyber Power Index 2020: Methodology and Analytical Considerations*, Belfer Center for Science and International Affairs, Harvard University, September 2020, https://www.belfercenter.org/sites/default/files/2020-09/NCPI_2020.pdf

Wæver, Ole, "Securitisation and Desecuritisation," in *On Security*, ed. Ronnie D. Lipschutz (New York: Columbia University Press, 1995).

Wæver, Ole, and Barry Buzan, "Racism and Responsibility: The Critical Limits of Deepfake Methodology in Security Studies—A Reply to Howell and Richter-Montpetit," *Security Dialogue* 51, no. 4 (2020): 386–94.

Walker, R. B. J., "The Subject of Security," in *Critical Security Studies: Concepts and Cases*, ed. Keith Krause and Michael C. Williams (Minneapolis: Minnesota University Press, 1997).

Wallis, Joanne, and Henrietta McNeill, "The Implications of COVID-19 for Security in the Pacific Islands," *Round Table* 110, no. 2 (2021): 203–16.

Walt, Stephen M., *The Hell of Good Intentions: America's Foreign Policy Elite and the Decline of US Primacy* (New York: Farrar, Straus & Giroux, 2018).

Walt, Stephen M., "US Grand Strategy after the Cold War: Can Realism Explain It? Should Realism Guide It?" *International Relations* 32, no. 1 (2018): 3–22.

Waltz, Kenneth N., "Reductionist and Systemic Theories," in *Theory of International Politics*, ed. Kenneth N. Waltz (Reading, MA: Addison-Wesley, 1979).

Waltz, Kenneth N., *Theory of International Politics* (Reading, MA: Addison-Wesley, 1979).

Wang, Haidong, "Estimation of Total and Excess Mortality Due to COVID-19," Institute for Health Metrics and Evaluation, October 15, 2021, http://www.healthdata.org/special-analysis/estimation-excess-mortality-due-covid-19-and-scalars-reported-covid-19-deaths

Wang, Philip, "China Tells Mines to Produce 'as Much Coal as Possible,'" CNN Business, October 20, 2021, https://edition.cnn.com/2021/10/20/business/china-coal-production-intl-hnk/index.html

Wang, Yuan-Kang, *Harmony and War: Confucian Culture and Chinese Power Politics* (New York: Columbia University Press, 2011).

Warner, Christopher G., *Implementing Joint Vision 2010: A Revolution in Military Affairs for Strategic Air Campaigns* (Montgomery, AL: Air University Press, 1999).

Warren, Aiden, *The Obama Administration's Nuclear Weapon Strategy: The Promises of Prague* (Abingdon, England: Routledge, 2014).

Warren, Aiden, "Regulating the Abstraction of Violence: Interventions and the Deployment of New Technologies Globally," in *Rethinking Humanitarian Intervention in the 21st Century*, ed. Aiden Warren and Damian Grenfell (Edinburgh: Edinburgh University Press, 2017).

Warren, Aiden, and Adam Bartley, *US Foreign Policy and China: Security Challenges during the Bush, Obama, and Trump Administrations* (Edinburgh: Edinburgh University Press, 2020).

Warren, Aiden, and Phillip Baxter, *Nuclear Modernization in the 21st Century* (Abingdon, England: Routledge, 2020).

Warren, Aiden, and Ingvild Bode, "Altering the Playing Field: The US Redefinition of the Use-of-Force," *Contemporary Security Policy* 36, no. 2 (2015): 174–99.

Warren, Aiden, and Alek Hillas, "Friend or Frenemy? The Role of Trust in Human-Machine Teaming and Lethal Autonomous Weapons Systems," *Small Wars & Insurgencies* 31, no. 4 (2020): 822–50.

Warren, Aiden, and Alek Hillas, "Lethal Autonomous Robotics: Rethinking the Dehumanization of Warfare," *UCLA Journal of International Law and Foreign Affairs* 22, no. 2 (2018): 218–49.

Warren, Aiden, and Joseph M. Siracusa, *US Presidents and Cold War Nuclear Diplomacy* (Cham, Switzerland: Palgrave Macmillan, 2021).

Watson Institute, "Costs of War," September 2021, Brown University, https://watson.brown.edu/costsofwar/figures/2021/WarDeathToll

Watts, Clint, "Disinformation: A Primer in Russian Active Measures and Influence Campaigns," Statement Prepared for the US Senate Committee on Intelligence Hearing, March 30, 2017, https://www.intelligence.senate.gov/sites/default/files/documents/os-cwatts-033017.pdf

Watts, Michael J., and Hans G. Bohle, "Hunger, Famine and the Space of Vulnerability," *GeoJournal* 30, no. 2 (1993): 117–25.

Wedeman, Ben, and Lauren Said-Moorhouse, "ISIS Has Lost Its Final Stronghold in Syria, the Syrian Democratic Forces Says," CNN, March 23, 2019, https://www.cnn.com/2019/03/23/middleeast/isis-caliphate-end-intl/index.html

Wells, Samuel F., Jr., and Mark Bruzonsky, *Security in the Middle East: Regional Change and Great Power Strategies* (New York: Routledge, [1987] 2019).

Wenham, Clare, et al., "Gender and Race on the Frontline: Experiences of Health Workers in Brazil during the COVID-19 Pandemic," *Social Politics* (2021), https://doi.org/10.1093/sp/jxab031

Whetham, David, "Drones and Targeted Killing: Angels or Assassins?" in *Killing by Remote Control: The Ethics of an Unmanned Military*, ed. Bradley Jay Strawser (New York: Oxford University Press, 2013).

White House, "Fact Sheet: President Biden's Global COVID-19 Summit: Ending the Pandemic and Building Back Better," September 22, 2021, https://www.whitehouse.gov/briefing-room/statements-releases/2021/09/22/fact-sheet-president-bidens-global-COVID-19-summit-ending-the-pandemic-and-building-back-better/

White House, *National Security Strategy of the United States of America*, December 2017, https://trumpwhitehouse.archives.gov/wp-content/uploads/2017/12/NSS-Final-12-18-2017-0905.pdf

White House, "Remarks by President Barack Obama in Prague as Delivered," press release, April 5, 2009, https://obamawhitehouse.archives.gov/the-press-office/remarks-president-barack-obama-prague-delivered

White House, "Remarks by Vice President Harris on the Indo-Pacific Region," August 24, 2021, https://www.whitehouse.gov/briefing-room/speeches-remarks/2021/08/24/remarks-by-vice-president-harris-on-the-indo-pacific-region/

White House, "Statement by the President on the Trans-Pacific Partnership," October 5, 2015, https://obamawhitehouse.archives.gov/the-press-office/2015/10/05/statement-president-trans-pacific-partnership

Wibben, Annick T. R., "Debates in Feminist Security Studies," in *Routledge Handbook of Security Studies*, ed. Myriam Dunn Cavelty and Thierry Balzacq, 2nd edn. (Abingdon, England: Routledge, 2017).

Wibben, Annick T. R., "Opening Security: Recovering Critical Scholarship as Political," *Critical Studies on Security* 4, no. 2 (2016): 137–53.

Wike, Richard, Janell Fetterolf, and Maria Mordecai, "US Image Plummets Internationally as Most Say Country Has Handled Coronavirus Badly," Pew Research Center, September 15, 2020, https://www.pewresearch.org/global/2020/09/15/us-image-plummets-internationally-as-most-say-country-has-handled-coronavirus-badly/

Wikileaks, *Afghanistan War Diary*, 2004–2010, 2010, https://wikileaks.org/wiki/Afghan_War_Diary,_2004–2010

Wilde, Jaap H. de, "Environmental Security Deconstructed," in *Globalization and Environmental Challenges*, ed. Hans-Guenther Brauch et al. (Berlin: Springer, 2008), 595–602.

Wilder-Smith, Annelies, and Sarah Osman, "Public Health Emergencies of International Concern: A Historic Overview," *Journal of Travel Medicine* 27, no. 8 (2020): taaa227.

Wilkinson, Claire, "The Copenhagen School on Tour in Kyrgyzstan: Is Securitization Theory Useable outside Europe?" *Security Dialogue* 38, no. 1 (2007): 5–25.

Williams, Michael C., "Words, Images, Enemies: Securitization and International Politics," *International Studies Quarterly* 47, no. 4 (2003): 511–31.

Williams, Michael C. and Keith Krause, "Preface: Toward Critical Security Studies," in *Critical Security Studies: Concepts and Cases*, ed. Keith Krause and Michael C. Williams (London: UCL Press, 1997).

Wilson, Cameron, "Why Are Australians Chanting 'Arrest Bill Gates' at Protests? This Wild Facebook Group Has the Answers," *Buzzfeed News*, May 11, 2020, https://www.buzzfeed.com/cameronwilson/lockdown-protest-australia-bill-gates-conspiracy-theories

Wilson, Jeffrey, "Adapting Australia to an Era of Geoeconomic Competition," Perth USAsia Centre, January 2021, https://perthusasia.edu.au/getattachment/Our-Work/Geoeconomics-Report/PU-184-Geoecon-210526-WEB.pdf.aspx?lang=en-AU

Windsor, Leah, et al. "Gender in the Time of Covid-19: Evaluating National Leadership and COVID Fatalities," *PLOS One* 15, no. 12 (2020): e0244531

Winter, Jana, "Exclusive: FBI Document Warns Conspiracy Theories Are a New Domestic Terrorism Threat," Yahoo! News, August 2, 2019, https://news.yahoo.com/fbi-documents-conspiracy-theories-terrorism-160000507.html

Wise, Paul H., and Michele Barry, "Civil War and the Global Threat of Pandemics," *Dædalus* 146, no. 4 (2017): 71–84.

Wither, James, and Richard Mašek, "The COVID-19 Pandemic: Counterterrorism Practitioners' Assessments," George C. Marshall Center, October 2020, https://www.marshallcenter.org/en/publications/perspectives/covid-19-pandemic-counterterrorism-practitioners-assessments

Wolfe, Patrick, "Settler Colonialism and the Elimination of the Native," *Journal of Genocide Research* 8, no. 4 (2006): 387–409.

Wolfe, Patrick (ed.), *The Settler Complex: Recuperating Binarism in Colonial Studies* (Los Angeles: American Indian Studies Center, 2016).

Wolfers, Arnold, "'National Security' as an Ambiguous Symbol," *Political Science Quarterly* 67, no. 4 (1952): 481–502.

Wolfsfeld, Gadi, Elad Segev, and Tamir Sheafer, "Social Media and the Arab Spring: Politics Comes First," *International Journal of Press/Politics* 18, no. 2 (2013): 115–37.

Wolfson, Elijah, "Ebola and Climate Change: Are Humans Responsible for the Severity of the Current Outbreak?" *Newsweek*, December 8, 2014, https://www.newsweek.com/climate-change-ebola-outbreak-globalization-infectious-disease-264163

Wolfsthal, Jon B., Jeffrey Lewis, and Marc Quint, *The Trillion Dollar Nuclear Triad* (Monterey, CA: James Martin Center for Nonproliferation Studies, 2014).

Wong, Julia Carrie, "Revealed: QAnon Facebook Groups Are Growing at a Rapid Pace around the World," *The Guardian*, August 11, 2020, https://www.theguardian.com/us-news/2020/aug/11/qanon-facebook-groups-growing-conspiracy-theory

Wong, Wilson, "Despite Court's Decision, Florida Withholds School Board Salaries over Mask Mandates," NBC News, August 31, 2021, https://www.nbcnews.com/news/us-news/despite-court-s-decision-florida-withholds-school-board-salaries-over-n1278107

Woodward, Alex, "Coronavirus: White Supremacists Planned to Use the Virus as a Bioweapon," *The Independent*, March 22, 2020, https://www.independent.co.uk/news/world/americas/coronavirus-terrorist-white-supremacy-fbi-bioterrorism-a9417296.html

Woolf, Steven H., et al., "Excess Deaths from COVID-19 and Other Causes, March–April 2020," *JAMA* 324, no. 5 (2020): 510–13.

"Working with DG ECHO as an NGO Partner: Forgotten Crisis Assessment (FCA)," DG ECHO Partners' Website, https://www.dgecho-partners-helpdesk.eu/ngo/financing-decision/dg-echo-strategy/forgotten-crisis

World Bank, "COVID-19: Remittance Flows to Shrink 14% by 2021," news release, October 29, 2020, https://www.worldbank.org/en/news/press-release/2020/10/29/covid-19-remittance-flows-to-shrink-14-by-2021

World Bank, "COVID-19 to Add as Many as 150 Million Extreme Poor by 2021," press release, October 7, 2020, https://www.worldbank.org/en/news/press-release/2020/10/07/covid-19-to-add-as-many-as-150-million-extreme-poor-by-2021

World Bank, "Flu Outbreaks Reminder of Pandemic Threat," March 5, 2013. https://www.worldbank.org/en/news/feature/2013/03/05/flu-outbreaks-reminder-of-pandemic-threat

World Bank, "GDP (Current US$)," 2021, https://data.worldbank.org/indicator/NY.GDP.MKTP.CD

World Bank, *Pandemic, Recession: The Global Economy in Crisis* (Washington, DC: World Bank Group, 2020).

World Bank, *Reversals of Fortune: Poverty and Shared Prosperity 2020* (Washington, DC: World Bank, 2020), https://openknowledge.worldbank.org/bitstream/handle/10986/34496/9781464816024.pdf

World Bank, *World Development Report 2011: Conflict, Security, and Development* (Washington, DC: World Bank, 2011).

World Commission on Environment and Development, *Our Common Future* (Oxford: Oxford University Press, 1987).

World Health Organization, "Air Pollution," 2021, https://www.who.int/health-topics/air-pollution#tab=tab_1

World Health Organization, "Attacks on Health Care in the Context of COVID-19," July 30, 2020, https://www.who.int/news-room/feature-stories/detail/attacks-on-health-care-in-the-context-of-covid-19

World Health Organization, "Coronavirus Disease (COVID-19): Climate Change," April 22, 2020, https://www.who.int/news-room/q-a-detail/coronavirus-disease-covid-19-climate-change

World Health Organization, "Global Influenza Surveillance and Response System (GISRS)," https://www.who.int/initiatives/global-influenza-surveillance-and-response-system

World Health Organization, "Health Security," https://www.who.int/health-topics/health-security#tab=tab_1

World Health Organization, "IHR Monitoring and Evaluation Framework," https://extranet.who.int/sph/ihr-monitoring-evaluation

World Health Organization, "International Health Regulations," https://www.who.int/health-topics/international-health-regulations#tab=tab_1

World Health Organization, "Violence against Women: Impact and Scale," 2021, https://www.who.int/health-topics/violence-against-women#tab=tab_2

World Health Organization, "What Is the ACT-Accelerator," https://www.who.int/initiatives/act-accelerator/about

World Health Organization, "WHO Coronavirus (COVID-19) Dashboard: Data Table," December 19, 2021, http://web.archive.org/web/20211219003041/https://covid19.who.int/table/

World Meteorological Organization, "State of the Global Climate 2021: WMO Provisional Report," 2021, https://library.wmo.int/doc_num.php?explnum_id=10859

World Organisation for Animal Health, "Rinderpest," https://www.oie.int/en/disease/rinderpest/

Worldometer, "China. Coronavirus Cases and Deaths," February 17, 2022, https://www.worldometers.info/coronavirus/country/china/

Worldometer, "United States. Coronavirus Cases and Deaths", February 17, 2022, https://www.worldometers.info/coronavirus/country/us/

Wright, Mike, et al., "State Capitalism in International Context: Varieties and Variations," *Journal of World Business* 56, no. 2 (2021): 101160.

Wyn Jones, Richard, *Security, Strategy, and Critical Theory* (Boulder, CO: Lynne Rienner, 1999).

Xiao, Alison, "Army to Begin Patrolling Sydney COVID Hotspots to Help Police Enforce Lockdown Rules," ABC News (Australia), July 30, 2021, https://www.abc.net.au/news/2021-07-30/adf-soldiers-to-arrive-in-sydney-covid19-lockdown/100336124

Xinhua, "China, Serbia Sign Memorandum on Space Technology," June 6, 2020, http://www.xinhuanet.com/english/2020-06/06/c_139117562.htm

Xu Wei, "China's Bigger Role in Offering Vaccine Stressed," *China Daily*, August 9, 2021, https://www.chinadaily.com.cn/a/202108/09/WS61106199a310efa1bd66771d.html

Xue, Ye, "China's Economic Sanctions Made Australia More Confident," *The Interpreter*, October 22, 2021, https://www.lowyinstitute.org/the-interpreter/china-s-economic-sanctions-made-australia-more-confident

Yablokov, Ilya, "Conspiracy Theories as a Russian Public Diplomacy Tool: The Case of *Russia Today* (*RT*)," *Politics* 35, no. 3–4 (2015): 301–15.

Yang, Dali L., "The COVID-19 Pandemic and the Estrangement of US-China Relations," *Asian Perspective* 45, no. 1 (2021), 7–31.

Yang, Samuel, "China Claims It's Leading the Way in 6G Mobile Tech Research, But the Reality Is Still Years Away," ABC News (Australia), June 22, 2021, http://web.archive.org/web/20220105051653/https://www.abc.net.au/news/2021-06-22/china-claims-its-lead-in-the-global-5g-rollout-and-6g-research/100165362

Ye, Min, "The COVID-19 Effect: US-China Narratives and Realities," *Washington Quarterly* 44, no. 1 (2021): 89–105

Yew Lun Tian, "China Defence Spending Gets Mild Boost amid Economic Caution," Reuters, March 5, 2021, https://www.reuters.com/article/us-china-parliament-defence-idUSKBN2AX07Z

Young, Karen E., "The Emerging Interventionists of the GCC," LSE Middle East Centre, December 2013, http://eprints.lse.ac.uk/55079/1/__libfile_REPOSITORY_Content_LSE%20Middle%20East%20Centre%20Papers_The%20Emerging%20Interventionists%20of%20the%20GCC.pdf

Young, Robert J. C., *Postcolonialism: An Historical Introduction* (Oxford: Blackwell, 2001).

Young, Robert J. C., *Postcolonialism: A Very Short Introduction* (Oxford: Oxford University Press, 2003).

Yousaf, Farooq, and Steve Wakhu, "Security in the 'Periphery' of Post-colonial States: Analysing Pakistan's 'Tribal' Pashtuns and Kenyan-Somalis," *Social Identities* 26, no. 4 (2020): 515–32.

Zaamout, Noureddin, "Post-colonialism and Security," in *The Palgrave Encyclopedia of Global Security Studies*, ed. Scott Romaniuk, Manish Thapa, and Péter Marton (Cham, Switzerland: Palgrave Macmillan, 2020).

Zakaria, Fareed, "The New China Scare: Why America Shouldn't Panic About Its Latest Challenger," *Foreign Affairs*, January/February 2020, https://www.foreignaffairs.com/articles/china/2019-12-06/new-china-scare

Zala, Benjamin, "Weighing Up the Balance: What Role for the Balance of Power in the Twenty-First Century?" *Cooperation and Conflict* 45, no. 2 (2010): 245–52.

Zalewski, Marysia, "Feminist International Relations: Making Sense . . .," in *Gender Matters in Global Politics: A Feminist Introduction to International Relations*, ed. Laura J. Shepherd (Abingdon, England: Routledge, 2015).

Zürn, Michael, *A Theory of Global Governance: Authority, Legitimacy, and Contestation* (Oxford: Oxford University Press, 2018).

Index